A NATURAL HISTORY OF WESTERN TREES

BY

DONALD CULROSS PEATTIE

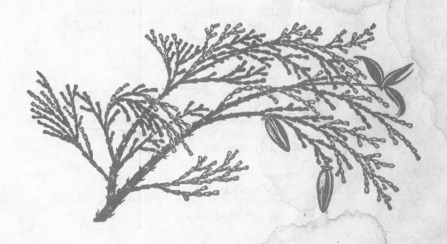

Companion to this volume

*A Natural History of Trees of
Eastern and Central North America*

_____

For Mary Tresidder

A Natural History of Western Trees

Copyright 1950, 1951, 1952 and 1953 by Donald Culross Peattie
Copyright © renewed 1978, 1979, 1980 and 1981 by Noel Peattie
Copyright 1953 by Paul Landacre

Introduction copyright © 1991 by Robert Finch

Library of Congress Catalog Card Number 80-12263
ISBN 0-395-58175-3 (pbk.)

Printed in the United States of America

FFG 10 9 8 7 6 5 4 3 2 1

CONTENTS

INTRODUCTION

by Robert Finch

Like most children in the Eastern United States, I grew up thinking that trees grew everywhere. This despite my school geography lessons and all the Westerns and Biblical desert movies I watched, for everywhere *I* went I saw trees.

I grew up in northeastern New Jersey, nobody's idea of a sylvan paradise. But even along the cracked sidewalks of my town, trees were always at hand, not just as shady presences but literally, and somewhat illicitly, *at hand*. Each spring my friends and I sought out the crooked-branched, black-plated trees that seemed to grow in almost every backyard, playground, or park. Climbing their rough trunks, we stripped the fruiting branches of their small hard green berries, perfect ammunition for the peashooters that appeared each spring in our corner store. It was decades before I learned that these "pea trees" were actually Wild Black Cherries.

No less useful were the stunted thorny trees we found in vacant lots. Their sprouts, shooting up among junk and trash, made superb bows for our Cowboy and Indian games, and their weird fruit — large, warty, globular green spheres filled with acrid-smelling milky pulp — were superb for summer snowball fights. We might have taken more pride in our archery had we known that this tree was highly valued as bow wood by the Osage Indians of Arkansas and Missouri, after whom it was named — the Osage Orange.

And there was the fall ritual of helping our fathers rake the nameless, numberless leaves into piles in the street and setting them ablaze in the crisp early darkness of October evenings — a memory that even now seems not just environmentally innocent but curiously and powerfully primitive.

Like adults, trees were presences we children were ready enough to use but did not bother to know personally. It was only when I began to recognize that they were not a universal phenomenon, that the temperate zone woodlands of my childhood were something of a global aberration that I began to be interested in trees as distinct individuals. When I did, Donald

Culross Peattie's *A Natural History of Trees* was among my earliest discoveries. I was initially attracted to it more for its vigorous narrative, sensuous descriptions, and contagious affection for its subject than as a source of factual information or as a field guide. Though *A Natural History of Trees* and *A Natural History of Western Trees* are excellent references, that is not their main strength nor the author's primary intention. As Peattie says in his Foreword: "A name is only a door open to knowledge; beyond lie the green ways of growing and, too, all that makes a tree most interesting and important to man. . . . To tell a little of these things is the main purpose of this book."

These volumes are above all collections of superbly wrought stories about trees; taken together, they tell one of the great environmental sagas in American history. In fact, these works might more accurately have been titled *A Natural and Human History of Trees,* for it is the long and intimate record of human and sylvan interaction on this continent that forms the focus of Peattie's great achievement. As Peattie says, "Nowhere else in the world . . . have trees so profoundly influenced the migrations, the destinies and the lives of human beings." We are a druidic race, both by heritage and by experience, and Peattie is one of our finest chroniclers. One can only regret that his plans for a third book, on the Southern Trees, never materialized; conspicuous by their absence in these two volumes are such magnificent species as the Southern Live Oak, the Southern Yellow Pine, the Bald Cypress, and the Catalpa.

Here one finds compendiums of colorful local names for trees; stirring accounts of our first encounters and relationships with hundreds of native species; stories of the historical, literary, and mythic significance of the great wilderness forests and of individual trees; and impressive, often appalling, narratives of the rise and fall of the great lumber industries. These books are a vibrant human document; through their pages flows a rich sap of heroes and villains, characters and comics, tragedy and romance.

Rereading these essays now, however, it seems to me that their most impressive quality is Peattie's ability to enter into an almost personal relationship with every tree he portrays. Though the two volumes describe more than four hundred species, there is not a single perfunctory account. His trees come across, not as abstract scientific flora, but as individuals, often gently imbued with an anthropomorphic will. The Hemlock, for instance, does not simply grow in rocky places, it "loves rocks; it likes to straddle them with its ruddy roots, to crack them with its growing, to rub its knees against a great boulder." Such descriptions do not sentimentalize trees; rather, they reflect the connection that we feel with them and the human responses they call up in us, as when, in the presence of the great Redwood groves, "you draw yourself up achingly, trying to find some undiscovered worth in yourself to add a cubit to mere manhood." Peattie *salutes* every species that he encounters, if not for its importance to human culture or its inherent aesthetic appeal, then, as in the case of the Pitch Pine, for the very fact that it "disdains even to be useful to man." He describes many remarkable individual trees (what botanists call "specimen trees," though he never uses the term) that have a special hold on the human imagination. Several species serve as springboards for what amount to sociological essays on American life. Peattie possessed an eye and an ear as fine as John Muir's for the religious and mystical feelings that certain trees evoke; he describes, for instance, the play of light and shade from an American Elm as "music without sound, a dance without dancers." In a two-page essay on the Balsam Fir he can, first, inspire admiration for the tree's remarkable resin, which makes a nearly perfect fixative for microscope slides, and then evoke a sense of nostalgia for its role as a Christmas tree, arriving "like a shining child at your door, breathing of all out of doors and cupping healthy North Woods cold between its boughs."

Nothing about trees seems beyond Peattie's interest or notice. Where else can you find a description of how a Saguaro cactus *sounds?* Or come on such wonderful throwaway lines as his comment that "several hundred pounds [of Mesquite gum] are exported annually to Australia, *for what purpose is unknown*"? Or find, along with descriptions of modern sawmills and paper-making processes, the assertion that "of all western Pines [the Ponderosa] seems to the beholder most full of light"?

It is in his treatment of the major tree species that Peattie's talents as a writer are given full expression. In the Eastern and Central North American volume his essays on White Pine, White Oak, Black Walnut, White Birch, American Beech, Sugar Maple, and dozens of others are rich, full-length portraits, skillful mixtures of geographic vistas, poignant elegies, botanical and cultural history, folklore, sylvaculture, ecology, humorous and sometimes bizarre anecdotes, and myth debunking (the famous Washington Elm in Cambridge, Massachusetts, was apparently only a slim sapling in 1775 when the general purportedly took command of the Colonial troops beneath its shade).

But it is with the Western trees that Peattie attains his loftiest achievements, particularly in the essays on the evergreen giants, which make up nearly half of that volume. The great Western monarchs — the Sequoias and Redwoods, the Sugar and Ponderosa Pines, the Sitka Spruces, Douglas Firs, and Western Red Cedars — compelled not only a greater and more dramatic scale of human enterprise than the Eastern trees, but also a new, and to some degree alien, set of emotional and psychological responses from Americans, including the sense that "such holy presences as these must be preserved." It was in the West, after all, that the great forest preservation efforts of this century were born.

At an environmentally enlightened distance of four decades, it is easy to criticize Peattie for what often seems a naive belief in American technology and "the greatest scientifically managed forests in the world." Though he is unflinching in his indictment of the lumber industry's exploitation of North America's irreplaceable wilderness forests, he also conveys the sense that we have learned from our mistakes, reflecting the nearly universal belief of the Eisenhower era (still alive and kicking today) that "properly managed" forests can accommodate *all* the needs of industry, recreation, wildlife, and broader environmental concerns.

Mistaken such faith may have been; naive it was not. While he may have believed in sustainable sylvaculture, he also recognized that it remained, in his day, an ideal rather than a reality. He delivers stern warnings to the forest industry and the Forest Service, and reminds us that not even the trees in our National Parks are necessarily forever safe. The conservation ethic Peattie espoused may not have been as radical as that of his contemporaries Aldo Leopold and Rachel Carson, but like them he knew that any enduring change in human environmental behavior must take place in individual sensibilities.

And it is in the celebratory spirit of books such as these, showing our affinity with our natural surroundings, that the basis for such change can be found. Rarely has American nature had a celebrant as broadly knowledgeable and as infectiously enthusiastic as Donald Culross Peattie. Though I have acquired several more up-to-date texts on trees, I still return to Peattie, not primarily to identify trees but to learn to identify *with* them — how they look and feel, how they have insinuated themselves into our consciousness as well as our lives. I open these pages, with their wonderfully evocative woodcuts by Paul Landacre, not to find "environmentally correct" attitudes, but to draw from their inexhaustible well of curiosity and affection.

Brewster, Massachusetts
February 27, 1991

FOREWORD

THE SYLVA of western North America is the most impressive and humanly significant in the world. For here grow the tallest of all forest trees and the densest stands of merchantable timber. Foremost in the minds of even those who have never seen our Pacific coast are the two Sequoias — the California Bigtree and the Coast Redwood — which for age, girth, and height are unsurpassed. But there are many other trees that closely rival them, such as the Sitka Spruce, the Douglas Fir, the Sugar Pine, the Western Hemlock, the Port Orford Cedar, each one the mightiest of its genus anywhere and in itself a magnificent natural resource. Altogether, the trees of the Pacific coast, from the fjords of Alaska to the fog belt of northern California, contain one-fourth of all the saw timber in North America and constitute a forest that, greater than the sylva of any other equal area on earth, crowns the continent with natural splendor.

In particular is this a region of conifers; no province of comparable size can boast anything like as many kinds of softwoods. And the conifers are the most generally useful and valuable of all trees. They furnish this land not only with dimension timbers of a size unequaled, and vast quantities of lumber in all sizes, but they answer such exacting needs as wood for airplane construction, for the sounding boards of musical instruments, pulpwoods of long fiber, veneers for plywood and prefabs, and cellulose in all but inexhaustible quantities for plastics, synthetic textiles, and hardboard. No wonder that the wood resources of western North America are the wonder and envy of the world.

Nor can the trees of the West be computed completely either in dollars or board feet of lumber. They are a benign presence, mighty and healing, for the many who come to them. Let one but speak the name of any of the greatest of the National Parks of the West — Sequoia, Yosemite, Rocky Mountain, Glacier, Rainier or Olympic —

and in the mind rise those titan forests, benison in the sweep of their boughs, in the breath of their sighing needles. As for our National Forests, they are the greatest scientifically managed forests in the world, straddling the mountain watersheds and crossing whole states with woodland wilderness. Even on the deserts are found strange and beautiful trees, mostly of tropical affinities, and many a roof in town and even city still keeps guardian boughs above it.

Trees have entered into the history of the West to an extent rather neglected by historians, absorbed as they are apt to be in political and economic events. In the first place, trees were, and remain in many regions, intimately connected with the lives of the Indians; the Canoe Cedar was to the Alaskan Indians in itself almost a way of life; so was the Mesquite to the desert tribes. Keen observers of Nature, the Indians knew their trees in every property, and lived by and with them in a way scarcely known to civilized man save in the brief decades of pioneering.

The first white explorers of the West, from Lewis and Clark and Father Serra to Frémont and the Pacific Railway surveyors, were companioned all the way by trees, and many of them, like David Douglas and Thomas Nuttall, were keen field naturalists who have much that is significant to tell us of the virgin forests. Those who came after them, to "settle up" the great spaces, could not, where the forests were dense, build a house, or even a fire, without considering the trees. Nowhere else in the world, not even in the densest tropical jungles or the vastest expanses of the Siberian *taiga* have trees so profoundly influenced the migrations, the destinies, and the lives of human beings. Even the cowboy, spurring the treeless range, from the beginning sat a saddletree made of a native western wood, and thrust his feet into stirrups of another, while he built his corral of a third, his ranch house of a fourth. His cattle, browsing the nutritious pods of a fifth kind of tree, so spread it by its seeds that in modern times it has gone on the march, invading the grasslands.

To tell a little of a few of these things — something, for instance, about the titanic growth of the lumber industry, something about the astounding discoveries of modern wood technology, a little about the Indians and their ethnobotany, with passing references to Western history and famous characters as associated with trees — is one aim of this book; no attempt has been made to treat any of these subjects exhaustively.

Another purpose is to assist in the identification of Western trees.

For until one knows the name of a tree one cannot ask questions about it, or trace it in books of reference, or, indeed, even think of it clearly. Named, it is a good companion throughout the days of high holiday in Western glory spots, serving to keep more truly alive the memories of that happiness. With a little study and familiarity it becomes possible to identify many sorts even from trains and planes, and such recognition richly peoples the scene, adding a deep new perspective.

The approach to tree identification is here made in two ways. The most instinctive, requiring no previous training, is by searching through this book for a picture resembling the specimen in hand. This is not an unsound method, providing that one thereupon verifies the resemblance by a careful reading of the description, which has been couched in language using the minimum of technical terms: such technical words as are employed are explained in the brief glossary. Secondly, field keys are provided, for the botanically minded, at the back of this book.

The present work deals only with native trees. No exotic species, such as the citrus fruits and the Eucalyptus, however common or important, can be included lest they overwhelm these pages, and the reader. For the same reason it has proved impossible to include any hybrids, natural or man-made.

The Latin nomenclature endeavors to follow the latest International Rules, and to keep abreast of the important recent revisions of genera by specialists. But this is not to say that every "earlier" name that someone has proposed for exhumation has been adopted. To do this would be to drift with every whimsical breeze of opinion, and arrive nowhere. In the matter of varieties of species, only a very few have been adopted. This is not to deny the botanical validity of the varieties ignored here. But based, as so many are, upon minute variations in the shape and pubescence of leaves, they are too hair-splitting, and of too uncertain permanence, to interest the general reader. The large Latin synonymy that has grown up through the years, owing to changing concepts of species and accidental duplication of names, has not been given space in the body of the text but is relegated to the Index where the interested student will find it cross-referenced to the name accepted in this book.

In the selection of English or common names, it has seemed best to give a generous, but not a complete, list for each tree. True, attempts have recently been made by some foresters to give each species a distinctive name not duplicated by any other species, but the effect, laudable in theory, results sometimes in putting forward as *the* "common name" a name which is in fact quite uncommon, or coined for the occasion and not in use anywhere. The correct common name of a tree, one may hold, is the name used by the man to whom you are speaking. As an example, a tree such as *Thuja plicata,* the Canoe Cedar, is called one thing by lumbermen, another by Indians, a third by ranchers, a fourth by foresters, a fifth by your woods guide, a sixth by nurserymen and landscape architects, and a seventh, perhaps, by the distinguished visiting professor of botany from the Yale School of Forestry. Obviously it were unwise to suggest to a man of any of these callings that you know better than he!

The circumscriptions of this book — the range which it attempts to cover — can best be understood by a glance at the map in the end papers. The boundaries furnished by the Pacific Ocean and the Arctic Sea are, of course, wholly natural, and the Mexican Boundary is completely familiar. On the east, the 100th meridian proved, upon much study, to be the most satisfactory dividing line in most of the United States. There are only about twenty species, out of more than two hundred, which cross this boundary between the western and the northwestern sylvas, and approximately the same number, though quite a different lot of species, do so in Texas where the western and southern floras just meet on the almost treeless plains.

Within this area is treated here every native species which, in the judgment of the author, reaches tree size. True that no perfectly satisfactory definition separates trees clearly from shrubs; the sharper one tries to make such a distinction, the more absurdities and contradictions one raises. In general, however, the author has fought to keep out of the book as many shrub-like species as possible, in order to let the trees rise clear. With these more than two hundred native species the author has been preoccupied for many happy years; it is his hope the reader may enjoy his own excursions among them.

D. C. P.

ACKNOWLEDGMENTS

Numerous persons have given of their expert knowledge by criticizing portions of the manuscript. The author is grateful to Mr. W. E. Crosby of Seattle, editor of *The Lumberman,* for reading the text of the conifers and making most valuable suggestions and corrections. Mr. John W. Duffield of the Institute of Forest Genetics, Placerville, California, critically read the material on Pines and Sequoias, while Dr. Philip G. Haddock of the College of Forestry, University of Washington, Seattle, reviewed all the rest of the book. Dr. Cornelius Muller of the University of California has read the text and the key to the Oaks and made valuable suggestions. Mr. Harold Gladwin of Santa Barbara, authority on Southwestern archaeology and tree-ring dating, kindly contributed several pages in his speciality for the essay on Pinyon Pine. Dr. William Dayton of Forest Service, United States Department of Agriculture, was so good as to assist in deciding on certain details in taxonomic botany. Mr. Weldon Heald of Portal, Arizona, collected Pine specimens for the author and furnished valuable notes, while Father Maynard Geiger (O.S.F.) offered his notes on the life and travels of Padre Junípero Serra. Through the kindness of the National Park Service, specimens were sent to the illustrator from many Western states.

For permission to use quotations, of more than 75 words, from various books and articles whose copyright is still in force, grateful acknowledgment is made to the following publishers, institutions, and authors when living: *Death Comes for the Archbishop* by Willa Cather (Alfred Knopf); *Adventures With A Texas Naturalist* by Roy Bedichek (Doubleday); *Piñon Country* by Haniel Long (Duell, Sloane and Pierce); *Sagas of the Evergreens* by Frank Lamb (W. W. Norton); *Trees and Shrubs of Mexico* by Paul C. Standley (Smithsonian Institution); *The Mountains of California* by John Muir (Appleton-Century); *The Wyoming Guide* (Oxford Press); "White Pine, My Lady of the North" by Nancy Rowen Warren (*American Forests*); "Remember 1910!" by Stanley Koch (*American Forests*); "Wood For American Archers" by A. E. Andrews (*American Forests*); "Douglas Fir" by E. H. Frothingham, Forest Service (U.S. Department of Agriculture); "The Trees and Forests" by Mary Tresidder, in *The Sierra Nevada,* edited by Roderick Peattie (Viking); "Uses of Plants by the Indians of the Missouri River Region" by Melvin Randolph Gilmore, Bureau of American Ethnology (Smithsonian Institution); *The Silva of California* by Willis Linn Jepson (University of California Press); *Silva of North America* by Charles Sprague Sargent, Arnold Arboretum (Houghton Mifflin); *The Border and the Buffalo* by John R. Cook, R. R. Donnelly and Sons (The Lakeside Press); *Fray Juan Crespí* by Herbert Bolton (University of California Press).

Professor Emanuel Fritz of the University of California kindly granted permission to quote from his writings on the Redwood.

Selections from this book appeared in advance of publication in the following magazines: *American Forests, Atlantic Monthly, Arizona Highways, Colorado Wonderland, Country Gentleman, Natural History, Nature Magazine, Pacific Discovery, Pacific Spectator, Reader's Digest, Sunset,* and *Westways.* The author is grateful to these distinguished periodicals for permission to reprint those portions of his book which they published.

THE SEQUOIAS
(*Sequoia*)

THESE TITANIC TREES, with lobed or fluted and massive trunks, possess two barks, a very thick, furrowed, fibrous and corky outer cortex and a close, firm, and thin inner integument. The short, stout branches give rise to lateral deciduous twigs. Foliage is of two sorts, that on immature trees and young shoots bristling all around the stem, and in outline very narrowly elliptical, while the leafage of mature growth is either scale-like and closely overlapping, or like a flattened needle and spreading; sometimes both forms appear on the same branch.

The minute, solitary, unisexual flowers appear from buds formed the previous autumn. Terminal in the axils of the upper leaves, the male flowers consist in numerous spirally disposed stamens subtended by closely overlapping bracts; each stamen terminates in a little umbrella-like connective from which are suspended the spherical numerous anthers. The female flowers, which are terminal on the twigs, form the aggregate conelets having 5 to 7 ovules in 2 rows borne naked in the axils of short bracts adherent to the woody keeled scales of the cone. The cone, pendulous and small, is formed of a few thick and woody scales which are enlarged at the outer end (surface of the cone) and are traversed on the end by a depressed line, and bear large deciduous resin glands. Even after the opening of the scales and the escape of the seeds (5 to 7 under each scale) on their membranous wings, the cones, which mature in the first or second season, may persist on the twig for several more.

The Sequoias are normally and, from a strict botanical viewpoint, correctly placed not at the beginning of the conifers but further on, following the Firs and preceding the Incense Cedars. However, in view of the great interest they arouse, and their indisputable kingship, as to size and antiquity, over all the western sylva, it has seemed permissible and appropriate to place them at the opening of this book.[1]

[1] The old genus *Sequoia* has recently been separated by Buchholz into two genera, *Sequoia* proper for the Coast Redwood and *Sequoiadendron* for the Bigtree. On philosophic grounds this is probably correct but in view of the vast literature on these trees wherein both are considered Sequoias, it has seemed best, in a book of this sort which makes no attempt at being a taxonomic revision, to retain *Sequoia* in its more classic and inclusive form.

*   *   *

GIANT SEQUOIA

Sequoia gigantea (Lindley) Decaisne

OTHER NAMES: Sierra Redwood. Gigantea. Mammoth-tree. California Bigtree.

RANGE: Western slopes of the Sierra Nevada in California, between 4500 and 8000 feet altitude, Placer County south to Tulare County, chiefly in some 26 isolated groves.

DESCRIPTION: *Bark* rich reddish brown, becoming on old trees 1 to 2 feet thick, very deeply furrowed, with rounded, very large ridges (4 or 5 inches broad), the fibrous outer scales purple-tinged, the inner ones bright cinnamon-red. *Twigs* slender, becoming, after the leaves die off, reddish purple and scaly. *Flowers* — male terminal on the branches, borne in large quantities all over the tree, female with 25 to 40 pale yellow, gradually pointed scales. *Leaves* ⅛ to ¼ inch long, overlapping on the twig, and, at least in their lower half, closely pressed to it (or longer and more spreading on leading shoots), rigid, sharp-pointed, concave on the upper surface, rounded on the lower, marked on both faces with bands of stomata. *Cones* 2 to 3½ inches long, 1½ to 2¼ inches wide, dark reddish brown, the deeply pitted scales thickened gradually from base to dilated apex, the long tip reflexed and marked above with resin glands. *Seeds* compressed, ⅛ to ¼ inch long, light brown, surrounded by a pair of united wings. *Wood* very light (18 pounds per cubic foot, dry weight), soft, weak, coarse-grained and brittle, turning dark on exposure.

The kingdom of the plants has a king, the Giant Sequoia or California Bigtree. It is, as a race, the oldest and mightiest of living things. Not even in past geologic times, apparently, were greater trees than *Sequoia gigantea.* Only the Bigtree's closest of kin, the Redwood of the California coast, approaches it in longevity and girth. In grace and height, indeed, the Coast Redwood, *Sequoia sempervirens,* is a queen among trees, a fit mate for the craggier grandeur of the Bigtree of the Sierra Nevada.

Constituting all that is left of the once widespread genus *Sequoia,* these two species have found asylum in California but they salute each other from widely separated mountain systems. The Redwoods inhabit

the north Coast Ranges where they are maintained in a coolhouse atmosphere by long baths in sea fogs, unviolated by storms. In contrast, the home of the Giant Sequoia, lying between 6000 and 8000 feet altitude on the western slopes of the Sierra, is Olympian, as befits this Jovian tree. There the winters have an annual snowfall of 10 to 12 feet, but drifts may pile up among the titans almost 30 feet deep — a mere white anklet to such trees. The summers are exceedingly dry; if rain does fall it is apt to come with violent thunderstorms and lightning bolts that have been seen to rive a gigantic Sequoia from the crown to the roots. Those who know the species best maintain that it never dies of disease or senility. If it survives the predators of its infancy and the hazard of fire in youth, then only a bolt from heaven can end its centuries of life. Perhaps, if this majestic tree had a will, it would prefer to go this way, by an act of God.

The province of the Giant Sequoias is measured out on the planetary surface between the 36th and the 39th degrees north latitude, a distance of 250 miles. But you will not happen upon any single Bigtree in this range, for it grows only in groves, to be sought out by pilgrimage. Each Sequoia grove has its associations and history, and thus they have all received names — the Giant Forest, the Mariposa, Calaveras and General Grant groves, to mention only the most famous and accessible. Others bear such suggestive titles as Lost Grove, Dead Grove, Surprise Grove, and Big Stump Grove. Some are so remote from roads and sightseers that they are seldom visited save by forest rangers on their rounds. In all, there are, by the most particularized classification, some 71 of them, or there were until several of the finest were ruthlessly destroyed with dynamite, axe, saw, and fire. It is certain that all have been discovered, and all too likely that Nature will never spontaneously create any more.

Stranger still, there seem to have been no more even long before the coming of the white man. At least, so thought John Muir who for years combed the mountains looking for traces of extinct groves and a more continuous distribution. Logs of Gigantea, which are now straddled by other living Bigtrees of great age, show no signs of decay in the heartwood after perhaps 10,000 years since they began to grow. So it should have been possible, surely, to find traces of Sequoia growth outside the present groves had there been any. But Muir's fruitless search drove him to conclude that in post-glacial times, at least, the Bigtrees had already found all the places where they could flourish.

Thus, to see the Bigtrees you must travel far and climb high. It is the better part of a day's run to them by car from San Francisco or Los Angeles, with an inescapable crossing of the flat San Joaquin Valley — in summer a furnace for heat. Then you wind for a long way through the foothills, among shadeless Digger Pines and Interior Live Oaks whose glittering foliage hurts the eyes. There it was that the Forty-niners toiled, in their lust tearing up the beds of rivers and sluicing down the very hills. But, serene above such ant-work of a day, stood the Giant Sequoias, undreamed of by the fevered Argonauts, holding themselves aloof with the confidence of a thousand years.

Up through groves of Black Oak and Blue, of grand Yellow Pines and Incense Cedars, you mount, up and up into the realm of White Firs, symmetrical with tier on tier of whorled boughs, the trunks as satiny as flesh. Somber Douglas Firs darken the late afternoon as with oncoming night. At last the Sugar Pines with rugged purple trunks, the mightiest Pines in all the world, close ranks about you.

It will be dusky, no doubt, when you reach the giant groves. And the forest will be still, yet watchfully alive. A deer may come to your outheld hand and put an inquisitive black muzzle in it. It will be a long moment before you realize that the vasty shadow behind the little doe is not shade but a tree trunk so gigantic that you cannot comprehend at first that this is a living thing. Were that great bole put down in a city street, it would block it from curb to curb. That mighty bough, the lowest one, is still so high above the ground that it would stretch out over the top of a 12-story office building. If it were cut off and stood in the ground, it would in itself appear as a tree perhaps 70 feet high, and 7 feet in diameter at the base. As for the crown, it is as lost to accurate measurement and comprehension as your head would be, seen by a beetle at your shoe.

Yet the trees conceal their true immensity by the very perfection of proportion. For each part — breadth at base, spread of boughs, thickness of trunk, shape of crown is in calm Doric harmony with the rest. There is no obvious exaggeration of any part, no law-defying attenuation. Even the enormously distended bases by which the giants grip the mountainside and brace the gigantic superstructure have a look of functional rightness, so that we hardly realize that they may be 100 feet in circumference.

On second view, by morning light, the impression of the Giant Sequoias is still not so much of outsize as of color and candor. The ruddy trunks, especially in the more southern groves, are richly bright.

The metallic green of the foliage is the gayest of all Sierra conifers'. In winter a Sequoia grove has the simple colors of a flag — a forest-soft red, white, and green. In summer the white ground is changed for the faultless blue of Sierran skies. The bright world is never shut away, as in the misty dimness of the Coast Redwood groves with their over-arching canopy. The sunlight here reaches right to the floor. The bracing air, a shining but invisible god, moves proud and life-giving in its temple. Instead of the hush of the Redwoods, you hear among the Bigtrees the lordly racket of the pileated woodpeckers at irreverent carpentry on Sequoia wood. The Douglas squirrels frisk up the mon-strous boles as familiarly as children on their fathers. Running out on the boughs, they cut the cones and then scamper 200 feet to earth, to despoil them of their seeds.

Sooner or later everyone asks which is the largest of all the Giganteas. Yet no pat answer should be given. For the tallest are not the greatest in girth, the thickest are not the highest. Further, trees that were felled long ago give indications that they were larger and loftier than any now standing. The General Grant tree is 271 feet high. The Boole tree, at 16 feet above the ground, is 25 feet in diameter — the record among standing trees — while the Hart tree is the tallest of all, at 281 feet 6 inches. These measurements were made in 1928–29 by a trained engineer with the best of instruments, but time does not call them final.

In the Calaveras North Grove lies prone the tree called Father of the Forest, inside whose hollow trunk a man rode horseback without

having to bend his head. In the Big Stump Basin are two truncated
witnesses of boles that were once 30 feet in diameter when their bark
was still on them. Of the same diameter was a colossus of the Calaveras
North Grove, traditionally believed the first Bigtree ever seen by a
white man. In accordance with the ebullience of our pioneering spirit,
it was speedily cut down and made into a dance floor where 30 couples
at a time could waltz.

The discovery of this tree was made one spring day in 1852 when a
miner from Murphy's Camp pursued a grizzly bear far up into tall
timber. When Mr. A. T. Dowd (for history has preserved the name
of this Nimrod) encountered the Bigtrees, his astonishment was so great
that he allowed the bear to get away. True, the Bigtrees seem to have
been sighted several times before by exploring parties, but as the journals and diaries that mention them were not published till long afterwards, hunter Dowd's discovery stands, like Columbus's of America,
as the first effective one. At any rate, his fellow miners came, incred-
ulous, and beheld 50 acres of what we now call the Calaveras North
Grove, covered with trees some of them 325 feet high and 19 feet in
diameter. The men departed, to spread the fame of the "Mammoth
Trees" as they were at first called. And within a month or so of their
discovery by Dowd, somebody now forgotten gathered specimens of
branches, leaves and cones which somebody else passed on, in June
of 1852, to the excellent Dr. Albert Kellogg, pioneer botanist of California. But Dr. Kellogg was a man of leisurely habits and did not
hasten to publish in a botanical way on the great discovery. In fact it
does not appear that he had roused himself to visit the Mammoth
Trees when, two years later, he showed his specimens to William Lobb
who had recently arrived to collect plants for a British nursery estab-
lishment. With swift initiative Lobb set out for the Calaveras Grove,
hastily gathered herbarium specimens, hurried back to San Francisco
and, without saying a word to any American scientists, took the first
boat to England.

There he turned his specimens over to John Lindley, an English botanist who rushed a formal botanical publication into print by December of 1853, naming the mighty conifer *Wellingtonia gigantea,* in
honor of Arthur Wellesley, Duke of Wellington and victor of Waterloo,
who was then still alive to be flattered by having the mightiest production of Nature named in his honor.

Loud was the patriotic anguish of the American botanists. But fortunately the generic name of *Sequoia* for the Coast Redwoods had been

published in Germany six years before *Wellingtonia*, giving it priority, and when it was realized that the Bigtrees too are Sequoias, Americans were satisfied. For the name was bestowed in honor of Chief Sequoyah, the great Cherokee who devoted his life to inventing an Indian alphabet and teaching others to read it.

It was a disappointed gold seeker, G. H. Woodruff of New York State, who climbed up into the Bigtree groves in the early fifties and threw himself down, homesick, upon his back. As he lay gazing into the green crowns, the cones snipped off by the chickarees came plumping down all about him. He began to examine them and shake out their seeds. Soon he had a great many and put them for transport in an empty snuff box. Back at camp he wrapped up the little box and prepaid a charge of $25 to send it east by Pony Express. So the first seeds reached the nursery firm of Ellwanger and Barry in Rochester, New York, and from them sprang up in 1855 four thousand tiny trees. They did not sell very fast in the eastern states, but in England where they were retailed, as Wellingtonias of course, they sold so rapidly that orders could not be filled. Botanical gardens in England, France and Germany wanted specimens. Cities planted avenues of Sequoias. Soon every man of wealth or title must have a specimen for his grounds. "The great event of the year 1864," wrote Tennyson's son in a memoir of his poet father, "was the visit of Garibaldi to the Tennysons, an incident of which was the planting of a Wellingtonia by the great Italian and ceremonies connected with it." Eventually Ellwanger and Barry paid over to the fortune hunter Woodruff the sum of $1036.60 as his share in the profits — on a snuffboxful of seeds!

Californians were even then unabashed in the claims they made for their state, including the age of Gigantea. They asserted that these trees were old when the Pyramids were abuilding. Even so eminent an authority (on fishes!) as Dr. David Starr Jordan assured the press they had endured 10,000 years. John Muir counted the annual rings on the biggest stump he ever saw and found over 4000, but not more. Even that can no longer be verified, and is suspect of error. Accurate ring counts in recent times have never put the age of any logged tree at more than 3200 years.

Yet surely thirty centuries of life are awe-inspiring. There is something comforting about handling a section of Sequoia wood that seems scarcely less living now than when it grew before the time of Christ. For the proof of its age is there under your naked eyes, the annual rings which you can tick off like dates on a calendar — the years and the decades, the centuries and the tens of centuries. Somewhere about two inches inside the bark of a tree recently cut will be the rings laid down in 1849, year of the gold fever, and of the still more feverish 1850. Yet nothing of moment is graven for that time on the wooden tablets of Sequoia history. And it is humbling to notice that those particular rings may be 15 feet from the center of the tree, the starting point of its growth. The calm deposition of the rings (rosy-pink spring wood ending in the sudden dark band of summer wood) has gone on millimeter by millimeter for millennium after millennium — advancing ripples in the tide of time.

Why, out of a world of trees, do these live longest? Why is a Cottonwood decrepit at 75 years of age, why does the Oak live three hundred summers? And since it can do so, why does it not endure a thousand? How does the Giant Sequoia go on growing, without signs of senility, until literally blasted from the earth by a bolt from heaven, a consuming fire, a seismic landslide or a charge of dynamite?

One answer may lie in the very sap, for that of the Bigtrees contains tannic acid, a chemical used in many fire extinguishers. Though fire will destroy the thin-barked young Sequoias, when bark has formed on the old specimens it may be a foot and more thick and practically like asbestos. The only way that fire can penetrate it is when inflammable material becomes piled against the base and, fanned to a blowtorch by the mountain wind, sears its way through to the wood. Even then fire seems never to consume a great old specimen, no matter how it devours its heart. And the high tannin content of the sap has the same healing action that tannic acid has on our flesh when we apply it to a burn. The repair of fire damage by a Bigtree is almost miraculous. It begins at once, and even if the wound is so wide that it would take a thousand years to cover it, the courageous vegetable goes about the business as if time were nothing to it.

So we might say that Gigantea lives long because fire and parasites seldom succeed in storming its well-defended citadel. We might say all this and more, yet there remains some quantum of the inexplicable, and in the end we are forced to admit that Sequoias come of a long-lived race — whatever that means — and so outlast the very races of man.

All this sempiternal life, all these tons and tons of vegetation, come from a flaky seed so small that it takes 3000 of them to make up one ounce. The kernel is but ¼ inch long, and inside it lies curled the embryonic monarch. There are commonly from 96 to 304 seeds to a cone, and the cones themselves are almost ridiculously small for so mammoth a tree. They do not mature till the end of the second season and not until the end of the third, at the earliest, do they open their scales in dry weather and loose the seeds which drift but a little way from the parent tree. Their method of transport is not only weak, but their viability is low; perhaps only half of the seeds have the vitality to sprout. And long before they do so, they are attacked, in the cone and out of it, by untold multitudes of squirrels and jays. Many do not fall upon suitable ground — mineral soil laid bare — but are lost in the duff of the forest floor. Of a million seeds on a tree in autumn, perhaps only one is destined to sprout when the snow-water and the sun of the late mountain spring touch it with quickening fingers.

First the sprouting seed sends down a slim spear of a root. Swiftly this makes its way down about two inches and puts out its suckling root hairs. Only then does the first shoot appear, bearing four or five baby leaves still wearing the jaunty cap of the seed hull. Within a week or ten days the blades burst apart and the infant bonnet is flung away. Only now the tiny seedlings face further perils. They are attacked from below by cutworms, above by armies of black wood ants. Ground squirrels and chipmunks, finches and sparrows cock a bright eye at them and pull them up for a toothsome salad. Deer browse them by the thousands. If a seedling survives its first year, it may face the centuries with some confidence.

Underground, the taproot is descending faster than the shoot goes up, but at six to eight years it stops and thereafter only lateral growth takes place. Eventually the side roots will become gigantic and spread out in all their ramifications over two or three acres. A tree 300 feet high has roots whose circle has a radius of 200 feet, and occasionally the roots are longer than the height of the tree.

Up into the light and air grows the princeling. The youthful leaves are soft, glaucous blue-green; the bark is still smooth and gray with no hint of red about it. The stocky shape of childhood gives way to a conical outline and the young tree stands clothed to the base in boughs that droop gracefully at the tip, of wood strong yet supple. These lower boughs help to brace the trees against the weight of the great snows of the Sierran winter which will drift higher than young trees and bury and bend them. When the snows melt, the striplings shake off the last loads from lithe arms and lift shining heads and they are "gey bonny," as Muir might have said in his Scots idiom, as they stand ranked close about some dewy, iris-spangled, deer-browsed meadow formed where one of their ancestors has fallen and blocked a stream to make a sedgy bog.

In the second century of life, the trees begin to assume a "pole form" — that is, with strong central trunk clear of branches for a long way, and a high peaked crown. Gone now are the drooping limber boughs of youth. In their place great arms begin to appear, leaving the trunk at right angles and then, bending up as if at elbows, lift leafy hands in a gesture of hosannah. The soft blue-green foliage is replaced by metallic green. The smooth gray cortex gives way to the richly red bark of maturity. At last it is furrowed thicker than the brow of Zeus, and in the gales its voice begins, these years (and hundreds of years), to take on the deepest tone in the world's sylva.

When a Giant Sequoia flowers the trees are loaded with millions of male and female conelets from as early as November to late in February. The greeny-gold pollen showers all over the giant's body and drifts in swirls upon the pure sheet of snows. A single tree will bear hundreds of thousands of cones when in the full vigor of its life.

Great age brings to the trees a diminished fertility — fewer cones, that is, but not less viability of seed. It sees the heroic self-pruning of the older boughs which at last break off of their own weight. Electric bolts may repeatedly strike the monstrous lightning-rod, topping it unmercifully. The once broad and symmetrical crown becomes broken and craggy. The tremendous strains of the superstructure have resulted in gigantic buttressing at the base. The whole tree is now as far past the manly beauty of its prime as that is past the pretty charm of its childhood. It is, after thirty centuries, practically a geological phenomenon.

In the wood corresponding changes take place with the slow passage of time. The fibers of young trees are supple and all the wood, for the first hundred years, is light yellow sapwood with dark orange bands of summer wood to mark the years. Only in the second century does the dark rose heartwood, deeply impregnated with tannin, begin to form, first a slim pencil that increases, in a thousand years or so, till it becomes most of the vast cylinder of the trunk. The wood at the base of an ancient tree is all contorted and tough with the compressions and strains of carrying some 600 tons of body above it. That at middle heights is straight-grained, rose-red and, when fresh, so wet that it sinks in water. At the top of the tree the wood is pink, and lightly buoyant.

All the properties of Sequoia wood save one are inferior to those of nearly every other timber tree in our sylva. Its chief virtue is that it lasts perdurably. In consequence, it was early sought out by lumbermen for shingles, shakes, flumes, fence stakes and poles. The giant groves promised ready fortunes, by the look of them. Stumpage that scaled at from 20,000 to 120,000 board feet per tree promised fair!

So logging railroads were hurried up the mountains, mills were set up, and the Lilliputian lumberjacks fell to work among these woody Gullivers. First a 6-foot platform was erected to clear the flaring buttresses, and on it stood two men to chop a cut; chips 18 inches long flew out, till a gigantic notch was cut. When this was 10 feet deep, the fallers took a 20-foot saw around to the other side of the tree, and for several days they dragged it back and forth, all the while greasing it to make it slip, and stopping to drive great wedges behind it lest the tons of wood above begin to settle and vengefully trap the saw. At the last a few heavy gluts were sledged home and the vast structure leaned, toppled, kicked back with a terrible lunge, then struck the earth with a cracking of limbs and a seismic shock that could be felt and heard a mile away.

In this wise was accomplished the destruction of the Converse Basin grove, probably finer than any now standing. Today in the Converse Basin there are few seedling Sequoias to give hope that this species will grow there abundantly again. Instead there are thousands of logs that were never utilized because they proved too big or costly to handle, millions of board feet gone to waste because the wood smashed to bits in its fall. The whole ghastly enterprise ended in financial failure, but not a failure of destruction. That was complete.

To the ruin of lumbering there was soon added a worse one, the fires deliberately set by sheepherders to improve the annual browse; these consumed thousands of young trees, Sequoias of the future. And this havoc was wreaked not upon private lands but upon the public domain. The long battle to save the Bigtrees was begun, so far as the Giant Forest is concerned, by Colonel George W. Stewart, a newspaper editor of Visalia, California, who roused public sentiment where there had been apathy. He was joined by one public-spirited citizen after another, by newspapers and magazines in California and finally in the eastern states. When fraudulent surveys and applications for possession of the Sequoia groves were made under the old Timber and Stone law, Colonel Stewart detected them and brought about suspensions of the applications. When a Secretary of the Interior lifted the suspensions, forty men of Visalia marched into the near-by groves to file private claims and so save the trees for the nation. Victory came in 1890 when Sequoia and General Grant National Parks were created. Even then, without a national park service to patrol these reserves, stockmen and timber thieves continued to violate the public domain, until John Muir's demand for a troop of cavalry to patrol the parks was finally acted upon by President Theodore Roosevelt. Today General Grant Park has been merged with the much larger Kings Canyon Park (the dream of Muir's life), and thus, with the inclusion of other fine Sequoia groves in Yosemite Park, the future of the king of trees seems assured. It seems so, but the forces that wish to unlock the national parks for private exploitation never sleep, and the vigilance of the forces of conservation must not do so either.

COAST REDWOOD

Sequoia sempervirens (Lambert) Endlicher

OTHER NAMES: California Redwood. Coastal Sequoia. Sempervirens. Palo Colorado.

RANGE: In the fog belt of the California coast though usually, at present, not at the shore but 1 to 30 miles east of it, in the lower Coast Ranges and intermountain valleys, from the Oregon boundary (and 8 miles north of it) south to Marin County, north of San Francisco Bay. Reappearing in the Santa Cruz and Santa Lucia Mountains and down to sea level at Big Sur.

DESCRIPTION: *Bark* of old trees very thick (3 inches to 1 foot), coarsely fibrous, fissured in rounded ridges with dark brown scales which are cross-checked and, when they fall, reveal the bright cinnamon underbark. *Twigs* spreading in two ranks to form a flat spray of foliage, slender, the leading shoot covered, a few years after the leaves no longer clothe them, with scaly bark. Leaves of mature shoots ¼ to ½ inch long, ⅛ inch wide, appearing to lie all in one plane on the twig, flat, needle-like or awl-shaped, usually tipped with a rigid, slender point, dark green and shiny above, the lower surface obscurely keeled and marked by 2 narrow bands of stomata; leaves on leading shoots and juvenile growth generally are half as long, broader, bristling around the stem in all directions; they turn rusty before dropping off. *Flowers* — male obtuse, green, composed of about 12 anthers, female terminal, green, with about 20 spirally overlapping scales tipped with acute, incurved points. *Cones* ¾ to 1 inch long, when unopened ½ inch broad, the scales enlarged from narrow claws abruptly dilated into the grooved disk-like limb of the scales. *Seed* light brown, ⅟₁₆ inch long, with a wing equally long. *Wood* light (26 pounds to the cubic foot, dry weight), soft, weak, easily split, close-grained, light red.

The Redwood, the ever-living Sequoia, *sempervirens,* is the tallest tree in the world. Not just occasionally taller, in individual specimens growing under unprecedentedly favorable conditions, but taller as a whole, as a race, a titan race. Also it produces logs with the greatest diameter amongst all timber trees. Only the Redwood's big brother, the California Bigtree, *Sequoia gigantea* of the Sierra Nevada is ever greater in girth, but Gigantea is not today in the class of prime timber tree.

True, too, that the Bigtree lives longer, but Redwoods live long enough to awe the mind. A Redwood has a normal life expectancy of 1000 to 1500 years. The oldest specimen whose rings have been counted is estimated to be 2200 years old; a section of this log is preserved, for the doubting, in the Richardson Grove, part of California's state park system. So that tree began to grow when Hannibal was taking his elephants over the Alps; it was more than 200 years old at the birth of Jesus.

In all the world there is no other forest growth like that of the Redwood. It is at once the tallest and the densest of stands — not dense like the jungle's tangled quantities of trees, lianas, and undergrowth, for the Redwood groves are spaciously open to your footsteps — but dense in sheer volume of standing timber. Instances are on record of a growth of 2,500,000 board feet to the acre, and from a single tree have been sawed out 490,000 board feet of lumber. Up in the Redwood country they show you churches and banks and wooden mansions, each built out of a single tree.

The Redwood forest stretches all the way from extreme southwestern Oregon southward for 450 miles. It is, however, a narrow belt, averaging only about 20 miles in width and lying sometimes close to the Pacific, again 30 or 40 miles inland from it, as it follows the wandering crest of the Coast Ranges from Oregon to the Golden Gate. A detached province of it lies south of San Francisco in the Santa Cruz Mountains, and another in the Santa Lucia Mountains south of Carmel. But it is in northwesternmost California that these trees grow tallest and most densely; there the growth is most ancient and the quality of timber best, where the precipitation runs as high as 100 inches. Such an annual drenching would do credit to a tropical rain forest, the more as it falls all in the winter and spring months. The summers are rainless, but even then the Redwood belt is almost nightly blanketed in heavy sea fogs, and though these burn off in the morning, they frequently roll back during the day to saturate the atmosphere in which grows so deep the vegetation carpet of the Redwood forest floor — all the evergreen mosses, and the ferns of a Carboniferous luxuriance. Nowhere is the Redwood separated from these summer fogs.

To see the heart of the greatest Redwoods of all, take U.S. Highway 101 north from San Francisco. For nearly 200 miles you travel through the brilliant sunlight of the dusty interior California summer. Fields are open or, if there are woods of Oak and Pine, the light fills all their glades; wild flowers are gaudy, jays are clamorous, the swift-running stream of cars a loud, metallic current. The eyes are tired of color, the ears of sound. Then suddenly you are enfolded in the first of the centenarian groves, and for the next 40 miles, to and through the Avenue of the Giants, you are seldom out of their ancient shade. The transition is like stepping into a cloister, one infinitely more spacious and lofty than any ever raised by man, and closing the door behind you upon the bright secular world. Young and old, every visitor falls abruptly silent; cars creep slowly, the drivers conscious of the sacrilege of speed. Sooner or later you stop altogether, get out and breathe deeply; you draw yourself up achingly, trying to find some undiscovered worth in yourself to add a cubit to mere manhood.

Your footfalls make no sound on the needles and moss that have lain there for centuries. Your body casts no shadow in that green, lake-like diffused light. The goose honking of a car, the calling of a child, fade into the immensity of silence. Time, the common tick-tock of it, ceases here, and you become aware of time in another measure — out of an awesome past. For this forest has stood here since the Ice Age, and here, together with this transfixed past, is the future too, for these immense lives will outlast yours by a thousand years or so.

But this solemnity is not like that of church or tomb; it is enlivened by the soft dispute of a stream with its bed, or the swirling, blurred whistle of the black-throated gray warbler so high in the clerestory of the woods that he cannot be seen. And now and then the treetops utter a slow, distant sea-hush, a sigh that passes, and then comes again, as if it were the breathing of a life beside which our lives are as a single day. At any time in the day the mist may roll silently through the forest aisles. It may rest on the forest floor, drenching the beds of oxalis and moss; it may wander, like the incense smoke in a temple, among the trees; it may move through their crowns, leaving the forest floor quite dry. But always the strong sun comes piercing through the fogs in beams of smoky light, slant shafts that fall with unerring drama upon some high altar log swathed in the emerald cloth of Hypnum moss or bearing aloft the great tuft of a translucent fern or a spray of the phantom orchis. Many of the wild flowers of the Redwoods — the oceanspray, the sugarscoop, the deerfoot, and the inside-out-flower — are pale and delicate and small of corolla, as if the great trees had used up all the bigness at the time of creation.

And they are mighty past telling. Their enormously swelled bases are buttressed with great lynx-like claws, as if the trees gripped the earth to keep their balance. The ruddy shafts rise up, unlike almost all other trees, with scarcely any discernible taper, the sides parallel as those of columns for a hundred feet or two hundred, till they disappear in the high canopy of branches. The effect of gigantism is increased by the burls often seen on the trunks. Many other kinds of trees also produce those lumpy swellings but the Redwood's burls are in proportion to the rest of the tree — as much as six and eight feet thick. The cause of these burls is not understood but the result is the production of a heavy, hard, dark wood figured with fantastic grain. Like a potato with its "eye," a burl contains buds, and the small burls sold by the roadside will, if you put them in a dish of water, send out a ferny sprout.

When a Redwood is cut down, the high stump often sprouts from the base, giving rise to a lovely circle of sister trees. Yet they are not truly daughters of the old tree but a continuation of the same life. Again, a fallen log may send up shoots resulting in a straight row of close-ranked trees which put down roots straddling the log. This too is a continuation of the same tree life, not a new generation from seed. So that it is nearly impossible to say where a Redwood life ends; rather it changes direction and grows on — as nearly immortal as anything under the sun.

From the beginning, a Redwood is beautiful. In its seedling stage, its childhood, it is straight, graceful, covered with a lovely foliage of needles rather like a Hemlock's, dark green and glittering above, delicately silvered with lines of stomata below. Unlike the Pines, the Redwoods do not go through an awkward age, but in young and middle life they retain all their grace, all their military straightness, as they crowd down to the curving banks of the rivers, climb the slopes of the Coast Ranges, fill the flats and benches of the terrain. At this stage a Redwood forest is dusky as you walk under it, owing in part to the crowding of the trees before competition has weeded them out, but still more to the dense shade cast by the accompanying California Laurel and the Douglas Fir. But time is all on the side of the Redwoods. In the fullness of it, the fast-growing young trees will crowd out competitors, by root and by crown, till they reach the stage that ecologists call a climax forest — one which cannot be displaced by another sort unless axe or fire violently intervene.

In the climax forest there are or were specimens that pile climax upon climax! The "Captain Elam Tree," that stood on the holdings of the Little River Redwood Company, was found by log scalers to have a diameter of 20 feet and a height of 208 feet, containing enough lumber to build 22 average-sized houses. It was cut down a few years ago. A giant in the Mill Creek woods is known to be 340 feet tall and 16½ feet through. The tallest of them all, the highest tree in the world, is the Founders' Tree, in the woods at the North Dyerville Flat. It is 364 feet high, yet so lofty are its neighbors that without the figures to prove it, you would not guess this chieftain to be greater than its brothers. The age of the Founders' Tree is not known, but it is probably less than that of a tree felled in 1943 by the Union Lumber Company on Big Flat, Mendocino County. The count of its rings tallied 1728 years. Its height was 334 feet, with a stump diameter of 21 feet 6 inches. With a power-driven 22-foot saw, this ancient was laid low.

The mind pauses over the fact of such a magnificent tree, felled and sawed up into lumber. The fact brings us sharply to the realization that behind, and not far behind, the Redwood Highway and its slim ribbon of parks preserved for the public, there lies by far the greatest part of the Redwood stand, which is in the hands of lumber companies or private owners who will presumably sell if the stumpage price is attractive enough. The Redwood lumber industry is one of the most active in the country, but the public sees far less of its activity than that of most industries; public roads do not wind through most of these holdings, and visitors in the region where giants are crashing to earth are in too much danger to be welcome. The truth is that this industry, according to its own statistics, is cutting into the Redwoods at a rate that is seldom less, in recent years, than 300,000,000 board feet a year, and sometimes rises to 600,000,000.

Backed by all the inventive genius of our people, this industry has overcome, with power-driven saws and modern tractors, the obstacles to lumbering among giants which looked almost insuperable to the pioneering fathers and grandfathers of the present owners of what are among the greatest sawmills in the world. There are now about 400 sawmills, large and small, in the Redwood country, as well as some 40 shingle mills, and in the period 1899 to 1948 the industry cut about 22,000,000,000 board feet — at least a third, perhaps more, of the amount now standing. Salesmanship which can be admired for its resourcefulness is taking orders right now for Redwood in Australia, New Zealand, Central America and the eastern states, as well as in the fast-growing timber-consuming state of California itself. Trees being felled as you read this will soon be railroad ties in Peru, or banana boxes of the United Fruit Company's subsidiaries.

Must we be proud of this, or indignant? It is easy to give a quick, emotional answer, depending on our economic persuasions or our esthetic faith. But if one were appointed an arbiter with sole responsibility to do perfect justice to every conflicting interest, one would have to walk all around the question, viewing every aspect. To do that is impossible in these pages. The best that can be accomplished is to sketch very briefly the story of the white man's discovery of this tree, his great need of it, and his finally awakening consciousness that this heritage of the ages calls for some responsibility in him.

On October 10, 1769, Fray Juan Crespí, chronicler of the Portolá expedition (the first exploration that the Spanish made by land of the California coast), recorded that on the Pájaro River (near present

Watsonville) the party traveled "over plains and low hills, well forested with very high trees of a red color, not known to us. They have a very different leaf from cedars, and although the wood resembles cedar somewhat in color, it is very different and has not the same odor; moreover the wood of the trees that we have found is very brittle. In this region there is great abundance of these trees and because none of the expedition recognizes them they are named redwood from their color." Then, in 1776, Fray Pedro Font, chronicler of d'Anza's expedition to San Francisco Bay, recorded that on March 26, they saw "a few spruce trees which they call redwood, a tree that is certainly beautiful; and I believe that it is very useful for its timber, for it is very straight and tall. . . . " On March 29, on the return journey, the party descried in the distance "a very high redwood . . . rising like a great tower." Next day they came up with it; Font measured it and recorded: "I found it to be . . . some fifty *varas* high, a little more or less. [Fifty *varas* is 137 feet 6 inches.] The trunk at the foot was five and a half varas [about 14 feet 9 inches] in circumference and the soldiers said they had seen even larger ones in the mountains." [1]

So the Redwood enters into recorded history, named on sight though never seen before, and, it is significant to notice, immediately appraised for its value as lumber. Time swiftly brought increasing appreciation. When saintly old Padre Junípero Serra, founder of California's chain of missions, knew that his end was near, he ordered the mission carpenter to build a coffin out of Redwood, and in this he was buried in 1784 at Mission San Carlos Borromeo at Carmel. When the roof of this abandoned mission fell in 1852, the burial place of the good Father could not be found in the ruins, but in 1882, or 98 years after the burial, it was rediscovered, the Redwood coffin in perfectly sound condition.

The Spanish settlers used a little Redwood for beams in their churches; the Russian colonists used rather more, to judge from the numerous sawpits and stumps around Fort Ross and Bodega Bay. The Muscovite church at Fort Ross, built in 1812 of local Redwood, stands to this day. But the first real assault upon Redwood came with the Gold Rush. As early as 1850 sawmills appeared on the hills south of

1 Font's *palo alto,* his "tall tree," is still standing; from it the town of Palo Alto takes its name. As it was once a council tree of the Indians, so it is sacred in the traditions of Stanford University students, who used to guard it, the night before the football game with the University of California, from being cut down (they said) by their rivals. It is figured on the seal of the university.

San Francisco, and soon Redwood was cut for houses, barns, fences; it was carried to the mining country for sluice boxes, rockers, sheds. In 1855 the first shipment by sea went from Humboldt County to San Francisco, and that mushrooming settlement soon became a city of Redwood houses. Wharf piles, piers, bridge supports and even curbs were soon built of Redwood. Redwood gutters and eave troughs for houses became common. Aqueducts and flumes for irrigation canals were early built from it, and for outfall sewers and wooden water pipes and conduits it was found to be peerless, for not only does it not decay but the longer water runs through it the smoother become the inside walls, while iron grows rougher with grit and accretions. Every part of the United States has at some time used Redwood pipes and flumes as parts of municipal water plants or in mines. Railroad water tanks of Redwood have been built all over the country. Because Redwood splits so evenly and lasts so long, shingles were early made of it. The pioneer children of California were rocked in Redwood cradles and, in school, learned from Redwood "blackboards" made from a single plank 4 or 5 feet wide and as long, of course, as necessary. And soon the Milwaukee brewers were using Redwood vats. Presently Redwood reached the South Seas, and pearl divers in the Society Islands were making boats, with outriggers, of three Redwood planks. A more versatile wood never invaded the lumber markets of the world.

This versatility rests upon the inherent properties of the wood. For Redwood is so durable in contact with the soil and fresh, though not salt, water that it is matched by few American woods. It has slight tendency to shrink or swell, and holds paint well, making it ideal for drawers, sills, sashes, and doors. Because it is so nearly immune to the attacks of termites, it is exported to tropical lands extensively, and in California a law requires that wooden uprights under buildings be made of Redwood sunk in concrete. Owing to its lack of resin it is highly absorbent of water; when the hoses are turned on a burning Redwood house, it soaks up the water promptly. Redwood imparts no flavor of its own to liquids stored in it; in consequence the wine industry in California early began to make casks of Redwood and continues to do so to this day. Though it is not a very strong wood, absolutely speaking, it is strong in comparison to its weight. So, for light trestles and bridge supports, it early came into use, and in World War II immense quantities of it were rushed into the Pacific theater.

Redwood is a joy to carpenters, so knot-free, straight-grained, and smooth as cake under the plane. So it goes into balusters, newels, porch rails, posts, columns, moldings, flooring and siding as well as uprights, beams, doors, and shingles. As a wood for fine paneling it is a beauty. The heartwood needs no coloring but its own natural soft rich hue. More, it has an inexplicable golden gloss of its own, an halation as delicate as the shimmer on a tress of blond hair. White Redwood is produced by some of the trees near Crescent City, marvelously clear of blemishes and knots. The rare black Redwood comes from trees with extremely dark heartwood and on account of its lasting qualities is sought for tanning vats which are set below the surface of the ground. Curly Redwood comes from stumps and is highly valued for flamboyant cabinet work. But the finest grade of regular commercial timber is cut in the forests of Humboldt County. It is very soft, with a satiny surface, whitish sapwood and a terra-cotta-colored heartwood, has a straight grain, seasons well, and commands the highest price.

Although Redwood accounts for only two per cent of the timber cut in the country today, it is plainly high on the list when it comes to quality. In multiple use it is all anyone could ask of any one species, though it is spared the ignominy of being reduced to pulp, for in that direction it is of almost no promise. In sum, this is a tree around which a great lumber industry was predestined to arise; this country and many others would be poorer far without it, and will not be denied the use of it while there is Redwood to cut and the price remains within bounds. The bark, once considered a dead loss, is now sold for insulating electric water heaters, cold-storage warehouses, fur vaults, butcher shops and dairies; it is used for sound-deadening and mattress filling, for fishing floats and cork jackets, soil mulch, and even cloth and felt hats.

The first to lumber the Redwoods, back in the eighteen-thirties and eighteen-forties, merely nibbled at the woods, dropping trees small enough to be handled with pole axes and whipsaws. By 1850 a side-wheel steamer, its paddlewheels turned into pulleys, powered a steam mill of sorts on the Mendocino coast. It is said that the Chinese of Mendocino utilized the incoming and outgoing tides to drive a water mill rigged up with a Muley perpendicular saw. Later, double-bitted axes came into favor. "Fallers, or choppers, as they are known locally, work in pairs," so the veteran logger H. I. Bower recalled before the Pacific Logging Congress in 1936. "An outsider is impressed by the number of tools a set of choppers carry around with them in a Redwood operation — two axes, two eight-foot saws, one twelve-foot saw, two dozen plates, one dozen shims, ten wedges, two sledges, one pair of gun stocks, one plumb bob, twelve springboards, six pieces of staging.

"Areas are felled as units. The chopping boss — bull buck — plans the strips. A set of choppers may work anywhere from a month to three months on a strip. The timber as far as possible is felled uphill, heavy leaners being an exception. The choppers' primary concern is to fall the tree with the least amount of damage.

"After determining the direction of the fall, smaller trees, called 'bedding,' are felled into the layout to build up the low spots. The undercut is now put in. The back cut is the next step."

If the tree is out of plumb — and it easily may be as much as 4 feet, at the top of its 300 foot length, though appearing straight enough to the unaided eye — the bottom of the cut may have to be raised one inch to "take out the lean," and then raised another to make it fall in the right direction. The slightest miscalculation may send hundreds of tons of wood crashing on the loggers.

For a Redwood in death, Walt Whitman himself has spoken

> Farewell my brethren,
> Farewell O earth and sky — farewell, ye neighboring waters;
> My time has ended, my term has come.
>
> *Along the northern coast,*
> *Just back from the rock-bound shore, and the caves,*
> *In the saline air from the sea in the Mendocino country,*
> *With the surge for bass and accompaniment low and hoarse,*
> *With crackling blows of axes sounding musically driven by*
> *   strong arms,*
> *Riven deep by the sharp tongues of the axes, there in the*
> *   Redwood forest dense,*
> *I heard the mighty tree its death-chant chanting . . .*
>
> Nor yield we mournfully, majestic brothers,
> We who have grandly filled our time . . .
>
> *Thus on the northern coast*
> *In the echo of teamsters' calls and the clinking chains, and the*
> *   music of choppers' axes,*
> *The falling trunk and limbs, the crash, the muffled shriek,*
> *   the groan,*
> *Such words combined from the redwood-tree, as of voices*
> *   ecstatic, ancient and rustling*
> *The century-lasting, unseen dryads, singing, withdrawing . . .*

The chorus and indications, the vistas of coming humanity —
the settlements, features all,
In the Mendocino woods I caught . . .

Whitman saw Redwood lumbering still in its heroic age of falling by hand, when teams of twenty yoked oxen dragged the giants down the skid road to the splash dams or the harborless coast where the great logs traveled by cable from shore to schooner, or put to sea as gigantic rafts of logs towed by small steamers. But in 1881 John Dolbeer, a pioneer operator among the Eureka Redwoods, brought out of his blacksmith shop an invention that made the bullwhackers guffaw. It was a sort of donkey engine with a vertical boiler, a horizontal one-cylinder engine, and a big drum on which to wind up the tentacles of steel cable. He made these fast to a gigantic log, then opened up his engine wide. The log came thrashing down the skid road faster than the bullwhackers could cuss an ox, and the smirks died from their faces, for their jobs were gone. Today, supertractors take the place of the donkey engine, and powered saws cut short thousand-year-old lives like guillotines. The tempo of felling has risen to a *presto furioso,* with larger mills cutting up to 600,000 board feet a day. Their storage sheds may roof over ten and twelve acres each.

This is not to say that all the logging practice in the Redwood region is bad practice. On the contrary, many, though still not all, of the operators are carrying on selective logging, with the minimum of destruction to young trees. Mature and overmature trees are logged, leaving the "young" (under 400 years of age!) the light and space and soil water which they were denied by their tyrannous elders. Waste has now been cut to a low minimum, a saving at the mills that means a saving of standing trees. Fire is fought like a demon. Diesel tractors have largely replaced the donkey engines and cable systems of the past, with a great saving in damage to young trees.

The Redwood industry with a view to reforestation has set up about 100,000 acres, to date, in tree farms. More important, the current practice of logging with diesel engines makes it possible to leave scattered "seed trees" for natural reforestation. Selective logging instead of clear-cutting is now the practice on the best-regulated private holdings. Immature trees 24 to 48 inches thick on the stump are left, with the result that by the time the operator has cut the last acre of his ownership, the immature trees will have become prime for cutting, and in the meantime, they will have reseeded the land with another crop.

Thus, says Professor Emanuel Fritz of the Department of Forestry of the University of California, the timber is cut on a maturity basis and the land is kept in continuous production. Speaking of the outlook, he says: "At the expected rate of logging, 500,000,000 board feet per year, it would appear that we are overcutting the growth by just that amount during the first year, because the virgin timber itself is believed to make no accretion in volume. In the second year we will appear to have overcut by 1,000,000 board feet, less the growth on the area cut the previous year. But if logging and growth on new cutover lands are projected forward 50 years it becomes less and less apparent that the forest area is being overcut. The cut in the fiftieth year will still be, for the purpose of this exposition, 500,000,000 board feet, but there would be accumulated [by that time] . . . 500,000 acres of cutover land . . . the annual growth on such an area of selectively logged cutover land should produce 500,000,000 board feet per year. This is equal to the annual cut. . . . "

Like a good scientist, Professor Fritz honestly acknowledges that this is the picture of what should be, and only in part the picture of what is. He points out that his "present rate of cut" is merely assumed for purposes of argument; no one can know that it will not increase as the population of the country increases. And the whole industry, not merely the best of it, must practice selective logging. To bring about sustained yield in the Redwood Empire, all operators, not just some of them, must leave the lands in such a condition that the Redwood's marvelous regenerative powers can assert themselves, instead of being left in such a state of ruin that no Redwood can grow there again in centuries, if ever.

It is true that virgin forest is not necessarily the best forest, from the point of view of lumbering; a fine, healthy, even-aged, second-growth stand is in many ways more satisfactory to log. But from the point of view of preserving forest grandeur that it has taken a thousand years to produce, virgin Redwood groves have values that belong to the world, and the future. How much of this old-growth Redwood is there left? The estimates vary. The Forest Service thinks there are only 31,000,000,000 board feet of it uncut, but the lumbermen believe it amounts to 50,000,000,000. Taking their more optimistic view, virgin Redwood would last just 100 years more at the present rate of consumption if only virgin timber were cut. But selective logging is our hope. New growth on lands selectively logged will, studies indicate, produce from 1000 to 3000 feet per acre per year.

Unfortunately the progressive elements in the Redwood industry have no coercive power over their brethren still operating on the cut-out-and-get-out philosophy, while singing the old canticle of "inexhaustible abundance." Nor can the federal government take a hand. It has no authority to prevent owners of forest land anywhere from recklessly destroying their own capital. It possesses very little Redwood land of its own today, though once, in the Redwood Empire, it was monarch of all it had never surveyed. For soon after California joined the Union, Uncle Sam began giving away this empire under the then popular persuasion that the main thing was to get the country "settled up." Trees everywhere were regarded as usurpers of land that should be raising corn and hogs; they were ambush hiding murderous redskins. So for the pittance price of homestead claims, we gave away the finest timber in the world, on the same terms as saw-grass swamps and alkaline deserts!

Worse still, too many of the homesteaders in the Redwoods made fraudulent entries. Russian sailors just off the ships, for instance, were brought by interested persons to the Land Office, their claims were written out for them, a dummy cabin (transportable from place to place) was stood up briefly on the claim, to comply with the law, and the "homestead" then changed hands, for a few dollars. At least one clerk in the Land Office confessed later to connivance in the theft, in this way, of millions of dollars' worth of Redwood timber and many others must have known what was going on and cynically closed their eyes. From one speculator to another these originally stolen claims then passed. The ultimate operator often had to pay a fair price for the trees he cut, but the profit had been taken by profiteers, to the great loss of the government, the consumer, and all the American people.

When the Forest Service and the National Parks were formed at last, they were given lands out of the public domain then remaining. By that time the Redwoods no longer formed a part of it. Thus, the preservation of the Redwoods has been the work of private individuals and the state of California through its park system. It all began with a trip through the Redwoods taken in 1917 by Dr. Henry Fairfield Osborn and Dr. John C. Merriam, the naturalists, and Madison Grant, an amateur scientist. The devastation they beheld caused them to found the Save-the-Redwoods League. Today, with headquarters in San Francisco, it has over 15,000 members, has collected the funds — $5,000,000 to match state money — to buy some 60,000 acres of the noblest Redwoods, and with a master plan of what it hopes ultimately to accomplish, it is constantly working to secure other tracts of matchless beauty. For instance, World War II was not yet over when the League went to work to set aside, by purchase, the National Tribute Grove, to express the eternal gratitude of the nation to the men and women in the armed services. Today this magnificent virgin wilderness has been secured to that high purpose by contributions from all over the country. And there is the Children's Forest — one of the League's most moving projects. Anyone can add to its existing acreage by a contribution; most gifts to it are made in memory of beloved children who have died. With meadows and streams, paths and bridges to enchant a child, the grove is a serene and smiling monument in which to enshrine such lost little lives. Other groves have been purchased, with funds given the Save-the-Redwoods League by such organizations as The Garden Clubs of America, and by individuals, to be preserved from the axe forever.

And it is moving, as one travels slowly through the flickering light and shade of the Redwood Highway, to realize that many of these groves were given, in part at least, by people who have never seen the Redwoods and perhaps do not expect ever to see them. For the members of some of the sponsoring organizations live in Iowa or Vermont, in Georgia or New York. The great majority of them are probably not persons of wealth at all. They gave anonymously, they gave purely, they gave to the future, to people yet unborn; they gave not only to the country but to the world. And they gave out of a deep religious feeling that the beauty and age and greatness that here have risen from the earth to tower above us are holy and shall not be profaned.

THE PINES
(*Pinus*)

PINES are recognized by their resinous wood and their needle-like leaves which are found in bundles of 1 to 5 and enclosed at base in a papery sheath which may be, sooner or later, deciduous.

The male flower is a long catkin usually grouped with several others on a terminal twig. Each cluster of stamens is surrounded at base by 3 to 6 scales. When ripe the anthers are bright yellow with abundant, buoyant pollen. The female flowers, found on last year's shoots, form short thick catkins furnished with papery bracts which soon disappear, and larger persistent fleshy scales which become the woody scales in the mature cone. At flowering time the scales of the female conelet open wide and receive the wind-borne pollen.

When pollinated, they close again and do not open until the seed is ripe, or in some cases until years afterward. About one year after pollination, fertilization takes place within the ovules, and the conelet, which has changed little till now, begins a period of rapid growth. The exposed tip of each cone scale is usually more or less thickened and shows the apex of the first season's growth in a scar or protuberance which is frequently provided with a prickle and transversely ridged with a keel.

✳   ✳   ✳

WHITEBARK PINE

Pinus albicaulis Engelmann

OTHER NAMES: Whitestem, Alpine Whitebark, Pitch, Scrub, or Creeping Pine.

RANGE: A timberline tree found at 3000 feet in the north to 11,500 feet in California. British Columbia and western Alberta to central Idaho and the mountains of western Wyoming and northern Utah; south on the Cascades of Washington and Oregon and through the Sierra Nevada to the headwaters of the Kings River. Also in the mountains of north-central Oregon and of extreme northeastern California, but lacking in the Olympic Mountains and on the island of Vancouver, and lacking throughout the Coast Ranges of the United States.

DESCRIPTION: *Bark* soft, whitish gray on young trees and smooth; on old trees broken into brownish white, narrow, thin, plate-like scales; inner bark red-brown. *Twigs* tough and thick, at first reddish brown, becoming white-gray. *Leaves* 5 in a bundle, 1⅓ to 2¾ inches long, or shorter and scrubby in exposed situations, densely clustered at the end of the twigs, dark yellow-green. *Flowers* of both sexes scarlet, blooming in summer. *Cones* short-stalked, purple-brown, 1½ to 3 inches long, unarmed, the very thick scales remaining closed and the wingless, hardshelled seeds (⅓ to ½ inch long) escaping only by decay of the cone. *Wood* with pale brown heartwood and whitish sapwood, soft, brittle, and weak, very light (26 pounds to the cubic foot, dry weight).

Perhaps the easiest place to see this alpine Pine, without roping any cliffs or setting your heart to pounding, is from the highway that loops around the perfect, snowcapped, volcanic peak of Mount Hood, in Oregon. For it occurs as low as 3800 feet above sea level at Government Camp and, in even better style, in a protected cove near Cloud Cap, at 6000 feet. This tree reaches a modest maximum of some 70 feet in height, with a trunk sometimes over 5 feet thick. The branches, which in youth leave the trunk at right angles, become ultimately uplifted to form a bushy crown. And there is then something quite Aspen-like about the tree, at least when seen in the distance, in those uplifted, limber boughs, in the thick, fluent tufts of foliage and, most of all, in the whiteness and smoothness of the bark and the way that

the trunks are apt to be a little crooked. Often several trunks spring up near together and lean slightly outward from each other, to form a slim, plumy grove.

There are two other Pines, the Limber and the Bristlecone, which have whitish bark *in youth*, but with age it turns brown and grows scaly and furrowed. On the contrary, the young twigs of the Whitebark are purplish; then they and the trunk turn white *with age*. The bases of very old trunks may become somewhat brown and scaly, and as the scales grow apart they reveal the reddish inner bark but, dominantly, the white bark shines through the forest in a way to make identification certain at a glance. This is a feature so striking in a Pine that one can hardly believe at first that it is natural. One feels as though the trees must have been decorticated by fire or beetle. But a close view, a touch of the hand on the bole, will show that this bark, firm and satiny and gleaming as flesh, is as natural as any Paper Birch's.

At first, as one ascends any of the Canadian and Montana Rockies, or the Cascades of Washington and Oregon, the Whitebark is found in the company of Western White and Lodgepole Pines, Alpine Larch, Alpine Fir, Alpine Hemlock, and Engelmann Spruce. One by one it drops them behind in its ascent, for of all the trees in its range it is the most completely alpine. And at last it stands, or rather creeps and struggles, alone, rooted in desolate mountain rocks, its limbs on the windward (western) side dismantled, its stem foreshortened to a height

of three or four feet, its limber branches so intertwined you can walk
upon them. There is little white bark to be seen on such a timberline
specimen and, as John Muir says, the tree seems to have been stopped
in its growth by a low ceiling. That ceiling is real if invisible. It is
determined by the shrieking gales — winds of the very planet's turning — and by the storms of sand; by the crushing load of ice and snow
which last at high altitudes sometimes nine months in the year.

"During stormy nights," Muir wrote, "I have often camped snugly
beneath the interlacing arches of this little pine. The needles, which
have accumulated for centuries, make fine beds, a fact well known to
other mountaineers, such as deer and wild sheep, who paw out oval
hollows and lie beneath the larger trees in safe and comfortable con-
cealment." [1]

Muir undertook to establish the age of some of these alpine trees.
One specimen had 255 annual rings, though only three feet high, and
another of the same height had 426. Yet its branches were still so
supple with youth that he could tie them into knots.

As soon as the snow melts, which is not till the middle of July in
alpine situations, the Whitebark Pine begins to flower, the male catkins bright rose-purple and very gay for such a hard-bitten creature,
the female catkins or conelets with bright scarlet scales. The young
cones grow but little for the first year after pollination and stand erect
the first winter; in the second summer they become horizontal and
grow rapidly for a few weeks till ripe, in August. They are then
chocolate-brown and borne in rigid clusters half hidden down in the
brush of stout, clustered needles. The scales are very thick and seem
glued together as if they would never open. Not until the cones dry
out in autumn will the pearly seeds escape. Though they have wings,
when in the cone, these remain attached to the cone scales. Ineptly
then the seeds merely fall to the ground under the parent tree.

This would seem a poor method of distribution, but there is at
hand a vicarious one. For hosts of Clark nutcrackers come every year,
with their harsh, rolling cries of *churrrrr, churrrrr.* With mighty beaks
these gray crows thrash open the green cones and extract the seeds.
Indeed, most of the crop falls victim to these Pine-loving birds, but
enough are wastefully flung around or perhaps voided without killing
the embryo, to spread the species across the gulfs that separate its
alpine groves.

[1] *The Mountains of California.* The Century Company.

LIMBER PINE

Pinus flexilis James

OTHER NAMES: Limbertwig or Rocky Mountain White Pine.

RANGE: A timberline tree, growing at 4000 feet in the north to 11,000 feet in the south. Mountains of southeastern Alberta, south in the Rockies (including the Bighorns of Wyoming, Black Hills of South Dakota) through Idaho and Colorado to western Texas and the mountains of Sonora and Chihuahua in Mexico; the mountains of Utah and central and southeastern Arizona; wide-spread in northeastern Nevada, recurring on high desert ranges of southern Nevada. In California on the central Sierra, the high desert ranges (the Panamints, etc), and, in southern California, the San Gabriels, San Bernardinos, and San Jacinto Mountains. Absent from the Pacific Coast Ranges proper (except Mount Pinos, Ventura County), and from the northern Sierra and Cascades. Rare in extreme northeastern California and extreme western Nebraska.

DESCRIPTION: *Bark* of old trunks thick, dark brown or almost black and covered with thin, irregular, abundant little scales; that of younger stems whitish gray and smooth. *Leaves* 5 in a bundle, 1½ to 3 inches long, often curved, very thick and rigid, dark yellow green and shining, densely tufted and forward-pointing at the ends of the short twigs to form a scrubby brush-like mass. *Flowers* — the male reddish, borne on spikes throughout the crown of the tree, the female bright red-purple in clusters

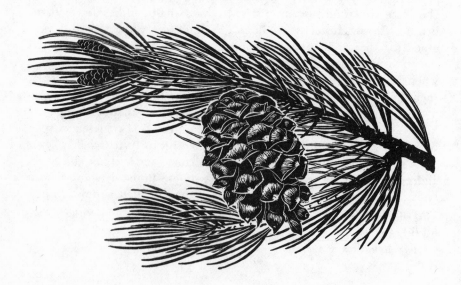

at the ends of the upper branches. *Cones* short-stalked, 3 to 10 inches long, with very thick unarmed scales, opening at maturity to allow the escape of the wingless light brown seed. *Wood* light (27 pounds per cubic foot, dry weight), soft, pale yellow, becoming red on exposure to the air.

U.S. Highway 30, the Lincoln Highway, between Cheyenne and Laramie, Wyoming, parallels the route of the Union Pacific Railroad where it makes its first climb over the Rockies. But the road is older than the famed route of those rails. "The first dim lines of this route were traced by the travois poles of Indians, on their way to obtain Mountain Birch for bows and arrows, or to participate in hunting. Fur brigades, with heavily laden carts, made the first wheel tracks; immigrants with ox-drawn wagons and loose stock, wore these tracks deeper. After an Indian uprising in 1862, the frothing horses and swaying coaches of the Overland Stage used this route instead of the Oregon trail through central Wyoming. . . . In the late 1860's, engineers and contractors laid the track of the first transcontinental railroad beside the old trail. Today the planes of great airlines hum overhead; at night, beacons flash their lights across the sky." [1]

And at the summit of the long grade up Granite Canyon, on this historic line of travel, stands The Old Pine Tree, called the most photographed object in Wyoming. An iron fence protects it now from souvenir hunters, and this is necessary, for this ancient of trees, of who knows how many winter snows, probably looked down upon the pageantry of trapper and settler, soldier and engineer. It has the appearance of growing out of a large granite boulder, the trunk forcing its way up through a great crack in the rock, while the roots are deep in the soil beneath the boulder. The story goes that when it was a struggling young life, back in the early days of the Union Pacific, firemen on the trains used daily to drench its roots. And so they kept it alive. The skeptic might say that it would have lived anyway; but the tradition proves at least that railroad firemen are a tenderhearted lot! The real point of the story is that The Old Pine Tree was a Limber Pine, and Limber Pines have a way of growing in dramatic places, taking picturesque attitudes, and getting themselves photographed, written about, and cared for, even to becoming the core of so entertaining a legend. This Pine so constantly occurs in the historically significant passes of the Rockies, that it was destined to link up with human history.

[1] *Wyoming:* American Guide Series. Oxford University Press.

Never by any chance does a Limber Pine look like just another Pine. You might confuse it with its timberline neighbors, the Whitebark Pines, because on young trees the bark is silvery gray, but eventually it turns brown and rough, and the cones are two or three times the length of those of the Whitebark Pine. Wherever it grows on high, wind-swept peaks and ridges, it is apt to creep along almost like a stunted shrub; much of the time it is half erect, or bent over at right angles, or developed on one side and not on the other where the wind blows keenest. Even when the elements are not too cruel to it, it is always eccentric in its form of growth. The stem is apt to be crooked, and always the lower branches (and many of the upper too) are extra-long, twisty as snakes, and with twigs so flexible and tough that without breaking they can sometimes be tied into a knot. If the trunk by any chance is straight, then it is apt to be strikingly short and thick, while the crown of the tree may be much broader than high, at least in ancient specimens, presenting an effect almost like that of the Parasol Pines of Italy. Sometimes trees only 10 to 18 feet high will have trunks two feet in diameter. Such a tree may well be 200 or 300 years old. The maximum dimensions reported are a height of 80 feet and a trunk diameter of 4 feet.

In the Wallowa Mountains the associates of the Limber Pine are White-barked Pine, Alpine Fir, and Mountain Hemlock. In the Sierra Madre, San Bernardino, and San Jacinto ranges of southern California, it grows only above 9,000 feet and up to 11,000 above sea level, and is most commonly associated with Lodgepole Pine — its exact opposite in habits of growth. It grows with Pinyon on the Panamint Mountains that look down on Death Valley, and in southern Nevada, where it is commonly called White Pine, it gives its name to the White Mountains. Before the days of railway transportation it was a valuable timber tree in White Pine County, in the Silver State.

Today lumbermen seldom trouble this adventurous mountain climber. Its refuges are too inaccessible, its lumber too knotty. Its true home, where it is most abundant and characteristic, is in the high Rockies of Wyoming and Colorado well above the zone of the Engelmann Spruce, and just below that of the treeless alpine turf with its brief carpet of wild flowers. Most of us climb to those places only in the summer months, and when we see the contorted forms of this timberline tree, we may be a little inclined to look down upon it, after the stateliness of Spruce and Fir and Yellow Pine below. But stop a moment and listen to the whistle of the mountain wind in its short, stubby, thick needles. Even on a fine summer day they give off a sharp whistling sound as the breezes of July run lightly through them. They are lifting their voices in a tale of their life that is all fierce endurance. For when we have gone to the valley and city, these trees will be enduring for months a degree of cold felt only passingly at lower elevations. The sort of winter wind that would get into the headlines of newspapers if it blew down below, blows here for days and weeks, raising the voices of the Pines to a high sustained keening note. Snows that would stop all traffic on our roads and streets weigh down its branches. But they do not break, for this is no ordinary Pine but a Limber Pine, whose long boughs and twigs can bend and bend without snapping. A tree better adapted to endure timberline conditions does not exist.

MEXICAN WHITE PINE

Pinus reflexa Engelmann

OTHER NAMES: Arizona White Pine, Ayacahuite Pine.

RANGE: From northern Mexico (Durango, Sonora, Chihuahua, Coahuila, etc.) north to western Texas (Guadalupe Mountains), central and west-central New Mexico, southeastern and east-central Arizona between 6500 and 10,000 feet above sea level.

DESCRIPTION: *Bark* dark gray, becoming on old trunks narrowly ridged, deeply furrowed, red-brown. *Twigs* gray-white, rather slender, covered at first with red-brown hairs. *Leaves* 5 to a bundle, 3 to 4 inches long, rather stiff, pale blue-green, only the lower surface marked by 3 or 4 whitish lines of stomata. *Flowers* reddish brown, the female clustered or in pairs, the male ⅓ inch long. *Cones* 5 to 9 inches long, opening early, their thick scales strongly reflexed, without prickles; cone stalks ⅓ to ⅔ inch long; seed nut-like, large (⅓ to ½ inch long), with a very short wing and a reddish brown thick shell. *Wood* clear yellow, close-grained, soft and light (30 pounds per cubic foot, dry weight).

It is an easy matter now to motor high in the Chiracahua Mountains of southern Arizona, where the Mexican White Pine grows. But anyone who knows his western history will still have a feeling that there is an Apache behind every one of the fantastic rocks, big as houses and churches, that crown the summit. For this was the home of the Chirachua band, one of the most implacable enemies of white men and all other Indians in the Southwest. Even after Geronimo and his followers had surrendered, there was one of them who escaped the prison train, near St. Louis, Missouri, and somehow made his way back to these his native mountains. This "bronco Apache," the unbroken Massai, hid out here for three years, singlehandedly maintaining his wild freedom against the United States and Mexico, stealing horses and, from the "tame" or reservation Apaches, women. The latter he strangled when he had done with them — all save one, a favorite whom he allowed at last to return to her people. It was while looking for horses stolen near here by Massai that Colonel Hughes Safford and Sergeant Neil Erickson found their way up a canyon and so discovered the wonderland of rocks that is today Chirachua National Monument. And here the Mexican White Pine, with the Chihuahua and Apache and Mexican Pinyon Pines, forms a forest unlike, in the species that compose it, any other Pine wood with which visitors from other states are likely to be familiar.

The Mexican White Pine, when growing in the sheltered canyons and at lower altitudes, has rather long, pale blue-green needles reminding one of the graceful eastern White Pine, but on the exposed rocks its stubbier tufts of foliage are like those of its close relative, the Limber Pine of the high Rockies to the north. When Mexican White Pine reaches full stature the tree may stand 60 to 100 feet high, with short, rapidly tapering, clear, straight trunk and a long, narrow, conical crown. The cylindrical cones are distinguished from all other Pines' by the strongly reflexed thin tips of the scales; since the cones are pendant, the reflexed scale tips are, by this inversion, seen as pointing upward when the cone is on the tree. From the cone drop at length the nut-like brown seeds tinged with red, each provided with only a very short wing, incapable, surely, of carrying the seed far, even in a mountain wind.

The hard, fine-grained wood, which is somewhat heavy for one of the soft Pine group, might well be worth the cutting if the tree were only abundant and grew in less inaccessible places. But it will never be a lumber species in this country and will always stand aloof and unenslaved to the will of our industrial race.

WESTERN WHITE PINE

Pinus monticola Douglas

OTHER NAMES: Silver, Soft, Fingercone, Mountain, Idaho, or Little Sugar Pine.

RANGE: Southern British Columbia and Vancouver Island, below 2500 feet, south to the mountains of northern Idaho and northwestern Montana, and through western Washington (sea level in the Olympics to 6000 feet in the Cascades), the Cascades of Oregon (2500 to 7500 feet), the northern Coast Ranges of California (4500 to 8500 feet), the Sierra Nevada (7000 to 11,500 feet) and, in southern California on the San Gabriel, San Bernardino, and San Jacinto Mountains above 8600 feet. Also in the Blue and Warner Mountains of eastern Oregon above 7500 feet, and in the Reno and Lake Tahoe region of Nevada.

DESCRIPTION: *Bark* of trunks silver-gray to almost purple and irregularly divided by narrow furrows and cross-checks into small oblong scaly plates. *Twigs* at first covered with a fine reddish down, later becoming hairless and red-brown. *Leaves* in bundles of 5, slender and twisted, 2 to 4 inches long, blue-green and furnished with a frosty appearance owing to the rows of white stomata on all sides of the needles. *Flowers* — male catkins yellow, in clusters of 6 or 7 on the lower branches, female catkins purple, borne at the ends of the higher branches. *Cones* 6 to 18 inches long, at first erect and green, becoming purple and pendulous on long curved stalks, the scales thin, flexible, without spines. *Seeds* reddish brown, only ¼ inch long but furnished with a membranous wing 4 times as long. *Wood* very light (24 to 30 pounds per cubic foot, dry weight), soft, easily worked and straight-grained, medium-weak, medium-soft, the heartwood pale brown, the sapwood nearly white.

Far removed from the experience and rounds of most of us, the queenly Western White Pine reigns over the "Inland Empire," as its inhabitants like to call it — the central parts of the northern Rockies, in the "pipestem" or "panhandle" and other northerly sections of Idaho, and adjacent parts of Montana, Oregon, and Washington. Even when you visit this region, on your trip from Glacier National Park, let us say, through the beautiful lake country of the Northwest, you may fail to distinguish this tree, splendid though it is, from its fellow conifers the Hemlock, Spruce, Larch, and Fir that make up the dense, the somber forest of the Empire, almost as lofty and as lush as that of the Olympic peninsula. For one thing, mature Idaho Pine (the lumberman's preferred name for it) has such a long stem clear of branches, carrying its crown to 100 feet overhead, locked in a dark arch with the crowns of the other trees, that from the ground you do not easily distinguish the bundles of 5 slender slim blue-green needles, nor the long, finger-slim, drooping cones which proclaim this tree a Pine, and one of the aristocratic White Pine group, at that. It is easiest, perhaps, to recognize this species by its bark, which is not furrowed even in age but is broken into many rather small and irregular but smooth blocks by narrow, shallow lines and cross-checks. The bark when fresh is purplish, but is soon weathered to a silvery color. If scoured by constant mountain winds, it may show cinnamon on the exposed side.

Yet though the living tree is known to so few of us it plays such a large rôle in our daily lives that every American handles its wood on an average of 2300 times a year! We are familiar with its weight (or rather its extreme lightness), with its color — or lack of it (for its sapwood is very pale) — and even with its faint, sweet smell. For this tree, almost exclusively now, yields us our wooden matches. Formerly they were made from the eastern White Pine, but as the first growth of that species approached exhaustion, the western species, its closest relative and similar to it in the physical and chemical properties of its wood, began (from about 1914 on) to bear the whole burden of matchwood production. This may not seem a great drain — a match is so slight a thing — but remember that 12,000 wooden matches are struck, by the American people, every second. That makes more than 103,000,000 in 24 hours. To produce a year's supply of matches, 300,000 mature pines must yield up their lives. If grown to a pure stand, they would cover an area 2 miles wide and 10 miles long.

Not all of any White Pine tree will do for the making of matchwood. A match plank, to be marketable, must yield sixty per cent or more of high-grade wood — that is, wood which has no diagonal, twisted, coarse, or hard grain, no knots, pith, compression wood, weak wood, or discoloration. Good match plank is sawed out into 2-inch thicknesses and cross-sawed into blocks exactly equal in length to that of a match stick. These are fed into machines where a row of some forty circular knives, flashing up and down at the rate of five strokes a second, slice off individual sticks on the down stroke, and on the up stroke they punch them into perforations in a steel plate. If you have noticed that one side of a match stick is usually rounded, you will understand that it is the squeezing of the stick into the perforation which gives it that shape. An endless belt then conveys the sticks through a paraffin bath to increase their inflammability; they pass next

through a chemical bath which shortens the afterglow, so that, once blown out, the ember will die quickly, not linger as a coal.

In almost all respects, the Western White Pine carries on the great tradition of the eastern White Pine as nearly peerless in its class as a softwood. Its best grades of wood are even-grained, light yet comparatively strong, remarkably free from warping and shrinkage. As a result, it is used in great quantities for window sashes, which must not warp with changes in the weather and should be so light that they can be moved at a touch, and for doors, panels, finish, columns, siding, shelving, sheathing, flooring, ceiling, and lattice and pantry work. Because of its lightness and freedom from resin and decay, it goes into window blinds and shutters. Because it takes paint and gilt so well and is light and smooth-grained, it is a favorite for picture frames, cabinet work, and veneer backing.

Much of the "knotty Pine" so popular now with interior decorators, especially if it is of a pale tone and with dark reddish knots, is Idaho White Pine. "Clear" — that is, not knotty — paneling of this species is also increasingly popular; it is almost without visible "grain," that is, the summer wood is scarcely darker than the spring wood and so presents a beautiful, light, satiny surface. The wood, moreover, is a joy to the carpenter, under his plane, so soft and smooth it is. For pattern-making it is ideal, since it can be cut across the grain with almost as much ease as with it. It seems a wood made by Nature for man's hand to fashion at his will. Straight and true, tractable, fine —

these are words one may apply to it both by analogy and quite literally. Only the virgin White Pine of the East, in its day, ever produced a softwood lumber of such refinement and versatility. But the eastern species was, half a century ago and more, ravaged and wasted. The western species has taken its place before the saw.

Wherever Western White Pine occurs on a commercial scale it is almost certain to be the most valuable timber tree in its region, no matter what its competitors. It fetches a higher price than Western Red Cedar or even Douglas Fir when growing side by side with them. The annual cut at the present time is running around 261,500,000 board feet a year, most of it in the "Inland Empire," but this rises at times to twice that amount. In British Columbia it would be probably the most valuable timber resource in that greatly forested province, if only it did not form so slight a percentage of the stand, and the same is true in California.

Yet Western White Pine lumber has but small market in the very regions where it grows. Its great reputation with buyers is in the eastern states, where the tradition of the eastern White Pine's marvelous wood still lingers. Eastern customers accept the western species as a satisfactory replacement for their native soft Pine in all the millwork enumerated above, and are willing to pay the high price of hauling the lumber across the continent. To reduce the cost of the rail haul, Western White Pine is usually kiln-dried near the sawmills. It is then shipped east, manufactured into all sorts of millwork and stock sizes of doors, frames, panels and the like, including "mail order" window sashes with their glass already set in them, and is then frequently shipped back to the West and sold to the housebuilder right in the "Inland Empire."

David Douglas, the great Scottish explorer-botanist who first discovered so many western trees, made this species known to science after he found it in 1825 growing on the slopes of Mount St. Helens, in what is now the state of Washington but was then unexplored "Oregon," a vast area neither clearly British nor clearly American. But the true home of this tree — where, at least, it occurs in its greatest abundance and finest dimensions — is deep in the interior of the northern Rocky Mountain system. And here it was that lumbering of this valuable timber began at a remarkably early date. For the year 1840 found Idaho still a howling wilderness, when that intrepid Presbyterian missionary, the Reverend Henry H. Spalding, employed his Nez Percé converts to dig a millrace from the Clearwater River and erect a sawmill, at his pioneering mission school of Lapwai, Idaho. The water-wheel for this mill was constructed of Western Red Cedar and Idaho White Pine, and the saw was obtained from the celebrated Dr. Mc-Loughlin of the Hudson's Bay Company post at Fort Vancouver. It was brought all the way from the fort to Lapwai, on horseback and in canoe, by Dr. Marcus Whitman, the medical missionary who was so soon to lay down his life as a martyr to the treachery of the Cayuse Indians. Spalding, who had with Whitman brought out the first wagons, the first printing press, and the first white women, over the Oregon Trail, was so horrified by the Whitman massacre that he became obsessed with a conviction that the Cayuse had been stirred to the act by the Catholic missionaries, and finally he left his sawmill, his school and mission altogether to stump the country with lectures on the subject. There is no evidence that the Catholic missionaries in-stigated, even indirectly, any such deed as resulted in the deaths of the saintly Dr. and Mrs. Whitman, and several others.

After Spalding's pioneering venture in White Pine lumbering, the business moved but slowly. The great bulk of the stand was almost wholly inaccessible for a long time, and the market was flooded with fine coniferous woods. But the approaching end of the supply of east-ern White Pine almost coincided with the building of the first rail-roads across northern Montana and Idaho — the Northern Pacific in 1881, the Great Northern in 1890, the Chicago, Milwaukee and St. Paul in 1908. These railways, at the start, offered special rates to home-steaders, and many special inducements to settlement in the last great forest frontier of this country. Some of the railroads themselves were owners of vast timber holdings, acquired from the government, in alter-nate sections of land on each side of their rights of way (as inducement for the great initial cost of laying the tracks), and these were disposed of to lumber companies and speculators. As the last century drew to a close, then, all the forces of exploitation were drawn up before the virgin stands. These forces included an approaching dearth of softwood lumber in the East, a "high" market, railway systems to take the wood to that market, a highly advanced technology of rapid lumbering and milling and seasoning, an influx of settlers and in-vestors on cheap land, an open-handed policy on the part of the gov-ernment, and the old frontier psychology of "getting rid of the woods and settling up the country."

Certainly the aboriginal growth of White Pine was temptation enough to set the saws to whining. There were areas in which sound trees, 150 years old or thereabout, cut out at 51,000 board feet to the acre. On the White Pine's preferred site of deep porous soils on gentle north slopes and flats, individual trees towered up 100 and 175 feet high, and produced boles as much as 8 feet in diameter at breast height. How beautiful such growth appeared before the destruction began is recalled in the memoirs of an Idaho settler who was about eleven years old, in 1901, when she first raised the curtain of the tourist train that was bringing her to her new home: "Trees surrounded us; tall, graceful trees; great trunks waving like timothy and exuding the exhilarating odor of pine. There were still mountains, but draped mountains, fold on fold of silvery green, a little darker than the breast of a teal, but with the same billowy sheen. As we wound around the shores of Lake Pend Oreille, the men gathered in an exclaiming group about my father, listening to his explanations of this splendor with avid interest. . . . Bay after bay swept by, green and blue and blue and green, drenched in the golden sunlight of a spring morning; and then, as we neared Hope, a startling sight met our eyes. Great trees lying prone, crisscross and tossed about, as if a tremendous tornado had swooped and slapped and slain. I heard the word 'slashings' for the first time and never can I forget its appropriateness. . . .

"Everyone was soon homesteading in the splendid Marble and Mica Creek district. . . . Logging was the only industry and at that time competition was brisk and haste the watchword. . . .

"Time passed. I married a homesteader who had just proved up. Homesteading was not farming in those days, but just a subterfuge to gain possession of timber. . . . The money from the sale of this . . . went into more timber and the financing of other homesteaders — a grubstake was tripled when the homesteader sold — and we used our stone and timber rights beside. Quick turnovers and more investments, and our stake was made. We were ready for a clean-up, all titles clear and the patents ready to turn over. The timber companies were planning a monstrous cut in the spring. Cruisers were making their final estimates, and thousands lay in the banks awaiting the word. We were jubilant. A new house and new clothes, a trip to the city, and a solid investment were the promises of the morrow." [1]

To understand what happened next, in that breathless, expectant August of 1910, we must leave the homesteader's young wife, Nancy Warren, and study the meteorological and political conditions prevail-

[1] Nancy Rovena Warren, "White Pine — My Lady of the North," in *American Forests,* September, 1928.

ing over Idaho for many weeks previous, for the murk about to en-
velop her was of vast extent, affecting hundreds of thousands of lives,
and great fortunes. Back in Washington, Congress in its wisdom had
just voted to deny the newly organized Forest Service any fire-fighting
funds. The winter over the northern Rockies had been normal
enough, but drought started in spring. The hills that year scarcely
grew green with grass before it was withered. Crops were seared, and
the forests became dry as tinder. All during June, July, and August,
dry electrical storms started small fires, while careless railroad crews
and wandering prospectors, loggers and homesteaders were responsible
for others. The force of the Forest Rangers was thinly scattered in the
Lolo, Coeur d'Alene, and Pend Oreille forests; there were no lookout
stations, then, few telephone lines, no firebreaks, few trails.

As the small fires increased to some 3000, a curtain of resinous smoke
spread over the whole region. Lights burned by day in people's houses.
Train conductors had to read the passengers' tickets by the light of
their lanterns. The oppressive air was strangely quiet — sounds seemed
to be swallowed up; birds staggered in their flight, and horses rolled
their eyes, straining at their halters. Then on the night of August 20,
the superheated atmosphere over the whole area, rising, sucked in
winds of hurricane force. Forest rangers were almost blown out of
their saddles; acres of timber went down like kindling. And the small
fires were whipped, in a matter of moments, into great ones.

Young Mrs. Warren stepped outdoors to get some fuel for the
evening meal, when she says, "a smoking twig fell at my feet . . . I
sniffed, but the air was usually laden with smoke. I looked at the
horizon and saw nothing. A blast of hot air swept my face — just that
and the smoking twig, but a sudden fear gripped my heart."

"On the Lost Horse Trail, deep in the Bitteroot Range, a forest
guard stirred uneasily in his sougans (a thin, generally shoddy, quilt).
Something pattered on the tent roof. . . . Wind was moaning through
the trees, dropping needles and refuse on the tent. . . .

"A few minutes later one of his crew . . . called him out. . . . A star,
he said, had fallen on the hillside across from the camp, setting a small
fire. The forest guard swung around into the wind. There on the
western horizon, a fiery glow lit the sky for mile after mile. He knew
then what the 'star' was and what it meant."[1]

Mrs. Warren had also, about the same time, and a hundred miles
away, seen a "star" fall. The church bell began to ring. Women

[1] Stanley Koch, "Remember 1910!" in *American Forests,* July 1942.

gathered in groups. Children were awakened. The fire rolled down
the hills like a gigantic curtain, while the able-bodied men hurriedly
plowed and shoveled a fire line on the forest side of the town. Water-
pipes were hastily laid and all the available fire-fighting apparatus was
called to the aid of the workers.

The "stars" that these two had seen, the blast of hot air that hit Mrs.
Warren's face, were but the perimeter phenomena of as frightful a
calamity as ever befell a forest. For as the thousands of small fires were
lashed by the winds into seething holocausts, an area hundreds of square
miles in extent became so superheated that the resins in the virgin and
mighty coniferous stands began to volatilize until great clouds of inflammable hydrocarbon gases were formed. And these, catching fire all
at once, simply exploded in one screeching detonation after another.
Tongues of flames shot into the sky for thousands of feet. Whole burning trees were uprooted and sent hurtling far ahead as gigantic brands.
Flames tore through the crowns of the forest at 70 miles an hour. Settlers' cabins, railway trains, towns, were suddenly engulfed in seas of
flame.

At Wallace, Idaho, the telegrapher for the Northern Pacific Rail-
road tapped out EVERY HILL AROUND TOWN MASS OF FLAMES WHOLE
PLACE LOOKS LIKE DEATH TRAP MEN WOMEN CHILDREN HYSTERICAL IN
STREETS LEAVING BY EVERY POSSIBLE CONVEYANCE.

The telephone girl at Avery, Idaho, where the St. Paul tracks cross
the Continental Divide, was broadcasting her warnings up to the moment when the line went dead — the poles leading to the telephone
office were down in flames. One refugee train with a thousand souls
aboard hid from the flames in Tunnel Thirty-two, while, outside, the
ties were burning and the steel rails buckling.

About ten miles from the burning town of Wallace, Ranger Edward
C. Pulaski, grandson of the Polish Count, Casimir Pulaski, who gave
his life for American Independence at Savannah, was in charge of a
crew of forty-three men, most of them volunteers. As the flames closed
in around this band from every side, Pulaski led his men into an
abandoned mine shaft. Two or three blankets had been salvaged in
the flight and wetting these in an underground trickle, Pulaski made
a fire curtain of them over the door of the shaft. As the heat and
smoke grew too intense for endurance, and the mine timbers began
to burn, men became insane and tried to dash outside. Pulaski held
them back with his revolver until he dropped, suffocated. But at the
words, "Come on outside, boys, the boss is dead," he revived to say,
"Like hell he is," and scramble to his feet. Five men died in the

tunnel before the flames passed. The survivors were led to safety by Pulaski through a landscape charred beyond recognition.

All through the national forests similar scenes of heroism and tragedy were being enacted. Not till the twenty-third of August did a general rain, with snow on the high peaks, descend in torrents and quench the holocaust that no power of man could have stopped. An area the size of Connecticut, in the aggregate, had been destroyed, 80 fire fighters had been burned to death, hundreds of homes destroyed, millions wiped out in fortunes large and small.

Supervisor Koch of the Lolo Forest set out to tramp the embers' wrath: "The still warm ashes were knee deep where once I had walked in cool forest aisles. For mile after mile, as far as the eye could reach, lay a smoldering, desolate waste. Stunned and heartsick, I never wanted to see the country again."

Mrs. Warren and her husband, their lives saved by the rains which came too late to save their little fortune, walked over the scene of their green hopes, that was now a blackened ruin. Then, as their eyes slowly swept the scene, they saw a fluttering tuft of pine, a single tree on a hilltop that by some miracle had, though scorched, not been killed.

It was from such as these that the burned-over area began its natural restocking. Today, nearly fifty years later, an even-aged stand of second growth has, in some places, entirely healed the dreadful scars of 1910, but in too many other spots, Aspen and Fir and other inferior trees are still in the slow process of making the ruined land habitable again.

There were many lessons taught by this, the worst forest fire in history. The most obvious and painful was that the lessons of Alpena, Peshtigo, Hinckley, and the other disasters in the eastern White Pine had not taught the succeeding generations a thing. Haste, recklessnesses, waste, greediness for quick profits, all played their part in the starting of the innumerable fires that went out of control when the high winds arose. And this responsibility, as usual, must be scattered over a wide field; it applied to great railway systems and to small landholders alike. The only force for conservation on the scene was the Forest Service, which before the fire was widely unpopular with lumbermen, stockmen, and prospectors, but emerged from the flames with enhanced reputation. A wave of popular indignation rolled over Congress when the fire was out, and rightly, for it too must share in the blame for the disaster.

Lumbering on private holdings in Idaho White Pine today is carried on along the scientific lines advocated years ago by Forest Service. At least this is true in the best-conducted operations. Slashings and other wood waste are reduced to a minimum and carefully disposed of before they become a fire menace. The lower limit of diameters of trees suitable for logging has been raised. Adequate numbers of seed-trees are left to restock the cut-overs. Thus an area logged in, say, 1926, will be available for a second cut in 1961 and, seed-trees again being left, a sustained yield of this high-grade lumber should continue into perpetuity, if fire and the insidious blister rust can be kept out.

To the lover of wilderness scenery, of course, these second growths, cut just when they are beginning to attain their full beauty, can never mean what the virgin White Pine means. For that we must look in the future to our national parks, and even there, even in the sanctuary of Glacier, we see the ravages of fire. In this semi-arid climate, with such highly inflammable and resinous trees, it will remain a danger always.

SUGAR PINE

Pinus Lambertiana Douglas

OTHER NAMES: Big or Great Sugar Pine.

RANGE: From the central Cascade Mountains of Oregon (2000 to 3000 feet, or on east side to 5000 feet) to southern Oregon (down to 1000 feet in the inner Coast Ranges and Siskiyous); at 4500 to 6500 feet in the desert ranges of southeastern Oregon; in California in the Siskiyous, Trinity Alps (1800 to 6000 feet), south on the northern Coast Ranges (but not in the coastal fog belt), especially in the Bully Choop and Yollo Bolly Mountains (2300 to 6000 feet) to northeast slopes of Mount St. Helena but not around San Francisco Bay; reappears (2000 to 7000 feet) in the Santa Lucia Mountains of Monterey and San Luis Obispo Counties. Found around Mount Shasta and Mount Lassen (3000 to 7500 feet) and southward in the Sierra Nevada (west slopes, 3000 to 9000 feet); in the high mountains of the Santa Barbara region, and from 4000 to 10,500 feet in the San Gabriel, San Bernardino, and San Jacinto Mountains of southern California. Also in the Lake Tahoe region of Nevada and from 8000 to 10,000 feet on the San Pedro Mártir Mountains of Baja California.

DESCRIPTION: *Bark* of trunks very thick, deeply and irregularly furrowed, with long plate-like ridges covered with cinnamon-red or purple-brown scales; these often weathered to a grayish brown. *Twigs* stout, at first pubescent and dark orange-brown, becoming dark purple-brown. *Leaves* 2½ to 4 inches long, in bundles of 5, stout, stiff, twisted, in color deep blue-green with a whitish cast. *Flowers* in early spring, the male yellow in clusters on young twigs; the female pale purple to light green. *Cones* at first erect, in the second summer pendulous, on stalks often 6 inches long, brown and attaining their full length of 11 to 18 or even 23 inches, and a diameter of 2½ to 3½ inches, the tips of the leathery, unarmed scales lustrous reddish brown, the inner part of the scale deep purple-brown. *Seeds* ½ to ⅝ inch long, nearly black, their dark brown wings twice as long. *Wood* light (22 to 25 pounds to the cubic foot, dry weight), soft, weak, not stiff, the heartwood pale reddish brown, the sapwood white.

The great genus of the Pines stretches around the north temperate zone and on mountains far into the tropics and numbers some 80 species. Many of them are of the highest use or the greatest beauty, and many of them attain splendid proportions. But there is one species, the Sugar Pine, that towers above them all. It is the king of Pines, undisputed in its monarchy over all others.

In magnificent dimensions the Sugar Pine ranks after the two Sequoias and the Douglas Fir; it is, therefore, the fourth greatest of all American trees in size. A specimen standing today in the Stanislaus National Forest, California, is 200 feet high and has a trunk circumference, at breast height, of 31 feet and 8 inches. Some of its neighbors in the mountains of California are almost as tall and mighty of bole, and it is quite possible that before the lumber mills began, over a century ago, the whirlwind destruction of the finest of accessible stands of Sugar Pine, there were other specimens larger still.

A grand old Sugar Pine 200 or 300 years old can stretch out its lower limbs high above the heads of many other species — the Incense Cedars, Yellow Pine and the Firs. Even in the company of the Big-trees, the Sugar Pines are not dwarfed but stand as worthy associates of the largest and oldest living things upon earth.

As you mount up the western slopes of the Sierra Nevada, you first meet the Sugar Pine at altitudes as low as 2000 feet in the north, but in the southern Sierra it scarcely occurs below 6000 feet, and on the high mountains of southern California it is first met with at 8000 feet and ranges up to 10,000 feet altitude. It thus occurs in what are the most grandly forested portions of this great mountain range, where the

rainfall is in the neighborhood of 40 inches and the snow at times may
lie 12 feet deep. But in summer, which is the dry season, this is the
most enjoyable part of the Sierra Nevada — a region of open groves
with very little underbrush but a wealth of wild flowers and small
flowering shrubs. Here mule deer step proudly and unafraid, through
the groves of the Sugar Pine; a lumbering bear goes by intent on his
business and not in the least hostile to man; the Douglas squirrel
dances and chitters on the boughs perhaps 100 feet overhead, the
needles are deep underfoot, and views of snowy peaks, canyons, and
waterfalls, open at every vista of the groves.

In this magnificent setting the Sugar Pine is at home. Its mighty
boles rise straight as the shafts of columns, but colored a rich purplish
brown and livened with tufts of the yellow-green staghorn lichen. The
incense of its needles and resinous exudations fills the aisles of this
forest temple. Overhead the majestic crowns of the Sugar Pines just
touch each other, making a vaulted roof that is airy and full of light.
Everywhere is a sense of light and space, of hope and time — time
enough to grow a kingly tree, a long time that has gone before you,
to clothe a mountain range thus nobly.

Young Sugar Pines are all alike in their slender, close-grown, conical
form. In winter their youthful limbs easily shed the snow, never
breaking under it. Before the season is done the drifts may have
sifted so high that the little trees are buried many feet under it and
many tons of weight may lie upon them. Yet the snow is the friend
of these trees, for, softly but firmly encasing them, it keeps them for
months of the year in a rigidly upright position, so that a crooked stem
is almost never seen in a Sugar Pine. Once started straight, the tree, as
it grows older, is able to keep the martial *tenue* it gained in youth. The
lower branches are self-pruned as the young groves grow older, with
the result that few Pines have so little limbage, or a larger bole so
clean of branches. At the top of the long stem an old Sugar Pine bears
a palm-like crown, though grander than any true palm's, for the
lowest limbs may be 40 feet in length — very fair trees in themselves
were they cut off and set upright. As it enters old age, the Sugar Pine
allows itself endless eccentricities. No two old trees look alike; each is
an individualist of the most rugged sort, grandly asymmetrical, dis-
daining the prettiness, the uniformity of Fir tops, or the winsome nodding of the tips of Hemlock. Instead, an old Sugar Pine's crown looks
storm-racked but indomitable, sometimes almost absurdly sprawling
or overreaching.

Yet this tree has its grace; for from the underside of the foliage, hang the swaying, slender cones, 15 to 26 inches long, green shaded with dark purple on the sunward side. After they ripen in September and October, their scales open and the winged seeds slip forth upon their errands through the forest. Now the color of the scales alters to a warm yellowish brown, and thus the cones remain swinging on the wind all winter and through the following summer. Fallen at last on the forest floor, they are still so big and beautiful that he who wanders a Sugar Pine grove for the first time is almost certain to pick up the first few cones he sees, convinced that he has come upon specimens of an unusual size. But he soon discovers that the woods are full of them and he drops his armful back to earth, conscious that he is in the presence of treasure so bounteous that he need not carry away any; that all he has to do, to be rich in the best things of earth, is to stay where he is, to breathe this air, to hear the sound of the wind in those great singing crowns, and rest his hand upon the serene boles.

It was the enormous cones of this tree which led to its first discovery by science. For David Douglas, pioneer botanist of the Northwest, was shown a single cone of this tree, when he was in the valley of the Columbia River in 1825, and the sweet seeds, too, which the Indians carried in their pouches for food. So great a cone could only come from a great tree, he reasoned, and with this single cone for clue, he set off from Fort Vancouver on September 20, 1826, when the present states of Oregon and Washington were under the British flag, holding few white settlers outside the forts, and hostile Indians and grizzlies roamed a land unknown, unmapped, unspoiled. Now let him tell his own story, which he wrote by the flickering light of a Pine torch, on what is now Sugar Pine Mountain, just west of Roseburg, Oregon

"THURSDAY, 26th. I left my camp this morning at daylight. . . . About an hour's walk from my camp I was met by an Indian, who on discovering me strung his bow and placed on his left arm a sleeve of racoon-skin and stood ready on the defence. As I was well convinced this was prompted through fear, he never before having seen such a being, I laid my gun at my feet on the ground and waved my hand for him to come to me, which he did with great caution. I made him place his bow and quiver beside my gun, and then struck a light and gave him to smoke and a few beads. With a pencil I made a rough sketch of the cone and Pine I wanted and showed him it, when he instantly pointed to the hills about 15 or 20 miles to the south. As I wanted to go in that direction, he seemingly with much good-will went with me.

At midday I reached my long-wished *Pinus* (called by the Umpqua tribe *Natele*), and lost no time in examing and endeavouring to collect specimens and seeds. New or strange things seldom fail to make great impressions, and often at first we are liable to over-rate them; and lest I should never see my friends to tell them verbally of this most beautiful and immensely large tree, I now state the dimensions of the largest one I could find that was blown down by the wind: Three feet from the ground, 57 feet 9 inches in circumference; 134 feet from the ground, 17 feet 5 inches; extreme length 215 feet. The trees are remarkably straight; bark uncommonly smooth for such large timber, of a whitish or light brown colour, and yields a great quantity of gum of a bright amber colour. The large trees are destitute of branches, generally two-thirds the length of the tree; branches pendulous, and the cones hanging from their points like small sugar-loaves in a grocer's shop. . . . Being unable to climb or hew down any, I took my gun and was busy clipping them from the branches with ball when eight Indians came at the report of my gun. They were all painted with red earth, armed with bows, arrows, spears of bone, and flint knives, and seemed to be anything but friendly. I endeavored to explain to them what I wanted and they seemed satisfied and sat down to smoke, but had no sooner done so than I perceived one string his bow and another sharpen his flint knife with a pair of wooden pincers and hang it on the wrist of the right hand, which gave me ample testimony of their inclination. To save myself I could not do by flight, and without any hesitation I went backwards six paces and cocked my gun, and then pulled from my belt one of my pistols, which I held in my left hand. I was determined to fight for life. As I as much as possible endeavoured to preserve my coolness and perhaps did so, I stood eight or ten minutes looking at them and they at me without a word passing, till one at last, who seemed to be the leader, made a sign for tobacco, which I said they should get on condition of going and fetching me some cones. They went, and as soon as out of sight I picked up my three cones and a few twigs, and made a quick retreat to my camp, which I gained at dusk. . . . The position I am now in is lying on the grass with my gun beside me, writing by the light of my Columbian candle — namely a piece of wood containing rosin."

The Sugar Pine takes its name from its sweet, gummy exudations. "The sugar," John Muir explains, "is to my taste the best of sweets — better than maple-sugar. It exudes . . . in the shape of irregular, crisp, candy-like kernels, which are crowded together in masses of considerable size, like clusters of resin-beads. When fresh, it is perfectly white and delicious, but, because most of the wounds on which it is found have been made by fire, the exuding sap is stained on the charred surface, and the hardened sugar becomes brown.

"Indians are fond of it, but on account of its laxative properties, only small quantities may be eaten. Bears, so fond of sweet things in general, seem never to taste it; at least I have failed to find any trace of their teeth in this connection." The sugar in this resin is said to be as sweet as cane sugar, but belongs to an entirely different class of the sugars known as pinitol. If you are a chemist it may mean something to you to learn that pinitol is a monomethyl ester of dextro-inositol.

No other Pine in the world has such length of trunks clear of limbs and with very little taper. Taken all in all, the delightfully fragrant wood with its lightness, satin texture, close grain, ease of working, and ability to take a fine polish makes it an outstanding lumber Pine. And no other produces so much to the acre. Small areas are known which will yield 100,000 to 200,000 board feet to the acre. So it is not surprising that from the earliest days of settlement in the Sierra foothills, the Sugar Pine was cut in preference to any other. Indeed, it was to cut Sugar Pine that John Sutter set up his famous mill at Coloma, where gold was discovered on a momentous day in 1848. And when the sudden influx of settlers brought a great demand for house timbers and shingles, the Sugar Pine answered best of all. Sugar Pine roofed the shacks of the Forty-niners and their followers and descendants.

The first shingles were, more exactly, shakes; that is, split, unshaved pieces of wood usually 30 inches long and from 4 to 6 inches wide, and often only ¼ inch thick, rived out by hand. Those early shake-makers were experts with the froe, but wastrels in the way they used this precious wood. Trees that would have sawed out at 10,000 or 20,000 feet of lumber were cut down by the shake-makers and oftentimes left to rot in the woods if it was found that their splitting properties were less than excellent. And even when they were outstandingly good, usually more than one-half of the tree was wasted. The shake-makers would go up in parties of two to four and make a camp in the pineries to spend the summer and, without stirring more than 300 yards, they could provide themselves with a season's work, for four or five giant Sugar Pines sufficed. Needless to say these were all stolen trees. Any sort of tree on government land was then considered to be the property of him who could get to it first and cut it down.

But though shakes might roof the early houses of California and provide siding too, large buildings and barns demanded structural timber, and so the sawmill early made its appearance. Sugar Pine was sawed, in the days of the Forty-niners, for flumes, sluice boxes, bridges, houses, barns, fences, and mine props. Like the shake-makers, the pioneer mill men simply stole thé government's trees, and soon more Sugar Pine was being cut in the Sierra than all other woods combined, for it was lighter and softer than the Yellow Pine, its nearest rival. Before railroads brought in lumber from other regions, ox teams were toiling up steep grades to altitudes of 4,000 to 6,000 feet and hauling off Sugar Pine for building and fencing material from the mountain mills to treeless valleys below, for a distance of as much as 100 miles. At the same time, the old shake-makers were giving way to shingle mills, only a little less wasteful than the crew they had displaced. Then, as the fruit industry developed in the Sacramento valley, Sugar Pine was cut for orange and raisin boxes. Sugar Pine wood, because it imparts no flavor to what it touches and is so light and handsome, has remained the ideal packing box for fruits.

As the White Pine of the East began to give out, toward the end of the last century, Sugar Pine came to replace it. For it has about the same weight per cubic foot and is sometimes considered preferable to White Pine for doors and sliding sashes since it shrinks and swells even less, and holds its shape better. White Pine was long considered the one ideal wood for pattern-making but Sugar Pine matches it today. Planing mills utilize it for molding and panels, railing and stair-work, doors, sash, blinds, and the decking of boats. Because of its freedom from odor, it is used for the compartments in which to store coffee, tea, rice and spice, and for druggists' drawers. Its straight grain qualifies it for service as the pipes in church organs, a rôle in which comparatively few woods are at all satisfactory.

When, roused to its duty by the stinging words of John Muir, the government at last began to take charge of its own forests in the Sierra Nevada, the first thing it did was turn out the wandering bands of shake-makers. Its struggle with the sheepherders was longer. It had been their wont to build corrals on the edges of the meadows by felling Sugar Pines in such a way that, stretched at length on the ground, they made a huge triangular or circular enclosure — all this, of course, as a trespass upon government land. Longest of all was the battle with the cattle ranchers who had for years been dropping Sugar Pine logs end to end to make fences to turn cattle. Regarding themselves as lords of the land, as pioneers who had won their way, as tenders of a vested interest with precedence over any other interests, they went armed, and took orders from government foresters only a little more respectfully than they would have taken them from sheepherders. Decades of tact, education, patience, and firmness were required to bring about the present and still precarious balance among the interests of the sheepherders, the ranchers, and the foresters, on the Forest Service's own lands.

And, even now, by far the largest part of the stand of Sugar Pine in California and Oregon is out of the government's hands and in those of lumber companies or private individuals who might sell whenever the stumpage price goes high enough. The national parks and the national forests protect the magnificent groves of Sugar Pine when these fall within their boundaries. But the countless visitors who each year motor or climb through the Sierra Nevada seldom realize that some of the Sugar Pines which they most admire are not within the jurisdiction of the government, and that their destiny is the sawmill — if not next year, then ultimately.

Knowledge of this fact rouses the emotions of us all, and it is meet and right that groves of great antiquity and beauty should be included in the bounds of national parks and national forests whenever possible. It is also right and necessary that there should be a lumber industry, and that a tree of such high utility as this one should be cropped in a scientific way which will permit a sustained yield from one generation to the next. Unfortunately that goal has not been reached yet by most lumber companies in the Sugar Pine region, and with some it is not even an ideal. At the present time the cut is still well in excess of the natural replacement, and until the two come into balance we can expect only increasing destruction of this superb tree and a corresponding rise in the price of its fine lumber.

BRISTLECONE PINE

Pinus aristata Engelmann

OTHER NAME: Hickory Pine.

RANGE: Mountains of Colorado, Utah, Nevada, northern New Mexico, desert ranges of eastern California (Panamint and White Mountains), and on the San Francisco Mountains of Arizona, between 7500 and 10,800 above sea level.

DESCRIPTION: *Bark* of old trunks red-brown and shallowly furrowed and ridged. *Twigs* stout, light orange becoming nearly black, bearing long tufts of foliage at the tips. *Leaves,* in bundles of 5, 1 to 1½ inches long, stout and usually curved, dark green and shining on the back (upper surface), marked on the lower by several rows of whitish stomata, usually crowded on the ends of the twigs and appearing brushed forward and commonly with sticky white exudations of resin. *Flowers* — male dark orange-red, female purple. *Cones* 3 to 3½ inches long, short-stalked with thick scales dark chocolate-brown at the ends, the umbo with a long, fragile, bristle-like prickle; often coated with exudations of shiny brown resin. *Seeds* ¼ inch long with long terminal wing, light brown and frequently mottled. *Wood* with pale brownish-red heartwood and thin pale sapwood, medium-soft, brittle and medium-light (35 pounds per cubic foot, dry weight).

Wherever a natural timber line occurs, throughout the mountains of the world, the trees grow more and more stunted as they approach that forest frontier, and their forms, crushed under the weight of winter's snow and ice, starved at the roots for soil and water in the brief growing season, become more and more fantastically gnarled. The vegetation seems beaten to its knees, and finally flung face down on the rock, to be stripped of upper foliage down to its white-barked limbs and whipped by the wind forever. In the Swiss Alps such growth is called the *Krummholz,* the "crooked wood." In Colorado, where there are more peaks above timber line than in any state in the Union, they call it by the name, at once poetic and accurate, of "wind timber." It begins at about 11,500 feet altitude on the north sides of Colorado Rockies, and runs up to 12,300 feet on the south sides.

For hundreds of miles wind timber follows these contours through the congested mass of Colorado's mountains. Most of it lies high above the roads and passes of the state, above the "parks" — tree-dotted mountain meadows so beloved of the summer vacationists — and so it happens that few ever see much of the Bristlecone Pine, that typically timberline conifer whose home lies higher than even that of the Limber Pine and Alpine Fir. On the mountain gales its winged seeds can be carried across valleys a mile deep or two, and many miles wide, to find lodgement in some distant crag. Enos Mills, the famous Rocky Mountain guide, tells of finding a timberline specimen only two feet high, growing in the most desolate situation he had ever seen, where he could not stand for the wind and could scarcely get his breath; yet it bore a single valiant cone. Probably, despite its small size, this tree was not precocious. It may well have been forty or fifty years old.

Indeed, a Bristlecone Pine no taller than a man may yield a record of more than 900 annual rings and more, and be even older than the tale they tell. For in some years the snows where it grows may not melt for several summers, and it is impossible that any growth could be made in such conditions. At best, the growing season is but three months in the year, and snow may fall on any summer day, while the average temperature for the year is but 2° F. above freezing. Yet there are hours of tranquil beauty in the wind timber. Long shafts of light from the setting sun still hold the wild gardens in a trance, while the valleys are already steeped in night and lights in the mining towns are coming on. The white-crowned sparrows and solitaires pour out their music to the alpine wilderness; Clark crows come, rollicking and squawking, to pick the seeds out of the cones, and bears paw up the trees, looking for marmots.

Yet even in summer life is hard for these trees, for the westerlies, having crossed the deserts of Utah and Nevada, carry an invisible weapon of sand, and with it they scour the bark right off the windward side of the trunk, flaying it to the white sinews of its sapwood. Famous examples of such Bristlecones may be seen in Hoosier Pass, Colorado, at 11,542 feet. Their short stature and broken crowns give no hint of their age, but their massive trunks tell a tale of centuries of indomitable will and struggle, and their buttressed bases seem to grip the thin soil with wildcat claws.

When the Bristlecone can find a foothold farther down the mountains, in more sheltered spots, or when grown in cultivation, it forms a symmetrical and even luxuriant tree. Young specimens are clothed to the base in numberless branches which themselves are completely clothed in very dark shining needles. Each branch gives off, at sharp right angles, tiers of short, stiff branchlets, Christmas-tree fashion. At last the tree may attain a height of 40 or 50 feet, and if crowded by others will retain for some time a handsome spire-like form. But it cannot forever restrain the picturesque eccentric in its nature, and before long the symmetry is broken by the shooting out and up of long snaggy arms.

The Bristlecone Pine was first collected by F. Creutzfeldt, botanist with the Pacific Railway survey through Colorado made in 1853. August 31 found the party commanded by Captain J. S. Gunnison, in what is now Saguache County, Colorado, threading its way up over the continental divide through Cochetopa Pass by the same route taken so easily today by the motorist on State Highway 14. "At our camp this evening," records Lieutenant Beckwith, the diarist of the expedition, "[the valley] is half a mile wide, covered with fine grass. . . . We passed, also a fine grove of cotton-wood half a mile in length in which the deer were bounding about in every direction, even passing between our wagons, which were separated by but a few yards. . . . The hills and mountains enclosing this . . . beautiful valley, vary in height from two to three hundred to twelve or fifteen hundred feet, *covered with a scanty growth of pine.* No mountain pass ever opened more favorably for a railroad than this. The grouse at camp are abundant and fine, as are also the trout in the creek, several having been caught this evening weighing each two pounds."

Of these Pines Creutzfeldt collected a single branch, without cones. Perhaps he meant to secure better specimens later; he had no presentiment, on that summer twilight, with the grouse booming and the deer jumping and the trout rising, of impending disaster. But on October 26, in eastern Utah, he and his commanding officer, with an escort of seven soldiers and two guides, detached themselves from the main party for exploration and were attacked by red hostiles before dawn. The "Gunnison massacre" was twelve hours over before the main party came to the scene. Gunnison's body had been pierced with fifteen arrows. After being slain the victims were mutilated; wolves had already dragged some of the bodies away and gnawed at all. Gunnison's papers and instruments were later recovered from the Indians by the intervention of Governor Brigham Young. And eventually Creutzfeldt's specimen of the Bristlecone reached Dr. John Torrey and Dr. Asa Gray, classifying plants in eastern herbariums far from the yells and knives of Utes.

FOXTAIL PINE

Pinus Balfouriana Greville and Balfour

RANGE: Mountains of California, on the inner North Coast Ranges (Siskiyou, Scott, and Yollo Bolly Mountains) at 5000 and 6000 feet altitude; in the southern Sierra Nevada from 9000 to 12,000 feet, around the headwaters of the Kings, Kern and Kaweah rivers; occurring only on the west slopes of the Sierra except at Cottonwood Creek at very high altitudes. Absent from the central and northern Sierra, Mount Shasta, Lassen Peak, etc.

DESCRIPTION: *Bark* of old trunks bright cinnamon-brown, with squarish plates; that of branches smooth and chalky white. *Twigs* drooping. *Leaves* 5 in a bundle, bright blue-green above, glaucous below, ¾ to 1 inch long, curved, stout, and densely clothing the ends of the branches. *Cones* 2½ to 5 inches long, 1¾ to 2 inches wide, slender when unopened, becoming terra-cotta-colored when expanded, the tips of the scales thickened, or low-pyramidal, with a shrunken, scar-like umbo and no prickle. *Seeds* blotched and speckled with dull purple, ⅓ inch long, their wings thrice as long. *Wood* yellow-brown, soft, medium-light (34 pounds per cubic foot, dry weight).

In the days when there were few roads of any sort in California, one region was as inaccessible as another, and botanical explorers, though few in number a century ago, expected nothing but hardships in the West, wherever they went. So that John Jeffrey, the Scottish explorer

and first discoverer of this species, made his way to the stands of this
tree on the Scott Mountains, as early as 1852. Jeffrey was always a
lonely man, collecting far out ahead of civilization, claiming few
friends. Thus he was not quickly missed when he disappeared forever,
having set out from San Diego to cross the Colorado desert in search
of new plants. He was either killed by Indians or died of thirst. No
trace of his end has ever been found.

The Foxtail Pine is likewise a solitary creature. Where it grows in
the southern Sierra, for instance, by glacial cirques, on land scoured
by ice, it has frequently no other trees to keep it company and some-
time not even shrub, or grass, or a tremulous alpine wild flower. In
such sterile soil, exposed to drought and cold and sun and wind, the
specimens of necessity stand far apart, solitary. And the harsh conditions under which this tree exists leave their imprint on it. Commonly much of the top is dead — the bark sloughed off — so that it
looks like the whitened skeleton of a deformed cripple. The gleaming
needles are all borne in a scrubby tuft at the tips of the twigs, like the
brush of a fox. The boles become with age immensely thickened in
proportion to the height of the tree; a specimen only 45 feet high may
have a bole 5 feet in diameter, at breast height, gradually tapered
above to the craggy tip. In middle life the limbs halfway up may sometimes grow disproportionately long. These become loaded with cones

that in youth are a dull blackish blue but when ripe a yellowish brown.

Even in the highest and most exposed situations, the Foxtail Pine does not take things lying down like most subalpine trees, but manages to stand essentially erect. It may lean, but it never sprawls. There may be a twist to its trunk, but its branches do not writhe. Wind and sand may roughen its naturally smooth and rather flaky bark to a dark brown or strip it half away, but somehow the indomitable vegetable survives.

MEXICAN PINYON PINE

Pinus cembroides Zuccarini

OTHER NAMES: Three-leaved or Stoneseed Pinyon Pine. Piñon.

RANGE: Highlands of central and northern Mexico to southern Arizona (at 4800 to 8000 feet altitude), southeastern New Mexico and the Big Bend region of western Texas.

DESCRIPTION: *Bark* scaly, reddish brown, irregularly furrowed and ridged. *Twigs* stout, orange-brown or gray-brown. *Leaves* usually 3 in a bundle, dark blue-green, the inner faces whitened with lines of stomata, the margins finely toothed, $1\frac{1}{2}$ to $2\frac{1}{2}$ inches long, slender ($\frac{1}{48}$ inch broad) usually 3-sided, rather straight, the basal sheath only partly deciduous. *Flowers* — male yellow, in crowded clusters; female dark red. *Cones* short-stalked or stalkless, 1 to $2\frac{1}{2}$ inches long and nearly spherical to egg-shaped before opening, the scales few with thick, shining, ruddy-brown tips, the unexposed parts pinkish, only the middle scales seed-bearing, the lower small and crowded. *Seeds* $\frac{1}{2}$ to $\frac{3}{4}$ inch long, with a hard shell, chocolate-brown and yellow-blotched on the undersurface, cinnamon-brown above, with oily sweet flesh; in falling from the cone leaving with the scale the rudimentary wing. *Wood* medium-heavy ($40\frac{1}{2}$ pounds to the cubic foot, dry weight), medium-hard, coarse-grained, brittle, with light yellow heartwood and thin whitish sapwood.

The Mexican Pinyon stands clearly distinct from the other three Nut Pines of the Southwest. Its needles, by comparison with the others' stout, stiff, scrubby ones, are much finer, more flexible, and longer; the margins of the leaves are minutely toothed, and the color of the foliage is a glossy blue-green except for fine white lines of stomata. When the needles, which are triangular in cross-section, are crushed, they give off a much more delicate aroma than the rank pungency of the other Pinyons. The shell of the nut is distinctly harder, and the bark, which is furrowed, is not braided by diagonal ridges.

As seen on Mount Lemmon, in the Santa Catalina Mountains above Tucson, Arizona, the Mexican Pinyon grows well above the zone of the cactus and the zone of scrub or chaparral, but below the crowning zone of the Firs. It keeps company with the strange Alligator Juniper,

the stately Arizona Cypress, the Mexican White Pine, the Chihuahua Pine, and the Arizona Yellow Pine. It is not so tall as they — generally not over 35 feet high, and never over 50, and flourishes, like the Netleaf and the Silverleaf Oaks, as an understory tree. In youth it forms a short-trunked tree, with ascending branches and compact crown. In time, however, it will become very broad-headed, with the lateral branches held out almost horizontally, like spreading arms.

Too rare in this country to be of importance as a food, except to little rodents and to birds like the thick-billed parrot, the nuts of this Pinyon are the commonest Pine seeds sold in the markets throughout Mexico, and are seen even in the capital city wherever Indian people come to market.

"The seeds," says Paul Standley, in *Trees and Shrubs of Mexico*, "are eaten in all regions where the nut pine grows and are highly esteemed. They are very palatable raw, but are improved by roasting, after which they possess a flavor unexcelled, perhaps, by that of any kind of nut. The seeds are placed in the mouth and the thin shells cracked with the teeth, and ejected without being touched by the fingers, an operation in which one may become very proficient by a little practice."

NEW MEXICAN PINYON PINE

Pinus edulis Engelmann

OTHER NAMES: Colorado, Mesa, Two-leaved, or Common Pinyon Pine. Piñon.

RANGE: Foothills and mesas from the Uinta Mountains of Wyoming south through Utah, Nevada and Arizona and from southern Colorado through New Mexico to western Texas, and south to Chihuahua.

DESCRIPTION: *Bark* of trunks superficially grayish but showing reddish brown in the irregular furrows between the shallow, diagonal ridges. *Twigs* rather limber though stoutish, at first light orange-brown becoming at last dark brown and then gray. *Leaves* usually 2 to a bundle, those on mature trees dark yellowish green, those on young trees blue-green, the inner faces whitened with lines of stomata, but with only three stomatic lines on the back, stiff, sharp-pointed, curving in toward the twig, only 1¼ to 2 inches long and thickish (½₄ inch), unequally 4-sided, the back convex, the bottom slightly concave, the edges not toothed. *Flowers* — male dark red, covering the tree, female on the ends of the twigs, purple. *Cones* few-scaled, shining yellowish brown when mature, 1¼ to 1¾ inch long before opening of the thick unarmed scales which are pale red-brown in the unexposed part, and raised-pyramidal at the apex, only the middle scales bearing seeds, the lower small and crowded. *Seeds* wingless, thin-shelled, pale yellowish with reddish-brown markings on one side, the other side dull red-brown, sweet-tasting and oily. *Wood* medium-heavy (40 pounds to the cubic foot, dry weight), narrow-ringed, hard but very brittle, with light yellowish-brown heartwood and nearly white sapwood.

When the traveler from the East first looks out of the train window upon the sun-baked hillsides of New Mexico, he sees a landscape of turquoise blue sky, silvery glint of snow-capped, far-off ranges, red, desertic earth molded into conical hills, and hundreds of little crooked Pine trees. These are Pinyons, the state tree of New Mexico, and the hundreds soon became thousands and, after a few hours, the traveler realizes they are reckoned by the millions. And that, though so wide-spaced that they show the earth between them or the tufts of pale straw-colored grama grasses, these little trees are part of a forest of vast extent, where only occasionally does one see the adobe villages of the Indians, or a Navaho shepherd girl watching her flocks, or a small copper-skinned boy astride a burro.

These Pinyon groves are forest in the original sense of the word —

the sense in which it is still often used in England — that is, wild or waste land, not cultivated or fenced, and not necessarily densely shadowed with trees. Indeed there is little shade in a Pinyon forest. The individuals are too far apart, their boughs are too few, their crowns too thin, their needles too scant. A well-grown man walking in a Pinyon grove may find he is taller than the trees. He looks out over their tops and sees mesas and *bajadas,* sometimes pueblos, and always farther ranges swathed in dark coniferous timber.

The Pinyon occupies a position in the foothills of the Rockies between the zone of the sagebrush or in the south the creosote-bush, both of which occur, as a rule, below 4500 feet altitude, and the Douglas Fir that usually begins at 8500 feet in this part of the world. The Pinyon's is a zone of steep gradients, and thus these little trees act as an important check upon erosion. It is a natural defense costing man nothing, built up by Nature with painful slowness. But when fire or too much cutting removes this defense, costly engineering will be required to replace it, and two or three centuries of growing are needed for the return of a Pinyon forest destroyed in a blaze of a few hours.

That dauntless soldier of fortune and scholarly nobleman, Cabeza de Vaca, was the first white man recognizably to describe, in 1535, this Pinyon and the native use of it, but thousands of years before this, the Indians had been eating Pinyon seeds, as they still do today. "In good years," says Haniel Long in his delightful book *Piñon Country,* "the crop may be worth a million dollars, and the pickers get perhaps a third of this amount. About four-fifths of the crop is sold outside the state, most of it going to the east side of New York. There the pushcart vendors sell the nuts to people who miss the Russian pine nuts and the Italian pistachios of their homelands. The piñon is a good nut, quite small, higher in protein and carbohydrates than pecans, but lower in fat. It keeps well; if unshelled it can go a year without turning rancid. . . .

"To gather them is an occasion for the whole family to work together, and if relatives are visiting, to get some work out of the relatives. Cars and wagons lie like beetles along the highways and byways. You hear people and children chattering not far away, with as much noise as the piñon-jays whose blue wings flash among the branches. The dwarf trees are suddenly a vineyard; the barren land turns fruitful and calls for pickers. Little children run from tree to tree picking up the nuts that have fallen. Sometimes they find the cache of a squirrel and get ten or fifteen pounds at a stroke. Against the dark green of the tree the cones are a beautiful henna inside and flare out in ever wider clusters of dark little coffee berries, until they literally bend backward. The taste is pine and sunshine and popcorn, and peanuts too in a way. Grown-up people spread a sheet underneath the tree and beat the nuts down with an old broom. They take along stout flour-sacks, and when they return to town in the October dusk after a long day and two meals in the open, the sacks are full, and they have made sure of one source of food for the winter.

"Even U.S. Americans become expert in cracking the shells with their teeth. But it takes an old Indian or native to show what can be done. Piñons go in one corner of the mouth and the shells come out the other. Sitting against a warm wall in the winter sun, people can keep it up for hours."

But man can obtain of this delicious crop only what the animals leave ungarnered. Weevils eat far too many, and so does the inevitable goat kept by every Spanish-speaking family in the Southwest. The wild turkey, the thick-billed parrot, Mearns's quail, all devour the seeds; so do porcupines, black bears, mule deer, the Hopi chipmunk, the Magdalena chipmunk, the rock squirrel, the antelope ground squirrel.

But there is one creature which, like the Indians of old, eats Pinyon nuts in preference to every other food. You see him as soon as you

walk out among the bushy *piñones,* the pinyon jay — really more of a
blue crow than a true jay — since there is no prospect where he does
not sail lazily over the Pines and Junipers, calling his name and that of
the groves of this tree. For his cry sometimes sounds wonderfully like
peen-yoney. All day long, this sea-blue bird so far from the sea is
rapping at the cone scales, extracting with hammer-like pecks one
sweet, fat seed after another. Probably he takes more nuts than all the
rest of the fauna, including man, combined, and he exults, with loud
crowing clamor, in his kingship over the endless pineries. Around the
watering places, or at nightfall when he roosts, or at nesting time when
he builds colonially, this bold piratical bird assembles in great flocks,
their uproar equal to that of the rookeries of eastern crows. But with
the dawn he scatters again, ranging far in search of his sweet, ancestral
diet.

The Pinyon is a notably resinous tree, liberally besprinkling with
gum or pitch any picnicker so incautious as to sit under it. Naturally
the Indians have long utilized the caulking properties of Pinyon pitch.
The Apaches made their baskets watertight with it; the Navaho still
do the same with their water bottles, and also use it to make a black
dye for their wool. And the wood of Pinyon has since prehistoric times
been used as a structural timber in the famed pit houses of the southwestern Indians. In words written especially for this book, by the
archaeologist Harold Gladwin, such construction is thus described:

"The pit, dug with the hands or a sharpened stick was, when completed, about 18 inches deep, 10 feet wide, and perhaps 12 feet long.
When this excavation was made, four post holes were set in and into
each a Pinyon trunk was stepped and packed around the base with
rocks and clay. With the four uprights in place, the Indian laid four
lighter Pinyon poles for stringers, lashed in place. For walls, Pinyon
branches were then set in the ground around the edges of the pit,
their tops inclined to lean against the stringers; a space was left for a
door and more branches were laid horizontally along the inclined
poles, followed by fine brush. To make the flat roof, long poles were
laid across the frame, then more branches and more brush, and when
this had been done, the whole house was covered with a thick coating
of mud, reinforced by bast and Juniper bark. From a study of the
annual growth rings of Pinyon timber in these ancient pit houses, it
has been possible to date these prehistoric American homes, and place
their building as long ago as 400–900 A.D."

Pinyon, which probably furnished much of the fuel to ancient Americans, is still the commonest firewood almost throughout the range of this tree. It burns with a smoky orange flame, steadily and with little sparking. The odor of "Pinyon smoke" curls its way into the heart. That aroma first became known to Anglo-Saxon Americans in the days of the Santa Fe Trail — the eighteen-forties — when the early traders set forth from the prairie "ports" — Westport and Franklin and Independence — for the then-forbidden pueblo of the Holy Faith, to carry to it Yankee manufactures, and bring back Spanish silver and Spanish mules. They say that those who, like Kit Carson, had once known the bells and the women and the "Pinyon smoke" of Taos could never stay away — come Kiowa, come Sioux, come Kansas blizzard or *calabozo*. As it was for those Americans a hundred years ago, so it is for us of this century. Pinyon incense is sold in boxes now — and one whiff of it will tempt you to ring up the city ticket office and reserve a place on the next westbound train.

In youth the Pinyon has a short, thick trunk, giving off branches from the very base; the crown of the tree is flattish or a low dome, and all the branches are twisted and bent low, so that the whole aspect of the tree then resembles that of some dwarfed but ancient Apple tree. The dense crops of cones — green the first season, but yellow-brown the second — give the impression that this species comes to a precocious bearing age; yet in fact a tree with a stem only six inches thick has probably seen a century of life, so slowly does it grow in the arid environment. A trunk a foot thick is probably one hundred and fifty years old, and still the hardy dwarf may live on, abundantly, dutifully fruitful, to the age of two and a half centuries. By that time the trunk will have pruned itself of the lower branches, and may be thirty feet high. It will have lost its Apple-tree appearance and sharpened its low crown into something more conical. But it will not have gained greatly in symmetry or stateliness. It will keep still those contorted branches, those bandy trunks, that stubby foliage which clings to the tree for five and ten years and gives out, when crushed, an aroma as of orange rind and turpentine. To the end, the Pinyon resolutely puts away grace and elegance, having no more use for them, in its hard-bitten existence, than some old Indian woman bowed with childbearing and the toting of the burden basket.

FOUR–LEAVED NUT PINE

Pinus quadrifolia Parry

OTHER NAME: Parry's Nut Pine.

RANGE: San Pedro Mártir Mountains of Baja California, irregularly north to the Santa Rosa and San Jacinto Mountains of Riverside County, southern California, at 4500 to 5500 feet altitude, chiefly on the eastern or desert slopes.

DESCRIPTION: *Bark* of trunks dark brown tinged with red, rough and shallowly divided into broad connecting ridges covered with short, thick, closely flattened scales. *Twigs* at first light orange-brown and coated with a pale pubescence, becoming grayish. *Leaves* usually 4 in a cluster, and 3-sided, ⅞ to 1½ inches long, 1⁄32 to 1⁄24 inch thick, incurved toward the twig, the margins not finely toothed, pale blue-green on the back, the inner faces with numerous whitish lines of stomata. *Cones* nearly globular in shape, 1¼ to 4 inches long, brown at maturity, the apex of the scale much thickened, keeled, and with a ridged knob, only the middle scales seed-bearing. *Seeds* ⅝ inch long, chocolate-brown with yellow blotches. *Wood* medium-light (35½ pounds per cubic foot, dry weight), soft, close-grained, very dense, pale brown or yellow.

There are four closely related Nut Pines or Pinyons in the Southwest, all having much in common — their small size and crooked stems, their love for desert mountains and mesas, their egg-shaped cones which require two seasons to ripen, and their sweet edible seeds in dark, mottled shells. When we try to separate the different kinds, we encounter difficulties; yet if we attempt to unite them in one species, we find ourselves trying to reconcile the contradictory. The present species, the Four-leaved Nut Pine, is the most poorly marked of all; at least it is very close to the New Mexican or Two-leaved Pinyon, and differs from it chiefly in that it predominantly shows four needles to a bundle and that the needles, in cross-section, are triangular. It is, further very distinct in its range, separated from the New Mexican Pinyon by a great expanse of desert. It is most abundant in northern Baja California, where it is an important article of food to the natives. Birds too are seen attacking its cones, and squirrels jumping through its branches, so that it does not grow, in its hard-bitten desert mountain environment, in vain.

ONE–LEAVED NUT PINE

Pinus monophylla Torrey and Frémont

OTHER NAMES: Gray, Frémont, Singleleaf, or Nevada Nut Pine.

RANGE: Foothills and lower slopes of desert mountains from southern Idaho through Utah and Nevada to northwestern and central Arizona, on the mountains of eastern and southern California especially on the east or desert sides, from 2000 to 4000 feet altitude, and in northern Baja California.

DESCRIPTION: *Bark* of old trunks roughly and irregularly furrowed with thin, close, reddish-brown scales. *Twigs* rather stout and light orange, becoming finally dark brown. *Leaves* usually solitary, gray-green, rigid, cylindrical in cross-section, sharp-pointed and awl-like, curved toward the branch, those on mature and fertile shoots ⅞ to 1¼ inch long and 1⁄12 inch thick, those on vigorous and leader shoots thicker and longer. *Flowers* — male dark red, in spikes, female short-stalked and purplish. *Cones* 1¼ to 2¼ inches long before opening, and greenish the first year, yellowish-brown the second, few-scaled, the scales concave, thick, 4-sided, knobbed at the apex, only the middle scales seed-bearing, the lower small and crowded. *Seeds* ½ to ¾ inch long, thin-shelled, dark chocolate-brown mottled with yellowish patches, with sweet oily kernels. *Wood* medium-heavy (37 pounds per cubic foot, dry weight), medium soft, weak, brittle, the heartwood yellowish brown, the thick sapwood paler.

"A man was discovered running towards the camp," records Captain John C. Frémont in his diary for January 24, 1844, "as we were about to start this morning, who proved to be an Indian of rather advanced age. . . . He brought with him in a little skin bag a few pounds of the seeds of a pine tree, which to-day we saw for the first time, and which Dr. Torrey has described as a new species under the name of *pinus monophyllus;* in popular language, it might be called the *nut pine.* We purchased them from him. The nut is oily, of very agreeable flavor, and must be very nutritious, as it constitutes the principal sub-sistence of the tribes among which we were now travelling."

Thus for the first time did this Nut Pine become known to the white man, or at least to a man of science — for Frémont was an excellent botanist, writer, and soldier of fortune, whether or no he will be adjudged by history as a good general and administrator. With his famous guides, Kit Carson and "Brokenhand" Fitzpatrick, he was, at this point in his trail-breaking explorations, on the east or desert side of the Sierra Nevada, seeking a pass through them to the interior val-leys of California.

Engaging as a guide the bearer of the Pinyon seeds, for the price of a piece of scarlet cloth and "other striking articles," Frémont and his little band started up the snow-fed creek that today we know as the west fork of Walker's River, "between dark-looking hills without snow; but immediately beyond them rose snowy mountains on either side, timbered principally with the nut pine. On the lower grounds, the general height of this tree is twelve to twenty feet, and eight inches the greatest diameter; it is rather branching, and has a peculiar and singular but pleasant oder."

On the twenty-ninth, Frémont and two companions found them-selves suddenly in the presence of an Indian party. "They seemed to be watching our motions, and like the others, were at first indisposed to let us approach, ranging themselves like birds on a fallen log on the hill side above our heads. . . . Our friendly demeanor reconciled them and, when we got near enough, they immediately stretched out to us handfulls of pine nuts, which seemed an exercise of hospitality. . . . The Indians brought in during the evening an abundant supply of pine nuts, which we traded from them. When roasted, their pleasant flavor made them an agreeable addition to our now scanty store of provisions. . . . The Indians informed us that at certain seasons they have fish in their water, which we supposed to be the salmon trout; for the remainder of the year they live upon the pine nuts, which form their great winter subsistence — a portion being always at hand, shut up in the natural storehouse of the cones." [1]

[1] *Report of the Exploring Expedition to the Rocky Mountains in the Year 1842.* By order of the Senate of the United States. 1845.

"This . . . is the Indians' own tree," says John Muir,[2] "and many a white man have they killed for cutting it down. . . . Tens of thousands of acres occur in continuous belts. . . . No slope is too rough, none too dry, for these bountiful orchards of the red man. . . . When the crop is ripe, the Indians make ready . . . old and young, all are mounted on ponies and start in great glee to the nut-lands, forming curiously picturesque cavalcades; flaming scarfs and calico skirts stream loosely over the knotty ponies, two squaws usually astride of each, with baby midgets bandaged in baskets slung on their backs or balanced; while nut-baskets and water-jars project from each side, and the long beating-poles make angles in every direction. Arriving at some well-known central point where grass and water are found, the squaws with baskets, the men with poles ascend the ridges to the laden trees, followed by the children. Then the beating begins right merrily, the burs fly in every direction, rolling down the slopes, lodging here and there against rocks and sage-bushes, chased and gathered by the women and children with fine natural gladness. Smoke columns speedily mark the joyful scene of their labors as the roasting-fires are kindled and, at night, assembled in gay circles garrulous as jays, they begin the first nut feast of the season."

Among all the Pines of the world, this one is distinguished by the fact that within each papery sheath there is contained normally but a single needle, and this is consequently round, not flattened on the inner face like needles crowded in a bunch. A single season's growth of these needles may remain on the tree as much as 12 years; never was there a Pine more reluctant to give up its reputation as evergreen. The cones ripen in the heat of the desert summer, in August, after their second season on the tree, then shed their curiously bean-like nuts, with shell so fragile it cracks between the teeth or fingers. The growth of this tree is painfully slow. A tree with a stem only 6 inches in diameter has already seen a century of arid seasons pass, and still its life course may not be half run. In youth the short thick trunks are capped by pyramidal crowns of rather straight and uplifted branches. An ancient Nut Pine, however, is almost unrecognizable, in shape, as the same thing, for the crown has become short and flat, and the branches are all twisted and bent low, and the years will but add to the gnarled look of this manna tree of the Mohave.

[2] *The Mountains of California.* The Century Company. 1913.

CHIHUAHUA PINE

Pinus leiophylla Schiede and Deppe
variety *chihuahuana* (Engelmann) Shaw

RANGE: Mountains of central and northern Mexico (Chihuahua, Sonora, etc.), southeastern Arizona and southwestern New Mexico, at 5500 to 8200 feet above sea level.

DESCRIPTION: *Bark* on mature trees as much as 1½ inches thick, blackish brown, the furrows deep and narrow and bright red-brown, the ridges broad and flat and covered with thin, closely flattened scales. *Twigs* slender, bright orange-brown becoming on older wood dull red-brown. *Leaves* in bundles of 3 (rarely 2 to 5) and 2 to 4 inches long, slender and pale bluish or grayish green and whitened on all sides by 6 to 8 rows of stomata; margins minutely toothed; the broad sheaths deciduous. *Flowers* — male yellow, female green. *Cones* on distinct, reflexed stalks often occurring in opposite pairs, 1½ to 2 inches long, at first light chestnut-brown and shining, becoming dark chestnut-brown, the scales thickened at the ends, and tipped at first with minutely recurved prickles which are soon deciduous. *Seed* ⅛ inch long with a thin dark brown shell and a twig ⅓ inch long. *Wood* weak, soft, and light though durable (34 pounds per cubic foot, dry weight), with light orange heartwood, and very thick pale sapwood.

The best place in the United States to see the Chihuahua Pine is in the Chiricahua National Monument, in southeastern Arizona. In this lonely spot rise many-colored cliffs, isolated columns, temple-like formations, balanced rocks, and others that look like the dolmens and menhirs of some vanished stone-worshipping people — this high in a range that rises out of grazing country. And here grows a forest predominantly coniferous, like that of all western mountains, but composed of species such as one seldom sees to the north, for its members are Mexican Pinyon, Arizona Yellow Pine, Apache Pine, Arizona Cypress, Cherrystone Juniper, Alligator Juniper, and the present species, which is often the dominant one.

The slow-growing Chihuahua Pine becomes 35 to 60 feet high and at most will have a trunk diameter of 2 feet. The trunks, very straight, are clear of branches for one-half or two-thirds of their length, and the branches themselves, usually rather ponderous, have a handsome upward trend, raising their arms to form a narrow conical crown. The foliage is usually a dull gray green or a pale bluish green, looking much lighter and less shiny than that of any of the other Pines, and dis-

tinctly thin and tufted. The flowers, unlike those of almost all other Pines, do not appear until July. And the cones take three years to mature after pollination. After a Chihuahua Pine has been cut, there is often a dense coppice growth of shoots from the stumps, a trait rare among the conifers. Indeed, the Chihuahua Pine is something of an anomaly, for it stands halfway in evolution between the soft Pine group and the hard Pines. As in the soft Pines, the sheath is early deciduous from around the base of the needles, but it is like the hard Pines in the character of its wood, which is not much inferior to that of the Western Yellow Pine. Primarily, however, this is a Mexican species, and its importance in the United States is slight. But to seek it out, where it lords it on the lonely ranges of the Mexican border, provides for the ardent student of western trees a memorable journey into that sunburnt land of Apaches and rustlers and the vanished smoke of burning wagon trains.

WESTERN YELLOW PINE

Pinus ponderosa Lawson

OTHER NAMES: Bull, Black Jack, Western Red, Western Pitch, Big, Heavy, Sierra Brownbark, Western Longleaf, or Ponderosa White Pine.

RANGE: Almost throughout the mountains of the western states at low altitudes in the north and increasingly higher in the south, from southernmost British Columbia, western Texas and the high mountains of southern California, occurring sporadically on the high plains of Montana and Nebraska, and high mesas of Arizona and Oregon, rare in southwestern North Dakota, absent from the desert ranges of California and Nevada, from the Coast Ranges of British Columbia and Vancouver Island, and the Olympic peninsula. Varieties are found on the mountains of Mexico.

DESCRIPTION: *Bark* of younger trees blackish or dark red-brown and narrowly furrowed, that of very old specimens with great broad, orange, or russet plates built up of many thin scales. *Twigs* orange-brown, with the odor, when broken, of orange rind. *Winter buds* brown and resinous. *Leaves* 3 (rarely 2 or 5) in a bundle, 5 to 11 (or exceptionally 15) inches long, dark green, thick but flexible, the leaf sheath persistent and distinctly fringed. *Flowers* — male 2 to 3 inches long and dark red in California, short and yellow in the Rockies, female dark red, in pairs or clustered. *Cones* 3 to 6 inches long, scarcely stalked, lustrous, light reddish brown or clay-yellowish, all but the small lowest scales thick, inwardly ruddy, distinctly 2-edged, with broad low-pyramidal tips armed with small slender recurved prickles. *Seed* ½ inch long, dull yellowish mottled with purple, with light purple-brown wings. *Wood* hard, strong, medium-light (29½ pounds per cubic foot, dry weight), fine-grained but coarse-textured, the heartwood orange-brown or reddish yellow, the very thick sapwood lemon-yellow to nearly white.

If you know your West at all, you know its Yellow Pine. It is found in every western state and parts of Canada and Mexico, from near to sea level in Washington to 10,000 feet in Arizona. In general, it chooses the life-zone that ecologists call the Arid Transition — the very range of conditions that man himself finds most agreeable and the eastern tourist most exhilarating. So the Yellow Pine grows most abundantly in the West's prime "Vacation-land" as the travel posters call it. Its dry and spacious groves invite you to camp among them. Its shade is never too thin and never too dense. Its great boles and boughs frame many of the grandest views, of snow-capped cones, Indian-faced cliffs, nostalgic mesas, and all that brings the world to the West's wide door.

Untold millions, for example, have taken that ride by train or car from Williams, Arizona, to the south rim of the Grand Canyon, through the flickering light and shade of the Western Yellow Pines. Wide-spaced as if planted in a park, stately of trunk, with colorful orange or cinnamon or buff-yellow bark, the Pines of that fine plateau are all of this one species. And they look so unlike any other western tree that there is no mistaking them.

If you get out of your car, you discover that no conifers are finer than these for a walk beneath their boughs — so ample and open their groves, so clean the forest floor of all save needles and grass and pungent sagebrush, with here and there a fleck of wildflower red or blue — some bugler pentstemon or lupine with its pouting lip. And the voice of these Pines is a grand native chanty. "Of all Pines," thought John Muir, "this one gives forth the finest music to the winds." If you have been long away from the sound of the Western Yellow Pine, you may, when at last you hear it again, close your eyes and simply listen, with what deep satisfaction you cannot explain, to the whispered plain-song of this elemental congregation.

And you will breathe again, with a long, glad inhalation, the cleanly incense of these groves, which is nothing so cloying or seductive as a perfume. It is an aroma, rosinous and timbern, that pervades much of the life of all the West, and many towns, like Bend, Oregon, and Flag-staff, Arizona, are perpetually steeped in its wholesome, zestful odor. Indeed, the town of Flagstaff takes its name from the incident, on the Fourth of July, 1876, when a group of scouts stripped a lofty pine of its branches and "with suitable ceremony" raised the American flag upon it, with rawhide strings. With time the gigantic flagpole became a landmark of the trail, known from Santa Fe to San Francisco. " 'Travel straight West, stranger, till you come to that flagstaff,' " im-migrants used to be told. " 'There's a good spring there, and it's warm alongside that mountain, and a good place to camp.' " [1]

Of all western Pines this one seems to the beholder most full of light. Its needles, of a rich yellow-green, are burnished like metal. When the shadowless summer winds come plowing through the groves, waving the supple arms and twigs, the long slender needles stream all one way in the current, and the sunlight — astronomically clear and constant — streaks up and down the foliage as from the edge of a flashing sword. Then, when the wind is still and the trees stand motionless in the dry heat, a star of sunlight blazes fixedly in the heart of each strong ter-

[1] *Arizona, A State Guide.* Hastings House. 1940.

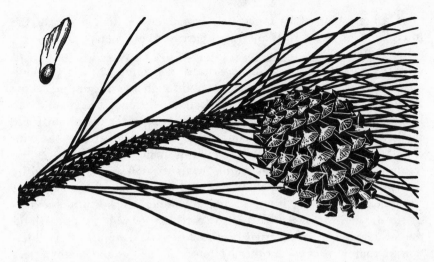

minal tuft of needles. Each tree bears a hundred such stars, each clump of Yellow Pines a thousand, and the whole grove blazes like a temple with lighted sconces for some sacred day. The Western Yellow Pine covers an area of 1,000,000 square miles on this planet's surface! And no tree that grows, and few works of man, one feels, could satisfactorily replace an acre of this, the foremost lumber Pine of all the West. Deep-rooted, aromatic and sparkling, the forest stands exultant, with the mule deer bounding through its aisles and overhead the ravens, jet and stertorous, cruising the timber from canyon rim to snowy range.

The Western Yellow Pine is a tree gregarious in high degree. It will associate with other species on occasion — Pinyon in the South, Lodgepole in the North and, with Douglas Fir in California. It tolerates the red-trunked Incense Cedar in the Sierra Nevada, and the White Fir, many-tiered and fragrant, in the Rockies. But best it likes to grow alone, to see nothing but its kindred to the horizon. It is not fastidious as to geology and soil, will thrive upon limestone or basalt, gravel or sandy clay-loam, or endure with little soil at all on cliffs and rocks. It mounts the cinder cones of the West's not long-dead volcanoes and gives shade even on the pitiless malpais, the pumic rock of old lava flows. It springs up freely on burned-over lands, but is seldom or never a true alpine tree. The high altitudes to which it goes in the southern Rockies are still squarely in the temperate zone.

The preferred habitat of this great tree is on level or rolling land. Even in the Sierra Nevada, it elects the floors of the U-shaped valleys carved out by glaciers, and, in the Rockies, silted-up beaver ponds.

Over a great part of its range it is found on the high plains of the interior, or on those lofty plateaus that the Westerner prefers to call mesas — taking from the Spanish pioneers the word for table. Most of this area is located deep in the interior of the country, where the summers are very dry. Indeed, as you travel through a vast forest of Yellow Pine in midsummer, when the air is like a furnace breath and the bunch grass is withered to straw, you marvel that trees of such size can grow under such desertic conditions. Yet remember that the winters have a heavy snowfall and the melt in spring does not run readily off these level lands; most of it sinks to the subsoil and is captured by the extensive root systems of this tree. No Pine has a more efficient equipment of roots, for it is deep and in its branchings almost as extensive as the limbage of the crown. So, searching for water, the roots and rootlets expand in an inverted hemisphere until they meet the subterranean competition of another Yellow Pine. Thus the mighty trees hold each other at a distance in those park-like groves that characterize it.

And mighty this tree certainly is. In the more arid Rocky Mountain states it does not grow so high as on the Pacific coast. Sixty to 125 feet is usual for mature specimens in the Rockies, with a diameter, at breast height, of 20 to 30 inches. On the coast, where the growth is much denser, owing to the greater precipitation brought from the Pacific by the prevailing westerlies, it is still greater in all its dimensions. Near Lapine, Oregon, one specimen was found to be 162 feet high, and 27 feet in circumference around the trunk. In Washington State, on the south slopes of that perfect, snow-capped cone, Mount Adams, stands a Yellow Pine 175 feet high, and 84 inches in diameter. But John Muir measured one tree 220 feet high, in the Sierra Nevada, with a diameter of 8 feet. With such a magnificent physique, its great plates of bark 4 and 5 feet long, its boles soaring, almost without taper till the lowest branches are reached, for 60 feet and more, its short heavy crowns of foliage, and the prodigious spread of its middle branches, well does this species merit the name of *ponderosa* suggested by David Douglas when that famous Scottish explorer of the Northwest wilderness first made it known to science.

But even before his day, it had been distinguished and admired by Lewis and Clark in their immortal journey from the mouth of the Missouri to the mouth of the Columbia and back. It first came to their attention when they noted "pine burrs," borne on the swift current of the White River where it reaches the Missouri in what we now call

South Dakota. Lewis, if not a trained botanist, was a keen observer, and he seems to have recognized that these were not such cones as he knew in his native Virginia; they promised great forests, somewhere far in the mysterious interior, and indeed we know now that they came from some of those outlying stands of Western Yellow Pine found on the high plains of westernmost Nebraska, or else from the Black Hills. The explorers, as they toiled up the Missouri into western Montana, undoubtedly collected specimens of the new Pine, which they speak of in their journal as the "longleaf pine," but unfortunately those specimens were damaged beyond salvation when they were buried at the foot of the Lemhi pass, and only those collected on the return journey were ever brought back to civilization. One of these was a specimen of *Pinus ponderosa* taken in 1800 near present-day Orofino, Idaho, where the canoes were abandoned and horses mounted for the crossing of the continental divide. It was Meriwether Lewis's intention to publish his extensive notes on natural history, and had he done so he might have named this great Pine, but violent death cut short one of the most promising careers in American history. His natural history notes were completely passed over when the expedition journals were first published; his specimens were shuffled through by Frederick Pursh the botanist, in search of novelties, but so superficially that this Pine was not even recognized as distinct and so, just as Lewis's friend Thomas Jefferson feared, it fell to foreigners to rediscover and name far too many of his pioneering "finds."

But the discovery and naming of a tree are small matters compared with the impressive story of the living tree itself, a monarch that expects to reign (man and fire and beetle permitting) for 250 to 500 years. A seedling just starting life has come even so far by a series of lucky accidents, for the seeds are a favorite with numberless animals like quails, squirrels, chipmunks, grouse, and those gray crows known as camp-robbers or nutcrackers. Even so, provident chipmunks are sometimes the friends of Yellow Pine reproduction. On the dry pumice soils of the upper Deschutes basin in Oregon, for instance, as much as 85 per cent of the seedlings come up in chipmunk caches that have either been forgotten by these little scatterbrains or have been left as a legacy by the demise of one of these misers. Foresters found one such hoarding in which 29 seedlings had sprung up, and similar clumps dotted the volcanic barrens. For some reason chipmunk-sown clumps are far more likely to survive drought in their early years than wind-sown seeds falling singly on the bitter waste. Where an old tree has fallen and then been burned in a ground fire, perfect hedgerows, 25 to 75 feet long, of Yellow Pine seedling will spring up, fertilized by the minerals in the ash.

The seedling is cruelly subject to heaving of the soil by frosts, to nipping by late spring frosts, to the long summer drought characteristic of most of the West, to browsing by mule deer which, in season, make it their favorite food. Bushes afford the youngster much protection from sun and wind so that sagebrush, bitterbrush, and squawcarpet are its nurses in youth. Later, Lodgepole Pines afford it protection without seeming to compete seriously with it as parent Yellow Pines would do.

The first effort of the little tree is to put down a taproot. This will be 7 to 12 inches long, while above ground only 2 or 3 inches of growth will be made by the shoot in the first year. But the second year more of a top is formed, and by the time it is eight years old the young tree will be about a foot and four inches high — a slow growth. Indeed, few first-class lumber Pines grow so slowly as this one unless it finds unusually favorable conditions such as prevail in the Sierra Nevada and the west slopes of the Cascades. Broadly speaking, Yellow Pine grows very slowly for the first 10 or 15 years; but for the next 75 or 100 years the growth is fairly rapid; exceptional trees will increase 2 feet in height a year and 1½ inches in diameter. At the age of 150 years the increment has fallen off almost completely; the tree is now mature and prime for lumbering, for from this point on only breakage and decay can be expected, in progressive amounts.

In its fiftieth year or so a Yellow Pine begins to bear cones in abundance. But time brings many changes in appearance. The bark of young boles is often furrowed, with slender blackish ridges, the inner bark in the crevices showing somewhat orange or yellowish. Lumbermen call this "blackjack," as though it were a different kind of tree. But "blackjack" bark gradually changes until it assumes those great smooth plates, sometimes 4 or 5 feet long by 18 inches wide, that give the old trees such a noble look. No other western Pine approaches this one in the thickness, the smoothness, the bright color of its bark. Only in the Pines of the Gulf states does one see the same sort of plated bark, on the Longleaf, Loblolly, and Shortleaf Pines. And this is for the very good reason that our Western Yellow Pine belongs to the same section (*Australes*) of the genus *Pinus* as do those southern trees, while no other western Pines do so, except the Jeffrey and Apache Pines. The long needles, too, remind one of the Longleaf Pine, and there is some similarity in the wood, so that the western and southern Yellow Pines compete fiercely in the eastern lumber markets.

That wood, which lumbermen prefer to call Ponderosa or even Ponderosa "White" Pine, makes a very high-grade lumber at its best — fine-grained and so light and soft-textured that it sometimes passes for true White Pine and is often so marketed. It is turned to almost every purpose to which Pine lumber anywhere can be put. In the Northwest many houses are built entirely of Yellow Pine — even the shingles, floors, trim, paneling, doors, and sashes and frames for windows. It is exported, even by the high expense of rail haul, all the way to the eastern states as a general all-purpose factory material in the production of stock sizes of doors, sash, finish, shelving, bevel and drop siding, pattern material, and rustic ceiling and flooring. Much of the "knotty Pine" so much in favor at present is Yellow Pine; it is known from Western White Pine paneling by its brownish, not dark reddish, knots.

In the early days of western settlement this wood was extensively employed for mine props and stulls and in some localities it met the whole demand. Quartz mills for crushing the ore from the mines utilized Yellow Pine for fuel, and a single mine would strip hundreds of acres of forest in a few years, to feed its uproarious stamp mills. Early railroads like the Denver and Rio Grande laid the rails of their heroic engineering through the Rockies on ties of Yellow Pine, and others set them in the sod of the high plains, in the days when buffalo were stopping the first trains and toppling the telegraph posts of Yellow Pine as they scratched their hides against them. Time has shown that Ponderosa is not durable in contact with the soil unless treated with preservatives and in case of a fire in a mine, its resins, when superheated, gave off gases that exploded. Its future is all above ground.

The outlook for Ponderosa Pine as a timber tree is good for a long time to come; that is to say, we are far from the end of it. But we are also far from bringing the rate of cut and of losses by fire, insects, and overgrazing into balance with the rate of reproduction. To be sure, the stand of merchantable timber is great, with 185,441,000,000 board feet. It thus ranks third in the country, exceeded only by Douglas Fir and the southern Yellow Pines. In cut, it ranks fourth — 3,650,000,000 board feet a year.[1] But the annual gross growth or replacement is only

1 The statistics include the Jeffrey Pine, which is not distinguished by lumbermen, but neither does it account for a large share of the total.

half as much as the yearly cut. One reason for this is the serious toll taken by insect damage. The Pine butterfly and the Pandora moth in their caterpillar stages defoliate the trees. The Pine-engraver beetles destroy young growth, and the Western Pine beetle and other coleoptera attack the bark. Laws and chemicals are arrayed against these insects, but their depredations are best halted by cutting timber before it becomes overly mature.

Ground fire is calamitous to young trees and regarded with too much indifference by the population because the flames never break into terrifying crown fires endangering lives and homes. Worse still is overgrazing. Cattle and sheep raisers were well established in the West before lumbering or forestry became common; they think of their rights as an eminent domain, something wrested by their own efforts from the Indians and practically assured by the Constitution. And the open, usually flat groves of the Western Yellow Pine, with their grass cover but little shrubby undergrowth, seem to the stockman as if made for grazing by a God who loves the cowboy. Scientific studies show, however, that heavy browsing of seedlings by stock is one of the worst, perhaps the most objectionable, of deterrents to satisfactory reproduction by this valuable and noble tree. Reduction in the number of cattle per acre, especially on lands stocked with seedling Yellow Pines, is the answer. It will not only aid greatly in the perpetuation of the forest but will bring about improvement in the stock.

Naturally, a tree with such an immense range of climates, altitudes, and soils (perhaps the greatest among all the Pines of North America) exhibits marked variations. Among them are:

Variety *scopulorum* (Engelmann) Lemmon, the ambiugously called Rock Pine or ROCKY MOUNTAIN YELLOW Pine, characteristic of the east slopes of the Rockies and sometimes found to the east of the mountains, on the Great Plains in Montana, Nebraska, etc. It is a smaller tree, both in stature (75 feet is about the average maximum), and in its organs. The leaves are only 5 to 7 inches long and sometimes only 2 to a bundle; they are somewhat curved and definitely more rigid and blue-gray than the Pacific coast form. The cones tend to be smaller (2 to 4 inches long) than those of the typical species.

Variety *arizonica* (Engelmann) Shaw, the so-called ARIZONA PINE, has usually 5 needles in a bundle (but the same tree may also bear bundles with 2 and 3 needles); the twigs are rather glaucous and the brownish, stalked, non-prickly cones are, on the whole, shorter than those of the true species, and the needles slenderer, but only by $\frac{1}{24}$ of an inch.

APACHE PINE

Pinus latifolia Sargent

OTHER NAME: Arizona Longleaf Pine.

RANGE: Mountains of northern Mexico (Durango, Sinaloa, Chihuahua, and Sonora) north through the Chiricahua, Dragoon, and Huachuca Mountains to the Santa Ritas of Arizona, and in extreme southwestern New Mexico.

DESCRIPTION: *Bark* of old trunks rugged and furrowed, divided into narrow plates, at first very dark, becoming yellowish in age; *Twigs,* ashy brown, rugged and stiff. *Leaves* in bundles of 3 or 4, or occasionally 5, close-clustered, stiff and stout, a shining clear green, somewhat glaucous, 10 to 15 inches long, $\frac{1}{12}$ inch thick, square or triangular in cross-section, the edges minutely toothed; leaf sheaths 1 to 2 inches long. *Flowers* — male yellow, female violet. *Cones* in pairs, or whorls of 3 to 5, short-stalked, hard and heavy, broadly egg-shaped or oblong-conic, somewhat reflexed, oblique, and slightly curved, 5 to 7 inches long, ochre-colored and generally lustrous, sometimes covered with an amber-like resin, the tips of the scales reflexed, with very marked transverse keel and tipped with a short slender but hard spine. *Seeds* dark coffee-colored, provided with a long brown wing. *Wood* light yellowish to white, smooth, fine-grained.

Doubtfully distinct from the Western Yellow Pine, the Apache Pine — at least in the days of its youth (the first hundred years, perhaps) — is certainly striking enough even at one glance to be known from any other western Pine, with its glittering needles 10 to 15 inches long, enclosed at base in a long papery sheath. Everyone who has ever seen the famed Longleaf Pine of the Southern states at once remarks the resemblance in foliage between the two trees. In advanced age, however, the Apache Pine replaces its magnificent foliage with shorter needles much like those of Western Yellow Pine, and the bark comes to look more and more like that of its relative.

But certainly in youth this is as handsome a Pine as any in all the West, even though it only attains about 75 feet in height, with a trunk diameter of 30 inches. It grows abundantly on the high mountains of southern Arizona, old "Apache country" where only 75 years ago — in the memory of many Southwesterners still living — Cochise and Geronimo were on the war path, leading the United States cavalry around in circles, raiding the ranches, torturing and slaughtering settlers, and running off horses and women.

The lumber of Apache Pine is reported to be of fine quality, but the tree grows in such inaccessible spots and is so largely included in national forest lands that it does not appear on the market.

JEFFREY PINE

Pinus Jeffreyi Greville and Balfour

OTHER NAMES: Bull, Western Black, Truckee, or Sapwood Pine.

RANGE: From southernmost Oregon south to the mountains of California at altitudes of 5000 to 9500 feet, generally on the east slopes of the Sierra Nevada; in the northern Coast Ranges it occurs almost at sea level, but on the mountains of southern California in isolated groves on high peaks: Big Pine Mountain (Santa Barbara County), Mount Pinos (Ventura County), Mount Wilson (Los Angeles County), Big Bear Valley in the San Bernardinos; on San Jacinto Peak to 9500 feet, Pine Valley in the Cuyamaca Mountains (San Diego County) down to 3500 feet. Also in the San Pedro Mártir Mountains in Baja California.

DESCRIPTION: *Bark* of old trunks hard, non-resinous, dark reddish brown, wine-color or tawny, deeply furrowed with rather narrow grooves. *Twigs* stout, on the first season's growth green overcast by a frosty or glaucous bloom, becoming on old wood brownish but retaining something of the bloom or cast; the odor of the twigs, when broken, like that of pineapple. *Leaves* 3 to a bundle, 5 to 9 inches long, coarse and stout, dark blue-green, marked on young trees at least by the powdery lines of prominent stomata. *Cones* 6 to 10 inches long, with numerous, closely compacted, stout scales projecting almost horizontally from the cone axis; prickles long and delicate, mostly deflexed, the points straight or slightly turned in, seldom protruding outward. *Seeds* ½ inch long, with an inch-long wing. *Wood*, light (32½ pounds per cubic foot, dry weight), straw-color and rather wide-grained.

The great mountain wall of the Sierra Nevada has two unlike faces. The western face, intercepting the moisture-laden winds from the Pacific, is well watered, and magnificently forested, and though the descent from the highest peaks to the base is great, the angle of the slope is not. In absolute contrast is the eastern face of this range of mountains. It forms, in places, one of the steepest, swiftest descents — almost a downward plunge — of the planet's surface. It faces the desert, and its slopes are arid. At first this side of the Sierra appears

much the less hospitable and charming, and it is certainly less accessible. But in time one comes to have a special affection for its dramatic
scenery, for its pure, cold lakes so secretively concealed, for the bracing dryness of its air, for its greater wildness and lack of milling throngs
of our fellow humans whom we are so glad to know are enjoying
themselves, with rights in paradise quite the equal of our own — and
so glad to put out of earshot and mind.

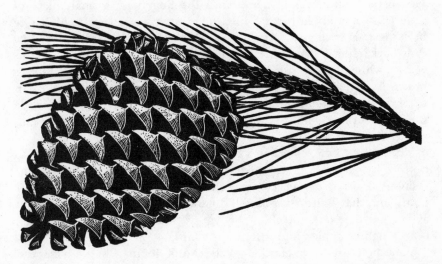

It is on the craggier, drier, lonelier side of the Sierra that the
Jeffrey Pine comes into its own. True that it is found on the western
slopes too, but in limited quantities; there reigns its close relative and
rival for our admiration, the Yellow Pine; on the eastern slopes Yellow
Pine seldom occurs; and Jeffrey Pine is the most impressive of all trees.

And certainly it is scarcely less imposing than Yellow Pine in its
dimensions. Under forest conditions it may shoot up 125 or even 175
feet high, with a trunk 5 or 6 feet in diameter. Its blue-green foliage
reflects the sunlight just like the yellow-green of the Yellow Pine, and
is even more densely tufted. The cones are much larger — 5½ to 11
inches long — and heavier, with the prickles backwardly hooked instead of standing out straight. The shape of the Jeffrey cones is that
of an old-fashioned beehive, and from the first the cone has a distinctly
purplish cast, becoming richly ruddy in old cones. Next to the three
truly gigantic-coned Pines (the Digger, Coulter, and Torrey), Jeffrey
cones are the largest in the West, so handsome that people gather them

as mementoes of glorious vacation days or even for sale to the impressionable tourist.

The bark of the Jeffrey Pine goes through the same evolution as the Yellow's; that is, in youth it is comparatively dark, and deeply furrowed with narrow, braided ridges, and becomes gradually smooth and divided into great plates. Experts tell us that the two species can be distinguished by the greater hardness of Jeffrey bark. Thus if you will tap an old Yellow Pine's plates with the fingernail, a small piece of scale will generally fall free, while the glossier, harder scales of Jeffrey bark are merely dented. Again, the inner surface of a scale of Yellow Pine bark, especially one from near the base of the trunk, is a sulphur-yellow while the interior of the scale, when you break it across, is brown or tan, and there are strong resin pits throughout the scale. In a Jeffrey bark scale, however, the interior shows deep reddish, while the inner surface is light creamy pinkish-brown or chocolate color and no resin pits are present.

The Jeffrey Pine, too, has a smell of its own, though one hard to capture by description. A broken twig of Yellow Pine has but a faint resinous odor of orange or tangerine rind. All are agreed on that point, and that Jeffrey twigs smell different. But there is no agreement as to what the odor resembles. Some say violets, some say pineapples, others mellow apples, and still others vanilla.

Some botanists have classified Yellow and Jeffrey Pines as one and the same thing; others have rated the Jeffrey but a variety; and certainly there are many intermediate, perhaps hybrid, specimens to confuse one. But a true Jeffrey Pine is distinguishable from very early in its life by foliage, leader shoot, buds, twigs and bark.[1] Older trees are known apart even at a distance, by the very port of their limbs. In the Yellow Pine the boughs are distinctly stout, often grotesquely bent and gnarled in very old trees, and comparatively short and straight in young ones; usually they are but slightly upturned at the ends. The Jeffrey Pine boughs are more slender, elongate, and straight, and distinctly upturned at the ends; also they are retained longer on the bole, so that the trunk of a Jeffrey Pine appears shorter, the crown longer and more symmetrical.

High on the Sierra Nevada there occurs sometimes a growth form of this species scarcely recognizable as the stately forest tree of lower altitudes, for it sprawls along the ground, lies flat on the rocks, cowers

[1] Kenneth H. Bradshaw. "Field characteristics distinguishing *Pinus ponderosa* and *Pinus Jeffreyi.*" *Madroño* vol. 6, pp. 15–18. 1941.

in hollows sheltered from the winds, and in every respect behaves like a true alpine tree — something the Yellow Pine will never consent to do. The picturesque specimen on Sentinel Dome in Yosemite, photographed by everyone who ever climbed to that windswept top with a camera, is a typical alpine aspect of the Jeffrey Pine.

The lumber from Jeffrey Pine is marketed as Yellow Pine and so closely similar are the two woods that no separate statistics are needed by the lumber industry. So we scarcely know how much Jeffrey Pine is being cut. Much of the stand is in the national parks and the national forests, and the inaccessible situations there in the mountains would always have made these trees unmerchantable. But on the high plateaus around Mount Shasta, and the basins of the McCloud and Pit Rivers, this tree grows in most tempting style, in vast stands of tall timber, and here the cutting has been long and heavy. You have only to notice, as you motor through that little-visited wild country between Shasta and Lassen Peak, the height of the sawdust piles, to believe that the toll is great.

DIGGER PINE

Pinus Sabiniana Douglas

OTHER NAMES: Bull, Gray, or Grayleaf Pine.

RANGE: Foothills of the eastern slopes of the Sierra Nevada and, intermittently, all around the mountainous rim of the Great Central Valley of California, in the Coast Ranges seeking the drier situations, occurring as low as 500 feet in the northern part, and, in the southern part, at increasingly higher levels (2000 to 5000 feet in Santa Barbara County).

DESCRIPTION: *Bark* of the trunk of old trees thick, with wide furrows, and irregular, braided, scaly ridges, dark brown or nearly black, the bright orange underbark showing between them. Twigs stout, pale and glaucous, the first season, turning nearly black the second. *Leaves* 3 in a bundle, borne drooping and very sparsely in tufts at the ends of the sparse twigs, 8 to 12 inches long, stout but flexible, not rigid, and pale blue-green or grayish because of the whitened rows of stomata on each of the three faces. *Flowers* — male yellow, female dark purple on short stalks. *Cones* ponderous, 6 to 12 inches long, 5 to 7 inches broad, thick, drooping on long stalks, becoming at maturity light reddish brown, the scales with very thick down-bent and keeled faces, these narrowed to fierce, stout, up-curved spines. *Seeds* ¾ inch long, rounded and plump below, compressed at the tips, dark brown to black with a hard thick shell and encircled by a wing ½ the length of the sweet, slightly resinous nut. *Wood* light (30 pounds per cubic foot, dry weight), soft, weak, brittle, close-grained, with red or light brown heartwood and thick white sapwood.

Among the Pines of California, so many of which are either grand and beautiful, or of the greatest economic importance, or both, the Digger Pine does not, at first, seem to stand high on any score. Its foliage, which droops, sad and gray, is all tufted at the ends of the twigs, and though the needles are so long, their number on a tree is so sparse that the Digger Pine has been described as "the tree that you can see right through." Just where the weary prospectors of old and the hiker of today would most enjoy some cooling shade, this tree gives practically none. As timber it is nearly in the worthless class; the wood rots quickly when wet, and when dry it warps so badly that the old-time California lumbermen used to say that "boards from the mill stacked outside to season will walk off the lot overnight." More, the trunks are very commonly forked near the base one or more times, so that instead of one clear trunk out of which boards might be cut, there are often several spindling and eccentric stems. Although the Digger Pine sprawls out over a great deal of room, it seldom becomes a very tall tree, and so is not able to bear its bushy form with any great dignity. The big cones with heavy prickles are curiosities, but they look outsize on the scant branches.

So it may seem surprising that David Douglas, the first discoverer of this tree, should have described it as "a noble new species" and "one of the most beautiful objects in nature," and that in sending it to Joseph Sabine, secretary of the London Horticultural Society, in whose honor he named it, he should have ventured to express the hope that in English gardens the Digger Pine would "exist and flourish when we shall cease to be, when we shall be gone forever." These words were written shortly after Douglas, who was then, in 1830, staying at San Juan Bautista Mission, had ascended the Gabilan Range where this tree still grows. He did not live to see this Pine established in England.

Yet David Douglas was a veteran plantsman, who had seen the most splendid conifers of the Pacific coast; he must have had good reasons for admiring these Digger Pines. And indeed the longer one travels about in its range — the inner Coast Ranges and the foothills of the Sierra Nevada — the more one comes gradually to understand why he admired it. From rating it practically as a clown of a tree, we come to appreciate it at last both for its strange, awkward grace, the subtle lightness and appropriateness of its form in the sunbitten localities where it grows, and for its association with much of the romance of early California. For it is one of the commonest trees along parts of the old Camino Real, the Spanish king's highway, along which are strung the Franciscan Missions; no less is it characteristic of the Mother Lode country, the site of the great gold rush of '49.

When you go to Sutter's Mill, on the American River, where gold was first discovered, you see the Digger Pine leaning out from the hillsides all around that fateful spot. And all through the wandering length of the Mother Lode country along California State Highway 49, it is the dominant Pine. In spring its feet are swathed in sheets of the sky-blue lupine and orange California poppies that touch those foothills of destiny with magic, and the romance of the old mining towns like Columbia and Mokelumne Hill, Jackass Hill, Chinese Flat, Angel's Camp, and all the rest of them is framed in the setting of this omnipresent Pine. It springs now on hillsides which still bear the scars of the mad rush for gold and encroaches upon the old graveyards of the Argonauts. If indeed you "can see through" this tree, it is ghosts that you see.

In the hot inner Coast Ranges the Digger Pine grows where, else, no tree at all might grow. It reaches its finest proportions where it crowns the steep, arid, conical hills between the Sacramento River and the higher Coast Ranges of California's North Country. Where it grew abundantly, in the southern coastal ranges, the Indians settled thickly, to live upon its sweet nuts; and so, because there were more souls to be saved where this tree grew, the good Franciscan fathers plodded their tireless sandaled way in its thin shade.

For the California Indian had the highest respect for this tree so despised by the white man. The sweet oily seeds were an important article of food with the native tribes, only slightly less so than that of the Oaks. The cones, when little and green, were also eaten; the Indians cut out the soft core and devoured it uncooked. Young buds and the inner bark in spring also furnished them with food, and they ate the rosiny, gummy exudations. When the white settlers ruthlessly cut down these trees, either to be rid of them or for whatever value as timber they had, the Indians did not always contain their grief and rage. They found it hard to follow the thinking of the white man, which seems to have run something like this: The Digger Indian (a contemptuous name by which the pioneers inaccurately lumped all California tribes together) used the tree as food; what is good for an Indian is beneath notice for a white man; *ergo,* the tree merited about the same respect as the Indians, who were dispossessed, when not enslaved, beaten, or killed.

One characteristic the Digger Pine has by which it can be often distinguished almost as far as it can be seen. For most trees when they grow on a hillside still grow vertically, and appear to march, erect, down the slope, but the Digger Pine has a most engaging and picturesque way of growing at right angles to the slope, so that it leans out from the hillside in partial defiance of gravity. Dignity such a habit may lack, and yet there is in it a sort of admirable conformity to contour. At any rate, such Pines give to the arid hills they clothe a distinctive appearance that in time becomes linked in the mind with the Californian's sunniest hours, when he turns to the inner Coast Ranges in search of wild flowers, old ranches, meandering back-roads, and all the sights and sounds of a gentler age.

TORREY PINE

Pinus Torreyana Parry

OTHER NAMES: Soledad, Lone, or Del Mar Pine.

RANGE: Known only from the California Coast at Del Mar, San Diego County, and the eastern end of Santa Rosa Island.

DESCRIPTION: *Bark* of old trees thick, deeply fissured, with irregular broad ridges covered with close purplish scales. *Twigs* very stout, the first season bright green, the second year bright glossy green, the third nearly black. *Leaves* 8 to 13 inches long in dense tufts at the ends of the twigs, in bundles of 5, stout, gray green, and marked with rows of stomata on the three faces. *Flowers* — male yellow in short dense heads, female on long, stout stalks. *Cones* massive, 4 to 6 inches long and about as thick, reflexed or spreading on long stalks, at maturity deep chestnut-brown, unsymmetrical, the scales much thickened at the outer end, and tapering to a sharp down-bent point but not armed with a spine. *Seeds* angled ¾ to 1 inch long, with thick, hard shell, the upper surface light yellow-brown, the lower mottled, nearly surrounded by the short dark wing. *Wood* soft, weak, brittle, light (30½ pounds to the cubic foot, dry weight), and coarse-grained, the heartwood light yellow, the sapwood thick and yellow or white.

Three miles north of the pretty seaside town of La Jolla, California, a wind-swept mesa drops away some three hundred feet to the Pacific.

The winter rains have clawed this soft tableland down into little barrancas that, joining, become considerable arroyos and these in turn unite to make canyons plunging seaward. In these V-shaped hollows, so that one looks from the mesa down into their crooked crowns, troop the Torrey Pines, the rarest in North America, perhaps in the world. For they are found as natives only on this one mesa, to the number of some 3000 specimens, and on Santa Rosa Island, off the coast of Santa Barbara, where there are perhaps 100 trees surviving from a day when what are now the Channel Islands were peninsulas standing out in the ocean, and this species was, very likely, abundant on the whole southern California coast. A changing shore, a shifting climate perhaps, have all but exterminated this curious species.

The Torrey Pine is strikingly unlike all others except its Californian relatives, the Bigcone and the Digger Pines. Its enormous cones, weighing a pound or more, are armed with great, stout, fiercely hooked scales — not a pleasant sort of fruit to have drop on your head. Its leaves show a dusty gray-green, and, up to a foot long, are confined to bristling tufts at the ends of its long, sinuous branches. No wonder that it was recognized, as soon as seen by a botanist, as something unique. And its first botanical collector was Charles Christopher Parry, physician, geologist, and botanist with the Mexican Boundary Survey, who, hearing of these Pines, the big sweet nuts of which the Indians ate, made his way up the coast from San Diego, in 1850, to see them. He named them in honor of Dr. John Torrey, his old teacher, the great botanist at Columbia University.

In the wild this species grows only 15 to 20 feet high, but the charm of the Torrey Pines lies rather in their strange unsymmetrical growth as they lean picturesquely from the sides of the arroyos and the front of the mesa. This asymmetry is due in part to the inherent tendency of the boughs of old trees to grow excessively, sprawling and winding near the ground. But the strangely sculptured forms are the result of the age-long punishment by the sea winds laden with fine salt spray, so that many of the trees seem to be flinging themselves upon the slopes of the mesa to escape it. Prostrate, or semi-prostrate, or excessively developed upon the leeward side and appearing as if blighted upon the windward, they take on forms so bizarre that no art save Nature's could achieve them. As a result, every tree in the grove is oddly individual and seems a spirit captured in a twisted form.

And not a little of the beauty of the Torrey Pines City Park, which includes the greater part of the mesa, is due to the setting of the trees, to the sweet solemnity here which, since the great artery of U.S. Highway 101 has been shortened and carried away from the Park, is broken now by few visitors save on holidays. Far down below, the shore stretches away, curved as a curlew's bill, in parallel bands of color, golden dunes, white fringe of breakers, green of the shoal water, rusty brown of the fringing beds of giant kelp, blue of the open sea fading off to a silvery horizon where the fog banks lie. Here are pungent odors, of the rosiny Pine themselves, of the minty sages, of the *yerba santa* with its blue trumpet-flowers and woolly white leaves. The wind blows winy here, and brings the silken thunder of the surf, and plays upon the Pines as on a wild harp. If this is a small beauty spot, only 1600 acres in extent, it is a subtle one.

Torrey Pines in Nature are very slow-growing, and yet not long-lived for conifers. A span of a century is usual, of two centuries rare. Their fertility is potentially great, but owing to the ravenous appetites of birds and rodents for their sweet seeds, the reproduction rate must be something like one in many thousands. The aridity and exposure of the position on the mesa are great; hence each tree is its neighbor's fierce competitor, and the stand has always been and will remain sparse.

Yet in cultivation, the Torrey Pine acts like a spirit released from an evil spell. In form and speed of growth a garden Torrey Pine is almost unrecognizable as a descendent of those stunted ancients on the mesa. A tree on the grounds of the University of California at Berkeley grew 4 feet a year for many years. A bud at the tip of a main axis was a foot in length while still in autumn dormancy. A gigantic specimen known as the Ward Torrey Pine grows in a village dooryard at Carpinteria. It was dug up, as a seedling, on Santa Rosa Island and replanted in 1894; by 1947 it was 101 feet high; the trunk was 5 feet thick, and the branches had a spread of 122 feet, with no end to its lustihood in sight. While the sparse needles of the wild tree cast almost no shade, this lawn tree is luxuriant of foliage and fully as umbrageous as one could ask any Pine to be. Everything indicates that the Torrey Pine could become one of the most magnificent ornaments of any country with the Mediterranean type of climate. It is a moderate success even now in New Zealand.

BIGCONE PINE

Pinus Coulteri D. Don

OTHER NAMES: Coulter, Nut, or Pitch Pine.

RANGE: Coast Ranges, from the Santa Lucia Mountains (Monterey County) and Mount Diablo, south in scattered groves at elevations of 3000 to 60000 feet to the Cuyamaca Mountains of San Diego County, and most abundant on the San Bernardino and San Jacinto Mountains.

DESCRIPTION: *Bark* of the trunk thick (1½ to 2 inches), dark brown or nearly black, the thin, closely scaly ridges broad, rounded, and braiding. *Twigs* very stout, in the first season dark orange-brown becoming, after a few years, black. *Leaves* tufted at the ends of the branches, 6 to 12 inches long, in bundles of 3, and 3-sided, stout, rigid, dark blue-green and marked on each face by numerous bands of stomata. *Flowers* — male yellow, female dark reddish brown. *Cones* light yellow-brown, massive, 10 to 20 inches long, 6 to 7 inches broad, pendant on short stalks, unsymmetrical at base, with broad, thick, wiry scales, armed with flat, broad, hooked claws ½ to 1½ inches long. *Seeds* compressed, ½ inch long, dark chestnut-brown, the thick shell encircled by the tapering wing which is an inch longer than the seed and over ½ inch broad. *Wood* weak, brittle, soft, and light (26 pounds per cubic foot, dry weight), the heartwood light red, the sapwood thick and nearly white.

Three Pines of southern California have outsized cones, but those of the Bigcone or Coulter Pine are larger than even those of the Torrey and Digger Pines. Fifteen to 20 inches long, and often weighing 5 to 8 pounds, the cones are armed with fierce talons. Visitors to California regard them as a curiosity, and take them home separately or by the sackful for the amazement of relatives or the ornamenting of the summer fireplace. One might expect the tree which produced such giant fruit to be itself a Goliath among Pines, and indeed this species does grow commonly 40 to 75 or even 90 feet high, with a fine spread of long lower branches, and trunks 1 to 2½ feet in diameter. But these dimensions are not impressive in a state which produces Sugar Pines, Douglas Firs, Redwoods, and Bigtrees — true forest monarchs which could stretch their lower limbs over the top of the average Bigcone.

However, where the Bigcone Pine grows, in the central and southern Coast Ranges of California, it does not have to compete with these species, and its greatest rival is the handsome Yellow Pine, from which it can be distinguished by its pale or yellowish green foliage, in contrast with the bright green mass of the Yellow Pine.

In the station where it was originally discovered in 1831 by Thomas Coulter, near the mission of San Antonio in the Santa Lucia Mountains, Bigcone is associated with the Santa Lucia Fir. On the west slopes of the Santa Lucias where they drop abruptly into the sea, the Bigcone holds its place grandly even in the presence of the Redwoods which stand in narrow files in the bottom of the canyons. On the driest and rockiest chaparral slopes, it sometimes has for neighbor the Knobcone Pine, but easily overawes that spindling tree. In the Sierra Madre and the San Bernardino Mountains, the Bigcone attains some of its grandest dimensions, and on the high mountain plateau in the San Diego back-country, its groves are favorite sites for cottages and summer resorts. Even when standing in groves, the Bigcone is still a tree of ample dimensions, with long benignant arms, heavy crown, thick-set trunks covered with a dark-hued bark so roughly broken as to form an irregular network of long fissures. Sometimes the bark loosens into long plates or scales.

The Indians seem to have eaten the seeds of the Bigcone Pine, but they always regarded them as inferior to those of the Pinyon and Digger Pine. Lumbermen are increasingly cutting this tree, though the wood is very knotty. The Bigcone shows less precocity, vitality, and ability to reproduce swiftly after fire than the Knobcone but is still far more vigorous than Yellow Pine. This is a tree that will be prized for ages to come for its grand, untamed, rustic strength and beauty. And always there will be the wonder of those mighty cones. Why did Nature go to such lengths as this simply to reproduce the tree? But Nature does not answer the "why" of things; she leaves that to the moralist, being herself preoccupied with *how* to do them.

BEACH PINE

Pinus contorta Douglas

OTHER NAMES: Western Scrub, North Coast Scrub, Sand, Shore, or Knotty Pine.

RANGE: Coast from maritime Alaska (as far north as Skagway) to that of Mendocino County, northern California, and, in Oregon and Washington, inland on the Coast Ranges and on the western slopes of the Cascade Mountains.

DESCRIPTION: *Bark* of trunks thick (¾ to 1 inch), deeply and irregularly furrowed and cross-checked into small oblong plates covered with numerous orange- or purple-tinged closely flattened scales. *Twigs* stout, at first orange, becoming dark red-brown and finally blackish. *Flowers* orange-red, the male in crowded short spikes, the female on short stalks, in pairs or clusters. *Winter buds* dark brown, resinous. *Leaves* 1 to 1½ inches long, very dark green and slender (½ inch thick) marked on each face by 5 to 10 rows of stomata. *Cones* ¾ to 2 inches long, light yellow-brown and shining, often unsymmetrical at the oblique base and deflexed on the twig, the scales thin, slightly concave, purplish within, their tips armed with deciduous, long, slender, more or less recurved prickles, those toward the base of the cone, on the upper side, developing into thick mammilate knobs. *Seeds* ⅛ inch long, oblique at the tip, with thin, brittle, red-brown shell mottled with black, and wing ½ inch long, widest near the base, gradually tapering toward the oblique tip. *Wood* medium-light (36 pounds per cubic foot, dry weight), hard, strong, brittle, coarse-grained, the heartwood light brown tinged with red, the sapwood nearly white.

On the fog-swept coasts of northern California and thence northward all the way to Alaska, on shifting sand dunes or on the rocky
headlands where the North Pacific's tremendous wintry anger is vented
in salt spray, there clings and crouches a spindly little Pine with dull,
dark, scrubby needles and contorted stems and boughs, known as the
Beach Pine. Sometimes its trunks writhe, prostrate, on the dunes and
beaches, and sometimes they are reduced to knee height or hip height,
and are thin as stalks of reed. Again, a little back from the first fury
of wind and spray, the Beach Pine may form a thick-set wood of a
scrubby growth, just too high to see over and not high enough to give
shade. Or there may be a lopsided development of thick-set foliage
upon the windward side, forming a sort of natural windbreak behind
which, when you are thoroughly exhausted and chilled from the buffet-
ing of the wind, you take a grateful shelter.

Follow the Beach Pine a little further inland and it becomes a
reasonably high tree, growing to as much as 35 feet, with a depressed
or irregular dark green crown. The slim, crooked trunks, up to $1\frac{1}{4}$
feet in diameter, are clothed in a dark rough bark, and an extremely
heavy crop of small tight cones is borne. These are usually prickly
when young, but the eroding weather of the north coast soon polishes
them smooth. If the stand is a particularly crowded one, the lower
limbs may be lacking, but if the Beach Pine has any space at all in
which to spread itself, there is a strange overdevelopment of thickly
set branches.

Seeing such scrub-like growth of Pine, one would scarcely suspect
the age to which the Beach Pine can attain. Trees two hundred years
old, and possibly three centuries, will in their long battle with the
elements scarcely have reached 40 feet in height. Such longevity is
probably made possible by the dampness of the climate which cuts
down the hazard from fire.

A tree with as many distinctive characteristics as these (most of them
on the grotesque side and quite unfitting the tree to be of any value
as lumber) would seem to be as sharply set off from other species as
one could wish. And yet by insensible gradation, as you follow the
Beach Pine away from the beaches into the high Coast Ranges, it
ceases to be a contorted Beach Pine, *Pinus contorta,* and turns little by
little into the Lodgepole Pine, a timber tree tall and straight. Many
have been the attempts to separate these two trees along specific lines,
but they all break down, and at best the two extreme forms are but
poorly marked varieties of the same thing. For they differ not at all in

flower and fruit and in foliage only in the greater narrowness and dark hue of the Beach Pine's needles. It is chiefly in the trunk and bark that one can find any differences. Habitats intermediate between beach and mountain produce trees intermediate in form.

LODGEPOLE PINE

Pinus contorta var. latifolia Engelmann

OTHER NAMES: Black, Spruce, Prickly, Jack, or Tamrac Pine. Tamarack.

RANGE: From the Nutzotin Mountains of eastern Alaska south through the Rockies of British Columbia and Alberta to Colorado and northern Utah, and on the east side of the Cascades in Washington and Oregon, south, at increasingly high altitudes (6000 to 10,000 feet) in the mountains of California: in the north, in the Trinity Mountains, Siskiyous, and Mount Shasta; abundant southward through the Sierra Nevada; on very limited areas high on the mountains of southern California: the San Bernardinos, San Gabriels, and rare at 10,000 feet on the San Jacintos. Also on the San Pedro Mártir Mountains of Baja California.

DESCRIPTION: *Bark* of trunks thin (¼ inch) and loosely, not closely scaly, and not deeply furrowed or cross-checked, the scales deciduous from old trunks. *Leaves,* about 2 inches long and ⅛ inch thick, dark green, stiff, twisted, 2 to a bundle, the margins minutely toothed. *Flowers, cones,* and *seeds* as in *Pinus contorta. Wood* soft, fine-textured, light (25½ pounds per cubic foot, dry weight), weak, easily worked, not durable, with pale brown heartwood and thick whitish sapwood.

As you cross the Great Plains of Montana or Alberta and reach at last the foot of the Rockies, you see that the slopes are swathed almost to their bases in a great zone of even-aged Pines. When living, the foliage of these Lodgepole Pines is yellow-green and thus paler than that of most conifers, though darker than the leaves of their twinkling companions, the Aspens. Frequently, though, hundreds of acres will be crowded with dead yet still standing Lodgepoles, killed by fire or the far more insidious beetle. But even these "ghost forests," as Westerners sometimes call them, are arresting and by moonlight cast an eery spell, and they but serve, these tree cemeteries, to accentuate by contrast how much of wiry vitality there is in the surviving stands. Often these look as if they had been sown from seed all at the same time — so uniform are they in height and dimensions, and this (for reasons to appear) is probably just what happened. Martially straight — straight and slim as poles — these Pines, if not individually noble, yet make, when densely grown over a vast tract of mountain slope or valley, an impression of forest grandeur, as great today as when Lewis and Clark in their toilsome journey by canoe up the Missouri first beheld their multiple dark lances.

But very different will be your impression if you have come from the magnificently forested Pacific coast — through the western gate of Glacier National Park, for instance — where gracious Hemlocks, giant Cedars, and Douglas Firs grow lushly. For there, when you emerge on the eastern slopes of the Rockies, the Lodgepole forests seem arid, monotonous, and spindling, and thin of shade. Campers and trampers who have tried to make their way through a dense Lodgepole stand, fighting against the dead branches to which it perversely clings instead of neatly self-pruning them like other trees, will find little good to say of the Lodgepole. For when one of these Pines dies it finds no room to fall decently down but, caught in the dead branches of its neighbors, it slants halfway to the ground. So an old Lodgepole grove is a perfect jackstraw pile, exasperating and exhausting to the explorer! Yet this is one of the most curious and significant of all western trees; it has played a great rôle in the lives of red men and white; its vast domain and numbers would be impressive even were it not rich in human associations. It is at the same time a forest weed and a commercial timber crop, a tinder box in case of fire and a phoenix after it. And, finally, it

is not one sort of tree but two, utterly unlike in every trait except botanical.

At different altitudes and under different conditions of crowding or freedom of growth, Lodgepole takes on these two distinctive forms. They do not differ in flower, cones, or leaves, but in the outline of the tree and the shape of the trunk they are strikingly unlike. Timberline trees, and those with ample room to develop, have nothing pole-like about them. Much nobler in aspect, they have no value as timber. So (and because it is much more abundant), consider first the typical form of the Lodgepole Pine, which is that of a spindling tree growing in a close grove; it may be 50 feet high yet possess a trunk only 5 or 6 inches thick — a true pole.

This form is due to the intensive crowding of the trees where they grow together and form a pure stand of this species alone. And that very crowding is due, in turn, to the behavior of the seedlings, and of the seeds which gave rise to those seedlings, and of the cones in which the seeds were borne. For the cones are often retained, unopened, on the trees for years, but sooner or later fire is almost predestined to sweep through a Lodgepole forest. This was true even before the coming of the white man, for the Indians probably started many fires, and certainly lightning, from the Rockies' abundant and savage summer storms, must for ages have started fires among these trees. The tinder-dry deadwood of the lower branches, the dead trees carried in the arms of the living, the thin bark of the living trees, and the resinous crops of successive seasons' cones feed a holocaust sometimes unappeased till every Lodgepole within reach of its wind-whipped breath is consumed to the roots.

Yet the seed life, sealed between the scales by a heavy coat of stiff resin, is not killed by the fire. Indeed, the resin is melted, the cones are roasted till their scales pop open, and out leaps the seed crop that has been dormant for years. Thus as many as 100,000 seedling trees will spring up on a single acre of burn. Most of them are destined to be crowded to death, but even so, a great number will survive to maturity and produce a dense stand. So, where the excessive light, heat, cold, drought, and lack of humus of a burned-over area would be fatal to many more aristocratic trees, the indomitable Lodgepole surmounts, indeed it thrives upon, these harsh conditions. If the Lodgepole is gravely subject to fire, it is incomparably adapted to survive and triumph over it. Further, since all the seedlings after a given burn will be of the same age, the stand will be remarkably uniform — which is ideal for the lumber industry, making cutting and milling easy. Many North American Pines are similarly adapted to natural reforestation after fire, and even in similar measure dependent on fire for release of the seed crop. But Lodgepole is the archetype of the fire forest, which is as distinctive a formation as the coniferous rain forest of the Olympic peninsula.

Few Pines grow more slowly than this one. It takes about a hundred years to produce a saw log of the smallest size — quite a while to wait for a pole to grow! A trunk 3 feet in diameter is probably the outside limit. And though such poles eventually grow to 50 or even 60 feet tall, that is nothing much in the great coniferous forests in the West. In compensation, there is the fact that Lodgepole may come of cone-bearing age at 6 years and seldom later than fourteen — a precocity that, linked with its fertility, is almost unparalleled.

Slow as is the growth of Lodgepole, this species has probably greatly increased its acreage in modern times. For with the increased incidence of fires and the heavy cutting of more valuable trees in so many parts of the West, the Lodgepoles have sprung up over vast areas once occupied by other trees. Moreover, the Lodgepole is a pioneer tree in the invasion of small, flat, springy meadows in the Rockies and the Sierra Nevada, such as grow when old beaver ponds fill up with silt, sedge, brush, and grass. Slowly but steadily the Lodgepole, encircling such meadows, will creep out upon them and on the flood plains of mountain rivers, such as the Merced in Yosemite Valley. Within the memory of persons still living, spots in the Yosemite which now support a close stand of Lodgepole were once open meadows bright with wild iris and browsed by deer. The cottages of Yosemite Lodge are set in just such a Lodgepole grove.

Both on a small and a large scale, then, the Lodgepole is an aggressive pioneer of a tree, much like its associate the Aspen. In the ecological succession of trees, Lodgepole should be ousted at length by such shade-tolerant trees as Western Hemlock, but sometimes one fire succeeds another so soon (as time is reckoned in the life of a tree) that Lodgepole, which is shade-intolerant and sun-loving in the seedling stage, tends to succeed itself decade after decade. Today, Lodgepole covers something like a million square miles, from Alaska to New Mexico and the Sierra Nevada, and much of this is burned-over land that would not be ready for over 100 years to support finer but less vigorous forest types. No one knows from year to year, in so vast an area, how many billion board feet of timber are standing in the form of this species, but there is little doubt that in sheer abundance the Lodgepole is the seventh most common tree in North America.

Lodgepole takes its name from the custom, among the Rocky Mountain Indians, of cutting the trunks into lengths 10 to 15 feet long, in the spring, and peeling off the bark. Then they would set out on their summer hunts, leaving the poles to season until fall. By that time these would have become light, and easily dragged or carried by the women into winter camp. Owing to the growth habits of the tree, these poles were nearly of the same thickness (or thinness) for their whole length. Such a pole 15 feet long may be only 2 inches in diameter and, when seasoned, would weigh only 7 or 8 pounds. Furthermore, it is extremely strong, stiff, and nearly impossible to split. When the red men wished to set up a wigwam these poles were arranged in a circle inclined inward to the top and there lashed together. On these poles were then stretched the buffalo hide which made the walls of the tepee.

Lodgepole sticks were also the favorite for the making of the travois, the litter or drag-sled which, in default of any wheels in the life of the Indians, were dragged by dogs or women. With a piece of hide stretched from the two poles, the travois became a platform to which bundles could be tied when the tribe was on the move. So great was the demand for poles of this particular tree that the Indians of the Great Plains, who had no trees or only the unsuitable Cottonwood or Willow, went all the way to the Rockies to cut Lodgepole Pines, or bought them by barter.

When the first white settlers began to move into Lodgepole country, this tree, more than any other, was a boon to their immediate wants. Its pole-like trunks made it ideal for fencing corrals, and of it the pioneer built his sheds, stables, and sometimes even his cabin. Later, when orchards began to produce fruit in the northwestern states, Lodgepole furnished a cheap and excellent material for fruit boxes. Then came a need for the first telegraph poles, and later for telephone poles, and again this species, when properly treated with preservative, proved ideal — straight growing yet of twisted sinew within.

From the earliest days of ranching in the West, Lodgepole served, too, for poles and rails in fences, for corrals, small bridges, cattle pens, sheds, and barns. For mine props it is a cheap and substantial timber; even wood that has been standing dead from fire for many years can be treated with creosote and thoroughly seasoned and, very light as it is, proves valuable in mines. When creosoted, Lodgepole crossties will serve a railroad bed without decay for many years; the very first railroads to enter the Rockies utilized Lodgepole ties. At Horse Creek, in the Wyoming Range, the forests are still levied upon for railway ties. "Lumberjacks fell the lodgepole pines for this purpose in winter, saw them to six-foot lengths, trim them with razor-sharp broad-axes, and then stack them near frozen streams. Pole ties, the most durable, are made from small trees and the tips of larger trees, with only two sides surfaced; slab ties are made of larger poles, split once, with three sides surfaced; quarter ties are made of poles, split into four segments, with four surfaces finished. An experienced trimmer can leave the surfaces of a tie almost as smooth as if planed. In early summer, the timbers are floated 15 or 20 miles to the Green River, where they are boomed (held back by cables stretched across the creek mouths), until the waters are at the best height for the drive to the city of Green River. The boomed timbers extend upstream for miles. If they jam when the booms are removed, men with spiked boots and long pikes walk out to the middle of the stream, upon the treacherous floor of sticks, and work them loose." [1]

In complete contrast to the Lodgepole that the lumberman knows — that is, the pole-shaped specimen of the dense, even-aged stand in the fire forest — is the high-altitude and timberline growth of what is, botanically, identically the same tree. These high mountain specimens grow not in pure stands, but scattered amidst Alpine Larch, Mountain Hemlock, Red Fir, and others. They wear a completely different expression from that of the close-packed typical Lodgepole, as different as is the behavior of a sheep in a flock kept in line by dog and herder, from a lone sheep brought up with children and dogs for playmates. For every close-grown Lodgepole is perforce like the others; every open-grown specimen is an extreme individualist. Shaped by the torque of gales, crouching from the lash of snows, or bent to its knees by mountain slides, its stems often look as if they had writhed as they grew. Comparatively small trees may be — and look — already old, their crowns preternaturally broad in proportion to the foreshortened stem, or lopsided or one-sided. The trunk may become so thickened and shortened as to have a bottle-like swelling at base — this in a Lodgepole! But if conditions are not too harshly arrayed against one of these trees it may attain, as in the high hanging valleys and "flats" of upper Yosemite, a rude nobility. One specimen measured there is 106 feet tall, with a bole 19 feet around.

These high mountain trees, like the grove trees, often retain their

[1] *Wyoming:* American Guide Series. Oxford University Press.

lower branches obstinately, but as living, not dead, wood; this gives such specimens a look of indomitable vitality. The bark of pole-like trees is a thin skin of a hue varying from the gray of ashes to the black of cinders, but in all cases without luster. The bark of the high mountain specimens is thicker, softer, with a warm, living, yellow-brown to ruddy hue, or even a charming pink tint, as if it kept some of the afterglow of alpine sunsets.

Fire probably plays but an infrequent part in determining the life span, the opening of cones, the occurrence or non-occurrence of seeding, in these open-growth mountain trees, and thus neighboring specimens are not even-aged but may be long tree-generations apart. Possibly the mountain trees are longer-lived, too, since less threatened with fiery death. The thick and crooked-boled individuals could never have been used for the poles of lodges or of travois, and no more would most of them be worth logging today, even if they grew in accessible spots.

Truly these trees have life stories quite as different from those of the pole-stemmed specimens, as they are unlike them in appearance, and they deserve a distinctive English name even if they cannot logically be granted a separate botanical one. But there seems to be none as yet, and, when it is given, let us hope it is not made known by revealed authority of some deus-ex-nomenclature, but is born out of the imagination and experience of the western people, just as was the name Lodgepole itself.

EASTERN JACK PINE

Pinus Banksiana Lambert

OTHER NAMES: Gray, Black, Black Jack, Scrub, Prince's or Banksian Pine.

RANGE: From southern Mackenzie and northern Alberta (almost to the base of the far-northern Rockies) in Canada southeastward between the prairies of Saskatchewan and Alberta and the tundras of Keewatin, throughout Ontario except the northernmost part and in Quebec north of the St. Lawrence, south in Nova Scotia, New Brunswick and Maine (only locally abundant) to northern and eastern Minnesota, locally on sterile soils to south-central Wisconsin, northeastern Illinois, northwestern Indiana, and southern peninsula of Michigan, rare in northern Vermont and northern New Hampshire.

DESCRIPTION: *Needles* sparse and scrubby, 2 to a bundle, flat on the inner face, short (¾ to 1½ inches long), thick, stiff, twisted, and dull dark green. *Flowers* — male flowers yellow, in short, crowded clusters, female dark purple, clustered. *Cones* incurved, dull green or purple, finally becoming shiny light yellow, 1½ to 2 inches long, remaining closed for years, the scales thick and armed with a delicate prickle which is usually deciduous. *Seeds* black, triangular, minute (1⁄12 inch long). *Bark* thin, on old trunks with irregularly branched and braided ridges bearing thick dark brown scales. *Wood* — heartwood pale brown, sapwood thick and white, weak, soft, and light (29 pounds to the cubic foot, dry weight).

In the northeastern states, Jack Pine is generally a runty tree, crooked and knotty, with heavy but weak wood, and nothing but the great scarcity of finer timber in recent years has made the lumberman deign to look upon a tree which in the heroic age of eastern lumbering was regarded as the veriest weed. But within the circumscription of the present book, Jack Pine, especially west of Lake Winnipeg and north of the Saskatchewan River, grows as much as 90 feet high, with trunks 2 feet in diameter. Some of the wood produced by these trees is nearly of the same hardness and weight as eastern Red Pine, and clear grades of its lumber are so similar in appearance and working qualities to Red Pine that they could probably pass for it, and doubtless that name has often been assumed for it. More and more, of recent years, heavy tongue-and-grooved Jack Pine planking has been used for roofing under a waterproof covering. Logs as small as 6 inches in diameter are cut into rough slack-cooperage stock and for packing cases. Jack Pine is being used today for pulp in the production of kraft paper, for which it seems peculiarly suited. Growing in dense stands as it does in Canada's Middle West, Jack Pine produces a fine straight timber, comparatively knot-free. So that it is of genuine value in western Canada, and by no means to be despised.

Furthermore this tree covers a vast area between the eastern foot of the Canadian Rockies and the Atlantic coast, scoured by ancient glaciers, sterile and inhospitable to agriculture, leveled again and again by forest fires, which would otherwise be almost barren. This, indeed, is one of the West's numerous fire forest types. For the cones, strangely hump-backed and retained for as much as 25 years unopened upon the tree, seem to thrive upon forest fires. The toasted cones open their scales and out come the wonderfully viable seeds, whose seedlings are able to endure the harsh exposure to light, cold, drought and wind, of a burned-over forest area. Where its nobler competitors would be quite destroyed by such a catastrophe, Jack Pine comes into its own. Growing very fast for the first few years, it may act as a temporary shelter for the tender seedlings of other trees. But in 15 to 20 years the species it has nursed will outstrip it.

KNOBCONE PINE

Pinus attenuata Lemmon

OTHER NAME: Narrowcone Pine.

RANGE: In the Coast Range mountains of southern Oregon and northern California (on the Siskiyou Mountains), Trinity Alps, Mount St. Helena summit, etc.), on the Santa Cruz Mountains, on Point Pinos, near Carmel, Monterey County, and the eastern slopes of the Santa Lucia Mountains, Monterey County; on Mount Shasta (4000 to 5600 feet); on the west slopes of the northern Sierra Nevada, at 1500 to 4500 feet, south to the south side of the San Bernardinos at 2500 to 4000 feet. Lacking otherwise in the southern Sierra Nevada and southern Coast Ranges.

DESCRIPTION: *Bark* of old trunks at base dark brown or tinged with purple, divided by shallow fissures into irregular plates bearing large, loose scales. Twigs slender, dark orange-brown the first season, growing darker. *Leaves* 3 in a bunch, 3-sided, 4 to 5 inches long (rarely 3 to 7 inches), with rows of stomata on all sides, firm, slender, rigid, and pale green. *Flowers* — male orange-brown, female clustered, often with several clusters on the shoots of the year. *Cones* unsymmetrical, 3 to 6 inches long, usually several in a whorl, clustered on short stalks and reflexed around the branch, and persistent, unopened, for many years, sometimes becoming imbedded in the growing wood; in color light yellow-brown, with thin scales of unequal sizes, those nearest the branch with slightly thickened tips armed with minute recurved prickles, those on the outside prominently swollen to transversely keeled knobs fitted with thick and flat incurved spines. *Seeds* black, compressed, ¼ inch long, the shell thin and oblique, the wings gradually narrowed to both ends, 5 times as long as the seed. *Wood* light (22 pounds per cubic foot, dry weight), soft, weak, coarse-grained and brittle, the heartwood light brown, the sapwood often tinged with red.

There can never be any difficulty in identifying the Knobcone Pine at a glance, because its cones occupy so unusual and conspicuous a position on the tree. Instead of being borne at the end of the branches and far out on twigs, like those of most Pines, they are pegged by a short stalk to the wood of the main trunk and branches. Rigidly attached and bent downward, they encircle the stems in whorls or clusters of 3 to 5 at a node, or abnormally seventeen! While unopened, they are remarkably long and narrow, very lopsided at base, and show a most curious development of the scales facing away from the branch and an odd warping or foreshortening of those on the side next the branch. They may remain upon the tree until the second or third or fourth year, when they expand, losing their narrowly conical form, and fall off after releasing their seeds. But more commonly this is not the case. The tree, on the contrary, tends to hoard its cones, sometimes until they are 25 years old, and the growth of the wood may actually engulf the base of the fruit, so that this has been called "the tree that swallows its cones." So they cling there as weathered knobs, awaiting the breath of fire — the destroyer of the parent tree and liberator of the next generation locked away in the prison of the unopening cones.

The seed will germinate in the most barren soils, and from the start the seedlings are hardy. So that the Knobcone Pine, like the Lodgepole, is distinctly a fire forest type — gravely subject to fire and yet marvelously adapted to reforestation after its ravages. About 85 to 160 seeds are formed in a cone. When a young field is springing up with Knobcones after a fire they stand, as Jepson says, "as thickly as stalks in a cornfield." Like the Lodgepole, the Knobcone begins to be fertile at a very early age, and trees only 5 or 6 years old will soon be covered with cones. Unlike the Lodgepole, this tree does not produce wood of any value commercially except as firewood. However, it has even more constitutional vigor, will grow in even more desolate situations, and is not nearly so subject to the attacks of beetles and fungi as the Lodgepole. In reforestation it may yet have a great role to play.

Twenty to 30 feet high, with trunks only 6 to 12 inches in diameter, the average Knobcone is an unimpressive tree among the great conifers of the West, but specimens in favorable situations may grow to be 60 or 70 feet high, with a trunk 30 inches in diameter. When given room to expand, the tree is generally forked and subdivided into a wide irregular crown, with a short trunk and slender branches coming well down to the ground. The thin foliage is usually rather faded in appearance, no matter what the age of the tree, and in general nothing much can be said for this species on the esthetic side. But if man does not admire it, Nature evidently does, for within the spotty range of this species it often grows abundantly. It thrives, where better trees would die, so that at least it may be called the best of possible trees where one finds it.

BISHOP PINE

Pinus muricata D. Don

OTHER NAMES: Pricklecone, Dwarf Marine, Obispo or Umbrella Pine.

RANGE: Coast of California, intermittently, from Humboldt County south to Lompoc (Santa Barbara County) and on the Pacific shores of Baja California near San Vicente, and on Cedros and Guadalupe Islands.

DESCRIPTION: *Bark* at the base of old trees often very thick (4 to 6 inches) and divided by deep fissures into narrow elongate ridges covered by thin scales. *Twigs* stout, in their first season dark orange, subsequently becoming orange-brown with a purplish tinge. *Leaves* in crowded clusters, 2 in a bundle, 4 to 6 inches long, dark yellow-green and rigid, *Flowers* — male orange, in elongated spikes, female short-stalked and whorled, 2 whorls on each fertile shoot of the year. *Cones* strongly reflexed, seated directly on the wood, in whorls of 3 to 7 around the twig, very unsymmetrical, about 3 inches long, at maturity shining, light chestnut-brown, the scales most unequal in size, those nearest the branch slightly flattened and armed with straight, slender spines, those on the outside greatly thickened into stout incurved knobs, sometimes armed with stout, flat, incurved prickles. *Seeds* ¼ inch long, triangular, with a thin, black, roughened shell, the wing four times as long as the seed. *Wood* hard, very strong, coarse-grained, and medium-light (39 pounds per ·cubic foot, dry weight), with light brown heartwood, and thick nearly white sapwood.

When the early lumbermen on the California coast pressed inland, with axe, saw, and ox team, sometimes they passed, near the shore, a tree to which they gave the contemptuous name of Bull Pine. Its stems were bandy, short, and pitchy. Its wood, though heavy, was weak, and certainly coarse-grained and knotty. When behind these shore Pines reared the majestic Redwoods, the Douglas Firs and Yellow Pines, Bull Pine was beneath the notice of a self-respecting logger.

Pitch Pine it was also called by the lumbermen and, where it grows on the Mendocino County flats, Swamp Pine. In Marin County, just north of the Golden Gate, it is often known as Umbrella Pine. For there it takes on, in billowy groves, a beautiful umbracular shape, not wholly unlike that of the Italian Stone Pines one sees in the backgrounds of Renaissance paintings. But the trees beside Mount Tamalpais look less premeditated and "set" than those beside the bay of Naples, more unkempt and wild, as befits a tree breathed on eternally by the prevailing westerlies off the North Pacific.

The accepted if not descriptive name of Bishop Pine owes its origin to the discovery of this species in 1835 by the young Irish botanist Thomas Coulter, who first collected it near the Mission of San Luis Obispo, that is, Saint Louis, the Bishop of Tolosa (Toulouse). Perhaps, too, one may see something rather like a mitre in the prickles that cap the cone scales. Or if both allusions seem a little far-fetched, there is the not very distinctive name of Pricklecone Pine to fall back on. But Bishop Pine is the name spread most widely on the books and officially adopted by the Forest Service.

Much of the year, on the north coast, the Bishop groves stand wrapped in the roiling fogs or keen winds. On the south coast its groves are far and few, sunbitten and lonely. Everywhere, as it clings to the seacoast, in these times turned hostile, this tree survives as a relic (so we learn from fossil cones of the Ice Age) on a shore where it was once widespread. In each of the localities where it occurs, Bishop Pine is molded by the hand of environment so variously that it hardly seems like the same tree. On the flats of Mendocino County it attains its greatest height, 40 or exceptionally 80 feet and, pressed on by other trees, each specimen tends to grow straight but with spire-like crown, and to be self-pruned of lower limbs. On the Purisima hills near Lompoc, on the other hand, it is clothed in boughs almost to the ground, for the trees are well-spaced on the dry hills, shallowly rooted in the diatomaceous rock that is light and white as chalk. On the sterile sands, clean and glaring, of the Mendocino White Plains, Bishop

Pine is only head-high, with spindling stems. On the Point Reyes peninsula, graveyard of ships, the Bishop Pine, wherever the full force of the Pacific gales can reach it through "wind passes" in the Inverness Ridge, is tortured into strange shapes, its boughs to windward whipped away, or bitten back by the salt spray.

But the true beauty of Bishop Pine is seen on the east or leeward side of this same Inverness Ridge, and at near-by Shell Beach, where the trees overhang Tomales Bay. Here, sheltered from the full force of the eternal sea winds, but with the hoarse voice of the surf, the bellowing of the fog horns, the clanging of buoy bells distantly audible most days in the year, the Bishop Pine forms lovely groves, with picturesquely twisted stems, and flat-topped or dome-shaped crowns that interlock, tree with tree. So each tree takes protection from its brethren and all together they achieve an air of inviolable serenity and a sort of pagan sanctity. Or where the winds find passage through breaks in the ridge, it prunes them into weird topiary effect so that their branches seem to stream to leeward like the pennant from a mast.

The most striking sylvical feature of Bishop Pine is the great crop of humpbacked and finely prickly cones clustered in whorls around the twigs and leader shoot. At least one whorl is produced on most fertile shoots each year, from the time the tree comes of bearing age. But the cones do not open the first, second, nor even the third or fourth year, but, green and tightly shut up, they cling on for fifteen years or so before opening. And even after the cones are opened, the tree hoards them like a miser for perhaps another fifteen or twenty years. The result is that many cones, if borne next to the main shoot or trunk, are engulfed in the expanding bark, and may even at last be included in the wood itself, their grave completely concealed by the bark.

A closely related species is the ISLAND PINE, *Pinus remorata* Mason, known only from Santa Cruz Island, California, and Cedros Island, Baja California. It is a slender tree 30 to 65 feet tall, the trunk seldom over 15 to 45 inches in diameter, having, at maturity, rather a flat-topped crown, and deeply furrowed bark. The needles are heavy, 2 to a bundle, dark green, 3 to 8 inches long, $\frac{1}{16}$ inch wide; the cones are practically symmetrical, egg-shaped, only 2 to 3 inches long, scarcely deflexed but standing at right angles to the branch, or nearly so, solitary, or in pairs, or borne in whorls up to 7 in number, each scale plane at the tip or slightly rounded and furnished with a slender, minute prickle. The seed is black, somewhat ridged and minutely roughened, cut obliquely truncate, with a rather stout wing. This Pine grows with the Island Live Oak, *Quercus tomentella*, the island blueberry, *Vaccinium ovatum*, the island manzanita, *Arctostaphylos insularis*, and other endemics of the Channel Islands of California, as well as the Pricklecone Pine and the Christmasberry. Fossil cones show that in Pleistocene (glacial) times this same assemblage of plants grew on the island and sheltered, as a forest, such extinct vertebrates as the island elephant, the dire wolf, the giant condor, and the last of the native North American horses. The tar pits at Carpinteria on the mainland coast of Santa Barbara County have also yielded cones of this Pine and its present plant, and former animal, associates.

MONTEREY PINE

Pinus radiata D. Don

RANGE: Along the California shore from Pescadero, San Mateo County, intermittently to Cambria, San Luis Obispo County, and on Guadalupe Island, Mexico.

DESCRIPTION: *Bark* of old trunks 1 to 2 inches thick, gray, with deep furrows and long irregular flat ridges, the inner bark showing in the

furrows as reddish brown. *Twigs* slender, limber, rather crooked, at first bright brownish and sometimes glaucous, soon gray. *Leaves* 3 (rarely 2) in a bundle, slender, flexible, bright, rich and shining green, 4 to 6 inches long, minutely toothed on the lower surface, rather densely tufted on the twig. *Cones* very short-stalked, reflexed, solitary or in pairs, or more often whorled, 3 to 7 inches long, unsymmetrical at base, with somewhat unequal scales, those on the side of the cone away from the twig enlarged, protuberant and knob-like, the umbos armed with a minute and deciduous prickle; color driftwood-gray overlying a dull yellowish brown. *Seeds* compressed, ¼ inch long with thin brittle shell and striped wing fully 1 inch long. *Wood* brittle, weak, coarse-grained, soft and light (28½ pounds per cubic foot, dry weight), the heartwood light brown to red, the sapwood thick and yellow or nearly white.

Probably no other American tree, certainly no western conifer, has been so abundantly planted all over the world as the Monterey Pine. Sometimes under that name and sometimes called Insignis Pine, it has been grown as an ornamental for well over a hundred years in England, especially the western and southern parts, and in Mediterranean Europe and in North Africa, while in South Africa and Australia it is planted as a valuable timber tree. In many of the cities, towns, and gardens of California, Monterey Pine is considered the best of possible Pines for shade and beauty, attaining in 30 or 40 years a height of 60 to 80 feet, with fine, sturdy boles, a magnificent sweep of boughs that is neither too symmetrical nor too eccentric, rich but cheerful green foliage, and scarcely any special demands in the way of watering or protection from pests. Moreover, the Monterey Pine, unlike most trees, produces a far more luxuriant growth away from its native setting.

And that setting is confined to three small localities, all within the fog belt of the central California coast. The first (that is, the largest and most famous of these), is the Monterey peninsula. Here, between the town of Monterey itself and over the interior hills of the peninsula, to Carmel, it forms its densest growth. It extends also inland some six or seven miles on the ridges above the Carmel valley, and again, south of the Carmel River, it is found at Point Lobos State Park and on a narrow strip of the ocean bluffs as far south as Malpaso Creek. Some sixty miles down the coast, there is a picturesque small stand of Monterey Pine on the Cambria hills. This is the southernmost outpost of the Monterey Pine today, and the northernmost is a grove just south of Point Año Nueve, close to the shore and just south of Pescadero. But in interglacial times the Monterey Pine was more widespread up and down the coast; its fossil cones have been found, along with the sabertooth tiger's fierce tusks, in the La Brea tar pits of Los Angeles, while up in northern Marin County other cone fossils were suddenly revealed by the San Francisco earthquake of 1906. But in the past, as now, Monterey Pine was strictly a maritime tree.

Yet though so closely tied to the coast, the Monterey Pine does not so often grow, as do the Monterey Cypresses, on rocks directly over-hanging the salt spray of high-tide mark. In such localities the Cypress seems better able to endure the harsh conditions. Or perhaps when the Cypresses attempt to spread inland, they meet opposition from the Monterey Pine. These are faster growing and perhaps in other ways more aggressive; so, by root below and shade above, they carry on a subtle warfare with their gnarled fellow conifers and keep them pushed to the very shore.

Like these Cypresses, the Monterey Pines, especially those within a mile of the sea, where the air is most often saturated with the thickest fog, drip with the misnamed Spanish Moss — in reality the lichen *Ramalina reticulata,* which gives the woods a gray and sorrowful look. Though it is not a true parasite (like the dwarf mistletoe that often attacks conifers), but merely a perching plant, the lichen harms the Pines mechanically by shutting out the light and blanketing the leaves, so that boughs are smothered and starved to death, and sometimes whole trees may die from the high cost of playing host to this depen-dant. But these wavering shrouds of lichen are an inseparable part of the solemnity of the groves, and belong there, for weal or woe, as naturally as the pouring fog, and the pervasive and ineluctable reek of some soil- or log-inhabiting mold that, especially at night and in the mist, exhales, as Robert Louis Stevenson called it, "a graveyard odor."

Sometimes when these Pines grow on dunes, their struggles with the shifting sand may result in half-buried trees with sprawling prostrate limbs. Again, their form, when they grow densely in groves, is apt to be spindling — the boles and crowns both unimpressive. It is only farther back from the sea, away from the fogs, the shifting sands, the shrouds of lichen, where these Pines begin to feel the unrelenting cheer of California sunlight and to associate with wide-spreading, normal Live Oaks instead of the tortured Cypresses, that the Monterey Pines begin to stand out as individual trees and take on their inherently ample and even lusty forms. Here the sun runs a glistering finger along the polished surface of the foliage tufts; here the bark grows thick, showing between the corky ridges a ruddy glow, and the air smells sweetly of this Pitch Pine's natural rosin. When given such

improved conditions — plenty of sunlight, depth of soil, and space —
an individual Monterey Pine will shoot up 80 and 100 feet high, cast
what is for a Pine a wide pool of shade, and begin to branch its trunk
with some ease. Yet just where this tree seems to reach its finest proportions, it stops abruptly short, apparently unable to live far, except in
cultivation, from the enslaving fogs.

Naturally so fine a tree in so striking a position came to the notice
of the very first explorers of the California coast. Only fifty years after
Columbus discovered America, Juan Rodríguez Cabrillo, in his bat-
tered little galleon, sailed past here and named the peninsula the Cabo
de Pinos, while Monterey Bay itself he called the Bahia de Pinos. But
a savage sea was running, the fogs were treacherous, and Cabrillo kept
his little bark well out to sea without landing. Not until Vizcaino in
the year 1602 anchored in the bay did any other European see our
Pines. Vizcaino surmised that they might furnish masts of any size, and
perhaps he had visions of launching a fleet here. At any rate, he
changed the name of the bay to do honor to the Mexican Viceroy, the
Conde de Monterey, and he named the peninsula the Punta de Los
Pinos. Then, having clapped these resounding monickers on the landscape, he too sailed away.

At last arrived the first overland expedition under Portolá, bringing
with it Padre Junípero Serra himself to found San Carlos Mission,
today popularly known as the Carmel Mission, amid the Pines. After
the sword and the cross came the Spanish settlers. And now the sound
of the axe was heard, the woods were set alight in order to provide
better browse for the white man's cattle, a great space was cleared in
the Pine groves for the Presidio, and from every direction the stately
Pine forest began to shrink. By the time Robert Louis Stevenson
reached Monterey, in the year 1879, the destruction had advanced far,
though not nearly so far as in our times.

Fires deliberately set for the purpose of burning off the woods, or
allowed to rage unchecked, are a thing of the past. And so, one would
have thought, would be the whine of the sawmills which for many
decades in the early period of American settlement laid waste these
unique and noble groves. But for a short time, beginning in 1946,
tractors and bulldozers went roaring and bucking through these lovely
groves. In one year three million board feet of timber were felled on
the Monterey peninsula, according to an author [1] who seems to have

1 Charles H. Stoddard, "Forestry in the Monterey Pines," *American Forests*, June,
1947.

thought it a grand accomplishment. An electrically driven mill with a 25,000 board foot daily capacity showed how swiftly these groves can still be exploited. Except for the small stand in Point Lobos State Park, all the Monterey Pines are still in private hands, to be managed as private owners see fit.

As a timber tree, the Monterey Pine is indeed tempting, and if we ever come to a day when we start planting commercial forest instead of living on our forest capital, this species should have a great future. The wood is hard, strong, tough, and durable away from soil. In the days of the Spanish Californians, selected trees were used in boat building. The cutting of the early American period was for flooring, the planking of wharves and in bridge construction. Its value as fuel is great, and formerly the Montereyans exported as much as 25,000 cords of fuel wood a year. Today it is used mostly locally, for building the bungalows among the Pines of the pretty seaside town of Carmel.

The reproduction of the Monterey Pine is, fortunately, abundant. The cones may remain upon the tree for many years, maturing their seeds, and sometimes only a forest fire will force the scales to open. Yet if fire is kept away, there will come a year when conditions seem just right, and then on some warm day in the fall when there is no wind to tear them off, the cones begin to drop off of their own accord. On the twig that is left there is a little pitch-lined pocket, and the stem of the cone will show the heavy drip of golden brown pitch. But often the cones open while still on the tree. This usually happens in the hottest weather, which in Monterey is autumn. One walking in the woods then may hear a great crackling and snapping like the first licking of fire through brush. But this is the sound of the cones bursting open and it may continue all through the night that follows the warm day. Once opened, the thick elastic scales look, when fresh, like so many (a hundred or more) flower petals. For they show under their tan tip a wine-red color with lacquer-like finish. Meantime, thousands of little black seeds have escaped. Each fluttering on its single wing, they glide or gyrate as far as the wind will take them into the forest. They are wonderfully viable,.and a seedling only four or five years old may be a tree ten or fifteen feet high. Fertility and hardihood have so far saved the Monterey Pine from all the assaults that have been made upon it.

One cannot leave this lovable tree without brief mention of the affinity which is shown for it by butterflies. Especially in the spring, thousands of the common but handsome monarch butterfly will settle on some favored specimen, and next year the same tree is likely to play host again to these fluttering guests. In the sunlight, giddy swarms of them drift around and over the tree. But if the chill fog comes rolling in, they hang from every bough and twig like bunches of brown oak leaves. It is not known why certain individual trees are so beloved by the butterflies that they are sought out by succeeding generations of these frail ephemeral creatures.

Literary historians have pointed out that the Monterey peninsula and its pines furnished the setting created by Robert Louis Stevenson for the immortal *Treasure Island*. The author, in 1879, was at Monterey and writing of it both in his letters and his essay "The Old Pacific Capital," and two years later published *Treasure Island* under its original title of *The Sea Cook*. Again and again are Pines mentioned in *Treasure Island*, as well as Live Oaks, and such Montereyan sights, odors and sounds as the bellowing of sea lions, the strange, fungoid odor of the woods, the gray and sorrowful appearance of the island groves, which is identified in his Monterey descriptions as given by the beards of Spanish moss. In fact, almost every plant and animal alluded to in *Treasure Island* is definitely identified with the fauna and flora of Monterey, and conversely almost every organism, even every natural sound and smell which Stevenson mentions from his sojourn on the peninsula is carefully inserted on his imaginary island.

THE LARCHES
(*Larix*)

THE LARCHES have straight central, mast-like trunks giving off tier upon tier of whorled branches with frequently pendulous branchlets that are studded with knob-like short-shoots (spurs). On these the slender, flat, keeled foliage is borne in spreading clusters of many needles of different length, or on fast-growing, leading shoots the needles are single, sparsely spiraling around the twig. Distinct rings of old leaf scars mark each season's growth on the short-shoots, while the long shoots are grooved and channeled by the scars of old leaf bases.

The blood-red buds on the tips of the short-shoots produce not only the leaves but the flowers, which appear in earliest spring before the foliage. The male flowers are composed of numerous stamens, arranged in catkins, while the female come in conelets, with vivid scales. The small cones, which ripen the first year, are erect on the twig, with leathery, woody scales each one of which is accompanied by a papery, bright-colored, extruded scale. After the winged seeds have fallen, the dead, blackened cones cling for years on the twigs, adding to the somber aspect of these northerly trees.

❋   ❋   ❋

WESTERN LARCH

Larix occidentalis Nuttall

OTHER NAMES: Western Tamarack. Hackmatack.

RANGE: Mountains of southeastern British Columbia south through the Cascades, Blue Mountains, and Wallowas of northern Oregon and the Bitterroots of Montana and Idaho, 2000 to 7000 feet above sea level.

DESCRIPTION: *Bark* of old trunks 3 to 6 inches thick, reddish cinnamon in color, deeply seamed and with massive ridges; on younger growth flaky-scaly. *Twigs* orange-brown, brittle and stout. *Leaves* 14 to 30 in a cluster, 1 to 1¾ inch long, light pale green, in cross-section, flaky, triangular, and distinctly keeled, turning bright lemon-yellow in autumn. *Cones* 1 to 1½ inches long, red-brown to purple-red, short-stalked, the scales white woolly and broader than long, distinctly shorter than the long-tipped exserted bracts. *Seed* ¼ inch long, with frail thin wings twice as long. *Wood* hard, heavy (46 pounds per cubic foot, dry weight), coarse-grained, strong and durable, the heartwood red-brown; sapwood thin and nearly white.

The home of the Western Larch, as one of the great lumber trees of the West, lies primarily in the region that likes to call itself the "Inland Empire" — west of the continental divide in Montana, and including northern and much of central Idaho. This is, too, a region of

fine lakes, such as Pend Oreille, Coeur d'Alene, Priest, Whitefish, Mc-
Donald, and largest of all, Flathead Lake. Around the shores of this
last, and up past Kalispell and the western slopes of Glacier National
Park, the Western Larch reaches its grandest size. Trees 200 feet high
were known, at least formerly, before the assault in force begun by the
lumber industry, half a century and more gone by, cut such wide
swathes in the virgin stands of Larch, Western White Pine, and Douglas
Fir. Even today one sees individuals 100 and 150 feet tall, the tapered
trunk rising straight as a flagpole, and the branches astonishingly short,
thus exaggerating to the eye the height of the tree. The branches are
also sparse, as are the needles.

As you travel today through the Inland Empire, you may feel at
times that you are gazing on an empire torn by war. Here a mountainside has been swept bare to the mineral soil by some dreadful holocaust of the past, and there lie the "slashings" of lumber operations, a
jackstraw pile of logs, with the very high stumps left by the logging
methods of a past generation. Second growth is coming up, though not
so swiftly or densely as in regions of greater rainfall, and from it still
stand forth the gaunt gray poles of trees swept by fire or decorticated
by the ravages of the beetle. But high above the second growth, out of
the slashings, tower scattered specimens whose bark perhaps was so
thick that it resisted injury by fire, whose years were too many to make
it likely that their wood was sound enough to pay for logging them.
And these reminders of the Larch forest's past greatness stand like
warriors who still keep their feet after a battle that has littered the
ground with their dead comrades. Seen through the clouds of a
gathering storm in the mountains, or through the drifting smoke-haze
of some fire, each one of these becomes, as you ride or tramp, a landmark that looms up ahead, is reached, passed, and falls behind, to be
followed by another sentinel ancient in years. There is an air of lofty
tragedy about these grand old trees, some of which cannot have much
longer to live, and we can only hope that the second growth will be
saved from fire and beetle, and lumbered, if at all, on a basis that the
future as well as the present will call sound.

True that there are fine and almost pure stands of Larch remaining
that have never been logged over — most of them now in the hands of
Forest Service which gives them a protection that they have seldom had
on private holdings where the annual cut continues at the rate of
some 26,000,000 board feet a year. But it is likely that there are no
stands that have never been burned over, for "never" is a long time;

and fires, in this region of violent electrical storms striking in some of the most inflammable, pitchy forests in the world, must from time to time have raged here with little to check them. Winds too, of hurricane violence, must have blown here in ages past, and have piled their own kind of slashings in their wake, so that scenes of natural devastation may well have opened to the Indian's eyes as well as ours. Yet somehow this, the king of Larches, has, like its fellow conifers, managed to reassert its reign over and over in the Inland Empire.

In youth the Western Larch is a pretty thing, far removed from the grandeur and grimness of some of the centenarian survivor specimens. The long, lithe branches of the young tree clothe it to the ground, and the rime of delicate foliage lights the twigs with a soft halo of pale green, paler than that of any other kind of western conifer, so that one can pick out Larch from as far away as colors can be distinguished. Then, when autumn comes and the sun shines through the golden foliage, the trees gleam for a while like the Aspens in an angelic light. When the needles drop, then of course the trees are left naked, a starkness the more barren and dead-seeming because we are accustomed to think of the needle-trees as evergreens. But the beautiful cinnamon-red bark gives this species more color than the other Larches show in winter.

Few softwoods have such hard and heavy wood, yet it is easily worked with tools and takes a good polish. So it goes into interior finish and even furniture. Its great durability under conditions likely to favor decay makes it valuable for railway ties and boat construction. This durability, and the perfect straightness and scant limbage of the trunk, have caused it to be cut in great amounts for telegraph poles. Much Larch disappears underground, for use in mines, and experiments indicate that the wood is suitable for pulping and would make a high-grade wrapping paper. But most of all is it used for rough lumber, that is, construction timbers where its strength and comparative cheapness recommend it. Western Larch is thus a valuable but not a precious or fine wood. It may be coarse compared with the highest grades of some woods, but it does heavy duty with an endurance that could not be expected of many another tree.

ALPINE LARCH

Larix Lyallii Parlatore

OTHER NAMES: Tamarack. Mountain Larch.

RANGE: From 4000 to 8000 feet above sea level, in the Rockies of southern Alberta and British Columbia, south to Glacier National Park and high peaks of the Bitterroots in Idaho and Montana. Also in the Cascades of Washington.

DESCRIPTION: *Bark* on old trunks ½ to ⅞ inch thick, red-brown or purplish, shallowly seamed, the ridges flat and flaky-scaly; on younger trunks smooth and ashy. *Leaves* in clusters of 30 to 40 or more, 1 to 1½ inches long, 4-angled, pale blue-green turning bright yellow in fall. *Cones* 1½ to 2 inches long, reddish purple, the cone scales broader than long and jagged at the tip, shorter than the bristle-pointed, purplish, exserted bracts. *Seeds* ⅛ inch long, with shining light red wings twice as long. *Wood* like that of the preceding species.

Concerning the Alpine Larch the fact which even most naturalists know best is that they have never seen it. And so scattered is its growth, so wild and inhospitable its favorite haunts at timber line in the Canadian Rockies and the little-visited east slopes of the Cascades of Washington, that most people would not know where exactly to begin to look for it. A good place — at least not requiring mountaineering feats or packing-in — is at the head of the stupendous V-shaped gorge of Icicle Creek which, though it lies at the entrance to the Mount Stuart wilderness, is traversed by a narrow 17-mile dirt road, passable in summer, that starts out from Leavenworth, Washington, just above the famous Wenatchee apple-growing district.

The scenery, the very atmosphere, of this more arid eastern slope of the great Cascade range is entirely different from the humid western slopes so well known to tourists, where the forests are somber and continuous, humid and almost tropically lush with ferns. On the east slopes — quite the contrary — the air is dry and hard, cold and bright. The rocks are bare and brilliant, eroded into profound gorges, violently uplifted into splintered ridges and toppling pinnacles. And there the mountains cup lakes of glacial melt, and wear, like bits of bright clothing, pale green meadows, spangled in the long days of the northern and mountain summer with a brief, enchanting flora.

Scattered like park trees through these meadows, clinging to the walls of gorges where it would seem roots could find neither water nor hold-fast, is found a crooked tree of stunted appearance, with its smooth gray branches remarkably scraggly and short, as if the elements had never given them a chance to develop far. They are, however, very tough, well able to endure punishment by gales and ice, even if they lack the grace of the long fragile boughs of the Western Larch, and indeed for nine months of the year the tree, being deciduous, stands naked, and looks not only dead but cursed and blasted by the god of storms. This is the Alpine Larch, a tree of which you could never believe it would have any pretty charms.

Yet the warm chinook wind melts the snows at last; lengthening days return to this northern country, and reluctant spring comes finally to the alpine passes and ledges. Then some morning the beholder is likely to see a fair sight when the morning light, shining through the dew that hangs in the fuzz of white woolly hairs on every twig of this tree, rimes it all in a silvery halo. Time now for the leaves to burst their woolly-coated buds on those curious knobs or spurs that roughen the Larch twigs. So a tender green will cover the branchlets, and the unlovely limbs for the brief summer season will be clothed in living beauty. When the cones, fringed with those surprisingly long slender purple scales, have matured and dropped in August, the leaves begin to turn color. From miles away their bright gold can be seen edging the arid timber line. Then they too fall, and once more the tree returns to its long winter sleep.

EASTERN LARCH

Larix laricina (Du Roi) K. Koch

OTHER NAMES: American, Black, or Red Larch. Eastern Tamarack. Hackmatack.

RANGE: Throughout the valley of the Yukon in Alaska and of the Mackenzie in Canada; from the base of the Rockies in Yukon Territory, across Canada between the prairies and the arctic tundra to Quebec, Labrador, and Newfoundland and the Maritime Provinces. South through Minnesota and Wisconsin to northern parts of Illinois, Indiana, and Ohio, northernmost West Virginia, Pennsylvania except the southeastern parts, extreme northwestern New Jersey, throughout New York State except Long Island and Staten Island.

DESCRIPTION: *Needles* numerous, in bundles, on short spear-like shoots, or solitary and spiraling around the stem on long shoots, triangular in cross-section, with the upper side rounded, the lower sides keeled, ½ to 1 inch long, bright light green. *Flowers* — male bright yellow, nearly spherical, seated directly on the twig, female oblong, the scarlet scales extended with long green tips. *Cones* ½ to ¾ inch long, with about 20 thin bright chestnut-brown scales. *Seeds* ⅛ inch long, with long chestnut-brown wings. *Bark* thin, bright reddish brown, scaly. *Wood* heavy for a conifer (38 pounds to the cubic foot, dry weight), hard, very strong, close-grained, and long durable.

The Eastern Larch, within the circumscriptions of this book, grows far beyond the ken of most of us, in the valley of the Mackenzie, following it all the way to the mouth of that river on the shores of the Arctic Sea. It follows, too, the Yukon in Alaska and reaches to the foot of the Rockies in northeastern British Columbia, climbing them to about 1700 feet. On the tundra and muskegs, and around old beaver ponds that are silting up, it delights to grow in boggy and quaking ground where, except in the dry summer months, its roots are constantly wet.

In winter, since all Larches are deciduous, these trees are some of the deadest-looking vegetation on the planet, with their black branches, and their stumpy short-shoots that appear seared by fire. But when the arctic spring comes, with that apologetic rush and will to please which well become the tardy, these same trees that one thought were but "crisps" begin, soon after the wild geese have gone over and the ice in the beaver ponds has melted, to put forth an unexpected, subtle bloom. The flowers are followed in a few weeks by the renewing foliage, and there is no more delicate charm in the North Woods than the moment when the soft pale green needles first begin to clothe the sternness of the Larch. So fine is that foliage, and so oddly clustered in sparse tufts, that Tamarack, as the lumberman prefers to call it, has the distinction of giving less shade than any other far-northern tree. Even in summer the sunlight reaches right to the bottom of a Tamarack grove.

The Indians used the roots of Tamarack for sewing the strips of Birch bark for their beautiful canoes. The best roots came from trees in beaver ponds, for they were especially tough, pliant, slender, and elongated. The white man has utilized Tamarack as the ideal wood for railroad ties since it is so durable in contact with the soil, and the mast-like trunks had only to be lopped of their branches to make telegraph poles. But in the West or, rather, Far North, Tamarack does not grow to large size and its stands are remote from railroads. In any other region it might be lumbered and the logs driven toward the mills on the streams, but the rivers of the Far Northwest flow for the most part toward the Arctic Sea away from the market. So the Eastern Larch will probably never be extensively lumbered up there, but for ages to come the rivers will pile its skeletons as driftwood on their desolate beaches.

THE SPRUCES
(*Picea*)

Pʀᴏᴅᴜᴄɪɴɢ soft white or reddish wood and straight, mast-like trunks with scaly rather than furrowed bark, the Spruces are conical trees with regular whorls of narrow, horizontal branches. Their aromatic needles are usually 4-sided and tipped with a pungent prickle. Borne separately, not in bundles, they crowd densely on the twig and, disposed in several spiral ranks, they bristle out in all directions, or if by curvature they bunch toward the top of the twig they do not, at any rate, form flat sprays of foliage as in Hemlock and Fir. They are not jointed by a stalk to the twigs but seated directly on minute woody knobs which remain, after leaf fall, as spiral roughenings on the branchlet.

The male flowers, found in the leaf axils, consist in many spirally arranged stamens to form a catkin. The short female catkins grow terminally on the twig, and are brightened at flowering time by numerous rounded or pointed scales. Always pendant under the bough, the cones have thin, leathery, persistent scales with still thinner papery bracts between them, which, however, are not longer than the scales. Maturity comes to the cones the first year; they soon open their scales and drop their small winged seeds. When the cone falls, it falls with its scales intact; they do not break away separately from the central axis as do the cone scales of Firs.

❈   ❈   ❈

ENGELMANN SPRUCE

Picea Engelmanni Parry

OTHER NAMES: White or Mountain Spruce.

RANGE: At 1500 to 5000 feet in the Canadian Rockies (central British Columbia southward) through the southern Rockies (10,000 to 12,000 feet) to southern parts of New Mexico and Arizona. Frequent in the Cascades and rare in Shasta County, California.

DESCRIPTION: *Bark* only ¼ to ½ inch thick even on mature trunks, purplish brown or cinnamon red and broken into large loose scales. *Twigs* stout, gray-brown or orange-brown. *Leaves* flexible, 1 to 1⅛ inches long, blue-green (only sometimes glaucous) without resin ducts, the tips not prickly to the touch, the lower needles tending to curve up and crowd to the upper side of the branch. *Flowers* — male dark purple, female bright scarlet. *Cones* 1 to 2½ inches long, with flexible, jagged-toothed, light chestnut-brown scales. *Seed* ⅛ inch long, black, with an oblique wing 4 times the length of the body. *Wood* straight- and long-fibered, soft, thin-layered, very light (21½ pounds to the cubic foot, dry weight), with light yellowish or yellowish brown heartwood and thick, paler sapwood.

The most dramatic tree of your first trip in the Rockies will almost certainly be the Engelmann Spruce. Your memories of it will be linked with the towering Grand Tetons, the long, forested valleys of the Yellowstone, the breath-taking beauty of Lake Louise, the park-like spaciousness, the exciting dry air, of Rocky Mountain National Park. And the meeting with a bear, glimpses of bounding deer, the insolence of crested jays, the racket of nutcrackers, the chill of high mountain lakes, the plop of a diving beaver, the delicious taste of camp food cooked in appetite-sauce, and mountain meadows glorious with lark-spur, columbine, and lupine — all these are part of your composite recollections of the realms where this fine Spruce grows. But you would not recall it as distinct from other trees had it not an inherent personality of its own. Fifty and 100 feet and more tall, it is, in dense forests, slender as a church spire, and its numbers are legion. So it comes crowding down to the edge of the meadow where your tent is pitched, to the rocks surrounding the little lake that mirrors its

lance-like forms upside down. And when the late mountain light begins to leave the summer sky, there is something spirit-like about the
enveloping hosts of the Engelmanns. Always a dark tree, this Spruce's
outlines are now inky, and its night silence makes the sounds of an
owl, or of an old moose plashing somewhere across the lake, mysterious and magnified in portent.

When daylight comes again the friendliness returns to the Engelmanns, and they are seen in the light of reality to be trees that are
merely dramatic by their very nature, with those short, dense, down-
sweeping boughs. But there is nothing impenetrable about their
groves, and little that is ever dangerous. Fragrant and glittering, the
hosts of this Spruce clothe vast areas in the Rockies with a beauty
equalled by no other western conifers save some of those on the Pacific
coast.

At high altitudes the Engelmann behaves like most other timberline
trees, and is dwarfed, straggling, naked on the windward side, and
even sprawling. It is not truly an alpine tree, however, since its real
home is lower down. When growing in the open, of course, it retains
its lower boughs more completely and takes on more ample outlines.

The commercial stand of Engelmann Spruce is reckoned at some
29,000,000,000 board feet. The wood is relatively strong, and yet
lighter in weight than White Pine. Millwork and interior trim are
sometimes worked up from Engelmann, but it is the very straight stems
that recommend it to its most common use — for telephone and telegraph poles.

Fire in this pitchy, close-growing tree may soon become a demon out
of all control, but Engelmann Spruce is a tree endowed with great

vitality and the necessary tolerance for recapturing what it has lost. For its seedlings are able to endure deep shade. So they come up under any and all other growth. Thus a forest may become so umbrageous that other tree seedlings do not thrive beneath their parents, but this Spruce's children continue to seed and come up year after year. They grow very slowly under such conditions, but they do not give up, and they can afford to wait, for some day old age, decay, windfall, or lumbering operations will remove their superannuated rivals. Then, when the sunlight reaches the young Engelmanns, and the roots of their tyrants wither away, these Spruces will put on a spurt of amazing growth and eventually Engelmann Spruce may take over entirely. But no other tree is so well fitted to succeed them as it is to succeed itself, year after year, so that the triumph of the Engelmanns is likely to be final till flames or axes or avalanches intervene.

COLORADO BLUE SPRUCE

Picea pungens Engelmann

OTHER NAMES: Blue, White, Silver, or Parry Spruce.

RANGE: From the mountains of western Montana and central Idaho (at 6000 to 9000 feet), south in Yellowstone and Grand Teton National Parks through the mountains of Colorado to New Mexico (Sangre de Cristo, Mogollon, and Sacramento Mountains, at 8000 to 11,000 feet) and from the Uinta and Wasatch Mountains of Utah to Arizona (Kaibab Plateau and White Mountains, 7000 to 11,000 feet altitude).

DESCRIPTION: *Bark* ¾ to 1½ inches thick on old trunks and then deeply furrowed and with rounded ridges, pale to dark gray and thin and scaly on young trunks. *Twigs* stiff, stout, orange-brown to gray-brown. *Leaves* 1 to 1¼ inches long, bristling from the trunk in all directions, blue-green and (especially on young trees in cultivation) silvery-glaucous, with a long pungent tip. *Flowers* — male yellow tinged with red, female pale green. *Cones* 2½ to 4½ inches long, lustrous chestnut-brown, with tough spreading scales having ragged margins. *Seed* ⅛ inch long, dark chestnut-brown, with oblique wing 4 times as long as the body. *Wood* knotty and brittle, soft, weak, light (23 pounds per cubic foot, dry weight).

He who has seen this tree only in formal cultivation in well-tended grounds has little notion of its wild beauty in the grandeur to which it is native. It is a popular tree indeed in the eastern states, where it is the most planted of western conifers, under the name of Blue Spruce or sometimes Silver Spruce, for it is no end admired by the suburbanite as a lawn tree, and the newly wealthy man likes to order it in quantity as a windbreak, or to line the curving approaches to his summer place. As a hedge, it is so close-growing and cruelly prickly as to be boy-proof and is indeed impenetrable to still smaller animals.

If you don't yet know it in cultivation, the nurseryman's catalogue is sure to carry a color picture of young specimens of this insistently pretty tree, displaying its charms of tier on tier of branches graduated in perfect symmetry from the longest boughs that sweep the ground to the slender but strong tip. Above all, the feature that brings the customers in off the street is the cast or bloom, like blue moonlight, upon the foliage of young trees and the tips of the new or summer growth of older trees. All specimens exhibit more or less of this glaucous beauty, for a time, but some more than others and these are carefully selected in seedling stage for they are in most demand and fetch the highest price. A very showy form called Silver Spruce has foliage tips of an argent frostiness and these are propagated by grafting them on stock of less silvery individuals. No wonder that Colorado has made this its state tree when it has spread its fame so far around the world.

But when the Easterner comes West, he does not find the middle slopes of the Rockies covered with neat blue symmetrical little trees like those on the lawn at home. Instead, dark cohorts, proud as lances, march up the noble slopes with a look unconquered, unrestrained. These trees are not consistently powdered with that look of stage moonlight; they are predominantly dark green, even somber, like most Spruces, with little blue about them except, for a brief season, the tips of the new growth or, here and there, a young specimen that is fairly azure or glaucous all over. And as the summer wanes the blueness on older trees tends to weather away, since it is nothing, after all, but a superficial waxiness or powder, and not at all the underlying color of the needles.

But let the Aspens turn from green to glowing gold, let them spend all that gold and shiver nakedly in the swift-driving snow, let the snow pile deep, and still proudly above it, though heavy laden with it, march these Spruces upon their sky-piercing conquest of the Rocky Mountain scene. In this wild state they are in beauty far above the mere symmetry of the lawn-grown specimens; here they have the proud look of fighters. For forest competition soon kills off the younger boughs, and the trunks become pole-like, the crowns carried high, and irregularly sculptured by the elements. Forgotten is the connotation with the lawn mower and the upholstered hammock. Instead, after a vacation in the West, you will have stored, beneath the flickering shade and in hearing of the seething murmur of the Colorado Spruce, some of your most treasured memories — of the flash and thunder of white water, of a line tautened by the rainbow trout, of a family of dippers teetering on the edge of the fall or plunging right under the flood. And when you go back east you will look on the cultivated specimens of the Blue Spruce with changed eyes. How all too blue the fancy-dress little things appear, how juvenile in their self-conscious symmetry, how stingy of shade, and voiceless in the wind!

WHITE SPRUCE

Picea glauca (Moench) Voss

OTHER NAMES: Skunk, Cat, or Single Spruce.

RANGE: From the Yukon valley of Alaska and the Rockies of Alberta, east to Labrador and Newfoundland and the Maritime Provinces of Canada; south to Montana, Minnesota, Wisconsin, northern Michigan, northern New York, Vermont, New Hampshire, and Maine. Also on the Black Hills of South Dakota.

DESCRIPTION: *Needles* erect and crowded, bristling, twisted to the upper side of the twig, incurved, blue-green or pale blue with a bloom, 4-sided, ⅓ to ¾ inch long, narrowed to the sharp tip. *Flowers* — male pale red under the yellow dust of pollen, female oblong-cylindric with red or pale green scales. *Cones* 2 inches long, pale green tinged with red, and shining, the scale thin and flexible and not ragged. *Seeds* ⅛ inch long, pale brown, with slender wings. *Bark* thin, with brown-tinged gray scales, not furrowed. *Wood* light (25 pounds to the cubic foot, dry weight), light yellow, soft, relatively weak, and straight-grained.

The White Spruce ranges across from the Atlantic to the Pacific and north almost to the Arctic Sea in Yukon Territory. But on the eastern slopes of the Canadian Rockies it attains (in the shape of the variety *albertiana* mentioned below) its greatest height. There it may produce a trunk 3 or 4 feet thick and tower up 150 feet — a tree worthy to compete with any other tree found there, and far grander than any in eastern Canada.

But, east or west, it is a rarely beautiful tree, as gracious in outline and form, with its great downsweeping boughs, its spire-like tips, its sparkling blue-green or pale green foliage with bluish cast, as its close kin the Black Spruce is somber, secretive, knotty, and spindling. In youth the White Spruce is as lovely an ornamental as one could ask, a Christmas tree for shape and brilliance. In age, of course, its top grows broader and less elegant, its trunks sturdier yet still mast-straight, still giving off tier on tier of whorled branches regularly graduated in length from bottom to top. When it grows in the open it is apt to keep its lower branches through life, and scattered trees of this sort give a park-like beauty to many spots in the far Northwest. Under forest conditions crowding of individuals produces a spire-like crown, with the trunk bare of branches for 50 or 75 feet or more. So common it is in the Yukon Territory that the Mackenzie River and its tributaries are often choked with naturally fallen logs, and its driftwood is piled high on the desolate beaches or swept to the delta in the Arctic Sea.

In eastern Canada White Spruce is an important pulpwood tree; in the West, with the mighty Sitka Spruce growing in such quantities and close to the seaports and railroads, the inferior White Spruce is scarcely touched as yet for this purpose, for it is safe in the remote interior where few railroads penetrate, and the rivers where the logs might be floated flow uselessly to the frozen North.

But as a lumber source White Spruce comes into its own in Yukon Territory and interior Alaska. There it is the finest timber tree. If it does not grow as large as farther south in Alberta, it still reaches 75 feet in height, with saw logs measuring up to 21½ inches in diameter above the butt. In view of the fact that some of these trees are growing at the Arctic Circle, such dimensions make of it a timber resource unequaled elsewhere in the Far North. The stand may not be dense in comparison with those of more favored regions, yet it often cuts out at 10,000 board feet to the acre. And communities like Fairbanks have an intense need of the White Spruce, for without it any other good building material or mine props would have to be imported at prohibitive cost. To some extent it is used for fuel, though Birch has a much higher caloric value and is preferred. But in exterior and interior finish of buildings White Spruce is *the* timber tree of the Far North.

At first the abundant growth met all the needs of the mining communities. But excessive cutting in the most available spots, and serious destruction by fire, have so depleted the trees near the settlements that most of the Spruce is now cut far from the mills, on the Salcha and Chena rivers, to be floated to the mills, cut into lumber, and shipped down the Yukon by boat, or across the mountains on the Alaska Railroad or even flown by plane to inaccessible mining communities. Valuable stands are now sought out, in little-explored regions, by airplane reconnaisance.

During the great building boom at Fairbanks in 1912, drives of several million feet of Spruce were attempted along the treacherous swift currents of the Tanana River, but nearly 2,000,000 feet of logs were lost. Now smaller drives are made, closely watched by the drivers in poling boats, and motor launches place shear booms at strategic points in the current. Even so, the log drives remain hazardous business. The logs, cut during winter temperatures as low as 50° below zero, are hauled by horses and tractors to be yarded along the rivers until the ice melts. Then the rafts have to be guided through winding sloughs and fanged rapids, past snags and drift piles and treacherous bars. Hundreds of pounds of dynamite are used to break up the jams, and the loggers, eating when they can, constantly wet to the skin, get little rest during the drive of a hundred and two hundred miles. Not in the most heroic days of White Pine lumbering in Maine and Michigan did loggers run such dangers, work under such hardships, or need the skill — acquired only through years — and the great strength and daring of the Alaska loggers.

Variety *albertiana* (Stewardson-Brown) Sargent is the form of the White Spruce commonly found in the Black Hills, the Rockies of northern Wyoming, Montana, Alberta and northward. Much taller than the species proper, it may grow up to 150 feet high, with a trunk of 4 or 5 feet and often a narrower and more pointed crown. The cones are somewhat shorter and broader than those found on eastern trees, but not more so than the cones of far-northern White Spruce.

BLACK SPRUCE

Picea mariana (Miller) Britton, Sterns and Poggenberg

OTHER NAMES: Bog, Swamp, Water, or Double Spruce.

RANGE: Newfoundland and the Maritime Provinces of Canada, west to Labrador, Mackenzie, and Alaska, and south to northern Minnesota, Wisconsin, Michigan, the Adirondacks, northern New England, the mountains of the Virginias and coastal swamps of New Jersey. Rare in the Great Smokies of Tennessee.

DESCRIPTION: *Needles* appearing brushed forward, ¼ to ¾ inch long, incurved above the middle, abruptly tipped with a sharp point, pale green and hoary above, shining below, 4-sided. *Flowers* — male dark red, female with purple scales, oblong-cylindric. *Cones* ½ to 1½ inches long, on strongly recurved stalks, dull gray-brown, the scales with irregular margins. *Seeds* ⅛ inch long, oblong, very dark brown with pale brown membranous wings. *Bark* not furrowed, thin, with innumerable gray-brown scales. *Wood* heavy for a conifer (33 pounds to the cubic foot, dry weight), soft, close-grained and weak, with reddish-tinged heartwood and pale sapwood.

Though the Black Spruce is mainly an eastern conifer, it is on the well-drained bottom-lands and low stony hills of Saskatchewan that it reaches its greatest height — sometimes 100 feet. It forms a spire-like, narrowly pyramidal tree there, with spindly trunk which eventually becomes clear of branches for a long way, and has a correspondingly high and narrow crown with short stiff branches. Where it grows in open groves on the Canadian prairies, the branches are long and pendulous, and the old trees are clothed almost to the base. In the Yukon basin it is never over 40 feet high and usually only half so tall. On the ill-drained, highly glaciated areas of the Far Northwest, it invades the muskegs, those small lakes and ponds that are gradually filling up with sedges and sphagnum moss. The detritus of the life and death of these aquatic plants has formed floating islands, and on them Spruce has grown without contact with mineral soil. These muskeg trees often bear cones when only two or three feet in height; however, two or three feet of growth may represent a long life. In such cases the cone-bearing branches are almost the only ones, and become "densely crowded near the top of the tree, while the trunk below is often destitute of living branches, although unshaded and growing far from other trees. These dense tufts of dark branches like plumes upon poles present a strange spectacle to the traveler who for the first time crosses the larger muskegs, especially at twilight, for he seems to be looking over a weird procession, stretching often mile after mile until lost in the distance." [1]

In eastern North America the Black Spruce sometimes climbs the mountains and after a century or more will be but two or three feet high, but with such tough old branches that the mountaineer can walk on them. In the Canadian Rockies it grows only 25 to 40 feet high at the most, with stems a foot thick in old age. In general, however, it is not well adapted to mountain conditions; at least it grows much more luxuriantly around bogs and Willow swamps in the Northwest. Its tree associates there are Yellow and Bebb Willows, Red Alder, Eastern Tamarack, Black Cottonwood, and Balm-of-Gilead.

Knotty, weak, coarse and soft of wood, crooked and short of stem, the Black Spruce has few attractions for the lumberman. No longer is chewing gum collected from the trees to make the forgotten Spruce gum of the lumbermen. Perhaps no one, any more, drinks Spruce beer. But pitch from this tree is still sometimes used for caulking the leaks in canoes in the Northwest.

No other tree, perhaps, can be so depressingly somber and monotonous as this — not in a grand and graceful way, like some of the conifers of the Northwest coast, but in a hard-bitten, subarctic way of which it is possible ultimately to grow very weary. The naturalist Robert Kennicott, writing from La Pierre's House, Mackenzie Territory, in 1862 told his family back under the Bur Oaks of Illinois: "I made myself melancholy by thinking of the bonnie oaks and other

[1] Ayres, "The Muskeg Spruce," in *Garden and Forest,* vol. 7.

trees I so well remember at The Grove while passing through some of these . . . everlasting forests of spruce. I used to like the evergreens best, but I fear the too constant view of spruces will give me a distaste for them. And oh! how I long to see even the bare branches and shaggy bark of the hickory."

WEEPING SPRUCE

Picea Breweriana Watson

OTHER NAME: Brewer Spruce.

RANGE: Siskiyou Mountains of California and the Coast Ranges of southwestern Oregon, from 4000 to 7000 feet above sea level.

DESCRIPTION: *Bark* of trunks thin, with long, thin, close scales, dull red-brown. *Twigs* switch-like, at first red-brown, growing dark gray-brown, coated for the first years with a fine pubescence. *Leaves* ¾ to 1⅛ inch long, ⅟₁₆ to ⅟₁₀ inch wide, rounded and dark green and lustrous below, but flattened and whitened by rows of stomata above, abruptly narrowed at tip but blunt, not prickly, to the touch. *Flowers* — male dark purple; female oblong-cylindric, the scales with reflexed margins, the bracts oblong, and fringed at the apex. *Cones* dangling on straight slender stalks, 2 to 4 inches long, rich deep purple or purplish green becoming light orange-brown at last, with broad thin scales which after

seed fall become flexible and markedly reflexed. *Seeds* ⅛ inch long, full and rounded, dark brown, their wings 4 times as long. *Wood* soft, medium-heavy (32 pounds per cubic foot, dry weight), close-grained, the heartwood nearly white to light brown, the sapwood almost indistinguishable.

Nature seems to have made some trees to serve man with endless uses, and others to hold the soil over vast areas, some to line riverbanks and some to shade the prairie and desert traveler. A few she made, one might say, for no other reason than to contribute to the higher things of life — to be extraordinarily beautiful, and very little else. And of these the Weeping Spruce is one. More, it is an exceedingly rare tree, and grows in some of the least accessible or most unvisited spots in the West. Indeed, it is confined to fairly high altitudes in the Siskiyou, Trinity, Klamath, and Marble Mountains of northwest California, and more rarely still in southwest Oregon. Not that these regions lack for roads; numerous highways cross them, but you travel down in the bottoms of deep valleys and gorges, the mountains towering so close that you see only their lower slopes and not their tops. Further, this is one of the snowiest spots in the United States, and the Weeping Spruce prefers to nestle in cup-like hollows at the heads of canyons on the cold north slopes, where the snow piles up 20 feet deep for full half the year, with lingering drifts to be seen in July or even into September — and almost time for the storms to return. Perhaps the easiest place to see the Weeping Spruce at home is on a trail of Castle Crags State Park, 4½ miles south, on U.S. Highway 99, of Dunsmuir, California, a wilderness of rocks haunted by memories of the Modoc War of 1855, and brightened by breath-taking views of Mount Shasta.

There it forms open and park-like groves, the trees with long-pointed slender crowns and heavily drooping branches, from which hang vertically the long slim twigs and the crop of slender conical cones. Altogether the growth-habit of the tree is sorrowful, as the dark foliage is somber. In many ways this species looks much like the favorite Norway Spruce so much cultivated through all our northern states. But for some reason Weeping Spruce has not responded well to horticulture, and until gardeners learn what it is that this strange tree requires, and can supply it, it will remain the most mysterious Spruce of the New World.

SITKA SPRUCE

Picea sitchensis (Bongard) Carrière

OTHER NAMES: Tideland or Menzies Spruce.

RANGE: Islands and sea slopes of the Alaskan Coast Ranges from sea level to timber line (up to 3000 feet), from Kodiak Island and the length of the Alaskan peninsula, all around the Kenai peninsula and south through the Panhandle (maritime southern Alaska) to the islands and Coast Range of British Columbia, from sea level to 4000 or rarely 5000 feet; in Washington mainly at the mouths and bottom-lands of rivers and extending up valleys to the foothills of the Cascades, 50 miles from the sea; in Mount Snoqualmie National Forest at 1800 feet in the valley of the Nisqually; in the Olympic National Forest only up to 1000 feet; confined to the coast in Oregon except in the Columbia valley where reaching the Cascade foothills, south to Mendocino County coast in northern California.

DESCRIPTION: *Bark* of old trees thin, deep purple or dark reddish brown, with big loose scales. *Twigs* smooth, at first pale green, becoming dark yellow-brown. *Leaves* ½ to 1⅛ inches long, flat, obscurely rigid, ⅟₁₆ to ⅟₁₂ inch wide, stiff and thick, straight or curved with the callous tips long and pungent, the lower surface dark green and lustrous, the upper whitened by bands of conspicuous stomata, bristling on all sides at right angles from the twig. *Flowers* — male dark red, at the ends of the pendulous lateral branches; female in the upper half of the tree, on rigid terminal shoots, the roundish, toothed scales hidden by the elongated bracts. *Cones* 2½ to 4 inches long, pendant, short-stalked, yellow green tinged with dark red at first, becoming shining pale yellow or reddish

brown, with thin stiff scales nearly twice as long as the slender bracts.
Seeds about ⅛ inch long, full and rounded, pale reddish brown, with
slender oblique wings 4 times as long as the body. *Wood* weak, soft,
(26½ pounds per cubic foot, dry weight), straight-grained, the heartwood
light brown tinged with red, the sapwood thick and white.

The greatest tract of unbroken forest in the United States is that
on the Olympic peninsula where the temperate rain forest (12 feet of
rain a year) clothes an area the size of Connecticut. There has been
heavy lumbering on the south and east sides of the peninsula, but
from timber line on the Olympics down the north slope to the Straits
of Juan de Fuca and the west slope to the Pacific Ocean, hundreds of
thousands of acres are virgin wilderness. A single auto highway
traverses it, and so vast is the forest that even traveling at 50 and
60 mph., hour after hour, you seldom see a house or slightest clearing
in the woods. Only trees — towering, majestic, dark coniferous forest
— their crowns interlocking till they shut out the sky. And the farther
you go on, the more the trees become an element like the sea without
shores, like the rocks when you go down in a cave, or like space,
when you think too long about the distance of the stars. If you have
companions, they and you have long since ceased to speak; you only
look in each other's faces and see there a reflection of your own awe,
as Western Hemlocks, Cedars, titanic Douglastrees, and great Lowland
Firs come rushing toward you, are passed, fall behind, and then seem
to spring reborn out of the horizon ahead.

But there is one tree here that seems grander than all the rest, for
it is on the Olympic peninsula that the Sitka Spruce attains its greatest
stature. Trees 200 feet high, with a diameter of 10 feet above the
much greater, swollen and buttressed bases, are sighted towering
above the rest of the forest, and some have been scaled by foresters at
280 feet. Such a tree has probably lived 800 years or more, but so
fast-growing is this species, especially for a Spruce, that trees 200 feet
high have been shown by their annual rings to have shot up to such
heights in a single century.

Yet the majesty of the Sitkas is not all in their size, but rather in
the noble bearing of the crowns, the monumental cleanly straightness
of their boles. The branches of this king of Spruces have an upward
sweep suggestive of strength and rejoicing; from these the branchlets
hang down in a beautiful weeping habit, and the twigs too, ending in
the pendant cones. The young tree, and the trees by the side of the
highway with room to expand, are clothed to the base in thick-set

numberless boughs. The ancients of the deep woods, on the contrary, have tall bare trunks — and what trunks! The strains and stresses above, perhaps, and the boggy nature of the ground beneath, have resulted in greatly swollen and buttressed bases, whence the roots start, claw-like, from the stem and grip the earth as if to balance the immense superstructure. Above, the trunks soar, columnar and incredible, to disappear in the canopies of crowding, lesser trees; their own crowns may be quite shut away from you, far overhead. But the voice of the varied thrush may drift down to you, where the bird in the Sitka's topmost branches faces the sunlight that never penetrates below.

Some women's beauty (say those who know about such matters), imperils them but their virtues never do. Just the opposite, Sitka Spruce, one of the most imperiled trees in all the American sylva, is in danger not because of its surpassing beauty but for its high qualities. For man has so many uses for this tree that the competition between its suitors is fierce. But whatever the outcome amongst them, it is the tree that suffers.

First, the general lumber industry has the highest regard for the properties and qualities of Sitka Spruce. Though soft it is strong, and has a uniform texture and a high affinity for glue and paint. This makes it ideal material for doors, especially overhead garage doors which must be so light as to move at a touch. The wood has little tendency to bleed through the finish, so it is excellent for interior trim and paneling, bungalow siding, and furniture. It does not split, warp, or crack, in the position of hatch covers for vessels, and being both light and strong is unexcelled for workmen's scaffolding.

One of the most select of all this great tree's uses is in the sounding boards of pianos and violins, and for the pipes of organs. A satisfactory sounding board must have qualities not found in every wood; indeed, resonance, in a high degree, and with fidelity to pitch, is found in few woods. Such a wood must be uniform in texture, and without irregularities in the grain, so that all parts of the wood, when vibrating, will respond equally. The annual growth rings should be narrow as well as uniform, to produce the greatest elasticity. The instrument builders of Europe long ago settled on the Norway Spruce for sounding boards. In this country, Sitka Spruce is found to yield most frequently the close-ringed, defect-free, straight and true boards.

Of all the woods in the world, Sitka Spruce has the highest strength-to-weight ratio. Many a wood is strong, but usually strength implies corresponding weight, and weight, in the last analysis, is a form of weakness. Many a wood is admirably light, and consequently cheap to ship and easy to handle, but usually it is weakish to very weak. Sitka Spruce of the best grades combines remarkable strength and toughness with lightness and freedom from cupping and warping under severe strains.

The simplest example of the need of lightness and strength combined is in a ladder; it must be light enough, even if exceptionally long, to be handled readily, but human life depends upon its strength. So the best ladders are Spruce ladders. Similarly, but with more lives depending on it, is the lightness of Spruce combined with strength in portable bleachers for sports events. But these must have an added quality — they must not splinter with use. To all these needs Sitka Spruce answers admirably. College racing shells, too, must be made of the lightest of possible woods having also strength. The seat of such a shell of Sitka Spruce, for instance, will carry a 200-pound man, yet it weighs only 1¼ pounds. As constructed by the famous builder, George Pocock of Seattle, the racing shells are built of Oregon-grown Spruce for its toughness and strength; pound for pound it is stronger than steel.

But airplane construction tests a wood to the last degree, and in two world wars, Sitka Spruce met the demands of heavier-than-air craft. Experience in combat has taught that wood has greater ability to absorb shock than has metal. When a metal propeller is dented it may develop an unseen fatigue crack that will explode later; not so with Spruce props. A bullet hole in wooden wing or wooden fuselage is repaired by plastic wood in a jiffy; repairs of holes in metal is a major operation involving time and resulting in additional weight. Gunfire through wooden planes results in no extensive tearing.

Going back to the field of plane production, manufacturers find the construction of a metal plane requires hundreds of hours of work by skilled riveters, welders, and metal workers. But wooden planes can be produced with a minimum of manpower in a minimum of time. Kiln drying of Spruce cuts the time required for curing the wood from two years to twenty-one days, and yields a better product.

The arguments for Spruce in wing beams, wing ribs, and as plywood are conclusive enough, but the amount of Sitka Spruce actually suitable to aircraft construction does not present so bright a picture. Strength, of course, is the first factor, and a strong wood is a straight-grained wood with a divergence of no more than 1 inch for every 15 inches; it must also be free of knots and blemishes. Such trees are not common at any time, and only about 12 per cent of logs are judged, after cutting, to be suitable. Of this lumber only 10 per cent is likely to prove acceptable when sawed out in boards. At best, one board foot in every fifty is of plane quality. So the search for air-worthy Spruce has been called the jewel trade of the lumber business.

The needs of planes for defense cannot be denied, and under the stress of national survival, the cut of Spruce has gone on, in the past, without thought to the wasteful methods involved. More, the drain of three fighting nations in the last wars has been leveled almost entirely upon Oregon and Washington Spruce, for wood grown in those states was considered superior. So intense was the demand, however, that Alaska sent her Sitka Spruce in rafts of a million board feet at a time, towed 900 miles along the coast to Puget Sound. But large though Alaska's Spruce resources, much of her stand is quite inaccessible and so is British Columbia's. Only in Washington and Oregon is this species growing where it is easy to cut and move, and even here the merchantable stand is but a fraction of the total growth that includes both immature and superannuated trees.

And still the list of uses of this versatile tree is not complete. For Sitka Spruce is today one of the continent's great raw materials for paper pulp. Indeed, you could not ask for a better conjunction of favorable conditions for industry in the Northwest, where the forests, the water power, the transportation, and the climate are all conjoined for a tremendous output. At Ocean Falls, British Columbia, for instance, ocean-going steamers dock just below the pulping mills which utilize the water power from a big dam holding back a long lake which, further, furnishes the immense quantities of pure water required for washing the pulp. On this lake are rafted the Spruce logs which have been cut in the heavily timbered mountains. And so dense is the growth of Spruce, so much does the mild rainy climate favor rapid replacement after logging, that it is hoped that the supply of pulpwood will be a self-renewing resource that will never give out, and the pulp plant and the town that depends on it will be permanent.

Here, as elsewhere in all modern pulping plants, the processes of converting Spruce logs into paper have been worked out to near perfection in mechanical efficiency. The logs are taken from the lake or river by conveyors and sawn into proper length and piled. When needed, the raw log material is mechanically conveyed to the mill where big steel revolving drums wear off the bark. The enormous machines hold the peeled "stick" against a grindstone turned by water power and kept cool by further large volumes of water.

The ground-up mass that results is a dirty slush which is then run through screens of successively finer caliber to strain out all coarse material. Now the water pulp must go to a Hollander or beating vat where it is whirled and further macerated with blades against an adjustable anvil. Then are added the fillers — clays and other substances to give polish and body to coated papers, and rosin, alum, and gelatine for sizing so that the paper will take ink without blotting. And, last, the dyes are added to tint the pulp the desired color.

But now the mass, with all its chemical elements added, must be dried by a machine that may measure 30 feet wide, 300 feet long, and 30 feet high, and weigh 2000 tons. Into it flows, day and night, every day in the year, a continuous stream of slush which is 199 parts water to 1 part solid pulp, and the problem is to expel the water and dry the pulp. First the mass is shaken on a screen so that the fibers will lie in every direction and not arrange themselves in the direction of flow — lest the ultimate paper product tear too readily in that direction. Then the screen and its watery sheet are run across suction boxes and through suction cylinders. Much drier now, the papery sheet is put through felt-lined wringers and mangles and then pressed between a series of some fifty enormous steam-heated rollers. Now the half-formed paper is sent between steel rolls that polish it and finally it is rolled up on a mandrel or core, like towel paper on a kitchen roll.

So effective are all the inventions that have been brought together at the pulping mill that the pulp travels sometimes at the rate of 1200 feet a minute, and a sheet of paper is unrolled which never stops, year in, year out, unless the sheet breaks.

The question arises, in view of all these demands, whether Sitka Spruce can stand the drains upon it. If it served any one of its masters exclusively — the pulp industry, the general lumber industry, or plane production — the answer might be a clear yes. But when for all uses the cut runs to 240,000,000 board feet a year in Oregon and Washington alone, while annual growth in that region amounts to but 21,000,-000 feet, it is plain that we are cutting Sitka Spruce more than ten times as fast as it is replacing itself. Of all the great industrial trees on this continent, Sitka Spruce stands in the most deadly peril, and under the stress of war or even preparation for war, the peril may be nearly doubled. The tree, as a species, is not in danger of extinction as a very rare and local species might be. But when the great stands of it are gone, no other tree will do its many jobs so well, since no other has quite the same strength-weight ratio or the high quality of fibers for pulp. We shall then have to wait for second growth, and it will be cut under pressing demand as fast as it matures.

There is one bright side to the picture, and that is the large amount of Sitka Spruce held in national forests and national parks. That in the parks can never be cut, under the present laws; Spruce in the national forests can be logged at the discretion of Forest Service whose regulations permit it to mark mature trees for falling; private companies then bid for the timber and are allowed to take it out under government supervision. Thus the Spruce in the national forests constitutes a national reserve which could meet a national emergency. But it should not, in the judgment of the conservative, be called on to help out private industry just because the lumber and pulping companies are running short. They will have to solve their own problems and bring into line the rate of cut with the rate of natural reproduction.

THE HEMLOCKS
(*Tsuga*)

HEMLOCKS are soft-wooded, densely conical trees, usually with gracefully nodding tips. The branches bear alternate twigs, mostly in one horizontal plane. The evergreen, dark, and glittering foliage is usually whitened beneath by glaucous lines of stomata; not collected in bundles, the needles, jointed on very short stalks to cushion-like woody bases, are borne singly but densely on the twigs, in 2 or 4 ranks, and are flat or angular and blunt-tipped. The solitary male flowers grow in the axils of last year's leaves, and consist in numerous spherical anthers; the female stand erect on the tips of shoots, with numerous nearly circular scales. The small reddish-brown cones droop under the boughs, and have only few, thin, flexible, roundish, and curved scales. After the seeds have fallen, the scales persist on the axis of the cone which falls without breaking. The seeds, furnished with resin vesicles, are flattened and much shorter than the membranous wing that surrounds them.

❋   ❋   ❋

WESTERN HEMLOCK

Tsuga heterophylla (Rafinesque) Sargent

OTHER NAME: Alaska Pine.

RANGE: Islands and seaward slopes of the Coast Ranges of southeastern Alaska from sea level to 2700 feet; in British Columbia, on the southwest coast of Vancouver Island and the Queen Charlotte Islands; on the Coast Range, and, inland, up to 5000 feet in the Selkirk and Gold Mountains; throughout western Washington from sea level to 5000 feet on Mount Rainier; throughout western Oregon, frequent on the west side of the Cascades but rare on the east and not known from the Siskiyous; confined in California to the fog belt of the north coast (Del Norte and Mendocino Counties; reappearing in Sonoma County).

DESCRIPTION: *Bark* 1 to 1½ inches thick on old trees, deeply seamed into broad, flat, connected ridges covered with close, thin, cinnamon-brown scales. *Twigs* slender, at first, pale yellow-green and clothed with long, pale hairs, later becoming dark reddish brown and for several years downy. *Leaves* ¼ to ¾ inch long, ⅟₁₆ to ⅟₁₂ inch wide, dark green and very shiny and grooved above, whitened beneath by conspicuous rows of stomata, rounded at the tip, abruptly narrowed below to the short stalk. *Flowers* — male yellow, female purple. *Cones* ¾ to 1 inch long, not stalked, the somewhat papery scales longer than the dark purple bracts. *Seeds* only ⅛ inch long, their narrow wings twice or thrice as long. *Wood* light (32½ pounds per cubic foot, dry weight), but hard and tough, the heartwood pale brown tinged with yellow, the sapwood nearly white.

Wherever the winds of the north Pacific come bearing eight and nine months of rain (up to 100 inches a year) followed by three months of bright but deliciously cool summer, the Western Hemlock grows. It comes down almost to the beaches of Oregon and extends far up the gorge of the Columbia — the grandest river scenery on the continent. Its delicate fronds of foliage wave in the breezes set up by the numberless and enchanting waterfalls of the Cascades whose slopes it climbs for a few thousand feet, as long as the climate stays mild and rainy. It swathes the bases of the Olympics, of Mount Rainier and Mount Baker, and is perhaps the most abundant tree around the intricate fiords of southeastern Alaska. Compared with some of its constant companions — Douglas Fir, Western Red Cedar, and Sitka Spruce — Hemlock is not one of the gigantic species, though its 100 to 150 feet of height would be considered so in the sylva of the eastern states. But abundant, almost omnipresent in its range, it certainly is. For Hemlocks seem, in the Northwest, to fill all the spaces not forcibly occupied by other trees, leaving scant meadows save where the ground is actually boggy or inundated by tidal waters. True, there are many places where other trees completely dominate the scene; there are spots where the Hemlock is quite lacking, or, again, where it seems for miles around to be the only tree. But in general it is simply the commonest, most continuously distributed, of the trees of the great coniferous rain forests of the Northwest coast.

Fortunate it is, then, that it is so beautiful a tree. In its early life, when it takes the form of a broad-based cone, its branches have a deliciously youthful gesture, as of uplifted arms. In age the reverse is true; the branches, becoming old and heavily laden with branchlets, bend down at the tips, and the twigs are often pendant too, so there is something of the "weeping" habit about a specimen 200 and 300 years old — or perhaps only half "weeping" — gracefully resigned, rather, to the burdens and the dignities of age.

The Western Hemlock is notable for the way that its long, lash-like leader shoot nods over at the tip, like the end of an old-fashioned buggy whip as it stood in its socket. Its needles, lying in a very flat spray, make a gracious shade. For, though small, they are closely set, and so are the spirals of boughs around the stem, of branches on the boughs, of branchlets on the branches and, in their turn, the twigs. The tiny needles by the millions thus cast some of the densest shade thrown by a conifer and, where the Hemlock grows thickly, the forest floor may not see many sunbeams from one month to the next.

The astonishing darkness under a close canopy of Western Hemlock plays an important role in forest ecology and succession. For Hemlock seedlings are able to endure the darkness forced on their early years by their parent trees, but the young hopefuls of other species are firmly shaded out. Thus where Hemlock once gets in, even as an understory and seemingly humble and unaggressive tree, it is really preparing to inherit the earth and, except for the intervention of fire or steel, it is likely to do so.

This was one of the reasons why the old loggers of the Northwest hated the Hemlock. It seemed to them that wherever they turned they met more of this "weed tree" than any other, and its lumber was supposed, on the analogy of Eastern Hemlock, to be well nigh worthless. True, its bark contains twice as much tannin as the eastern species, but the cost of hand labor in the Northwest is and always has been so high that there is no prospect that Western Hemlock bark will ever compete with the tannin materials coming in from Argentina and other countries. As for the logs, if one were cut by mistake, the old-time mill foreman refused to scale it; he just quietly sawed it up and sold it with Douglas Fir, with as much sense of sin as you feel in passing off a Canadian 25-cent piece that has been passed off on you.

Then, toward the turn of the century it was realized that the Western Hemlock is not a bad lumber by any means, since it is strong, fine-textured, straight-grained, stiff, free of pitch, saws off easily without splintering, and holds nails well. So it is a good lumber for studding, drop siding, ladder stock. Flooring of Western Hemlock takes a polish almost like a hardwood; indeed, it hardens and darkens with age. Interior paneling, furniture, sash and door millwork are all served by this species, which is shipped as far as Japan and through the Panama Canal to ready markets in the eastern states.

With dramatic suddenness, in the nineteen-thirties, Western Hemlock leapt to the fore as one of the most important industrial woods in the world. Inventions which had been worked out twenty-five and fifty years before, chemical theories long known but till then little applied, caught up with this abundant and versatile tree. At the same time a lot of ill-founded assumptions fell to the ground. For, it appeared, the fast-growing Western Hemlock was just as capable of producing paper pulp as the slow-growing Spruces which, it had always been asserted, were the only trees that yielded the right sort of cellulose. That sort is alkali-resistant and is referred to in industrial chemistry as alpha cellulose, and Western Hemlock has it in abundance.

The staple of its fibers is long and strong, and it can be easily separated from the other wood elements — primarily the lignin or gluey material — and economically prepared for market. This is done by "digesters" which, in the case of Hemlock, often employ the sulphite process, invented in this country by Tilghman in 1866–67. A "cooking liquor" of calcium bisulphide and sulphurous acid is ingeniously put together on the spot and heated to 250° to 300° F. Into this is fed the Hemlock; in the fierce chemical fire of the digester everything except the cellulose fibers will be eaten away. The digested wood — "the batch" — is a pulpy, dingy slush, which must be screened and then washed in quantities of pure running water till every trace of acid and of non-cellulose is sluiced from the precious fibers. These then go to the bleaching plant where chlorine turns the pulp to an almost snowy white. The finished pulp — now a heavily surcharged yet still partly liquid mass — travels in pipes to the paper plant, if paper it is to become. But Hemlock first and foremost supplies the alpha cellulose that goes into the making of cellophane, rayon yarns, and plastics.

Within one generation, rayon — at first called "artificial silk" — has stampeded the textile markets of the world, throwing a scare into the wool, silk, and cotton businesses by its cheapness and attractive appearance. True that many sources of fiber, including some that are completely inorganic, contribute to the total rayon output of the world. But Western Hemlock is one of the great sources, and yields rayon yarn by the Viscose process patented back in 1892. Essentially, the process consists of placing the pulp sheets in a box with strong caustic soda which is later squeezed out by wringers; then the flaky "crumbs" of pulp that remain are heated with carbon bisulphide. The result is "xanthate," a viscous solution with a texture and hue something like mucilage. This is then forced through a threaded nozzle, much as the spider and the silkworm force the products of their silk glands through their spinnerets, so that the silk emerges as a strong but fine thread. Indeed, the threaded nozzle is also called a spinnerette (and thus spelled, in distinction from the insects' organs), and its holes correspond in number and size to the desired caliber of fiber. Constant improvement in rayon has resulted in a yarn that is finer and stronger than any natural silk. At the same time the price has steadily climbed down while the production has mounted. As a result, the child of the poorest parents can wear pretty, dainty rayon clothing that, a short while ago, was a murmuring Hemlock in the somber forests of the Northwest. As the child peels the cellophane wrapper from the sanitarily packaged food she eats, she is handling another product of wood cellulose, that may, in all likelihood, have come, too, from Western Hemlock.

Many are the sources of our plastics — all the handles, kitchenware, steering wheels, composition "leathers," safety films, Lucites, substitutes for tableware, lenses, buttons, and the like, to which in one generation we have become so accustomed. But those made from wood cellulose are superior in toughness, strength, resilience, and brilliance, and Western Hemlock is the commonest source of much of them. The cellulose pulp is very inexpensive to cast in steel dies in any desired form, and to tint or color before the casting. Then the pulp is solidified in the die, by high pressure and heat, and the product is complete without any further finishing, coloring, or tooling — all ready to sell.

Fortunately Western Hemlock is an abundant resource. Washington, Oregon, and British Columbia possess something in the neighborhood of 161,000,000,000 board feet of this species — four times as much as the supply of that next-most-important pulp wood, the Sitka Spruce. The cones may be small, and not beautiful like the long cones of Mountain Hemlock, but their seeds fly far on those wings and are bounteously produced. They germinate well, whether they fall on the soil or in deep moss, or even on the trunks of fallen trees which they straddle with their roots. There is reason to think that the natural replacement of this species is well in excess of the present cut, which indeed is not increasing because so many other softwood trees are now known to be capable of producing pulp and are coming to share the burden of the cut. So often have we boasted in the past of our inexhaustible resources, only to see them sadly depleted, that it would be rash to claim that Western Hemlock, though favored by its native climate of a long growing season and tremendous rainfall, will hold out forever. But in the foreseeable future its great stands are in no danger of becoming exhausted, while the possibilities of further progress in plastics and synthetic textiles are all but limitless.

MOUNTAIN HEMLOCK

Tsuga Mertensiana (Bongard) Carrière

OTHER NAMES: Black Hemlock. Hemlock Spruce.

RANGE: Southeastern Alaska, southward through the Coast Ranges of British Columbia as well as in the Selkirk Mountains in the interior; on the Olympics and Cascades of Washington, the Cascades and Siskiyous of Oregon, the Siskiyous, high Sierra, Mount Shasta and Lassen Peak in California; also in the Bitterroots of Montana and Idaho and the Blue Mountains of Oregon. Descending to near sea level in Alaska; ascending to 10,000 feet altitude in the Sierra Nevada.

DESCRIPTION: *Bark*, even on rather young trees, early broken and rough; on old trunks hard, thick, red-brown or purplish brown, deeply furrowed between the narrow rounded ridges. *Twigs* short and dense, at first light red-brown becoming gray-brown and scaly. *Leaves* ½ to 1 inch long, in cross-section semicircular, the upper surface often keeled or grooved, pale bluish green, bristling from the twig in all directions or crowded (as if brushed) toward the upper side of the twig. *Flowers* — male purple, drooping on slender stems; female green or purple, the scales shorter than the bracts with their narrow tips. *Cones* 2 to 3½ inches long, purplish to yellow-green, the scales, at maturity, spreading at right angles to the axis, or even reflexed. *Seed* ⅛ inch long, the wing 4 times as long. *Wood* weak, soft, light (28 pounds per cubic foot, dry weight), and fine-grained, the heartwood pale brown or red, the sapwood thin and white.

The West has so many alpine species of conifer that at first you may think you will never learn them apart, yet each one has distinctive qualities. The Mountain Hemlock can be told from all others as soon as you are close enough to lift a spray of foliage under your palm and observe the beautiful star-shaped pattern made by the needles when you are looking directly down upon the axis of the shoot. For the short-shoots or leaf-bearing twiglets are apt to be massed at the upper side of the branch, and as the needles are clustered at the ends of the shoots and bristle around in all directions, numerous, gleaming, slender "rays" shoot out from the tip of the shoot. This is true, at least, of sterile shoots; those bearing the cones have the needles all brushed forward, as it seems, toward the tip of the twig, giving a slim, lash-like appearance to each long shoot.

A young Mountain Hemlock is all feminine grace, with a long slender leader whose tip nods over. The limbs, even in quite large and

mature trees and under the close conditions of forest growth, will clothe the tree almost to the base. Long and slender, the arms are held out like a dancer's, and the smaller branches curve gracefully out and away and down, like the fingers of a hand extended but relaxed, and all the twigs are clothed in the bluish green of the softly shining foliage. When the tremendous snowfall of the high peaks of the Cascades descends upon the Mountain Hemlock it bends with a lithe young strength beneath the burden, all its boughs, twigs, and ultimate twiglets drooping farther and farther till at last the load may be spilled to the ground. Then the bough, released, bounds up again into place, or sometimes the whole of a little tree will be relieved at once, during a thaw in bright sunshine, and suddenly spring up, shaking itself and seeming to laugh with its bright foliage.

Such is the appearance, such the life, of a Mountain Hemlock growing, let us say, well up on the slopes of Mount Hood, Oregon, where the climate is good for skiers, but seldom severe. A little farther down, where conditions are milder still, and the rainfall and soil ample, it may grow 100 feet high, with even more airy grace in its gestures. But an ancient Mountain Hemlock at timber line in Alaska, or growing on the muskegs with nothing but desolate tundra or the cold sea of air between it and the Pole, is not recognizable as the same thing. The trunk, creeping along the rocks or struggling erect, may be no higher than a man. Such boles are apt to be immensely thick in proportion to the height. Gone is the slender, spire-like crown, the whiplash leader.

Instead, the crown may be completely blunt, a very low dome shape that is often broader than high. Such strangeness in the proportions is a requisite, as Lord Bacon said, of "excellent beauty." Or if you will not allow that these timberline specimens have beauty, they represent at any rate some four to five centuries of indomitable living in the face of desperate obstacles.

THE DOUGLAS FIRS

(*Pseudotsuga*)

CHARACTERIZING these trees are the densely conical growth habit (or spire-like under forest conditions), the deeply furrowed thick dark bark of old trunks, the slender more or less horizontal whorls of branches which form tiers of broad flat sprays of foliage. The leaves, borne singly, not in bundles, and on short stalks, are flat and often somewhat curved, the tip blunt or acute but not pungently pointed, the upper surface grooved and the lower marked with numerous rows of stomata and having a strong midrib. In the axils of the upper leaves are borne the egg-shaped acute leaf buds whose inner scales mark the twigs in falling with ring-like scales. The male flowers, scattered along the branches, are oblong-cylindric in form, with many spherical anthers; the female, found in the axils of the upper leaves or terminal, are composed of spirally disposed, rounded, ovule-bearing scales which, shorter than the sharply 2-lobed bracts, terminate in slender tips that are but an extension of the midrib. The pendulous cone, which matures in one season, is oblong-egg-shaped in outline, with dark brown, rounded, concave, rigid scales between which are extruded the much longer papery bracts that end in rigid, slim, woody points. Nearly triangular, full and rounded, the seeds are enfolded by their long wings on the upper sides which are dark-colored while the lower face of the seed is pale. The horny outer seed coat encloses a thick papery inner coat.

This genus bears distinct resemblance to the Hemlocks in their stalked blunt leaves, in the fact that the leader shoot (tip of the stem) is often nodding, in the pendant cones and persistent cone scales, but the seeds do not have the resin vesicles of Hemlock seeds. Douglas Firs have resinous wood, while that of Hemlocks is non-resinous.

Resemblance to the Balsam Firs is seen in the ultimately rough, deeply furrowed bark with resin pockets or blisters, and, in some species, in the extruded bracts between the scales of the cone, but the cone is not borne erect as in Balsam Firs, nor do the cone scales fall off one at a time.

To Spruces, these trees seem related in the drooping branchlets, the foliage bristling all around the stem, the small drooping cones with persistent scales and the seeds without resin vesicles. But the Douglas Firs have trident-like protruding bracts between the scales of the cones. This last is the feature which distinguishes them from all other conifers; some, like the Balsam Firs and the Larches, show protruding bracts, but none are tridentate.

❀   ❀   ❀

COMMON DOUGLAS FIR

Pseudotsuga taxifolia (Poiret) Britton

OTHER NAMES: Douglas, Yellow, or Red Spruce. Oregon Pine. Douglastree.

RANGE: The true species found from the head of the Skeena River in British Columbia southward through Washington and Oregon (Coast Ranges and Cascades, from sea level to 7200 feet) and in the mountains of California, south on the Sierra Nevada to the headwaters of the San Joaquin, and in the Coast Ranges south to the Santa Lucia Mountains of Monterey County. The variety *glauca* (*q.v.* below) found from Tacla Lake, British Columbia (latitude 55° north) southward for 2200 miles through the Rockies at 4000 to 11,000 feet altitude, in Alberta, Montana, Wyoming, Idaho, Utah, Colorado, Arizona, and New Mexico to western Texas and the highlands of Mexico; also in the Black Hills of South Dakota, the Big Horns of Wyoming and, somewhat rarely, on the mountains of eastern Nevada.

DESCRIPTION: *Bark* of young trunks whitish gray and smooth except for numerous resin blisters; later becoming red-brown and very scaly, and in old age very rough, thick, and deeply furrowed, with broad, heavy ridges between the furrows. *Twigs* slender, at first orange-brown, soon becoming gray-brown. *Winter buds* sharp-pointed, long-conical, ¼ inch long, and shining brown or bright red. *Leaves* ¾ to 1¼ inches long, more or less flattened, the upper surface grooved, the lower whitened with lines of stomata, and spirally disposed around the twig. *Flowers* — male orange-red, female reddish green. *Cones* hanging on long, stout stems, 2 to 4½ inches long with thin, rigid, rounded scales shorter than the long-exserted tridentate bracts. *Seeds* ¼ inch long, light shining reddish brown above, white-spotted beneath with a rounded terminal wing. *Wood* light (32 pounds per cubic foot, dry weight), and rather soft, variable in color (reddish or yellowish heartwood) and thickness of the whitish sapwood, and in closeness of grain, the springwood wide and weak, the summerwood dense and stronger.

When the immortal frigate *Constitution* first put to sea in 1798, she carried as masts three lofty White Pines felled in the state of Maine. But when in 1925 these had to be removed, there was left no White Pine in all the eastern states tall enough to replace those glorious sticks. From the Northwest came, instead, three towering shafts of

Douglas Fir, and these "Old Ironsides" bears in her decks today where she rides in honor at the dock of Boston Navy Yard.

Thus has White Pine fallen from first place among the timber trees of the continent; thus has Douglas Fir (which no American had ever seen or heard of when the keel of the *Constitution* was being laid), risen to the position of premier industrial tree of the world. For it was to this great western conifer that the lumber industry turned when, at the close of the last century, the end of virgin eastern White Pine was in sight. Luckily for them and us the noble species which took its fallen sister's place is quite as versatile in fulfilling a hundred vital uses and many fold as abundant.

And it is mightier in stature. Towering up to heights as great as 220 feet, with sometimes 100 feet of trunk clean of branches, arrow-straight, and with almost no taper below the crown discernible to the naked eye, an ancient Douglastree may be 17 feet in diameter. This tree is thus the tallest and most ponderous in North America, save only the two Sequoias. And except in their presence it is almost everywhere in its immense range the most majestic species, as it is the most commercially important.

One fourth of all the standing saw timber in the United States is Douglas Fir! In volume cut it surpasses any other one species. It occurs in every western state, and in parts of Canada and Mexico. Its somber shape, its serrated crowns and sharp lance-point tips and long swaying boughs become printed like a lasting eidolon on all our memories of the Pacific Northwest. And even deep in the desert states of the Southwest we meet it again, on high peaks, with gratitude for its dim, cool groves, after the glare and heat of the rocky wastes below.

Yet this important and abundant and beautiful tree has never had a universally accepted common name. Formerly in this country it was known as Oregon Pine and is still so called abroad. In Canada, and commonly in the lumber trade in this country, it is simply called Fir — *the* Fir, since no other can approach it in economic importance. In the literature of forestry it has wavered between Douglas Fir and Douglas Spruce, though it is no Spruce and no true Fir, as botanists see matters. Some years ago the Forest Service officially settled on "Douglasfir" and if this impaction seems to you to clear up matters, you may use it with the blessings of the Government Printing Office. The least misleading of proposed names is Douglastree, since it leans on no analogies and still does honor to that noble pioneer among explorer-botanists of the Northwest, David Douglas. In the pages that follow, this name will be used for the living forest tree, but for its logs, lumber, and wood products, the lumberman's name of Douglas Fir (or Fir for short) seems best.

The veriest beginner will have no difficulty in distinguishing a Douglastree in the field by its cones, for between their soft, broad scales are thrust out ribbon-shaped bracts that look like 3-forked tongues. Many species of *Abies,* the true Firs, also have extruded bracts, but they are never trident-like. With experience one comes to recognize Douglastree in the field from almost as far as it can be seen, by subtle points and traits. The dense, compact crowns, the lusterless, dark-blue green of the foliage (relieved only for a few weeks by bright new growth), the darkly, deeply furrowed old boles, the mast-like stems, and the grand down-sweeping of the boughs, all go to make up the character of this species.

But one feature there is which is peculiarly distinctive, and that is the way that numberless long slender twigs, clothed in a spiral of needles, hang vertically from the branches. Though the general habit of the tree is not what gardeners call weeping, these long pendants have a sort of sorrowful grace. When the summer winds blow lightly through the forest they stir this shawl-like fringe in an idle, ferny way; when winter rains come driving through the forest, level and endless from the storm-bound Pacific, then these long pennants lie out waving upon the gale in a way that gives the whole tree a wild and streaming look.

To see a growth of virgin Douglastree in all its venerable grandeur — for these trees may live 500 to 1000 years — perhaps the most impressive of easily accessible spots is on Grouse Mountain which rises behind the fine seaport city of Vancouver in British Columbia. A highway takes you up in hawk-like, soaring swoops, and from the excellent hostel at the road's end a footpath leads you directly up into the undisturbed and solemn stand where Douglastrees of towering height mingle with Hemlocks and Cedars only a little less tall. It is very dim and cool under the close canopy; seldom does a sunbeam reach to the forest floor where the mosses seem not to have been trodden since the Ice Age. And everywhere you look the great shafts of the Fir close up the aisles with their dark, deeply furrowed bark. From time to time the mountain wind goes seething through the high canopy above you, as if the whole forest were breathing as one ancient organism. And, if you are still, you will hear a spirit voice. It seems to begin far away at the auditory horizon and to bound toward you — a "bump . . . bump . . . bumpadump" — as if some creature were knocking on the great Fir trunks as it approaches. This is the call of the blue grouse for which the mountain is named, and as each bird utters it the next one takes up the proclamation. So the sound approaches, passes right by you — for the nearest bird is probably right over your head in some grand Fir, close to the trunk — and goes bounding into the distance. Somehow the stentorian bird seems the very voice of this profound and aboriginal wilderness and its cry, once heard, will be linked forever with your memory of Douglastrees.

Once, presumably, the entire Northwest was more or less covered with wilderness like this. It marched right down to the shores in the days of 1792 when Archibald Menzies, a naturalist of the famous Vancouver expedition that explored the Puget Sound region, saw, first of European scientists, the "impenetrable stretches of Pinery," among them the Douglastree that then bore no name. Menzies, who was also the first to collect specimens of the Coast Redwood and so many other great western trees, brought back herbarium specimens of the Douglastree and on their basis Lambert, the leading English authority on conifers, published the new species — as a sort of Pine! Then, when David Douglas reached the mouth of the Columbia in 1825, he saw from the deck of the ship "a species which may prove to be *P. taxifolia*" — the

tree that was to be named for him and carry that name, in a hundred useful products, to the ends of the earth. Proceeding inland, Douglas began to measure some of the gigantic logs of the tree he knew as *Pinus taxifolia*. The largest specimen he could find was 227 feet long and 48 feet in circumference. He wished to collect seeds, but found trouble in procuring them from such lofty trees; his buckshot would not reach the cones so high overhead and his hatchet could not cut down such lusty giants. When he finally procured seeds, he set out on a race for the coast, knowing that the ship *Dryad* was soon to sail. Only a day was left him to pack his collections of a year, which included 125 pounds of seeds, but he got his cargo aboard in time, and from those seeds grew the first European trees of this forest monarch. Soon Douglas's life would be cut short by a cruel death on the Hawaiian islands where he fell into a trap pit set for wild animals, and was trampled to death by a bullock.

Douglas's host, Dr. John McLoughlin, the celebrated Hudson's Bay Company agent, in 1828 erected the first sawmill on our Northwest coast and began the cutting of Fir. But it was not until the lumbering of eastern White Pine had laid waste the virgin growth of that species that the great days of Northwest logging really began, toward the close of the last century. Some firms came as a unit, bringing their lumberjacks with them; one old Maine firm transported its mills in sections around the Horn. Many bought up great blocks of forest from the railroads which had received them from the government as grants to compensate them for building transcontinental lines into country almost uninhabited. Other companies bought up large tracts from homesteaders, and in Oregon there was even a thriving business done by one government clerk in making false homestead entries which then went to lumber companies for a song; eventually he and some much bigger fish went to prison.

Indeed, lumbering in the Northwest in the early days was often a "two-fisted" business, in which one would say that neither the lumber barons (who came to be known as tyees) nor the lumberjacks, had learned a thing from the wastage, the fires, the boom-and-bust days, and stump counties of eastern history. Nothing, that is, except greatly increased efficiency at whirlwind exploitation. But that was in a cruder age, in the days when labor troubles went to the shooting stage, when pirates on Puget Sound stole whole rafts of timber and secretly sawed up the logs after obliterating the brands (each legitimate company had its own, like cattle ranchers), when fires burned over forests the size of many a European principality, when the Forest Service was jeered at and obstructed, when saloon bars in the coast towns were a mile long and brothels were big as hotels. Those days are gone. Progressive companies now hire their own trained foresters and follow practical conservation. Well-located lumber towns have become permanent cities, with fine schools, churches, hospitals, parks. Employees are usually married, own their homes, eat the best of food, sleep in clean beds. Fire is fought like the Devil. Those who wish to read more of the sociology and business history of this raucous saga with the prosperous and respectable ending should turn to *Holy Old Mackinaw* and *Green Commonwealth* by Stuart Holbrook, *The Great Forest* by Richard G. Lillard, and *Time, Tide and Timber* by Edwin Truman Coman.

The geographical setting of the Douglas Fir industry shows why the Northwest was destined to become the lumber capital of the world. For that region is the tidewater country around Puget Sound, Georgia and Juan de Fuca Straits, and the lower Columbia and its big tributary the Willamette, occupying an extensive area in British Columbia, Vancouver Island, Washington State, and Oregon. True that this region was, for a century and more after its discovery by mariners, trappers and explorers, remote from the lumber markets of the world. But the coming of transcontinental railroads, and still more the Panama Canal, changed all that, and made it possible to sell Fir to the eastern United States and even Europe.

More important still has been the lay of the land, much of it being level or nearly so, and thus making transport from timber to mill inexpensive. The intricacies of Puget Sound, and the waters between Vancouver Island and mainland British Columbia, have made possible the movement of great log rafts, some of which have gone to sea as far as San Diego. The great harbors permit ocean-going vessels to dock right at the mill yards. The small harbors have proved ideal for the location of a host of small mills (and at one time for sheltering the log pirates).

But most important of all has been the climate, with rainfall up to 100 inches a year and over, and a mild winter, permitting a long growing season. In very wet mild climates all trees grow swiftly and very densely, grow tall and mighty in bole, and tend to live long. But the inherent greatness of Douglastree made it king in the Northwest tidewater. Add to this one lucky fact: this king in size is also, by the physical properties of its wood, a timber tree of the very highest grade, with potentialities for multiple use in our complex civilization undreamed of by the first tyees who saw in it only its dimension timbers in abundance.

From the beginning, the task of getting those giants out of the big woods has called upon all the skills, courage, and inventive genius gained by the fallers and buckers in a hundred years of experience with eastern Pine. Undercut notches as much as five feet deep are first chopped by these living Paul Bunyans. Then on the opposite side of the tree the long falling saws are started on Herculean work, with steel wedges driven in to keep the tons and tons of living wood from settling on the saws, until at last only a thin pivot between the undercut and the saw supports the fatally swaying monarch.

" 'Timber! Timber!' the fallers loudly warn everyone of danger," writes a veteran of Northwest logging, "and with a few final blows on wedges they withdraw their tools and place themselves on each side of the severed stump. With increasing velocity the top describes an arc, the trunk hinging on the uncut wood of the undercut and saw cut. Faster and faster, with mounting crescendo of sound through nearly five hundred feet of an arc, the top sweeps to the ground, shattering the smaller trees in its way and finding its resting place with a thud, roar and rush of wind that shakes the earth for hundreds of feet and sets all the other trees to swaying as though an earthquake had shaken the forest." [1]

The next task is to get the big sticks out of the woods and here ingenuity and invention have made their greatest progress. First came the old skid roads, with logs laid on the ground to act as rollers stretching from deep timber to the nearest splash-dam or logging railhead, or even to the mill, with long strings of oxen dragging the giant sticks till the rollers smoked with the heat of friction and the air was blue with the oaths of the bullwhackers. But the arrival of the donkey engine to drag the logs by a steel cable wound on a great drum so speeded up the delivery of timber that it came too fast for the mills. Then the mills grew so vast that a speed-up (workmen call it high-balling) in log delivery was called for. This was met by the "high-lead," where logs shot along on cables slung high over the tops of the forest. This operation demanded a great spar on which to rig the pulleys and cables, and this in turn brought into existence the high-rigger, the most spectacular kind of logger ever known, a steeplejack of the big sticks who at some point 100 to 200 feet up the trunk saws off the top of a giant tree that is to act as a spar. Then a block weighing

[1] Frank F. Lamb. *Sagas of the Evergreens.* W. W. Norton Company.

up to 1½ tons is fixed at the top of the spar; through this will pass the cable. Rigging slingers then hook the steel chokers to the logs to be dragged to the foot of the spar tree. Chasers hook them to the main line; the flagman waves to the whistle punk who blows signals for starting, stopping, and backing-up by the donkey punchers at the engine's levers — and off sails a giant on its giddy course.

Today the donkey engine has grown into something as great as Babe, the Big Blue Ox, for it is a giant powered by diesel, steam, or electricity. In its grip logs weighing fifty tons are moved like jackstraws; ropes of braided steel fly at a thousand feet a minute through the forest; in eight hours a single crew has been known to handle 10,000,-000 pounds of Fir.

The need of cutting areas where the merchantable timber is scattered has summoned from the farm and battlefield the track-laying tractor which tows the great logs from stump to dam or truck. Yet this 150-horsepower slave is under the control of one man, the cat-skinner, who can take his monster up steep grades, through deep mud and among big rocks, pushing down trees six to eight inches thick which obstruct his path, till he finds his way to the spot where the fallers are bringing down the giants. Arrived at the mill, the logs are dumped by crane into a storage pond, then pulled by an endless chain to the head saw, a band of thin steel running over two large pulleys at the rate of twenty-five miles per hour. The approaching log is handled by a "nigger" which flips it over from one face to another to receive the shearing cut of the saw. Then the big cuts or cants of lumber have next to be cut into the desired finer and precise dimensions. So they are raced over rollers and run onto a platform where they are slid sideways past a battery of circular saws. These can be raised or lowered by a man in a cage who plays upon a bank of keys like a skilled pianist. Finally the lumber, cut and dressed to order, green or seasoned, marked for grades by experts, is lifted by an automotive spider that runs out over the wood, straddles the piles with its wheeled legs, raises the lumber under its throbbing body and bears it off like a predatory creature, to drop it right into waiting railroad car, or storage pile, or on a wharf or in the hold of a ship.

Out of this complex called a modern sawmill still come Fir timbers measuring up to 24 by 24 inches wide and thick and 100 feet long. And dimension timbers remain today of outsize importance in the Fir business, just as they were back in the days when the Mormons cut trunks of huge Fir, in the mountains, and brought them down to Salt

Lake City to arch over the roof of their great fane, the Tabernacle. Enormous Fir timbers and masses of solid wood are more than ever called for in structural beams and trusses for big buildings, docks, trestles, bridges and spans and for planks in the floors and ceilings of factories. Also, in the construction of reinforced concrete buildings there is a demand for wooden forms into which to pour the concrete which shall be both long and strong, and able to hold rigidly in place the heavy masses of restless, wet concrete. For this purpose Douglas Fir's superiority is recognized at home and in distant lands.

Taking the place of eastern White Pine, Douglas Fir is now a favorite with carpenters and architects, since the wood does not warp or pull its nails, for sills and posts, beams, floor and ceiling joists, roof rafters, floor boards, and studding. Kiln-dried Fir makes a beautifully figured, easily finished interior woodwork, both in vertical and flat grain.

Thousands and thousands of miles of railroad track in the West are laid on Douglas Fir ties which can be cut from second-growth trees, since large dimensions are not needed. Beside the tracks march telegraph and telephone poles of whole Douglastrees. Fir makes, too, a hot firewood, inflammable even when green; the mills commonly sell off their slabs and waste for this purpose in the Northwest. The bark, once considered a total loss, is now ground up and then variously treated to serve as a soil conditioner, as absorbent filler in plaster acoustical products, as a substitute for the expensive and sometimes unobtainable natural cork, as soles for shoes, in radio recording for electrical transcriptions, and patented inventions which have already passed 500 in number.

In World War II Douglas Fir, more than any other tree, played a vital rôle. Every man in the service knew it well, for his foot locker was generally made of it. He crossed rivers on pontoon bridges of Douglas Fir, and if he was wounded he was carried from the field on stretchers whose rails were, very likely, of this strong yet light wood. Fir went into the tanks for gasoline storage, at advanced bases. It was a favorite wood for the Pacific huts that housed our soldiers all the way to Japan. Every few minutes, 24 hours a day, factories completed another Pacific hut; it was then shipped in knock-down form to the remotest atoll or Aleutian isle.

Both in war and peace, the most revolutionary thing that has happened in the field of structural wood is the rise of the plywood industry. Though many trees may be made into plywood, Douglas Fir has taken, and will probably always hold, the lead. Plywood is not exactly new, since its basic principle was known to the Egyptians. Nor is it a complex process involving a reconstruction of the very fibers of cellulose into something unrecognizable as wood, as in the case of plastics. Plywood is simply a glue-up of thin sheets of wood, usually kiln-dried. The extremely thin wood is cut from the log by a rotary veneer knife which unrolls from the log a continuous sheet of wood, as one unrolls paper towelling. This is the veneer, which is then sliced by guillotine knives into the sizes desired. When the veneer is to be used structurally, as in the case of Douglas Fir, it is built up in layers (commonly 3-ply), each layer or ply lying with its grain at right angles to the pieces above and below. This gives a resistance to splitting that makes plywood stronger than steel of the same weight. Any householder who ever thought to make kindling wood out of pieces of plywood left by carpenters by swinging an axe on them has found that he and his axe are worsted. Nails and screws can be put in the very edge of plywood without any possibility that they can tear loose under strain, or that the wood will split.

Of course a bonding agent is required to unite the plies, and this is one of the marvelous modern glues, united under heat and pressure with the plies. These glues are even stronger than the wood, and new glues with special properties are appearing on the market. Glue and ply together form a structural system that can be extended to any length, bent into any shape. As a result, synthetic structural timbers are now made of ply, which even so titanic a tree as Douglas Fir could never produce in the forest. Great hangars, and arches for enormous warehouses and halls are made of glue and wood almost as thin as paper which yet surpass steel in strength, lightness, and cheapness. Plywood has proved ideal, too, for the Navy's lifeboats, saving a ton of steel on each boat, and floating 7 inches higher out of water than its steel counterpart. Plywood also goes into coastal patrol and torpedo boats, into PT and assault and landing boats. In the field of prefabricated housing, which has revolutionized the building business, plywood is the magic name, and Douglas Fir is in the lead for a dozen reasons. One of the least important of them economically, but esthetically pleasing, is the beauty of the grain; this is not destroyed by the veneer knives or lost in the bonding, but stands out, as vivid and handsome as that of Yellow Pine, in plywood paneling in your room.

Can even the great stands of a Douglas Fir withstand the demands presently made by the greatest of all lumber industries? It is said that in some thirty years one-half of all the virgin Fir in Washington and Oregon has been lumbered, and in the neighborhood of railroads and highways it is all gone. Lands cut over by wasteful methods in early days have too often reverted for delinquent taxes to the counties — but as desolate stump lands from which even the hardiest lumberjack or tyee averts his eyes. True that plywood may eventually take away some of the drain upon virgin timber, since trees of great dimensions are not needed for it, but that will happen when the profitable virgin growth is still scarcer, and will merely mean that second growth will be cut as fast as, or even before, it wholly matures.

On the bright side — and it is brighter than for almost any other important tree now being cut — there is the tremendous regenerative power of Douglastrees. They are fertile; they are vigorous; they are very fast-growing. These inherent qualities are favored by the reliable and abundant rainfall and the mild climate. True, under virgin conditions a forest tract dominantly Douglas Fir in one tree-generation is likely to be supplanted in the next by the far less valuable Western Hemlock. The reason for this is that a heavy stand of old Fir is too shady for its own seedlings, which are light-demanding while the seeds of Hemlock will sprout in the dimmest woodland light, and their saplings shoot up and eventually take over. But when a tract in the Northwest is thinned by selective cutting or clean-cut (completely razed of all trees), then Fir seedlings rejoice, but Hemlock's are sun-smitten. So Douglas Fir will succeed itself over and over if repeatedly cut — providing, always, that the cleared areas are small enough to allow for natural reseeding from neighboring strips of woodland, and that fire is kept out of young growth.

Young Firs under favorable conditions come on lustily. We can count even now upon 4,700,000,000 board feet a year of renewed growth on cut-overs in this country, if they are well managed. The lumbermen promise themselves an eventual increment of 7,400,000,000 feet annually. That will still be short of the present cut and loss, however, and there is no reason to think the present cut will not increase as our population and industrial civilization increase. But the losses to fire could be cut, and the most progressive lumber companies are now carefully managing their cut-over lands and planting where planting is needed. They believe that they are already started on a cycle of balanced cut and regrowth which will keep them in business on their own present acreage forever.

The Rocky Mountain phase of the Douglas Fir differs from that of the Pacific coast in slight and subtle ways and has been designated as variety *glauca* (Mayr) Sudworth. The foliage in the Rocky Mountain variety is often bluish green, almost like that of Colorado Blue Spruce, while that of the Pacific coast tree is a very dark green, appearing at times almost black against the sky, or at least very somber except for the bright yellow-green growing tips. However, the bluish or glaucous hue is by no means constant in the Rocky Mountain trees. It may be pronounced in some individuals and lacking in others in the same locality.

The cone of the Rocky Mountain trees is smaller, fewer-scaled, and more uniformly conical in outline than that of Pacific coast trees. "Its bracts project more and are strikingly reflexed, often standing out at right angles from the cone axis. Cones of the coast Fir are from 2½ to 4½ inches long and about 1 inch broad, while those of the mountain form are rarely over 3 inches long, though they often have a breadth of 1 inch.

"Though no distinction has yet been made on the basis of the minute structure of the wood, lumbermen who have sawed both forms testify to differences between them in grain or in ease of working . . . The [Rocky] mountain form produces a red wood, with usually a large proportion of summerwood. It is neither as straight-grained nor as easily worked as the coast fir, but it is highly valued for its strength and its durability in contact with the soil, in which respect it surpasses the other species with which it grows." [1]

The Rocky Mountain form is much more tolerant of drought, much less tolerant of shade than the coast tree, and grows more slowly. This appears to be true not only under the different climatic conditions of the Pacific coast with its heavier rainfall and mild winters and the Rockies with their more arid conditions and hard winters, but holds good even when the trees are grown side by side in Europe.

---

[1] E. H. Frothingham, "Douglas Fir: A Study of the Pacific coast and Rocky Mountains forms." U.S. Department of Agriculture, *Forest Service Circular* 150. 1909.

BIGCONE DOUGLAS FIR

Pseudotsuga macrocarpa (Vasey) Mayr

OTHER NAME: Bigcone Spruce.

RANGE: On the cool sides of southern California canyons, 2200 to 7000 feet above sea level, chiefly in the San Gabriel and San Bernardino Mountains, but widely distributed in favorable locations from the high mountains of eastern Santa Barbara and southwestern Kern Counties south to the Mexican border and beyond to the San Pedro Mártir Mountains of Baja California. Absent from the Sierra Nevada.

DESCRIPTION: *Bark* of old trunks up to ½ foot thick, dark reddish brown, deeply furrowed with broad scaly ridges between the furrows. *Twigs* slender and pubescent at first and dark reddish brown, becoming smooth and gray-brown. *Leaves* ¾ to 1¼ inches long, dark bluish gray-green, incurved above the middle, with a slender callous tip, lying all in one plane (by a twist in the leafstalk). *Flowers* — male light yellow and sheathed at base in the shining bud scales; female with pale green bracts tinged with red. *Cones* short-stalked, 3 to 6 inches long, at maturity rich dark brown, the scales thin, concave, broadly rounded at the tip and rather broader (1½ to 2 inches) than long, but little exceeded by the narrow extruded bracts whose midrib terminates as the flexible, flattened tip. *Seeds* ½ inch long, wrinkled, the upper surface nearly black, the lower pale brown. *Wood* hard, strong, close-grained, light (28½ pounds per cubic foot, dry weight).

The Bigcone Douglas Fir is but a poor relation of the Common Douglastree, distinct enough from it botanically, but, with almost all of its limited stand included in national forests, it never enters into lumbering or commercial use. Its home is on the sides of sheltered ravines and canyons, and on the cool north slopes of the mountains of southern California, and you see it growing in fine style — from 30 to 90 feet high and with very long, swaying, handsome branches — as you take any of the roads that lead from Pasadena, Claremont, and San Bernardino, up into the Sierra Madre ranges which keep the north winds away from the orange groves and resort cities at their southern bases. Up there, this tree keeps company with Bigcone and Yellow Pines, and wears much the same grand, somber air as the true Douglas Fir which it replaces entirely in the south. Its wood, though tough and hard, is coarse and in all respects inferior to that of Douglas Fir.

THE BALSAM FIRS
(*Abies*)

THESE TREES of superb form, with their lance-sharp tips and regular tiers of whorled branches, have trunks which go up through the tree, from root to tip, straight as a pole. On the upper, cone-bearing branches the needles bristle out in all directions, but on sterile branches they may lie flat in one plane, like those of Hemlock. Again, like Hemlock needles, Fir needles are usually flattened, not squarish, and generally blunt, not usually prickle-tipped, and they are whitened beneath by two pallid lines. The upper surface is deep green, grooved and lustrous.

From large bud scales appear the flowers in the axils of last year's leaves. The male flowers cluster abundantly on the lower sides of branches above the middle of the tree, showing scarlet or yellow anthers; the female are always borne on the upper sides of twigs. Consequently the cones are carried erect. The thin leathery scales are closely overlapping and broadly rounded at tip but narrowed at base to a claw. Often the papery bracts between them are longer and hence extruded. Finally the scales drop one by one, leaving the axis of the cone erect on the twig, like a spike. The winged seeds are furnished with conspicuous resin vessels.

*   *   *

EASTERN BALSAM FIR

Abies balsamea (Linnæus) Miller

OTHER NAMES: Balm-of-Gilead Fir. Blister, Fir, or Silver Pine.

RANGE: Yukon Territory and northern Alberta, east across Canada to Newfoundland, and south to northern and eastern parts of Minnesota and Wisconsin, northern Michigan, throughout northern New England, the Berkshires, eastern New York, and south on the mountains to southwestern Virginia. Rare in northwestern Connecticut and northeastern Iowa.

DESCRIPTION: *Needles* on cone-bearing twigs appearing brushed up to the top of the twig and only ½ inch long, but twice as long on horizontal shoots and lying all in one plane, shining dark green above, silvery below, blunt or acute but never prickle-tipped. *Flowers* — male yellow or purple, female pale yellow-green. *Cones* dark rich purple, 2 to 4 inches long. *Seeds* ¼ inch long; the light brown wings a little longer. *Bark* thick, smooth or thinly scaly, rich brown, with many resin blisters. *Wood* light (26 pounds to the cubic foot, dry weight), soft, weak, coarse-grained and swiftly decaying, the heartwood pale brown, the sapwood thick and yellowish white.

The Eastern Balsam Fir enters the circumscriptions of this book in a zone between the prairies and the tundra of Alberta and Saskatchewan, extending northwestward on the plains of British Columbia and Yukon Territory. It never mingles there with any other *Abies* except, close to the Rockies, with the Alpine Fir, which is known instantly by its pencil-slim outline, while the Eastern Balsam is more broadly conical. The needles of the alpine species appear brushed upward on the twig; true that those of the Eastern Balsam sometimes do so too, but only on the upper, cone-bearing twigs; sterile and lower branches have 2-ranked needles that lie all in one plane. Far more does this species keep company with the White and Black Spruces, which much resemble it in shape. But the Spruces have prickle-tipped needles and pendant cones; our tree has blunt needles and erect cones.

Seldom seen in the West except by trappers and Indians, the Eastern Balsam can never mean here what it does to the people of eastern Canada and New England where it is the only Fir. Nor has the lumberman ever had any use for this tree except to make himself a sweet-smelling mattress laid on a springy frame of Spruce boughs. In the East this is one of the best-loved of Christmas trees; where it grows in the Far Northwest there are a million Christmas trees to every Christian inhabitant. In the East the deliciously aromatic needles are sewed into small pillows and sold as souvenirs to city folk on vacation. In the West the very airs in the forests are balsamic.

For success in the eternal forest battle for survival, this tree depends upon its adaptability, the speed of its growth and its fertility. The seeds which fly through the wods on trim bright wings are many, though the grouse and red squirrels and pine mice devour them, just as moose and deer browse on the foliage.

The blisters yield what is called Canada balsam, a sort of resin employed in the manufacture of varnish and as a fixative and preservative for mounting specimens on glass for the microscope.

ALPINE FIR

Abies lasiocarpa (Hooker) Nuttall

OTHER NAMES: Balsam or White Fir. White or Mountain Balsam Fir.

RANGE: Coast Ranges of southeastern Alaska from sea level to timber line (3000 feet), and southern Yukon Territory, in the Rockies and east slopes (not west) of the Coast Range of British Columbia and Alberta, south through the Rockies of Idaho, Montana, Wyoming, Colorado, Utah, and Nevada, to southern Arizona and New Mexico (Tunitchta Mountains, Pecos Baldy), at or near timber line (10,500 feet in the southern Rockies); also in the Olympics of Washington, the Cascades of Washington and Oregon and the Wallowa Mountains of eastern Oregon, and the Trinity Mountains of California.

DESCRIPTION: *Bark* of old trunks essentially smooth, thin, pale grayish white, only intermittently and narrowly scored with brownish fissures which reveal the reddish inner bark. *Twigs* rather stout, at first clothed in pale rusty pubescence, finally smooth and silvery gray. *Leaves* 1 to 1¾ inch long, ½₂ inch wide, the tip blunt and notched, deep blue-green, that of the new season's growth with a silvery tinge, upper surface with 8 or 10 rows of stomata seen as whitish lines above the middle of the blade; the whole tuft of foliage on each twig appearing as if brushed upward, nearly erect, due to a twist in the leaf stalk. *Flowers* — male

dark blue or violet, female with broad short purple scales and long, slender-tipped, strongly reflexed bracts. *Cones* usually densely clustered, 2¼ to 4 inches long, 1¼ to 1½ inches thick (or broader after the scales begin to loosen) the very thick scales wedge-shaped at base, at first deep purple, gradually growing paler with weathering, the exserted bracts abruptly contracted to a slender tip. *Seeds* ¼ inch long, ivory brown, with very large shining brownish purple or violet wings. *Wood* light (21½ pounds per cubic foot, dry weight), weak and soft, the heartwood pale brown or nearly white, the sapwood whitish.

The outline of the Alpine Fir, so outstandingly slender and martially erect and rigid, is the most dramatic statement made by any native tree. The Engelmann and Black Spruces, when crowded for space, may take on such a cathedral-spire form, but given room they will expand; under all circumstances the Alpine Fir, at least in all but the lower third of the tree, keeps this pencil-slim form. Not the Lombardy Poplar or the Italian Cypress is more ejaculatory in the landscape. And they are but horticultural sports of trees which normally have wide-spreading boughs. The Alpine Fir comes by its outline naturally, through the extreme shortness of all but the lower branches. Its statement in the subalpine and subarctic scenes is that of an exclamation point!

And the scenery where, in the United States, the Alpine Fir grows most triumphantly, is something to exclaim over. For though it grows so widely, from Alaska to the Colorado Rockies, this tree displays its

beauty to the most striking advantage where at high altitudes it rings round those snow-capped and extinct volcanic cones — eleven of them, and each more than a mountain, each a majestic spirit — that soar above the Cascade ranges of Washington and Oregon. Greatest is Mount Rainier, a peak that rises up from almost sea level to 14,409 feet, which, in relative height of peak above base, makes this the highest, as it is the most beautiful, peak in the United States. Indeed, it is more than any ordinary peak; in its vastnesses it is the equal of a great range. Scores of waterfalls leap from its sides; twenty-six great glaciers glitter on its flanks, and trees beyond all estimating swathe it round.

Among these the most striking and yet fitting is the Alpine Fir, which frames all those views so beloved of the photographer, of long, flower-spangled meadows leading toward the great cone that seems, in its clearness and abruptness, about to break as a white wave. Indeed, it would require a tree of the most dramatic shape, of almost incredible symmetry, to draw attention to itself in all this splendor. Yet so eye-taking is the Alpine Fir that even in photographs of Mount Rainier and Mount Hood, Mount Olympus, Mount Baker, and the rest, it wrests attention away from the sensational peaks, so that people who have never seen the West inquire its name. They do not say, "That is a mountain I would like to climb," but rather, "That's a place I would like to camp" — in just such a meadow, with just such a view, amid such trees.

Many kinds of trees that love the mountain heights must for long seasons bear great weights of snow. Some, like the graceful but weak-tipped Douglas Firs and the Hemlocks, bend under it, especially while young, till they look like sheeted ghosts all doubled up, or crouching, as if convulsed either with mirth or with pain, but scarcely recognizable as trees. Not so the Alpine Fir. No matter how immature it is, it is already rigid as a mast, with tier on tier of whorled, perfectly horizontal branches that are too short and stiff to bend. Many other conifers have flexible needles, but those of this Fir are at once stiff and all, as it were, brushed upward to the top of the twig. So the foliage instead of being a flat spray, as in the Eastern Balsam Fir, is a spiky bed on which the snowfall is speared and held in cottony tufts. If it is to escape these leafy fingers it will have to melt; the sturdy needles refuse to yield to it and spill it.

Around the mountain meadows in the United States the Alpine Fir will grow to some 50 or 75 feet in height, at the most. At timber line it may be only 3 or 4 feet high, yet it is still erect — a miniature of its greater self — and never prostrate like so many alpine trees. But it is in north-central British Columbia that Alpine Fir attains its greatest stature, up to 175 feet. Here, where it is the only true Fir, it grows so closely, so loftily, and casts such a somber shade that Theodora Stanwell-Fletcher, who has probably written more of it than any other author, speaks repeatedly of it, in her book, *Driftwood Valley*, as forming a "jungle." No Indian camps, she says, seem ever to be pitched in the shadowy depths of its groves — so dank and deeply drifted in winter, so windless and mosquito-haunted in summer.

The late northern or mountain spring brings to the Alpine Fir many touches of subtle color to lighten its coniferous solemnity. The tips of new foliage are gleaming silver. The male flowers are a dark blue, turning violet, the female violet-purple. With the coming of the brief summer, the deep purple cones mature; as the hot weather beats upon them, silvery blobs of resin drip from the scales. When the cones open in the fall, they loose ivory-gray seeds that twirl away upon large, lustrous-purple or violet-tinged wings. Usually gray, the bark of the trunk is sometimes chalky white. In its youth, big resin blisters are found upon the stem, but these disappear in age and the bark becomes quite flinty.

The lumberman has little use for the soft, weak, coarse, non-durable wood. According to Mrs. Stanwell-Fletcher, even the Northwest Indians find trouble in making a fire with Alpine Fir. But mountain sheep, Richardson's grouse, and Cascade pine squirrels devour the seeds.

Variety *arizonica* (Merriam) Lemmon, the Corkbark Fir, differs from the typical Alpine Fir in having soft, corky, thick bark made up of large, overlapping yellowish-white scales; the cones are longer and narrower than those of the Alpine Fir, the scales at base halberd-shaped. This variety, which is found at 8000 to 10,000 feet altitude in the mountains of southern Colorado, northern and southwestern New Mexico, and central and southeastern Arizona, grows 50 to 75 feet tall, with a trunk up to 1½ feet thick. Within its range and on the thin gravelly or rocky soils where it grows, it may accompany or replace Alpine Fir.

LOWLAND FIR

Abies grandis (Douglas) Lindley

OTHER NAMES: Grand, White, Silver, Yellow, or Stinking Fir.

RANGE: Vancouver Island and the adjacent mainland of British Columbia, west to the Rockies of Montana and Idaho, and south in the Cascades to Oregon and in the Coast Ranges to Sonoma County, California; also on the mountains of the eastern parts of Oregon and Washington.

DESCRIPTION: *Bark* of old trunks deeply but narrowly furrowed, with long, flat, pale brown or ashy ridges, that on young trunks smooth and ashy brown splashed with chalk-white. *Twigs* slender, yellow-green or orange-brown. *Leaves* flat, blunt or notched, shining dark yellow-green, and grooved above, whitened below by 2 lines of stomata, those on the lower or sterile branches distant, 1½ to 2 inches long, 2-ranked to form a flat spray, those of the fertile branches a little shorter and more crowded and seeming to bristle all around the twig or to point upward. *Flowers* — male pale yellow, female light green. *Cones* 2 to 4½ inches long, 1 to 1⅓ inch thick, green-purple to yellow-green, the scales broader than long, and much longer than the short-tipped bracts. *Seeds* ⅜ inch long, pale yellowish brown with straw-colored wings. *Wood* light (22 pounds per cubic foot, dry weight), soft, fairly strong, coarsely but straight grained, heartwood light brown with pale yellowish sapwood,

All the western Firs are beautiful trees, and many are grand. But the Lowland Fir is grandest of all, fulfilling honestly the boastful Latin of its name of *Abies grandis*. In the great coniferous rain forest that covers the lowlands of the Olympic peninsula, the Puget Sound region, the tidewater country around the mouth of the Columbia, the Lowland Fir rises like a tower for 150 to 200 feet, and exceptional trees have been measured which were 250 to 300 feet high, with trunks up to 6 feet in diameter. Such individuals rank with Douglas Firs, Sitka Spruces, and Redwoods in their majesty, and even lesser specimens stand out handsomely in the rain forest. In the "Inland Empire" or forested area of northern parts of Idaho and Montana, the Lowland Firs are not great in dimensions, but at all times they are beautiful. The foliage, on the upper surface, is a dark but glossy green; on the under surface it is almost silvery white. The cones, looking rough-hewn but handsome, are so big that though they are borne chiefly near the top of the tree, they show conspicuously and still further carry the honor of this Fir's specific name.

Like so many Firs, this species has big resin blisters under the bark of the young growth, and when you cut down a little Lowland Fir for a Christmas tree you may get a shot of balsamic gum right in the face. The needles when crushed have a sweet, balsamy aroma that steals forth into the room when the tree is being decorated. The wood is too soft, yet too heavy in proportion to its little strength, to make first-class lumber. Pulpwood offers its only commercial future, and there are so many finer pulping species in the woods that Lowland Fir is little felled for any purpose, and is usually left in the forest to make music and distill incense.

WHITE FIR

Abies concolor (Gordon and Glendenning) Hoopes

OTHER NAMES: Balsam, White, or Silver Fir. White Balsam. Fir.

RANGE: Cascades and Siskiyou Mountains of Oregon, south in the high Coast Ranges of northern California, and throughout the Sierra Nevada (4000 to 8000 feet) and in the high mountains of southern California from the San Rafael Mountains of Santa Barbara County south through

the San Bernardinos (up to 10,000 feet altitude) and the San Jacintos to Baja California; and in the Rockies from the Wallowa, Blue, and Warner Mountains of eastern Oregon, and in Idaho west and south, through the mountain systems of Utah and Colorado, Arizona, and New Mexico to the highlands of Sonora and Chihuahua; on some of the desert ranges of Nevada; rare in Wyoming and Montana.

DESCRIPTION: *Bark* of old trees very massive, hard, horny, up to 6½ inches thick, rough ashy gray, with deeper furrows and big, wide ridges, that of younger trees smooth and gray. *Twigs* rather thick, smooth, at first yellow-green, becoming gray-brown. *Leaves* silver-blue to silvery green, on lower branches 2 to 3 inches long, sharp at tip, flat, straight, remote and 2-ranked along the twig, those on fertile branches only ¾ to 1½ inches long, curved, thick, the upper surface keeled, crowded and standing or curling erect. *Flowers* — male dark red or pink, female with rounded wide scales. *Cones* 3 to 5 inches long, purplish or olive or dark yellow-green, the scales wider than long, and longer than their short-pointed bracts. *Seeds* ⅓ to ½ inch long and yellow-brown; wings rose-colored. *Wood* soft, weak, coarse-grained, very light (22½ pounds per cubic foot, dry weight).

Of all the western Firs, the White Fir is the most widespread. You see it abundantly on the mountain slopes just above the floor of Yosemite Valley, its beautiful, light gray and smooth bark shining between its tier on tier of regularly whorled branches, its deep green or almost silvery gray needles cheerfully matching the clear mountain sunlight. In Colorado it lines the exciting mountain drives, and crowds into the canyons where the streams come seething down. A particularly noble grove of it is seen in North Cheyenne Canyon, one of the favorite tourist sights in the neighborhood of Colorado Springs. Always the springing boughs, the symmetrical broad cone of the outline, have a look of strength and health and the ability to grow almost anywhere in the drier mountains of the West, and endure all that the Rockies and Sierra Nevada can bring of snow and storm, and long dry summers. Balsamic fragrance breathes from them, squirrels bound in their branches, grouse devour their seeds, porcupines commit lamentable depredations on their bark; the black-tailed and mule deers are highly dependent on them for food and you may practically count on seeing some of these beautiful creatures, sooner or later, in any good growth of White Fir.

There are no complete statistics on the amount of logging of this tree, for it is cut along with all the Firs without botanical distinction. It would make a good pulp wood, but is not needed now in that well-supplied market. Its lumber "compares favorably" with Eastern Hemlock, which is faint praise, and holds paint and nails well when used for boxes or construction lumber in small houses.

Rather does the future of this tree lie in its value as an ornamental. It takes with the most accommodating good nature to cultivation, developing pretty charms not nearly so visible in the wild. It will even survive and make growth in the dense shade of older, higher trees and of city buildings. So, long life to it — and may it attain wherever it grows its full fine stature of 100 and even 200 feet.

SILVER FIR

Abies amabilis (Douglas) Forbes

OTHER NAMES: White, Red, Amabilis, or Lovely Fir. Larch.

RANGE: Extreme southeastern Alaska, from sea level to 1000 feet altitude and on the Coast Ranges of British Columbia up to 4000 feet, and on Vancouver and the Queen Charlotte Islands; in the Olympic peninsula of Washington, 1000 to 6000 feet above sea level, and on both sides of the Cascades of Washington and Oregon (2000 to 7000 feet) south to Crater Lake.

DESCRIPTION: *Bark* ashy gray blotched with large chalk-white areas, smooth and unbroken except on old trunks which are seamed, scaly, reddish brown and broken into small plates at the very base. *Twigs* stout, softly pubescent in the first season and light orange-brown, becoming dark purple and at last reddish brown. *Leaves* of the lower

crown branches and sterile branches flattish and bluntly pointed or
notched at the tip, about 1¼ inches long, scattered (not dense) in a
plane, and grooved and dark shining green above, the lower face silvery
white with 6 or 8 bands of stomata between the prominent midribs and
inrolled margins; leaves of the upper crown shorter (about ¾ inch long)
and stout (not flattish), growing densely and erect on the twigs and acute
to a point, while those of the leader shoots are scattered and very sharp-
tipped. *Flowers* — male red, female with broad rounded scales and
shining dark purple rhombic bracts gradually narrowed to a broad point.
Cones 3½ to 6 inches long, 2¼ to 2½ inches in diameter, and dark
velvety purple, with broad round scales twice as long as the reddish,
rhombic, slender-tipped bracts. *Seeds* ½ inch long, dull yellowish brown
with light brown and shining wings. *Wood* light (26½ pounds per cubic
foot, dry weight), soft, weak, the heartwood pale brown, the sapwood
nearly white.

Silver Fir is a beautiful name for a beautiful tree which reaches its
most magnificent development in the Olympic Mountains that, seen
from Vancouver Island or the historic straights of Juan de Fuca, seem
to rise like shining angels right out of the sea. But their eternal snows
do not come down to the water's edge, as they appear to do. Their
bases and middle slopes are swathed in a forest whose virginity is still
unravished. And here the Silver Fir towers up as much as 200 feet.
Such a tree will have a diameter of 3 to 5 feet through the bole, but
the impression — due to the exaggerated height, and the spire-like
thinness of the crown in forest-crowded trees — is of a wondrously

slim straight pole. Such trees would seem to be a great temptation to
the logging foreman, but he knows that their wood is soft, weak, and
low in resistance to decay. It is cut only for the sidings of small houses
and for crates; it makes a good pulp, and is being increasingly cut for
this purpose.

There are so many Firs in the West that it takes an expert, sometimes, to tell them apart and even he is not always prepared to identify
a specimen at first glance. (Indeed no one need be ashamed of stating
that he cannot name a given tree, of whatever sort, without waiting
for the season to complete the flowering and fruiting of the annual life
cycle.) The Silver Fir in youth sometimes looks much like the Alpine
Fir, with its exclamation-point outline. But it is distinguished, once
you have a fruiting branch in hand, by the way its needles grow in 4
irregular ranks, the lower pair appearing brushed upward from below,
the upper pair brushed forward along the twig, giving the whole upper
surface of the spray of foliage a ruffled appearance; the lower surface
of a spray feels flat and smooth in the palm. The shining silvery undersides of the needles give this tree its name. As for the cones, they are
ponderous and big, and almost as handsome as flowers when mature,
with their purplish scales. Every two or three years there are large
seed crops, but the viability of the seeds is brief, the failure of the
seedlings common. Because of its beauty, Silver Fir has often been
cultivated, especially in Europe, but after exhibiting the pretty charms
of its youth, it is apt to pine away or, at least, fail to develop into the
grandeur of its sisters in the far-off, shining Puget Sound region.

NOBLE FIR

Abies procera Rehder

OTHER NAMES: Red Fir. Larch.

RANGE: Mountains of the western parts of Washington and Oregon,
south in the Coast Ranges to the Siskiyous, and in the Cascades to
Crater Lake (from lake level to rim).

DESCRIPTION: *Bark* on old trunks bright red-brown under the thickly
appressed scales, and divided, by cross-checks as well as vertical furrows,

into numberless long irregular plates. *Twigs* slender, forward-pointing, reddish-brown. *Leaves* curved and grooved, pale or deep bluish green, with a silvery tinge, densely massed and stiff, appearing to grow erect on top of the twig, those of the sterile branches and of saplings 1 to 1½ inches long, ⅟₁₆ inch broad, flattish, the apex blunt and notched, those of the fertile and upper crown branches only ½ to ¾ inch long, very stout, 4-sided, with sharp, callous, spine-like tips, those on leading shoots 1 inch long, flat, rigidly pointed, and scattered. *Flowers* — male reddish purple, female with short, broad, rounded scales and elongated bracts with tips abruptly bent. *Cones* 4½ to 6 inches long, 2¼ to 3 inches thick, with broad purple or olive-brown scales which are almost completely hidden by the pale green, spatulate and reflexed bracts with their fringed ends and midribs extending as long points. *Seeds* ½ inch long, dull reddish brown, about as long as their pale brown wings. *Wood* hard, strong, and light (28½ pounds per cubic foot, dry weight), the heartwood light brown streaked with red, the sapwood darker.

The Noble Fir takes its name from a Latin designation, *Abies nobilis,* which it wore for a long time, till it was discovered that the name had been pre-empted by another species. It was David Douglas, himself a noble fellow and first discoverer of so many of our western conifers, who started giving the western Firs their complimentary titles and his botanical friends in England continued them. So we hear too of *magnifica, grandis, amabilis* (lovely) and *venusta* (beautiful). Quite distinctive common English names have come into existence for most of these, but the literal translation of *nobilis* has persisted. Let the

lumberman, if he thinks he must, call it and sell it as "Larch." To all the rest of us, who love the majestic Cascade Mountains, snow-capped, forest-swathed, laced with the loveliest waterfalls in all the world, this tree will always remain Noble Fir.

After all, a Fir that towers up 100 and 200 feet tall, with trunks that become, in 600 or 700 years of life, 3 to 6 feet in diameter, is all that one could ask in the way of sylvan nobility. Even very average specimens are 50 to 75 feet high, and their port is nothing less than superb, with tier on tier of regular whorls of strong branches flung out from the mast-straight stem, bark and foliage gleaming in the crystal summer air, the whole tree radiating light and balsamic fragrance, speaking of strength and health. In age, in the deep woods, the lower limbs die and a very long clear pole is left, with a short conical crown, but even this retains the utmost dignity and lofty beauty.

In the hand the Noble Fir's needles are seen to be distinctly curved at the tip, a clearly distinguishing trait, as well as grooved on the upper face, and all the foliage appears brushed upward from below, so that a spray of it lies smooth when lifted from below, but prickles stiffly with a hundred points against the palm when pressed from above. Even the cone is noble — big and heavy, with the sharp-tipped, bright green, papery bracts completely enwrapping it in spiral lines. By the coming of heavy autumn weather the seeds are loosed and the great cones shatter, dropping scale by scale, but the central axis of the cone still stands erect like the metal core of some antique candelabrum. The older a Fir of this species becomes, the more seeds it seems to produce, but their span of viability is short and the rate of germination low. Seedlings do not develop well in dense shade; they love the sunny slopes and so are generally associated with the middle altitudes of their mountain home and not with the dark Hemlock and Douglas Fir zone of sea-level forest.

A tree that makes so fine and straight a growth as this one has naturally attracted the attention of the lumber industry for many years, for flooring, interior finish, doors, window sashes, boats and boxes. But scientific research in wood has shown that Noble Fir has almost the same qualities as Sitka Spruce for airplane construction. The R.A.F. Mosquito bombers of World War II were accordingly built of Noble Fir frames, with Birch wing covering. As a result, foresters have now begun extensive plantings of Noble Fir to augment the limited stand of commercial saw timber of this species which is calculated at 8,000,000,000 board feet.

CALIFORNIA RED FIR

Abies magnifica Murray

OTHER NAME: Silvertip Fir.

RANGE: High mountain slopes (4000 to 9000 feet) in the Cascades and Siskiyous of southern Oregon, and high peaks of the Trinity Alps, the Salmon, Siskiyou, Klamath and Yollo Bolly Mountains of northwestern California; also Mount Shasta and Lassen Peak, and southward through the Sierra Nevada to the headwaters of the Kern River system.

DESCRIPTION: *Bark* on old trunks thick, deep red-brown, with narrow, rounded, zigzag or braided ridges, separated by diagonal, deep, rough furrows; younger bark smooth and chalky white. *Twigs* forward-pointing, stout, in the first season yellow-green, becoming ultimately smooth, shining, and silvery gray. *Leaves* ⅝ to 1¼ inches long, 4-angled (the angles on the upper sides rounded) or flattish, more or less curved, and dark blue-green, the new growth of the season pale green and much whitened, those from the lower part of the tree wider at the blunt tip than at base, and more nearly flattish, and appearing to grow in 2 dense upright lines from the upper side of the twig, those from the crown branches narrowed to a sharp tip, stouter and more nearly 4-angled, and densely crowded toward the top of the twigs. *Flowers* — male dark reddish purple; female with short rounded scales and oblong pale green bracts tinged at tip with red. *Cones* 6 to 8 inches long, dark purplish brown, the scales 1½ inches wide, narrowed to a heart-shaped base. *Seeds* ¾ inch long, dark reddish brown with shining rose-red wings. *Wood* weak, soft, light (29 pounds per cubic foot, dry weight), the heartwood light red-brown, the sapwood thick and darker.

As you mount the western side of the great Sierra Nevada, in California, the trees grow larger and grander, instead of lesser, until on the high shoulders or plateaus of the range they reach a maximum — which falls off rapidly as, at higher elevations still, timber line is approached. The reason for this splendid growth is that for every 1000 feet in elevation, in the northern and central Sierra, there is an addition of 200 inches of annual snowfall. And, in a climate with such aridity as California's, snowfall is the mountain forests' principal source of water. For instance, on these high tablelands ("flats" as the mountain people call them) at 7000 to 8000 feet above sea level, 30 feet of snow a year may be received, and records in excess of 60 feet are not unknown for some years. This snow, instead of sliding down as would happen at higher elevations, or melting swiftly and rushing down the streams, at lower elevation, lies long on the flats, and as it

melts sinks, in large part, into the soil. So it nourishes the roots of a snow forest (to coin a word comparable with rain forest). It is quite distinct from the wind timber of alpine situations, distinct in the species that compose it, and distinct in physiognomy and port. Alpine trees are lashed by a fierce wind which keeps them crouching, growing eccentrically or completely stunted; it lashes their bark with sand, while ice breaks their limbs. But Sierra snows, though so deep, are gentle — warm and unstirring as a blanket, life-giving and with no effect upon the form of the trees unless to help, perhaps, to keep them growing straight, in the days of their youth, with a beautiful erectness they never lose in later life.

Such a forest is perfectly exemplified at Snow Flat, three thousand feet above the floor of Yosemite Valley, and here the king of trees is the Red Fir. At lower altitudes it mingles with White Fir and Yellow and Sugar Pines, and hardly attains its full grandeur. But up in the flats it leaves these trees behind and grows alone — or just tolerating the pink-boled mountain form of Lodgepole Pine — in nearly pure stands. It is perhaps not so high here, as when pressed upon by other forest trees and forced up, by competition for light, to 250 feet — but it looks a great deal happier, like a man standing on his own ground where he knows he is right, and cannot be bested. You will think you never really saw Red Firs before; you will ask yourself why you never appreciated them until now and why, indeed, they are not famous as Cedars of Lebanon or Himalayan Deodars, as they stand there, each tree holding the other at a reserved distance, yet all looking like brothers, a band of kindly giants. Their lower boughs sweep down with a splendid gesture of benignance; the shorter upper ones are lifted as if they rejoiced. Here and there storms have broken their tops, but even then they have a craggy appearance.

The finest thing of all about the tree is not the crop of big, erect, purplish-brown cones that look as if a crystaline balsam had been spilled over them from above, nor the fragrant, dark blue-green foliage, nor the crop of purplish, pendant male flowers that bloom in April while icicles still hang from the twig tips, but the great trunks and richly colored bark. In old specimens this becomes very thick; it is deeply furrowed as the brows of old gods; it is a rusty red, richer in tone than that of the Bigtrees, the Junipers, or the Incense Cedars, all of which have reddish bark. Red Fir may be named from the hue of its lumber, but the name fits the living trunk most aptly. Be the sky never so blue, or the snow so white, that deep rich red is the color

you will remember from the flats and the noble groves upon them —
that and the dry wine of the high mountain air, the *screep* and twang
of the nuthatches spiraling around the trunks, the sight of an old bear
pawing for ants among the rotted wood, and the carpet of larkspur
and lilies.

The lumberman is turning increasingly to this Fir in the Mount
Shasta region and in southern Oregon. But from early days in California campers have had their own uses for it. "It is from this tree,"
says John Muir, "that mountaineers always cut boughs to sleep on
when they are so fortunate as to be within its limits. Two rows of the
plushy branches overlapping along the middle, and a crescent of
smaller plumes mixed with ferns and flowers for a pillow, form the
very best bed imaginable. The essences of the pressed leaves seem to fill
every pore of one's body, the sounds of falling water make a soothing
hush, while the space between the grand spires afford noble openings
through which to gaze dreamily into the starry sky. Even in the matter
of sensuous ease, any combination of cloth, steel springs, and feathers
seems vulgar in comparison."

Muir loved the Red Fir groves best in autumn: "Then the noble
trees are hushed in the hazy light, and drip with balsam; the cones are
ripe, and the seeds, with their ample purple wings, mottle the air like
flocks of butterflies; while deer feeding in the flowery openings between the groves, and birds and squirrels in the branches, make a
pleasant stir which enriches the deep, brooding calm of the wilderness, and gives a peculiar impressiveness to every tree." [1]

Red Fir has a life expectancy of some two hundred and fifty years,
perhaps exceptionally a hundred more. This is not great compared
with that of some other forest giants of the Sierra, and so one sees
many dead trees among the groves — not standing dead (always a
dismal sight) but promptly and decently fallen. Even in death they
are grand and arouse no pity like the logs of a lumbered-over or
burned-over tract, but only call forth, each one, a tribute; here, we say,
another monarch has fallen, but only to make room for the hosts of
shining youngsters that spring up about their parent's feet. Decay of
the wood is swift, but the bark, though so soft, is thick and resistant.
As a result the groves are quite littered with brightly colored chunks
of it. And so great is the quantity that for more than eighty years the
famed "firefall" of Yosemite has burned Red Fir bark every summer
night, and twice weekly in the autumn.

[1] *The Mountains of California.*

This is one of the grandest sights of Yosemite — a cascade of fire and embers and sparks thrust over the edge of a thousand-foot cliff at Glacier Point. In the day a pile of Red Fir bark some three feet high is raked together. It is lit about six in the evening and, as seen from Camp Curry in the valley floor, glows through the dusk like a red star on the brow of the cliff, gradually brightening.

A few minutes before nine, when crowds have gathered, and all outdoor lights are extinguished, a long hail is sent up from the valley — "Hello-o-o-o-, Glacier!" Then, from 3254 feet above the watchers, sails down the alpine echo, "Hello-o-o Camp Curry!" Then comes the answer "Let the fi-i-i-i-re fa-a-a-all!" And from high in the dark sky rings out the cry "A-a-a-all ri-i-i-ight!" Then the Firefall Man with a long iron-handled pusher thrusts the glowing pyre over the edge of the beetling cliff, and a cascade of light spangles the dark mountainside, the coals glowing brighter as the wind of their descent blows on them like a great bellows. Sometimes the firefall is a delicate ribbon, twisting thinly in its fall, sometimes it fans out at base or blows this way and that like the water of Bridalveil. Always it is a beautiful end to the last of a great tree's life.

Variety *shastensis* Lemmon, is distinguished by the rounded, bright yellow bracts which are so long they frequently cover nearly half their scales. It is found on Mount Shasta, the Scott and Trinity Mountains, and occasionally in the southern Sierra Nevada.

SANTA LUCIA FIR

Abies venusta (Douglas) K. Koch

OTHER NAMES: Bristlecone or Silver Fir. Fringed Spruce.

RANGE: Santa Lucia Mountains of Monterey County, coastal California.

DESCRIPTION: *Bark* of old trunks thin, light russet color outside, with clear brown underbark, irregularly fissured and covered with closely appressed scales. *Twigs* stout, smooth, at first glaucous, light reddish brown. *Leaves* shining dark yellow-green above, the lower surface whitened with lines of stomata, keenly pointed, flat and long (1⅓ to 2 inches), those of the lower sterile branches appearing to grow in 2 ranks along the sides of the twig, and to lie in one horizontal plane, while those of the middle and upper crown grow very densely erect and seemingly all from the top of the branch. *Flowers* — male light yellow, abundantly produced from the middle of the crown to the top, female borne at the tips of the top branches, with yellow-green, long-tipped bracts. *Cones* 2¾ to 3½ inches broad, smooth, with thin, pale purple-brown scales and pale yellow-brown bracts with very long, flat, rigid tips. *Seeds* ⅜ inch long, dark red-brown, with shining pale reddish brown wings. *Wood* coarse-grained, heavy (42 pounds per cubic foot, dry weight), but not hard, the heartwood light brown tinged with yellow, the sapwood paler.

"You will begin to think," wrote that braw Scot, David Douglas, pioneer botanist-explorer of the Pacific coast, to Sir William Hooker at Kew, "that I manufacture Pines at my pleasure." Yet a new species, if not a true Pine as we now recognize the genus, he found at this time (1832), as spring was coming to the Santa Lucia Mountains, that part of the Coast Range between Monterey and San Luis Obispo. The tree he discovered was the Santa Lucia Fir, the rarest of its genus in the world, confined to a few heights inaccessible on those wind-swept summits that hang above the ocean, some of them not visited in many years together.

As you motor today up the San Simeon Highway (California State Highway 1), with the wrinkled Pacific crawling 500 feet directly beneath you, you can see that the tops of the Santa Lucias are covered now by grass and now by dark coniferous forests. But to reach those groves the easiest way, which is still arduous, is to enter from the other side of the mountains, on roads successively rougher, steeper, narrower and less maintained. Indeed it proves simplest to provide yourself with a guide from the U.S. Forest Service. But of course there were no guides in Douglas's day, unless one of the Fathers or neophytes of Mission San Antonio showed him the way. The Franciscan Fathers of the mission had long utilized the balsamic resin from this tree in religious ceremonies, and indeed called the tree *incienso*. The grove which Douglas visited was probably the one high on Twin Peaks well above the limit of the Redwoods. Here the Firs cling to the granite walls, troop down the canyons, and, park-like, dot lonely Pine Valley.

So distinctive is the Santa Lucia Fir that it can be recognized from afar by its outline, for the crown is that of a tall, narrow spire, ending in an exceedingly sharp point. Usually the pitchy cones are borne only at the top of the tree, and in alternate years the crop of them is very heavy, so heavy that though they are technically borne erect they bend the branches down and so seem to hang from the tree. Certainly they are most striking, with their very long slender bracts extruding like fringe or bristles from between the cone scales.

Usually standing well apart, the Firs attain to the full their natural dimensions and are generally clothed to the very base in branches, each tier of them longer than the tier above, to form a tree of the most superb symmetry. No wonder that, in regions which can grow it, this is one of the most prized conifers, imparting to estate grounds an air of dignity and spaciousness, yet from every needle reflecting light and cheer.

THE INCENSE CEDARS

(*Libocedrus*)

Scaly or shreddy bark, spreading branches, flattened twigs lying all in one plane, and flat sprays of closely overlapping, scale-like foliage that invests the alternately forking twigs characterize these aromatic, resinous, and stately trees with their naked buds and durable, fragrant wood. The foliage is disposed in 4 ranks on leading shoots, forming a distinctly squarish twig, but on older growth is strongly compressed and apparently 2-ranked, thereby forming a flat spray; on seedling plants the foliage may be needle-like and bristling around the twig in all directions.

The flowers are unisexual, terminal, and solitary; the male flowers possess 12 to 16 stamens, each filament bearing 4 nearly spherical anthers. The female flowers consist in 6 short-pointed floral scales of which only the middle pair bear ovules. These scales become the 6 scales of the cone, the lowest pair thin and reflexed, the middle pair thick and spreading, the upper pair erect and confluent. Occurring in pairs at the base of the fertile scales of the cone, the seeds are provided with thin, markedly unequal wings.

The Incense Cedars most closely resemble the Arbor-vitæ trees (*Thuja*) but differ in having only 6 cone scales of which only the middle pair bear ovules, while the leaves appear to be in whorls of 4 instead of opposite pairs.

*　　　*　　　*

INCENSE CEDAR

Libocedrus decurrens Torrey

OTHER NAMES: White, Bastard, or California Post Cedar.

RANGE: Both east and west slopes of the Cascade Mountains in Oregon, from the foothills to 6600 feet, and southward through the Sierra Nevada, and Coast Ranges of California (3000 to 9700 feet) to the San Pedro Mártir Mountains in Baja California. Also in Nevada (Washoe County).

DESCRIPTION: *Bark* bright cinnamon red-brown at base of old trunks, scaly, thick. *Twigs* stout, lying all in one plane on the bough, short side branchlets much flattened. *Leaves* scale-like, pale green, ⅛ inch long or on leader shoots ½ inch long, lying close to the stem except for the spreading callous tips, arranged in 4 ranks on the twig, in alternating pairs, those on the sides of the twig keeled and glandular on the back, gradually narrowed toward the tip, and nearly covering the top and bottom pair which are flattened and abruptly pointed. *Flowers* on the ends of short lateral branchlets, the male abundant, bright yellow, ¼ inch long, the female subtended at base by 2 to 6 pairs of leaf-like scales and composed of 6 light yellow-green, slightly spreading flower scales. *Cones* drooping ¾ to 1 inch long, light red-brown, the scales leathery-woody. *Seeds* ⅓ to ½ inch long, the hilum pale, the inner coat penetrated by resin chambers and a red balsamic liquid. *Wood* light (25 pounds per cubic foot, dry weight), soft, close-grained, the heartwood light reddish brown, the sapwood thin and nearly white.

Many a person who comes to the Sierra Nevada looking for his first sight of the Giant Sequoia or California Bigtree is likely to think he has seen one when he first beholds the Incense Cedar. For it has a ruddy, thick, and deeply furrowed bark, a ponderous and heavily buttressed and fluted trunk, and a lofty carriage such as we have learned, from pictures and descriptions, to associate with the mighty Sequoia. More, both trees have scaly leaves that closely overlap upon the twigs. But much as the two trees resemble each other, and closely as they are related, they must not, need not, be confused.

In the first place, the Bigtree is seldom found below 4000 feet above sea level. The Incense Cedar is found all the way down to the western foothills of the Sierra Nevada — with the Digger Pines in the old

Gold Rush country. Nor does it form groves, as Bigtrees do, but occurs scattered among the Pines. The bark is a rich, bright cinnamon-red, not a reddish-brown like the Sequoia's. Thick though it is, the bark is much less massive than that of its gigantic brother; it is more stringy, less spongy; its furrows are far narrower and its ridges too. An Incense Cedar may live 1000 years, exceptionally, and grow to be 150 feet high, but never will it endure 3000 winters, or tower up 300 feet. Once you have seen a genuine Bigtree, you will never again mistake an Incense Cedar for it.

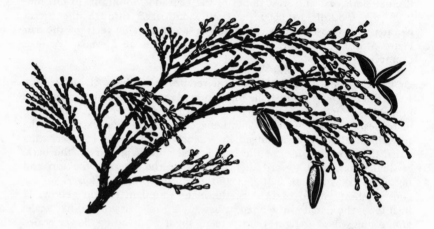

The comparison, of course, is all against the Incense Cedar, when it comes to majesty and hoary age. But it is not fair to compare anything with a Sequoia, which is a god among trees. Judged by ordinary mortal standards, Incense Cedar is a splendid species, with its flat sprays of foliage which reflect the clear Sierra sunlight, its colorful trunks, its limber boughs full of grace. In youth it forms a strictly tapered crown from the broad base to the slender spire-like top, the lower branches sweeping downward in ample curves, the topmost ascending sharply to form a feathery tip. The years and the centuries change the grace of youth for a craggy strength, with irregular big boughs starting out at right angles from the trunk and then sending forth, as if from bent elbows, short ascending branches. The crown becomes broken — perhaps even dead at the tip — but only gains in picturesqueness thereby. Of the "plumes" of an Incense Cedar's foliage, John Muir says: "No waving fern-frond in shady dell is more unreservedly beautiful in form and texture, or half so inspiring in color and spicy fragrance. In its prime, the whole tree is thatched with them, so that they shed off rain and snow like a roof, making fine mansions for storm-bound birds and mountaineers." [1]

"In the fall," writes Mary Tresidder,[2] "the edges of the flat sprays are picked out with the immature green pollen buds, like the old-fashioned scalloped edges of embroidery we used to do. Then in December these pollen cones ripen and shed their golden pollen, and many of the local inhabitants have attacks of hay fever and long for the first storm to settle the pollen dust." The little pale green female flowers appear on the tips of last season's growth. Then, in the late summer, the flowers having been fertilized, the slim cylindrical cones hang gracefully from the tips of the branchlets, each scale enclosing one or two tiny seeds that go sailing away on the September winds. Highly tolerant of shade or sun, the seedlings spring up abundantly. In spite of fire dangers and dry-rot, a prevalent disease, this species seems able to stay on top of any perils and hardships in its life, for it is holding its own well, at least in the national forests and parks. On the floor of the Yosemite Valley it is, with Yellow Pine, a dominant species, whose hosts, at once so virile and so smiling, shine in every prospect. Even to remember them, from afar, is to see again the windblown tresses of Bridalveil Fall, to hear the clamor, half harsh, half sweet, of the jays, smell the tang of the dry exciting air, the incense-laden breath of this lovely tree.

Abundant though this Cedar is on federal lands, it has, on privately owned holdings, been exploited for almost a century, though never lumbered separately but only in connection with general cutting of conifers. The remaining stand is estimated at 9,700,000,000 board feet. During the war years from 1940 to 1943 the cut reached a peak of 30,000,000 board feet a year. From the durable wood are turned out door and window frames, because of its lightness and the quiescence of the wood once it is well seasoned; it is cut for cedar chests on account of its odor, for shingles and railway ties because of its great durability. And, from the earliest settlement of the Great Central Valley of California, it has been employed for fence posts in large quantity. Unfortunately the post industry rejects the creamy sapwood, which may constitute more than half the woody cylinder, leaving it to waste and rot, for only the long-lived heartwood is acceptable to the trade.

When the commercial supply of pencil wood from Eastern Red

1 *The Mountains of California.*   2 *The Sierra Nevada.*

Cedar came to an end, half a century ago, it was to the Incense Cedar that the pencil-makers principally turned. The western tree has all the needed properties for a good pencil wood; it is soft but not too splitty, and can be sharpened in any direction with equal ease. Voracious though the demand for pencils, the Incense Cedar can probably stand up under the assault. The actual lumbering operations are on a small scale. Pencil trees are usually selected and felled singly by farmers and other landowners. The log is then cut into sizes that are later reduced to pencil blocks 7¼ inches long, ³⁄₁₆ of an inch thick and 2⅝ inches wide. From this, 7 pencils of standard size can be struck out at the factory where the blocks are surfaced and groved on one side, the graphite leads then inserted in the grooves between two blocks, and the pair glued together. Then the blocks are slit between the grooves and turned, polished, and painted as desired.

THE ARBOR-VITÆS

(*Thuja*)

THESE are slightly resinous and aromatic trees, with massive and buttressed trunks, thin branches, and heavy crowns, living to a great age and with correspondingly durable wood. The branchlets incline to be gracefully pendulous and to lie all in one plane, making flat sprays of foliage. Completely clothing the twigs in 4 ranks, the leaves are scale-like and closely overlapping. The sexes occur on different branches of the same tree, the flowers solitary and terminal on the twig. The few-scaled cones are leathery and erect and mature the first season. The thin-coated seeds are winged.

* * *

CANOE CEDAR

Thuja plicata D. Don

OTHER NAMES: Giant or Western Red Cedar. Shinglewood. Arbor-vitæ.

RANGE: Maritime Alaska (from Portage Bay southward), in British Columbia on sea slopes of the Coast Ranges and inland, on the southern Selkirks and Gold Mountains, up to 6000 feet altitude; in Washington on the Olympics to 4000 feet, on the west slopes of the Cascades from sea level to 4000 feet, and on the Canadian Rockies from Alberta and eastern British Columbia south to the Bitterroots of Idaho and Montana, at 2000 to 7000 feet above sea level, and south through the Coast Ranges of Oregon and the west slopes of the Cascades to Crater Lake up to 7500 feet above sea level, and in the fog belt of California (Del Norte and Humboldt Counties).

DESCRIPTION: *Bark* of trunks thin (½ to 1 inch), bright cinnamon-red to grayish brown, stringy and fibrous, the frequently twisted ridges running without a break the length of the trunk but connected by many stringy, diagonal ridges. *Twigs* in drooping sprays, slender and flat, invested by the foliage. *Leaves* dark yellow-green and shining, scale-like, in pairs alternately crossing at right angles, those on the upper and lower surfaces flat, those on the edges keeled or rounded. *Flowers* dark brown, male with 3 to 6 alternating pairs of stamens, female (on separate twigs) with 8 to 12 thin, fine-topped scales of which only 6 are fertile. *Seed* brown, ⅛ inch long, the wings at its sides as wide as the seed. *Wood* coarse-grained, soft, light (23½ pounds per cubic foot, dry weight), brittle, and very easy to split, dull brown often strongly tinged with red.

On a June day in 1805, near Armstead, Montana, the Lewis and Clark expedition buried the boats in which they had come, against the relentless current of the Missouri, a thousand toilsome miles and more. Now began their crossing of the continental divide, their goods packed upon the horses purchased from the Shoshones. Then they must find a navigable stream, on the westward slope where so many are unnavigable and perilous, that would carry them in boats down to the great Columbia and so to their goal, the shores of the Pacific. And near that stream, to build those boats, they must find growing a tree fit for the purpose.

To make the needed pirogue or dugout, such a tree must be of great size, big enough to carry not only men but food, trading goods, and all sorts of equipment. Its wood must be the lightest possible, for buoyancy and ease of portage around the rapids. It must, since they had but simple tools with them, be soft in texture, straight-grained, with easy splitting qualities. And it must not decay in water. Lewis and Clark could not know of any such tree awaiting them, for no white man at that date knew anything of the sylva of the wilderness which we now call northern Idaho. Yet the success of the expedition depended on such a tree; already destiny had provided the passes, the Shoshones with their pack horses and, most marvelously, the Indian girl Sacajawea, found a thousand miles from her birthplace at the moment they needed her most, to become their loyal and dauntless guide.

And now, as the hungry and exhausted men toiled through the gigantic jackstraw timbers of Idaho's primeval forests, the captains sighted, on September 20, "an Arbor-vitae" — one they noted as "very common and grows to a great size, being from two to six feet in diameter." Next day their journal remarks that "the arbor vitae increases in size and quantity as we advance," down toward the open valleys of the Clearwater. So on the twenty-fifth William Clark, with the Nez Percé chief Twisted Hair, set out to find a promising grove of this new great tree. Near the present town of Orofino, Idaho, he located his boat timber, and here the party felled the trees whose stumps were still pointed out as late as 1900. With fire, mallet, and crude chisel, they fashioned four large pirogues and a smaller one, "to spy ahead." And on the morning of October 7, the fateful and illustrious band set out upon the last stage of the outward journey, downstream to the Pacific, borne in the great boles of the Giant Canoe Cedar, which lumbermen today call the Western Red Cedar.

Those virgin forest conditions produced in this Cedar enormous trunks such as we see today too seldom; in the early days trees were known as tall as 200 feet. But the lumbermen have left us a small race, and a specimen now regarded as a challenger is one near Lake Quinault, in Olympic National Park, which has a circumference of 62 feet and 8 inches, above the immensely greater base all swollen and buttressed and fluted as it is. In general, trees with trunks 8 to 10 feet in diameter are considered large, in our times, while a trunk with a 3-foot diameter is mature merchantable timber, in the eyes of the lumberman. If the tree grows too old, its magnificent proportions are,

for the logging foreman's purposes, too apt to be spoiled by a decayed
heart inside the shell of the bark with its ruddy armor of long, twisted
fibrous strips.

But the camper, the hiker, the motorist, the tourist who explores
coastal British Columbia and southeastern Alaska by boat, does not
view the Canoe Cedar in terms of board feet. To him it is a tree of
the utmost grandeur, its boughs sweeping from the narrowly conical
crown nearly to the ground (for even in dense stands the lower limbs
are not always self-pruned by reduced light but may be held tenaciously). Young limbs lift upwards joyfully; old ones spread downward
and outward with majestic benevolence. And over all glitters the lacy
foliage in flat sprays that are forked and forked again, drooping parted,
like the mane of a horse, from the axis of the branchlet in a gesture
of strong grace.

On Vancouver Island the Canoe Cedar reaches its greatest dimensions — so gigantic, even in our day, that they place it among the
greatest conifers of the world. But on the Queen Charlotte Islands, on
the Olympic peninsula and all around Puget Sound, on the mainland
of British Columbia and on the islands and along the fiords of southern Alaska, the Canoe Cedar is scarcely less imposing. And it was there,
where the mountains fall precipitously to the sea, where the glaciers
glitter on the mountain flanks, and somber forests of Hemlock, Spruce,
Fir, Cypress and Cedar march down to the very shore, that from
ancient times there dwelt the Indian tribes who raised the famed
totem poles, carved of trunks of the Canoe Cedar. And all the inter-
communication of the villages of these tribes — the Tlingits, Haidas,
and Tsimshians who were never conquered by the cruel Russians —

was in canoes of Cedar. No other Indians ever exhibited such artistic skill and technical mastery in wood-working of all sorts as these, and indeed it is said that the canoe reached its highest expression among these peoples. Their family canoes were from 20 to 25 feet long, fit to transport a whole household, complete with provisions and gear and trading supplies, a load that might comprise two tons. Even longer and stronger, yet still carved from a single trunk, were the voyaging canoes, sometimes as much as 65 feet in length, bearing three masts and sails and a mainstay-sail, and capable of carrying some thirty or forty people. So wondrous were these craft, so perfect in their lines, that — tradition states — models were carried away by the Yankee sailing masters of the late eighteenth century, and these furnished to the designers of the Boston and Salem clippers the lines of the fastest and fairest American ships ever moved by the wind.

Of Cedar wood these warlike people made helmets, dagger handles, bows, arrow shafts and spear poles. Chieftains' carven batons, medicine men's rattles, and carved and painted household boxes were all fashioned from this beautiful wood that splits so easily and evenly, and takes color so well. The coast Indians built their potlatch houses (feasting halls) of Cedar uprights and stringers lashed together with bark of the same tree. Rough Cedar planks were hewn out laboriously for the sidings of the house.

But it was into their totem poles that these proud people poured their artistic genius. The Indian artist, before the white man brought him steel tools, worked with cutting edges of jadeite and shell, yet he was able to achieve anything he desired in representation. If the legends and figures to be represented were many, he had to solve the complex problem of superimposing them. He did so with ingenious skill, and so clever are his simulations that the straight beak of the raven, the curved hook of the owl's beak, the shaggy hide of the bear, the springing legs of the frog are perfectly recognizable. The totem carver worked from no preliminary model; like the Greek sculptors of old he carried the whole design in his head and attacked his materials directly with his tools. The fine marks of those tools give to the old genuine totemic wood much of its vigor and texture; only in spurious modern imitations is there a smooth surface.

Many carvers achieved great reputations, remembered long after their deaths; they traveled from village to village, accepting commissions, and their fees were so great that a family frequently ruined itself to pay a famous artist. For the totem pole was not merely a form of genealogy and heraldry; it was frequently a funereal monument and might enclose in its base the sacred ashes of ancestors. Further, it embodied what the Indian considered history — not politics and war but such matters as the origin of the world and of mankind. Humor of a sort was not lacking in some of these columns; thus if a man owed another a debt that was not collected, a special pole would be erected by the creditor to tell the world about it in mocking symbolism, and this would continue to taunt the defaulting neighbor till the debt was paid. As a form of receipt, the creditor then destroyed the pole.

The prehistoric Cedar poles were comparatively small affairs because the cost of carving a huge tree with primitive implements would have been prohibitive. Metal axes, saws, drawknives, froes and other European implements changed all this and in the nineteenth century the Indian artists were able to produce gigantic poles that dwarfed their villages. But this was the burst of glory before the end. The same outside influences that brought the tools of a more advanced technology brought disruption and decimation to the coast Indians. Alcohol, smallpox, and venereal diseases rotted the magnificent physique of these great peoples; a taste for the white man's luxuries caused a neglect of their tribal arts. And education under the missionaries turned many earnest red souls against the ancestral religion. They began to pull down and destroy their totemic columns, or to turn out debased and insincere imitations, colored gaudily with modern commercial paints, for the tourist trade. Whole villages were abandoned when families sought employment in the white man's settlements, and under the tremendous rainfall of the coastal area, the poles began to molder away, just as the very memory of the carving art and the knowledge of its religious symbolism faded in the Indians' minds. One hundred and twenty-five poles were counted, in 1916, by a visitor to the deserted village of Tuxekan, and fewer than half were sufficiently preserved to be worth moving.

Then the Forest Service began to undertake the restoration of the vanishing art. Aged men who had been apprentices to master carvers in boyhood were found and set to work; their assistants were teen-aged Indian boys who showed a marvelous aptitude for learning though they had never handled a stone adze before. For only the primitive tools were used, only the original dyes, derived from native roots, berries, ferns, clays and ores. The ancient legends were again collected, the ruined models pieced together and studied, and finally Saxman Totem Park was established near Ketchikan, Alaska, where more than 50 reproductions of authentic poles preserve in Cedar wood the art and history of the gifted coast tribes.

And much of the life of those tribes, from their beginning, was braided with the life of the Canoe Cedar. The fiber of its inner bark furnished them with their chief textile and cordage materials — sufficient indeed for everything in their lives. Their blankets and clothing were composed of twisted twine or cord of Cedar bark fiber for the warp, while the woof was worsted spun from the wool of the mountain goat and dyed with brown, yellow, black, and white, to make superb totemic patterns. Woven hats of Cedar bark fiber, shawls and girdles of the same material, added to the costumes of men and women. Rope was regularly made from Cedar bark, and provided (in default of nails or, rather, superior to any nails) the lashings that joined pieces of wood in all sorts of construction. Cordage of Cedar bark made the dip nets and drag nets of these great fishermen, and their women wove it into bags and baskets for every use.

The white man has found so many uses of his own for the Western Red Cedar as to place it among the six premier coniferous woods of North America, and probably among the dozen greatest timber trees of the world in quantity cut, while in the more intangible matter of quality it is equally high. The only serious defect of Red Cedar is that it is not strong enough for heavy usage, but for house construction it is quite sufficient. It has a beautiful soft, close, straight-grained texture, making it a joy to work with the plane, and finishes to a satiny smooth surface. It takes and holds enamels, paints, and stains with the half-dozen best of lumbers, and has superior glueing qualities for the production of laminated wood. A natural preservative oil in the heartwood makes it immune to decay to an unexcelled degree, without the use of artificial preservatives. It is thus superfluous to paint Cedar to preserve it from rot, for even under severe climatic conditions it does not deteriorate when left in a natural state. The coloring is extremely attractive, the almost pure white sapwood contrasting beautifully with the dark reddish-brown to yellowish heartwood. When weathered by the elements, Red Cedar turns to a driftwood-gray.

In the Pacific Northwest, this is a favorite wood for home-building, and indeed it is exported to every state in the Union, partly on account of its freedom from the pitch that makes Pine such a "hot" wood to live with, and so inflammable, and partly because it is among the lightest of all lumber when dried, and hence inexpensive to ship by rail. For mountain cabins, motor lodges, and the like, knotty Cedar makes a handsome rustic interior finish, but more elegant effects are produced by clear lumber. The rich yet cheerful and varied color, the exquisite surface, the attractive figures of its flat-grain finish, make it as charming a panel wood for bedroom, dining room, or library as one could ask. As siding for the exterior of the house, as molding, door and window stock, its popularity is immense, and thus it has frequently taken the place of the old eastern White Pine in the construction of frame houses. One of its attractive properties in home building is its insulating qualities when used for shingles, roof boards, sub-flooring, siding and sheathing; it tends to keep the house cool in summer and warm in winter.

The famed durability of Western Red Cedar makes it a wood of the first class for flumes and mud sills and tanks, for barn boards and feed platforms, greenhouse wood, hotbeds and nursery equipment in general — all of which are constantly exposed to changing weathers, to water, soil, and all the seeds of decay. Beehives are often built of Red Cedar, and silo doors, fence posts, well curbing and stop gates. Because of its lightness and resistance to water decay Red Cedar is claimed, by its promoters, as the world's foremost material for boat construction, from the college team's racing shells to the millionaire's pleasure cruiser.

Everyone knows something about the heartwood of this magnificent tree — whether he knows it by name or not, he has tested its weight or, rather, its lightness; he has seen its characteristic dark ruddy color and smelled its delicious odor; he has fingered its soft, coarse grain, its ready splitting properties, and has often harkened to its characteristic pitch and timbre — when raindrops play upon it. For it is the leading shingle material of the United States, probably of the world. In America, 80 per cent of all shingles are made of Western Red Cedar. The large size of Red Cedar shingles, their freedom from knots, their fine straight grain, make them incomparable. On the score of durability they are equally satisfactory. On San Juan Island in Puget Sound, the roof of a house built in 1856 was covered with Red Cedar shingles which were still intact in 1916.

The introduction of the shingle-sawing machine has speeded production and correspondingly reduced the price, turning out the excellent commercial thin-tipped, thick-butted shingle in lengths of 16, 18, and 24 inches, ½ inch thick at the butt, and 4 inches wide or more as desired. Shingles are sold in bundles of about 250, and 4 bundles are enough to cover 100 square feet. An ingenious machine buncher speeds the process of modern production still further and a good "shingle-weaver" can pack 80,000 a day. But hand-riven shakes, such as our ancestors knew, have never gone completely out of fashion, and, if you can afford them, they give a roof an individual and hand-wrought appearance that is not to be expected of any machine-made product.

The Northwest shake-maker is a very specialized artisan, almost an artist. His tools are axe, saw, and froe or splitting blade and his raw materials are usually salvaged from logging operations — old ones more than new, because old-time loggers were more wasteful and left more good wood and high stumps. Usually the shake-maker builds himself a cabin in the midst of the big-butted stumps, and there he is likely (since he generally is an old man) to find enough shingle wood to work on the rest of his life. If he has a family, his sons help, and their wives and sisters tie the shakes into bundles. First, logs are sawn and then split into bolts of a size easy to handle and are trucked to the shed where the work can go on under all weathers. The shake-maker's implement, the froe, is perhaps the only hand tool that has not been changed through the centuries from the original model. It is a blade 14 to 20 inches long, and 3 inches wide, the butt end terminating in a metal ring or eye through which passes a wooden handle. The bolt of wood to be split is stood on end on a block, the froe is placed a half-inch from the edge of the bolt, and then the handle of the froe, which is held firm in the right hand, is struck a blow on the butt by a club of Vine Maple, held in the left hand. The blade bites into the Cedar and a shake is neatly split off along the grain. Rough defects are then trimmed off usually by womenfolk. Then, when he has a truckful of shakes, the artisan drives to the local lumber yard, and sells for cash. With it he buys a twist of strong chewing tobacco, a supply of black-eyed peas, some kitchen ware and fixin's for his wife, and then returns happily to his stumps and froe, content in his life which is that of a specialist who earns little, perhaps, but is not replaceable by more ambitious men.

THE TRUE CYPRESSES

(*Cupressus*)

THESE ARE TREES with aromatic wood and foliage and scale-like leaves which are minutely fringed, when seen under a lens, and on old and fruiting branches persistent for years and closely overlapping on the twig in alternate pairs (that is, 4-ranked), thus forming a more or less 4-sided slim sprig. The leaves on young trees and vigorous sucker and leader shoots are usually at least twice as large as those of fertile branches, with spreading and often prickly tips, and are frequently glaucous; this foliage is short-lived and soon turns brown at the base of the twig and is finally pushed off by the expanding bark. Seedling leaves are needle-like, remote, and spreading. The twigs (except in *Cupressus Macnabiana*) do not lie all in one plane but arise all around the branch.

The minute flowers are unisexual, the male and female catkins or conelets produced on different branches of the same tree. The male flowers are borne profusely on the tips of densely leafy branchlets, in short, angular-spherical catkins, each scale with 2 to 6 spherical and finally protruding anthers pendant under an enlarged connective; the color of the male flowers is greenish yellow, fading brown. In the female flowers the numerous bottle-shaped, erect ovules are borne in several rows at the bottom of the fertile scales which open to receive the wind-borne pollen and then close again. Generally the female flowers are solitary on the tips of stubby, very leaf-thickened branchlets, though these are often closely aggregated, and at first appear merely like new growth but soon form a light green conelet.

The erect, nearly spherical, tardily opening cones consist in the few ripened scales of the female flowers, now much thickened toward the surface of the cone and flat-faced at the apex, but often with a central boss or short point. Two years are required to mature the cone, and it may cling on, after opening, for many years more. The numerous irregularly shaped small seeds are compressed at the edges, with frequently a wing-like margin, yet are probably ill adapted to wind distribution.

✻   ✻   ✻

MACNAB CYPRESS

Cupressus Macnabiana Murray

RANGE: Irregularly scattered on the west slopes of the Sierra Nevada (Aukum in Amador County, Grass Valley in Nevada County at about 2500 feet; Texas Hill and Indiana Creek in Yuba County) and, in the north-central part of California at Whiskeytown, Shasta County and the Betty May Mine, Trinity County; thence south in the inner northern Coast Ranges at Hough Springs and Reiff in Lake County, and at Aetna Springs, Napa County; also near Ukiah in Mendocino County.

DESCRIPTION: *Bark* of old trunks gray, fibrous, and seamed by narrow furrows into a network of braiding, regular, flat ridges. *Twigs* slender, 4-angled, flexible, dark brown or, immediately after leaf fall, purple-red, lying all in one plane to make a flat spray. *Leaves* aromatic, $\frac{1}{12}$ inch long, a deep dull grayish green, sharp-pointed, with a minute blister-like gland on the back of each scale. *Cones* green the first season, then rich reddish brown under an ashy cast, and finally ashy gray, 1 inch or less long, the 6 to 8 scales with horny points. *Seeds* 75 to 105 to a cone, brown with a slightly glaucous surface. *Wood* soft, close-grained, medium-light ($34\frac{1}{2}$ pounds per cubic foot, dry weight).

Among all the true Cypresses of North America this one is unique in having flattened branchlets always lying all in one plane, to form a "spray" as in Arbor-vitæ, instead of bristling all around the twig as in most other species of *Cupressus*. Only a species from the vale of Kashmir, and the Funeral Cypress of China, have these flat sprays of foliage. More, the needles of Macnab Cypress are very fragrant, more so than those of any other species. The bark too is most distinctive, becoming on old trees a dark chocolate-brown markedly furrowed with deep narrow seams and a network of flat connected ridges between which lie diamond-shaped interspaces. In general, the appearance of this tree is of a dull gray-green becoming, as winter approaches, a lifeless gray. In the following spring when the male flowers bloom in profusion, the tree shines with a vivid yellow-green for a few weeks.

A young tree starts out with a strong central leader shoot but soon, by accident or because the lateral shoots grow faster, it takes on a bushy form, and as time goes on, growth at the side is so much greater than strictly vertical growth that the tree looks like a great overgrown bush, broader than high in the crown, with a very short stem. Even this will be concealed as the old boughs begin to bend to the ground to form at last a tree with a hemispheric outline.

Macnab Cypress was first discovered by William Murray when he was exploring California in the eighteen-fifties for the Royal Botanic Garden at Edinburgh. Probably he found his specimens near Whiskeytown in Shasta County, California, on Whiskey Creek, about five miles west of the historic mining community of Old Shasta. To this day there is quite a grove of these strange, sad-looking dome-shaped Cypresses growing there in the sterile, nearly white soil, with Knobcone Pine and Interior Live Oak. One by one, other localities have been discovered, as mentioned above in the statement of the range of the tree. And all these localities have intensely dry and hot summers, with the result that in the course of time they have for the most part been swept by fires. This species is especially inflammable, so that groves with mature trees up to 30 feet high are rare. Many cut stumps show that the ranchers have sought out this Cypress, because of the durability of its wood, for fence posts, though probably in no other way is it of any practical value.

The Macnab Cypress was received in England a century ago with great enthusiasm by horticulturists. But it has never been accorded much honor in its native state. At the Rancho Santa Ana Botanic Garden in southern California where perhaps it misses its serpentine rocks, it has been tried and found subject to so many ills that it is regarded as horticulturally worthless. This is not to say that it is not a picturesque part of the scene in the hot foothills of the old mining communities where it grows natively.

MODOC CYPRESS

Cupressus Bakeri Jepson

OTHER NAMES: Baker or Siskiyou Cypress.

RANGE: Known only from the Siskiyou Mountains of California and Oregon.

DESCRIPTION: *Bark* at the base of old trunks reddish or gray-surfaced, and partially curling loose in irregular layers; that of younger trunks almost like that of the Cherry. *Twigs* fine and congested on the slender branchlets. *Leaves* more or less glaucous, pale gray-green, about $\frac{1}{16}$ inch long, rather acutely and sometimes abruptly pointed, keeled on the back, the dorsal resin pit visible even on very young foliage, and located well above the middle of the leaf. *Cones* composed of 6 or 8 scales, spherical, less than $\frac{1}{2}$ inch long, gray-brown or, in age, weathering to silvery gray, and slightly warty from the numerous resin pockets. *Seeds* numbering 50 to a cone, often somewhat compressed and glaucous.

In Miocene times — some 19,000,000 years ago — northeastern California seems to have cracked open in a hundred places, and out came pouring black lava, as fast as blood from a cut. Basalts and andesites flowed out for centuries and millennia, to a depth of thousands of feet. And though even the last of these flows was congealed ages agone, you will today, as you motor through sparsely inhabited Modoc, Shasta, Lassen, and eastern Siskiyou Counties, great piles of black clinkers, old fumaroles, stacks of jagged rocks, and choppy seas of knife-edged frozen lava still unsoftened by much erosion, barely blessed in many places with vegetation — only tufts of sad sagebrush and withered bunch grass.

It is in these forbidding lava beds, and there only, that the Modoc Cypress grows in typical pure form. And at present only two groves of it are known, although in country so difficult to traverse, so seldom entered even by the California botanists, that it may be other groves will yet be found.

In these rare stands the Modoc Cypress grows up to 40 feet high, with a broad crown 18 or 20 feet across, and a slim trunk not over 2 feet thick. Being spaced well apart, in that bleak soil, these trees have a chance to develop fairly symmetrically, nor does fire come often to those lonely regions to destroy them. So the Modoc Cypresses hold firm their place, awaiting their few visitors.

A variety of *Cupressus Bakeri* called the SISKIYOU CYPRESS (subspecies *Matthewsii* Wolf) is found in two groves in the Siskiyou Mountains of northwestern California and southwestern Oregon. It differs in being ultimately a taller tree, 45 to 90 feet tall, with the cones larger ($\frac{5}{8}$ to $\frac{7}{8}$ inch in diameter), the surface usually light gray-brown and conspicuously warty but with inconspicuous umbos on the scales. The foliage is perhaps less dusty gray in appearance, more of a light gray-green, and in every way this would seem to be a handsomer form.

The Siskiyou Mountains are among the least explored and wildest

country in the Pacific Coast states, and are notable too for their great
snowfall, sometimes claimed as the heaviest in the country. The Siskiyou Cypress, therefore, grows under conditions surpassing in winter
severity those of any other Cypresses throughout the world. " . . . Temperature drops to zero degrees F. or even below on occasion," says Dr.
Wolf. "In this same region . . . but a short distance to the east in the
vicinity of Dry Lake Lookout, I found that in December, 1940 the
ground above 4000 ft. remained continuously frozen despite the fact
that in mid-day the air temperatures rose to nearly 40 degrees F. It is
probable, therefore, that the Siskiyou . . . cypress . . . trees stand in
frozen ground for several months each winter. . . . However, the summer months in the Siskiyous and on Goose Nest Mountain are hot and
dry, and some of the trees on the south slopes may be subjected to
temperatures of over 90 degrees F." [1] Obviously the Siskiyou Cypress
suggests the possibilities of growing it as an ornamental in regions
with much more extreme climates than are suitable for such famous
horticultural Cypresses as the Italian, Funeral, Monterey, and Smooth-
barked Arizona species.

[1] *The New World Cypresses* by Carl B. Wolf. 1948.

ROUGHBARK ARIZONA CYPRESS

Cupressus arizonica Greene

OTHER NAME: Arizona Cypress.

RANGE: In southern Arizona (Mount Lemmon, at about 3500 feet), the
Chiricahua Mountains (5000 to 5500 feet), the Dragoon Mountains, on
the Chisos Mountains of Brewster County, Texas (at 6000 feet); south
to extreme northeastern Sonora, the Sierra Madre in Chihuahua, and
the Sierra de Parras in Coahuila.

DESCRIPTION: *Bark* at base of young trunks smooth, cherry-red, and peeling away in thin, curling, papery plates; that on older trunks dark brown
or blackish and broken into irregular small oblong or squarish plates, or,
on very old trunks, thick, gray to nearly black, fibrous or shreddy, and
deeply furrowed between the longitudinal ridges. *Twigs* evenly distributed all around the branch. *Leaves* dull gray-green except on young trees,
when glaucous blue-green, about $\frac{1}{12}$ inch long, sharply acute, keeled or
ridged on the back, with or without an active and open or obsolete resin
gland. *Cones* at first green then very glaucous gray, becoming in their

season dull gray to brown or purplish, about 1 inch thick, composed of
6 to 8 warty-surfaced scales of which the face is angular with a distinct
umbo. *Seeds* brown, 90 to 120 in a cone, thin, oval to roundish, with a
small wing. *Wood* soft, easily worked, light (30 pounds per cubic foot,
dry weight).

The "show" excursion in the neighborhood of the fine old city of
Tucson, Arizona, is up the slopes of Mount Lemmon, high peak (9180
feet) of the Santa Catalina Mountains. On the lower slopes you drive
through a fantastic natural garden of cacti, yuccas, aloes, Mesquite,
ocotillobush, and Acacias, but as you climb the Prison Camp road
(where police cars are always prowling) through Bear Canyon, you re-
enter the more natural and familiar world of the conifers accompanied
by such deciduous species as Alders, Willows, Ashes, and Sycamores in
the canyons, and such broadleaved evergreens as the Arizona White
Oak and the Emory Live Oak. But the needle-leaved trees, though they
look and smell like coniferous forests elsewhere, are made up of very
different species from those one knows in the northern Rockies and
California. Here grow such unfamiliar Pines as the Mexican Pinyon,
the long-leaved Arizona Yellow, and the Chihuahua. But the two
dominant conifers are the Juniper with bark like an alligator's hide
and the Rough-barked Arizona Cypress.

Here, and in such other characteristic stations as Stronghold Canyon
in the Dragoon Mountains, and Bonita Canyon in Chiricahua National Monument, the Arizona Cypress makes a handsome growth. A
dense to somewhat openly branched tree, it grows 30 to 70 feet tall,
with a straight central trunk as much as 3 feet thick. Old trees have
very thick rough bark, gray to dark brown or blackish and divided
into squarish irregular plates between the deep furrows. This is com-

pletely unlike the bole of the Smooth-barked Cypress, with which this species is so badly confused in horticulture. The smooth-barked tree has strips of silvery bark that peel naturally away to reveal a mahogany-colored inner bark, and while young specimens, and young branches of the present species, show this pretty feature, the old trunks are never exfoliating and never red.

It is in its youth that this tree shows to its greatest advantage. The foliage is then a shining glaucous blue-green, and the form is compact yet bushy. So it makes an ideal Christmas tree for the Southwest. Its possibilities in this way were first realized by the veteran nurseryman Leslie N. Goodding who received, in 1917, an order for 40 pounds of seed of this tree from the Transvaal government of the Union of South Africa. From all over the world other orders began to come in for this fast-growing, fair-featured tree so valuable for checking erosion in dry countries. But, too, it possessed features as a Christmas tree, Goodding saw, that made it ideal: its needles did not shed or wither so rapidly as those of Firs, or prick the hands like Spruces; the cones make beautiful .tree ornaments when gilded, while the tree itself, with its lovely foliage, needs no doctoring of any sort to make it a radiant presence in the house. As a result of his introduction of the Arizona Cypress into the Christmas trade, it now outranks every other tree in the Southwest, selling five times as well as its nearest competitor. It is also planted extensively for this seasonal market, coming readily from seed and growing very rapidly. The limitations on its culture are that it requires from 15 to 20 inches of rainfall a year and cannot endure winter temperatures that remain long below 15 degrees above zero.

PAIUTE CYPRESS

Cupressus nevadensis Abrams

RANGE: Known only from the drainage of Bodfish Creek, and, at 4000 feet, on Red Hill in the Paiute Mountains, all localities in Kern County, California.

DESCRIPTION: *Bark* of lower portions of old trunks gray-brown and fibrous, narrowly furrowed, and with slender, flat ridges; that of upper portions somewhat cherry-red to brownish, seldom peeling. *Twigs* slender, distinctly 4-sided, standing out in all directions. *Leaves* about $\frac{1}{16}$ inch long, soft gray-green, glaucous and often coated in white resin, sharply acute, keeled, and with an active resin gland, located well above the middle, this visible even on the newest leaves of youngest twigs. *Cones* $\frac{5}{8}$ to $1\frac{1}{4}$ inches long and rather narrower, composed of 6 or 8 minutely warty-surfaced scales which the first year are rich light brown with conical and pointed bosses, but the second year silvery gray and glaucous, the points weathered away. *Seeds* about 90 to the cone, rich light tan, with conspicuous winged margin.

Far in the southern end of the Sierra Nevada of California in the hot, dry Paiute Mountains scantly dotted with ghost towns grows the Paiute Cypress, in the company of Digger Pine, Oneleaf Nut Pine, California Juniper, the blue-leaved Douglas Oak, and that curious little relative of the conifers, the Mormon-tea, *Ephedra*, while stately yuccas with spires of white bloom six feet long and more light up in early summer the rather desolate landscape with torches called Our-Lord's-candle.

Most of the California Cypresses tend to be rare and local in their occurrence, but none more so than this one, which was discovered in 1915 by that dean of California botanists, Leroy Abrams. He drove south along the road between Bodfish and Havilah for about 3 miles to the summit of a grade, then turned off on an unsurfaced clay road, utterly impassable in wet weather, for 2½ miles. And there he came on thousands of specimens of this conical tree, its foliage in summer, when Abrams first saw it, a dusty gray-green, though in spring when the rains are ending it is a fine glowing green. Flowering takes place in February and March and at that time many of the specimens, ac-

cording to the ranchers, appear as golden trees, powdered over with untold numbers of yellow male flowers.

The trunk of the Paiute Cypress is furrowed and provided with
stringy, long, vertical, braided strips of fibrous outer bark. But little
is seen of the trunk from a distance, so tenaciously do the old boughs
hang on, so that the tree seems clothed almost to the base. It grows
up to 30 feet in height, with a trunk 2 to 2½ feet thick. Young trees
are narrowly conical and compact but old trees are more broadly
conical and open. Like most of the native Cypresses, this one has long
been used by the ranchers in the vicinity for fence posts, since it lasts
for years in contact with the soil.

A related species the CUYAMACA CYPRESS, *Cupressus Stephen-
sonii* Wolf, differs in that the seeds are over ⅕ of an inch long, with
a wing rather broad (in proportion to the width of the seed), the
surface of the seed not at all glaucous. The resin glands of the leaves
are inactive. It resembles *Cupressus glabra* in its smooth peeling bark
but has much less glandular leaves. This species, described in 1948, is
known only from a few scattered trees on the headwaters of King Creek
on the southwest side of Cuyamaca Peak, San Diego County, California. These trees were first noticed by the late Bert Stephenson of
the Forest Service, for many years District Ranger at the Descanso
station, when he was fighting a forest fire. This species grows 30 to 50
feet high, producing a glaucous gray-blue-green foliage which when
crushed emits a lemon-like odor, and dull gray or brown spherical
cones about 1 inch in diameter, the scales with warty surfaces.

SMOOTH ARIZONA CYPRESS

Cupressus glabra Sudworth

OTHER NAMES: Smooth or Arizona Cypress.

RANGE: Central Arizona, from Oak Creek Canyon (Coconino and Yavapai
Counties) to the Mazatzal Mountains, East Verde River, and Natural
Bridge (Gila and Maricopa Counties) at 4000 to 5000 feet altitude.

DESCRIPTION: *Bark* of young trunks smooth, cherry-red and exfoliating annually in thin, externally silvery gray layers or plates; that of old trunks sometimes close-barked at base, sometimes furrowed and cross-checked into little warty plates. *Twigs* slim, at first dark gray or brownish, later turning cherry-red. *Leaves* on fertile branches closely appressed, ½ to ¾ inch long, keeled or ridged on the back, with a conspicuous resin gland, dusty gray-green or, on young specimens, glaucous blue-green and whitened by copious resin from the glands. *Cone* ¾ to 1 inch long or rarely 1½ inches, and nearly as wide. *Seeds* about 100 to a cone, light to very dark brown.

A more beautiful conifer than this one, for cultivation in the hot dry climate of the Southwest, you could not ask, and so think untold numbers of California and Arizona gardeners. The young trees have an elegant, spire-like outline almost as compact and decisive as that of an Italian Cypress, but the foliage is not somber like that of the Old World tree with its funereal associations, but a blue-green so heavily covered with a glaucous bloom (and with whitish exudations from active glands on the leaves) that it seems bathed in silvery moonlight. Or it may appear a dusty gray, if the light is dull, but perfectly consonant in this with the hues of the desert. The greatest beauty of all is found in the texture and colors of the soft bark. Externally the thin, Birch-like layers are a gleaming silvery gray, but constantly this is found peeling and curling back in strips to reveal an inner bark of a gleaming cherry- or mahogany-red.

Old trees may lose their very slender outlines; the beautiful silvery bloom of their foliage will eventually wear off, and the bark at the base of very old trunks may fail to peel away. But what the specimens lose in youthful charm they gain in sturdiness as they grow 45 to 60 feet tall, with a spread of 15 to 36 feet and trunks 1½ to 3 feet thick.

Because it is so very resistant to prolonged summer droughts, high desert winds, alkaline soil, and exposure to light, the Smooth Arizona Cypress has been planted throughout southern California except within the range of the coastal fogs where it does not do well. Probably the finest and most extensive planting in the country is that bordering U.S. Highway 6 from Saugus to Newhall, in interior Los Angeles County. At an age of 40 years, these trees are 30 feet high and except perhaps for some irrigation in their earlier stages, have never received any care. On the Mohave desert between Victorville and Palmdale one meets this tree frequently, still flourishing even on abandoned ranches where, long since, the Pears have died. In the Pomona and San Fernando and San Bernardino valleys this is a favorite windbreak tree. In the neighborhood of Phoenix, Arizona, it is constantly used in parks and grounds of splendid estates.

Yet in the wild this charming tree is little known, since it is confined to a strip about 80 miles long, on the drainage of the Verde River, which includes famous Oak Creek Canyon, the flanks of the Mazatzal Mountains, and Natural Bridge, all in central Arizona. Its tree associates there are Alligator, Rocky Mountain, and Utah Junipers, Pinyon and Western Yellow Pine and such deciduous trees as Ash and Sycamore. There, on mesa and mountainside and canyon wall, this Cypress forms a fine open-type forest. But the trees are much less conventionally charming than those in cultivation. When springing up in thickets they may be nothing more than canes with a few branches bearing a cluster or two of cones at their tips. But with ample room they spread to make, eventually, a broad-headed tree, impressive in dimensions as desert trees go. In Oak Creek Canyon, with a setting of huge red sandstone cliffs and rocks eroded to a gigantesque sculpture, its beauties are set off superbly.

Before it was described as a new species, in 1910, this tree was seen many times by botanical explorers without being recognized as distinct from the rough-barked Arizona Cypress. Probably it even reached cultivation in England as early as 1888, but it was cultivated there, as it is commonly offered here by nurseries, under the incorrect name of *Cupressus arizonica,* which is in reality a less beautiful tree. No American Cypress holds out more future to gardens and highway planting than this one. True that in the past the Monterey Cypress has been planted in great amounts, here and abroad, but it is not adapted to the same sort of conditions, requiring as it does a much more tempered climate where the choice of ornamentals is boundless. The destiny of Arizona Smooth Cypress is in desertic lands where any sort of tree is a boon, and a beauty like this one is unmatched.

TECATE CYPRESS

Cupressus Forbesii Jepson

OTHER NAME: Forbes Cypress.

RANGE: Santa Ana Mountains (Orange County, California); Guatay Mountain and Otay Mountain, San Diego County, and Mount Tecate on the U.S.-Mexican boundary; also El Cañon de Pinitos (70 miles south of Ensenada) in Baja California.

DESCRIPTION: *Bark* of trunks exfoliating, leaving a clear brown or rich cherry-red smooth surface, sometimes only partially peeling away, and persisting as grayish shaggy scales with curling edges. *Leaves* light rich (never glaucous) green, only about ½ inch long, acute but rather blunt-tipped, rounded or ridged on the back, the resin gland slightly darkened but inactive except on the larger leaves of vigorous young shoots. *Flowers* — male abundant, their catkins blunt, ⅛ to ⅙ inch long, slightly 4-sided, of 8 to 14 scales; female about ¼ inch long, usually abundant, sometimes congested into clusters of 15 or 20, composed of 8 to 10 scales. *Cone* about 1¼ inches long and nearly globular in shape, dull gray to brown. *Seeds* plump, rich dark brown.

The chief interest in most of the California Cypresses is not in the trees as they are found in the wild, for they are almost all of limited occurrence. Rather are our Cypresses significant for their possible value in horticulture. The rapid growth, the beautiful form of many, their usefulness not only as ornamentals but as windbreaks for gardens and orchards, their cooperative submission to clipping and trimming into hedges, their endurance of wind and heat, drought and hard soils, all mark them out for careful experimentation, such as is being given them at Rancho Santa Ana Botanic Garden in southern California.

And, according to the records kept there, the Tecate Cypress, which has been tested by nearly 10,000 plantings at the garden and else-where, is the best of substitutes for the overplanted and now often diseased Monterey Cypress. The Tecate Cypress sprouts from ripe seed in about 38 days — three times as fast as some of the other species tested. At Riverside and Chatsworth, the Tecate survives searing desert winds that wither the leaves right off citrus and Eucalyptus trees. With proper space, drainage, and a little irrigation, it does splendidly as a windbreak and clipped hedge plant. Though it does not grow as tall as the Monterey Cypress it grows as rapidly; though it is not immune to the noxious canker disease, it is more so than the Monterey Cypress. Its optimum conditions, however, do not lie in the same localities; the Monterey tree does best within reach of the sea fogs; the Tecate Cypress shuns them and rejoices in interior stations.

In youth Tecate Cypresses are narrowly conical and very compact trees, with upright branches clothing the trunk to the ground, and with a light, rich green foliage, which in late summer grows dull until the dry season is ended by the autumn rains. But age brings a lowering of the branches from their erect position, till the lowest are horizontal. Now the crown is broad and shade-giving — a fine tree when not crowded. If specimens are planted too near together, however, the lower branches die from lack of light and the skinny pole bears but a spindling spire of foliage at the top.

The most remarkable feature of the tree is the bark. This may be, and usually is at some early stage, a mass of brownish scales but so loosely attached they are that the very winds can blow them off. The trunk then looks as peeled as a Eucalyptus stem, but revealing an inner bark which is sometimes a dull red and again a strange pea-green, so that the bole appears as multicolored and blotched as that of a Sycamore.

MONTEREY CYPRESS

Cupressus macrocarpa Hartweg

RANGE: Known in native growth only on the sea coast at Carmel, California, in two groves, at Cypress Point and Point Lobos. Widespread in cultivation.

DESCRIPTION: *Bark* of young trunks dark red-brown, becoming thick, fibrous and ashy gray on large old trunks, irregularly furrowed into broad connecting and braided ridges which bear slender persistent scales. *Twigs* after leaf fall covered with thin, flaky, dark red-brown bark. *Leaves* only

⅟₁₂ inch long, rich bright green, never bluish or glaucous, without a resin gland but marked on the back with a shallow pit and 2 grooves. *Cones* clustered on stout short stalks, 1 to 1½ inches thick, consisting in 4 or 6 pairs, of scales with broadly thickened bosses, at first green, then brown, weathering to gray before their very tardy opening. *Seeds* about 140 to the cone, plump, dark brown with white hilum, with a rather prominent wing-like margin. *Wood* very durable, hard, strong, and heavy (39 pounds per cubic foot, dry weight).

The most spectacular beauty on all the coast of California is the rocky, forest-clad shore that winds between Monterey and Point Lobos, including Pebble Beach, Cypress Point, and Carmel. To the south rise the grand Santa Lucia Mountains, bearing their Redwoods and Firs and plunging in fearsome cliffs into the sea. To the north, Monterey Bay curves gracefully off to the misty Santa Clara coast. Now the fogs roll in dramatically, pouring through the forest aisles like wraiths hurrying to Judgment, while the foghorns blow a raucous Gabriel trump, the buoys toll as if for drowned mariners, the surf thunders hollowly, and the bellowing of the sea lions on their island rocks is a savage Cerberus barking. And now the fog lifts, the sun bursts out on silken blue sea and curdy rollers, the pungency of pine and sage is steeped from the hillsides, the white-crowned sparrows' "sirr-*sweet*-see" rises drowsily where they sway upon grass stalk and golden poppy. Soft and ancient sound the bells of weathered old Carmel Mission where lies buried Padre Junípero Serra, the first of white men to love this spot and plant the Cross upon its shores.

In this romantic setting, and only here — always within half a mile of high tide, and along a few winding miles of shoreline — grows natively the Monterey Cypress, perhaps the rarest, certainly the most fantastic tree of North America. This species is in fact confined to two

groves, the one at Cypress Point north of Carmel, and the other at Point Lobos State Park, just south of it. The number of individual trees in them has been rather precisely estimated by Harry Ashland Green who found (in 1929) that there were 7850 trees in the main grove at Cypress Point and 2700 in the strip of shoreline along the Seventeen Mile Drive through Pebble Beach.[1] The other grove at Point Lobos is much smaller and contains far fewer trees. Yet from these two stands have descended all the specimens, running into untold numbers, which are now grown in Europe, Australia, New Zealand, and South America, as well as up and down the coast of California in every garden and city park, and on many a ranch where this tree forms, with its intricate growth and adaptability to pruning, a solid windbreak to protect the precious citrus crop.

But a Monterey Cypress cultivated away from its spray-bitten native cliffs is but a tamed thing, fast-growing, obedient to the gardener's will, and handsome, though not superior, to other Cypresses. It is indeed so far from the bewitched forms of the wild tree as not to be recognized as the same species by anyone but a specialist. For it is the sea wind and the salt spray and the close, colonial habit of a Cypress wood's growth that account for all these fantasies in form comparable only with the tortured shapes of trees at timber line, or with that style in Japanese gardening by which trees, after years of being deliberately pot-bound, bud-nipped and otherwise mistreated, take on a gnomish and perverse distortion. But, however bizarre, the native Monterey Cypresses have no appearance of unnaturalness, for Nature shows her hand in every contortion of the twisted and incredibly stunted and thickened or flattened trunks, in the sinuous, flattened buttresses that spring from the base of the trunks and snake their way down the sea cliffs, in the long arching of the lower limbs, in the massed intricacy of the twigs, in the sculpturing of the flat-topped crown, which may be ten and twenty times as wide as it is high. Sometimes it is also tilted, like a great hat worn aslant; if the stem leans over the cliff toward the sea, the crown will usually lean backwards toward the sward of the rocky shore or mesa. If the wind is too constant, and the brine too abundant, the trunk may sprawl along the ground, and the branches and their foliage lie as a mat to leeward. Often many will grow together thus, crouching with their backs to the lash of the salt winds, but presenting landward an impenetrable natural hedge.

[1] *Madroño*, vol. 1, pp. 197–98 (1929).

A result of the excessive growth of the tree on one side is the development of heavy, fluted, swollen, and asymmetrical butts. Asymmetrical is a weak word, indeed, to describe the contours of such boles. When these specimens have been felled, the outlines of their cross-sections look like pieces from a jigsaw puzzle, and the annual growth rings are compressed here, expanded there, until they become illegible as indicators of the age of the trees.

Little indeed is known of their ages, but what can be determined scientifically does not substantiate any claim to antiquity like the Sequoias'. Two centuries is perhaps the average, three extreme. It is rather the hard lives that they have lived which have aged the Cypresses early, for those specimens growing farthest from the sea approach most nearly the appearance of the lusty normal forms of the cultivated examples, with symmetrical outlines and a straight central leader.

The appearance of utmost eld which is seen among the seaside fantastics is increased by the long trailing beards of dripping gray "moss" — really a lichen, *Ramalina reticulata* — which clothe almost all the old specimens. Forever stirring in the sea wind, they waver not like healthy foliage but with the listless despair of cobwebs. The *Ramalina* is indeed an enemy of the Cypresses, for it smothers its foliage and, always gaining headway, eventually kills the tree without actually parasitizing it, but by a sort of suffocation. It is, however, valuable to the bird life of the Cypress groves. Not only does it provide shelter, but the majority of nests are composed of this gray-green and mournful growth — the bush tit's pendent, ball-shaped nest, and the homes of the Hutton vireo and the tuneful linnet.

On many of the trees, particularly those at the tip of Point Lobos, a mysterious ruddy or orange glow lights up the tip of the branches. At sunset it would be mistaken for the natural color of the sun's last rays. But it is there at all hours. Approach the twigs closely and you find that they seem infested with a sort of rusty, cobwebby, dry, felted, fungoid mass. This is no natural part of the tree but a living organism and, like the beards of lichen, a perching not a parasitic plant. Strangest of all, this is a filamentous alga with the odd faculty of being able to grow out of water although the air is so saturated with wind-borne spray and prolonged fogs that its humidity is high indeed. Technically this alga, *Trentepohlia*, belongs to the great class of the green algæ, but its green pigments are masked by a red-orange layer which functions, perhaps, as a reserve food store supplemental to starch. So abundant is *Trentepohlia* on the trees that its color may locally dominate the landscape — the only case, maybe, where anything so lowly as an alga does so.

A dead Cypress lasts as long as a live one or nearly so, for its wood is remarkably resistant to decay, and when dead the tree is if possible more picturesque than when living; its bark sloughs off, the foliage browns and drops from the twigs; these too are torn away; then the sea winds and the sunlight scour the great bole and boughs to a bone-like whiteness, and so the ghostly thing remains standing, a gesticulating skeleton. More birds are seen on dead cypresses than on living, for a leafless tree forms a favorite lookout for flycatchers, woodpeckers, and hawks. Sometimes gulls rest upon them too.

Under the Cypresses it is always strangely dim and damp; the footfall is hushed by the bed of needles accumulated through centuries, a moist, not a dry bed, for this is the belt of almost daily fogs. Very few birds save the hermit thrush forage down there, and humans, as they wander, are apt to fall silent in some awe. Then the sound of the surf, the bellowing of the sea lions, and the chittering of pigeon guillemots invade the hush of the groves; and the glimpses of the blue and breathing ocean, the swift angelic flight of terns and gulls, seen through the aisles and boughs, are like the bright outside world framed by a window slit in the dimness and damp of some ancient building.

Little wonder that the Monterey Cypress has accumulated legends about it. If they had arisen in medieval Europe, they would take a turn to the supernatural; but in our times and in this location they drift into the pseudoscientific. Some will have it that these are Cedars of Lebanon, and were brought hither by the Franciscan Fathers when the Carmel Mission was founded. Others, perhaps confounding the Cypress with the Cryptomerias so common in Oriental temple grounds, would prefer to believe that they were carried here across the Pacific by Buddist monks who came, presumably, by way of the wonderful land of Mu!

The truth of it is that the first European scientists to see our trees recognized them immediately as a new and distinctive species. In June, 1846, just when the American flag was being raised for the first time on the soil of California, a young botanist, Karl Theodore Hartweg, in the employ of the London Horticultural Society, set out from Monterey for a botanical ramble over Huckleberry Hill, having decided that the disturbed political conditions between Mexicans and Americans made it unsafe to botanize far from his quarters. His footsteps led him to the Cypress groves. "Here I found . . . *Cupressus macrocarpa* . . . attaining a height of 60 feet, and a stem of 9 feet in circumference, with far-spreading branches, flat at the top like a full-grown Cedar of Lebanon which it closely resembles at a distance." This is the first valid botanical naming of our tree, yet several years before Hartweg's arrival, the Monterey region had been botanized by such great collectors as Archibald Menzies, David Douglas, and Thomas Nuttall. How could they have missed the most striking tree of the region? Perhaps they collected specimens which were lost or misplaced, yet they do not even mention the Cypress in their diaries and correspondence.

In cultivation this tree is easily germinated from seed. It sprouts in the open nursery bed within two or three weeks and the seedlings shoot up fast as weeds. For many years they have been sold at nurseries at ten to fifteen cents each, and as a result the symmetrical but somber and rather uniform shape of the cultivated tree has sometimes been repeated to triteness. Yet most of the land surface of this world can never have the Monterey Cypress. For it retains this much of its maritime heritage: that out of the reach of damp sea winds it will not thrive. Even in central California it lives only a few years, then pines away for lack of the very winds that flog it till it writhes into forms that might, as Robert Louis Stevenson said of them, "figure without change in a circle of the nether hell as Dante pictured it." [1]

Closely related to the Monterey Cypress and, like it, growing in native state only around Carmel, California, is the GOWEN CYPRESS, *Cupressus Goveniana* Gordon. It differs in having slender, and not harsh, branchlets, smaller cones (less than 1 inch long), the seeds dull, not shiny. Either a shrub or a bushy tree, with bright green foliage with a yellowish cast, quite unlike the dark blue-green of Monterey Cypress, it may reach 25 feet in height. This species has been found only on Huckleberry Hill above Cypress Point, on the Seventeen Mile Drive, and 1 mile east of Point Lobos State Park, on a hill above San Jose Creek.

[1] "The Old Pacific Capital," in his *Travels and Essays*.

MENDOCINO CYPRESS

Cupressus pygmæa (Lemmon) Sargent

OTHER NAME: Pigmy Cypress.

RANGE: On the coast of Mendocino County, California.

DESCRIPTION: *Bark* of trunks thin, fibrous and shreddy, gray-brown. *Twigs* of the season long, slender, thickening and branching the second season and, by the time the foliage is shed in the third season, becoming clothed in smooth brown bark. *Leaves* very dark dull green, on fertile shoots very small (⅟₂₄ to ⅟₁₂ inch long) and closely appressed, a dark, closed resin gland seen on leaves of the second season's growth. *Cones* at first green, changing the second season to a rich tan, and then ⅝ to ⅚ inch in diameter, becoming gray as the cones weather on the tree and the umbo wears away. *Seeds* about 130 to a cone, flattish, brownish or shiny black, often as broad as the stiff narrow wing.

The Mendocino Cypress takes its specific Latin name of *pygmæa* from the diminutive stature of the first specimens discovered, on the famed Mendocino "white plains" or "barrens" around Fort Bragg, far up on the fog-swept coast of northern California. Not only does this Cypress grow there no more than 3 feet high, with a trunk only ½ to ¾ inch thick, but the Bishop Pines too are reduced to mere runts, the Beach Pines look like so much reed or cane, and the Chinquapin, one of the noblest of trees, is dwarfed to a mere scrubby semblance of its better self. Yet not far off stand the mighty Coast Redwood, the Lowland Fir well sustaining its name of *Abies grandis,* and full-size specimens of Douglas Fir. The reason for the cretin stature of all the trees on the white plains seems to be the nature of the soil — or lack of it. Everywhere is found a white sandstone which forms a hardpan incapable of absorbing much of the rainfall which collects in pools while the rainy season lasts but evaporates without ever sinking into the ground. Then when the dry season comes the roots of the trees there have almost no gound water supply on which to draw. More, the surface soil, derived from the white rock, comes to lie as a coating of cement-like dust on every leaf and twig, held there by the pervading dampness of the pouring fogs. Thus, with one of the heaviest rainfalls in California, the white plains are — for purposes of the vegetation — almost a desert, but a desert where the sun shines little, the days seldom get warm. No wonder that even a Cypress should be a pigmy under such conditions.

Yet under better ones, and not far off, this species grows up to 150 feet in height, with trunks 3 feet thick, and a spread of the crown of as much as 45 feet — very creditable for a plant that bears the name *pygmæa!* The habitat of these large trees is in low damp swales that are covered with water for days at a time during the rainy season.

The Mendocino Cypress, like its Monterey cousin, early develops a long, whip-like leader shoot, and it grows nearly as fast as the Monterey Cypress, but puts forth much less wood in the way of branches, is more straggly in consequence, and is seriously subject to the canker disease. Unable to endure conditions unlike those of its native home (harsh as they seem to us), it pines away in most places where it has been planted.

SANTA CRUZ CYPRESS

Cupressus Abramsiana Wolf

RANGE: Santa Cruz Mountains (1600 to 2500 feet altitude), Santa Cruz County, California.

DESCRIPTION: *Bark* of trunks rather thin, gray and either fibrous and shreddy or broken into vertical strips or plates. *Leaves* rich light bright green, 'acute but blunt-tipped, closely overlapping on fertile shoots and forming slightly 4-sided sprigs of foliage, developing, after a season, an inconspicuous non-functional resin gland. *Cones* at maturity ¾ to 1¼ inches long and spherical or a little elongated, the scales becoming a rich lustrous brown with the umbo only a slight hump. *Seeds* angular, flattened, about 60 to the cone, brown and either slightly glaucous or slightly shiny, with a narrow hard wing.

The Santa Cruz Cypress is found along that lonely stretch of California State Highway 1, between Santa Cruz and San Francisco, and at three stations only. In all cases the growth is quite restricted in extent and the trees occur in but a thin and scattered way, not forming any real groves. Usually these trees spring from white sand in granitic soil, between 1600 and 2500 feet above sea level, and in general well above the usual height of the fog belt that bathes so much of this stretch of the coast.

When well-grown this species rises to 30 feet, making a symmetrical and conical growth, the slim trunk clothed with branches nearly to the ground, with a straight central leader and a thin gray bark which is generally smooth and only with age broken into vertical strips or plates. The foliage is of a bright, light, rich green.

In cultivation this tree does well and should make a good windbreak for northern California, in the opinion of Willis W. Wagener who has done so much work with native Cypresses at Santa Anita Botanical Garden, but it is so susceptible to the Cypress canker that it cannot be successfully grown in southern California.

SARGENT CYPRESS

Cupressus Sargentii Jepson

RANGE: Coast Ranges of California, from extreme northern Mendocino County (Red Mountain) and Cooks Springs, Colusa County, south through Lake, Napa, and Marin Counties, reappearing on Cedar Mountain, Alameda County, in the Santa Lucia Mountains of Monterey and San Luis Obispo Counties; on Zaca Peak (at 3000 feet) in the San Rafael Mountains of northern Santa Barbara County.

DESCRIPTION: *Bark* of old trunks gray or dark brown or almost black, thick, and fibrous, splitting into vertical strands. *Twigs* of the season thickish, rounded, stiff and harsh. *Leaves* dusty gray-green, sometimes with a bloom, $\frac{1}{12}$ inch long and broad, rather blunt, the small resin pit, when present, inactive except on the foliage of vigorous leader shoots. *Cones* in the first season changing from green to brown, in the second season to a rich glossy brown weathering to dull brown or gray, ultimately $\frac{3}{4}$ to 1 inch long, with 6 to 10 scales bearing sometimes conspicuous umbos. *Seeds* about 100 to a cone, dark brown but glaucous, the marginal wing thin.

The distribution of Sargent Cypress (entirely in the Coast Ranges of California) is more extensive than that of any other North American species of this fine genus save one. You may come upon it in such famous situations as the northeast base of Mount St. Helena (familiar from Robert Louis Stevenson's *Silverado Squatters*), or Mount Tamalpais, a mecca of botanists and hikers which stands just north of San Francisco in Marin County, or on Cedar Mountain in Alameda County, close to Mount Hamilton where the Lick Observatory stands. Or you will see it at Los Burros Mine, near the Mission San Antonio de Padua, where Father Serra hung his bell upon an Oak bough and called the Indians to prayer by it, and on the mountains just behind the fantastic "castle" of William Randolph Hearst near San Simeon.

Dry rocky outcrops, mountain ridges, and brushy hillsides are its home, where the rainfall averages around 25 inches a year, mostly in the winter months. In general, Sargent Cypress grows only 30 to 45 feet high, but on the slopes of canyons or ravines it may be considerably taller — up to 75 feet high. In youth it makes a beautiful, thickset, symmetrical tree with a straight leader coming to a spire-like point — a perfect cone. With age this form is broken up, as the lower branches die away and the whole crown broadens and grows rather flat, till a Pine-like outline is attained. Trees on mountain slopes, as those on Tamalpais, are inclined to be short, flat-topped and broad in the crown, and distinctly picturesque if not beautiful.

And beauty just misses the foliage, which though thick and healthy is a dull green as if lightly coated with dust, while the male cones are often produced in such profusion as to give the trees a yellowish cast. About 100 seeds are borne in each female cone, and so though this species is very susceptible to chaparral fires, the abundant and viable seed resows the area, with the result that it is soon found to be coming up to Sargent Cypresses of a uniform density and height. And though fires frequently sweep the chaparral, so ample is the reproduction and so swift the growth of the young shoots that they generally reach bearing age before another fire occurs.

THE FALSE CYPRESSES

(*Chamæcyparis*)

THE MEMBERS of this group are long-lived trees with aromatic, resinous foliage and wood, the trunks (in old specimens) swell-butted and fluted, with nodding shoots, spreading branches and flattened and very slender branchlets that lie all in one plane, closely invested by the scale-like leaves, so that the foliage forms a flat spray. The leaves, closely overlapping, are like those of *Thuja* in occurring in alternate pairs — a flat pair on the upper and lower side of the twig almost enfolded by a keeled pair along the sides; leaves of seedlings are quite unlike those of mature shoots, since they are long, slender, sharp-pointed and spreading, and occur in whorls of 3 or four. When the foliage of a *Chamæcyparis* grows old (after 3 or 4 years) it turns rusty or brown and may persist, more or less woody and seemingly a part of the twig, for some time. The minute flowers open in early spring from buds formed the previous autumn, with the sexes on separate branches of the same tree. The small spherical cones, erect on the twigs, consist in club-shaped scales, their broad ends facing outward. The seeds are provided with wings but lack resin vesicles.

*   *   *

ALASKA CEDAR

Chamæcyparis nootkatensis (D. Don) **Spach**

OTHER NAMES: Yellow Cedar. Yellow, Nootka, Alaska or Sitka Cypress.

RANGE: From sea level on the Islands of Prince William Sound, Alaska, up to 3000 feet altitude on the Coast Ranges of British Columbia, and south along the Cascade Mountains to the mountains of Siskiyou County in northern California.

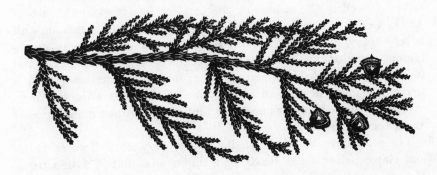

DESCRIPTION: *Bark* of trunks thin, separating on the surface into loose, big, thin scales irregularly fissured with numerous diagonal ridges connecting the larger ones, in color light gray tinged with brown. *Twigs* all in one plane on the branch, stout, at first light yellow sometimes tinged with red, becoming by their third season bright red-brown, and ultimately gray and smooth. *Leaves* in flattish sprays, dark blue-green, prickly to the touch, ⅛ inch long, scale-like, closely flattened to the twig, or on vigorous leader shoots twice as long and with tips spreading and acute. *Flowers* — male yellow, growing on side branches of last year's growth, consisting in four or five stamens; female found near the tips of the upper branchlets, liver-colored. *Cones* at maturity deep russet brown under a conspicuous whitish bloom, very small, ½ inch thick. *Seeds* of the same color as the cone, 2 to 4 in number under each fertile scale, with thin reddish wings as wide as the seed. *Wood* resinous and aromatic, very close-grained, brittle, hard, and light (30 pounds per cubic foot, dry weight), the heartwood clear bright yellow, the thin sapwood nearly white.

The Alaska Cedar can be one of the most beautiful yet most sorrowful of western conifers. Its long, lithe leader shoot bows its head — sometimes bent nearly double in a young tree — and its dull dark bluish-green foliage is evergreen for two years, then turns a rusty brown. The dead foliage is not shed, however, for another year, leaving the whole tree more or less tinged with the hue that, for vegetable life, is the color of mourning. The great, long lower boughs of trees grown in the open sweep deeply down, till they may touch the ground, then lift in a wide upward curve with a majestic gesture, but from the branches the twigs swing pendent, and from the very long whip-like twigs the flat sprays of foliage droop so persistently that they appear almost wilted. So the whole tree has something of a weeping habit, though not in the exaggerated form of a Weeping Willow. Rather does it look, even in summer, as if it were weighted with snows.

And indeed in the islands off the coast of British Columbia where Alaska Cedar attains its greatest size — 90 to 150 feet — the snowfall is very heavy, and so is the rainfall. Where the tree grows in mountainous situations the winds and the ice loads break it mercilessly and it loses the beautiful symmetry seen in more protected spots and is frequently more dead than alive — one of the least attractive trees among all conifers. Or it may, near timber line, sprawl ignominiously along the ground.

The growth of the Alaska Cedar is often very slow. Two centuries may elapse before a tree reaches saw-timber size, that is, with a trunk 15 to 20 inches in diameter. Only in infrequent years, and at irregular intervals, is a good crop of seeds produced. Slipping from the cones, in the autumn gales, they glide far on their little wings, but probably the number that struggle through to success is not great.

Much of the standing timber of this tree is found in country too rough and inaccessible for lumbering, but where it can be profitably cut it is eagerly sought and exported as far as Japan. What may be the toll of the lumber industry upon this tree is not definitely known, for though the lumberman does distinguish it by name — he prefers Yellow Cedar as its title — he seldom lists it separately in statistics. The wood is certainly a fine one, probably the hardest of all trees rejoicing in the loosely given name of Cedar, and the grain straight and so regular that it takes the highest polish. It is also sweetly, resinously aromatic and highly resistant to decay; logs that have lain for decades in the forest are perfectly sound under the green winding sheet of moss.

The handsome yellow boards work up into furniture and interior finish of high quality. For boat-building this is a first-class wood in decking, railing, and interior paneling. It makes a fine wood for pattern blocks. Because it is both a very light and very stiff wood (one of the rarest of combinations), and wears smoother, not rougher, with use, it was from prehistoric times the favorite material for the making of those paddles by which the Indians of the Northwest coast propelled their famous canoes of Western Red Cedar, as the Haidas, Tlingits, and Tsimshians pursued the sea otter, the sea lion, and the seal, or carried war to the very gates of Old Sitka in the days of the cruel Russian *promyshlenniks*. From its trunks they also cut their ceremonial masks, highly colored and often inlaid with copper and abalone shell to represent teeth that could be made to snap and eyes that could be made to roll — to the mingled terror and delight of beholders.

Like its relative the Port Orford Cedar, the Alaska Cedar in cultivation has produced a large number of handsome or far-fetched forms, some of them sold by nurserymen under the name of Retinospora. So this tree, one of the less-known, least domestic of all the trees of the Northwest, has made its way around the world as a garden pet, proving hardy in England and the eastern United States.

PORT ORFORD CEDAR

Chamæcyparis Lawsoniana (Murray) Parlatore

OTHER NAMES: White or Oregon Cedar. Lawson Cypress. Ginger Pine.

RANGE: From Coos Bay, southwestern Oregon, south along the Pacific coast, ranging inland about 30 miles, to the mouth of the Klamath River, northern California; inland, also, on the Siskiyou Mountains of Oregon and California, and around the headwaters of the Sacramento River, south of Mount Shasta.

DESCRIPTION: *Bark* at the base of old trunks very thick (6 to 8 inches), divided by deep narrow seams into long, loosely stringy, slender ridges, connected by narrower diagonal ridges, the outer fibrous strips easily separating and displaying the unweathered rich red-brown of the underbark. *Twigs* closely invested by the foliage, mostly lying in one plane on the branch and rather remote. *Leaves* on lateral shoots 1/16 inch long, scale-like, flattened to the twig, bright green, and conspicuously glandular, those on leading shoots ⅛ inch long and somewhat spreading. *Flowers* — male bright red, female with dark spreading scales each bearing 2 to 4 ovules. *Cones* very numerous but small (½ inch long), at first bright glaucous green, becoming when ripe red-brown with a pallid cast, the tips of the scales boss-like and reflexed. *Seeds* ⅛ inch long, light chestnut-brown, 2 to 4 under each fertile scale, with thin wide wings. *Wood* resinous and aromatic, light (29 pounds per cubic foot, dry weight), strong, hard, easily worked and durable, the heartwood light yellow, the sapwood paler but hardly distinguishable.

Shining and gracious in youth, gigantic and glorious in age, possessed of a fragrant wood of great beauty and scores of the most valuable uses, the Port Orford Cedar has but one defect with which it can be reproached: there isn't — and never has been — enough of it!

Even under aboriginal conditions it was not exactly a plentiful tree, confined as it always was to a rather small range, from Coos Bay, on the Oregon coast, south to the rugged Siskiyou Mountains of northern California, with a few stations around the head of the Sacramento River. Even then it was by no means continuous over that range, occurring only in a spotty way. Yet sometimes the virgin growth was very dense, and the trees, towering up to 175 or even 200 feet in height, with 150 feet of the trunk clear of branches, produced sometimes as much as 100,000 board feet of high-grade lumber to the acre. Estimates place the total stand of the original growth at 4,000,000,000 board feet, which sounds like a lot until we compare it with the existing stands of other lumber trees. The Western Yellow Pine, for instance is, even today, 45 times as abundant as the entire aboriginal stand of Port Orford Cedar.

But from the first discovery of the big stands of this timber in 1855, man and fire have assaulted it relentlessly. A disastrous fire in the Coos Bay region at an early date wiped out a vast but undetermined amount. Next, sawmills were at work, and schooners were anchoring off the rocky, harborless coast, to be loaded with Cedar logs carried by a high line from the cliffs to the decks.

The demand for Port Orford Cedar, as soon as it became known in eastern and foreign markets, grew swiftly and remained steady. For it is scarcely excelled in the manufacture of venetian-blind slats, mine timbers, railway ties, millwork. Its ginger-like odor is reputed to be repellent to moths, so that it has gone into the making of clothes chests and presses. Because it is resistant to acids, it has been used for storage battery separators. Latterly it has been in demand for plywood for aircraft construction and for veneer generally. From the first it was valued in boat building; Sir Thomas Lipton ordered all his cup-challenger yachts built of Port Orford Cedar.

The wood is light in color — elegantly so — and takes well both a high polish and stains and paints. For this reason it has become a cabinet wood, which can be finished in imitation of Mahogany, Oak, and other precious woods. In its own right it early began to enjoy a reputation as a casket wood, not so much in its native land as in far-off Cathay and Nippon. Its lightness, satiny texture when finished, its pungent odor compared by some to ginger, by some to roses, and the fact that it ranks, in contact with the soil, with the most durable of all woods, singles this Cedar out for a casket wood, and when we reflect that — according at least to a solemn tradition among small boys — a Celestial dies every time you draw a breath, one can see that the Oriental market for Port Orford Cedar would be high. Sometimes one wonders if there is not almost as much of it underground in Asia as there is above ground here.

For the mills have eaten and eaten into the limited supply, spurred on by a rising market, until today the stumpage price of this tree exceeds that of every other wood in Oregon, our greatest lumber state. Oregon coast towns such as Coquille, Marshfield, North Bend, Bandon, Parkersburg, and Port Orford itself, became for a time at least booming lumber towns, which also specialized in the building of all-Cedar ships. On the streets of these settlements mingled the roistering lumberjacks, shipbuilders, dockhands, sailors from many strange ports, coal miners from the Marshfield beds, and, for many years, the inevitable pigtailed coolie whose memory is preserved only in the Chinese cemetery on Marshfield's Telegraph Hill.

Some of the above settlements have now become ghost-towns or nearly so, for they cut themselves out of all reason for existence by laying waste the Cedar without thought to the future. Others have prospered as they diversified their interests. For Bandon, once known as the prettiest town in Oregon, a special fate was reserved. It was founded by Lord George Bennet, an Irish peer, who made things more homelike, in the eighteen-seventies of the last century, by naturalizing the Irish furze or gorse, and as the majestic stands of Cedar were cleared away, it took hold in fine style on the logged-over lands, and was much admired, in spite of its thorns, for its golden pea-like flowers. By 1936 Bandon was a pretty beach resort at the mouth of the Coquille River surrounded by a sea of gorse, and on the hot dry night of September 26 much of the population was at the motion-picture theater seeing a film prophetically titled *Thirty-Six Hours To Live*. Suddenly on the edge of town there was a flash of flame like an explosion. The tinder-dry gorse caught fire for miles around in a matter of a few moments, and a sea of flames thirty feet high rolled toward the town. Fireproof buildings burned like berry crates. The loss of life and homes was so appalling that one scarcely cares to mention what had happened to the precious resource of the Port Orford Cedar. It wiped out thousands of acres of second growth of this species and probably blasted all hopes of restocking many more acres, though it did not reach the old growth or virgin stands.

But logging, there, has proved the equal of the worst crown fires. The stand of merchantable Port Orford Cedar had sunk to 1,140,000,-000 board feet in 1938, and in 9 years of further cutting the figure has dropped to 745,000,000 board feet. The virgin timber cannot last more than a quarter century at the present rate of cut. Second growth, what there is of it, is the only hope.

In 1938, the U.S. Forest Service set aside the Port Orford Cedar Experimental Forest, on the South Fork of the Coquille River, for purposes of regeneration and practical forestry. The tract is so situated that it will be safe from inroads of fire and logging. And well it is that this should be so. Today 69 per cent of this precious timber is in private ownership, which means that its destiny is the saw mill whenever the stumpage price is attractive enough to the land owners, while

15 per cent is held on the Oregon and California Railway revested grant lands managed by the Department of Interior. Only 16 per cent is in the hands of Forest Service. Very small tracts are owned as parks by the state of Oregon.

The best way to see this tree of almost legendary fame is to follow U.S. Highway 101 between Reedsport and Gold Beach, Oregon, where the Pacific comes rolling in with heavy thundering surges, pushing foam castles up the black sand of the beaches, shooting up in geysers against the isolated stack rocks, and sending its cold briny breath deep into the forest. Grand Firs, mighty Douglas Firs, Sitka Spruce, and waving Hemlocks march down from the Coast Ranges to the steep-pitched meadows — brief carpets of sunlight and flowering that end at the ocean cliffs. And here, along the roadsides and on the steep wooded hills, rises a tree that you may take at first for Western Red Cedar, so alike are the two in their flat sprays of foliage. But Western Red or Canoe Cedar (Arbor-vitæ to the garden-minded) has the foliage shining yellow-green on the upper surface, dull green below. Port Orford Cedar, which is notably finer, thinner, and in every way more ferny of frond, is a dull blue-green above and often flecked with a frosty whiteness below. In young trees, or trees grown in the open, the limber, zigzag branches clothe the specimen to the base. But the forest monarch, which may have lived 600 years, will have an awesomely long straight trunk covered with a soft, fibrous, fluted bark, and a very narrow crown of branches which droop with a grand but sorrowful gesture.

By exploring in your car up many roads — the more unpromising the better — you may find at last some limited grove of ancients, whose lonely isolation tells the story of their vanished monarchy. And you will want to cut a twig just to smell that spicy odor, one of the strongest and most lingering given out by any commercial wood — the odor that, in the old sailing schooners that bore the fresh-cut Cedar across the Pacific, grew and grew upon the sailors till they were almost mad with it.

Though always on the rare side in the wild, and growing steadily rarer, this tree, under the horticultural name of Lawson Cypress, is widespread in the gardens of the world, partly for its natural beauty, and partly for another sort that to a forester at least is more or less unnatural. For this, like all the six species of *Chamæcyparis*, is given to the production, under cultivation, of freaks, sports, and showy variations such as never exist in the wild. Eighty such have been described for Lawson Cypress — forms with silver-tipped or golden-tipped foliage, and columnar forms, sprawling forms, weeping forms, glaucous forms, blue forms, glittering forms — bearing such over-dressed Latin names as "elegantissima" and "erecta glauca." More, this and other species of *Chamæcyparis* sometimes produce in the seedling stage abnormal needle foliage something like that of a Balsam Fir or Yew, and if offsets of these freaks are propagated, they continue to produce throughout life this abnormal showy foliage. When this is combined with, for instance, a dwarf but narrowly conical and compact habit, the ultimate in artificiality is obtained, and under the name of "Retinospora" (which is more gardener's Latin and not a recognized botanical genus), such plants are dearly beloved by the architect. For they look formal and expensive against the stone walls of a fashionable church or outside a city mansion. But a Port Orford Cedar springing straight and aboriginal from the wild Oregon soil is a nobler sight to anyone who loves a tree as God made it.

THE JUNIPERS
(*Juniperus*)

THESE ARE aromatic trees with durable, close-grained, soft wood and thin shreddy bark. The scale-like leaves occur in pairs or threes on the twig; the minute flowers (with the sexes borne on separate trees) appear from buds formed the previous autumn, in small lateral catkins, the male with numerous stamens in pairs or threes, the female with 2 to 6 pairs of pointed scales each bearing on its inner face a minute ovule-bearing scale. The female flower scales fuse, after fertilization, into a succulent pulp surrounding the bony seeds and enclosed in a skin, thus forming a berry-like fruit.

*   *   *

UTAH JUNIPER

Juniperus osteosperma (Torrey) Little

OTHER NAME: Desert Cedar.

RANGE: Mountains of southeastern Idaho and southwestern Wyoming throughout Nevada and Utah at elevations of 5000 to 8000 feet, to the desert (eastern) slopes of the Sierra Nevada and northern slopes of the San Bernardinos and on the Panamint Mountains above Death Valley; on mountains, mesas, and high plains of northern and north-central Arizona.

DESCRIPTION: *Bark* of mature trees finely divided by narrow deep furrows, into long, thin, fibrous ridges, ashy gray weathering to whitish. *Twigs* slender, stiff-looking, yellow-green, covered after leaf fall with a thin, light, red-brown, scaly bark. *Leaves* about ⅛ inch long on mature shoots, pale yellowish green, scale-like and in opposite pairs making 4 rows, or in whorls of 3 making 6 rows on the twig. *Berries* about ⅓ inch long, red-brown covered with a bluish white bloom, prominently roughened at the top by the persistent tips of the flower scales, the skin tough, the flesh strongly aromatic from the presence of numerous resin canals. *Seeds* 1 or rarely 2 to a berry, sharply angled and prominent-pointed, with conspicuous scale-like hilum. *Wood* durable but brittle and soft, medium-light (34½ pounds per cubic foot, dry weight), and much less aromatic than that of most Junipers, with light yellowish-brown heartwood and thick white sapwood.

On the very edge of the opened book of the Grand Canyon — page upon page of red stone tablets receding away into the purple shadows of a billion years of time gone by — perches the Utah Juniper. Now erect of stem, with crown symmetrically intact, now aslant over the awesome chasm, with storm-torn, broken head, and stem contorted as by the whirl of the winds themselves or lightning-riven and stripped to the white bones of half its bark — this indomitable tree dares the south rim of the Canyon for miles. And when you step gingerly to the edge and look down into the vast emptiness, you see this Juniper far below you, dotting the bridle trail, clinging to perilous ledges, springing out of crevices in the rocks, sprinkling the giddy slopes of talus, a symbol of undefeated life in an abyss of death. From this only silence wells up to you, a silence as of outer and infinite space, where interplanetary gales could blow and make no sound. But when you stand by a rim Juniper you hear the whistling of the wind in its sharp-angled foliage, a high thin vibration of an elemental harp, and it is a comforting sound; it is a sort of message from green life, in all this dead geology. Yet in its way the living tree, the older and craggier it grows, seems the most consonant of possible trees with this, the most stupendous site in all the world.

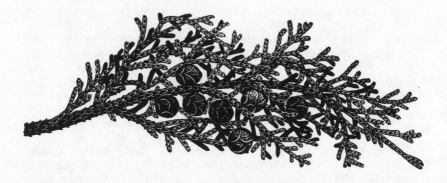

South of the Grand Canyon, from Ashfork, Arizona, for mile upon mile, the Utah Juniper forms an open forest, below the belt of Pinyon and Yellow Pine, looking handsome and vital, with its dark green masses in contrast with the gray-green of the sagebrush. And indeed everywhere in the Great Basin — between the Rockies on the east and the Sierra Nevada and Cascade ranges on the west — this tree is likely to be the most abundant, as it is the most widely distributed, at least in the life-zone called the Upper Sonoran. It dots the mesas, descends the canyons, climbs the mountains. In its namesake state of Utah it is as characteristic a settler as the Mormons, and in its venerable age sometimes reminds you of an old patriarch of the sect — rugged and weathered and twisted by hardship, but hard too to discourage or kill. Utah's famed Cedar Breaks (breaks meaning great natural ampitheaters in mountain and mesa) take their name from this tree, and so does historic Cedar City. It is the Chief Inhabitant, amongst trees, of Bryce Canyon National Park, that "petrified sunset," as it has been called. No other tree, it seems, is so well fitted as this one to endure the arid, wind-blown, sand-swept land of Deseret.

Like most desert trees, the Utah Juniper is unimpressive in height, for it seldom grows more than 20 feet tall, and it is extremely slow of growth. A trunk with a diameter of no more than 6 to 10 inches may show an annual ring count of 145 to 250 years of life, and some of the ancients near the Grand Canyon with trunks 3 feet thick have been claimed as trimillenial. This may be doubted, but old they certainly are, as they are grand, with their broken, leaning crowns, their contorted stems, and heavy coats of long fibrous bark strips which are generally so weathered by sun and sand that they are whitish instead of their natural brown.

Almost every Utah Juniper is heavily infested by parasitic mistletoe, so much so that these tufts of pale yellowish green foliage — a sickly color appearing more dead than alive — are a characteristic feature of this tree. The lusterless lead-white of the mistletoe's berries mingles with the Juniper berries, red-brown washed by a soft bluish-gray cast, and both are highly attractive to western birds.

The short, branched, contorted stems of Utah Juniper have never allured the lumberman, though fence posts are made of the durable wood and it makes a fine fuel that burns, however, without the fragrance of some of the other species. But in the lives of the desert Indians, from ancient times, this tree has figured importantly. In the Gypsum Cave dwellings of the prehistoric red men in Nevada, M. R. Harrington discovered that Juniper bark had been used extensively for cordage. The vanished race, pedantically called the Basket Maker II people, manufactured an unfired clay pottery which was molded in baskets and given a strengthening of Juniper bark, just as we make bricks with straw. Basket Maker II infants were carried in cradles of Juniper bark bound with yucca fibers, and the bark went into the making of sandals and was woven into bags. In the famed pit houses of the Southwest, Juniper bark was used as a thatch under the earthen covering of the roof, and as a cordage to lash the wooden uprights of the house to the stringers. On the walls of the pit houses were hung coverings of Juniper bark matting.

In a side valley of the Grand Canyon today lives the small tribe of Havasupai, a people of the Yuman stock. In the life of the Havasupai the Utah Juniper figures from babyhood to the grave. When the child is born he is covered with Juniper bark which his mother has rubbed very soft for his tender skin, then swaddled in a blanket and placed in a Juniper cradle. From the bark are fashioned the dolls with which he first plays, and he sleeps on an oval mat of the bark. When he is weaned, he begins to eat the berries of the Juniper, and in winter he is warmed at a fire which has been made by his father's starting a spark in tinder of the dried bark. When he reaches puberty, the

Havasupai boy carries a slow-match or spill of twisted Juniper bark, running toward the dawn as far as he can with it, touching his ankles, knees, wrists, and elbows with the fire, to keep him, so goes the belief, from getting rheumatism. Then he throws the slow-match over his head so that he will be able to recall forgotten articles when he sets out from camp. When he marries, the young Havasupai brings his wife to a bed of Juniper bark.

The closely related Yavapai Indians give a woman a drink of tea of Juniper leaves after the birth of her child, to promote muscular relaxation following the violent contractions she has endured, and later she will be "fumigated" with smoke of the leaves laid on hot coals. If the Havasupai is wounded, he uses Juniper gum as we use "New-Skin," to make a protective membrane over the sore until it can heal. When a Navaho dies, the two men who attended him to the last back carefully away from the grave, sweeping their tracks with Juniper boughs so that deathliness shall not follow them from the grave.

CALIFORNIA JUNIPER

Juniperus californica Carrière

OTHER NAMES: California White Cedar. Sweet Berry Cedar.

RANGE: Inner Coast Ranges of California from Lake County (foothills to 4000 feet above sea level) south to the Tehachapi Mountains and thence northward through the foothills and lower slopes of the southern Sierra Nevada, especially the desert (eastern) slopes up to 5000 feet altitude; common on the desert (northern and eastern) slopes of the Sierra Liebre and San Bernardino and San Gabriel Mountains (occasional on the seaward or southern slopes, as at Pasadena) and on both sides of the Coast Ranges in San Diego County to the Mexican border; reported from the San Pedro Mártir mountains of Baja California.

DESCRIPTION: *Bark* scaly, red-brown beneath the gray-weathered surface. *Twigs* stout after leaf fall, with thin scaly bark of a pale ashy-brown hue. *Leaves* ⅛ inch long on mature shoots, grouped in whorls of 3 on the twig, keeled and conspicuously glandular-pitted on the back, pale yellowish green (not gray-green or ashy). *Berries* ¼ to ½ inch thick, with the loose, papery, and extremely thin skin dark red-brown under a whitish bloom, the flesh dry, mealy, and fibrous but sweet and without resin cells. *Seeds* 1 or 2 to a berry, angular and irregularly grooved but not pitted.

Wood fine-grained, soft, brittle, splitting easily, medium-light (39 pounds per cubic foot, dry weight), slightly aromatic, pale brown tinged with red.

Much of the time the California Juniper is only a big brushy shrub, where it grows with the splendid Yucca called Our-Lord's-candle, on the mountainous fringes of the western Mojave desert. But not infrequently it rises to be a tree from 20 to 30 feet high, with a conical crown, and a single, short trunk that may be 20 inches in diameter. In old trees — the life span may be as much as 250 years — the branches often become large and greatly distorted. The value of California Juniper is found in its ability to thrive in the hot, dry hills of the inner (eastern) face of the southern Coast Ranges. When rain falls here it comes all at once, in a few weeks of winter or an occasional summer thunderstorm, and on the scantily covered clays it works with destructive force of erosion. The California Juniper is the largest tree or shrub throughout much of this area, and its power to check erosion is inestimable.

DROOPING JUNIPER

Juniperus flaccida Schlectendahl

OTHER NAME: Drooping Cedar.

RANGE: Northeastern Mexico to the Chisos Mountains (at 6000 to 8000 feet) of western Texas.

DESCRIPTION: *Bark* ½ to 1½ inches thick, firm, separating into long, narrow, loosely attached scales, red-brown beneath, but on the surface weathered gray. *Twigs* drooping, slim, with bright cinnamon-colored, loosely scaly bark. *Leaves* on mature shoots in pairs alternately at right angles, ⅛ inch long, the long points somewhat spreading at tip and prickly to the touch, the margins minutely toothed, the back with or without glandular resin pits, light yellow-green. *Berries* ⅓ to ⅝ inch thick, dull brown under a glaucous bloom, with close firm skin and thick, resinous, dry, and hard flesh. *Seeds* 4 to 12, irregularly shaped, ⅛ to ¼ inch long. *Wood* hard, heavy, durable, the heartwood clear yellow-brown, the sapwood thick and white.

The Drooping Juniper is chiefly a Mexican tree, found at present in but one region in the United States, namely the Chisos Mountains of western Texas, in the crook of the Big Bend, as they call the country where the Rio Grande makes a long dip to the south, then turns north again on its course to the Gulf. On those mountains, some of the most dramatic and rugged and least known in North America, the Drooping Juniper is common, growing on dry rocky benches, slopes and ridges, and equally in the deep, gravelly and sandy soil at the bottoms of well-watered canyons. Formerly, according to the testimony of old stockmen in the Big Bend country, the Drooping Juniper was much more common in the Chisos range than now, but about 75 years ago large amounts of the biggest trees were cut for timbering the mines of Boquillos, Mexico. For the fragrant wood is very long-lasting and resistant to the decay attendant on posts in mines.

The Drooping Juniper is strikingly unlike any of its kin in its distinctly "weeping" habit, the twigs and sprays of foliage hanging with a flaccid grace. The trunks are slender for a Juniper and straight, and though the tree is not tall — 25 feet at the most — a tree it is distinctly, never tending to a bushy habit like so many of our western species.

ALLIGATOR JUNIPER

Juniperus Deppeana Steudel

OTHER NAMES: Mountain, Thickbark, Oak-barked, or Checker-barked Cedar.

RANGE: Mountains of central and southeastern Arizona, central and southwestern New Mexico, and western Texas and south to northern Mexico (Sonora, Chihuahua and Coahuila).

DESCRIPTION: *Bark* dark red-brown, 1 to 4 inches thick, and broken up, Oak-like, by cross-checks as well as furrows, into numberless small flat-topped plates, 1 or 2 inches square. *Twigs* slender, 4-angled and pale blue-green; after leaf fall covered with thin, light, reddish brown, close bark. *Leaves* of mature growth bluish green, scale-like, scarcely ⅛ inch long, in opposite pairs. *Berries* ½ inch thick, dark red-brown more or less overcast with a whitish bloom at least during the first season, with thin skin and thick, dry, mealy flesh. *Seeds* 4, pointed. *Wood* close-grained, soft, brittle, aromatic, durable, medium-light (36½ pounds per cubic foot, dry weight), the heartwood clear light yellow sometimes streaked with red, the sapwood thin and whitish.

Gallant Dr. Samuel Washington Woodhouse, the surgeon-naturalist who first collected specimens of the Alligator Juniper, back in the days 1851) of Captian Lorenzo Sitgreave's exploration for a route from the Zuñi pueblo of New Mexico to San Diego, California, worked under difficulties, to say the least. The Navahoes were on the war path, and terrible thirst and near starvation plagued the party on the dread Gila desert. While warming himself by a fire in Arizona, he was shot through the leg by the arrow of a Yavapai Indian. But even before the expedition got well under way he had been bitten in the hand by a rattlesnake which he thought he had killed. The surgeon applied to his bite tourniquet and suction, *"aqua ammonia fortis,"* swallowed "pulv. doveri grs. x, mass hydg., and ext, collocynth comp." and on the advice of an old Westerner got dead drunk on snakebite whiskey and brandy. Yet he lived — to the age of 83, dying in 1914, last of the old Army surgeon-naturalists — but was denied the use of his right hand throughout most of the expedition.

At Camps 19 and 20 (between Bill Williams Fork and the San Francisco Mountains), Woodhouse records, "found the rough-barked cedar and I procured specimens with the fruit . . . About this camp a beautiful species of phlox [1] was growing quite abundantly . . . saw numerous wild turkeys, Steller's jay. Deer plenty. On the edge of the mountains the air is filled with a sweet perfume from the *Fallugia paradoxa"* (Apache-plume). Captain Sitgreaves too alludes in his diary to the tree and the beauty of the scene when all the West was bright with virginity and danger; "Oct 21, Camp No. 19. Occasional patches of white clover were again met with, and the singular cedar first seen when crossing the Zuñi mountains. The trunk is large and

1 *Phlox Woodhousei* Torrey.

low, with wide-spreading branches, and the bark, several inches thick, is corrugated like that of the oak. The camp overlooked a wild picturesque cañon. Tall pines, oaks, and the low, spreading cedar were mingled so as to produce a park-like effect." [1] A fine old steel-engraving plate illustrates the "park-like" country, with the earliest of all pictures of this, the king of the western Junipers.

For the Alligator Juniper may grow as much as 60 feet high and produce a trunk 4 to 6 feet in diameter. If the tree has room to expand it does not usually grow so high, but at all times it has a very decisive single stem, much unlike many of the more bushy species. The portion of the trunk clear of branches even in old trees is not great, but the parasol-like breadth of the crown of old trees makes it look even shorter than it is, and this must explain how Sitgreaves could call it a "low cedar."

If all the Junipers were as easy to distinguish as this one, they would not be the distracting lot that they are in the West. The chequered bark is unique, and its resemblance to a saurian hide has well earned for it the name of Alligator Juniper. So apt is the description that if you have ever heard of the existence of such a tree you identify it upon your first sight of it.

[1] Lorenzo Sitgreaves, "Report of an expedition down the Zuñi and Colorado rivers." *U.S. Senate Executive Document,* 33d Congress, 1st Session. 1854.

SIERRA JUNIPER

Juniperus occidentalis Hooker

OTHER NAMES: Western Juniper. Yellow or Western Red Cedar.

RANGE: Low hills and high plains of southeastern Washington (where rare), canyons, bluffs, mesas and foothills of northeastern and central Oregon (Blue, Maury and Warner Mountains, Klamath River basin, Powder River Mountains), east slopes of the Cascades, rare on the west slopes, not present in the Coast Ranges; in Idaho only in extreme west-central portion; in California from Mount Shasta and Lassen Peak southward the whole length of the Sierra, at increasingly high altitudes (2500 feet in the north to 10,200 feet above sea level in the Mineral King region); on the desert ranges (Panamints, north slope of Telescope Peak above 9000 feet), on the north Coast Ranges (Siskiyous and in the Trinity Mountains); in southern California at 9500 feet in the San

Bernardino Mountains and 10,000 feet on Mount San Antonio in the San Gabriels; reported from the highest summits of the San Jacinto Mountains and the San Pedro Mártirs in Baja California. In Nevada only in the Lake Tulare region.

DESCRIPTION: *Bark* firm, stringy, shallowly furrowed into long flat ridges connected by a network of diagonals, light cinnamon-brown, ½ to 1¼ inches thick. *Twigs* rounded and stout and, after leaf fall, papery-scaly and bright red-brown. *Leaves* scale-like, ⅛ inch long, gray-green, distinctly gland-pitted on the back, and fringed with fine teeth, occurring in threes or in pairs alternately at right angles, flattened to the twig or, on vigorous young shoots, with spreading tips. *Berry* blue-black with a bloom, ¼ to ⅓ inch in diameter; flesh thin and resinous, skin tough. *Seeds* with bony shells ⅛ inch long, 2 or 3 in each fruit, acute, deeply pitted or grooved on back, flat on inner face. *Wood* durable, medium-light (36 pounds per cubic foot, dry weight), soft, and brittle, the heartwood pale reddish brown, the sapwood thick and white.

The traveler leaving Yosemite National Park by the road over the Tioga Pass (9971 feet above sea level) motors up and up through one of the most magnificent coniferous forests in the world, to just above timber line at the top of the pass. But as he descends the precipitous eastern slopes of the Sierra Nevada, he encounters no such sylva as those mountains bear on their western flanks which intercept the rain-bearing winds from the Pacific. Instead, far as the eye can see from the roadway, stretches the Nevada desert, gray with sagebrush or whitened with alkali playas, only the intense, enameled blue of Mono Lake gleaming in it like a lost jewel. All about the twisting road are barren rocks, thinly dotted with scrubby growths or a few unprofitable-looking alpine trees. But one tree there is — the Sierra Juniper — which seems undaunted by the winters' snows, the summers' droughts, the winds that never cease to blow, the lack of soil, the acidity of the granite crags. It is a tree that seems positively to rejoice in the most inhospitable situations and, with a flair for the dramatic, to fix itself upon isolated pinnacles of rock, or overhanging giddy chasms, there to outlive the generations of men. John Muir believed that it could endure 2000 years, though only half that much is allowed it by most dendrologists. But the poet of the Sierra is right when he says that it is a tree that "dies standing, and wastes insensibly out of existence like granite."

Along the road from Tioga Pass to Mono Lake these Junipers are frequently but 8, 10, and 15 feet high, yet their flat-topped or broken crowns may be as broad or broader, while the trunks of aged trees are fantastically chunky in proportion to the height; columns 25 and 29 feet in circumference at 4 feet from the ground were measured by John Muir. These trunks are picturesquely furrowed and buttressed and fluted, giving them an air of Jovian age and nobility, the bright cinnamon-red of the stringy outer bark standing out as handsomely as some freshly broken surface of mineral or rock in contrast with the hoary or ashen green of the tufts of foliage. And these craggy trees develop immensely long, thick roots; these go straddling the rocks in all directions, clinging for support like the claws of a great beast, and seeking in every cranny for some thread of water. Commonly the root system visible to the eye is nearly as extensive as the rest of the tree, and seems like an inverted or mirror image of the stem and branches and crown.

In more favorable situations, on level land, with a better ground water supply, the tree attains what is its more normal if less picturesque form. The trunks are far more slender and but little fluted and furrowed; the crown is narrower and more symmetrical, the root system hidden beneath the soil. Heights up to 60 feet are sometimes reached, on the high plateaux of northeastern California, but never with any great length of trunk clear of branches. In consequence, the wood is always too knotty for ordinary lumbering purposes, but the great durability of it does make it ideal for fence posts, and for that purpose it has been cut as needed by ranchers for many decades, yet will continue to furnish good posts through the foreseeable future.

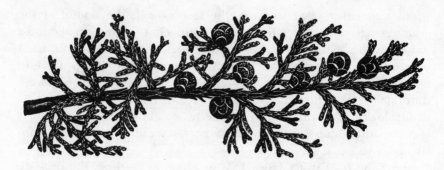

CHERRYSTONE JUNIPER

Juniperus monosperma (Engelmann) Sargent

OTHER NAMES: Oneseed Juniper. New Mexico Cedar.

RANGE: Mesas and mountains from Utah and western Colorado to eastern
Nevada, Arizona, except the southwestern section, and Texas (Panhandle,
Big Bend, and Edwards Plateau). In northern Sonora and Chihuahua.

DESCRIPTION: *Bark* thin, soft, ashy gray, deeply and narrowly furrowed,
with flat, stringy, and fibrous ridges. *Twigs* slender, 4-angled but after
leaf fall becoming roundish, loosely scaly, and red-brown. *Leaves* on
mature growth in alternating pairs or rarely 3 in a whorl, scale-like, ⅛
inch long and acute, slightly spreading at the tips, otherwise flattened to
the stem, gray-green, the back thickened and rounded and usually
glandular, and fringed on the edge with minute teeth. *Berries* copper-
colored or rarely blue, under a glaucous bloom, ⅛ to ¼ inch thick;
flesh thin. *Seed* 1 (rarely a pair) often 4-angled and marked at base by
a little 2-lobed hilum. *Wood* durable, rather heavy (44½ pounds per
cubic foot, dry weight), and hard, with yellow-brown to red-brown heartwood and white sapwood.

"One evening in the autumn of 1851 a solitary horseman, followed
by a pack-mule, was pushing through an arid stretch of country somewhere in central New Mexico. He . . . was trying to find his way back
to the trail. . . . The difficulty was that the country in which he found
himself was so featureless — or rather, that it was crowded with features, all exactly alike. As far as he could see, on every side, the landscape was heaped up into monotonous red sand-hills . . . exactly the
shape of Mexican ovens, red as brick-dust, and naked of vegetation except for small juniper trees. And the junipers, too, were the shape of
Mexican ovens. Every conical hill was spotted with smaller cones of

juniper, a uniform yellowish green, as the hills were a uniform red."

Thus, in the opening pages of *Death Comes for the Archbishop*, does Willa Cather describe the Cherrystone Juniper's interminable monotony. It is not a dreary repetition, since this is rather a bright tree and likely to yield from its growth the flashing blue of a pinyon jay, the call of a Gambel quail, the slinking form of a coyote, a handful of mistletoe, an unexpected burro, or an even more unexpected Indian urchin. But reiterant it certainly is — in form, in color, in sun-baked fragrance.

It is hard, if possible at all, to think of another southwestern tree that, unaccompanied by another species, covers so vast an area — uncalculated thousands of acres of the old Spanish country. Again, it may have a single companion, no taller, no more varied, than itself, the Pinyon. Together these two come to haunt all our memories of the red hill country of New Mexico. And they are happy memories, full of the high curved turquoise of her skies, full of sweet aromas, of the startling liquid voice of thrashers, of the spell of the pueblos, their art and their deeply religious bronze-skinned peoples. He is lost to simplicity who complains of their monotony. What is more monotonous than the streets, the buildings, the gray, damp, low-skied days to which he is apt to return from the country of the Juniper? Many a time we would gladly exchange all that to see again the conical spires of this evergreen rising from the ruddy domes of the little hills down Santa Fe way.

The very air of the old town of Santa Fe entices the visitor, transporting him, from the world of speed and noise, to an older and sweeter way of life, where travel is at the burro's pace, where the commonest sounds are the tinkling of the *acequias* that slide and glitter through gardens and streets, the clangor of old bells with much silver in their copper, and the soft commingling of Spanish and Indian tongues. For in place of gasoline fumes, Santa Fe's soft dry air is pervaded by the smell of Pinyon smoke, blent with the odor of the *enebro* wood, as the Spanish-speaking people call the Juniper — a mingled perfume, sweet as the curling smoke from some church censer.

And you sniff it everywhere, upon the airs — not only in the narrow *calles* of Santa Fe and Taos, but throughout the pueblos of the southwest and in the long-settled, warm, Spanish-speaking part of Colorado. For the Indians and the Spanish-Americans, even in the towns, often cook by wood fires, in those outdoor bake ovens of clay that look like old-fashioned skeps. For heating, the wood of true Pinyon pine is pre-

ferred by many people, but Juniper is employed in cooking, because
of the intensity of its heat and its glowing bed of coals. It has, however, the disadvantage, in an open hearth, of throwing sparks and is
used there chiefly to clean out flues and chimneys, according to Haniel
Long, the distinguished author of *Piñon Country*.

Twenty and thirty years ago if you went walking in the Pinyon- and
Juniper-clad hills around Santa Fe you were almost certain to meet the
head of a donkey bobbing toward you on the trail; then you saw the
big faggot of *enebro* on his back, fixed there on a wooden saddle frame,
and behind him paced an old man, or a small boy, carrying a stick for
the better correction of the burro's innate sin of sloth. This was Santa
Fe's fuel supply — perhaps four dozen crooked sticks of dead and seasoned wood at a time, advancing at the slowest rate that the burro
could manage. It followed, therefore, that there had to be more than
one old man and donkey, and indeed the woods were full of them, all
wending their way from the surrounding hills to the little adobe city.
It was the same around Taos and every other town wherever the
Juniper grows and the Spanish tongue is spoken; the streets, between
the adobe walls, especially toward twilight, were filled with the clatter
of burdened donkeys. They delivered the wood directly to the householder's gate in the wall, without any middleman to take away the
pleasures of the courteous greeting from the vendor, of the buyer's pat
on the little burro's flank, a word or two in his cocked ears, and a
Vaya con Dios as beast and man depart. Today trucks go rattling out
on the roads and the wood is delivered without picturesque accompani-
ments.

Cherrystone Juniper grows up to 60 feet high or even more, but generally it is much shorter; often the tree is as broad as high, and usually
there are several forks from near the base; in any case the trunk, however thick and old, is always short, sometimes with branches coming
out close to the ground and resting their tips upon it, or, again, the
trunk is bare of branches below, revealing its picturesque contortions.
With age the trunk becomes fluted and buttressed, covered with twisting strands of soft fibrous bark. Some specimens are believed to be 500
years old. A trunk only 5 to 7 inches in diameter represents, in general,
a life of 175 to 195 years, while trunks 10 to 12 inches thick have
yielded 315 to 375 annual growth rings.

Probably the most fantastic and ancient specimens, certainly the
most exclaimed-over and photographed, are those in The Garden of
the Gods, that stage set of geologic drama, that playground of centuries

of erosion and droves of summer tourists, with Pikes Peak for a back-drop. Here, amid fantasies in upturned sedimentary red rocks, are ancients of this race of trees with trunks twisted and crowns lopsided as if to rival the most extravagant whimsies of this unearthly spot. The Juniper known to the Garden guides as "Methusaleh" has several enormous stems all forking from the ground and leaning out from each other, much like the trunks of a Crack Willow, each one seemingly mighty enough to be the bole of a fair-sized tree, each top with a crown of rich green foliage that, with the red of the rocks and the white of Pike's snows, paint the Garden in elemental splendor. "Methusaleh" is claimed, or rather guessed, to be 900 years old. There may be grave doubt of that many, but several centuries at least must have produced such a growth. Although the ground around it is littered with bark strips and dead and broken boughs, there is promise still of indefinite life in this grand old specimen.

The Navaho eats the berries of this Juniper in the winter or fall when they are ripe. In times of food shortage, these people chew the inner bark. When the snow is deep, branches are lopped off for the sheep to eat. Wool is dyed green with the bark and berries by the Navaho weavers. The Navahos say that the beautiful margins of their baskets are an imitation of the overlapping of Juniper leaves. To this day in the Navaho war dance a stick of this Juniper is carried. All the twigs except a small bunch at the tip are first pruned away and with it is bound a bunch of rabbitweed or snakeweed. Prayer sticks, war bow, and bows for the canopy of the papoose cradle are made by the Navaho of the wood of this tree, and they use it as charcoal for smelting their famous silver jewelry.

The wood is close-ringed, and in consequence hard and dense. Like that of most Junipers it is, if properly seasoned, strongly resistant to decay, and is used locally for ranch fence posts, though there is never enough clear lumber to make boards of it. A pity, since it has a delicious Cedar-like fragrance, and handsomely contrasting ruddy heartwood and clear pale sapwood.

The female trees are sought for their berries by the Hopi chipmunk, quail, fox, rock squirrel, and deer. Both sexes yield browse to New Mexico's omnivorous goats — but what does not?

WEST–TEXAS JUNIPER

Juniperus texensis van Melle

OTHER NAMES: Mountain or Rock Cedar, Mountain Juniper.

RANGE: Trans-Pecos and Big Bend country of western Texas,' and in canyons of the Texas Panhandle. Sonora, Mexico and probably also in adjacent parts of New Mexico.

DESCRIPTION: *Bark* ashy gray, soft and fibrous, peeling in longitudinal strips. *Twigs* rather slender, reddish-brown and loosely scaly. *Leaves* light yellow-green, in opposite pairs or whorls of 3, scale-like, flattened (except at the spreading tips) to the twig, rounded and often glandular on the back. *Flowers* with the sexes on separate trees or in separate catkins on the same tree. *Berries* globose to conical-ovoid, ⅜ to ⅝ inch long, as green as the foliage when they first appear, becoming when ripe nut-brown or yellowish brown or more rarely rose-red or bright reddish brown, turning as they grow old to a dull gray or grayish brown or purplish gray, never bluish or glaucous. *Seeds* 1 to 2 (rarely 3) to a berry, marked with 3 to 5 longitudinal grooves, and a large hilum.

Not distinguished and described until 1952, this species is at the present writing so new that little is certainly known about it as a separate entity. Its wood has not been analyzed for any physical and chemical properties; its distribution is still, probably, imperfectly known, and references to it, in literature, are concealed under the names of the Cherrystone Juniper, the Mexican Juniper and perhaps other Junipers of western Texas. Specimens of this species in herbaria show that botanical explorers have been collecting it since the sixties of the last century without recognizing it as distinct, and so it is generally mislabeled in exsiccates.

The Texas Juniper forms a low bushy tree, usually about 18 feet high, but in narrow canyons and crowded among other trees it is often considerably higher. Generally it has two main forks beginning low down and ascending more or less widely, with ramified branches, to form an open, broken, broad or dome-shaped crown. Very commonly the tree is much broader than high, except in crowded conditions, when it may become slenderly conical.

The fruits ripen the second year, from autumn to early spring, but often cling on the tree, gradually losing their color and turning dull gray, but not their resinous juiciness through the following summer. They are eaten in fall by Townsend solitaires, those birds of modest plumage and exquisite voice. Of course they are silent when feeding among the Junipers in the autumn, but anything is blessed that nourishes these birds whose hermit-like song, warbling and long sustained, is one of the most mysterious and unexpected voices in all the West.

The favorite site of the Texas Juniper is in the lonely, grand, arid mountain chains of Texas west of the Pecos River — in the great bend of the Rio Grande. It grows on the Chisos, Guadalupe and Davis Mountains, in the Sierra Diabolos, and quite generally in Big Bend National Park. Its common associates in the Park are the Cherrystone, Alligator, and Weeping Junipers. From the last two, West-Texas Juniper is distinguished by the fact that its branches are not "weeping" and its bark is not marked off into small corky segments like the hide of an alligator. From the Cherrystone Juniper, which it most closely resembles, it must be distinguished solely by its berries and seeds. The berries show no slightest trace of gray or bluish bloom; they are less coarsely wrinkled than those of Cherrystone Juniper and are much less juicy. The berries of West-Texas Juniper are also a little smaller, only $\frac{3}{8}$ to $\frac{5}{8}$ inch in diameter, while those of Cherrystone Juniper are $\frac{1}{8}$ to $\frac{1}{4}$ inch thick.

In the lower, rolling country just east of the Llano Estacado or Staked Plains, West-Texas Juniper is said by van Melle to be the only Juniper to be seen. But it creeps up into some of the deep canyons of this Panhandle region, notably Palo Duro Canyon, scene of fierce battles with the Comanches after the Civil War. The Palo Duro forms a "system of canyons nearly sixty miles long and a thousand feet in depth, varying from a few hundred yards in width to extensive bad lands fifteen miles across. It furnished shelter from the northers of the bleak plains and water and grass sufficient for many thousands of cattle. Its cottonwood, wild china, hackberry and cedars had been fuel and shade for Comanche camps from time long past, and a *comanchero* told Goodnight that he had once seen 12000 Indian horses grazing therein." [1] Here of Cedar (that is, Juniper) logs Goodnight built his first two-room house and so abundant then were the Cedars that in 1880 Goodnight agreed to repay the suttlers who brought out from Dodge City six months supply of food, feed, and 67 miles of barbed wire, by allowing them to cut Cedar. So handsomely did they reimburse themselves that the old cattleman was sick at the sight of their devastation. Yet he had enough Junipers left to build corrals and fences for the whole of the great JA ranch.

[1] *Charles Goodnight* by J. Evetts Haley. University of Oklahoma Press, 1936.

ROCKY MOUNTAIN JUNIPER

Juniperus scopulorum Sargent

OTHER NAMES: Mountain Red Cedar. Weeping Juniper.

RANGE: From British Columbia (frequent in the Rockies, rare in the Coast Ranges and on Vancouver Island), and the Rockies of Alberta (where rare), south in the American Rockies to the mountains of western Texas and south-central Arizona, at increasingly high altitudes (4000 to 8000 feet above sea level), and in the mountains of eastern and central Washington (rare on the Olympic peninsula), eastern Oregon and most of the mountains of Utah and some of those of eastern Nevada. Also on high plains, buttes, mesas, and bluffs lying east of the mountains in Montana, the Dakotas (western halves), and western Nebraska.

DESCRIPTION: *Bark* weathered grayish outwardly, red-brown underneath, stringy, seamed, and with braiding and twisted ridges. *Twigs* slender, 4-angled and, after leaf fall, pale brown, smooth, round, and sometimes pendent. *Leaves* in pairs alternately at right angles, ⅛ inch long, dark or gray-green, with smooth margins and only obscurely pitted. *Berries* ¼ to ⅓ inch in diameter, clear blue under a glaucous cast; skin thin; flesh resinous, sweet. *Seeds* 1 or 2 (rarely 3) to a berry, angled and sharp-pointed, with bony shell. *Wood* soft, smooth-grained, light, with heart-wood bright red streaked with white and thick white sapwood.

The Rocky Mountain Juniper is very closely related to the famed Eastern Red Cedar, and the early western explorers did not distinguish it in their reports, as they sighted it on the eastern flanks of the Rockies all the way from Alberta to Texas. Many Westerners still call it Mountain Red Cedar — a name that is or might be claimed by so many other species that it had best be dropped. Its home is on low mountain slopes, in canyon bottoms on sandy or gravelly soil, and on dry exposed mesas and the talus of those cliffs and escarpments that, like the risers of stairs, lift one behind the other in the long approach to the Rockies from the plains — old Blackfoot, Arapahoe, and Comanche country. In exposed situations this forms but a bushy tree 10 to 20 feet high, with a rather narrow, rounded crown of large long limbs that hug the stem or at least rise rather steeply upwards. In this one sees at once a resemblance to the Lombardy-Poplar-like form of the Eastern Red Cedar. In sheltered canyons specimens may grow up to 30 feet in height, with the ends of the branches and twigs sometimes drooping or even pendent, giving the tree a Weeping-Willow-like form. Such trees are often called Weeping Juniper.

The wood is closely similar to that of the Eastern Red Cedar, which is to say that it is extremely handsome, bright rose-red streaked with yellowish white. It has the same Cedar fragrance, the same good working qualities, and would doubtless make a good pencil wood. But the trunks are not straight enough, nor tall and thick enough nor sufficiently knot-free to make a fine lumber tree like the Eastern Juniper.

EASTERN JUNIPER, *Juniperus virginiana* Linnæus, also called Eastern Red Cedar, reaches the circumscription of this work in western parts of Kansas, Nebraska, and the Dakotas (except the Black Hills). It forms a tree usually not over 40 feet tall in these regions, with a frequently lobed or buttressed or fluted short trunk and thin, light brown or reddish bark separating into long narrow strips. The leaves on mature branchlets are closely overlapping in opposite pairs with the margins not fringed or cut, but dark blue-green or glaucous, those on young branchlets spreading, sharp-tipped and light yellow green. The

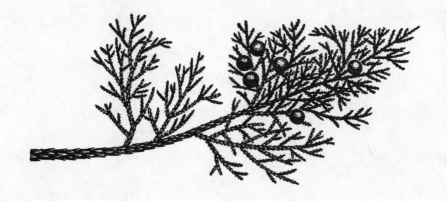

fruit, ripening at the end of the first season, is ¼ to ⅓ inch thick, pale green at first, becoming dark blue and covered with a whitish bloom, the skin thin but firm, the flesh sweet and resinous and with 1 or 2 (rarely more) seeds. It is found in our area chiefly along banks of streams and in ravines, and sometimes along roadsides, and is also considerably cultivated as a dooryard, cemetery, and windbreak tree.

THE YEWS
(*Taxus*)

THE YEWS possess scaly (not furrowed) dark bark, very hard, heavy, strong, pale, and durable wood, and wide-spreading, slender, mostly horizontal branches. The evergreen foliage is needle-like, the leaves borne singly in two spiral ranks; the upper surface is rounded or keeled and dark green, the lower pale, with rows of stomata in minute nipple-like projections, the margin of the leaf slightly curled under. The flowers are unisexual with only one sex on a given tree, and surrounded by the numerous persistent bud scales — the male in globular heads and consisting in the naked stamens united into a column, the connective between the united anthers umbrella-like and partly concealing them; the female flowers are solitary and consist merely in a single ovule borne on a bract or scale in the axil of a leaf of the preceding year. The solitary seeds are not borne in a cone but are imbedded in a cup-shaped disk (aril) of bright-colored pulp.

✻ ✻ ✻

WESTERN YEW

Taxus brevifolia Nuttall

OTHER NAMES: Pacific Yew. Mountain Mahogany.

RANGE: In Alaska only on islands off the southeast coast; seaward slopes only of the Coast Range of British Columbia, and on Vancouver and the Queen Charlotte Islands, and inland to the Selkirk Mountains; south in the Rockies of Montana and Idaho, and the Blue Mountains of Oregon; in the Coast Ranges from the Olympics to the Siskiyous, Trinity Mountains, Redwood belt, and inner Coast Ranges (Lake County) of California; also in the Santa Cruz Mountains, south of San Francisco; in the Cascades of Oregon and Washington up to 6000 feet altitude, in the Western White Pine belt, and southward through the Yellow Pine belt of northeastern California and the west slopes of the Sierra Nevada to Tulare County, up to 8000 feet.

DESCRIPTION: *Bark* very thin, of papery, purple, easily detached scales, the underbark clear rose or reddish purple. *Twigs* slender and drooping. *Leaves* often curved, slender-stalked, ½ to 1 inch long, 1/16 inch wide, dark yellow green and keeled above, paler below with lines of stomata and incurved margins. *Flowers* — male, pale yellow, of 4 to 8 stamens; female in the axils of the scales of short branches, the ovule erect and seated in a ring-like disk. *Seed* about ⅓ inch long, with a much depressed hilum, and surrounded by but free from the scarlet, succulent, aril-like disk which is open at the apex; outer seed coat thin or fleshy, inner thicker and woody. *Wood* hard, very strong, heavy (40 pounds per cubic foot, dry weight), the heartwood bright red, the sapwood thin and light yellow.

On the Olympic peninsula, that great block of land that lies between Puget Sound on the east and the Pacific on the west, with the eternal snows of the Olympic range shining at the heart of it, the Western Yew reaches its best development, growing up to 75 feet in height. But big as this is for a Yew, it is fairly lost in the lowland forests of the peninsula, first because it is not a common tree even there, and further because all its coniferous neighbors are so gigantic — Douglas Firs, Grand Firs, Sitka Spruces, Western Red Cedars and mighty Hemlocks. These make the most somber, unbroken, and utterly overwhelming forests on the North American continent, and in their midst the Yew must be sought out with a knowing eye.

To recognize it, look for a tree with flat and prickly-tipped needles, for the Sitka Spruce is the only other species locally present which has such. But the needles of the Sitka Spruce bristle stiffly all around the twig, while the Yew's are soft and lie all in one plane. And there are other distinguishing features, such as the beautiful, peeled-looking bark, whose papery purplish scales are always curling and sloughing away to reveal the flower-like clear rose of the inner bark. The trunk is usually fluted and twisted and often unsymmetrical; in dense forests, however, it is straight and slender though usually clothed in fine down-sweeping branches right to the ground. Sometimes it grows so densely, as around Lake of the Woods in Oregon, as to form veritable jungles. Slender whip-like twigs depend from the boughs, giving a "weeping" appearance, and the whole tree has a sort of wood-sprite grace, mingled with mystery in the very dark mass of foliage — quite the most somber of all the western trees, but lightened, when seen from below, by the silvery white undersides of the needles.

Only the female trees, of course, bear the berry-like, coral-red fruit, which is really an aril, that is, a mass of fleshy pulp with an open pit in which is lodged the seed. That pulp is sweet and mucilaginous and is devoured by birds which may carry the seeds far before voiding them, their viability quite unimpaired. One would think that this would make the Yew abundantly successful, but the amount of fruiting is scarce, and seedlings are comparatively rare. More, growth in the darkness of these woods is very slow, and a trunk only 12 to 20 inches in diameter is probably 140 to 245 years old.

The Yew of Europe, *Taxus baccata,* often lives a thousand years and some specimens are known to be two thousand years old, but no authenticated counts of annual rings in our tree show anything like such sempiternal life. In Europe the Yew is the time-honored wood for bows, so stiff and strong it is, and before the invention of gunpowder, a good supply of Yew was as important as steel as a raw material of war-making. As a skill and a hunting sport, archery has never completely gone out of fashion, even in the New World, and naturally the Western Yew, as the largest of its genus in North America, has been sought out by the bowyers, as it was by the Indians from ancient times. In some parts of the Northwest, there is quite an artisan industry of Yew bow production. As a bow wood, our Yew is good but not, upon trial, as reliable as Osage Orange, the premier native bow wood of the continent. The experts tell us that our native Yew sometimes "casts" and "crisals" (warps, and fractures across the grain) in hot and cold weather respectively, and sometimes "explodes" — breaks up — under strain. It is however a first-class material for canoe paddles, wearing smooth as Ebony with use, and its strength, hardness, beautiful rose-red heartwood and clear yellow sapwood make it suitable for small cabinet work. But so scarce is the Western Yew that it will never be found in the statistics of the leading commercial timbers.

THE TORREYAS
(*Torreya*)

THIS GENUS is characterized by furrowed bark and whorled or opposite and drooping branches and linear, evergreen, fetid foliage, with
pale bands of stomata on the lower surface, the upper dark green, with
the margins curved under. The flowers are unisexual with only one sex
on a given tree — the male crowded in the axils of adjacent leaves and
consisting in 6 or 8 whorls of 4 stamens, each stamen with 4 pollen
sacks united into a half-ring on the expanded stalks; female flowers are
found scattered on shoots of the current year's growth, the solitary
ovule lying in and at length enclosed in a fleshy, urn-shaped, aril-like
disk. At the end of the second season the fertilized ovule takes the
form of a drupe-like fruit, the thick seed coat woody, its inner layer
folded into the thick white albumen, and ultimately enclosed in the
enlarged, dark green or purple aril or disk which is composed of flat,
separable, thin fibers. At maturity the fruit splits longitudinally into
2 parts.

❋　　　❋　　　❋

CALIFORNIA NUTMEG

Torreya californica Torrey

OTHER NAMES: Stinking Cedar. California Torreya.

RANGE: California, on the Coast Ranges up to 3600 feet, from Mendocino to Lake, Marin, and Santa Cruz Counties, and on the west slopes of the Sierra Nevada from Tehama County to Tulare County, up to 6000 feet.

DESCRIPTION: *Bark* thin, with loosely scaly, interbraiding ridges checkered with small plates by numerous cross-furrows, and irregularly seamed, the outer layer soft and weathered to an ashy or yellowish brown, the under-bark gray-brown tinged with orange. *Leaves* flat and slightly curved, 1 to 3½ inches long, ⅟₁₆ to ⅛ inch broad, dark yellow-green and lustrous above, paler beneath with bands of stomata. *Flowers* — male, small, bud-like, female ¼ inch long, borne on the lower side of the branches, from the bases of new leaves of the seasons. *Seed* 1 to 1½ inches long, its coat greenish and more or less striped with purple. *Wood* soft, close-grained, light (29.66 pounds per cubic foot, dry weight), the heartwood clear yellow, the sapwood thin and nearly white.

The California Nutmeg is no true Nutmeg but a member of the Yew Family and takes its name from the resemblance of the wrinkled seed coat to the nutmeg of commerce. The greeny and purplish fruits — really arils — look much like olives as they hang from the boughs of

female trees, while the leaves might make one think these little trees, when barren of fruits, were some sort of Fir. Prickly-tipped and rather large, these needles lie all in one plane in a manner not lacking in grace. But when bruised they give off, as does the bark, a fetid odor that has earned for this odd little tree the name of Stinking Cedar.

In youth and middle life the tree is a fine broad-based cone in shape, with branches arranged in tier on tier of rather formal whorls around the usually crooked trunks, clothing them to the base. With age, and under crowded forest conditions, the lower branches vanish, leaving a long clear trunk and a curious dome-like crown. The bark is characteristically cross-checked and scaly-ridged, and soon weathers to a dull grayish color. Trees in the moist Redwood forest become 90 feet high, but as a rule they are much smaller, and by contrast with the grandeur of the Sierran forest, for instance, they seem mere dwarfs, quite unimpressive, but not without charm as their needles glister in the warm light of the lower mountain slopes. Perhaps the most accessible of places to watch for this little tree is on the Arch Rock road by which one leaves Yosemite National Park for Mariposa and Merced.

This long-lived little tree produces a strong wood, once used by the California Indians for bows, with long-lasting qualities, a charming color, and a fine grain, and doubtless it would make a good cabinet wood if the trees were not so small and so rare or widely scattered.

THE WASHINGTON
PALMS
(*Washingtonia*)

THESE LOFTY TREES, the only genus of Palms native to the western
states, have stout columnar stems terminating in a heavy crown of
large, palmately lobed leaves. The leafstalks are long, two-edged, and
thorny.

The bisexual flowers are enclosed at first in boat-shaped spathes and
borne on an elongated spadix, the blossoms jointed to their disk-like,
thick stalklets. Tubular and papery, the calyx is slightly 3-lobed at
apex; the corolla possesses a fleshy tube only half as long as its lobes.
Inserted on the tube of the corolla, the filaments of the stamens are
free from each other. The 3-lobed ovary has 3 long slim styles which
are stigmatic, not on the apex but on the sides. The fruit takes the
form of a short-stalked, small berry, containing a solitary seed.

Like all Palms, these differ from most other sorts of trees in having
an unbranched stem and a solitary growing-point — a terminal bud
in the center of the crown of tough, evergreen leaves — and in having
no woody cylinder and no annual growth rings, since the woody fibers
are scattered as long, thread-like fibro-vascular bundles through the
pithy tissue of the stem. True bark is not developed by the Palms,
only a sort of rind.

*　　　*　　　*

DESERT PALM

Washingtonia filifera Wendland

OTHER NAMES: California Fan Palm. Arizona, Washington, or Fanleaf
Palm. Overcoat Palm. Wild Date.

RANGE: *Bases* of the desert (eastern) side of the San Jacinto Mountains
of Riverside County, California (Palm Canyon, Palm Springs), and base
of the southeastern end of the San Bernardinos (Twentynine Palms),
south irregularly in the desert canyons of eastern San Diego County to
Baja California and Sonora; also in mountain canyons just above Yuma,
Arizona.

DESCRIPTION: *Rind* bark-like, thick, pale cinnamon to dull light red-
brown, marked by narrow seams. *Leafstalks* 3 to 6 feet long, 1 to 3
inches thick, 2-edged, the cartilaginous orange-colored margins armed
with 2 rows of hooked spines of various sizes. *Leaves* 3 to 6 feet long
and usually not quite as broad, fan-shaped, deeply slashed into stiff,
ribbon-like, sharp-tipped divisions, 2-cleft at the ends, the margins separating into numerous drooping threads; after death becoming deflexed
by their stalks. *Flowers* borne in great compound clusters, 8 to 12 feet
long, which appear from the axils of the upper leaves; regular, perfect,
but minute; corolla with funnel-form tube and 6 petal-like lobes; stamens
6 in number. *Berry* ⅓ inch long, the skin black, the flesh thin and dry;
seed ¼ inch long, ⅛ inch thick, russet.

On its many merits, the Washington or California Fan Palm has
made its way around the gardens of this world wherever a palm can
be grown, and under glass in colder climes. In Hawaii and Algeria
it is now so familiar in the landscape of cultivated districts as to seem
like a native. Indeed, in Hawaii it has received a thoroughly native-
sounding name, the Hula Palm, in allusion to its skirt-like thatch of
dead leaves hanging beneath the crown of living ones, like the grass
skirt of a Polynesian dancer. The same appellation has been applied
to it in Florida, where it is now a familiar garden and street tree. On
the Riviera it is highly prized. No other palm indigenous in this
country has proved so popular in cultivation. Yet in the wild it has
always been a rare species within the borders of the United States.
Until Palm Springs (which takes its name from this tree) became a

winter resort, in the second decade of this century, few indeed, except bands of Indians and old "desert rats" or wandering prospectors, had ever seen it growing natively, with an artless dignity, a wild, desertic fitness, that it never wholly possesses in the flashy horticulture of subtropical cities.

The chosen habitat of the Desert Palm, as it is called where it is native, is, though so restricted, one of the grandest on the continent. For this tree inhabits the canyons at the foot of the eastern or desert side of the Coast Ranges in Riverside and San Diego Counties. From elevations of over 11,000 feet, in the San Jacinto Mountains, where Lodgepole Pines stand all winter amid glittering snows, the surface of the planet here drops abruptly for two vertical miles to the floor of the intensely desertic Coachella Valley. Portions of this chasm lie below sea level, as if a great block of the earth had slipped out of place and sunk deep. And this indeed is probably the case; the Gulf of California, our American Red Sea, is doubtless but a portion of the same deep planetary crack, now filled with ocean water; and fossil oyster beds and old shorelines around the Coachella Valley show that in former geologic times the Gulf was here, or there was at least a landlocked salt lake, a sort of Dead Sea, of which the enameled blue of the Salton Sea is a recent manifestation.

Around the shores of this vanished sea are dotted the scattered colonies of our palm. They are found at the bay-like bases of the canyons, between the waterless capes of the San Jacintos' buttressing ridges. They cling to last waterholes in the Little San Bernardino Mountains which enclose the Coachella Valley to the east. All the way down the inner face of the Coast Ranges to the Mexican boundary, and beyond, into lower California, colonies of Palms cluster wherever there are mountain walls to give them shade, for part of the day, from the fierce desert sun, and springs or streams or the least slow seepage to nourish their deep, far-traveling roots. A few of these groves, near the popular resorts, are visited yearly now by many thousands of people, but most of them are still little accessible. In profound desert loneliness they catch, each morning as the planet rolls eastward, the first fierce rays of the sun, spilling it in swords of light from the ribs and finger-like lobes of their fronds. Each year they produce, all unseen, their great compound bunches of creamy flowers, and ripen their black cherries, and drop their horny seeds. They have no company but the trade rats and lizards that scuttle under the thatch of dead leaves around the stem, and the liquid raptures of the canyon wren who nests behind the thatch, or the rolling whistle of orioles that hang their nests from under the living fan fronds upon threads made of the long fibers of the leaves themselves.

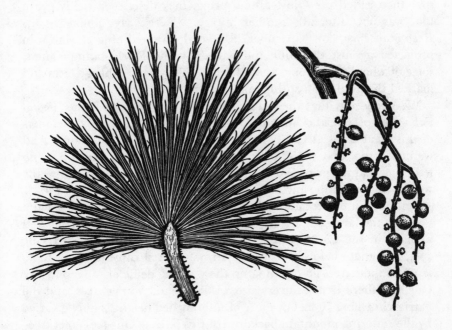

Yet though so rare a tree, the Washington Palm was early discovered by Europeans. On March 29, 1769, the Franciscan Father Juan Crespí, chronicler of the Portolá expedition, observed it 30 miles north-north-west of Vallicola, Baja California, near the future site of Mission San Fernando. He speaks of camping here, after a desolate *jornada*, under the grateful shade of a grove of fine Palms, and since Washingtonias are the only Palms growing there, no doubt can be entertained of their identity. On May of the same year, the immortal Padre Junípero Serra mentions Palms at the same spot. So, contrary to widely received opinion in California, the "Mission Fathers" (Franciscans) did not bring the Palm here from the Holy Land, or from Spain.

In 1848 Colonel William Hemsley Emory, "Bold Emory" as his fellow West-Pointers named him, soldier, explorer, engineer and astronomer, brought the Mexican Boundary Survey party safely across the terrible wastes of then-unknown desert roamed over by Indian hostiles. At last the sun-scorched, saddle-sore and foot-sore party, parched with thirst, saw from the Little San Bernardinos the towering, barren rock wall of the San Jacintos, and as they crawled across the Coachella Valley toward the mouth of Carrizo Creek Canyon, at a spot then called the Ojo Grande spring, they descried a shady grove that was not, after all, another mirage. "Here," says Emory in his *Reconnaissance,* "on November 29, several scattered objects were seen projected against the cliffs and hailed by the Florida campaigners, some of whom were along, as old friends. They were cabbage trees and marked the locale of a spring and small patch of grass."

We know now that these trees were not the Cabbage Palms (*Sabal Palmetto*) of Florida, but our own Desert Palms, the only members of this great tropical family native to the western United States. And we know, too, that the Ojo Grande spring of Emory's day is now no less than Palm Springs, one of the glossiest pleasure resorts in the world, where motion picture stars come to acquire a desert tan.

Only ten minutes' automobile ride from Palm Springs lies Palm Canyon, the largest of all the groves of Desert Palm in California, and perhaps in the world. Your car mounts a steep hill, to the parking area, and there below you lies a narrow watered canyon where thousands of these trees go trooping up the winding defile of the mountain. One sees there trees of every size, seedlings and young trees, and old patriarchs whose 70 feet or more of unbranched height is only dwarfed by the towering mountain backdrop of this setting. One sees erect trees, and trees picturesquely canted at all angles. In the desert sunlight the fronds flash proudly. They stir in the canyon draft with a soft lisp and clash. And, deeply cut as the leaf blades are, into palmate lobes like the fingers of the hand, the narrow, flexible segments move separately and seem to twinkle glittering, beckoning digits. The long marginal filaments, streaming and curling in the wind, add the final touch of airy grace.

By moonlight these trees are especially magical — palms indeed seem meant for the moon and warm winds — and then this desertic portion of the planet, its barren features unsoftened by water, seems indeed like some lunar landscape, save for the proud difference of the Desert Palms, waving life's green banners. Travelers who have been among them during one of the desert's rare but violent summer storms speak of the stiff whistling of the thrashing, living fronds, the hollow drumming of the driven rain upon the armor of dead leaves.

Like other palms, and unlike the conifers and hardwoods, these desert trees have peculiarities that account for their strange ways and habits, almost topsy-turvy to the rules that apply to growth in other trees. Growth, for instance, is all by the great terminal bud. If this be killed — as when the Indians cut it out and roast it — the whole tree will die as surely as a man with his head cut off. This bud gives off all the leaves that the tree will ever bear in the course of its life, and looking down on top of a palm from the mountainsides, one sees leaves in all stages of development, the innermost the youngest, the middle the full-grown, and the outermost beginning to fade and finally hang, head downward, against the stem. For this Palm does not cast its leaves when they die but retains them tenaciously as a dry persistent coat of armor about the stem. Indeed, if not burned or cut away, this shard may enclose the trunk right to the ground like a trouser-leg or pantalette. When seen thus in cultivation, our palm is apt to look dingy and unkempt in contrast to the polished formality of city parks and estates of the rich, wherefore gardeners sometimes cut away the dead, reflexed foliage. But this leaves the tree looking skinned and top-heavy, and, having lost its chief distinction, it now owns no superiority over other and more gracile palms.

Yet in the wild this thatch has a look of rightness and dignity, and its weathered colors harmonize naturally with the desert's tints. The Indians used sometimes to burn off the leaves in the belief (perhaps not unfounded) that a heavier crop of the sweet edible berries would result. The fire permanently blackens the stem but does not otherwise injure the tree, for palms have no true bark to lose, no all-vital cambium layer under their rind to be killed. And indeed a fire-seared Desert Palm has a picturesqueness of its own, in the wild, and speaks of the days when it was to the wandering bands of desert tribes what the Date Palm means to the Arabs and Bedouins. For where it grew it was a sign of water and herbage. Its berries and buds or hearts-of-palm fed the hungry; its seeds were ground into a flour. The leaves were used to thatch the Indian's shelters, and the threads from the foliage served to bind the cordage of the women's baskets. A band of Indians who found a good palm grove had no reason to hunt further for a settlement site, and even today the famous Palm Canyon grove serves the Agua Caliente Indians on whose reservation it stands, for at the gateway an Indian collects a coin from you for his tribe.

It is possible that the Indians sometimes planted this species beyond its primitive range. For instance, the grove at Twentynine Palms, on the Mohave Desert, is not only out of the seemingly normal range of the species, but it is associated with so many archaeological remains that one suspects strongly that this is a plantation rather than a natural grove. Certainly it is a strangely magnetic one, what is left of it, inevitably drawing the visitor to the little oasis where, amid Cottonwoods and Mesquite, these northernmost representatives of the species stand.

Everyone who visits the grove at Twentynine Palms remarks a grave, a small mound ringed about, like a child's play-place, with white quartz stones and honored only with a nameless wooden cross. Here is buried a young girl, who was being brought out on the desert for her health, by her mother, a poor woman hoping to reach the Virginia Dale mines to serve as a cook. When the young spirit left the body, February 10, 1903, the woman turned to the palms as the only beautiful things in all that waste where she could bear to leave her child. Two old desert rats dug the grave and made a narrow coffin; they and an Indian band sang such songs as they knew or thought appropriate; a Bible was produced from somewhere and "an educated mining man" read from it. Then the desert earth was thrown upon the box. For many years the Indians and prospectors laid wild flowers on Mary Whalen's grave. Now only the old Palms could remember how long the woman looked back at them as she was led away.

THE YUCCAS
(*Yucca*)

THE TROUGH-SHAPED, rigid, erect leaves, sharp and bristling as bayonets, are clustered near the ends of the club-like branches, at least in such species as are of tree size, or at the tops of unbranched stems. The corky, bark-like rind of the tree Yuccas is furrowed and checked in age, like that of ordinary trees, unlike that of the Palms. But, like the Palms and unlike other trees, Yuccas have no woody cylinder, only fibro-vascular bundles running like long tough threads through the pithy tissue. Unlike the foliage of Palms, the Yucca leaves are simple, not palmately or pinnately compound, but after persisting for several seasons they die and become deflexed as a thatch around the upper parts of the stem, just as in the Desert Palm.

The waxy, perfect flowers appear in large branched clusters from among the topmost leaves. Each blossom opens for a single night and is fertilized (except in the case of one species) by moths. The tulip-like flowers, cup-shaped and creamy or greenish white, have 6 petals and petal-like sepals, 6 stamens with fleshy club-shaped stalks, and a 6-sided greenish white ovary terminating in an ivory-white triangular style. The fruit takes the form of a 6-celled, 6-angled pod with an inner and an outer wall. The numerous compressed seeds are thin and black.

*　　　*　　　*

JOSHUATREE

Yucca brevifolia Engelmann

OTHER NAMES: Yuccatree. Yucca Palm. Yucca Cactus. Tree Yucca. Joshua Yucca. Joshua.

RANGE: Irregularly scattered on the higher gravel slopes skirting the deserts of California, southern Nevada, southwesternmost Utah, and eastern Arizona, and at the bases or on the talus slopes of various desert mountains and in mountain passes, usually between 2000 and 6500 feet above sea level.

DESCRIPTION: *Rind* of the stem bark-like, gray or reddish brown, rough, broken by narrow deep fissures and cross-checks with conspicuous plates. *Leaves* clustered at the ends of the branches, the creamy or greenish base firmly attached, the blade 7 to 12 inches long when fully grown, narrow, rigid, straight, the upper surface flattened, or concave at tip, the lower convex and sometimes keeled, the keel often toothed, both surfaces pale blue-green or sage-green and glaucous; the margin thin, narrow, horny, lemon-yellow and edged with sharp, short, straw-colored teeth; tip dark reddish brown at base, straw-colored at apex, and sharpened to a rigid stiletto-like point. *Inflorescence* densely crowded in a branched cluster, the main branches heavy, fleshy and brittle; bracts abundant, those at the base of the central branches rubbery and spiny-tipped, the others successively smaller and at first cream-colored tinged with rose or purple, soon becoming papery and dry. *Flowers* 1½ to 2¾ inches long, the petals and petal-like sepals fleshy, brittle, dull greenish yellow to sage-green or rarely cream-colored, united at base, free above, never fully spreading even at height of blooming; stamens 6, the filaments stiff, flattened against the ovary at base, club-shaped at the tip, pistil 1 to 1¼ inches long, the ovary with 3 deep fissures; style short and thick, terminating in 3 small, erect stigmas. *Fruit* spongy or dry, spreading (not drooping) on the crowded axis, in compact clusters, the individual fruits 2½ to 4 inches long, 1¾ to 2½ inches thick, plump throughout, the apex tipped with the persistent remnants of the style, and surrounded, while the fruit is still green, by the persistent remains of the petals, sepals and stamens; fruit eventually reddish brown or nearly black; seeds large, thin, and very numerous.

Tradition has it that the Mormons gave the Joshuatree its name. Certain it is that in 1857 Brigham Young, wishing to concentrate the power of the Latter-day Saints in Utah, summoned a Mormon colony from San Bernardino, California, to join him. They left by way of the Cajon Pass, and just on the other side of it, as they made their way down toward the Mohave River, they passed through one of the most impressive Joshua forests in the country, near present-day Victorville. We can still see what they must have beheld — a wide-spaced grove, running far as the eye can see to north and south, of the strangest tree in North America. From a distance, indeed, a Joshua looks more like the blasted skeleton of a tree which had grown all awry, for it spreads abroad no shade-giving foliage. On close inspection it is found that leaves there are, but they appear to have been hurled by a sword-thrower into the short trunks and branches. And what leaves — a desert gray-green, rigid as a dagger, with as sharp a point, and with formidable sawtoothed edges! Around the older parts of the stem and trunk the dead foliage is reflexed as a sort of palm-like thatch.

But if these trees gave no shade to the desert-crossing Mormons, they were at least full of expression. For the thick rigid branches come out at right angles to the trunks, and are often bent again, as if at the elbows. So the trees seemed to the Mormons to be gesticulating, as if to wave them on their way, and the shaggy, hoary leaves added the look of some bearded Old Testament prophet. More, the Saints kept encountering these groves as they went, for this Yucca, though so erratically distributed, does recur at certain altitudes through the Mohave, and in the deserts of southernmost Nevada and southwesternmost Utah. Thus the Saints' fancy grew to a sort of mystical certainty that this gesturing prophetic tree was leading them to the promised land of Deseret and, filled as Mormon pioneers were with biblical imagery, they named it the Joshuatree.

There are some who love it from the moment they first behold it, silhouetted, perhaps, against some desert sunset sky, with the snows of far-off peaks still flashing their signals, and the twilight filled with the last cry of the day birds — the ash-throated flycatchers and plaintive Say phoebes — while nighthawks sweep the skies with pointed wings and the burrowing owls begin to pipe from their holes in the sand. At such a moment the Joshuas lose their gauntness and take on a spiritual quality. With every day that you stay among them they come to seem friendlier and the one right tree in their place. When you set off again across the treeless spaces of the great Mohave, you greet each rare recurrence of these great Yuccas as a Bedouin greets a palm grove.

But for others the first sight of this vegetation is abhorrent and the

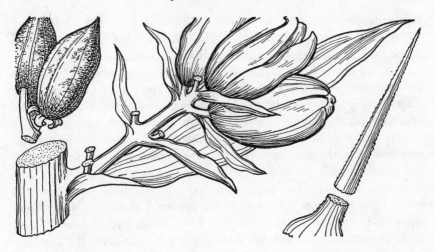

strangeness never wears off. Thus Captain John C. Frémont, the first English-speaking traveler who ever (so far as written record goes) noticed them, found these Yuccas, with "their stiff and ungraceful forms . . . the most repulsive tree in the vegetable kingdom." True that Frémont had just come out of the San Joaquin Valley, in the days when it was still one vast meadow of wild flowers, still laced with streams from the Sierra snows and dotted with park-like groves of Oaks. Then as, crossing the Tehachapi Pass, he descended upon the vast, sere wastes of the Mohave, the sense of contrast was brutal. Yet the year was at the spring, and even he admitted that the desert too had its beauties; streaks of purple sand verbena, of orange poppy, and blue gilia carpeted the Yucca groves, and his troop galloped swiftly through the air heady with perfume.

Most of Frémont's botanical collections on this, his second expedition, were lost when a mule bearing his specimens fell down a cliff into a river. No scientist sighted the Yucca forests again for ten years, when the War Department sent out reconnaissance expeditions to survey railway routes to the Pacific. The party which explored the route later taken by the Santa Fe, under two young Army officers (later to become famous), Lieutenants Whipple and Ives, reached the Victorville Yucca forests in March, 1854, and the surgeon-botanist of the expedition, Dr. John Bigelow, collected specimens still without flowers. Not until 1871 did the flowers become known to science.

And what strange blossoms! They belong to the lily family, but have the texture of creamy leather, breathing forth an odor like that of mushrooms. Flowering is most irregular; there is a little every spring, but there come "Yucca years," when all the trees of a given region will, for unexplained reasons, bloom heavily at once. Quite as curious are the fruits, the size of an ostrich egg, with a rind half dry and capsular, half berry-like and spongy. Once they are ripe, they drop quickly and, light as they are, may roll and tumble before the desert winds, shaking out seeds as they go.

The young shoot of a Joshua is a simple unbranched affair, making very slow growth, and very reluctant about producing its first bloom. But when flowering does occur at the tip, the terminal bud thereafter dies; then the first branch puts forth, a few feet below the point of flowering, and when this branch has flowered the same thing takes place again; so the Yucca forks, and forks again, dichotomously, and thus comes naturally by its gesticulating appearance. But the fantastic asymmetry is due in part to the loss of branches by self-pruning. In time the branches may be so many and so far from the stem that they weigh the main boughs down, and at last the branchlets point to the ground and may finally touch the desert sands. No one knows how old a Joshua may live to grow, and desert enthusiasts sometimes claim thousands of years, knowing they cannot easily be disproved since a Yucca does not, any more than a Palm does, produce concentric annual rings of wood. But one can distinguish the infancy, youth, middle life and old age of these trees by the amount of the branching. Patriarchs may have a hundred branchlets, and develop a trunk 4 feet in diameter, and heights up to 40 feet are known.

Under the desert sands there is a corresponding root development. Roots both grow down vertically and spread horizontally in the search for moisture, and underground runners send up the many sprouts one sees about vigorous trees. The ultimate rootlets are red, and from them the desert Indians used to obtain a dye for their patterned baskets. There is, however, no great taproot or powerful cordage of roots to anchor this topheavy vegetable in the soft, shifting sand. As a result, one sees a great many down trees, toppled over in some desert gale.

Like Palms, Joshuatrees have no solid cylinder of wood. As the pith — always a juvenile tissue — tends to disappear with the years, the stems are apt to become hollow. But this is not to say that there is no woody tissue; there are bundles of wood fiber around the hollow center, just as in a bamboo stem. These suffice to give the tree an efficient structural system, for the hollow cylinder, as engineers know, is stronger in proportion to its weight than a solid one. For this reason Joshua wood has been used for surgical splints, since it is at once light and strong, and even for the posts of desert pioneers' houses. At one time paper was made of the fiber, and a pulp mill was started in Los Angeles. Several Eastern and British newspapers bought up some of the paper stock, but fortunately it proved of poor quality. For it would not have taken long to destroy almost the entire stand of this rare tree, once serious pulp-logging operations started.

The distribution of the Joshuatree is erratic; there are many areas where one would expect it yet does not find it; and where it is found the next nearest grove may be a hundred miles away. All this suggests that it is a species once more widespread, which has endured many losses and is lucky to survive at all. In general it occurs only where there is enough rainfall, or rather enough run-off from regions with 10 to 15 inches of annual precipitation, to support its thirsty roots and the water requirements of its ponderous stems and branches. The snows of the San Bernardino and the San Gabriel Mountains, melting in spring, course briefly down in freshets to the foothills where the Joshuas grow in a zone of their own below that of Oneleaf Pinyon and Juniper, but above that of the treeless wastes of creosotebush, and here and east of the little San Bernardinos and in Antelope Valley are found the only extensive forests of the Tree Yucca. But small groves recur in passes and on the benches of what are known as the "lost ranges" of the mountainous Mohave desert.

In a region, such as the Mohave, which has frequently only one species of tree, it is not surprising that that tree should be a center of life for much of the fauna. So in Joshua branches and trunks, the red-shafted flicker and the cactus woodpecker drill holes for their nests. After these are abandoned they may be taken up by screech owls, bluebirds, Bewick wrens, titmice and ash-throated flycatchers. With the long fibers of the leaves, the Scott oriole suspends its nests from the branches of the Joshuatrees. Wood rats often climb the trees to gnaw off the spiny leaves with which to make their nests impregnable.

One animal there is which seldom leaves the shelter of the Joshuas for any cause — the desert night lizard, a species of *Xantusia*. It lives under the thatch of dead leaves, in cracks of the rind, and inside decayed and fallen branches — for Joshuas are forever dropping their boughs. Because of its nocturnal habits, and because confined to the Yucca trees, it was formerly thought to be a very rare animal; at least

it was rare in collections. But the California herpetologist Van Den-
burgh has found that every fourth or fifth tree examined yielded from
one to four specimens of this little saurian. He reports that when
exposed to the light it turns a pallid color, in keeping with the desert,
but shows no inclination to escape by running down holes in the
sand, preferring to return only to the patriarchial shelter of the Yucca.
In the dark it quickly turns dark again, like a chameleon.

Extinct now is a mammal which, like the lizard, was closely bound in
its life history to the Joshuatree. This is the giant ground sloth,
Nototherium, whose remains — skeletons, desiccated hides and hair,
and even the fossilized dung — were discovered in 1930 in Gypsum Cave
near Las Vegas, Nevada. Analysis of the dung showed that it consisted
of 80 per cent, by volumetric measurement, of Joshua leaves, readily
identified by their saw-toothed edges. At the present time Joshuas are
as extinct as the ground sloth in the neighborhood of Gypsum Cave,
and only grow 3000 feet higher up. This, too, seems proof that the
Joshua once inhabited a greater range, either in Glacial times or in
Recent times just following the Pleistocene.

But of all the creatures linked with the Mohave's Joshuas the most
famous is the Yucca moth, *Pronuba* (*Tegeticula,* by the latest nomenclature). Its life history was discovered by that celebrated early American entomologist, Charles Valentine Riley. With his old-fashioned
lantern Riley watched the strange rites of the Pronuba and found that
the female lays her eggs in the ovaries. But it is essential that the
ovules should be fertilized, if a ripe supply of fruit tissue is to be at
hand for her larvæ. And, as if she understood the principles of pollination, she gathers loads of pollen and crams them down on the
stigma — the female receptive organ of the flower. Thousands of
species of insects pollinate flowers, lured there by the odor, and myriad
are the floral mechanisms for catching or lifting off the pollen brushed
on the insect bodies. But there is no other known instance of an insect
which seems to pollinate the flowers deliberately. Say if you like that
her act is some sort of reflex and not the product of forethoughtfulness
like that of a human intellect. But what stimulates the reflex to such
an elaborate and careful ritual? More, the Yucca flowers appear dependent on the Pronuba moth for fertilization. Probably no other
insect visits them. A more complete symbiosis between a flower and
animal could not be found.

With time, a belated appreciation of the strange beauty of the
Yucca forests has come to the public and, as resorts and guest ranches

multiply on the western edge of the Mohave, they are commonly located in Joshua groves, and the trees are protected and individually valued for their fantastic qualities. The federal government in 1936 established Joshua Tree National Monument, containing 1344 square miles of desert and Yucca forest, a region so wild that it still retains some of its aboriginal fauna, which includes the desert bighorn sheep and the mule deer. You reach it most easily from Twentynine Palms, where the Monument headquarters are located. But the roads are still few and sandy, and subject to sudden washouts from summer thunderstorms. Unfortunately there are many enclaves of privately owned land within the periphery of the Monument — tracts that might be sold at any time that the desert's mineral wealth attracted the attention of mining interests. The status of a National Monument is quite different from that of a National Park which cannot be exploited unless an act of Congress actually alienates the land from Park status; but a Monument can be opened up to commercial development at the discretion of the Secretary of the Interior. As to the wonderful Joshua groves in Antelope Valley, where Frémont rode so long ago, they are at the present time entirely in private hands, and neither the state of California nor the rich county of Los Angeles has seen fit as yet to take a step toward preserving them, beyond evincing a willingness to accept them as a gift.

THE WAX MYRTLES
(*Myrica*)

THE LEAVES of Wax Myrtles are alternate and, in the tree-sized species at least, simple and evergreen, the old leaves gradually deciduous as the new thrust out in late spring or early summer. In falling, the leafstalks leave elevated semicircular scars on the twigs. The inconspicuous flowers are borne in short or globular catkins in the axils of leaves of the year. The catkins may be wholly female or wholly male, or female above and male below, but are always without sepals or petals and are instead provided with small scales, each one, in the male flowers, bearing a set of 4 or more stamens on its thickened base, while in the female flower the scales subtend the ovary with its short style which is divided into two thread-fine stigmas. The fruit takes the form of a waxy drupe with dry flesh and a thick-walled stone containing the seed.

❋   ❋   ❋

CALIFORNIA WAX MYRTLE

Myrica californica Chamisso

OTHER NAMES: California Bayberry. California Myrtle.

RANGE: Dunes, hills and streambanks, close to the sea, from Puget Sound to Santa Monica, California.

DESCRIPTION: *Bark* of trunks smooth, compact, externally light brown or gray, but the inner bark dark red-brown. *Twigs* stout, at first clothed in loose woolly hairs and dark green or light red-brown, becoming in the second season darker and finally ashy gray and much roughened by the elevated scars of old leafstalks. *Winter buds* with loosely overlapping acute, dark red-brown, woolly-hairy, persistent scales, which become ½ inch long when full grown. *Leaves* 2 to 4 inches long, ½ to ¾ inch wide, thin but firm, dark glossy yellow-green above, the lower surface flecked with minute dark glands and marked by a narrow, curled-under margin. *Flowers* subtended by small but conspicuous bracts, those of the two sexes on the same plant, the male in simple oblong catkins about 1 inch long, the female in shorter catkins in the axils of upper leaves, intermediate catkins containing male flowers above, female below; stamens in each male floret numerous with dark purple anthers soon turning yellow; ovary with bright red-purple styles. *Fruit* in short, crowded spikes, a dry drupe, minutely warty and dark purple under a coat of grayish wax. *Seed* minute, pale reddish brown. *Wood* heavy (42 pounds per cubic foot, dry weight), very hard and very strong, close-grained, brittle, the heartwood light rose, with thick, paler sapwood.

All up and down the coast of Oregon and northern California, wherever there are boggy meadows bordering the estuaries of little streams behind the dunes, you find the Wax Myrtle. Sometimes it grows in the dune sand with Beach Pine, and sometimes besides the streams with Alders, but always it is a graceful, softly shining little tree with pretty mottled bark much like an Alder's, and leaves much like a Willow's, but hard and evergreen and marked below with tell-tale dark glandular dots. The flowers are noticed only by the trained observer, and the fruits, covered with translucent resinous globules, are not showy like those of its famous relative the eastern Bayberry. Only 24 feet high at most, with much-branched and crooked stems, this is anything but a showy tree. Yet one comes to be fond of it, if not for any great beauty then for its associations, for it is linked with memories of vacation days on the Oregon coast — with the thunder of the North Pacific's green and curdy surf, with the commingled smell of salt and Pine, the aching blue of the summer sky, the trill of warblers, and the curl of the looping black highway.

The first discoverer of the western Wax Myrtle was Adelbert von Chamisso, who, despite his German-sounding name, was a French nobleman who found himself on a Russian ship, the *Rurik,* when it dropped anchor in San Francisco bay in 1805. As a young man he had fled from the French Revolution to Germany, mastered the German language, and written poetry in it. He was the author, too, of the famous story of Pieter Schlemihl, the man who sold his shadow to the Devil. And though possessing so imaginative a mind, he was also an excellent systematic botanist, and so was chosen by Count Nikolai Petrovitch Romanzoff to accompany the Kotzebue exploring expedition to Russian America, which then extended down the coast of California to Fort Ross. Among Chamisso's discoveries were the far-famed California Poppy, and the Wax Myrtle, both of which he probably collected on the site of the Presidio in San Francisco.

THE POPLARS

(*Populus*)

Poplars are fast-growing, short-lived, tall trees with bitter and astringent bark, light, weak wood, thick, brittle, pithy twigs, and restless foliage. Frequently the big, scaly, more or less gummy buds give off a marked aroma. Prominent leaf scars generally roughen the thick twigs. Long-stalked, alternate, and deciduous, the leaves are seldom more than twice as long as broad, and often broader than they are long.

Frequently appearing well before the leaves, the flowers are wind-pollinated and grouped in long catkins, with the sexes on separate trees. Each male floret consists in 8 to 30 or more stamens; the female floret is an ovary with two stigmas. From the flask-shaped, thin-walled seed pod escape the minute, short-lived, innumerable seeds, which are borne on the wind by their cottony down.

*   *   *

WESTERN TREMBLING ASPEN

Populus tremuloides Michaux, variety *aurea* (Tidestrom) Daniels

OTHER NAMES: Quaking Aspen. Quaking or Aspen Poplar. Popple.

RANGE: In Alaska north in the Yukon Valley to the latitude of the Arctic Circle, south slopes of the Endicott Mountains (to 2000 feet), west nearly to the Bering Sea and south to the inland side of the Coast Range and to its seaward side at Cook Inlet, Kenai Mountains, base of the Alaskan peninsula. In Yukon Territory and British Columbia west to the inland slopes of the Pacific Coast Range and noted on Klondike, Stewart, Liard, Stikine and other rivers. East to the high plains of Saskatchewan, the western parts of the Dakotas and Nebraska, and south in the Rockies to the mountains of western Texas, southern Arizona and the northern parts of Nevada, and California, to the northern Coast Ranges and from 5000 to 10,500 feet in the Sierra Nevada and the high mountains of southern California. Also in northern Mexico.

DESCRIPTION: *Bark* of trunks at first thin and smooth, nearly white and often variegated with greenish or yellowish areas, becoming on old trunks nearly black at base and roughened by horizontal bands of wart-like thickenings, and deeply divided into broad, flat ridges broken on the surface into small, appressed, plate-like scales. *Twigs* clear reddish brown and very shiny the first season, flecked with scattered lenticels. *Winter buds* slightly resinous, with smooth, not downy, red-brown scales. *Leaves* on flattened yellow stalks, thick, 1½ to 3 inches long and broad, the upper surface a bright, clear, shining green, the lower very pale, the margins thickened, the veinlets obscurely meshed. *Flowers* in catkins 1½ to 3 inches long, the male florets with 6 to 12 stamens, the female with a short style and 2 erect, 2-lobed, red stigmas. *Fruit* a narrowly concave, 2-valved, curved capsule ¼ inch long. *Seeds* ½₂ inch long, light brown. *Wood* light (25 pounds per cubic foot, dry weight), soft, weak, and brittle, the heartwood light brown, the sapwood very thick and greenish or silvery white.

The Trembling Aspen is the most widespread tree of North America, ranging from Atlantic to Pacific across Canada, and in the western United States it extends, at increasingly higher altitudes as one goes south, through all the great mountain systems to Mexico. But, a small tree in the eastern provinces and states, it can never mean — there where it is but one of hundreds of hardwoods — what it does here in

the West. For here it is actually a finer tree, up to 90 feet tall in some
favored localities; in many regions of the Far North, it is the only
hardwood to break the somber monotony of the vast coniferous forests.
In the Rockies, it grows in the very spots most sought by the vacation-
ing camper — in the high, dry, cool places, commonly close to clean,
rushing water. It is apt to form open, sunny groves, where the snow or
the night damps and chill do not linger, and the breeze sweeps away
the insects. Sweet, dry grass carpets the floors of these groves, flecked
with the blue of lupine and wild flax, of larkspur, columbine, and
monkshood (where else are there so many blue wild flowers as in the
Rockies?). Where the deer bound, where the trout rise, where your
horse stops to slather a drink from icy water while the sun is warm on
the back of your neck, where every breath you draw is exhilaration —
that is where the Aspens grow.

The least observant city-dweller quickly notices Aspens and learns
to identify them on sight. Their boles, except at the roughened, darkened base of very old trunks, are smooth as flesh and chalky white just
tinged with green. Unlike the bark of the Birch, Aspen bark never
peels in thin layers but is always compact and thick. Aspens resemble
their relatives the Poplars and Cottonwoods, but those have very sticky
buds, while Aspen buds are only slightly resinous. So there is no
other tree in the West that can be confused with Trembling Aspen.

And above all there is the tremble that gives them their name.
Father De Smet, the early missionary to the Northwest, relates that the
coureurs du bois had a superstition that this tree furnished the wood
of the Cross, since when it has never ceased to quake. If you prefer to
look for a scientific reason, there is one: the leaves of the Aspen are
hinged upon leafstalks longer than the blade and flattened contrary
to the plane of the blade, with the result that the leafstalk acts as a
pivot and the foliage cannot but go into a panic whispering every time
the slightest breeze flows down the canyon. Cottonwoods and Poplars,
too, rustle their leaves, but not all of them have that right-angle pivot
of blade and stalk. And with a little experience one can distinguish,
even without seeing the tree, the light, soft rustle of Aspen leaves from
the coarser rustling of the heavy-leaved Cottonwoods. As Aspen foliage
moves it twinkles brilliantly, for each shiny surface acts like a little
mirror to flash sunlight in your eyes.

The color of Aspen foliage, too, is distinctive — in spring and summer a pale green, compared to the Cottonwood's darker green, in
autumn the clearest shining gold in contrast to the dull butter-yellow

of Cottonwood. So you can pick out from afar the zones of Aspen, or its clumps, and groves, and the long river-like streaks where it seems to pour from the edge of a plateau like the north rim of the Grand Canyon, down the draws and gulches. And as if it wished to be seen to the utmost advantage, it is commonly found chattering and displaying its vivacity, its white limbs and green or golden mane of foliage, against the dark unmoved conifers. Engelmann and Blue Spruces, White and Alpine Firs, Douglastree and Lodgepole Pine are its constant companions in the Rockies, and in the Far North it associates with somber White and Black Spruce.

In all the West there is no tree with such brilliant autumnal foliage. This might seem to be faint praise, since the West is lacking in the great range of color seen in the East; but the West is so rich in the gold of the Aspen's coin-shaped leaves that it can afford to forget what it lacks of copper and bronze. And Western Aspens are more brilliant than the same tree in the East, for the dry, crystalline atmosphere lets the sunlight through them like a clear, sustained blast on angelic trumpets. The foliage shines for miles; thus as you cross the deserts in October, still hot and sere, you can see the gold band of Aspens in the sky, where they top the mountain peaks. But better it is to ride some horse trail up into the meadows where the Mormons graze their sheep in summer or walk an old lumber road through the Aspens in fall, and let the golden glory rain tranquilly down around you.

As you go, you may notice on the usually smooth bark of the Aspens curious deep pits and long slashes. These are made by the claws of bears who stretch up to their fullest height to achieve them. And to see just how high that sometimes is may make you take a quick look over your shoulder. Yet if the slashes are bordered by a rim of black, corky scar tissue, then those marks were made long ago. If Bruin passed this way recently there will be no black borders; the green cambium layer may show under the bark, or the sapwood, freshly exposed and white, will be moist still. Opinions differ as to the motives behind this ursine writing on the Aspen's inviting page of bark. Some think bears sharpen their claws in this way, and others, on the contrary, that bears intentionally so dull their claws. Many believe that old bears mark up the trees as a proclamation of foraging or courting rights in a certain bailiwick and that rival bears, seeing how high the marks reach, can tell whether they dare issue a challenge.

The number of animals which eat Aspen buds or bark makes a long list. It is an important food of the snowshoe hare and the moose; black bears, cottontail rabbits, porcupine, and deer include Aspen in their menus. Grouse feed on it abundantly at certain seasons and so does the boomer or mountain beaver (which is not really a beaver but a forest pest related to rats). Sheep, goats, and cattle are so fond of Aspen shoots and sprouts that where they are allowed to browse heavily little Aspen reproduction takes place. In the days when elk were abundant in Colorado they sometimes killed whole groves of small Aspen by overbrowsing.

But the real Aspen-worshiper is the true beaver. The inner bark, though bitter as quinine to our palates, is his favorite food, preferred to that of Cottonwoods, Willows, or Alders. Every sensible beaver lays up large stores of Aspen cuttings for his winter supply, anchored to the bottom of the pond by mud. Since it grows so handily by streams, Aspen is also the commonest tree cut down by those chisel teeth, for the making of the dam that will back the stream up into a moat where he can set his lodge. Tree-falling by beavers is more industrious than clever, but once the tree is down the beavers show endless ingenuity in snaking and skidding the poles to the stream; if necessary, canals are dug by these little lumbermen and the Aspen logs are then driven, as loggers say, to the pond. In time the pond may silt up; the beavers then leave, but on the new-made ground the Aspens spring up quickly.

In the first forty years of the nineteenth century, beaver fur was at a premium, for every gentleman in Europe and the eastern United States had to have a beaver hat. So it was beaver, more than any other fur-bearing animal, that brought the white man and the half-breed or *coureur des bois* as the first explorers of the West, long before the days of the cowboys, before the gold rushes, before the Indian wars. And wherever those hardy "Mountain Men" and Hudson's Bay Company's employees went, they looked out for Aspen, for it was beaver-sign. The best method of trapping the beaver was to breach a hole in the beaver's dam, set an Aspen stick in the break, and attach the stick to a trap. The beaver, swimming out to repair the dam, instinctively seized the Aspen stick; the trap fell on his leg and carried the little flat-tail down under water where he drowned. And it was commonly in the delicious Aspen groves that, annually, the Mountain Men appointed their rendezvous; there they brought their beaver pelts, and while waiting for the St. Louis supply train, would trade with the Indians for beaver and girls. Around the campfires of Aspen logs you could have seen, in that far-off Homeric age of the West, the weather-seamed faces of Jim Bridger, Kit Carson, "Brokenhand" Fitzpatrick, Jedediah Smith, Bent, Beckwith, St. Vrain, the Sublettes, Bonneville and Ashley and Vanderburgh. It is natural, therefore, that all the early accounts of western exploration mention the Aspen, over and again, and always with love for the beauty of its groves.

Aspen flowers bloom in earliest spring, their mouse-gray buds bursting from the shining chestnut scales. By the time the first delicate haze of foliage puts out, about a month later, the wind-pollinated flowers have turned to fruits, and the minute seeds, in immense quantities, float away on their coating of fluffy down. Sometimes this will accumulate in the corner of a corral to the depth of several feet, and the air may be filled for a while with millions of these shining argosies. Streams backed up by a log jam or beaver dam may have the surface covered with a thick cottony layer. Of course only the female trees bear seed, and many of these have a high degree of infertility, so that it is but a fraction of the Aspens in a region which do all the work.

Many of the seeds, too, are abortive — without a viable embryo. All are very short-lived. An Aspen seed must sprout almost as soon as it finds lodgment or it will not grow at all. And in the dry springtimes of many portions of the West the climatic conditions are hostile to such an event; there Aspen reproduction is largely from root-sprouting or suckers. Aspen is very susceptible to fire damage at all stages of its growth, but if the trees are killed by crown fires, the roots will soon send up a host of suckers which actually make faster growth than the shoots of seedlings. They are, however, shorter-lived, and if an Aspen is forced to sucker repeatedly, owing to crown fires, its suckers grow progressively feebler. Seedlings, having the vitality that comes with sexual reproduction, are naturally strong, but very susceptible to ground fires.

Harmful though fire is to Aspen, it is also the chief factor in the abundant success of Aspens over large areas. For Aspens do far better than most of their competitors in the intense sunlight of the tract cleared by fire; their seeds thrive in mineral soil such as may be laid bare by a humus-destroying ground fire. Thousands of seedlings spring up on burned-over and logged-over lands and, though only a fraction will survive, they will form those groves which make such excellent nurseries for other trees. As if designed to be nurse trees, Aspens, after a precocious burst of speed, begin to flag after fifty years or so — just when other trees, slower to get started, begin their period of greatest growth. In the next half-century Aspens are likely to be shaded out by their competitors and, their life expectancies being in any case short (100 years or exceptionally 200), they often give way to conifers, their good work done. In the Far North, though, and high on the Rockies, where the harsh climatic conditions bear more heavily on other trees, the hardy Aspens may form permanent stands.

The wood of Trembling Aspen will never be of value to the lumberman; it is not strong enough for structural purposes, its grain is commonly twisted and cannot be dependably seasoned; more, by the time most Aspens have reached saw-log size they are already infected by heart-rot fungi, species of *Fomes*. But whole logs of Aspen have been cut for log cabins; the Mormon pioneers made furniture of it in Utah, and its white wood recommended it for the kitchen utensils of their wives. But, though weak in many senses, it is also tough, like Willow — tougher far than most Pine; so from early times it has been used for barn floors and fence posts, corral posts and siding, and the stalls of horses, for it stands up against the kicking and gnawing of horses without splintering. It is used for snake rail fences and has been extensively cut for mine props; the poles have even been pressed into service to carry telephone wires.

And Aspen wood has certain qualities that recommend it above all other woods. Its peculiar shredding properties make it ideal for excelsior, extensively used in the West for packing watermelons, avocadoes and cantaloupes, and as padding for furniture, coffin cushions, and as an absorbent or filter in air-conditioning units for cars. Aspen excelsior is in great demand for wallboard, making a good soundproof and insulating product with the appearance of compact "shredded wheat."

The fibers of Aspen wood are too short to make a strong paper but when mixed with the stronger Spruce pulp they are ideal for book and magazine papers, for the wood is inexpensive to start with, cheap to log and peel, and easy to bleach and to size so that the paper will take printer's ink.

Pulpwood logging begins in early spring because at this season, when the sap runs, the bark is easy to peel. When the peeling season is over, the logs are cut into 4-foot lengths and hauled or sledded to the railroad. If they are to be driven downstream, the intact logs are usually floated with Spruce, since green Aspen is likely to sink. Large mills, using the soda process, produce about a ton of paper an hour. A cord of Aspen bolts will yield about 1000 pounds of pulp.

Despised once as the veriest weed of a tree, Popple, as the pulp loggers prefer to call it, has sprung up on lands logged over for more valuable timber trees in such abundance that many erstwhile deflated lumber boom towns are returning to prosperity. And when Popple is cut over it may, under good conditions, reproduce itself, quite unaided, within 50 years. So what seems a shallow-rooted, short-lived tree, driven like a vagabond from site to site as other species crowd upon it, may prove to have as much value, in the aggregate, as many a species of more solid reputation. All this — and charm as well!

The VANCOUVER ASPEN, variety *vancouveriana* (Trelease) Sargent, differs in having the leaves harsh to the touch and dark green on the upper surface, the female catkins 2 to 2½ inches long, with the rachis, stalklets, and disk densely long-hairy, and the capsules on stalklets ¼ inch long instead of ⅛₂ inch. It is found on Vancouver Island and around the shores of Puget Sound generally, and occasionally in the Willamette Valley of Oregon.

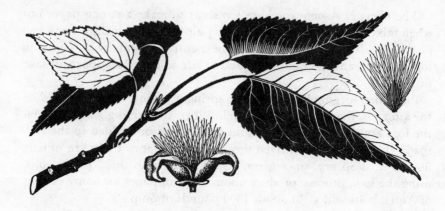

BALSAM POPLAR

Populus balsamifera Linnæus

OTHER NAMES: Tacamahac. Balm-of-Gilead. Rough-barked Poplar.

RANGE: Alaska, from 165° west longitude eastward almost throughout the interior and south to the head of the Lynn Canal; valley of the Mackenzie, east to Hudson Bay, Labrador, Newfoundland, and Nova Scotia; south to Idaho, Colorado, the Black Hills, the Turtle Mountains, northwestern Nebraska, Minnesota (except the corn belt), central parts of Wisconsin and Michigan, and to northern New England. Of scattered occurrence throughout New York State, rare in western Pennsylvania, in Iowa, northern Nevada, and British Columbia.

DESCRIPTION: *Bark* of trunks thin, light brown, smooth or warty, and in old age gray, furrowed, with broad, round ridges. *Winter buds* saturated in sticky, aromatic gum, the terminal bud large. *Twigs* of the season red-brown, becoming shiny the first winter, yellow-green the following spring, the lenticels bright orange. *Leaves* on rounded stalks, at first gummy, becoming dark green and shiny above, but paler or rusty or whitened with a bloom on the lower surface, 3 to 5 inches long, ½ to 3 inches wide. *Flowers* in long-stalked catkins, the female becoming 4 or 5 inches long. *Seed pods* small, light brown. *Wood* soft, weak, light (22 pounds to the cubic foot, dry weight), with pale brown heartwood and thick bands of white sapwood.

Those who have ventured beyond the great North Woods, out on the arctic prairies, where all the rivers fall into the polar sea or Hudson Bay, tell us of the surprising beauty of the isolated groves of Balsam Poplar there. As known in the western United States, it is only one

Poplar among many, nor does it attain, in the southern parts of its range, its greatest size, for there it is only 40 or 50 feet high, and dwarfed by its setting of mountain canyons. But out on the tundra of the Far North it may be the only tree, as it accompanies the lonely canoeman all the way, like a friend, and under favorable conditions it will grow to a height of 100 feet, with a long, cleanly, pole-like trunk and a slender crown with strongly ascending branches. In the endless monotony of arctic and subarctic scenery such a tree looms like a noble tower. It gives shade where none could be expected; it gives fuel — however inferior — where otherwise none could be had. Even the rustling of the leaves is most companionable when all else is silent. And the odor of the gummy buds in spring fills the stern arctic airs with fragrance.

Balsam Poplar delights to grow upon low and repeatedly inundated bottom-lands — riverbanks and sandbars, borders of bogs and swamps. So streams like the Athabasca, the Peace, and the Mackenzie, as they eat at their banks or change their course in flood, are continually sweeping down great trunks of the Balsam Poplar on their turbulent floods, to bleach as driftwood upon their estuaries and the unvisited shores of the arctic sea.

A fast-growing tree, whose trunk may attain 6 or 7 feet in diameter, this species, like so many other Poplars, acts as a nurse tree, preparing the way for the seedlings of Spruce. But as the Spruce grows tall it creates about itself and on the forest floor a dark, cold environment, completely hostile to the future seedlings of the sun-loving Balsam Poplar. So that it is driven away by the brood that it nurtured, and on its far-flying wings the seed must seek a new home.

The forester's name for this tree is Balsam Poplar, but to the pulp loggers of the North Woods it is Balm-of-Gilead (though the horticulturist means by that quite a different variety). Sometimes the loggers call it Balsam, which is confusing to say the least, or again they may designate it simply as Bam — a corruption, presumably, of Balm. Yet when it goes to market this wood often loses identity in the general designation of Popple, and so the cut of this particular species cannot usually be distinguished statistically on the ledgers of the wood-using industries.

A wood so quick-growing, so abundant on otherwise useless logged-over and burned-over lands and so soft amongst hardwoods, is nearly ideal for pulp, especially in the manufacture of magazine stock. Slim poles of young growth will do as well as large old trees, where pulp is the only consideration, and if the stand is cut over frequently it tends to keep on reproducing itself instead of giving way, at length, to Spruce.

The lumberman too has an interest in Balsam Poplar, but prefers large trees which yield broad, clear planks. Though so soft and weak a wood, Balsam Poplar is remarkably tough in proportion to its light weight. This makes it valuable for deal for boxes and crates, and for cutting into thin veneers for berry baskets. It is not even despised by the furniture manufacturers, as a core for costlier surfaces, and fine excelsior is made of its easily shredding wood.

BLACK COTTONWOOD

Populus trichocarpa Torrey and Gray

OTHER NAMES: Balsam or Balm Cottonwood. Balm.

RANGE: Kenai peninsula on the south coast of Alaska, and southern Yukon Territory, south throughout British Columbia (except the north-eastern part), Vancouver Island, Washington, northern and western Oregon and widespread in California going up to 10,000 feet in the Sierra Nevada, and generally not below 3000 feet in the mountains of San Diego County. Also in northern and western Idaho, northwestern Montana, in Nevada in the Tahoe region and on the high mountains of northern Baja California.

DESCRIPTION: *Bark* of young trunks greenish and smooth, that of old trunks very thick, deeply and sharply furrowed, with pale gray, broad, rounded ridges. *Twigs* rather slender, for a Cottonwood, commonly with narrow, projecting ridges at first red-brown, becoming in the second season dark gray and flecked by many orange lenticels and greatly roughened by the big, thick, raised leaf scars. *Winter buds* ¾ inch long, ¼ inch broad, curved, long-pointed and orange-brown, the 6 or 7 scales covered by an aromatic resin. *Leaves* 3 to 6 inches long, 2 to 4 inches broad, thickish and somewhat leathery, the upper surface dark green and smooth, the lower markedly veiny, pale green to silvery-white or sometimes rusty brown; the stalks long and round in cross-section. *Flowers* — male in dense, long, heavy catkins, each floret with 40 to 60 large light purple stamens; female in loose catkins with hoary ovary and 3 short styles with lobed stigmas. *Fruit* a nearly spherical, green, thick-walled, 3-valved capsule ⅓ inch long, in a long loose drooping spike. *Wood* light (23½ pounds per cubic foot, dry weight), soft and weak, with dull brown heartwood and thin white sapwood.

The Black Cottonwood is generally considered the largest Poplar in North America, perhaps in the world. Commonly it grows from 80 to 125 feet high, with rugged columnar trunks 3 and 4 feet in diameter. And in the early days specimens 200 feet high, with boles 7 and 8 feet thick, were reported from the region where it grows best — on the islands, bottom-lands, flats, benches and banks of the great Columbia River system. Fringing all those streams for mile upon mile, it comes to dominate the landscape, which is saying much, for this is the most impressive river scenery in all the West.

And when the great drafts blow up and down the Columbia gorge — the cool indrafts of sea wind or the hot exhaling breath of the interior basin east of the Cascades — they go plowing through the riparian forests. Then the Black Cottonwood comes into its full beauty, for on one side the leaf blades are darkly glittering, on the other almost silvery white with rusty veins. If you look down on this scene from the hills and highways, the trees seem, like the sea, to break into white-caps before the wind. Then, as the breeze dies down, they regain for the moment their green composure. In autumn the foliage turns a clear lemon yellow or a dull yellowish brown, never so beautiful as the Trembling Aspen's, but rich for all that.

This tree is called a Cottonwood and there is no disputing with a popular name whether ideally accurate or not. But in fact it belongs, like the two following species of "Cottonwood" as well as the one preceding, to a group of the genus *Populus* known as the Balsam Poplars or Tacmahacs whose distinguishing traits are their round or

4-angled, but not flattened, leafstalks, their great sticky, shining buds with a strong balsamic odor, their narrow or at least long-pointed leaf blades with rounded (not truncate) base, and their straight single trunks bearing upright branches to form a long crown. Amongst them the Black Cottonwood is by all means the most beautiful, and may be distinguished from other western Balsam Poplars by the narrow projecting ridges along the twigs. The common name of Balsam Cottonwood expresses this relation to other Balsam Poplars, and sometimes lumbermen call it simply Balm.

When the trunks grow large enough to make it profitable to cut them, as in Oregon, the logs yield clear wide lumber; some 7,000,000 board feet a year are cut for crates, sugar barrels, woodenware, for all of which uses the lightness, whiteness, and cheapness of the wood recommend it, where its softness and weakness are no disadvantage.

NARROWLEAF COTTONWOOD

Populus angustifolia James

OTHER NAMES: Black, Bitter, Mountain, Willow, or Willow-leaved Cottonwood. Narrow-leaved Poplar.

RANGE: Streambanks, generally between 5000 and 10,000 feet altitude, from southwestern Alberta south in the Rockies and on the high plains to western Texas and eastern and central Arizona and the mountains of Sonora and Chihuahua, Mexico. Also on the high plains of western Nebraska, the mountains of eastern and central Nevada, and in eastern Washington.

DESCRIPTION: *Bark* of young trunks smooth, thin, light yellow-green, becoming at the base of old trunks much thicker and shallowly fissured into broad, flat ridges. *Twigs* slender, flecked with pale lenticels, light yellow-green at first, becoming orange by the end of the first season, then pale yellow and finally ashen. *Winter buds* long-pointed and very gummy, with 5 thin concave scales, the terminal buds ¼ to ½ inch long. *Leaves* 2 to 3 inches long, ½ to 1 inch wide (or twice as large on sucker shoots), thin and firm, the upper surface bright yellow-green, the lower, paler beneath with stout yellow midrib, the veins arching and uniting below the thickened and slightly curled-under margin; leafstalks round in cross-section. *Flowers* in dense short-stalked catkins, with light brown, papery lobed bracts; male flowers with 12 to 30 big red stamens, the female with cup-shaped disk, the style terminated by 2 oblique stigmas. *Fruit* a thin-walled, 2-valved capsule ¼ inch long. *Seeds* ⅛ inch long, brown and hairy. *Wood* light (24 pounds per cubic foot, dry weight), soft and brittle, the heartwood pale brown, the thin sapwood nearly white.

To look at the foliage of the Narrowleaf Cottonwood, one would scarcely know it for any sort of Poplar, for the leaf blades are almost like some Willow's, both in their slenderness and their finely toothed edges. But most Willow twigs are beset with stipules — little leaf-like appendages at the base of the leafstalk — while Poplars never bear them. The buds of the Narrowleaf Cottonwood, especially in spring, are coated with a heavy resin exhaling a strong balsamic odor, proving that this is one of the Balsam Poplar group, and no Willow at all.

Reaching heights of 40 to 60 feet, with a narrowly pyramidal crown of strong, upright, slender branches, Narrowleaf Cottonwood is a fine handsome hardwood as it grows in groups or singly along mountain streams and moist flats, at 4800 to 9000 feet above sea level in the Rockies. It was first observed by Lewis and Clark on June 6, 1805 as they toiled up the Missouri on their immortal journey and came on "a species of cottonwood with a leaf like that of the wild cherry." On June 12 they mention that a narrow-leaved Cottonwood is mixed with the broad-leafed kind (*Populus Sargentii,* we would call it now) that had formed the principal timber of the Missouri. And they observed the whitish undersurface of the leaf blades and the fineness of the serrations of the margin, and add that the beavers seemed to prefer the narrow-leaved species because of its "deeper and softer bark." Marvelously keen and reliable observers of trees were these two, especially Meriwether Lewis who, at Thomas Jefferson's suggestion, studied botany while preparing himself for the momentous expedition. Many were the new species he discovered in those two years in the West, and only his untimely death by murder or suicide robbed him of the honor of naming this tree and many other new species.

As yet the lumber industry has taken no interest in the soft weak wood of this tree, though it is locally cut in the ranching country for fence posts and corral poles. But its hardiness and swift growth, in a region often hostile to trees, has caused it to be extensively planted in Rocky Mountain towns, as a street tree, where with a little irrigation it has become a handsome ornamental.

FREMONT COTTONWOOD

Populus Fremontii Watson

OTHER NAME: White Cottonwood.

RANGE: From the Sacramento Valley and inner Coast Ranges of northern California, south through the central and southern Coast Ranges and the water holes and streams of the Mohave Desert to northern Baja California; also in southern (rarely in northern) Arizona and southwestern New Mexico to the Sierra Madre of Sonora and Chihuahua; also in western Nevada and southwestern Utah.

DESCRIPTION: *Bark* of young trunks gray-brown and smooth, on old trunks thick, dark, deeply furrowed and boldly ridged. *Twigs,* round, in cross-section, pale yellow at first, then turning yellow-gray, only slightly roughened by the 3-lobed leaf scars. *Winter buds* hairless, the terminal buds ⅓ to ½ inch long and light green. *Leaves* 2 to 2½ inches long, 2½ to 3 inches wide, thick and firm, light yellow-green; leafstalks flattened at least in the the lower half, 1½ to 3 inches long, without glands. *Flowers* — the male in dense catkins 1½ to 2 inches long, each floret with 60 or more big red stamens, the female catkins sparsely flowered, the ovary with 3 broad stigmas. *Fruit* a thick-walled 3-valved capsule ⅓ to ½ inch long, and only very short-stalked in a compact drooping spike. *Seeds* ⅛ inch long, light brown and hairy. *Wood* with light brown heartwood and thin whitish sapwood (29½ pounds per cubic foot, dry weight), soft, brittle, liable to crack, and not durable.

The Frémont Cottonwood is a true Cottonwood, for it belongs, like all the following species, to the section of the genus *Populus* having, generally, leaves as broad as or broader than long, triangular in shape, and usually with a truncate base and a translucent margin,

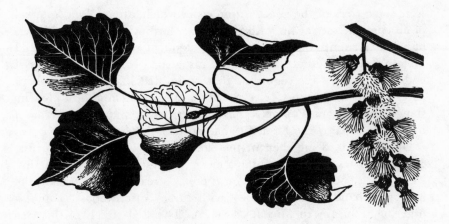

while the leafstalks are flattened in a way that keeps the foliage spinning in every light breeze. More, Cottonwoods, which are typically trees of riverbanks and water holes, are inclined to fork near the base into several equal trunks; as a result, all will be outward-leaning and the crown of foliage will be very broad, casting a wide pool of shade in summer. So, sign of water in the arid lands, fuel in an unwooded country, shade where shade is needed most, Cottonwoods are mentioned more often than any other vegetation in the literature of early exploration in the open Far West.

Most of the pioneers, though men of epic courage and ability, were not botanists, and to them any Cottonwood was just a Cottonwood. But John Charles Frémont, whose courage was seriously impugned by those who traveled with him, who proved his incompetence as a soldier and governor, who was styled "The Pathfinder" but seldom found a path in all the West not already known to traders, trappers, and Indians, was quite a genuine scientist. He was an excellent topographer, geologist, and mathematician, a good linguist, and a very fair botanist. Carefully he wrote up every night, by the flickering campfires that must soon be extinguished for fear of Indian attack, his notes on the vegetation. And on the night of January 6, 1844, near Pyramid Lake in present-day Nevada, he makes the first note of the tree that was to bear his name:

"Taking with me . . . [Kit] Carson, I made a thorough exploration of the neighboring valleys and found in a ravine in the bordering mountains a good camping place where was water in springs and a sufficient quantity of grass for a night. Overshadowing the springs were some trees of the sweet cottonwood, which, after a long interval of absence, we saw again with pleasure, regarding them as harbingers of a better country. To us they were eloquent of green prairies and buffalo." The reference to "sweet" Cottonwood is not an adjective of endearment, but a recognition that these trees had an inner bark palatable to his mounts. Certain other species of *Populus* — for instance the Balsam Poplars — have bitter bark, and these Frémont habitually calls by the French Canadian name of *liard amère*.

On April 10, being then in the San Joaquin Valley of California, Frémont writes again: "Turning a few miles up toward the mountains, we found a good encampment on a pretty stream hidden among the hills and handsomely timbered with large cottonwoods (*populus,* differing from any in Michaux's Sylva). The seed vessels of this tree were now just about bursting." From this we may assume that Frémont traveled with the heavy three-volume *Sylva* of François André Michaux, illustrated with Redouté's beautiful plates, and had the habit of making comparisons between that early classic and any specimens he met.

Leaving the San Joaquin Valley, Frémont set out on the Mohave desert to look for the reputed river of "San Buenaventura" and he struck it in the neighborhood of present-day Victorville, California. "The morning of the 22d of April was clear and bright and a snowy peak [San Antonio — "Old Baldy"] to the southward shone out high and sharply defined. . . . We travelled down the right bank of . . . a clear bold stream, 60 feet wide, and several feet deep. . . . It is well wooded . . . with willows and the beautiful green of the sweet cotton-woods. As we followed along its course the river, instead of growing constantly larger, gradually dwindled away, as it was absorbed by the sand." So much for the stream (now called the Mohave River) which was supposed to flow from California to the Mississippi! But if Frémont had disproved the existence of a great river he had discovered a great Cottonwood — *the* Cottonwood of all Arizona and southern California — Frémont's Cottonwood.

Growing from 50 to 100 feet high, with diameters of 1½ to 4 feet through the bole, this is an astonishingly large tree to find in such arid country. However, the spots it chooses are not in themselves truly arid, for it succeeds only along permanent streams and around water-holes. Where the streams are intermittent, it ventures for a while, but usually gives up.

When you stand on the rim of the Grand Canyon, the line of green that you see at the very bottom is made up of Frémont Cottonwoods, and this species follows the mighty river to its great, muddy delta where it empties into the lonely Gulf of California. There this riparian tree is forever being swept into the stream as the braided channels shift and eat at their banks. But forever the tree comes back, undismayed and determined.

Throughout the year Frémont Cottonwood maintains a changing drama of beauty; in earliest spring the catkins ripen on the naked wood, and the bees collecting pollen may make an uproar among the male flowers. When these fall, they litter for a brief while the pools, the cattle trough, and the streets of the western towns where they are so much planted. But the female catkins, of course, remain on the trees till the necklace-like strings of pods burst open and the seeds on their fluffy down float away. Then once again the litter is deep — a sort of snow that flies through the air in spring all around the ranches, the rivers, the towns, catching in the window screens, drifting in the corners of the corrals, and giving a sort of wild autumnal air to the days that are really lengthening and growing steadily warmer.

In the meantime the leaves have come out, and for a while they shine a brilliant, pale, cleanly green that gradually darkens and becomes glittering. Then, if not stripped away by the tussock moth, they spread their great pools of shade. And with every hot summer wind there comes from the dense crowns a mocking sound as of rushing water — a sudden gushing forth of some secret spring, that stops again as suddenly as it began, when the dry wind fails.

In fall the leaves turn yellow — not a beautiful translucent gold like Aspen's but still very welcome in desert lands that else would scarcely know autumn hues at all. About this time the buzzards begin to gather in great flocks in the Cottonwoods, stretching their naked necks and heads, silently, somberly congregating before their migratory flights. Early in the autumn mornings they unlimber their great black wings, and soar up in circles, to scout all the desert for its toll of dead.

Then when winter comes, and sunlight is needed for the traveler, the Cottonwoods stand naked. But their upper bark shines whitely against the winter skies, and the twigs, long before spring, begin to glow with a fresh pale yellow tint. And now show forth the tufts of sickly-green mistletoe that parasitizes the Cottonwoods even to the extent, sometimes, of killing them.

The tree's own twigs are forever competing with each other and killing their brothers. So there is a perpetual self-pruning going on in a Frémont Cottonwood's crown, with a corresponding litter beneath the trees. These bits make ideal kindling for the campfire of the old "desert rat," and he gathers them while he turns his burro out to graze on the *cienaga* cactus and to drink at the water hole.

The Mohave Indians once had their own uses for this tree, in the days when they painted themselves with ocher, clay, charcoal, and oil. For the women's skirts (their only garments, which did not even reach their knees) consisted, behind, of a mass of strips of the inner bark of Cottonwood hung from a string passing around the hips, while the front was made gay with twisted cords of vegetable fiber dyed in various colors.

To the Spanish pioneers this tree was the *alamo*, and most of the cities of northern Mexico are planted, at least around the inevitable plaza, with double rows of it; under its gracious shade at dusk walk the girls in couples and threes, in one direction, while the boys circulate in the other, with comments and glances exchanged in this grand right-and-left. Commonly the Mexicans and the Spanish-speaking people of the southwestern states pollard the Cottonwoods each year, in order to obtain a perpetual supply of fuel, and this gives their trees an odd, squat look. We gringos usually prefer trees to assume their natural shapes, but to the Latin peoples a tree exists to serve man, *por Dios,* and is often made to serve him by being bent to his will quite out of its primitive shape.

PLAINS COTTONWOOD

Populus deltoides W. Bartram, variety *occidentalis* Rydberg

OTHER NAMES: Western or Sweet Cottonwood. Sargent Poplar.

RANGE: New Mexico to Alberta, in the foothills of the Rockies, and east through the panhandles of Texas and Oklahoma, to eastern parts of Kansas and Nebraska (to the Missouri) and the Dakotas.

DESCRIPTION: *Bark* of the trunk thick and pale and equally divided into broad, rounded ridges. *Twigs* stout, angular, light yellow. *Winter buds* downy, light orange-brown. *Leaves* on flattened stalks, furnished with one or two small glands where stalk and blade join, the blade 3 to 3½ inches long, and ½ inch broader than long, thick, heavy, pale green and very shiny. *Flowers* — male catkins 2 to 2½ inches long, female catkins becoming 4 to 8 inches long. *Seed pod* ⅜ of an inch long, thin-walled. *Wood* dark yellowish brown with thick, nearly white sapwood.

The Plains Cottonwood is, upon the average, somewhat smaller (from 50 to 75 feet tall) than the Eastern Cottonwood, *Populus del-toides* proper, but occasionally it grows as much as 90 feet high, with trunks 4 to 6 feet thick. From such mighty boles were made the Missouri River pirogues, in the period of westward venture from 1860 to 1870. Hollowed out with fire, these primitive river craft were often 4 feet through, and two of them, placed side by side and solidly lashed together, could carry a burden of 10 to 15 tons.

It is difficult to realize that Cottonwood could have value as a forage for horses on the vast pasturage of the grass plains, but in winter the grass, of course, is covered with snow, and the Indians — so Josiah Gregg tells us in his *Commerce of the Prairies* — taught the early white trappers and explorers to feed their horses on the sweet inner bark. General Custer alludes to this in his fascinating memoirs:

"During the winter campaign of 1868–'69 against the hostile tribes south of the Arkansas, it not infrequently happened that my command while in pursuit of Indians exhausted its supply of forage, and the horses and mules were subsisted upon the bark of the cottonwood tree. In routing the Indians from their winter villages, we invariably discovered them located upon that point of the stream promising the greatest supply of cottonwood bark, while the stream in the vicinity of the village was completely shorn of its supply of timber, and the village itself was strewn with the white branches of the cottonwood entirely stripped of their bark. It was somewhat amusing to observe an Indian pony feeding on cottonwood bark. The limb being usually cut into pieces about four feet in length and thrown upon the ground, the pony, accustomed to this kind of 'long forage,' would place one forefoot on the limb in the same manner as a dog secures a bone, and gnaw the bark from it. Although not affording anything like the amount of nutriment which either hay or grain does, yet our horses invariably preferred the bark to either, probably on account of its freshness." [1]

Among the trials of pioneering life in the West was "gyppy" water — drinking water impregnated with gypsum and other alkalies, resulting in severe gastric disorders. Cottonwood sometimes provided a remedy when snakeroot was lacking. Thus Charles Goodnight, the great Texas cattleman, recalls that the cowboys "would get the inside bark, boil it to a strong tea, and drink liberally. It is a hell of a drink, a wonderful astringent, and a bitter dose. But it is a sure shot." [2]

From this, the chief tree of the prairies, the Omaha Indians made the sacred pole, which they regarded somewhat as the ancient Hebrews did the Ark of the Covenant. And Cottonwood bark was employed as a fuel for roasting the clays used in making paints for heraldic and symbolic painting of the skin, while a yellow dye was made from the leaf buds in early spring. Indian children used to make Cottonwood leaves into toy wigwams:

"They split a leaf a short distance down from the tip along the midrib; at equal distances from the tip they tore across from the margin slightly; then, bending back the margin above the rents for the smoke flaps, and drawing together the leaf-margins below the rents and fastening them with a splinter or a thorn, they had a toy tipi. These they made in numbers and placed them in circles like the camp circle of their tribe." [3]

In the days when the veritable great tipis rose thus, the days too of the prairie schooners, immigrants sighted their way, on the Santa Fe trail and the Oregon trail, from one grove of Plains Cottonwoods to

[1] George A. Custer, *My Life on the Plains*, 1875.

[2] Quoted in *Charles Goodnight, Cowman and Plainsman* by J. Evetts Haley, University of Oklahoma Press, 1949.

[3] Melvin Randolph Gilmore, "Uses of Plants by the Indians of the Missouri River Region," *Twenty-Third Annual Report*, Bureau of American Ethnology. Smithsonian Institution (1911–1912).

the next, sure that there they would find water, fuel, and shade in the burning day. For this Cottonwood grows naturally in low moist ground, in the vicinity of streams, water holes, and old buffalo wallows. Upon that shelterless sea of grass four hundred miles wide, these Cottonwood groves were the wayside inn, the club, the church, the newspaper and fortress, when the wagon trains drew up in a circle beneath the boughs. Whether the traveler "nooned it" or by night sent the sparks of Cottonwood logs flying to the stars, here he was sure to meet other travelers, and with them exchange the vital news of the trail. And these trees, whispering among each other, must have heard the talk of women, exchanging the immemorial secrets of their kind.

RIO GRANDE COTTONWOOD

Populus Wislizeni (Watson) Sargent

OTHER NAME: Wislizenus or Valley Cottonwood.

RANGE: Mountains of central Colorado and southeastern Utah south to the Big Bend country of Texas and a short distance over the border in Mexico.

DESCRIPTION: *Bark* of trunks thick and pale gray-brown, deeply furrowed and with broad, flat, connecting ridges. *Twigs* stout, round in cross-section, hairless, at first light orange-brown, becoming gray later and roughened by the old, raised leaf scars. *Winter buds* ⅛ to ⅜ inch long, brown, shining, downy and gummy but not fragrant. *Leaves* 2 to 2½ inches long, 3 inches broad (or on sucker shoots larger), thick and leathery, the upper surface shiny yellow-green, the lower paler; leafstalks flattened, 1½ to 2 inches long, slim and smooth, without glands. *Flowers* in catkins 2 to 4 inches long, the male florets with numerous short-stalked stamens, the female with light red, long-fringed disks. *Fruit* a thick-walled, 3- to 4-valved capsule ¼ inch long, on very long slim stalks, in a loose, branching, pendant cluster. *Seeds* light brown and hairy-tufted. *Wood* soft, brittle, light, warping and checking badly in seasoning.

The Rio Grande River and its tributaries from Colorado to Chihuahua are bordered by groves of this fine Cottonwood which forms *bosques,* as the Spanish-speaking New Mexicans call them, of sometimes large extent. Along white water in the New Mexican mountains, the Narrowleaf Cottonwood, really a Balsam Poplar, is seen. But the

present species is, in most counties of the state, the only true Cottonwood, and its habitat is chiefly along the lower valleys, the slower
waters. So it is called Valley Cottonwood, to distinguish it from Mountain Cottonwood, the narrow-leaved species. And you see it all over
the state, as an ornamental in the streets of the towns and around the
plazas; almost every school playground is sheltered by it; it is planted
around the railway stations and the hogans and pueblos of the Indian
reservations, and it shades the ranch dooryard, corral, and drinking-
trough. It grows, too, in verdant lines along the *acequias* — the irrigation ditches. Whether the human dwelling came to the kindly tree or
the tree was set out by loving hands we seldom can know, or need to.

In any case, the Rio Grande Cottonwood is beloved wherever it
grows, and even the casual traveler, looking out from automobile or
train window, readily sees why. For, amidst the range lands, the deserts,
or the monotonous foothills clad in stunted Pinyon and Juniper, hot-
looking and stingy of shade as they are, the Cottonwoods — growing
50 to 100 feet high — seem very lofty. Their shade is delicious in the
long summers, and in winter they yield fuel to the outdoor ovens and
little triangular fireplaces. The liquid whisper of their foliage is sweet
to hear, and its autumnal hue of lemony gold is very fair against the
bald blue of the skies. Even in winter the Cottonwoods shine forth
whitely against a grayer sky. One could not ask a more thoroughly

domestic tree. What if its life is short, when it sprouts so freely, and seeds so abundantly? The white down goes sailing through the airs in late spring, collecting in drifts on the streets, in the fences, in the ponds and the window screens, and floating down the tinkling irrigation ditches to find new homes.

Rio Grande Cottonwoods have a large bird population. Flocks of Treganza blue herons roost and sometimes nest in them, and all the hawks use them for look-outs. From their boughs the Arizona hooded and Bullock orioles hang their pendent nests, keeping up a rolling tuneful music. Naturally the hollow trunks of old trees are favorites with the Gila woodpecker and the red-shafted flicker whose "if-if-if-if-if-if" is heard during the season of raising the nestlings and its "wick-up-wick-up" at all times. In abandoned woodpecker and flicker holes the many kinds of owl will nest, as well as nuthatches and bluebirds, while the beautiful little violet-green swallows make their lodging in an old hollow Cottonwood bole.

Horses gladly gnaw at the sweet inner bark of the Rio Grande Cottonwood. If the logs or poles are debarked they will not swiftly decay and so make good posts and ceiling beams for adobe houses for, despite the weakness and warping of planed Cottonwood boards, there is no objection to solid poles of it in adobe structure.

The first discovery of this species was made by Frederick Augustus Wislizenus, a German physician and naturalist who settled in St. Louis but at the very early date of 1839 was already venturing far into the mountains of Wyoming and Colorado. Those were the days when you had to brush aside the Arapahoes and rattlers, the buffalo and fierce Sioux, to travel. Yet in 1846 this doughty European joined a merchant caravan going out on the old Santa Fe trail and, leaving it at the end of its journey, he continued south along the Rio Grande to Mexico, seeing much, surely, of the Cottonwood that was to be named for him. War had by this time been declared between Mexico and the United States, and Wislizenus was taken prisoner, but paroled to collect specimens within 2 leagues of his place of detention. At this time, or perhaps a little sooner, he collected the specimens that, more than 20 years later, were named by his fellow citizen of St. Louis, George Engelmann, in his honor.

The PALMER COTTONWOOD, *Populus Palmeri* Sargent, is a tree found in stream canyons of the Chisos Mountains and along the Rio Grande in the Big Bend country of western Texas, as well as in

Uvalde and Palo Pinto Counties, Texas. It has flattened leafstalks with glands near their junction with the leaf blades, slender twigs, thin, ovate and finely toothed leaves 2½ to 5 inches long, 1½ to 2¼ inches broad, and very thick pale bark on the old trunks divided by deep furrows into narrow ridges. It grows to a height of 60 feet, with a trunk as much as 3 feet thick, the smooth pale branches erect and forming an open conical head, the small branches horizontal or drooping.

THE WILLOWS
(*Salix*)

Willows are fast-growing trees, with bitter, astringent, aromatic bark, soft, light wood, with commonly a shrub-like habit of forking almost from the base. The vivid and limber twigs are frequently jointed near the base and so snap off easily. In our species the leafstalks are short and the alternate leaves are generally narrow and long (more than twice as long as broad) and turn yellow in autumn. In falling, the leafstalk marks the twigs with prominent scars. The sexes occur on separate plants, in elongated catkins; the sex organs are set on disks, provided with nectar glands. Thus Willows are insect-pollinated, though probably also wind-pollinated. The stamens are few in number and the ovaries bear 2 recurved, short, 2-lobed stigmas. The fruit is a flask-shaped seed pod containing numerous seeds winged with silky down.

In no case, except Hawthorns, is it so difficult to distinguish between trees and shrubs as in the case of Willows. All the tree species are also frequently shrubby; many of the habitually shrubby species are occasionally 20 to 25 feet tall. In our circumscription only the following are regularly of tree size, but one may occasionally find that other species are too, for example *Salix Coulteri, S. lucida, S. lutea, S. ligulifolia, S. Tracyi, S. melanopsis, S. Mackenzieana, S. alaxensis, S. Piperi, S. amplifolia.*

*   *   *

VALLEY WILLOW

Salix nigra Linnæus, variety *vallicola* Dudley

OTHER NAMES: Dudley, Goodding, or Western Black Willow.

RANGE: Interior northern California (Shasta and Tehama Counties) south along the western foothills of the Sierra Nevada mountains and in the Great Central Valley along streams, to the mountain valleys of the southwestern part of the state (where rare) and along the valley of the Colorado River (where common) to southern Nevada; almost throughout Arizona below 4000 feet; along the Rio Grande in western Texas and southern New Mexico. Also in northern parts of Sonora, Chihuahua, and Baja California.

DESCRIPTION: *Bark* of old trunks rough, thick, deeply furrowed, with narrow connecting ridges, very dark brown or sometimes nearly black. *Twigs* slender and easily separable from the branch, light orange or grayish. *Leaves* 1½ to 3 inches long, ¼ to ½ inch wide — that is, 6 times as long as broad — often slightly curved and commonly much larger on vigorous new shoots, dull green and, at maturity, hairless, with fine glandular teeth, stalks ⅛ to ¼ inch long. *Flowers* in narrowly cylindric, pubescent catkins that are 1 to 2 inches long, and borne terminally on leafy pubescent branches; scales yellow, hoary-downy; stamens 5 to 11 in each male floret; ovary with distinct, 2-lobed style. *Fruit* a light reddish brown capsule ¼ inch long and usually pubescent.

The Valley Willow was first collected as early as 1845 by John C. Frémont on one of his famed expeditions that were one third survey, one third filibustering, and one (and the best) third scientific. Sometimes it is a mere shrub, especially where the stream that laves its roots is a mere creek, but when it grows on the banks of a large river able, like the Sacramento, Colorado, and Rio Grande, to maintain a considerable volume of flow the year around, this tree grows 20 to 45 feet high. Commonly it is forked from the very base, with two or more widely spreading stems and a broad, loose, irregular crown. Only if crowded by other trees will it consent to stand up straight and make a compact growth.

The Valley Willow is known from all others in its wide range in the Southwest by the fact that its twigs, when pulled, snap off easily and neatly at the base, while other southwestern Willows tear raggedly when pulled. Indeed, the twigs are definitely articulated at base, just as are the bases of the leafstalks of deciduous trees in autumn, when the time comes for Nature to set them adrift. The autumn leaf, however, has no further destiny but to die. The articulated twigs of the Valley Willow, on the contrary, are quite capable of striking root wherever they are washed up by the streams of the Southwest. In this way the Valley Willow has spread along all the streams of California's Great Central Valley (whence the name). It is abundant on the lower reaches of the Colorado, after it leaves the Grand Canyon and takes its sluggish way to the Gulf of California; it extends up the Colorado's tributary in Arizona, the desert-crossing Gila, and many of the Gila's tributaries, far up into the mountain headwaters. Even beside the Mohave River is it found — that stream that is fed by the melting of the winter snowcaps of the Sierra Madre of California and flows eastward to die in the coruscating soda of an alkaline playa in the midst of the desert. How this Willow crossed a great mountain range, or a fierce desert to border the lonely Mohave with its shade, it would be hard to imagine except in terms of very different conditions in the geologic past.

To the desert traveler the sight of Willows is an infallible water-sign, and all the old accounts of early exploration, railway surveying, and Indian campaigning in the Southwest are full of grateful references to the Willow. To the desert Indians especially was this a valuable tree, and it still is. For though Willow wood is notoriously weak and practically worthless as fuel, it has properties of pliancy and splitting that timber trees do not possess. The Papago Indians, driven by their neighbors into the waterless Gila desert, had very little of this Willow and were — and still are — accustomed to trade for it with the more fortunate Pimas of the Tucson area. Or, when they make their annual trip to help the Pimas pick their cotton, or to assist in harvesting their wheat, they take the occasion to gather it.

For they have much use for the Valley Willow. With splints of it they weave baskets so tight that they hold water without caulking; indeed the Willow wood, as soon as wetted, swells up and closes even the minutest openings in the weave. The twigs have to be peeled the same day they are cut or the bark will adhere. They are then split lengthwise with the aid of a basketry awl and dried in the sun before being carried home for use. Very fine splints are often turned into long fibres and these serve the Indian women for a tough thread for sewing the baskets, which have a natural sweet odor when dry.

The EASTERN BLACK WILLOW, *Salix nigra* Marshall, barely reaches the circumscription of this book in western parts of Kansas, Oklahoma, and the Panhandle and Big Bend country of Texas. It differs from the Valley Willow in having reddish or grayish purple twigs, and in the bright green leaves which are 3 to 6 inches long and very narrow (only ⅛ to ¾ inch wide); that is, they are 8 to 24 times as long as broad. The fruiting capsules are hairless. The flowers appear after the leaves. The eastern Black Willow is the largest of all Willows when growing in rich bottom-lands of the Mississippi Valley; it may reach 150 feet in height there, but is usually not a fourth so tall on the periphery of its range.

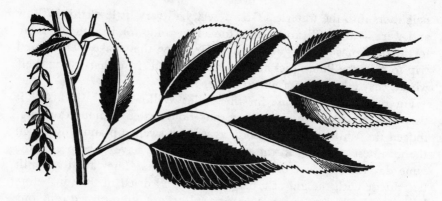

PEACH WILLOW

Salix amygdaloides Andersson

OTHER NAME: Almond Willow.

RANGE: Southern parts of British Columbia, Alberta and Saskatchewan, eastward to the north shore of Lake Superior, to Montreal, south through northern and western New York State to the Ohio Valley, throughout Missouri, and southwestward to the Panhandles of Oklahoma and Texas; widespread throughout the northern Rocky Mountain states to northwestern New Mexico, southern Utah, and eastern parts of Oregon and Washington; also in southwestern Oregon.

DESCRIPTION: *Bark* thin, reddish brown, divided by irregular furrows into flat braided ridges with thick plate-like scales. *Twigs* dark orange or red-brown and shining, marked with scattered pale lenticels. *Winter buds* dark chestnut brown, shiny, minute, and unsymmetrical. *Leaves* 2½ to 4 inches long, ¾ to 1¼ inches wide, pale green and shining above, pale and whitened with a bloom below, with stout orange or yellow midrib and prominent veins and meshed veinlets, teeth fine and numerous; stalks ¼ to ⅘ inch long, slender and twisted. *Catkins* 2 to 3 inches long, with yellow scales. *Seed pod* light reddish yellow, ¼ inch long. *Wood* soft, close-grained, light (28 pounds to the cubic foot, dry weight), with light brown heartwood and thick, nearly white sapwood.

The Peach Willow, named for the shape of its handsome blades, so like the foliage of the Peach, grows 60 or 70 feet tall, with a fine single straight trunk up to 2 feet thick, and straight, ascending branches. Not a frequent tree in the eastern states, it begins to be abundant around the mouth of the Ohio River, where it grows with its big sister species, the Black Willow. But the farther one goes toward the Rockies, the more Peach Willow tends to replace Black Willow along the Missouri and all the shallow braided streams tributary to it, and all the rivers that flow from the Rockies to the Gulf of Mexico.

The flowers appear at the same time as the leaves but grow more rapidly. With its gleaming leaves and general air of cleanliness and sprightliness, it is a vivid note in western river scenery wherever it occurs, and it holds innumerable banks from washing away. It is readily identified even from afar by its pendulous branchlets, giving it a somewhat weeping appearance.

Lewis and Clark in their toilsome journey up the Missouri must have seen this glittering foliage around every bend a thousand thousand times. Still fresh, still shining in the western winds that blow it, it speaks to us softly of the heroes — uncouth, Homeric and immortal — who must have rested, panting, in its shade.

The WRIGHT WILLOW, *Salix amygdaloides,* variety *Wrightii* (Andersson) Schneider, differs in having distinctly yellow or yellowish brown branches, and shorter, very narrow leaves ¼ to ⅛ inch wide, 1½ to 2 inches long, with very gradually narrowed bases and very long drawn out tips, the upper surface yellow-green, the lower much paler, with the margins very finely toothed. It grows along the Rio Grande near El Paso, and in Potter and Ward Counties, western Texas, and westward rather commonly throughout New Mexico except the northwestern part. This is the common narrow-leaved Willow of New Mexico, at lower levels, occurring along streams, *acequias,* and flood plains.

RED WILLOW

Salix lævigata Bebb

OTHER NAMES: Smooth, or Polished Willow.

RANGE: Northwestern California (Siskiyou and Del Norte Counties), south in the Coast Ranges and Great Central Valley to San Diego and Imperial Counties; along the Colorado River and its tributaries from Yuma, Arizona, north to southwestern Utah and along the Gila and San Pedro Rivers and their tributaries in central and southern Arizona.

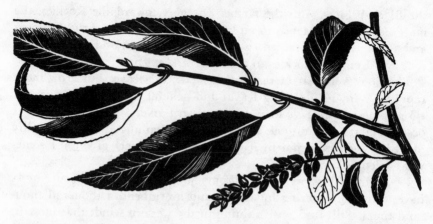

DESCRIPTION: *Bark* of trunks dark brown and deeply divided into irregular, connecting, flat and scaly ridges. *Twigs* slim, bright red-brown or orange. *Winter buds* pale chestnut-brown, rather blunt, ⅛ to ¼ inch long. *Leaves* 3 to 7 inches long, ¾ to 1½ inches wide, dark blue-green and shining above, pale and glaucous below, with a broad, flat, yellow midrib and a short, stout, grooved and minutely downy stalk; margins curled under, and obscurely toothed. *Flowers* in slender, lax, cylindric catkins that are 2 to 4 inches long and borne on leafy twigs; scales attached at their center, palely hairy; stamens usually 5 to 6 to a male floret; stigmas with broad, spreading, notched lobes. *Fruit* an elongated, conic, long-stalked capsule about ¼ inch long. *Wood* soft, light (30½ pounds per cubic foot, dry weight), the heartwood light brown tinged with red, with thick, nearly white sapwood.

Unlike most Willows, this one does not take readily to the banks of the slow, warm rivers, but likes to have its roots laved by living streams, white water, rippling or seething as it hurries out of the mountains of California. Consequently the Red Willow is the commonest of its kind along those mountain-born streams, the American, the Consumnes, the Mokelumne, the Tuolomne, the Stanislaus, and the Merced, whose sands once carried flakes of gold and nuggets washed down from the Mother Lode. There were, and are, Red Willows right on the bank of John Sutter's millrace on the American River, and Thomas Marshall must have pushed his way through them as his footsteps led him to the fateful discovery, that January day in 1849.

Then, when the Forty-niners came, these little trees must have shaded the backs of their necks, where they toiled in the furnace breath of the summer heat, with pick and pan. Under its shade they wrote their letters home and, womanless, washed and mended their clothes. But it served them in no other way, for such Willows are no good for fuel or timbers. Had they been, they would soon have vanished under the axe.

Instead, it is the Argonauts who vanished, this Willow that remains. There is no gold left in the streams now; after the white men had come and gone, the Chinese arrived, and with oriental patience amassed a fortune from the gleanings, and when the Celestials too departed, the Digger Indians (who gave the streams so many of their odd names) crept down out of the hills and with unfevered fingers turned over every last stone looking for yellow sands. Then they too vanished.

The white men brought with them from the eastern states the Black Locust and planted it where it still stands in grass-grown Coloma (the town that sprang up on the site of Marshall's discovery). The Chinese brought the Tree-of-heaven, still shading the few remaining houses smothered under old roses and honeysuckle. The Indians are remembered by the gray Digger Pines on the hills round about. But the Willow represents something more aboriginal than any race of man.

It is not an impressive tree, for it is usually only 15 to 25 feet high, with a short trunk and irregular broad crown, and at most grows to 50 feet. Its foliage, darkly gleaming above, silvery blue below, hangs still, with none of the brook-like fretting of the Cottonwoods. But there is gold about it yet. It comes pouring out from the trees in the canary-like trills of goldfinches and yellow warblers, and most of all in the explosive song of the long-tailed chat that, like some unsatisfied Argonaut, lingers always along those treasure-haunted streams.

YELLOW WILLOW

Salix lasiandra Bentham

OTHER NAMES: Waxy or Western Shining Willow. Western Black Willow.

RANGE: From the Arctic Circle and the valley of the Yukon (Alaska and Yukon Territory), south throughout valleys of British Columbia, Washington, Oregon and California to Baja California, and eastward to central Saskatchewan, western parts of Idaho and Nevada, southern parts of Utah and Colorado, northern parts of Arizona and New Mexico.

DESCRIPTION: *Bark* dark brown, shallowly fissured and cross-checked into broad, flat, scaly plates. *Twigs* rather stout, at first dark purple, or deep red, densely or sparingly hairy and often glaucous, later shiny and dark purple, reddish brown, yellow or orange-yellow. *Winter buds* light chestnut-brown and shining near the top, pale below. *Leaves* 1½ to 4 inches long, about ½ inch wide, dark green and shining above, pale or glaucous below (or green in some varieties), teeth fine and numerous. *Flowers* in narrowly cylindrical catkins 1 to 3 inches long, with palely pubescent scales; stamens 5 to 9 in each male floret; the style with short, slightly notched lobes. *Fruit* a light brown capsule ¼ inch long. *Wood* soft, brittle, medium-light (28 to 30 pounds per cubic foot, dry weight), the heartwood pale brown, the thick sapwood nearly white.

To identify the Yellow Willow in the field, look for the glandular-warty leafstalks and the long narrow leaves which take, commonly but not invariably, an odd sideways or oblique direction. In general the leaves are darker green than those of other Willows.

This is the commonest tree Willow of the Willamette Valley in Oregon, forming long lines along the streams and clustering about the sloughs and ponds, just the way the eastern Black Willow does in our middle-western states. It is abundant in the Great Central Valley of California and the foothills of the Sierra. Along the lower reaches of the Sacramento River (which remind one of the Delta country of the Mississippi by reason of the levees, the low-lying farms, the soft, heavy air), this becomes a fine tree, 40 or 50 feet high with one or more leaning stems.

The saddletrees of the Spanish Californians used to be made of this species and of the Red Willow, and were even exported at one time to

Mexico and Texas. Today it is of no known use except to dapple with its shade the streams of most of the western states and much of western Canada and Alaska, and to help in holding their banks in time of freshet and flood.

Several varieties have been described over its vast range. Variety *caudata* Sudworth has bright yellow or orange-yellow branchlets and very long-tipped leaves, green on both sides. It is the common form of the Rockies and interior regions of Oregon and Washington. Variety *lancifolia* Bebb is the form found from Alaska to northern California in the coastal regions. Its twigs and the lower surfaces of young leaves are covered with gray or rusty hairs.

BONPLAND WILLOW

Salix Bonplandiana Humboldt, Bonpland and Kunth, variety *Toumeyi* (Britton) Schneider

RANGE: Chihuahua and Sonora, Mexico, north to Sycamore Canyon, near Flagstaff, Arizona, and in the mountains of southwestern New Mexico. Also in Baja California.

DESCRIPTION: *Bark* dark brown or nearly black, and divided by narrow deep fissures into broad, flat, scaly ridges. *Twigs* slender, smooth, flecked with occasional pale lenticels, at first light yellow, becoming shiny brown and, in the second year, pale orange-brown. *Winter buds* long-pointed, curved, bright red-brown and shining, ¼ inch long. *Leaves* thick and firm, with a marked sidewise twist and curve, 4 to 6 inches long, ½ to ¾ inch wide, thick and firm, heavily mesh-veined below, shiny yellow-green above, the lower surface silver-white with incurled margins, the leafstalk stout, reddish and grooved. *Flowers* in erect, short-stalked, slender, cylindric catkins borne on leafy branches, the male catkins 1 to 1½ inches long, with usually 3 stamens to a floret, the female somewhat shorter, with club-shaped stigmas. *Fruit* a light reddish-yellow pod.

The visitor to the famed canals of Xochimilco, near Mexico City, notices, as he drifts along in his boat — buying flowers and paying for music from the natives' *canoas* — a kind of tree that he takes to be a Lombardy Poplar, on account of its very compact, pencil-shaped outline. But the boatman will tell him that it is no *alamo* but a *sauce* or an *ahuejote*, that is, a Willow — *Salix Bonplandiana*, to be botanically precise, named for Aimé Bonpland, the great French collaborator of Baron Humboldt. Whether or not the form (variety *Toumeyi*) of this tree first discovered in our country by E. A. Mearns, the naturalist, in southern New Mexico in 1893, is a distinct species, or only a variety, or not distinct at all, is a matter for botanists to argue. To the laymen it seems different enough, at least, for a variety, for instead of making a compact growth it forms a fairly broad crown. Its branches are quite erect and close to the trunk at the start, but they gradually spread out and at length are somewhat drooping. The leaves are narrower and less deeply toothed, and the catkins shorter, than in the typical species of central Mexico. Usually only attaining 25 feet at the most, along the streams of Arizona, this tree occasionally stands full 50 feet tall and makes a fine show with its foliage that is glittering above and whitish beneath. Alone amongst the Willows of the United States, this one is evergreen, retaining its leaves, or most of them, until the following spring. Though thickish, they do not, however, become hard like the blades of most broad-leaved evergreen trees.

SANDBAR WILLOW

Salix Hindsiana Bentham

OTHER NAME: Hinds Willow.

RANGE: Southwestern Oregon south to Baja California, in the flood beds of the Coast Range, the Great Central Valley, and the Sierra foothills up to 3000 feet altitude.

DESCRIPTION: *Bark* of mature trunks gray and furrowed. *Twigs* short, densely silvery-woolly at least in the first year. *Leaves* ¾ to 1½ inches long, ⅛ to ¼ inch wide, usually the margins not toothed or with only a few remote glandular teeth, or minutely toothed, bluish green under a gray silky-hairy pubescence which is sometimes deciduous. *Flowers* in numerous, paired, or solitary catkins ⅝ to 1½ inches long, on leafy stalks ¾ to 1½ inches long; the scales with long soft hairs; each male floret with 2 stamens, the filaments pubescent; ovary hairy, the stigmas deeply 2-lobed and recurved. *Fruit* a silky-woolly capsule.

Sometimes only a shrub, the Sandbar Willow may grow 25 feet high, with a single, tree-like, gray trunk, colonizing the banks of the major streams of the Great Central Valley of California. More, it increases by

stolons (underground, root-like stems) so rapidly as to clog the irrigation canals that, fed by the Sierra's snows and streams, are the life-
blood of the southern part of the Valley. As a holder of banks and
levees this Willow is highly efficient, but its virtues become the faults
of a weed in these artificial streams.

The flowers appear after the leaves, which in spring are extremely
silky with a dense coat of gray glistening hairs; the twigs, too, are
similarly clothed. No other Willow in the Valley has leaves that are
so short-stalked (less than ⅛ inch), and this serves to distinguish it
from most of its Willow neighbors.

SILVERLEAF WILLOW

Salix sessilifolia Nuttall

OTHER NAMES: Softleaf or Sandbar Willow.

RANGE: Vancouver Island, southwestern British Columbia and the Puget
Sound region and Whitcomb Valley in Washington, south to the upper
valleys of the Willamette and Umpqua Rivers in Oregon; not in the
mountains.

DESCRIPTION: *Twigs* silky-woolly. *Leaves* 1 to 2 inches long, ½ to ¾ inch
wide (or larger on vigorous summer shoots), sharply and minutely
toothed, pea-green or sage-green and densely to sparsely woolly on both
surfaces. *Flowers* in solitary or paired or triple catkins 1½ to 2½ inches
long, with densely hairy, deciduous, yellow scales, each male floret with

2 anthers with hairy filaments; ovary hairy, with deeply 2-lobed stigma. *Fruit* a hairy capsule. *Wood* soft and light (27½ pounds per cubic foot, dry weight).

The upper surface of the leaves of this little tree (it grows 25 feet high at the most) is a pale pea-green or sage-green, the lower is silvery-silky. When the wind sets the foliage (which is not unlike that of the Olive tree) to flashing, then the extensive thickets in which it grows on riverbanks, sandbars, and along irrigation canals in the Columbia and Willamette Valleys, make a charming sight. To this is often added the voice of the Cottonwood which delights to grow, with its woman-tongued foliage, in the same groves.

The flowers appear after the leaves and so attract slight attention. A distinguishing feature of this Willow is the fact that the foliage is seated almost directly on the twig, with practically no stalk.

COYOTE WILLOW

Salix exigua Nuttall

OTHER NAMES: Sandbar, Slender, or Slenderleaf Willow.

RANGE: Southern Alberta and the valley of the Fraser River in British Columbia, south along almost all the streams of the western states (except the Coast Ranges of Washington and Oregon), to western parts of Nebraska, the Big Bend country of Texas, and Baja California, Mexico.

DESCRIPTION: *Bark* of trunks thin, grayish brown, fissured. *Twigs* slender, smooth, brown. *Leaves* 1½ to 3 inches long, only ⅛ to ¼ inch wide (or larger on summer shoots) often slightly curved, minutely glandular-toothed above the middle, upper surface bluish green, the lower covered with minute silky white hairs. *Flowers* in catkins 1 to 2 inches long, with hoary-pubescent scales; male florets with 2 stamens each and filaments hairy below the middle; female with hairy ovary and stigma lobes seated directly upon it. *Fruit* a hairless capsule. *Wood* weighing 30 pounds per cubic foot, dry weight, with pale reddish-brown heartwood and thin grayish white sapwood.

In most parts of its wide range the Coyote Willow is but a slender, weed-like shrub, but in eastern Washington, on the borders of the Palouse and other rivers, it becomes a slender-stemmed tree about 20 feet tall. Coyote Willow is distinguished by very narrow leaves, ⅛ to

¼ inch wide (or about sixteen times as long as broad), so that in general this species may be known from other Willows at a glance. The blades are strikingly silvery-silky on the lower surface.

Seeding abundantly, the Coyote Willow also reproduces by creeping rootstocks that send up, from a single plant, scores or hundreds of stems to form extensive, reedy thickets. No other tree is so quick to establish itself on the sandbars in the arid interior parts of the West. True that the life of this Willow is only 20 to 50 years. But in that span the Cottonwoods and other more valuable trees move in and take possession of the sandbars pioneered by the little Coyote Willow and gradually transform them into good forested bottom-lands for which the travelers in the old days of exploration in the Northwest were very grateful.

YEWLEAF WILLOW

Salix taxifolia Humboldt, Bonpland and Kunth

RANGE: Guatemala northward through Mexico to the mountains of western Texas, southwesternmost New Mexico, and southeastern Arizona (3500 to 6000 feet).

DESCRIPTION: *Bark* of trunks light gray-brown, divided by deep seams into broad flat ridges. *Twigs* slender, in the first season hoary-downy, becoming reddish, or purplish brown and later roughened by the raised leaf scars. *Winter buds* dark chestnut-brown, ⅟₁₆ inch long and broad. *Leaves* ⅓ to 1⅓ inches long, ⅟₁₂ to ⅛ inch wide, pale gray-green, with a short silky pubescence, at least below, and with thickened, slightly curled-under margins. *Flowers* in dense, oblong cylindric catkins ¼ to ½ inch long, the scales on their outer surface hoary-downy; 2 stamens in each male floret, the ovary with deeply notched stigma lobes. *Fruit* a bright red-brown, more or less hairy capsule about ¼ inch long.

No other American Willow has such small leaves as this one — only ⅓ to 1⅓ inches long. A pale sage-green, and almost without teeth along the margins, the leaf of this species is about as modest and inconspicuous as one could ask. Indeed, when you take the magnificent drive up in the Chiricahua National Monument in Arizona, you have to watch sharply along the canyon streams to detect this retiring species, with its sad green foliage, which grows 30 to 40 feet high but melts into the forest background. Yet it is an attractive tree when seen by itself and appears to have been adopted into the gardens of old Mexico, for it was there that this species was first seen by the great naturalist, Alexander von Humboldt, in Querétaro more than a century ago. It was first discovered in this country by Charles Wright, an eminent collector of his day, near El Paso, in 1849. It is, in this country at least, decidedly a mountain species, preferring the banks of rushing streams rather than the slow constant rivers of the plains. Here it associates with the Arizona Sycamore and Walnut.

The early foliage is covered by fine, soft white hairs; these disappear from the dull upper surface but usually continue to clothe the lower. The flowers, which do not appear until long after the leaf, are disposed in very small, short, thick catkins, quite unlike those of most Willows, and are borne only terminally on the twigs. Owing to the lateness of flowering, the fruiting is also late, and capsules are still disbursing their seeds in November.

ARROYO WILLOW

Salix lasiolepis Bentham

OTHER NAME: White Willow.

RANGE: Eastern Washington and eastern Oregon, south through the valley of the Klamath River, northern California, through the foothills of the Sierra Nevada, and in the Great Central Valley, and on the Coast Ranges to southern California and Santa Catalina Island, south to the Sierra de Laguna, Baja California; and from Idaho south through Utah and Nevada to the mountains of southeastern Arizona (Cochise and Pima Counties, at 6000 to 7500 feet altitude).

DESCRIPTION: *Bark* of old trunks dark and broken into irregularly braiding, flat, broad ridges roughened with lenticels, that on young stems and branches light gray-brown, smooth and thin. *Twigs* stout, clothed at first in hoary woolly hairs and bright yellow or dark reddish brown, becoming darker and smooth. *Winter buds* light brownish yellow, flattened and with thin wing-like margins. *Leaves* 3 to 6 inches long, ½ to 1 inch wide, at maturity thick and leathery, the upper surface dark green, the lower pale or glaucous, margins curled under and intact or obscurely toothed; the slender veins arched and united within the slightly thickened and curled-under margins. *Flowers* in erect densely flowered

catkins about 1½ inches long, the male catkins ½ inch thick, each male floret with 2 stamens more or less united by their filaments; the ovary smooth, dark green, long-pointed, with broad stigmas; scales dark-colored, clothed with crisp white hairs. *Fruit* a light reddish-brown capsule ¼ inch long. *Wood* soft, close-grained, light (35 pounds per cubic foot, dry weight), the heartwood light brown, the sapwood thick and nearly white.

Another name for this shrub or small tree (which grows up to 25 feet tall or, exceptionally, 40 feet) is White Willow. This is given it on account of the light hue of the trunk and limbs and perhaps also because of the foliage which is whitish beneath. But that is a name pre-empted by a famous European Willow common in American gardens. And Arroyo Willow suits the present species well when it climbs the mountains in small canyons. It attains tree size, however, chiefly along the larger streams near sea level.

An easy place to observe this species is on the very spot where it was first discovered, in 1846 or 1847, by Theodor Hartweg, the German horticultural collector, who first found so many California trees. And that spot is near the mouth of the Carmel River, below the lovely old mission of San Carlos Borromeo, where rest the bones of Junípero Serra. You may know this tree by the pale gray or pale brown bark of the trunks and older limbs which is often blotched with nearly white areas. The smooth bark of younger stems and limbs is a beautiful pale green.

There is a handsome contrast between the very dark yellow-green of the smooth upper surface of the foliage and the silvery and often silky lower surface. When the sea wind or the valley breeze sets the foliage to dancing, all of a happy California day is in the flashing, alternating colors. Among these Willows, too, you are likely to hear, from dawn to dusk, in season, a continual twittering and whistling of green-backed and willow goldfinches, tule warblers, yellow warblers, pileolated warblers, warbling vireos and long-tailed chats. Mostly associated with streambanks, the blithe little choristers and their music become linked at last in the mind with the flashing of the bordering Willows' foliage, the long, sun-steeped summer days, the muffled thunder of the surf beyond the dunes, the very odor of the Willow bark itself (acrid and tannic), and of the bottom-lands where these Willows grow — a stagnant smell, half sweet, half heavy.

BEACH WILLOW

Salix Hookeriana Barratt

OTHER NAMES: Shore, Coast, or Hooker Willow.

RANGE: Coastal dunes and borders of ponds and salt marshes, Vancouver Island southward along the shores of Puget Sound, to Humboldt County, northern California.

DESCRIPTION: *Bark* of trunks thin, light reddish brown, only slightly seamed, with closely flattened, plate-like scales. *Twigs* stout, with large, scattered, orange lenticels and at first hoary-woolly, becoming in the second season merely pubescent and bright red. *Winter buds* ¼ inch long, dark red and pale-pubescent. *Leaves* 2 to 6 inches long, 1 to 3 inches wide, thin and firm, the upper surface bright yellow-green and shining, the leaves pale and glaucous and hairy, especially along the midrib and the slender arched veins and the conspicuously meshed veinlets. *Flowers* in erect but rather lax and more or less curved catkins about 1½ inches long with yellow and hairy scales; stamens 2 to a male floret with long, free, hairless anthers; ovary stalked, hairless, with a long bright red style. *Fruit* an oblong-cylindric capsule about ¼ inch long. *Wood* soft, close-grained, light (33½ pounds per cubic foot, dry weight), the heartwood light brown tinged with red, and whitish thin sapwood.

The Beach Willow is most readily known from all others of its genus by the fact that the leaves are fully half as wide as long; all other Willows have blades more than twice as long as broad; even if, in appearance, they seem not so, a ruler soon shows this to be the case. The leaves of Beach Willow are densely woolly beneath even at maturity — another distinctive feature.

Although the Beach Willow is frequently but a shrub, it grows on the Oregon coast to be a tree 30 feet high, with a single short trunk, sometimes 18 inches in diameter. It forms a broadly rounded head and, like so many western Willows, it is handsome when the wind caresses it, with its mass of foliage whitish beneath and dark green and shining above.

BEBB WILLOW

Salix Bebbiana Sargent

OTHER NAME: Beak Willow.

RANGE: Cook Inlet and eastern interior Alaska and southern parts of Yukon and Mackenzie Territories, south almost throughout British Columbia and Alberta to eastern parts of Washington and Oregon, and eastward to the western and southern shores of Hudson Bay and the valley of the St. Lawrence River, to the Maritime Provinces and Newfoundland; south through the Rockies to Colorado, northern New Mexico and Arizona (where ascending to 10,000 feet, as a shrub) and to Nebraska, Iowa, southern Michigan, northern Pennsylvania and Long Island.

DESCRIPTION: *Bark* of trunks thin, olive-green, gray tinged with red, or reddish, only slightly divided by shallow seams with plate-like flattened scales. *Twigs* slender and at first hoary-woolly, in the first winter dark orange-brown or reddish purple and roughened by raised leaf scars as well as flecked with scattered lenticels, becoming in the second year paler and reddish brown. *Winter buds* bright chestnut-brown, ¼ inch long, full and rounded on the back. *Leaves* at maturity 1 to 3 inches long, ½ to 1 inch wide, the margin without teeth or only remotely and irregularly toothed above the middle, thick and firm, the upper surface dull green, the lower blue or silvery white and covered with a pale rusty pubescence, especially along the midrib and principal veins and conspicuously raised and netted veinlets. *Flowers* in catkins terminal on short leafy branchlets, with scales yellow below and rosy at tip and covered with long pale silky hairs; male catkins thick-cylindric, ¾ to 1 inch long, densely flowered, with 2 stamens to each floret; female catkins oblong-cylindric, loosely flowered, 1 to 1¼ inch long, the ovary with long silky white hairs and broad-cylindric, long-beaked, long-stalked green capsule.

The Bebb Willow, when conditions are favorable, makes a luxuriant bushy growth up to 25 feet in height, with stout ascending branches that form a broad round head. But in the region west of Hudson Bay it is a shrub with intricate twisted branches and reclining stems that creates impenetrable thickets over a vast and desolate domain. In Colorado it ascends the Rockies to 10,000 feet; it ranges into the Arctic and yet is found as far south as Arizona. In the St. Lawrence valley and all the most thickly settled parts of the northeastern United States, it dwells as successfully with man as on the wild banks of the Mackenzie. One reason, it may be, is that the Bebb Willow is no timber tree. There is no reason why anyone, except an Indian making himself a wickiup, should ever cut it down. Absolute uselessness to man seems to be one of the most valuable assets a tree can possess!

But the cottontail rabbit has a use for this Willow, as he has for so many others. In winter hunger he ekes out his hunted and timorous existence by gnawing on the bitter inner bark. If he girdles the tree, it will die. But Nature is apparently very fond of Willows, just as she is of rabbits, since she has made so many of them, and for every one that a rabbit kills, more, many more are forever springing up.

The difficulty in distinguishing any Willow from others seems, at first, all but insurmountable, yet in a given region there are but a few Willows of tree size, and each of these has its earmarks by which it may be known. The Bebb Willow has these points which, taken in combination, serve to identify it: It belongs to a group of Willows whose leaf margins are intact — without teeth or with only rare or obscure ones. The upper surface of the blades is pubescent, not shiny, the lower very veiny. The catkins are not stalked but are borne directly on the naked twig. The flowers appear after, not before, the leaves, and are bracted by dark persistent scales.

FIRE WILLOW

Salix Scouleriana Barratt

OTHER NAMES: Scouler, Nuttall, Mountain, or Black Willow.

RANGE: In wet, or dry upland, situations from sea level to 10,000 feet above it, southern Alaska (Cook Inlet) and valley of the Yukon at Dawson (Yukon Territory), south through the Rockies to northern

New Mexico and the White and Santa Catalina Mountains of Arizona; in the Black Hills of South Dakota; abundant in Washington and Oregon, and, in California, following the Sierra Nevada far south and up to high elevations, and in the Coast Ranges to the San Bernardino Mountains of southern California.

DESCRIPTION: *Bark* of trunks thin, divided into broad flat ridges, dull gray to very dark; that of the branches commonly whitish. *Twigs* stout, the pale pubescence early deciduous or, in southern California, persistent, flecked with scattered yellow lenticels, yellow or dark orange, becoming in the second year dark red-brown and much roughened by old leaf scars. *Winter buds* ¼ inch long, orange, the scales with wing-like edges. *Leaves* smooth on both sides, 1½ to 4 inches long, 1½ to 3½ inches broad, thick and firm, the upper surface shining, dark yellow-green, the lower paler or glaucous, with thin arched veins and conspicuously meshed veinlets. *Flowers* in erect oblong-cylindric catkins, the male about 1 inch long, over ½ inch thick, each floret with 2 free stamens on hairless stalks; the female catkins 1½ inch long, ½ inch thick, the stigmas notched; scales dark, with long white hairs. *Fruit* a light reddish brown, pale-pubescent capsule, ⅓ inch long. *Wood* soft, close-grained.

Far more than most Willows does this species tend to stand up straight, instead of leaning, nor does the short trunk usually fork from the base as so many other Willows do. Instead, a single erect stem carries an unusually high crown of foliage, and under forest conditions the crown may be distinctly narrow. Indeed, this species, unlike most of its sisters, is one which delights to grow in the deep woods with Alders and Maples, and it climbs high in the mountains (to 10,000 feet) but is then only a shrub. It reaches its largest size at sea level in the neighborhood of Puget Sound and is there sometimes seen 50 feet high with a trunk 1½ feet in diameter.

The name of Fire Willow derives from the admirable habit of this tree of springing up after forest fires. Quickly it covers the tragedy of burned-over areas, much.as do Trembling Aspen and Fire Cherry.

Well before the leaves appear, in the generally tardy spring of the regions where this northern Willow grows, the catkins bloom on the naked wood like the famed Pussy Willows of the eastern states. In their first season the twigs bear crescent-shaped, glandular-tipped, leaf-like stipules about ¼ inch long, and these serve the purposes of identification at the start, but they are soon deciduous. If the wood of this Willow has no commercial value, the foliage, at least, forms an important browse for western stock in many localities where it grows.

SITKA WILLOW

Salix sitchensis Sanson

OTHER NAMES: Satin, Coulter, Velvet, or Silky Willow.

RANGE: Cook Inlet and Kodiak Island, Alaska, south to western Montana, southeastern Oregon (Blue Mountains) and along the coast from Alaska to southwestern Oregon and the northern Coast Ranges of California and the Sierra Nevada from Placer County to Nevada County at about 6000 feet altitude, and south to Santa Barbara County.

DESCRIPTION: *Bark* thin and broken into irregular, closely flattened, thin, reddish brown scales. *Twigs* brittle at base, at first hoary, then red-brown or orange becoming dark brown to black, and dull or slightly shiny. *Leaves* 1½ to 2¾ inches long, ½ to 1 inch broad, the upper surface dull green with impressed veins, covered beneath with a short, appressed, velvety, shining white pubescence and marked on the undersides with thin arched veins and meshed veinlets. *Flowers* in dense slender catkins up to 3 inches long; the stamen solitary in each male floret with violet anther and hairless filament, the stigmas short, erect, not notched. *Fruit* a capsule about ¼ inch long, light red-brown and pubescent. *Wood* soft, close-grained, light (31½ pounds per cubic foot, dry weight), the heartwood pale red, the sapwood thick and nearly white.

The Sitka Willow is known at once by its leaves which are broader above than below the middle — so spatulate, indeed, that they hardly seem to belong to a Willow at all, as we think of Willow foliage in general. More, the twigs are distinctly brittle at base, snapping off neatly when pulled, not tearing raggedly. True that this trait is shared by a few other species, but they do not have the spatulate leaves of the Sitka Willow.

The foliage, dark and shining green above, and whitish and silky or velvety below, is indeed handsome when the summer winds, sweeping up the gorge of the Columbia, play with its bicolored charms, for it is chiefly along that majestic valley that the Sitka Willow attains its finest dimensions. On sandy bottom-lands near Portland, for instance, it sometimes grows 35 feet high. Usually the trunk is leaning or crooked, or remarkably eccentric, after the customary slipshod, picturesque fashion of Willows, but occasionally it grows quite straight. The crown is rounded, dense and leafy, casting a fine pool of flickering shade over the stream. But if you are standing beneath the tree, the whitish undersides of its foliage prettily reflect the play of light upon the ripples, almost as in a mirror.

THE WALNUTS

(*Juglans*)

Walnuts have strongly aromatic leaves, bark, and fruits, and thick, round twigs whose pith occurs in overlapping flakes (easily seen by splitting the twigs lengthwise). The terminal buds have two pairs of opposite, rather open scales, the inner conspicuous. In falling in autumn, the leafstalks mark the twig with 3-lobed elevated scars.

The alternate, deciduous leaves are pinnately compound and consist in numerous (11 to 23) leaflets; the veins near the margin tend to recurve and mesh. The flowers occur in separate catkins on the same tree, the thick, heavy male catkins appearing on the last season's wood of the branch, with 8 to 40 stamens in each floret; the female catkins are few-flowered, borne at the ends of the shoots of the season; each ovary with a finely feathered stigma.

The fruit consists in a leathery, woody husk enclosing the nut which is hard-shelled, the shell furrowed and sculptured and opening by two natural sutures; the oily seed or kernel is 2-lobed between the ruminations of the inner wall of the nut and enclosed in a thin, papery, veiny coat.

*   *   *

ARIZONA WALNUT

Juglans major (Torrey) Heller

OTHER NAME: Nogal.

RANGE: Mountains of north-central Mexico (Durango and Chihuahua) north through western New Mexico in canyons and along streams, to south-central Colorado (valley of the Rio Grande), and north-central Arizona (Oak Creek, near Flagstaff), at 3500 to 6800 feet.

DESCRIPTION: *Bark* of mature trunks dark brown, or blackish, thick, scaly, deeply fissured. *Twigs* at first coated with rusty pubescence, becoming at the end of the first season red-brown and flecked with small pale lenticels, and the second season ashy gray and roughened by the large, pale, elevated, 3-lobed leaf scars. *Leaves* in over-all dimensions 8 to 12 inches long, with pubescent slender stalks and rachis bearing 9 to 13 (rarely 19) thin yellow-green leaflets the largest of which are 3 to 4 inches long and 1 to 1½ inches wide (the lowest pairs smaller). *Flowers* — the male in slender pubescent catkins 8 to 10 inches long, with hoary, pale yellow-green, 5- or 6-lobed calyx, and with 30 to 40 stamens bearing yellow anthers. *Fruit* 1 to 2½ inches thick, with a thin, rusty-pubescent husk having a small sharp point; nut thick-shelled, black or dark brown, a little broader than high and slightly compressed and seamed with deep longitudinal grooves. *Seed* small and sweet-tasting. *Wood* hard, coarse-grained, not strong, dark, satiny brown.

The Arizona Walnut, so called in English, is known as *Nogal* to all the Spanish-speaking people on both sides of the Border. But that, of

course, is simply Walnut in our language, and the two famous towns, separated only by a fence on the international boundary, called Nogales are named from the Walnut groves in the canyons round about, and in the bottom-lands, the draws, washes and gravels and adobe clays. On the drier sites the stems are spindly and sometimes numerous from one root, but when founded in good bottom-land near a permanent stream, this tree may grow 45 to 50 feet tall, and produce a fair-sized bole though the trunk is never clear of branches very high up; it soon divides into a number of large erect main boughs, or the forking may begin almost at the ground so that each tree is in itself a little grove. The branches have a smooth rather pale bark that shows with a certain elegance and cheer when the leaves are off the trees, in the brief southwestern winter.

The thick-shelled nut is much like that of the eastern Black Walnut's in its dark color and wrinkled surface, and the small kernels have much the same delicious rich flavor. The wood, too, is nearly as beautiful as the valuable eastern Black Walnut's, and nothing but the scattered nature of the growth, the small size of the trees and the rough country in which they grow saves this species from the process of search and seizure carried on against the eastern tree.

Reproduction is rather sparse, despite irregular periods of heavy fruit-bearing. Only scattered seedlings come up, amongst all the nuts that are borne off by flood waters and rodents who hoard them underground. In situations where such agencies occur seldom or not at all, the entire crop of nuts will fail to produce any seedlings, from year to year, and one can only wonder how these groves ever got their start. The seedling, once germinated, makes almost no growth above ground until it has spent several years exploring with its taproot and lateral roots all the possibilities for water in the subsoil. But once the little tree takes hold on life, it has an expectancy of some 300 or 400 years.

TEXAS BLACK WALNUT

Juglans rupestris Engelmann

OTHER NAMES: Little or River Walnut.

RANGE: Banks of streams in limestone regions, central and western Texas

(Big Bend country and Panhandle) to western Oklahoma and eastern New Mexico. Also in Coahuila, Mexico, and probably in Chihuahua.

DESCRIPTION: *Bark* of mature trunks thick, dark, deeply furrowed and scaly-ridged. *Twigs* coated at first with a pale scurfy pubescence (which may persist 2 or 3 years), in the first winter orange-red and marked by pale lenticels, finally turning ashy gray. *Winter buds* (the terminal ones) ¼ to ½ inch long, often compressed, oblique and narrowed at apex, and coated with pale woolly hairs. *Leaves* in over-all dimensions 9 to 12 inches long, with slender and pubescent stalks and rachis, having 13 to 23 thin, light green leaflets each 2 to 3 inches long, ⅓ to ⅔ inch wide. *Flowers* — male in slender catkins 3 to 4 inches long, with light yellow-green calyx and about 20 yellow stamens in each floret; female flowers thickly coated in russet pubescence, the stigmas green slightly tinged with red. *Fruit* ½ to ¾ inch thick, the thin husk covered with rusty pubescence; nut thick-shelled, deeply seamed with longitudinal grooves between the simple or forked ridges. *Seed* small and sweet. *Wood* heavy (42½ pounds per cubic foot, dry weight), hard but not strong, the heartwood rich dark brown, the sapwood thick and white.

Texas Walnut has the dark furrowed bark of the eastern Black Walnut but the slender, almost ferny fronds of a Pecan. It makes a bushy tree with short, crooked, leaning trunk and lower branches coming out very close to the ground. On some of the rich bottom-lands of Oklahoma and central Texas it grows — or once it grew — to a height of 30 feet, with trunks 14 to 18 inches in diameter. But most of those fine specimens were cut long ago for the sake of their beautifully figured dark wood, much like that of the eastern Black Walnut. Today one seldom sees a big specimen, and most trees are only 8 to 15 feet high, and 6 to 18 inches thick in the trunk. In poor sandy soil, under very

arid conditions, it may send up many slender stems growing from a common rootstock.

Yet in desert mountain ranges and on arid plains it is sometimes the one tree, clinging to the dry washes where it receives moisture only in the flashing floods that follow a summer cloudburst. This is the time when its seeds are distributed by the rushing waters. Otherwise it must depend for distribution on rodents who bury the seeds and then conveniently forget them.

If the seed lives to germinate, it sends down a deep taproot and many branching rootlets searching everywhere for soil water, in the meantime scarcely bothering to make much growth above the ground. But once a thread of water has been tapped, in the porous limestone this tree prefers, aerial growth begins. Very intolerant of shade, the seedling does well in the blazing sunlight of the Southwest.

The fruiting is abundant, though the nuts are the smallest of all walnuts and the kernels correspondingly so. Mexicans and Indians find them sweet, but the English-speaking Americans seem never to bother with such miniscule fruit.

SOUTHERN CALIFORNIA WALNUT

Juglans californica Watson

RANGE: Streambanks, canyons and foothills of the coast region of California, from Santa Barbara County and the Ojai Valley (Ventura County) and the San Fernando Valley, to the Santa Monica Mountains; along the southern base of the San Gabriel and San Bernardino Mountains (up to 4000 feet), and on the hills about Whittier and Puente to the canyons of the Santa Ana Mountains in Orange County.

DESCRIPTION: *Bark* of old trunks roughish, nearly black. *Twigs* at first coated with a scurfy-rusty pubescence, becoming by the end of the first season reddish brown and marked by pale lenticels, and by the second season gray. *Winter buds* coated in rusty-woolly hairs. *Leaves* in overall dimensions 6 to 9 inches long, with glandular-pubescent stalks and rachis, and 11 to 15 (rarely 19) smooth leaflets 1 to 2½ inches long, ½ to ¾ inch wide. *Flowers* — male in slender catkins 2 to 3 inches long, with minutely downy calyx and 30 to 40 yellow stamens in each floret; female flowers with yellow stigmas. *Fruit* ⅓ to ¾ inch thick, the husk thin, dark, and downy, the nut deeply scored with longitudinal grooves.

Seed sweet and small. *Wood* rather coarse-grained, medium-heavy (39 pounds per cubic foot, dry weight).

The Southern California Walnut, a modest tree seldom over 50 feet high, is quite distinct from the Walnut of northern California. Its nuts are much smaller, very hard-shelled, smooth-surfaced, and not at all furrowed. The trees are inclined to fork from the base, with outward-leaning trunks, not in the least like the strong, single, cleanly shaft of the northern species. Sometimes there is a single stem — occasionally 4 feet in diameter — but the bole is seldom clear of branches high up; on the contrary, long, thick branches shoot out and soon come to rest on the ground, making a dome-shaped crown that reminds one in general of the Live Oak's outline.

The intensive settlement of southern California has perhaps made this species scarcer than it was, but its localities have always been few and scattered. These· are in canyons or ravines, as if this deciduous hardwood were clinging to all the shadow and coolness and moisture it could find in the bright aridity of this region. As soon as the summer droughts begin, the delicate-looking foliage is apt to turn to a dull gold or crisp brown, and by early autumn it may have dropped entirely. One is grateful for the shade of the frond-like foliage while it lasts, but one cannot help feeling that this is a tree which must be left over from a different climate and now fights a losing battle with its environment.

NORTHERN CALIFORNIA WALNUT

Juglans Hindsii Jepson

OTHER NAME: Hinds Walnut.

RANGE: Banks of the lower Sacramento River, along Lafayette and Walnut Creeks in Contra Costa County, and near Walnut Grove; on the east slope of the Napa Range, near Wooden Valley, California. Now naturalized in many parts of the State.

DESCRIPTION: *Bark* of trunks gray-brown, vertically seamed into narrow, flat, smooth plates. *Twigs* at first thickly coated with hairs, becoming merely downy and reddish brown and flecked with small pale lenticels, and in the second season darker, nearly hairless, and roughened with small leaf scars. *Winter buds* coated with hoary wool, the terminal ones ¼ to ⅓ inch long, flattened, and rather swollen at the acute apex. *Leaves* in over-all dimensions 9 to 12 inches long, with slender hairy stalks and rachis, and 15 to 19 leaflets, each 2½ to 4 inches long, ¾ to 1 inch broad, at maturity bright green and shining above, furnished below with tawny hairs along the midrib and principal veins and with tufts of pale hairs in the axils of the veins. *Flowers* — male in slender catkins 3 to 5 inches long, the calyx and bracts scurfy-pubescent, each floret with 30 to 40 stamens; female flowers with ovary thickly coated in hairs, and bearing a yellow stigma. *Fruit* 1¼ to 2 inches in diameter, with thin, dark, softly pubescent husk; nut somewhat flattened at the end, faintly grooved. *Seed* sweet and small. *Wood* heavy, hard and coarse-grained, with dark brown and sometimes mottled heartwood and thick pale sapwood.

This is a tree which its discoverers found always associated with the sites of old Indian villages; its forest home, if any, has never been certainly known. It was originally confined, so far as the oldest records go, to three localities: the valley of Walnut Creek in Contra Costa

County, the banks of the Sacramento River, particularly at Walnut Grove, and Wooden Valley east of Napa. All accounts of old settlers say that the aboriginal trees on these sites were very fine, with single trunks up to 6 feet in diameter, the boles straight and clear of branches for 50 feet. But the finest of them were early felled for lumber by pioneers from the eastern states who, familiar with the valuable Black Walnut there, at once appreciated the worth of this western species. So only a few great specimens still remain.

But, as the beauty as well as the wood value of this rare hardwood became recognized, communities began to preserve the groves where they found them and steadily to increase them, and today, as you drive through the flickering light and shade of State Highway 21, through the Walnut Creek district just east of Berkeley, it is this native Walnut, more than any other tree, which keeps off the blazing summer sun and gives an eastern air to this pretty region. And cultivation has carried this friendly tree to many California cities as a street tree, and up into the old Gold Rush country of the Sierra foothills.

The nuts are larger than those of the Southern California Walnut, but the kernels are still hardly worth eating, compared with those of the eastern Black Walnut or the commercial English Walnut. However, 95 per cent of California's 3,000,000 English Walnut trees are now grafted on *Juglans Hindsii,* for it is far more immune to drought, gophers, and the Oak root-rot, a serious fungus pest.

THE HOP HORNBEAMS
(*Ostrya*)

THESE ARE Beech-like but small trees with simple alternate deciduous leaves. The male catkins in winter stand naked, without scales, each male floret composed of 3 to 14 crowded stamens. Each female flower has a closed calyx surrounded by united hairy bracts which become enlarged, inflated, and bladdery, hence the resemblance to hops. The fruit is a nut which is flattened and obscurely ridged longitudinally and quite enclosed by the veiny, pale, thin, bladdery scales. These are clothed at base with sharp, rigid, stinging hairs. At maturity the cluster of fruits is suspended on a hairy stem.

*   *   *

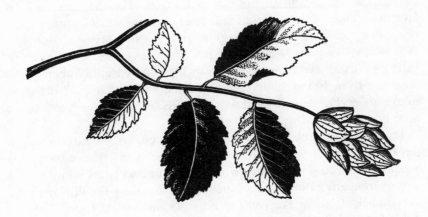

CANYON IRONWOOD

Ostrya Knowltoni Coville

OTHER NAME: Western or Knowlton Hop Hornbeam.

RANGE: Grand Canyon of the Colorado (6000 to 7000 feet); in Oak Creek Canyon, south of Flagstaff, Arizona; on the Grand River (Grant County, Utah), and in southeastern New Mexico and adjacent mountains of western Texas.

DESCRIPTION: *Bark* thin, separating into plate-like, loose scales, pale gray tinged with red, the inner bark bright orange. *Twigs* slim and round, at first dark green and hoary-woolly, becoming hairless, warty and dark brown and flecked with many pale lenticels. *Winter buds* small, pointed, scaly, dark red-brown. *Leaves* deciduous, 1 to 2 inches long, 1 to 1½ inches wide, tough but thin, dark yellow-green and hairy above, the lower surface paler and softly pubescent. *Flowers* appearing with the leaves, the male in clustered, drooping, slim catkins, each floret with 3 to 14 stamens attached to the base of a red and green bract, the female in erect, loose, terminal catkins, the ovary enclosed in a hairy, sack-like involucre. *Fruiting heads* cone-like, drooping, of a few loose papery, baggy, hop-like bracts enclosing the small, 1-seeded, flat, wingless nut. *Wood* heavy, strong and hard, with light red-brown heartwood and thin sapwood.

At the Grand Canyon in 1889 Frank Knowlton, the distinguished paleobotanist with the United States Geological Survey, ventured down the Hance trail. There he encountered an Ironwood or Hop Hornbeam, recognized by its fruits like hop bags — a type of tree he never expected to find in the Grand Canyon. For the Eastern Hop Hornbeam, one of the daintiest and most characteristic of Appalachian types, does not come within two thousand miles of Arizona. But, just as Knowlton suspected, this was a new species. And a very attractive little tree it was, and is, with slim (6-inch), usually leaning stems growing from 10 to 40 feet high. The slender branchlets give off the same sprays of beechen foliage as the eastern tree, letting through abundant light but keeping off the burning sun.

This pleasing little tree has proved oddly elusive. A careful search was made for it some years after its discovery, in the type locality, but no specimens could be found there; thus it threatened to join the mysterious company of lost trees. Later it was found by the distinguished astronomer, Professor Percival Lowell, in beautiful Oak Creek Canyon, Arizona. And finally it was relocated in the Grand Canyon, under both north and south rims, by Dr. Vernon Bailey, the ornithologist, who had been with the Geological Survey party of 1889. Several hundred trees are now known to grow on the Kaibab and Bright Angel trails, and colonies have been discovered at widely separated points in the Southwest, all the way to western Texas.

The catkins bloom in April, and in autumn the foliage turns dull yellow. The wood, like that of the eastern species, is very hard, but the trees are so rare that no commercial development is in prospect for this little species.

EASTERN IRONWOOD

Ostrya virginiana (Miller) K. Koch

OTHER NAMES: Eastern or American Hop Hornbeam.

RANGE: From the Black Hills of South Dakota eastward across the northern peninsula of Michigan to southern Quebec and Cape Breton Island, south to northern Florida (but not on the coastal plain of the South Atlantic States), thence west to eastern Texas (but not in the Delta country of Louisiana and not on the Gulf coast), and west to eastern parts of Oklahoma and Kansas.

DESCRIPTION: *Bark* thin, grayish brown, with numberless fine, flaky, plate-like little scales, often with a discernible twist. *Twigs* tough, slender, switch-like, at first light green becoming by midsummer smooth, shiny, and light orange; dull dark brown after the first winter. *Winter buds* light chestnut-brown. *Leaves* 3 to 5 inches long, dark, dull, yellow-green above, paler beneath, thin in texture but remarkably firm and tough. *Flowers* — male catkins becoming about 2 inches long at flowering time, their scales green with a red tinge; female catkins small, green tinged with red, hanging on very slender stalks. *Fruit* of very small nuts appearing as if enclosed in papery bags. *Wood* very heavy (almost 50 pounds to the cubic foot, dry weight), extremely hard, the heartwood light brown, the very thick sapwood white.

The Eastern Ironwood enters the circumscriptions of this book only by its extension across the plains of Nebraska and South Dakota to the Black Hills of South Dakota and Wyoming, where it is found in Rapid, Elk, and Spearfish Canyons. At best it is but a small tree, 30 to 40 feet high, with slender trunk and pendulous, often contorted branches that form a rounded crown. Its foliage is dainty and charming, turning a soft dull gold in autumn, and in summer shutting out all the heat of the sun but only a little of the light. There is something Birch-like about the bark, but it is more scurfy than papery. The distinctive feature is found in the hop-like scales that surround the nut and make it look as though the fruit were enclosed in little papery bags.

Ironwood is extremely hard — harder than Oak, Ash, Hickory, Locust, or Persimmon. In proportion to its great strength, its heaviness is not disadvantageous. But the trees are of such small size that they are never lumbered commercially, and only locally would they be used for mallets, axe handles, and levers.

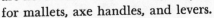

THE BIRCHES
(Betula)

Birches have resinous smooth bark, marked by long narrow lenticels, which commonly peels in thin papery plates; on old trunks the bark often becomes deeply furrowed at the base. The branches are slender and rather erect on young trees; on older ones they become pendulous. The twigs are switch-like, and very tough, and covered by the leaf scars of many previous years. Decidedly slender and elongated, the scaly winter buds are usually somewhat sticky when pressed between the fingers. Birch foliage is alternate and deciduous, with more or less heart-shaped blades and sharp teeth along the margin.

The male catkins appear in bud in summer in the axils of the last leaves of a twig; during the following winter they stand erect and naked; in early spring they lengthen and droop, the scales becoming orange or yellow in the lower part, lustrous brown in the upper, and in midspring they flower. Each male floret has a 4-lobed membranous calyx as long as the 2 stamens. The female catkins are thicker, terminal in the spur-like lateral branchlets, the florets without calyx, but the scales overlapping, of light yellow hue often tinged with red, becoming brown and almost woody. In autumn the scales are deciduous, with the nuts, from the central axis of the cone-like fruiting head (strobile). The minute seeds are wind-borne by the wing-like margins on the outer coats of the shell inclosing the flattened nut.

＊　　　＊　　　＊

PAPER BIRCH

Betula papyrifera Marshall

OTHER NAMES: Canoe, White, or Silver Birch.

RANGE: Newfoundland and Labrador, west to southern British Columbia, northern and eastern Washington State, northern Idaho, northeastern Oregon, eastern Wyoming and central Colorado, south to Long Island, northern New Jersey, northern Pennsylvania, around the shores of the Great Lakes, the northern parts of Illinois and Iowa and southern Minnesota.

DESCRIPTION: *Bark* smooth, peeling into papery thin layers, the outer bark soft, dull, pure creamy white, gray or dark reddish brown or orange; at the base of old trunks furrowed and dark brown or nearly black, inner bark dull orange with long, horizontal, bright orange, raised lenticels. *Twigs* at first green flecked with scattered orange lenticels, becoming the second year dark orange-brown and shiny, hard, and limber. *Winter buds* dark chestnut-brown, ½ inch long. *Leaves* not drooping on their stout yellow and glandular stalks which are ½ to ¾ inch long, thick and firm, dull dark green and smooth above, pale yellow below and flecked with black glandular dots, 2 to 3 inches long, and 1 to 2½ inches broad. *Flowers* — male catkins 3 to 4 inches long, slender and greenish with bright red styles. *Fruiting heads* 1 to 1½ inches long, ⅛ inch thick, drooping on slender stalks, the scales not downy except on the margins. *Nut* 1/12 to 1/16 inch long, elliptical, and much narrower than its slender encircling wing. *Wood* medium-hard, medium-strong, of medium weight (39 pounds to the cubic foot, dry weight), tough and close-grained, with light brown heartwood tinged with red, and thick whitish sapwood.

The geographical distribution of the Paper Birch in western North America has never been worked out completely, so numerous and so subtle are the differences between some of its forms; so few, comparatively, the collections made in the great Northwest wilderness. What is usually taken as the typical or at least the original type of the species, as seen in the Eastern States, is a tree with freely peeling, creamy to pinkish bark, varying occasionally to pale orange, and with leaves 2 to 3 inches long, 1½ to 2 inches wide, the base rounded or wedge-shaped, while the scales of the female catkins have three short, almost equally broad lobes. This tree appears to be found, within the circumscriptions of this book, in the Black Hills of Wyoming and South Dakota, in the Turtle Mountains of North Dakota, and along the Niobrara River in Nebraska, and at one locality (Boulder) in Colorado.

In the mountains of western Montana, northern Idaho, southern parts of Alberta and British Columbia, northern and eastern Washington, and the Wallowa Mountains of eastern Oregon there is found another form, variety *subcordata* (Rydberg) Sargent. It differs in having slightly smaller leaves which are slightly heart-shaped at base, while the scales of the female catkins have a long slender lobe and two short broad lateral lobes. Near the Pacific coast the bark of this tree is more often gray or brown than white, but in the rich woods of Glacier National Park, where it grows very densely and very tall — up to 80 feet — the bark is commonly as beautiful a milk-white as that of the eastern trees. These differences, marked enough in extreme specimens, are, however, both vague and technical; for all practical purposes, the true species typical in the East, and the common variety in the West, belong to one variable species and will be so considered below.

Paper Birch delights in the company of somber and militarily erect conifers, as if to set off its dryad-like charms of exfoliating soft bark, of daintily pendulous branchlets, of light green and vivacious foliage. It loves to grow around the cold clear lakes of the Northwest, where its smooth limbs will be reflected in the water, like a bather's. If it ascends in mountain woods, it never chooses arid and windy and sunbitten spots, but deep forests in sheltered canyons and valleys, with cool moist soil and great rocks all about. Gladly it laves its roots in white water, and will have naught to do with the slow, warm, muddied streams where Cottonwoods hold the banks.

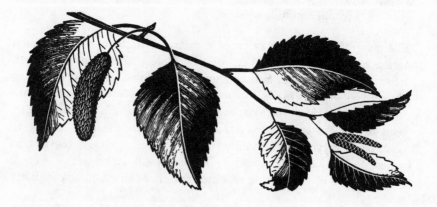

Formerly the Algonquian Indians used to make canoes of the bark
of this Birch, sewed with the long tough cords of Tamarack root and
stretched over a frame of White Cedar, while the thread holes and the
seams were caulked with resin of Pine, or Balsam, or Balm-of-Gilead.
Frail though Canoe Birch may seem to us, the Indians trusted their
lives to it as they shot the rock-fanged rapids. And it was the easiest
of canoes to portage, for a craft weighing only 50 pounds was strong
enough to carry twenty times that amount.

Birch wood furnished the Indian with snowshoe frames. The bark
served him sometimes as a covering for the tepee or lodge. Rolled into
a spill it constituted a taper or punk stick to keep away mosquitoes.
It made a sort of paper for kindling a fire. A moose-calling horn of
bark was carried by all the red hunters in the North Woods — a
straight tube about fifteen inches long and three or four wide at the
mouth, tied about with strips of more Birch bark.

The inner bark of the Canoe Birch is a favorite of the beaver, when
Aspen fails. Deer and moose browse the twigs in winter; the buds are
eaten by grouse. Sugar can be tapped from this Birch, as from Maple.
Thus, to each North Woods inhabitant man or beast, Birch is life-
sustaining.

To the delight of children and summer vacationists, the peeling
bark makes a sort of woodland writing paper. But when you strip the
outer layers from a living tree they will not be replaced. Instead, bands
of an ugly black scar tissue come to encircle the tree, and we see entirely too much of this around resorts. If you want to write on Birch
bark, hunt for a down tree; there are always plenty lying in the woods.

Many Paper Birches support a heavy growth of mosses on the side
of the trunk toward rain-bearing winds. When a Birch dies, its wood,
though so hard in life, decays very swiftly, and the tree topples in the
first winter wind or may even fall by itself with a solemn crash. But
the mosses seem then only to redouble their growth, completely covering the form once so lovely of limb, and giving it at last a fair green
grave.

Variety *kenaica* (Evans) Henry, the ALASKA COAST BIRCH, differs in its slender leafstalks which are ¾ to 1 inch long, and in the
broadly oval and not at all long-pointed leaf blades. It forms a little
tree 20 to 30 feet tall, on the coast of Alaska from Cook Inlet, the
Kenai peninsula, and Kodiak Island south to the head of the Lynn
Canal.

BROWN BIRCH

Betula occidentalis Hooker

RANGE: Southern British Columbia and northeastern Washington to northern Idaho and northwestern Montana.

DESCRIPTION: *Bark* thin, smooth, lustrous and light orange-brown or, in exposed situations, sometimes nearly white, separating into thin, papery layers which in falling reveal the light orange underbark. *Twigs* when they first appear, clear light yellowish brown, minutely downy and abundantly dotted with minute glandular specks, later becoming smooth and free of glands and hairs and very shiny. *Winter buds* bright orange-brown, their light brown inner scales becoming in spring ¾ inch long. *Leaves* inclined to hang from their stalks, 2½ to 4 inches long, 1 to 2 inches wide, firm and thin, dull deep green above and paler beneath, marked at maturity with only a few of the dark resinous dots that cover the young leaves; midrib and principal nerves yellow like the stout, glandular, downy leafstalks which are about ¾ inch long. *Flowers* — male catkins in spring 3 to 4 inches long, ¼ inch thick; female about 1 inch long, 1⁄16 inch thick, with long-tipped bright green scales. *Fruiting heads* pubescent, about 1½ inches long and ½ inch thick or less, spreading or erect rather than drooping on stout short stalks, the scales with a long narrow claw, and broad, short, forward-pointing lateral lobes, the middle one long and narrow. *Nut* oval, nearly as wide as its encircling wing. *Wood* soft, brittle but strong, medium-light (37½ pounds per cubic foot, dry weight), with light brown heartwood and thick, paler sapwood.

As you travel through the magnificent valley of the Fraser River in British Columbia, or the Skeena all the way to Hazelton, your eye is caught by a tree which lines the banks of these fine streams and their tributaries, and springs up, too, along the very highways, as if planted. If in some cases it is indeed set out as a roadside tree, no better choice could be made, for this is the Brown Birch, the tallest of all Birch trees in the world. At least in the lower Fraser Valley it commonly attains heights of 80 and 90 feet, and 120 feet have been recorded, with a trunk diameter up to 4 feet, which makes this the second largest hardwood in all the Pacific Northwest, exceeded only by the great Balsam Cottonwood. In its occurrence in the United States it is not so tall, nor so great of bole; and it is not nearly so common a tree. Rather must the Brown Birch be considered primarily a British Columbian tree, for there only does it reach great size and grow in abundance.

One of the favorite sites for seedlings of this tree is on stumps. The young roots sink down eagerly into the moisture of the stump and nourish themselves in the decaying wood. Finally all the stumpwood is consumed and the young Birch is found growing lustily inside the hollow cylinder of the old stump's bark — like a tree planted in a tub. Thus does an old life become a new one, after the wise economy of Nature.

YUKON BIRCH

Betula neoalaskana Sargent

OTHER NAME: Alaska White Birch.

RANGE: From central parts of Saskatchewan and Alberta north to the mouth of the Mackenzie and throughout the Yukon basin in central Alaska; through northern British Columbia to the Pacific (North Sound) and along the south Alaskan coast to the Kenai peninsula.

DESCRIPTION: *Bark* of trunks thin, usually dull reddish brown or sometimes superficially nearly white, hard and firm but separable into thin, plate-like scales; the underbark light red, with many slightly raised, long lenticels. *Twigs* slender, reddish brown and smooth, and conspicuously covered with minute, resinous, gland-like specks, as are also the young leaves. *Winter buds* egg-shaped, obtuse at the gradually narrowed tip, ¼ inch long, with light red-brown outer scales and very small rounded but oblong and papery inner scales. *Leaves* 1½ to 3 inches long and as wide or even a little broader, thin, dark green above and lighter beneath, on slender bright red stalks 1 inch long. *Flowers* — male catkins clustered, scarcely stalked, 1 inch long, ⅓ inch thick, the scales bright red with yellow margins; female catkins slender, glandular, 1 inch long, ⅛ inch thick. *Fruiting heads* more or less drooping on short stout stalks, 1 to 1¼ inch long, ⅓ inch thick, the scales with slender tapering claw, and broad, forward-pointing, lateral lobes; the middle lobe slender but no longer than the lateral. *Nut* oval, narrower than its wing.

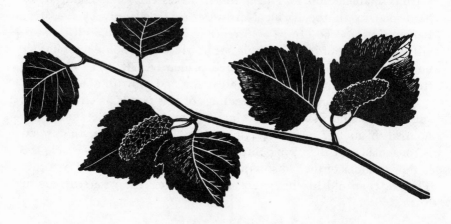

Interior Alaska and much of Canada's far Northwest would have a hard time getting along without this Birch. For in this region of bitterly long and cold winters, the Birch furnishes the best part of the fuel for houses, shops, public buildings, and when summer comes, melting the ice on the Yukon — Alaska's greatest highway — it is Birch, not coal, that fires the ravenous boilers of the steamboats. Now, good fuel wood must, first of all, have a high caloric value, and on this score Alaska Birch far excels Spruce, Larch, Aspen, and Poplar. It must be abundant, cheap to cut and haul, quick to dry, and not too valuable for other purposes. On every one of these scores, Yukon Birch would top the list where it grows. It is no disadvantage that a fuel wood tree should be small in stature and have slender pole-like stems, like this, which grows 30 feet high at the most and 6 to 18 inches in diameter; quite the contrary, a tree with these modest dimensions is easy for the lone woodsman to cut down and haul without help; the logs can be sledded or floated to market, sawed in 4-foot lengths and piled in ricks. They do not need, as a rule, to be split lengthwise but can be thrown directly on the fire. The bark of this Birch is inflammable rather than fire-resistant, hence it ignites the log almost as readily as paper, and every bit of a well-seasoned Birch log burns to a small white ash. Truly, the Birch is the anthracite of the Yukon country.

Banks of streams and lower hill slopes with moist gravelly soils are the commonest sites of this little tree. It climbs sturdily up to timber line (1600 to 2000 feet) on the plateau of the Kenai peninsula, along with White Spruce and Balsam Poplar. The tree forms a rather narrow head, with its slender erect branches and pendulous branchlets — suggestive, as with so many Birches, of feminine grace, especially when its pale green foliage is seen against the perpetual background of somber conifers.

WATER BIRCH

Betula fontinalis Sargent

OTHER NAMES: Red, Spring, or Rocky Mountain Birch.

RANGE: Central British Columbia east to western Alberta, and south, along stream courses, through the Rockies, high plains, and high on the desert ranges, to northern Arizona and New Mexico, east to the Black Hills of South Dakota, and west to northeastern and east-central California. Not near the Pacific, nor on the Coast Ranges, nor the western side of the Cascades and Sierra Nevada.

DESCRIPTION: *Bark* thin but not separating into papery layers, glossy dark bronze, smooth, and characterized by large pale horizontal lenticels becoming, on old trunks, 6 to 8 inches long. *Twigs* at first glandular and pale green, becoming dark red-brown and flecked by horizontal lenticels. *Leaves* 1 to 2 inches long, ¾ to 1 inch wide, thin and firm, the upper surface dull dark green, the lower minutely glandular and light yellow-green, the veinlets rather conspicuously meshed, the leafstalks glandular-dotted, light yellow, stout, ⅓ to ½ inch thick. *Flowers* — male catkins 2 to 2½ inches long, chestnut-brown; female green, with bright red styles, about ¾ inch long. *Fruiting heads* cylindrical, 1 to 1½ inches long, drooping, or spreading on long glandular stalks; scales with a short claw, the middle lobe a little longer and nearly as wide as the forward-pointing lateral lobes. *Nut* oval, minutely downy toward the apex, nearly as wide as its wings. *Wood* soft, light but strong, the heartwood light brown, the sapwood thick and paler.

As you mount up in the Rockies from the arid and burning sage-brush plains, into the zone of Pinyon and Juniper, you will see, quite surprisingly, a beautiful little Birch tree that reminds you, as all Birches will, of cooler climes and lusher forests. Indeed, this tree may venture out in the sagebrush as if to meet you more than half way. For the Water Birch clings to the cold mountain streams; as long as it can have its roots coolly laved, it dares the shadeless plains, the searing winds, and may follow streams whose destiny, in the Great Basin, is to die in the desert or reach only some soda lake — content with them, apparently, as long as the water keeps swiftly moving and runs the year around. So you see long double lines of the Water Birch, straight or winding as the descent of the water courses may determine, like streamers from the mountain forests.

Then, as you continue up the mountains into the zone of Yellow Pine and Aspen, you find that the Water Birch is in its preferred home. Here it grows taller — up to 25 feet high or, in the Grande Ronde Valley of eastern Oregon, 30 to 40 feet tall. Here its little leaves flutter almost as vivaciously as the Aspen's. Here its feet are set, by preference, in the cool, perpetually moist muck around mountain springs — hence the Latin name of *fontinalis*. In narrow gorges where tumbling waters dash from wall to wall, the Water Birch manages to squeeze in too, clinging to the rocky walls, its foliage blowing in the canyon drafts and often drenched with spray, and its half-bared roots washed and washed by the singing stream.

In its delicate carriage, with its narrow crown of slender branches, with its drooping twigs, Water Birch makes the same general impression of feminine grace as does the European White Birch (*Betula pendula*) so often cultivated on the town lawns. But it does not have the white bark of the cultivated Birch or of the famed Paper or Canoe Birch. On the contrary, it is a bronze or copper color (whence the name of Red Birch) with a beautiful metallic sheen when very fresh; or at most it is a light gray, but never chalk-white. More, the Water Birch's bark does not peel in thin, papery strips. This sets it aside from almost every other western Birch.

A closely related species is the DAWSON BIRCH, *Betula East-woodæ* Sargent. It is a little tree only 18 to 20 feet tall, found in swamps near Dawson, in Yukon Territory, where it forms dense thickets with shrubby willows. It is reported also as a shrub, near Jasper, Alberta. The bark of the trunks is chestnut-brown flecked with conspicuous horizontal white lenticels; the slender red twigs are thickly sprinkled with round white glands. The dark green veiny leaves are only 1 to 1¼ inches long, ¾ to 1¼ inches wide. Hanging on short stalks, the fruiting heads are but ¾ of an inch long and ⅛ inch thick, the smooth scales with very short base and forward-pointing lateral lobes, the middle lobe a little larger.

THE ALDERS
(Alnus)

THE ALDERS have close and astringent bark, and bear very straight-veined, toothed, broad, deciduous, alternate and simple leaves and few-scaled or naked buds. The flowers, in unisexual catkins, expand with or before the leaves (in our species) but make their first appearance in bud during the preceding season. The male catkins are pendulous, the individual floret with 4-parted calyx and 2 to 4 stamens, subtended by two small bracts. The female flowers, which are borne erect in a cone-let, have no calyx, but each ovary is subtended by 2 to 4 minute bracts and surmounted by 2 styles. After fertilization the conelet ripens into a little open cone-like structure (strobile) with woody scales from which are released the seed-like little nuts with thin wing-like borders.

※ ※ ※

SITKA ALDER

Alnus sinuata (Regel) Rydberg

RANGE: From the Arctic Circle, southward throughout Alaska, the Yukon, British Columbia, Washington, and Oregon, except the sagebrush desert, to the mountains and coast of northernmost California; also in northern Idaho and extreme northwestern Montana; usually a shrub in the United States and Canada, of tree size chiefly in southeastern Alaska. Also in Siberia.

DESCRIPTION: *Bark* thin and blue-gray, with red inner bark. *Twigs* slender, at first orange-brown and glandular, becoming smooth and light gray, flecked with numerous pale big lenticels and roughened by elevated leaf scars. *Winter buds* dark purple, ½ inch long, minutely downy. *Leaves* 3 to 6 inches long, 1½ to 4 inches wide, thin, the upper surface yellow-green, the lower paler and shiny, the midrib downy. *Flowers —* male catkins becoming in spring 4 to 5 inches long, the calyx lobes not as long as the 4 stamens in each floret; female catkins ⅛ inch long, in long clusters, on long stalks. *Cones* ½ to ¾ inch long, ⅛ inch thick, with scales thickened and truncate at the tip, the nut oval, as wide as its wings.

The Sitka Alder grows all the way to the Arctic Circle in Alaska, and along the Yukon forms extensive and almost impenetrable thickets. There it is only a small tree, and on the high mountains of Cali-

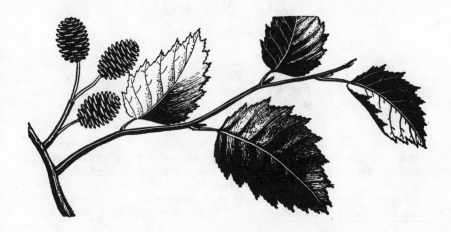

fornia, too, it is scarcely more than a shrub. But in Oregon, above 3000 feet, in moist mountain meadows, it is commonly 20 to 30 feet tall, and sometimes as much as 50 feet, with a trunk 14 inches through. Yet you seldom see a straight trunk; almost always the stems are more or less crooked and leaning. The Sitka Alder grows to timber line in Alaska, and in Oregon continues up to the zone of heavy winter snows. These so weight it down for six or eight months of the year that in the short summer it scarcely ever manages to recover an upright stature.

You may know this Alder from all other Alders in its range by the fact that the upper surface of the leaf is distinctly shiny, while the other species have dull foliage. Older trees possess a fine polished and mottled gray bark almost like marble. The flowers bloom in the spring with the unfolding of the leaves and not, as with most Alders, before them.

Sitka Alder is too little a tree to be useful directly to human needs. But all stream-side trees have their value, since they hold the banks against erosion and, with their roots and their litter of deciduous leaves, they give to the soil that sponge-like quality which holds precipitation when it falls, and emits it slowly and regularly in the form of numberless springs. So that an Alder helps to preserve the constancy and purity of a trout stream in the Northwest quite as much as the stream nurtures the Alder.

OREGON ALDER

Alnus rubra Bongard

OTHER NAME: Red Alder.

RANGE: From Yakut Bay, Alaska, south along the coast and on the islands and Coast Range of Alaska and British Columbia through western Washington and Oregon, and along the coast of northern California.

DESCRIPTION: *Bark* thin and roughened by minute wart-like excrescences, light ashy gray or even whitish, or at the base of very old trunks seamed, with narrow, flat, and sometimes connected ridges; underbark bright red-brown. *Twigs* at first light green and coated with hoary-woolly hairs, becoming the second season bright mahogany-red and shiny and in the third year ashy gray. *Winter buds* dark red, clothed in a scurfy pale

pubescence. *Leaves* 3 to 3½ inches long, 1¾ to 3 inches wide (or larger
on sucker shoots), the upper surface deep yellow-green, the lower coated
with rusty pubescence especially near the heavy yellow veins. *Flowers* —
male catkins in red-stemmed clusters, becoming in spring 4 to 6 inches
long, ¼ inch thick, with orange-colored scales and yellow calyx shorter
than the 4 stamens of each floret; female catkins ⅓ to ½ inch long, ¹⁄₁₆
inch thick, with dark red scales and bright red styles. *Cones* erect on stout
orange stalks, ½ to 1 inch long, ⅓ to ½ inch thick, with scales thickened
and truncate at the ends; nut roundish to broadly oval, surrounded by a
thin wing. *Wood* light (30 pounds per cubic foot, dry weight), soft,
weak, brittle, and close-grained, the heartwood light brown tinged with
red, the sapwood thick and white.

Every trout and salmon fisherman of the Northwest coast, surely,
knows the Oregon Alder. For from Alaska to the Redwood belt of
California it overleans, with its flickering, beechen shade, almost every
trout pool, laving its roots in the clear, cool water. And since it grows
most abundantly near the sea it is sure to be found on almost all the
salmon runs, where the great king salmon comes up from the ocean
to find the fresh waters where it was born, there to spawn and there to
die. More, the true Chinook angler will have his catch cooked over
this Alder's coals, just as the epicure of hams insists on Hickory smoke
to flavor them.

True, there are other creek-side Alders of tree size, but this species
is known at once by its concave-convex leaves, the margins somewhat
curled under, and by the markedly paler undersides of the blades.
When forest wind or ocean breeze sweeps through the boughs, the
undersides flash silvery, like some Willows'. And always there is the
reflection on the undersides of this Alder's light canopy, of water, running, or wind-whipped, or troubled into concentric ripples where a big
fish has plopped — crawling silvery ring on ring of light, like music
of which the sound is inaudible, only the nimble rhythm running on.

Everywhere that it grows this tree is associated with water, whether
plunging mountain streams, or the mouth of a creek wandering to the
sea, or the stagnant swamp behind some long lagoon sheltered from
the tumbling, hoarse-voiced open water by a gleaming sandspit. In
such a location grows what is perhaps the most beautiful grove of this
tree on all the Coast; you see it from the shores of Tomales Bay, in
Marin County, California, as you drive along State Highway 1. On the
other side of the long narrow bay, over on the Point Reyes peninsula,
these Alders grow for miles, their pale trunks shining almost white as
some Birch's, out of the inner gloom of the dark wood, gracefully lean-

ing or picturesquely contorted, clear of branches nearly to the top where their domes of foliage interlock, crown with crown, to form a high canopy. One longs to walk in these groves, but distance lends them their greatest enchantment. The ground where they grow is boggy, the groves are trackless, the air is stagnant and full of mosquitoes; best to admire them from across the water and pass on.

It is in the Puget Sound region that this Alder attains its greatest height — 100 to 120 feet, with boles 1 to 3 feet thick — a very respectable tree even in the company of the great Brown Birch, the Black Cottonwood, the Douglastrees and the Grand Firs with which it associates. But even when the trees are only 30 and 40 feet high they never lose their feminine charm, with that pale bark, those gracile stems commonly growing in sisterly groups and leaning picturesquely away from each other.

The bark is the loveliest feature of the tree. It is, in youth, a soft grayish white, quite as pleasing as any Aspen's or Beech's bark and almost as lovely as a Birch's, though it never peels. As the trees grow older, irregular low lumpy growths appear on the boles; these are generally blackish. And the very rainy or foggy climate of this Alder's range induces long lines of dark green moss to grow, especially on the north and west. The resultant mottling of colors is exquisitely subtle and harmonious. One could not ask for a lovelier sylvan presence than this.

Lumbermen prefer to call this the Red Alder — a most misleading name to the student in the field, for no Alder has so white a bark. But scratch that bark with your penknife and you will find that inside it

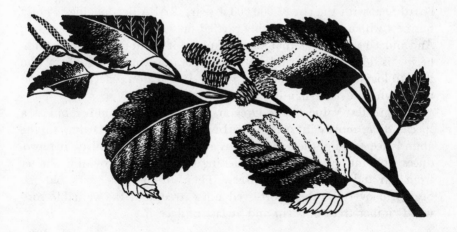

is a rich red. The wood, too, turns reddish brown on exposure to the air or, if cut in autumn, a pale golden yellow. This is no disadvantage, however, for most of the cut Alder is destined to be stained darker, in imitation of Walnut and Mahogany. It is a hardwood of many fine qualities; if properly seasoned and stored it does not warp or check appreciably in any plane. Though it has no fancy figure, it sometimes shows fine pith-ray flecks, similar to the clash of quartered Oak. The wood is highly shock-resistant and in the position of a beam or post is not too far behind Douglas Fir in strength. For high-grade veneer panels it is the equal of Yellow Poplar and Basswood, and for turned parts of furniture better than Red Gum. It takes paint, enamel, glue, and nails well, and its only fault is that it decays so rapidly in contact with the weather and the soil.

Formerly Red Alder was considered by lumbermen fit only for fuel (it is a good one) but the Northwest furniture companies began less than fifty years ago to realize that they need not import eastern hardwoods for all of their work, and today more Red Alder is cut than any other Northwest hardwood, including trees with such famous reputations as Oak, Birch, Maple, and Poplar. It is sometimes used as a 3-ply or 5-ply laminated wood, but in general it is manufactured into medium and cheap grades of furniture — that is, the sort made of solid, not veneered wood, such as kitchen chairs. The total amount of demand for such furniture is high, even if the styles are utilitarian and the prices low. Dozens of other uses are found for Red Alder, from ladder rungs to the inner soles of sports shoes.

The expanding business in Red Alder is limited only, but importantly, by the limited amount — perhaps only some 2,000,000,000 board feet, with the cut 23,000,000 a year. Red Alder logging is not a business which can be profitably carried on as a continuous operation. And indeed most mills that saw and plane it do not lumber it. Lumbering is done by thousands of small operators, mostly ranchers who turn to logging for a few months in the slack season, selecting trees on their own lands and hauling them to market.

The greatest value of the Oregon Alder is not as lumber but as a species that moves in swiftly on burned-over lands. Owing to the abundance and lightness of its seeds and their high viability, it reproduces well and grows swiftly, enriching the soil and providing shelter from sun and wind for other trees. Then, in 50 to 80 years, old age begins to overtake this short-lived nurse tree, and the valuable softwood timber trees outstrip and at last replace it.

MOUNTAIN ALDER

Alnus tenuifolia Nuttall

OTHER NAME: Thinleaf Alder.

RANGE: Southern Yukon, south through the Rockies of British Columbia and Alberta to Colorado, Utah, extreme northern parts of Arizona and New Mexico, also in Nevada, the Cascades of Washington and Oregon, the Sierra Nevada of California (at 6000 to 7000 feet). Also in central Saskatchewan and reported from Baja California. Not in the Coast Ranges.

DESCRIPTION: *Bark* thin, bright red-brown, the surface, on old trunks, broken into closely appressed scales. *Twigs* slender, at first pale brown and flecked with bright orange lenticels, and pubescent, later smooth and gray or light brown. *Winter buds* bright red and minutely downy. *Leaves* 2 to 4 inches long, 1½ to 2½ inches broad, firm but thin, the upper surface dark green, the lower pale yellow-green with a strong orange midrib. *Flowers* — male catkins becoming in spring 1½ to 2 inches long, with 4 stamens in each floret longer than the calyx; female catkins cone-like, dark red-brown, ¼ inch long. *Cones* ⅛ to ½ inch long with 3-lobed scales; the nut nearly circular, the wing a mere thin border.

Mountain Alder grows at the heads of mountain streams, where the ground is mucky around the springs, and in the gulches of mountain peaks, and around clear, cold mountain lakes. Ordinarily it is only a shrub 10 to 15 feet high at maturity, but at its best, in the mountains of Colorado and northern New Mexico, it becomes a small tree up to 35 feet high, always with very slender and bandy stems. In age the trunks change from gray to brownish red and become lightly flecked with thin scales.

The distinguishing mark of this Alder is in the very jagged margins of the leaf, which look as if raggedly torn into lobes, the lobes again jaggedly toothed. The winter buds are bright red, not dark red or purple as in other species, and the leaves are not glandular-dotted. The only species with whose foliage this Alder is likely to be confused is the Sitka Alder; but its leaves are shiny above, while those of Mountain Alder are dull.

The Mountain Alder is too small a tree to be turned to commercial use, yet it has served man in its day. The early explorers and pioneers soon learned that the presence of this species denoted running water, while the liquid whisper of a Cottonwood may be a delusion; Cottonwoods sometimes flourish handsomely along the courses of intermittent streams which actually run only a few weeks in the year. But the Mountain Alder must lave its roots in eternal streams whose waters it helps, with its shade and its humus, to keep cool and pure. So this Alder passed into the true legends of the West as the friend of the explorer and settler.

CALIFORNIA ALDER

Alnus rhombifolia Nuttall

OTHER NAMES: White or Western Alder.

RANGE: Southern British Columbia, south through the Cascades and eastern parts of Washington and Oregon (but not in the Coast Ranges of these states), south through western and central California (and to 8000 feet in the western slopes of the Sierra Nevada) to the Cuyamaca Mountains of San Diego County.

DESCRIPTION: *Bark* of old trunks thickish, gray, and irregularly furrowed and scaly-plated. *Twigs* slim and at first light green and pubescent, becoming smooth and dark orange-red and flecked with small scattered lenticels. *Winter buds* slender, dark red with pale pubescence. *Leaves* 2 to 3 inches long, 1½ to 2 inches broad, dark green and shining above, the lower surface bright yellow-green, minutely downy, with somewhat reflexed margins and broad yellow midrib. *Flowers* — male catkins becoming in spring 4 to 6 inches long; female catkins in short pubescent spikes. *Cones* ⅓ to ½ inch long with thin scales lobed at apex, the nut broadly oval with narrow wing-margins. *Wood* light (25 pounds per cubic foot, dry weight), weak, soft and brittle, with light brown heartwood and thick whitish sapwood.

From British Columbia to the mountains back of San Diego, California, this is the common creek-side Alder except close to the sea from San Francisco northward, where the Red Alder is dominant. It forms long lines of vegetation along the interior streams, dense groves 50 to 60 feet high around the heads of mountain gulches, either in pure groves of its own composition or mixed with Cottonwood and Ash along the lower streams. On steep north slopes its companions are the aromatic Laurel and the dark-leaved Maple; the three of them together cast a deep, cool shade where ferns grow lushly in the dim, windless environment. The trunks, straight and pole-like, are a softly mottled gray almost like that of a Beech, and very beechen is the emerald-green foliage.

In the brief period of cold weather in California the leaves of this Alder drop from the trees, and it is then, in January, that the catkins bloom on the naked twigs. To look down then from some mountainside on the green-gold of the Alders all in bloom for miles up and down the creek is one of the loveliest floral sights of the year in the California Coast Ranges; yet it is little seen because of the season, little appreciated because many people demand that flowers shall be a matter of brilliant petals, of garden pets marshaled in rows and borders. Yet flowers these catkins are, of course — male flowers which, being wind-pollinated, have of necessity immense amounts of buoyant pollen to loose upon the chill airs. A slight tap on a flowering twig will send a whole nebula of fertility to floating in the air, a golden haze that slowly drifts away, only by chance to find the little female flowers so neatly packed in small cone-like clusters.

After the flowers, come the tender young leaves — making a palest green, almost silvery, halo upon the crowns of all the trees. Summer brings full leafage, and the green foliage lingers up to Christmas time; then, without ever turning any particularly fine color, the leaves drop.

ARIZONA ALDER

Alnus oblongifolia Torrey

OTHER NAMES: Mexican or New Mexican Alder.

RANGE: From the mountains of eastern Sonora and western Chihuahua north through southeastern and central Arizona to the Grand Canyon region, and in southern and western New Mexico, generally between 4000 and 6000 feet altitude.

DESCRIPTION: *Bark* smooth and thin, light brown tinged with red. *Twigs* slim and at first orange-red, becoming gray or dark reddish brown, roughened with leaf scars and flecked with small but conspicuous pale lenticels. *Winter buds* smooth and shiny red. *Leaves* 2 to 3 inches long, about 1½ inches broad, the upper surface dark yellow-green, the lower surface paler and sprinkled with black glands. *Flowers* — male catkins becoming in spring orange-brown and 2 to 2½ inches long, the 2 or 3 stamens longer than the calyx, the female catkins ⅛ to ¼ inch long and light brown but the stigmas bright red. *Cones* ½ to 1 inch long with thin truncate scales; but broadly oval and narrowly margined.

The home of the Arizona Alder (which is equally New Mexican) is generally above 4500 feet above sea level, in the zones of the Ponderosa Pine and of the Oak woodlands, as in famed Oak Creek Canyon. Like almost all the other Alders it loves a rushing stream to cool its roots, and the head of cool canyons where the shadows lie long. But this species, which thrusts farther south into the desert states than any other Alder (going right over the Border into Mexico), is especially delightful when you come upon it after a long trip across the burning deserts and a long climb through the arid lower slopes of mountains like those around Tucson. As slim as young Birches, as cool as broad Beeches, as tall, sometimes, as 60 or even 80 feet high, the Alders form delicious groves, with the tinkling of the streams forever making music.

THE EVERGREEN
CHINQUAPINS
(*Castanopsis*)

Alternate, simple, unlobed, evergreen leaves, furrowed bark, smooth twigs bearing buds with many overlapping scales, and flowers in erect catkins characterize the members of this genus. The clustered, scurfy-stalked catkins arise from the axils of leaves of the year and bear, usually, numerous male florets at the top of the spike and a few female at the bottom, or the catkins may be wholly male, with the female flowers in much shorter catkins, or solitary, or in pairs. The male florets consist in 10 to 12 stamens with elongate stalks and oblong anthers inserted on the thickened receptacle and surrounded by a bell-shaped, scurfy-coated, minute, 5- or 6-lobed calyx. A minute aborted ovary is seen in the male flowers. The female flowers have an urn-shaped, hoary-woolly calyx, with 6 lobes, an ovary with 3 spreading styles ending in minute stigmas, and some abortive stamens that are seated on the thin disk. Usually the female florets are in clusters of 3, each cluster surrounded at base by an involucre of overlapping scales. The fruit takes the form of 1 to 3 nuts enclosed in the involucre of the female flower clusters which become at fruiting time bur-like, enlarged and prickly. The nuts, which are often softly hairy, are marked at one end by a large circular depressed scar, and at the other bear the remnants of the style; the seed is starchy, like that of the Chestnuts.

*　　　*　　　*

WESTERN CHINQUAPIN

Castanopsis chrysophylla (Douglas) A. De Candolle

OTHER NAME: Goldenleaf Chestnut.

RANGE: From the Hood's Canal region of the Olympic peninsula and Skamania County, in the Cascades of Washington, south on the western slopes of the Cascades of Oregon up to 5000 feet, in the Trinity Mountains of northern California up to 10,000 feet and southward on east and west slopes of the Coast Ranges of California to the San Jacinto Mountains (8000 to 10,000 feet) in the south; on Mount Shasta in the Yellow Pine belt (3000 to 6500 feet), Lassen Peak, the west slopes of the Sierra (in the Jeffrey Pine belt in the south) to the South Fork of the Kern River, and appearing on the east or desert side above Lone Pine at 6000 to 9500 feet.

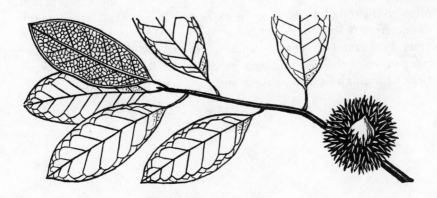

DESCRIPTION: *Bark* of mature trunks thick, deeply seamed and made up of very wide reddish brown plates, showing the brilliant red inner bark between them; bark of branches and younger trunks thin, smooth, and dark gray. *Twigs* rigid, coated when they first appear with bright golden scurf, becoming by the first winter dark reddish brown and subsequently darkening. *Winter buds* crowded near the end of the twig, with papery thin light brown scales, their edges curled back and fringed with fine hairs. *Leaves* evergreen, thick and leathery, 2½ to 3½ inches long (or more on vigorous shoots), ½ to 1¾ inches wide, the upper surface deep shining yellow-green, the lower coated, like the leafstalks, with shiny golden scales. *Flowers* white, in erect catkins, 2 to 2½ inches long and crowded at the ends of the twigs, some catkins wholly male, others with the female florets at the base of the male catkins, the calyx hoary-downy. *Fruit* a single, obtusely 3-angled, shiny light brown nut almost enclosed by a spiny 4-valved bur, and containing the dark purplish red, sweet seed. *Wood* light (34½ pounds per cubic foot, dry weight), fairly hard and strong, the heartwood light brown tinged with red, the sapwood paler.

In June all the Chinquapins burst into bloom, and each tree is covered with a wealth of creamy white blossoms. Set off against the sumptuous dark mass of foliage, the compound clusters of white spikes light up the whole tree as if they were branched candelabra on a Christmas tree. It is only the male flowers which are conspicuous and despite their beauty they have a drawback in their strong seminal odor. Though flowering is so abundant, Chinquapin fruiting is strangely shy. A well-plumped-out edible nut is hard to come by, and though the kernels are sweet to the palate, what a task to extract them from their spiny prisons! Most people would rather put a coin in a slot and get a handful of stale peanuts.

In the forests of Mendocino County, California, the Chinquapins often rise, strong and massive, 70 to 90 or 100 feet high, with a trunk diameter of 6 feet, and a probable age of 500 years. Such venerable years, such grand dimensions would be impressive if the most constant companion of the Chinquapins were not the Redwood, which grows twice as high and thrice as thick and lives four times as long!

THE TAN OAKS

(*Lithocarpus*)

THESE TREES are intermediate between the preceding genus, the Chinquapins, and the following, the Oaks. They resemble the Chinquapins in having foliage with straight unbranched veins running from midrib to the tip of the marginal teeth (in our species), and female flowers at the base of the catkins, below the spike of the male flowers, and in the cup or husk of the nut which is somewhat burry; but the Tan Oaks differ from Chinquapins in having the husk of the nut a mere cup, like an acorn cup not enclosing the nut. The Tan Oaks resemble the true Oaks in their acorn and cups, but differ in having stout and round (not slender and 5-sided) twigs, in the winter buds with only a few scales, in the persistent rather than deciduous stipules, and in the catkins erect and dense instead of drooping and stringy like those of Oaks.

Tan Oaks possess marked astringent properties in the deeply furrowed bark and the hard brittle wood. A thick down of clustered and branched hairs covers the buds, young twigs, and stipules; these last, remaining several years, often surround the buds in the axils of the upper leaves. The evergreen foliage is never truly lobed, as so many Oaks are, and in our species, though resembling that of Chinquapins, is toothed, the veins not, however, running out beyond the margins as bristles, the way those of Chestnuts do. The male flowers, in clusters of 3, consist in 10 stamens in a 6-lobed calyx and an abortive hairy ovary; the female flowers, which occur, a few only, at the base of the upper catkins, possess a 6-lobed calyx which, in turn, is enclosed in the many scales of the involucre (the future cup of the acorn). Three slender green styles that are stigmatic on the inner surface surmount the ovary, and a few aborted stamens may be found in the female flowers. The fruit matures at the end of the second season. A large pale circular basal scar marks the outside of the thick shell; within, the shell is downy and contains the red-brown seed.

*   *   *

TAN OAK

Lithocarpus densiflorus (Hooker and Arnott) Rehder

OTHER NAMES: Chestnut, Peach, Bur, Sovereign, or California Tanbark Oak.

RANGE: Southern Coast Ranges of Oregon (from the Umpqua River southward) and from sea level up into the Douglas Fir forest, to 5000 feet, on the west slopes of the Trinity Mountains, and south throughout the Redwood forests to Big Basin on the San Francisco peninsula, going inland in the north Coast Ranges only in the Napa Mountains to Mount St. Helena; in the Santa Lucia Mountains to 5000 feet, chiefly with Redwoods, rarely on the inner ranges (as high on Frémont Peak, San Benito County), and south to the Cuesta Pass (San Luis Obispo County), to 2000 feet, through the mountains of Santa Barbara County to Mount Pinos (9000 feet) and peaks above Ojai, in Ventura County. In the Sierra Nevada, from the Feather River basin at the north, southward along the western foothills and lower Yellow Pine zone (2000 to 5000 feet altitude), to Placer County.

DESCRIPTION: *Bark* of old trunks thick, firm, dark gray, and cut by narrow seams and cross-checks into broad, smooth, squarish plates. *Twigs* at first invested by a dense but deciduous wool of branched hairs, later smooth, and deep brown tinged with red, often overcast by a glaucous bloom. *Leaves* evergreen, 3 to 5 inches long, ¾ to 3 inches wide, at maturity thick and leathery, the upper surface light green and shining, the lower pale bluish and with traces, in the axils of the veins, of the tawny tufts of rusty pubescence that clothes the young leaves. *Winter buds* with loosely overlapping scales, the outer narrowest. *Flowers* stout-stalked, the catkins 3 to 4 inches long, the male catkins in crowded clusters. *Acorns* solitary or in pairs on a downy stout stalk that is ½ to 1 inch long, the nut light yellow-brown, shining and smooth after losing its scurfy pubescence, ¾ to 1 inch long, ½ to 1 inch thick, seated in a shallow cup which is coated within by short, soft, shining, ruddy hairs, and composed outwardly of rigid, spreading or recurved and often gland-tipped scales. *Wood* hard, strong, brittle and close-grained (42½ pounds per cubic foot, dry weight), with reddish brown heartwood and dark brown sapwood.

There is not a more admirable hardwood in all the West than the Tan Oak, a tree with a magnificent bole and sumptuous foliage — evergreen and darkly glittering above, and a beautiful silvery white beneath (from the dense coating of snowy wool). Long erect spikes (catkins) of white flowers light up the tree like candles at Christmas; and the fruit, a long, strong, darkly polished acorn, stands erect in a handsome burry cup. Young trees have mottled pale grayish and smooth bark; old ones are ruggedly checked into plates and outwardly brown, though the inside bark has a reddish tint. And finally there is the striking stature of this tree imparted by the great central (and most un-Oak-like) trunk that rises, mast-like, giving off spirals of mighty branches. In forest-grown trees the trunk is bare of branches a long way, with a very long, narrow crown; trees grown in the open have short, massive boles, and boughs almost to the base, which sweep boldly out, giving the whole tree an appearance of permanence and solidity.

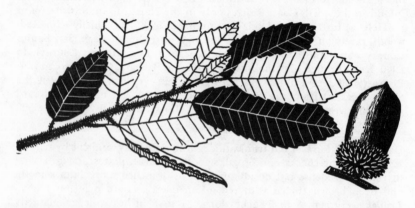

Trees 70 to 90 feet tall are frequent and some, growing in competition with Redwood, are little less than 150 feet high. But the acknowledged ancient of all is a specimen growing on exposed ridges at Rock Spring, 2000 feet above sea level on the slopes of Mount Tamalpais, in Marin County, California. Though only 65 feet in height, it is no less than 18 feet, 11 inches in girth, with a spread of limbs of 60 feet. From the base of this specimen sprawl out, above ground, scores of powerful roots, braiding, gripping the earth to balance the great superstructure.

The home of the Tan Oak is consistently in the Redwood belt of the north California coast; where it goes farther north or south than the Redwoods it swiftly becomes a rarer and shorter tree. But it will follow the Redwood well inland from the sea, wherever the sea fogs reach. Formerly it was felled in great quantities on account of the high tannin content of its bark — a commerce now all but dead. Tanning materials from foreign countries can be imported for less than the cost of hauling the bark out of the woods under present-day California labor conditions. And this is well, for the methods of tan barkers have always been wasteful. Today the Tan Oak, with any luck, grows undisturbed to its full tally of years — perhaps 500 — seldom troubled even by the lumbermen. For the fine hard wood, which might be used for furniture, cannot be profitably logged, owing to the inaccessibility of the scattered trees.

Formerly the Indians of Mendocino and Humboldt Counties used to make a flour of the acorn, first grinding it and then washing it in hot water to extract the bitterness, then cooking a mush of it; hence white pioneers used to call this Squaw Oak. There are still a few Indians left in the North Country woods, but probably they get to the store, like everybody else, and buy devitalized wheat flour over the counter.

THE TRUE OAKS
(*Quercus*)

OAKS ARE usually ponderous and heavy-wooded trees, with scaly or furrowed bark, and more or less 5-angled twigs and consequently 5-ranked leaves. The winter buds are clustered at the ends of the twigs, with numerous chestnut-brown scales, which in falling mark the twig with ring-like scars.

The flowers of all our species bloom in spring, with or after the appearance of the leaves. The male catkins are slim, stringy, drooping, and appear in clusters from buds in the axils of the leaves. Each floret consists in 2 to 6 stamens with yellow anthers, seated in a minute calyx which is usually 4- to 6-lobed nearly to the base. The female catkin is a solitary few-flowered spike appearing in the axils of leaves of the season. The tube of the 6-lobed calyx is adherent to the ovary and more or less completely enclosed in a cup of overlapping scales which finally become the cup of the acorn. The acorn is a nut marked at base by a large pale circular scar, with a thick shell.

The Oaks have extremely variable foliage, even on the same tree, where the leaves of a seedling or a sucker shoot may be quite different from those of the mature tree. There are also frequent wild hybrids which produce leaves intermediate in form between the parents. So many of thse hybrids have been described that they are now as numerous as the true species; to include them here would be beyond the bounds of the present work. The same is true of the many species which are predominantly shrubby but occasionally reach tree size. These are too numerous for inclusion. Among prominent examples are *Quercus turbinella*, *Q. reticulata*, *Q. undulata*, and *Q. Vaseyana*.

VALLEY OAK
Quercus lobata Née

OTHER NAMES: White, California White, Swamp, or Weeping Oak. Roble.

RANGE: Valleys of western and central California; at the foot of the Sierra Nevada (up to 2000 feet) from the Pit River on the north to the Tehachapi Mountains on the south; inner Coast Ranges north of San Francisco Bay and general in the southern Coast Ranges except close to the sea, south to the valleys of the Santa Susana and Santa Monica Mountains and Pasadena; also on the Channel Islands and Santa Catalina; absent from some parts of the Great Central Valley, but common in others.

DESCRIPTION: *Bark* of old trunks very thick (5 to 6 inches) and divided by deep furrows into broad, flat ridges, broken by numerous cross-checks into short, warty, light gray plates with close scales. *Twigs* slender and at first ashy or brownish and clothed in dense silky hairs, becoming smooth and paler the second season. *Leaves* deciduous, 2½ to 3 or 4 inches long, 1 to 2 inches wide, the upper surface dark green and pubescent, the lower pubescent and lighter, with pale, stout midrib and yellowish primary veins. *Acorns* solitary or in pairs, almost without stalk, at first glossy green, becoming bright chestnut-brown, and usually enclosed for ⅓ their length in the cup which has much thickened, palely downy, chestnut-brown scales with knobby surfaces, the lower ones with long free tips. *Wood* fine-grained, brittle and hard (46 pounds per cubic foot, dry weight), with light brown heartwood and thin paler sapwood.

To say that the Valley Oak is the monarch of all the deciduous Oaks of the West is almost enough to identify it. For you take one look at an old specimen's great bole, its magnificent crown, the width and the depth of its pool of shade, and you realize that it is king in its class. True, there are more precise and botanical ways of recognizing this species. First, there is the shallow but heavily knobby cup which holds the long, slender acorn shaped like a pointed cartridge shell. There is the pale gray bark broken into small cubes; there are the deeply lobed leaves, the lobes rounded or blunt, the sinuses between them narrow but rounded, not acute, at apex. And mature trees commonly have long, almost vine-like twigs that trail in weeping sprays. These traits, taken all together, typify this great species.

In many ways — in the light green foliage, the light gray bark, the mighty spread of limbs — the Valley Oak resembles its close relative the Eastern White Oak, *Quercus alba,* greatest of Oaks in the Northeast. Only a little more distantly related is the Norman or English Oak, *Quercus Robur,* king of all its clan in Europe. No wonder that the Spanish, when they settled California, thought this was indeed the Oak of their homeland, and called it *roble.* Or that Captain George Vancouver, exploring the Santa Clara Valley in 1796, thought it had been "planted with the true Old English Oak." For all three species belong to the blood-royal of the genus *Quercus.*

The name of Valley Oak was not the first applied to our tree, but it became fixed because it is so apt. For a valley tree this is. Its principal home, originally, was in the wide Sacramento Valley, near the rivers. It once clothed all of Napa Valley and the Santa Clara, on the south bay shore below San Francisco. Even far north in Mendocino County it reaches magnificent proportion, in Round Valley. In the vale of Eshom, along the north fork of the Kaweah where that stream comes singing out of the Sierra, it attains the rank of Oldest Inhabitant. The famed San Fernando and Pasadena Valleys are its southernmost outposts. In the Four Creeks country of the Kaweah delta there were once 400 square miles of Valley Oak Groves.

The reasons for this Oak's preference for valleys are found in what they may have to offer of deep loam and (for California) a high water table — from 10 to 20 or 40 feet below the surface. Flood plains and deltas of streams likewise favor it, for they are subject to inundations, especially the welcome spring rise which comes just when the new leaves are peeping out, pink and silky. In such a situation the Valley Oak need not fear the long, hot, arid summers of these interior valleys. Indeed, it invariably avoids the seaward slopes with their cool fogs and breezes. One mountain range between itself and the sea — as in the Santa Ynez Valley — will suffice, but that one must be there — perhaps to keep out the cold, moist breath of the ocean.

One of the outstanding characteristics of the Valley Oak groves is their open spaciousness. The trees almost invariably stand well apart from each other — held off, no doubt, by competition of their root systems in a wide search for water. Yet they are gregarious trees, almost never found out of sight of many of their fellows unless the axe and plow have intervened. They grow tolerantly with Live Oak and

Sycamore, the three trees forming beautiful harmonious contrasts, like notes in a sweet chord. But more commonly Valley Oak associates only with its own kind in these spacious groves, of which Vancouver wrote with some surprise "We entered a country I little expected to find in this region. For about twenty miles it could only be compared to a park. . . . The underwood, that had probably attended its early growth, had the appearance of having been cleared away, and had left the stately lords of the forest in complete possession of the soil, which was covered with luxuriant herbage, and diversified with pleasing eminences and valleys; which with the range of lofty rugged mountains that bounded the prospect, required only to be adorned with the

neat habitations of an industrious people, to produce a scene not inferior to the most studied effect of taste in the disposal of grounds."

In the course of its naturally long life — 300 years or more, if no accidents occur and no fatal disease supervenes — a Valley Oak changes its shape fundamentally. Four stages are described by Jepson, that lifelong student of this tree. In youth when it is but 10 to 20 feet high it owns a compact, cylindrical form, called the pole state, and this it assumes even when growing in the open with full opportunity to expand. In the Elm-stage, at heights of 30 to 60 feet, a thrifty Valley Oak will have a vase-shaped crown of ascending branches while the trunk is hidden more than half way to the ground by the down-sweeping of recurved branches. At this time the whole tree is very twiggy and, in consequence, densely leafy. At 100 years of age, and for the next 200, a Valley Oak is in the weeping stage. That means that from the branches there trail numerous long, whip-like or vine-like branchlets which sweep almost or quite to the grass, swaying in the valley's hot summer breeze with a gracious indolence. The tree has now attained its sturdiest yet most beguiling appearance. The last stage, when winter storms and decay have wracked and broken it, has been called second youth; the tree puts out a fresh effort and a pole-like growth results, with short, straightish, half-erect branches.

That specimens of great size or historic interest should occur is only natural in such a long-lived tree whose preference it is to grow where man too best flourishes. Perhaps the first to become famous, at least among English-speaking Californians, was the "Forty-niner's Tree" which gave the name to the community of Big Oak Flat, a flat being, in the vocabulary of the Sierra Nevada, a high mountain valley. This tree is said to have had a diameter of 11 feet, and was so sacred to the Argonauts of Forty-nine that they passed a camp ordinance to protect it. Nevertheless they themselves destroyed it, according to the story, when their mining operations caused the land to slip, carrying the tree down with it. Not far beyond this tree, at the ghost town of Second Garotte, seven men were suspended, by the neck, from the Hangman's Oak, for having stolen placer gold from the sluice boxes.

The most famous Valley Oak of all is the mammoth "Hooker Oak," near Chico, California, named in honor of Sir Joseph Hooker, the director of the Royal Gardens at Kew, England. In company with Asa Gray of Harvard, he visited this tree in 1877 as the guest of its owner, General Bidwell. Hooker pronounced it the largest Oak in the world, though we know now that it is not. Yet magnificent it is as it stands 110 feet high, has a trunk approximately 8 feet in diameter, and casts a pool of shade 150 feet across. Four titanic main limbs start forth not many feet above the base; each gives rise to a score of branches big enough to be a very fair-sized tree; some of these dip at their tips to the earth. Surrounded now by a beautifully landscaped park, this mighty spirit-tree is justifiably the pride of the city.

In contrast to the grand stature of the Valley Oak is the uselessness of its wood. To the disappointment of the pioneers it proved worthless to them, not only for boards but even for small tools; it is hard but brittle; it is heavy but weak. Its sapwood is apt to be eaten out with the Oak-root rot, and it decays rapidly in contact with soil and water so it is not good even for fence posts. In their disgust the early pioneers called it "Mush Oak."

The acorns, however, meant a great deal to the California Indians. Frémont, in his famed Second Expedition of 1844, found "an Indian village, consisting of two or three huts; we had come upon them suddenly, and the people had evidently just run off. Their huts were low and slight, made like beehives in a picture, five or six feet high, and near each was a crate, formed of interlaced branches and grass, in size and shape like a very large hogshead. Each of these contained from six to nine bushels. These were filled with the long acorns already mentioned, and in the huts were several neatly made baskets, containing quantities of the acorns roasted. They were sweet and agreeably flavored, and we supplied ourselves with about half a bushel, leaving one of our shirts, a handkerchief, and some smaller articles in exchange."

Naturally many animals beside man eat the sweet acorns — the gray squirrel, for one, and the California woodpecker. An epicure for the mast of this tree is the band-tailed pigeon, a fine game bird now growing rare. If you are fortunate you may still see a flock of these beautiful creatures as they come, banking and wheeling, incredibly swift, through the groves, uttering their hoarse cry of *hoop-a-whoo*, their wings whistling like escaping steam, and their bodies gleaming in opal hues as they rock in their headlong flight. But if no bandtails appear, you will almost certainly see another handsome denizen of the Valley Oak groves — the yellow-billed magpie, forever swooping among the trees in its jet-black, snow white, and metallic green, the individuals chasing each other about like boys at play, uttering their harsh *qua* or expressing unutterable things with tails so long they wag the bird.

The Valley Oak has many foes and is losing ground before them. The worst is man, although he has no use for its timber. For the Californian farmer clearly understands that Valley Oaks grow on the most arable land, level for plow and tractor, with rich soil and high water table. So this noble old tree has been cut and burned ruthlessly to make way for wheat and fruit. The California realtor and promoter makes unerringly for Valley Oak groves when he can, and indeed such groves are fine places for human habitation, shaded in

summer but open to the sun in winter. Yet something always happens
to the Oaks when residences appear. Many are cut down for house
sites; others have their roots cut for water and sewer mains and gas
lines whose inevitable leakage poisons the roots. Wells are sunk,
lowering the water table beyond the reach of the deepest roots.
Streams are diverted away, their waters conducted uselessly to the sea
or expended on irrigation projects at some distant point. Too often
the result is that, though one sees beautiful old Valley Oaks still surviving here and there where realty development goes on apace, as in
the San Fernando Valley, there is no new growth coming on, and the
loss of each old tree is irreplaceable.

Throughout the season this Oak presents a gentle drama which
evergreen trees do not offer — the tender haze of color when leaves and
catkins first appear, in late spring, the beauty of the long summer
shade, which is not dim and stuffy like that in a dense growth of young
Redwood, Douglastree and Laurel, but luminous and breezy — letting
in the light but not the full heat of day. The trees hold their
leaves until December and never turn any gorgeous colors, but while
the bare trunks and limbs in winter stand naked their grand, male
beauty of form comes out, the bark pale against the clouds filled with
the promise of rain. These Oaks are very late to leaf out, despite the
precocity and warmth of Californian springs. But this is advantageous,
for, the winter's rains being over and gone, says the Psalmist, the
flowers appear on the earth. The bare boughs have let the sunlight
freely through, and the dark loam absorbs its warmth swiftly. Then
the year brings forth its sweetest children, those displays of wild flowers
that are the singular pride of California. Acres of lavender lupine,
close as the threads of a carpet, stretch between the benignant bare
Oaks, away over dale and hill, drifted with the *nievatas* ("little snows"
— a sort of white forget-me-not) and burning with the orange fire of
the poppy. At such a moment one can behold California as it was in
its primeval innocence and dignity, before tractor and realtor, fool's
oat and filaree altered so much.

OREGON WHITE OAK

Quercus Garryana Douglas

OTHER NAMES: Garry, Western White, or Pacific Post Oak.

RANGE: Southeast coast of Vancouver (Nanaimo, southward) and along the Fraser River on the mainland of British Columbia; in Washington, generally below 3000 feet altitude, islands of Puget Sound, north end of Olympic peninsula, and Mount Rainier region, south on the west slopes of the Cascades to Oregon where it occurs chiefly in the Columbia River and Willamette Valleys, ascending the east slopes of the Cascades (to 3000 feet) at the north, and, in the south, on the lower slopes of the Siskiyous; in California on the Coast Ranges (but not near the sea or in the fog belt) south to Marin County and on the Santa Cruz Mountains south of San Francisco.

DESCRIPTION: *Bark* of trunks light gray or brown and shallowly fissured, with broad scaly ridges. *Twigs* stout, dark or light brown and downy through the first winter, then smooth and bright reddish brown and finally ashen. *Leaves* deciduous, 4 to 6 inches long, 2 to 3 inches across, the upper surface dark glossy green, the lower pale green, thick and firm with slightly thickened margins rolled under and stout yellow midrib giving rise to straight primary veins. *Acorn* 1 to 1¼ inches long, ½ to 1 inch thick, enclosed only ⅓ or less of its length in the cup with downy, thin, free scales having frequently elongated tips. *Wood* very tough, close-grained, strong and hard (46½ pounds per cubic foot, dry weight), the heartwood light brown, the sapwood nearly white.

The Oregon White Oak goes farther north than any of its tribe on the Coast, and is the only valuable timber Oak of the Northwest. A short time ago it was but little cut for lumber, though ranchers had long fenced in their rangelands with it, under the name of Post Oak, because it splits easily and its heartwood (but not the sapwood) lasts so long in contact with the soil. But in recent years the tempo of serious cutting for lumber has risen sharply, as the hardwood business becomes active at last in the West. Some 246,000,000 board feet a year are being sawed of it now, for furniture, cabinetwork, interior finish, construction, buildings, and agricultural implements. It has long been known as a wonderful fuel and shipbuilding material.

The acorns may not be edible by white man's standards, but David Douglas, in an unpublished manuscript, wrote: "The acorns are greedily sought by bears. By several of the native tribes they are gathered in the months of August and September, and deposited in pits on the margins of lakes and streams so that they are completely covered by water, in which state they lie till the following winter, when they are taken out and without any other preparation than simply wiping, they are eaten as an article of food. The smell is disagreeable and, as might be expected, they are far from being of a palatable flavor."

The place to see this noble tree is in the great valley of the Columbia, where, on islands and rich bottom-lands, it attains its finest dimensions, 75 to 90 feet in height, and as much as 5 feet through in the sturdy boles. The largest trees are probably 500 years old and they have a correspondingly craggy dignity, with great broad crowns of foliage. This is a dark, smooth shining green above, contrasting handsomely with the pale downy undersides.

In general, Oregon White Oaks tend to rise in spacious groves, with grassy glades between them — "opens," the country people call them — where the deer step slowly, if you are standing still, or bound if you move, followed by their springing fawns. The wise farmer of Oregon's Willamette Valley leaves a few of these great trees in his fields and pastures, in gratitude for the shade they give him and his stock. Many a ranch house do you see under its benignant boughs, looking indeed small, but blessed.

The chief beauty of the Oregon White Oak is in the light hue of the bark, almost bone-white sometimes. The great trunks, of a winter twilight, when the leaves are fallen, may stand out almost like cemetery slabs, with a strangely ghostly effect, but by day their pale bark has a look of cool elegance. Sometimes, where the fog or rainfall is heavy, the trunks and boughs are rimed with emerald moss which follows every twist of the gnarled branches till they look like something out of a Grimm fairy tale.

ROCKY MOUNTAIN WHITE OAK

Quercus Gambelii Nuttall

OTHER NAMES: Gambel, Utah, Scrub, Shin, or Mountain Oak. Bellota. Blackjack.

RANGE: From extreme southwestern Wyoming south in dry foothills and on canyon walls, throughout Utah, western Colorado and Nevada (except the western parts) to the mountains of western Texas, and through Arizona except the western and southwestern borders, to Sonora and Coahuila.

DESCRIPTION: *Bark* gray-brown, thin, rough and scaly. *Twigs* stout, at first downy and red-brown, becoming orange-brown. *Leaves* deciduous, 2½ to 7 inches long, 1½ to 3½ inches broad, thick and firm, the upper surface dark green and smooth, the lower pale and pubescent. *Acorn* ½ to ¾ inch long, usually solitary, enclosed for ½ its length in the cup which bears small but thick and palely pubescent scales. *Wood* hard, very heavy (52½ pounds per cubic foot, dry weight), and close-grained.

This little Oak (for, very slow-growing as it is, it is never more than 50 feet in height and more commonly 15, 20 and 25) is *the* common deciduous Oak of the greater part of the Rocky Mountain system. At the Grand Canyon it is the little tree you see growing in intricate bandy-legged chaparral clumps among the lofty Western Yellow Pines, right to the rim in many places. And it is one of the Oaks that give lovely Oak Creek Canyon, in central Arizona, its name.

Oak Creek Canyon lies south of Flagstaff, and was formed by faulting of the rock formation in the basic Coconino sandstone. The rushing of the creek through this fault, and the winds bringing sands from the Painted Desert to cut the sandstone, have carved out the canyon, an immense rift filled with geologic fantasies in purple and red cliffs, cap rocks of black lava, ledges of orange-yellow, russet buttes and saffron seams. And through it all Oak Creek churns and rushes along narrow declivities and down scores of little falls, the wind of its passing setting the fern beds to trembling, its spray drifting over the yellow columbine and lavender primroses, the blue asters and vermilion Indian paintbrush. Here, with Canyon Ironwood, Sycamore, Cypress, and Aspen, grows the White Oak in finest style, developing its branches, putting forth its sweet, softly green, roundly lobed leaves. And here, in autumn, it turns its most gorgeous colors, sometimes yellow but often a brilliant light red — a color almost never borne by a western Oak.

Young William Gambel, an ornithologist discovered by Thomas Nuttall and adopted as his assistant, first found this lovely little Oak when in his twenty-third year he joined a party of trappers, and in 1844 reached Santa Fe with them. In the few years of life that remained to this promising naturalist he discovered perhaps 100 new species in the West. But he never got used to the terrible exertions, the strange foods of the explorer in those days, and after a perilous crossing of the Nevada desert, and the Sierra Nevada in the winter of 1849, he arrived, on improvised snowshoes, at Rose's Bar, Plumas County, California, with a raging typhoid of which he swiftly died. He was buried near by, but when the Forty-niners discovered hydraulic mining they sluiced the whole hillside down; his bones, like his specimens back East, were scattered to oblivion.

At the Grand Canyon and commonly elsewhere, Gambel Oak, as it is alternatively called, has a habit of growing in dense colonies of a few to thirty individuals, if that is the way to speak of the shoots thrown up from a far-creeping subterranean system which might be compared to the rootstock of some fern that sends up frond after frond. But the underground stems of the parent Oak expand radially, forming a roughly circular colony, all the shoots living attached to the common system.

To livestock the foliage tastes sweet. Cattle browse it lightly, and your horse, if you are on a camping trip, will appreciate it highly. The acorns too are sweet and very fattening. Hogs devour them and goats will take them moderately. But the real enthusiast for this Oak is the Arizona wild turkey, which gobbles the acorn mast voraciously. Add, of course, the merry, frisking squirrels, while for the Rocky Mountain mule deer Gambel Oak foliage forms a large percentage of their summer browse.

BUR OAK

Quercus macrocarpa A. Michaux

OTHER NAME: Mossycup Oak.

RANGE: Manitoba and the Black Hills of South Dakota south to central Texas, east to southern Ohio, southwestern New Brunswick and southern Nova Scotia, and southward through New York State to Maryland, northern West Virginia, Kentucky, northwestern Tennessee, and Arkansas.

DESCRIPTION: *Bark* of old trunks thick, grayish or reddish brown, flaky, deeply cut into wide fissures dividing broad straight ridges with more or less flat surfaces. *Twigs* greenish gray, turning light orange, and the following year dark brown with somewhat corky ridges. *Leaves* 6 to 12 inches long, 3 to 6 inches broad, thick, firm, the upper surface shiny dark green, the lower silvery green and downy; deciduous. *Acorns* ¾ to 2 inches long, half buried in the strikingly fringed cup. *Wood* medium heavy (46 pounds to the cubic foot, dry weight), hard, tough, close-grained, with dark brown heartwood and thin paler sapwood.

The Bur Oak, one of the noblest and most characteristic trees of the Middle West, just reaches the circumscriptions of this book in western Nebraska. In Illinois the Bur Oak is found on upland ridges, but far out on the Great Plains it is driven by scanty water supply down into the bottom-lands. If not quite a riverbank tree like Willow and Cottonwood, it is seldom seen, out here, far from the streams, where it forms small groves.

This ponderous tree is called the Bur Oak on account of the heavily ringed cups of the acorns that look almost like the burs on a chestnut, but of course are not prickly. A grand old Bur Oak suggests an out-door mansion, a house in itself, for it is often broad rather than tall, and its mighty boughs, starting straight out from the trunk at right angles, may extend horizontally 50 or 60 or 70 feet, bending with the weight of their own mass to the very ground, so that within their circle is a hollow room, its grassy floor littered with acorns, with the sloughed-off corky bark of the boughs, with the deep bed of leaves, and the birds' nests of many a summer, the gold of many a flicker's wing.

Extensive studies have been made upon the root systems of the Bur Oak and they show that the taproot is comparatively short; like the trunk above ground it soon gives rise to a large number of wide-spreading, horizontal primary branches, which in old systems are almost as thick as the great main lower boughs of the tree above. The primaries send off obliquely slanting secondaries in still greater number, and these give rise to tertiaries, which in turn send down numberless sinkers or slim roots that travel straight down. For all these thousands of sinkers there are tens of thousands of still finer rootlets called obliques, and on these are clustered the millions of fine capillary or thread-form rootlets. These capillaries may be very long, and in their following of veins of water not only do they penetrate as widely as the widest spread of the great boughs and almost as deep as the tree is high, but others turn upward and reach nearly to the

surface of the soil and so catch all the moisture that falls from light showers but never penetrates more than a few inches. It follows, however, that a tree with so mighty a root system has one serious competitor which can fight it with its own weapons, and that is another Bur Oak. So, perforce, Bur Oaks keep a respectful distance from each other; they hold each other off, not so much by their wide-spreading branches as by the fierce competition of their root systems.

In autumn the leaves turn a soft dull yellow. Then the fox squirrels go rippling through the boughs, gathering mast, while on the prairies the wild grasses turn to tawny. Then, Indian summer over, the leaves fall very early, and the Bur Oaks take on the closed-up steely look of so many eastern hardwoods. Spring comes late to the Great Plains, and it has been here some time before the Bur Oaks finally consent to leaf out again. But though so slow to bud, they are slow to die, and may live out two centuries and three.

YELLOW OAK

Quercus Muehlenbergii Engelmann

OTHER NAMES: Chestnut or Bray Oak.

RANGE: In the Chisos, Davis, and Guadalupe Mountains of western Texas and on the Edwards Plateau, south through the mountains of Nuevo Leon and Coahuila, and west to the mountains of southeastern New Mexico.

DESCRIPTION: *Bark* of trunks thin and broken on the surface into brown scales with papery white margins. *Twigs* slender, markedly fluted, smooth or somewhat scurfy, light brown at first and with prominent lenticels, becoming gray or reddish brown in age, with a gray bloom. *Leaves* deciduous, 3 to 6 inches long and 1½ to 4 inches wide (or sometimes much smaller, only 2 inches long and ¾ inch broad), the margins with regular, large, rounded scallops, upper surface dark green, dully shining, the lower light green, hoary with sparse, closely flattened, clusters of branched hairs, the veins as many as the teeth and passing in to them, raised, as are the meshed veinlets, on both surfaces. *Acorns* 1 to 3 on usually short stalks, ⅝ to ¾ inches long, ⅜ to ⅝ inch in diameter, about ⅓ included in the hemispheric to deeply cup-shaped saucer, the scales roundly thickened and hoary-haired at base, the tips thin, closely flattened, and blunt.

Called Yellow Oak in the West, the eastern form of this tree is known as Chinquapin Oak. It flourishes in shaded, moist canyons high up in the mountains. Its leaves here are a little broader than those of the eastern trees, but there seems otherwise no good reason for separating the Big Bend specimens from those of the eastern states.

In the East this tree, with its wonderfully strong, tough wood, has played an important rôle, first as the best obtainable fuel for the old river steamboats, the best of tight cooperage for barrels to hold liquid merchandise, then as ties or sleepers for the early railroads. In the West it is too inaccessible to be turned to use. But you may still admire it for its nearly white bark, and for its lovely foliage, each crinkly blade handsome in itself, but on a windy day superb in the mass, when the leaves are spun around, contrasting now their darkly gleaming upper surface, then their flashing whitish lower surface.

BLUE OAK

Quercus Douglasii Hooker and Arnott

OTHER NAMES: Western White, Mountain White, California Rock, Iron, Jack, Post, or Douglas Oak.

RANGE: Foothills of the California Coast Ranges from Mendocino County south to the Santa Ynez Mountains of Santa Barbara County (at 550 to 4000 feet above sea level), in the neighborhood of Mount Shasta and Lassen Peak, and southward on the west slope of the Sierra Nevada (500 to 4000 feet) to the Tehachapi Mountains and on the desert (north) slope of the San Gabriel Mountains.

DESCRIPTION: *Bark* pale and covered with small scales. *Twigs* stout, very brittle at the joints, clothed at first in short, dense, hoary downiness, and dark gray, becoming later ashen or gray-brown. *Leaves* deciduous, 2 to 5 inches long, 1 to 1¾ inches broad, at maturity firm, thin and stiff, pale bluish above, the lower surface yellow-green, with conspicuously meshed veinlets and covered with a short pubescence. *Acorn* solitary or in pairs, ¾ to 1 inch long, ½ to ⅓ inch thick, shiny green turning in drying dark chestnut-brown, with a short zone of hoariness at the apex, barely enclosed at base in a cup of reddish-tipped, palely pubescent scales. *Wood* strong but brittle, hard and heavy (55½ pounds per cubic foot, dry weight), with dark brown heartwood that, on exposure, becomes almost black, and thick sapwood of light brown hue.

The old Gold Rush country of the Mother Lode, transversed today through its wandering length by the California highway so appro-

priately numbered 49, is lined almost throughout its length with this
rugged tree. For this is an arid region, though crossed by the many
streams that are fed by Sierra snows and rains, and the Blue or
Douglas Oak is a lover of aridity. It so shuns water that, it is related,
irrigation ditches cut too near hillside trees will gradually kill them,
though its constant associate, the Interior Live Oak, profits by the
added water content of the soil. Perhaps the Live Oak only lives here
because it cannot, for some reason, compete with other trees in more
well-watered situations. But the Blue Oak dwells in the hot dry foothills of the western slope of the Sierra Nevada of its own free will,
one would say, and in popular tradition shies from water like a mad
dog.

There is a brief period in spring when the winter rains are over,
the foothills have not yet begun to heat up, and all the world is one
mass of wild flowers — silken white mariposas and blue lupine, lavender harvestbells and orange poppy — stretching between these wide-
spaced trees, when the environment seems idyllic. But soon the flowers
fade, the grass is dried to burnished straw, the old mining towns sleep
beneath their roses and Trees-of-heaven, and the long dry summer has
set in. Now the Blue Oaks put out their full foliage, and it has a hot
look, like an opalescent blue-green haze, shade though it is. And not
even under its foliage is there any real relief from the heat, which wells
up from the rocks and earth and straw; only the glare is obviated when
one stops for a picnic under its boughs and amidst their litter.

For Blue Oaks are forever losing their limbs. The wood, though
hard, is brittle, and the winter storms break the old limbs when over-
weighted by becoming too long. Though heavy, the wood is weak
with a special susceptibility to attacks of dry rot and other fungi,
rotting off the boughs and eating out the heart of the trees. Of course
all this litter of broken limbs makes easy gathering for fuel, and the
caloric value of the wood is high. But the pioneer Californian used
to fear the wood too, for great masses of the mycelial threads of the
punk fungus, hidden under the bark, would often be lifted lightly,
while burning, by the updraft and, shooting out of the chimney, fall
as a brand on the roof of the cabin. He had more confidence in its
value for fence posts, and over the years great quantities of it have
been used to enclose the ranches.

Yet with all its failings, the Blue Oak is a picturesque, craggy,
grand tree, with beautiful pale bark and sturdy trunks. It gives, at
least, far more shade than its companion the Digger Pine which casts

almost none at all. And its blue leaves become associated in the mind with the lure of Route 49 and its miles of curves and grades, with the romance of the country once so feverishly inhabited by the gold diggers, now one of the quietest spots in the Golden State, where the rapping of woodpeckers on the Blue Oaks and the haunting clamor of crows may be the loudest sounds you will hear for hours on end.

MESA LIVE OAK

Quercus Engelmanni Greene

OTHER NAMES: Engelmann Oak.

RANGE: Hills of San Diego County, California, 15 to 20 miles east of the sea, and northward irregularly as at Oak Knoll, Pasadena, San Marino (where abundant) and San Gabriel, to Kern County; also found in northern Baja California.

DESCRIPTION: *Bark* of old trunks thick, light gray, deeply fissured and cross-checked into small plates, separating on the surface into thin close scales. *Twigs* rigid and stout, at first brown under the hoary down, later becoming gray or light brown and smooth. *Leaves* evergreen, thick, blue-green above and light yellow-green beneath, 1 to 3 inches long, ½ inch wide, dark chestnut-brown streaked with darker stripes, becoming light brown with weathering, enclosed for ½ its length, or less, in the cup which is covered with light brown scales coated with a pale down. *Wood* strong though brittle, hard and very heavy (58½ pounds per cubic foot, dry weight), with nearly black heartwood and light brown sapwood.

In the back-country of southern California, around Palomar and Hemet, and at the foot of the Sierra Madre, around Altadena and Glendora, this curious Oak is often the dominant one, on mesas and low arid hills. It probably passes, with most observers, for a Coast Live Oak, for its main lower limbs have the same habit of coming out nearly at right angles to the short bole, making a big, irregular crown. Its leaves are distinctively thick and very deep blue-green on the upper surface. The foliage is not strictly evergreen, though it is on the tree all winter; that is to say it does not last several years; the leaves begin to fade at the end of the first winter and are shoved off in spring by the new growth. At that time the crown of foliage is decidedly mangy and thin and the shade likewise. About all one can say for this Oak is that it makes fine fuel and that it holds the soil well in a region none too well provided with native trees.

MEXICAN BLUE OAK

Quercus oblongifolia Torrey

OTHER NAMES: Blue or White Oak.

RANGE: Central and southwestern Arizona, and western Coahuila.

DESCRIPTION: *Bark* ashy gray and broken into small, nearly square, plate-like scales. *Twigs* rigid and slender, at first downy and light red-brown, becoming in subsequent years ashen. *Leaves* thin but firm, blue-

green or in winter mauve above and paler beneath, 1 to 2 inches long, ½ to ¾ inch broad (sometimes larger on vigorous shoots), and with conspicuous meshed veinlets. *Acorn* usually solitary, ½ to ¾ inch long, ⅓ inch thick, at first shiny chestnut-brown, soon weathering to dull light brown, enclosed for ⅓ of its length in the cup which is composed out-wardly of red-tipped, hoary-downy scales and within is light green. *Wood* brittle but strong, hard, and very heavy, the heartwood nearly black, the thick sapwood brown.

Out on the desert southwest of Tucson, Arizona, you travel for miles and hours over the dusty washboard ranch roads, up over arid low hills, and down across the broad sandy washes, the monotony broken by catching now and then a sight of a vermillion flycatcher flashing past, and always having in view Baboquivari Peak looking like the high but lopsided crown of a Mexican sombrero. And the Live Oak that you see there, alternating with Mesquite thickets, is the Mexican Blue Oak. Its foliage is not so much blue as an unearthly mauve, as strange a color as is worn by a western tree. In winter it turns a sort of rusty bronze or cuprous, and falls in spring, a month or two before the new leaves appear. Gradually one comes to grow fond of this Oak with its pale trunks, as much for the odd lure of this desolate country as for any inherent beauty. Standing 16 to 25 feet high, it makes a broadly spreading crown often much wider than tall, and it casts shade of a sort beneath which it is good to stop, in your weary traveling, especially if you have brought any cooling drink to wash down your food so swiftly dried in that burning atmosphere.

ARIZONA WHITE OAK

Quercus arizonica Sargent

RANGE: Central and southeastern Arizona and southern New Mexico, south in the mountains of Sonora and Chihuahua.

DESCRIPTION: *Bark* of trunks ashen, deeply furrowed with broad ridges broken into thick, long, plate-like scales. *Twigs* stout, at first reddish brown and invested with dense tawny-woolly hairs, later becoming smooth and darker. *Leaves* 1 to 4 inches long, ½ to 2 inches wide, firm and rigid, dull dark blue-green above, the lower surface duller and covered with thick tawny minute down, the midrib broad and yellow, the margins curled under; reticulate veins very prominent. *Acorn* usually solitary, ¾ to 1 inch long, ½ inch thick, dark chestnut-brown and shining, soon weathering to a light dull brown, and enclosed for ½ its length in the cup, the scales of which are red-tipped and lightly downy, those below the middle of the cup thickened and rounded on the back. *Wood* close-grained, hard, strong, and extremely heavy (63 pounds per cubic foot, dry weight), the heartwood dark brown, the thick sapwood paler.

The Arizona White Oak shares, in its native State, with Emory Oak the *encinal* or great Live Oak zone, in canyons, on mountainsides and rocky spots in the high range land, well above the desert lowlands and well below the zone of the Yellow Pine and the Gambel Oak. Decidedly it is Arizona's biggest Oak, growing up to 60 feet high in well-shaded and watered canyons, and with a magnificent spread of its heavy lower boughs that come out nearly at right angles to the bole. So that, with its rounded crown, this species makes a grand dome-shaped mass of leafage very striking in the arid spaces of the high country down along the Border. The leaves fall in spring, a month or two before the new leaves appear. The acorns are bitter, and there are no published records that any animals devour them except that rare summer bird of the Border counties, the thick-billed parrot.

GRAY OAK

Quercus grisea Liebmann

OTHER NAME: Scrub Oak.

RANGE: Eastern Arizona to the mountains of western Texas (at medium and upper altitudes of all the mountain ranges) and south in the mountains of Coahuila and Chihuahua, Mexico.

DESCRIPTION: *Bark* of old trunks dark gray and deeply furrowed. *Twigs* slender, scarcely fluted, dark gray and somewhat hoary with yellowish hair for several years. *Leaves* deciduous, about 1¼ (rarely ⅜ to 2) inches long and ⅝ (rarely ⅜ to 1¼) inches wide, leathery but thin, blue-green, scurfy with branched white hairs below and to a lesser extent above, the upper surface appearing polished if the pubescence is rubbed off, the margins untoothed or occasionally toothed toward the outer end. *Acorns* paired at the end of a pubescent stalk, about ½ inch long, ⅛ inch in diameter, about ⅓ included in the shallowly top-shaped cup.

The Gray Oak is named from the sad, dusty gray-blue of its foliage, which is the more set off by contrast with the slickly gleaming yellow-green of Emory Oak's fresh-looking leaves, for the two, at least in western Texas, are strangely inseparable companions. Generally speaking, Gray Oak is a low, scrubby tree, growing in open canyons and on open slopes, in orchard-like thickets, with bandy stems and crooked boughs, looking much like old Apple trees. Growing very slowly, these trees at last, under favorable conditions, attain a height of 60 feet.

Gray Oak is the dominant tree of the *encinal,* the Live Oak formation, of western Texas, more or less densely covering all the mesas and gentler slopes of the mountains, and forming what the Texans call mottes, from a French word meaning a clump or knoll. These mottes are, in general, close round-topped thickets, the tallest trees at the center, and the outer rings successively and evenly lower, down to the size called scrub. The mottes invade the grassy slopes, providing in summer a welcome shade to the toiling botanist who, unlike most Westerners, is sometimes seen voluntarily afoot.

TOUMEY OAK
Quercus Toumeyi Sargent

RANGE: In Arizona on the San Francisco Peaks, Coconino County (where rare), in the mountains south of Prescott, and in the southeastern part of the state, in the Santa Cruz and Mule Mountains (where abundant). Also in the mountains of northern Mexico.

DESCRIPTION: *Bark* thin, dark brown or nearly black, and broken into thin, close scales. *Twigs* slender and, when they first appear, bright reddish brown and clothed with pale woolly hairs but covered in the second season with a thin nearly black bark broken into little warty scales. *Leaves* evergreen, thin but firm, small (½ to ¾ inch long, ⅓ to

½ inch wide), light blue-green and glossy above, the lower surface paler, with fine pubescence and inrolled margins. *Acorns* not stalked, in pairs or solitary, ½ to ⅔ inch long, ¼ inch thick, glossy light brown and with a ring, at base, of fine pubescence, seated for about ¼ their length in a cup with light red-brown scales coated with a pale woolly pubescence, the inside of the cup pale green and downy. *Wood* light brown, with thick paler sapwood.

West of the once hell-roaring town of Tombstone, Arizona, lies a broad desert valley, and beyond that rise the Mule Mountains, named for two peaks resembling mule's ears, but more beautiful than their name suggests! Their splendors come out best at sunset, when they glow with Indian browns and reds. And here it is that the Toumey Oak was first discovered, in 1899, and here it is still seen at its best, though it has also been found in the Dragoon Mountains to the east of Tombstone. When it rises above shrub height, it forms a tree as much as 33 feet tall. Its extremely small leaves cast but little shade, numerous as they are, for this is a true desert tree and like so many others of its kind it gives the minimum of shelter from the sun in places where the sunlight is at a maximum.

EMORY OAK

Quercus Emoryi Torrey

OTHER NAMES: Black, Black Jack, or Desert Live Oak.

RANGE: Mountains of central and northern Mexico to northern Arizona and northern New Mexico and the Big Bend country of western Texas.

DESCRIPTION: *Bark* of old trunks thick and deeply furrowed, dark gray and scaly-plated. *Twigs* rigid, slender, at first bright red and downy, then smooth and dark brown. *Leaves* 1 to 1½ inches long, ½ to 1 inch wide, thick, rigid and leathery, dark green above, paler below. *Acorn* ½ to ¾ inch long, at first light green, becoming dark brown or nearly black, the thin shell lined within by thick woolly hairs and enclosed ⅓ or ½ its length by the cup, which is light green and minutely downy within and outwardly covered with papery, light brown, softly pubescent scales. *Wood* close-grained, strong but brittle, hard and very heavy (57½ pounds per cubic foot, dry weight), with dark brown or nearly black heartwood and thick light brown sapwood tinged with red.

For centuries before the Spanish-speaking people, settling in our Southwest, began to call this tree *bellota*, the Indians had been grinding its sweet acorns for meal, for these are as a rule sweet, even eaten out of hand without boiling. The Apaches, especially, were fond of them; by a strange coincidence the great area, from western Texas to the mountains of southern Arizona and northern Sonora, where the Apaches had their strongholds or carried on their raids, almost exactly coincides with the range of this species.

In Apache Pass, of ghastly memory — but now so silent and deserted — this is the dominant tree. Its low, dome-shaped masses dot the grass and rocky slopes where once an emigrant train was stopped and the people tied to the wagon wheels and burnt. It is a tranquil monument to those tragic sites where the Butterfield stage was attacked so many times that, in spite of a special bonus for making the run, few drivers ever lived to collect it. Or where a rash second lieutenant's treachery to the great Apache chief, Cochise, under a flag of truce, started all these atrocities. They are gone, the soldiers and Apaches, gone from Fort Bowie, and Fort Crittenden, gone from the Dragoon Mountains, and from Cochise's stronghold where he was persuaded by a mail inspector, Tom Jeffords, to make a peace he faithfully kept. Cochise is buried somewhere there (only Tom Jeffords, of all white men, ever knew exactly where) and though his tribe still comes back to the Dragoons to gather acorns, those nuts that fall in the stronghold are always left, according to legend, in reverence to his spirit. Here with only the sound of the creek trickling through the arrowweed (the straight-stemmed *Pluchea* of which the dread Apache arrow shafts were made), the Apache's Oak stands proudly, its zigzag twigs as tough to break as sinewy savage arms, its leaves in the brilliant Arizona sunlight glittering almost painfully, or under a full moon twinkling like lance-points.

The Emory Oak is the dominant tree of the Arizona *encinal* (Live Oak formation), occupying mostly upland sites — canyons, rocky hills, mountainsides, high range land. It thus stands well above the range of the Mexican Blue Oak, found on the low deserts, but below that of the Gambel Oaks, deciduous trees found high in the mountains of the Border counties, in the temperate zone. Its foliage, though hard and seemingly evergreen, drops in spring a month or two before the new leaves appear.

Epicures and gourmandizers of its generous crop of nuts are the Mearns, Gambel, and scaled quails, while the rock squirrel and the Gila chipmunk fill their pouches greedily with them or store them when the fancy takes them. The foliage furnishes browse to deer.

CANYON LIVE OAK

Quercus chrysolepis Liebmann

OTHER NAMES: Maul, Goldencup, Iron, Canyon, Hickory, or Golden-leaf Oak. California, Blue, Mountain, or Spanish Live Oak.

RANGE: From extreme southwestern Oregon south throughout the Coast Ranges of California from the foothills (but not close to the sea) to 4500 feet in the northern counties, and from 1000 to 6500 in the southern, and along all the western slopes of the Sierra Nevada from the foothills to 6000 or 9000 feet; common on the mountains of southern California (San Gabriels, San Bernardinos, etc.) above 2500 feet altitude and up to 7000 in the San Jacinto Mountains; south to Baja California and, in shrubby form (*Quercus Palmeri* and *Quercus Wilcoxii*), in southern Utah, central and southeastern Arizona, and Sonora.

DESCRIPTION: *Bark* of trunks gray-brown tinged sometimes with red, and even in age smooth and unfurrowed. *Twigs* slender, at first downy, becoming light brown or ashy gray. *Winter buds* with chestnut-brown, minutely downy scales. *Leaves* evergreen, at maturity 1 to 4 inches long, ½ to 2 inches wide, leathery and thick, the upper surface smooth and bright yellow-green, the lower with incurled margins, and more or less tawny-downy, often becoming smooth and blue-green and often glaucous, those on old trees or boughs with untoothed margins or nearly so, those of young growth with several spiny teeth, Holly-like in appearance. *Acorn* ½ to 1 inch long and about as broad, light chestnut-brown, the inside of the shell thinly downy, the cup thick, broad-brimmed, with little triangular scales and often silvery-hoary or tawny-downy. *Wood* tough, close-grained, very strong, hard, and heavy (53 pounds per cubic foot, dry weight), the heartwood light brown, the sapwood thick and dark brown.

No other western Oak has so many folk names as this one; its beauty, its variability, and its usefulness account for that. But the name of Canyon Live Oak heads the list for the proper reason that canyons and mountain slopes are what it loves best. It will ascend to 9000 feet in the Sierra Madre above Pasadena, or come down almost to sea level in the North, if it can find the cool, rocky gulches that it loves. But it is not a tree of the broad valley floors, like the Valley Oak, nor of the hot dry foothills like the Blue Oak. The deeper the canyon, with sharp walls and the competition of tall conifers, the taller this Oak becomes. Trunks straight and clean of branches for 20 to 40 feet are

seen under such conditions, and the total height of the tree is likely then to be 60 to 100 feet, with trunks 2 to 3 feet thick. Sometimes an old specimen will have a trunk 5 feet through, and will maintain its columnar girth almost without taper for 35 feet. In more open situations however, Canyon Live Oak will grow less in height, but send forth from near the base mighty branches that, successively dividing, form a great dome-shaped crown sometimes 125 feet across, its periphery trailing to the ground to form a majestic hemisphere. Both these open-grown trees and the loftier, more slender ones of the forest are superb, always picturesque, always deep of shade and benignant of aspect.

The color of the foliage is one of the great beauties of this Oak. It is a bright yellow-green above, and below either covered with a golden fuzz, whence the name of Goldenleaf, or smooth and lead-covered, moonlight-blue, or even silvery. The foliage is strangely bewildering in its variability; one tree — usually a young one — may produce leaves with spiny, Holly-like margins, and another bear blades with their margins completely intact. In general, these are older trees. However, the same twig will often bear both kinds of leaves. The acorns are equally variable in size and shape, and the many varieties that have been based on acorns and leaves, though some are doubtless valid enough, are of purely botanical interest. The bark is striking for its thinness and its pale smoke-gray color that shines through the glades and canyons. With age it becomes checked and flaky, resembling then that of the White Oak of the eastern states.

This is, moreover, a stouthearted tree, with wood so tough and strong and shock-resistant that from early times it has been used for the slugs or bucks — pointed wedges with iron-rimmed heads — for splitting Redwood ties. With the axe-swinging pioneers it was a favorite for the heads of mauls, whence the widely used name of Maul Oak. For mauls, young sound trees were usually selected. The strong crotches made fine compass timber for ships, in the days of wooden shipbuilding; in the time of wooden carriage and wagon building Canyon Live Oak was always sought for axles, wheels, and poles. As a fuel wood it is unsurpassed on the West coast in caloric value.

ISLAND LIVE OAK, *Quercus tomentella* Engelmann, is a species found on Santa Rosa, Santa Cruz and Santa Catalina Islands, off the coast of southern California, and on Guadalupe Island, Mexico. It is closely related to the Canyon Live Oak, *Quercus chrysolepis* (q.v.), and resembles it in general stature. It differs in its proportionately broader leaves (2 to 4 inches long, 1 to 2 inches wide) which, when toothed, have the teeth wavy-scalloped rather than small and sharp. The acorn is broader at the base, and full and rounded at the tip, enclosed only at base by the cup with its chestnut-brown free scales almost buried under a thick coat of hoary-woolly hairs.

The Island Live Oak grows on steep canyon walls and on mesas facing the sea and swept by the ocean winds. Its chief associates are the Island Pine, *Pinus remorata,* and island manzanita, *Arctostaphylos insularis.*

COAST LIVE OAK

Quercus agrifolia Née

OTHER NAME: Encina.

RANGE: Coast Ranges of California from Sonoma County south to Baja California, Mexico, from sea level (except in extreme southern California), up to 4500 feet altitude in the mountains above Santa Barbara, Pasadena, and in the San Jacinto Mountains.

DESCRIPTION: *Bark* of old trunks very thick, dark gray and even in age only slightly furrowed but broken into irregular plates. *Twigs* fine, numerous, dull gray to reddish brown and coated with short downy hairs for 2 years. *Leaves* ¾ to 4 inches long, ½ to 3 inches wide, evergreen, hard, thin, convex and dull green above, concave and somewhat lighter and almost shiny below with tufts of rusty hairs in the axils of the principal nerves, or sometimes coated below with clustered or thick hairs. *Acorn* light chestnut-brown, shining, ¾ to 1½ inches long, ¼ to ¾

inch thick, the shell lined inside with a thick coat of woolly hairs, as is the cup which bears papery scales that are downy near the base of the cup. *Wood* brittle, hard and heavy (51½ pounds per cubic foot, dry weight), the heartwood light reddish brown, the sapwood thick and darker.

The Spaniards' name for the Coast Live Oak was *encina*, the word given to the evergreen Oak or Ilex of the Mediterranean world, and the word encina persists today as a name for streets, suburbs, homes, estates and ranches, throughout coastal California. Indeed, the Coast Live Oak was one of the two first trees of California to be described so clearly that we can recognize them. For specimens were collected in 1791 by the Malaspina Expedition, the first and only scientific reconnaissance which the Spanish government made in California. When the exploring ship was anchored in Monterey Bay, two officers went ashore and brought back with them a branch of the Coast Live Oak and another of the Valley Oak. These were turned over to the botanists of the expedition, who subsequently published scientific descriptions of leaf, flower, and fruit, although they had never, apparently, been ashore to see the trees themselves. So they gave no idea of the magnificent form of this species, of its abundance, or the great rôle that it played in the lives of the Spanish Californians. All of which goes to show that the first publication of the scientific name of a tree may be a barren thing, while the true discovery of a tree is something that comes with the years.

When in 1770 that beloved founder of California's chain of missions, Padre Junípero Serra, landed at Monterey Bay, he planted his cross under a great Live Oak close to the shore, and here he said his first mass on the Monterey peninsula and founded San Carlos Mission. Later, in order to withdraw the young Indian girls from the covetous eyes of the Spanish soldiers, he moved his mission to its present site at Carmel. But that great Oak remained in the memory of all the old Montereyans as the first Christianized spot in that part of California. and succeeding generations venerated it as their most historic tree. Already ancient when Serra preached beneath it, it died branch by branch until only its stump was left; and when even that vanished it was replaced in 1896 by a monument.

Once again the Live Oak appears in the story of good Padre Serra when, soon after the Carmel Mission was begun, he set off with Fathers Miguel Pieras and Buenaventura Sitjar to establish, 25 leagues to the south, the Mission of San Antonio de Padua, in the foothills of the

Santa Lucia Mountains. In a fine grove of Oaks, Father Serra caused the goods to be unpacked; among them were the bells of the unbuilt mission. These he caused to be suspended from a Live Oak, and the sight of them so excited him that he rang them in the liveliest manner, shouting, "Hear, O Gentiles! Come! Oh, come to the holy church of God! Come, oh come, and receive the faith of Christ!" [1] His companions protested that there was no one to hear, yet as Serra was saying mass, a redskin "Gentile" appeared, attracted by the bells. He remained through a sermon he did not understand, left loaded with presents, and returned bringing a crowd, with gifts of Pinyon nuts for the friars. Thus was this mission founded beneath the boughs of the Oaks.

In our own time the Coast Live Oak is the American tree best known all around the world, if not known by name. For no other is so often seen in motion pictures. Sometimes it serves as Sherwood Forest for the exploits of Robin Hood, again as Bagworthy Forest in *Lorna Doone,* or it is even made to pass as the woods which the Pilgrim Fathers faced around Plymouth! In a way, Robert Louis Stevenson foresaw all this when he described the twisted trunks, the tangled growth of Live Oaks around Monterey as "woods for murderers to crawl among."

Dramatic, romantic, pictorial and picturesque (to choose but a few possible adjectives), the Coast Live Oak certainly is. For it seldom grows tall and straight; almost inevitably its trunks lean this way or that, its long sinuous branches twist and turn, and eventually with a down-sweeping gesture will come, in old trees, to reach the ground. So that every Coast Live Oak is an extreme individualist, utterly unlike every other in the world, and yet the sum and total of all its many variations adds up to a composite picture of ample grace, of grace combined with strength, that make it recognizable at a glance as distinct from any other tree within its natural range.

A fine old Live Oak is a leafy mansion, a spacious house of a tree. A grove of such, dotting the plains or filling a valley, or hanging with leaning trunks upon some Coast Range hillside, is always the most lovable and livable part of any scene in California reached by the sea breezes. Whenever he can, the Californian prefers to make his home beneath an old Live Oak's shade or in a grove of Oaks. When a Californian says "the woods" he usually means an Oak woodland, or at

[1] Fr. Zephyrine Engelhardt, *San Antonio de Padua, the Mission of the Sierras.* 1929.

least a hardwood growth. When he says "the forest" he commonly means dense coniferous stands, timber land, usually found in the mountains.

On headlands swept by cold sea winds, the Coast Live Oak will be sculptured by the elemental forces into fantastic forms, or its boughs or even its trunks may writhe along the ground. On steep mountainsides, these trees may cling to the canyon like a living river of green. On the gentler hills, gently the trees conform to the waving contours and slopes. Upon a plain, the trees grow taller, interlocking their branches in a natural evergreen vault. Growing singly amidst the wild oats, the Live Oak expands to its full dimensions, a great circle, and something more than hemispherical in form.

A well-grown Coast Live Oak will reach 75 feet in height, but it is not in height that this tree impresses, but rather in its spread and girth. One tree measured in the Angeles National Forest had a spread of 130 feet, with a trunk more than 12 feet in diameter, and there may be others unmeasured even more majestic in proportions. The Napa Valley, in California's vineyard country, the Santa Clara Valley, the inner slopes of the Lompoc hills, and the Ojai Valley, are especially famed for the number and grandeur of their Coast Live Oaks. It was the beauty of the Live Oaks that first made the San Fernando Valley celebrated. Fame brought hundreds of thousands of settlers, and to give them living space a large part of the Oaks have been cut down!

The wood of the Coast Live Oak is moderately strong, hard and heavy, yet it has never furnished any considerable quantity of timber to the hardwood trade, owing to the eccentric growth and shortness of the main bole and the frequent habit of branching from near the base. Furthermore, large specimens which theoretically should furnish considerable lumber are apt to be partially hollow, owing to the attacks of termites and dry rot. Yet in the early days of California, the crotches were valued for ship knees and other sorts of compass timber for marine construction. In one respect the wood is almost incomparably fine, and that is for fuel. There are only a few other trees, and almost none in the West, with the heat value of a cord of seasoned Live Oak. Its logs burn with an intense and steady flame, not throwing off sparks or exploding, but forming a lasting bed of coals and giving out a sweet and subtle odor.

As a result of its high fuel value, this wood was in great demand in the days of the sailing ships, and as these came in increasing numbers after the immigration from the eastern United States began, the Spanish Californians along the coast cut back their Live Oaks ever faster, in response to the tempting prices offered by the sailing vessels. In Santa Barbara, for instance, most of the plain between the old Presidio and the Santa Ynez Mountains was originally covered with magnificent Oaks above whose tops rose the towers of the old Mission, but faster than the growth of the town went on the selling of these delicious groves for fuel wood for the ships that anchored off the harborless port. In 1855 the Council enacted an ordinance prohibiting the cutting of trees or shrubs belonging to the city. But, as much of the wooded land was privately owned, the destruction went on apace, and in 1859 the *ayuntamiento* (city council) levied a tax for the benefit of the city treasury on the countless wagonloads of wood that went creaking towards the beach. Its original Oak groves swept away, the town of Santa Barbara is now replanted with exotic trees, and the noble Oak groves persist only in Mission Canyon, Montecito, and some of the hillsides of Hope Ranch.

A similar story could be told for California towns up and down the coast — first a reckless destruction of the trees, followed by a belated appreciation of the fact that, for homesites of the highest class, no showy Palm, no lofty Eucalyptus, no golden Acacia or flowery Jacaranda, can take the place of the native Oaks. Unfortunately, the practice of diverting streams at their source for use in irrigation ditches, of sinking numberless wells which lower the natural water table in the soil, and the laying of drainage pipes, have all combined to strike literally at the very roots of the Live Oak's life. Fine old trees are dying far sooner than they should, and seedlings, which have always played against long odds, are finding their chances of survival poorer and poorer. In no other part of the United States are human population and building increasing so rapidly as in the range of the Coast Live Oaks. So that the future of this lovely tree is dark indeed, unless it is widely realized by home owners, real estate promoters, and town councils, that every Oak is a precious asset.

INTERIOR LIVE OAK

Quercus Wislizeni A. de Candolle

OTHER NAME: Wislizenus Oak.

RANGE: Foothills and valleys especially away from the coast in California, in scattered groves of the inner Coast Ranges from the neighborhood of Ukiah in the north, to the mountains of San Diego County and Baja California, Mexico; and from Shasta County south through the foothills of the Sierra Nevada (where abundant) all the way to the Tehachapi Mountains.

DESCRIPTION: *Bark* of old trunks thick, furrowed, with rounded, broad, connecting ridges separating on the surface into thick dark brown scales tinged with red. *Twigs* rigid, slender, light brown the first season and thickly coated with hairs, becoming gradually darker and smoother. *Leaves* evergreen, flat (not concave-convex), 1 to 1½ inches long, ⅔ inch wide at maturity, leathery and thick, the upper surface dark green and shiny, the lower pale and dull, hairless and with prominently meshed veins. *Acorns* light chestnut-brown, ¾ to 1½ inch long, ⅓ inch thick, minutely downy at tip, the shell lined within by a thin coat of pale hairs, the cup ½ to 1 inch deep, light green within and minutely downy, outwardly light brown. *Wood* strong and very heavy (49 pounds per cubic foot, dry weight), the heartwood light brown tinged with red, the sapwood thick and paler.

The Interior Live Oak is strikingly like the Coast Live Oak in appearance — which is in a way the highest praise — and only technical points differentiate them. Fortunately for the non-botanical, the two seldom meet, as is expressed by their respective names. If, in the foothills of the Sierra Nevada, you meet an evergreen Oak growing out on the hot grassy slopes with Digger Pine and the deciduous Blue Oak, it is an Interior Live Oak and your troubles of identification are already over.

The hard, heavy wood has never been lumbered, because of the way that the trees grow — not forced upward by forest competition into long clear trunks, but always full of great limbs almost to the ground. The result is a beautiful, dome-shaped mass, 30 to (rarely) 70 feet high, and often twice as broad as high; this makes a mansion of shade to the hot and dusty traveler. But such a tree would be hopelessly knotty and yield few clear board feet. The worth of the wood is all for fuel, and its caloric value is extremely high.

Coming from the coast, with its own beautiful Live Oaks, and rushing as fast as possible by car up to Yosemite Valley or Lake Tahoe, we may give the Interior Live Oaks in the hot, little-inhabited foothills but a glance, taking them for granted. Not thus did they look to their first scientific discoverer, Captain John Frémont, as he descended upon the Great Central Valley after a long and terrible crossing of the Sierra Nevada in winter. For many months he had seen only deserts and snows. The world of sunlight and green grass and gentle hills into which he descended that third of March 1844 seemed to him a paradise. "At every step," he writes, "the country improved in beauty; the pines were rapidly disappearing and oaks became the principal trees of the forest. Among these the prevailing tree was the evergreen . . . *live oak*. . . . The country is smooth and grassy; the forest had no undergrowth; and in the open valleys of rivulets, or around spring heads, the low groves of live oaks give the appearance of orchards in an old cultivated country."

CHISOS RED OAK

Quercus Gravesii Sudworth

OTHER NAME: Spanish Oak.

RANGE: Mountains of Coahuila, Mexico, north to the Chisos and Davis Mountains of western Texas.

DESCRIPTION: *Bark* light brown tinged with red, deeply furrowed and covered with light, close scales. *Buds* with dull reddish-brown scurfy scales. *Twigs* slender, fluted, reddish brown. *Leaves* 2 to 4 inches long, 1½ to 3 or 4 inches wide, typically 2- or 3-lobed on each side, with short triangular acute lobes and rounded sinuses between them, the upper surface dark green and dully shining, lower surface copper-green and dull with distinctly raised and netted veins, the chief nerves running out beyond the margin as bristly tips. *Fruit* biennial, solitary or paired, on a very short stalk, the cups deeply top-shaped, with light brown, scurfy appressed scales, and the acorns oval, light brown, and minutely silky all over, ½ to ¾ inch long and not quite so broad.

In the desolate grandeur of the Chisos Mountains, far down in the Big Bend country of western Texas, the Chisos Oak in autumn bursts into a glorious display. For miles there are solid masses of scarlet foliage, in a zone between 5000 and 8000 feet. In general it is on the moist, northward-facing slopes that this tree does best — the zone of the Western Yellow Pine, the Pinyon and the Gray Oak. If found on more arid slopes, it seeks the shade of deep canyons. Except for its autumn colors this is not an impressive tree, for it grows at the most only 45 feet high.

Quercus graciliformis C. H. Muller is a species which forms groves of small trees along Blue Creek Canyon in the Chisos Mountains of western Texas, the only locality known for it. It bears deciduous leaves 3 to 4 inches long, ¾ to 1¼ inch wide, with 8 to 10 bristle-tipped teeth with deep, rounded sinuses between them, glossy green above, duller and coppery beneath, the stalks deep red at base, dorsally flattened and very slender. The acorns are solitary or paired, egg-shaped-acute, about ¾ inch long, ⅜ inch thick, densely fine pubescent, and enclosed only at base by the cup with its light brown, partially hoary scales.

Probably the chief charm of this little tree, which is often shrubby but may reach 25 feet in height, is in the shimmering leaves. Suspended on very long stalks, they spin in every wind almost as gaily as an Aspen's.

SILVERLEAF OAK

Quercus hypoleucoides Camus

OTHER NAMES: Whiteleaf or Mexican Oak.

RANGE: Mountains of Sonora and Chihuahua, Mexico, north to central and southeastern Arizona, southern and southwestern New Mexico, and the Big Bend country of western Texas.

DESCRIPTION: *Bark* nearly black, deeply furrowed, the ridges with thick, plate-like scales. *Twigs* rigid, stout, at first hoary, becoming black or red-brown under a glaucous bloom. *Winter buds* with thin light chestnut-brown scales. *Leaves* thick, leathery, evergreen, 2 to 4 inches long, ½ to 1 inch broad, with a few coarse teeth at the apex, and margins rolled under, the under-surface covered with thick, whitish, woolly hairs, the upper dark green and gleaming. *Acorn* ½ to ⅔ inch long, dark green and often striped at first, turning light chestnut-brown, with thick shell which is hoary-downy at the tip, outwardly, and within lined with thick woolly hairs; cup thick, with light chestnut-brown scales clothed toward the base of the cup with silvery pubescence. *Wood* very heavy (50 pounds per cubic foot, dry weight), very strong, and hard, the heartwood dark brown, the sapwood thick and lighter in color.

When this little tree rises above shrub size, it grows in shaded and well-watered canyons up to 60 feet high, but usually it is much less, with rounded and spreading crown. In shrubby form it makes thick clumps. Its habitat is between 5000 and 7000 feet in the Southwestern mountains, where it delights to grow with Sycamores and Cottonwoods. The one beauty of this species is in the foliage, very thick and leathery and shining on the upper surface; in lovely contrast is the lower surface, covered with a dense white wool.

CALIFORNIA BLACK OAK

Quercus Kelloggii Newberry

OTHER NAMES: Kellogg or Mountain Black Oak.

RANGE: Mountain slopes and valleys from the Mackenzie River (western Oregon) south on the Coast Ranges of California to the Cuyamaca Mountains (San Diego County) and through the Sierra Nevada to the foothills of the Owens Valley.

DESCRIPTION: *Bark* of old trunks nearly black or very dark brown, with thick, irregular plates and broad ridges. *Twigs* at first very downy and bright red, becoming dark red-brown and smooth by the second winter. *Winter buds* with chestnut-brown, hairy-fringed, close scales. *Leaves* deciduous, at maturity thick and firm, light yellow-green and lustrous, 3 to 6 inches long, 2 to 4 inches wide. *Acorn* 1 to 1½ inches long, ¾ inch broad, light chestnut-brown, the cup with thin, glossy chestnut-brown scales. *Wood* hard, strong, brittle, medium-heavy (40 pounds per cubic foot, dry weight), the heartwood bright red, the sapwood thin and lighter in tone.

The California Black Oak is strikingly unlike all other deciduous Oaks in the Golden State, for its broad thin leaves are jaggedly lobed, with the veins running out beyond the leaf margins as fine bristles. It is found widely in the interior of the state; there is much of it in the fine, rugged San Diego "back country," along with Bigcone Pine; it grows away up in the northeastern part of the state, beyond the Sierra and on the edge of the sagebrush plains. It flourishes on the mesa lands above the Owens Valley and comes near enough to the sea to reach the historic town of Sonoma, where it was first discovered. But it is never seen in sight of the Pacific, avoiding the fogs, the Redwood belt in the North, the Coast Live Oak country in the South.

Black Oak grows 35 to 80 feet tall, with a graceful crown of mostly erect or ascending main branches. The bark is very dark, almost black, giving it its name, and the leaves on the upper surface glitter brilliantly in the California sunshine. In spring the foliage, in leafing out, is a beautiful bright pink or crimson for several weeks. In autumn the leaves turn yellow. The wood is strong but heavy and not long-lasting. Ranchers in the eastern part of the state cut it for fencing, and burn it for household fuel. Poor though its quality, the rising price of lumber has drawn this wood to the mills, where by combining air and kiln drying, some fair quality lumber is turned out.

But it has one admiring friend, the California woodpecker, who finds its acorns, bitter to our palates, exactly to his taste. True that he eats the nuts of many other Oaks, notably the Coast Live Oak, but the Black Oak appears to be a favorite. This handsome redhead devours what he can hold of acorns, and lays up great stores of them, like a squirrel. Instead of burying them in the ground, however, he drills holes, like a sapsucker, in the Oak's bark, and with apparent forethoughtfulness does so well in advance of the autumn crop. Then he drives the acorns into the prepared holes, shoot or pointed end first, and generally hammers them in till the blunt or root end is flush with the bark. Thus it is impossible for squirrels to extract them. Only a woodpecker could get them out again. Sometimes nobody seems to claim them, for you see Black Oaks riddled with irregular drillings, each with its imbedded acorn, unchanged for years. Oddly enough, woodpeckers only store the nuts when the crop is a scant one; in bumper years they simply gorge and don't bother to lay up treasure. If the crop is a complete failure, the birds may sometimes be seen thwacking pebbles into place!

THE ELMS
(*Ulmus*)

Eʟᴍs have scaly and furrowed bark, and simple, alternate, stalked, deciduous leaves which are usually unsymmetrical at the often very oblique base, with toothed margins and straight veins. From axillary buds near the base of the branch appear the small bisexual flowers on long, jointed stalks. The calyx, regular in form and 4- to 9-parted, encloses the 4 to 6 stamens; free from the calyx, the ovary is solitary and bears 2 styles. Fruiting takes the form of a samara — that is, a nutlet enclosed in a papery husk which is broadened into a sort of wing; the wings, light brown and more or less deeply notched at the apex, are veiny with meshed nerves.

*   *   *

WHITE ELM

Ulmus americana Linnæus

OTHER NAMES: American, River, Water, or Soft Elm.

RANGE: Extreme western parts of Nebraska and the Dakotas eastward through Manitoba to southwestern Newfoundland, south to central Florida and central Texas.

DESCRIPTION: *Bark* ashy gray, deeply fissured and broadly ridged and covered with thin scales. *Twigs* slender. *Flowers* borne on long slender drooping twigs, in 3- or 4-flowered, short-stalked clusters. *Fruits* small, greenish and reddish, with little round wings. *Wood* medium-light (35 pounds to the cubic foot, dry weight), medium-soft, medium-weak as a beam, but very tough and difficult to split and coarse-grained, the heartwood light brown, with thick, lighter-colored sapwood.

The White Elm, one of the most beloved, beautiful, and historic trees of the eastern states, extends far westward along the rivers of the Dakotas and Nebraska, reaching all the way to the base of the Black Hills that are crowned with Douglastrees and Western Yellow Pines. So that it enters the circumscriptions of this book as a native tree, by clinging to the moist soil of the banks of the great rivers and the narrow bottom-lands of the small streams where the farmer does not often pass the plow. Here it keeps company with Willows and Cottonwoods, competing well with them, for its little wafer-like fruits are ripe in early spring and ready to float on every puff of wind, by the thousands, on their glider-like wings. He who looks up may often see these tiny air fleets flashing in the sunlight as they take their way. And doubtless the waters spread them too. The seeds germinate readily, and with a high percentage of viability, and the seedlings come up in shady sites and sunny, not so much indifferent to environment as ready to profit by any where the moisture content of the soil is high.

This tree takes several forms; there is what is called the Oak form, with heavy, more or less horizontal branches, and there is a "weeping" form and a "feathered" form; but typically the White Elm is vase-shaped. In this, the most prized of all its outlines, the main trunk separates at fifteen to thirty feet above ground into several almost

equal branches. At first these diverge slightly and gradually, but at a
height of about fifty to seventy feet they begin to sweep boldly outward so that they form a great dome on the periphery of which the
branches arch and the branchlets droop. Thus a great old Elm appears
like a fountain of vegetation — the trunk as the primary jet gushing
upward and forking as it rises, then the jets again forking, the forks
spreading out and falling as if by gravity in a hundred branchlet
streams that become a thousand streamlet twigs and a million drops
of spattering foliage. So, because of its fundamental architectural
form, this is the ideal street tree; its branches meet across the road
in a vaulted arch that permits the passage of the highest vehicles. As
a dooryard tree, it hangs above the roof like a blessing — clean of
branches under the crown but shading the roof like a second air
chamber above it. On a college campus a colonnade of Elms is a
living stoa.

The historical associations of this noble tree, with such names as
George Washington, Abraham Lincoln, Thoreau, Daniel Boone and
other great Americans, are so many that they cannot be touched on
here. But it is not surprising that a tree with such a reputation should
have been carried West at an early date, across the great plains in
the prairie schooners and around the Horn in the old sailing vessels.
Today the Elm is a favorite of western college campuses all the way to
southern California; it is a prominent street tree of Colorado Springs
and numberless other western towns; in subtropical Santa Barbara it
shares the parkways with palms and Eucalypti! Far removed from
the dread Dutch Elm disease that is presently ravaging the eastern
specimens, its future as the friend of the Westerner seems bright.

THE HACKBERRIES
(*Celtis*)

THE HACKBERRIES are trees or shrubs with more or less warty bark and scaly buds, with alternate, deciduous, veiny leaves frequently obliquely unsymmetrical at base, and crisscrossed with veinlets. The flowers appear soon after the unfolding of the leaves on branches of the year, the male flowers in small dense clusters, the female solitary or in few-flowered clusters from the axils of upper leaves. The greenish yellow deciduous calyx is divided nearly to the base into 4 or 5 lobes; there are no petals. The 4 to 6 stamens are inserted on the margin of the disk at the center of the flower. The ovary of the female flower, green and shining, is topped by a short style divided into several lobes. Flowers of each sex contain the rudiments of the organs of the other sex, and usually some bisexual or perfect flowers are found. The fruit takes the form of a drupe, or stone fruit, with thick firm skin, thin flesh, and a thick-walled, bony nutlet.

✳   ✳   ✳

TEXAS HACKBERRY

Celtis lævigata Willdenow, variety *texana* (Scheele) Sargent

OTHER NAME: Sugar Hackberry.

RANGE: Central and western Texas to southern New Mexico and western Oklahoma. Also in northeastern Mexico.

DESCRIPTION: *Bark* thin, pale grayish, not usually warty. *Twigs* slender, red and smooth or gray-brown and pubescent, marked by elevated leaf scars and pale, oblong lenticels. *Winter buds* minutely downy, chestnut-brown, small (1⁄16 to 1⁄8 inch long). *Leaves* with untoothed or sparingly and irregularly toothed margins, often semi-leathery in texture, 1½ to 3 inches long, ¾ to 1½ inches wide, the upper surface dark green and smooth or granulated above, the lower with scarcely prominent or meshed veins, the veins and midribs hairless or sparingly pubescent though furnished with small tufts of hairs in the axils. *Flowers* on slender hairless stalks, 1 to 3 together in the leaf axils, the calyx greenish yellow and divided into 5 papery lobes which are hairy-tufted at the tip. *Fruit* a berry-like drupe, nearly spherical or short-oblong in shape, ¼ inch in diameter, with dark orange skin and slightly wrinkled nut. *Wood* close-grained, not strong, soft, and heavy, the heartwood light yellow, the thick sapwood nearly white.

This is at best but a little tree, seldom growing over 25 feet high, and half shrubby in its habit of growth. Its preference is for rocky bluffs and the sides of draws, the stony and gravelly soils of washes and, in the Texas mountains, for deep gorges like Oak Canyon in Big Bend National Park. On the plains of the Texas Panhandle, where three species of *Celtis* grow, this one is considered the commonest. It is also planted as a shade tree and has the advantages of being rapid-growing and not exacting in its requirements. But it splits easily in wind storms and is subject to the same disfigurements by mistletoe, witches' broom, cockscomb gall, and powdery mildew as the other species. But, like them, it has its place in the economy of Nature; its little berries feed the hungry birds and rodents, and its far-seeking roots hold the gullies and arroyos in an arid region subject to sudden and erosive rises of water after thunderstorms.

Probably the seeds are distributed, as in the case of other Hackberries, in part by birds who void them unharmed after eating the berries, and partly by the stream waters. For the berries float easily in water and, spherical in shape or nearly so, they roll on and on with the current without catching in the first obstruction they meet. The finally effective one will bring the fruit to the shore at last and there the little life is safely implanted on some bank all ready to begin its modest career as a riparian tree.

THICKLEAF HACKBERRY

Celtis occidentalis Linnæus, variety *crassifolia* (Lamarck) Gray

OTHER NAME: Bigleaf Hackberry.

RANGE: Canyons of the Big Horn Mountains of Wyoming and the Black Hills of South Dakota, and from southern Minnesota and eastern North Dakota south along streams to the Texas Panhandle, eastern Texas, and east to the low valleys of the southern Appalachians and Dallas County, Alabama.

DESCRIPTION: *Bark* dark brown, rather thick, smooth or more or less roughened by irregular warty excrescences or by long ridges. *Twigs* slender, light brown at first, becoming darker and ridged and flecked with oblong pale lenticels; pith finely chambered at the nodes. *Winter buds* chestnut-brown, ¼ inch long. *Leaves* thick, coarsely toothed, rough to the touch above, long-hairy beneath; 2½ to 3½ inches long, 1½ to 2 inches wide, the midrib and veins on the lower surface, silky-hairy; leaf-stalks only ¼ to ½ inch long, far shorter than the flower stalks and fruit stalks. *Fruit* a drupe about ⅛ inch thick, nearly spherical, on stalks ½ to ¾ inch long; skin thick, tough, dark purple, the flesh thin, dark orange; stone slightly wrinkled. *Seed* pale brown. *Wood* coarse-grained, not strong, rather soft, and heavy, the heartwood clear light yellow, the thick sapwood nearly white.

Commonly 50 to 60 feet tall and, when well-watered and protected, sometimes twice that height, fast-growing if short-lived, with a broad head of shade, this Hackberry would seem ideal as a street tree for those arid, wind-blown, almost shadeless parts of Texas included in the circumscription of this book. Especially so since it is a native there, in the draws and on the escarpments of the broken country of the Panhandle, on the ·blackland prairies and the wide Edwards Plateau. And indeed at one time its virtues were so long and thoroughly extolled by a prophet known as "Hackberry Jones" that it became the most planted tree of the aforementioned region.

"My father," relates Roy Bedichek, "embraced the hackberian faith. In the enthusiasm of a recent conversion he set out a row of saplings on each side of the walk leading from our front gate to the house, a distance of about two hundred yards. In summer these trees required water, not to make any growth but barely to stay alive. It was my job in droughty periods to supply the moisture from a cistern . . . so in the blazing sun of July and August I was often wet-nurse to forty hack-berries, supplying bucketful after bucketful to slake their many-rooted thirst . . . I . . . thus [became] a kind of human waterworks. Eventually I rebelled, saying in my heart that I didn't care if they did die — which, by the way, they did before any one of them ever cast a shade as big as a horse blanket. . . . Had my father known then what I know now, that the Hackberry demands a constant if tiny water supply such as is furnished by seams in limestone . . . he would have saved himself expense and me much vexation of spirit.

"During periods of excessive rainfall these hills become full of water which is held in the natural seams, the stone itself being impervious. The hackberry fits in here perfectly. It is a surface feeder and its roots range far and wide. They are a pest to our city water departments, for they seek out leaks in water pipes and crowd into them like thirsty cows about a watering trough. They have a nose for sewer pipes also and wreck them. They disrupt a watered lawn; they sprinkle tough sprouts all over the place, some of which take to your oak and to other shade trees, clinging with such leechlike grasp that you often have to wound your tree to dislodge them.

"Even in the act of dying, especially in domestication, the hackberry's habit is unpleasant and inconvenient. It dies by inches and sheds its corpse about piecemeal for several years. When its days are done, I like a tree, like little dog Rover in the nursery rhyme, to die all over." [1]

But the Hackberry, says the distinguished Texas naturalist, is a valuable tree on its native heath — or rather on the wooded hillsides, where it is more effective than any other species in producing natural check-dams by its roots across the ranch roads which, otherwise, soon erode into gullies. Those road-crossing roots, jolt the vehicle as they may, stand up against torrents of water in the rainy season, bitter drought in the dry, and chewing by the iron tires of agricultural implements.

Robins and cedar waxwings too may be grateful to the Hackberry. For when other forage gives out they come into the streets of towns planted with Hackberry, at the end of winter (always a starvation time for vegetarian birds), and make out very well with the little berries still clinging to this leafless tree.

[1] *Adventures With a Texas Naturalist.*

NETLEAF HACKBERRY

Celtis reticulata Torrey

OTHER NAMES: Palo Blanco. Western Hackberry.

RANGE: From northeastern and southern-central Arizona eastward throughout New Mexico, the Panhandle and Big Bend country of Texas to the Ozark region of Oklahoma and north-central Texas.

DESCRIPTION: *Bark* thick, ashen, rough, with prominent, short, connecting ridges. *Twigs* slender, red-brown, pubescent in their first season, smooth in the second. *Leaves* 1½ to 3 inches long, ¾ to 1½ inches wide, thick, dark green and usually rough on the upper surface, the lower yellow-green (but not pale) and with very prominent meshed veins which are sparingly long-hairy; the stalks stout, densely pubescent, ⅛ to ¼ inch long. *Fruit* a drupe hanging on pubescent stalks ⅛ to ½ inch long, with orange-red or yellow shiny skin, nearly spherical, ¼ inch long. *Wood* soft, weak, medium heavy, the heartwood light brown striped with yellow, the sapwood thick, pale yellowish gray or greenish yellow.

Netleaf Hackberry is a bookish if officially accepted English name for a tree that is called, where it grows best, in the Spanish-speaking parts of the Southwest, by the name of Palo Blanco, "white tree." Probably this name is in allusion to its wood; the sapwood is indeed very light and in general the trunk is all sapwood; only late in its relatively short life does a slim cylinder of heartwood form. There is marked resemblance to Elm wood, and perhaps Hackberry sometimes passes as Elm, when it is manufactured for boxes, crates, barrels, baskets, and cheap furniture. It is most commonly cut by the ranchers, who use it for fence posts. But it is also made into door sills and the treads of steps which are claimed, by its proponents, "not to squeak." What a boon this must be to many a Southwest Cinderella, stealing up stairs after the witching and parentally final hour!

This Hackberry grows, in the famed Cross Timbers of Texas and Oklahoma, as a modest component of the woods where Post Oak and Blackjack are dominant. In the mountains of western Texas, it takes to the Pinyon and Juniper belt. On the Panhandles of Oklahoma and Texas it sometimes stands alone out on the range lands. In New Mexico it seeks the desert washes — the gravelly beds of intermittent streams. With stout ascending branches it forms an open and irregular head. It may grow 30 feet high but is often much less impressive; its trunks are spindling and often crooked, and sometimes they are reduced to the form and height of a straggling shrub.

The Navaho Indians eat the berries, fresh or ground, under the name of *tjilxajih* which has the reasonable meaning of "chewing it." Of the wood they make tubes for bellows, while the leaves are boiled with the branches, to make a dark brown or red dye for wool.

Like all the other Hackberries of our region, this one is woefully subject to the attacks of a mite, *Eriophyes*, with the result that the twigs proliferate into abnormal bunches of unsightly naked shoots, called witches' brooms. This infestation is so nearly universal that it almost permits one to pick out a Hackberry at a distance, especially when the leaves are off and the naked tree has to show its sad deformities. Mistletoe, too, parasitizes the branches, flourishing with its sickly greens all through the crowns. A powdery mildew infects the leaves, and a gallfly stings them. Commonly almost every leaf will have big, ugly excrescences from these attacks, in shape something like a cock's comb. This greatly reduces the palatability of the foliage as browse for the stock of the ranges. All these pests are more or less universally found on all our western Hackberries.

Like the other Hackberries this one sometimes achieves a local and anonymous fame as "the unknown tree" that no one can recognize, that it "stumps" the experts to name, that "baffles science." The most baffling trait of our Hackberries is not any oddity but a complete lack of any. The general shape is what women call shapeless; the bark is undistinctive; the foliage vaguely reminds one of many other trees; the flowers are so insignificant as to be beneath the notice of anyone above the rank of botanist and the little berries are as quietly misleading as a cheerful liar, for they suggest some choke cherry rather than a member of the Elm family with its dry, papery, wafer-like fruits. And why, you may have wondered, do we call this tree a Hackberry? "Hack" would seem to have no current meaning, but philologists tell us it is a corruption of the Scottish "hag" (witch) berry. That name in Europe, however, is applied to the sour bird cherries. Apparently when the early colonists from Britain met the first "unknown tree" they transferred the name of Hackberry to it and it now has been made to stick for all the genus *Celtis*.

CANYON HACKBERRY

Celtis Douglasii Planchon

OTHER NAME: Douglas Hackberry.

RANGE: Discontinuous; in Washington and Oregon, east of the Cascades and along the Columbia Valley. In Idaho, Big Willow Canyon. In Nevada confined to the southeastern corner of the state. In California found in Hackberry Canyon, along Caliente Creek, Kern County; at Independence, Inyo County; in a canyon north of Banning, Riverside County; canyons on the north side of the Clark Mountains, eastern Mohave desert; and Thing Valley, Laguna Mountain, San Diego County; in Utah, in the canyons of the Wasatch Mountains; in Arizona in the Grand Canyon of the Colorado. In Colorado on the eastern foothills of the Rockies. Also reported from the Texas Panhandle, and Cedros Island, Lower California.

DESCRIPTION: *Bark* of trunks gray or reddish brown and rough. *Twigs* at first red-brown and marked by small gray lenticels, becoming gray and smooth. *Leaves* 2 to 2½ inches long, 1 to 2 inches wide, coarsely toothed, unsymmetrically heart-shaped at base, marked with a network of veins on the pale lower surface which become conspicuous late in the season, the upper surface rough to the touch. *Flowers* on slender stalks, greenish, minute, the calyx with 5 dry papery lobes fringed at apex. *Fruit* a shining light orange-brown berry ⅓ inch in diameter, swinging from the axils of the leaves on pendulous stalks.

The Canyon Hackberry is not a rare tree where it is found at all, but it is certainly, as seen from the details of its range given above, of very spotty occurrence. One may know great sections of the West intimately without knowing this tree, so localized are its stations. It would seem, from its distribution, to be a tree more widespread once, perhaps in a wetter age like the last Glacial one, before the West became again a predominantly arid country. Yet it does not occur at all on the rainy Northwest coast, but keeps to the arid interior, even remote desert ranges at points hundreds of miles from the next station. In the Columbia Valley it does not commonly make its way down to the streams and become a riverbank tree like some of the Hackberries of the Mississippi Valley, but stays, as if perversely, up on the dry rocky hillsides. There it is but a little stunted and scraggly tree sometimes only 15 feet high and quite as broad across its short crown. But when it is planted near water it shoots up to 40 feet, with a trunk as much as 30 inches thick. Its leaves under such thrifty conditions no longer look pale and limp, but firm and deep green.

The Papago Indians appreciated this tree even though the white man has little use for it. The Papagos of the Baboquivari Valley made sandals of the bark, which comes off in convenient smooth slabs. And the little berries are edible, if anyone wants to gather them, and even the fierce Mescalero Apaches once did so. It seems that some of the more sedentary and ill-nourished desert Indian tribes still do. The colony of trees found on the Havasupai Indian Reservation, deep in a side canyon of the Grand Canyon, may have been planted there; at any rate they are a boon to this poor tribe. And hungry desert birds devour the berries on their travels; little mammals are glad to find them.

THE MULBERRIES
(*Morus*)

THESE TREES have scaly bark, and slender, roundish branchlets; the growth is by prolongation from one of the upper axillary buds. In falling, the inner scales of the winter buds mark the base of the twig with ring-like scars. The leaves, alternate and deciduous, are 3- to 5-nerved at base and may be unlobed or unequally 2-lobed (mitten-shaped) or 3-lobed at the apex. The flowers appear from the axils of deciduous bud scales of the lower leaves of the year; the female are densely clustered. The familiar Mulberry fruit consists in a mass of thin-skinned fruitlets with juicy thick flesh surrounding the tiny nutlets.

*   *   *

WESTERN MULBERRY

Morus microphylla Buckley

OTHER NAME: Mexican, Texan, or Small-leaved Mulberry.

RANGE: Central Texas and the Big Bend Country westward through southern New Mexico to the Santa Rita Mountains of southeastern Arizona and to the canyons of the Colorado Plateau, northern Arizona.

DESCRIPTION: *Bark* of trunks thin, pale gray or slightly tinged with red, smooth or, at base of trunk, deeply furrowed, with scaly ridges. *Twigs* at first coated in soft white hairs, soon becoming smooth or nearly so, and, in their first winter, light orange-red and marked by small, horizontal, nearly round, elevated, concave leaf scars and small lenticels. *Winter buds* nearly 1 inch long when fully grown, with thin, light chestnut-brown, shiny scales with papery edges. *Leaves* about 1½ inches long, ¾ inch wide, heart-shaped or rounded or truncate at base and simply acute at tip or occasionally 3-lobed at the apex (the lateral lobes rather short, the middle one long), at maturity firm and thin, the upper surface dark green and often roughened by minute granular wartiness, the lower surface paler, either smooth or rough to the touch, and hairless or softly pubescent, but the broad orange midrib usually stiff-hairy: veinlets conspicuously meshed on the lower surface. *Flowers* with the sexes usually on separate trees, the male in many-flowered short spikes with dark green calyx deeply divided into roundish, reddish-tipped lobes, the stamens with bright yellow anthers; female flowers in very small, few-flowered spikes, the calyx unequally divided into thick rounded dark green lobes, the ovary green, smooth, with short stigmatic lobes. *Fruits* ½ inch long, sweet and juicy, turning from red to dark purple or blackish, the fruitlets (drupes) ⅛ inch long with thin fleshy skin and light brown stone (nutlet). *Wood* hard, close-grained, heavy (48 pounds per cubic foot, dry weight), with dark brown or dark orange heartwood, and thick, pale sapwood.

If the red man's cultural life had evolved as long and as far as that of Europe and Asia, this native Mulberry might have become an important fruit tree, for the Southwest Indians often cultivated it. There is, for instance, a grove of these trees to be found deep in a side canyon of the Grand Canyon of the Colorado, where the little Havasupai tribe carefully tend and harvest the trees, having brought them, doubtless, from afar. But the intervention of the white race with its highly advanced technological and horticultural civilization overtook Amerind culture back in its New Stone Age, so that this promising little fruit is still a primitive species, horticulturally speaking, a wildling of the stream sides, the canyons and washes of the Southwest desert, and the rocky talus below cliffs, at 2000 to 6000 feet above the sea.

The catkins appear in April with the leaves, soon followed, on the female trees, by the oblong, short clusters of little fruits. These are at first red, then purple and finally, when juicy and edible, nearly black. Birds, of course, devour them, and so do many small animals. But the white man, with all his cultivated fruit trees at his command, has never tried to improve the fruits by selection and breeding. Surely, in view of the tree's hardiness, this would be worth some experiment.

The Papago Indian bow was made of Mulberry. A new stick, 5 feet long and 2 inches thick, was cut at the time of the rainy season, the bark removed, protuberances rubbed down with a stone, and then the last quarter of the stick at each end tapered to 1 inch diameter by scraping with a stone. The ends were then notched for the string. Next, the bow was bent by laying it in hot ashes, with stones placed on and around it so as to bend up the ends at a gradual rate. Then the bow was strung with deerhide made smooth by running it through a hole bored in a Saguaro rod.

THE OSAGE ORANGE
(*Maclura*)

THE GENUS *Maclura,* characterized by the presence of milky juice, possesses very tough, stiff wood, spur-like, thorny twigs, alternate, simple, deciduous, and stipulate leaves, and thick, fleshy roots covered by exfoliating, bright orange-colored bark. The sexes are borne on separate plants, the minute flowers having each a 4-parted calyx and no petals. The stamens have flattened, light green filaments infolded, in bud, above the middle with the anthers inverted, back to back; when the flowers open, the filaments fly erect and are then exserted from the calyx. Male flowers are borne in slender spikes and the female in drooping small spherical heads. The individual fruits take the form of compressed drupes with thin flesh enclosing a nutlet; these, joined by the uniting of the thickened and elongated calyces, form a compound fruit rather larger than an orange and filled with milky juice. Growth is by elongation from axillary buds.

*　　　*　　　*

OSAGE ORANGE

Maclura pomifera (Rafinesque) Schneider

OTHER NAMES: Bois d'arc. Bowdark. Bowwood. Mock Orange. Osage. Prairie Hedgeplant. Yellowwood. Hedge Apple.

RANGE: Native in southeastern Oklahoma, southwestern Arkansas, northwestern Louisiana, eastern, south-central and western Texas. Widely naturalized from cultivation in the eastern and southern states.

DESCRIPTION: *Bark* of trunks deeply furrowed, showing pale orange between the dark orange, braided, scaly ridges. *Twigs* short, stout, tough, at first green often tinged with red, and softly downy, but becoming smooth and light brown tinged with orange and finally paler, flecked with bright orange lenticels, and containing orange pith; often spine-bearing. *Winter buds* commonly sunk in the bark and covered by a few conspicuous chestnut-brown scales. *Leaves* shining, deciduous, 3–5 inches long, 2 to 3 inches wide, on slender stalks, the margins untoothed, the veins arching at the end, and with a fine network of veinlets. *Flowers —* male in spikes 1 to 1½ inches long, green, with 4 stamens opposite the 4 lobes of the calyx; female flowers in dense spherical heads drooping on short axillary stalks on the new shoots, the calyx divided to the base into 4 green, unequal-sized sepals which invest the compressed green ovary that bears a slender style covered with white stigmatic hairs. *Fruit* compound, saturated with milky juice, green, large, heavy, warty-surfaced, consisting of a great number of thin-fleshed imbedded drupes which enclose the seed-like brown nutlets. *Wood* extremely hard, tough but flexible, coarse-grained, and heavy (48.22 pounds per cubic foot, dry weight), the heartwood bright orange, turning dark on exposure, the sapwood very thin, pale yellow.

In past geologic time there were many species of *Maclura;* now there is only this one, in all the world, so that *Maclura* is today a monotypic (one-species) genus, in the Breadfruit family. Even this one is now greatly restricted in its native home, for in inter-glacial times it seems to have grown, to judge from fossils, as far north and east as Ontario; today it is confined to the southern states west of the Mississippi. Or it was, when first discovered by scientists; it is now abundantly grown for its many fine qualities far beyond its original home and has become widely naturalized east of the Mississippi and in the Missouri Valley. As a native plant it enters the circumscriptions of this book in trans-Pecos Texas, notably at Bois d'Arc Spring, in Big Bend National Park.

The name of Osage Orange derives from the big, green, spherical and heavy fruits — rather larger than any orange, and with the mammillate surfaces quite different in texture and in color. Yet the comparison has survived all the onslaughts of common sense; and the word Osage, at least, was once appropriate since it was among the Osage Indians of Arkansas and Missouri that this tree became famous as a wood for bows, so strong it is — stronger than White Oak — and tough, tough as Hickory. The early French explorers of the Mississippi Valley named it *bois d'arc,* meaning bow wood, and this is sometimes corrupted to Bowdark.

For a bow wood, Osage Orange is in first or second rank with archers, amongst all native trees. It is by many considered more reliable than Yew, and the beauty of its grain, often stained in the heartwood with red, makes it the pride of fanciers. It takes time for a bow, like a violin, to become sweet and mellow, it seems, for one amateur, A. E. Andrews, tells us concerning a bow in his collection:

"One osage bow was blood-streaked when worked down so green that the sap oozed out on the scrapers. In seven months that bow was made, seasoning as it formed. In four years the blood-shots disappeared and the bow gained in strength of draw. At four to five years it seemed at its strongest and its color was brown. At the age of ten, it still shoots with a clean, quick, mellow smoothness." [1]

The reputation of the Osage's own bow wood spread widely among the Plains Indians. Prince Maximilian of Wied-Neuwied found that the Montana Blackfeet had prized bows of Osage Orange, which they obtained by barter. The Kiowas too appreciated it. A band of them seen by Lieutenant Whipple on September 8, 1853, on the Llano Estacado "carried superb bows of bois d'arc, ornamented with brass nails, silver plates, and wampum beads. The arrows were about 28 inches in length, with steel points and tinted feather trimmings. The quiver and belt, of wolfskin, were wrought with beads." [2]

John Bradbury, the Scottish traveler on our Great Plains, tells us that the price among the Arikara Indians of a bow made from this wood was, in 1810, a horse and a blanket — a very high charge indeed, but as the Arikaras had no Osage growing in the treeless Country, Bowwood was to them a precious timber. "Many of the war clubs," Brad-

[1] "Wood for Archers," *American Forests,* October 1940.
[2] *Pacific Railway Reports.*

bury adds, "are made of the same kind of wood, and have the blade of a knife, or some sharp instrument, fastened at the end, and projecting from four to six inches, forming a right angle with the club." Not a weapon to be treated with contempt!

Because of its great strength, Osage wood early proved one of the finest for railway ties, and nothing but its scarcity prevents it from being widely used for that purpose still. "In 1873 we procured from Texas," Bernet Landreth wrote in 1893 to Professor Sargent, "some railroad ties of Osage Orange, and had them set out in the road-bed of the New York division of the Pennsylvania Railroad alongside of oak, chestnut, and catalpa. The soft woods were all torn out in two or three years, but the Osage Orange, after twenty-one years, is still in place, after having been turned several times, and still as good as the first year." [1] Pavement-blocks were formerly extensively made of Osage Orange, and it was in high demand for wheel stock. The first chuck-wagon ever built, according to a well-founded tradition, was that invented by Charles Goodnight, the most famous Texan cattleman, and it was built of seasoned *bois d'arc,* in order to withstand the terrible usage of bumping over the far-flung Goodnight empire that covered much of the Panhandle in early days.

The fame of the Osage Orange spread gradually from the early *voyageurs* of the lower Mississippi Valley, who knew it well, to the English-speaking pioneers. It was first mentioned, in our language, in President Jefferson's message to Congress (1806), quoting from an account of it by two British explorers who had seen it two years before at the post of the Washita, Arkansas. They alluded to its probable value as a hedge plant. When that excellent botanist and ornithologist, Thomas Nuttall, found it a few years later growing luxuriantly on rich bottom-lands of the Red River, he named it in honor of his friend William Maclure, geologist, librarian, and philanthropist of the famed little town of New Harmony, Indiana.

At an early date, in the nineteenth century, Osage Orange began to be cultivated in the southern states as a natural hedge plant. For this it has every qualification, with its ability to grow thick-set, as gardeners say, with its scattered thorns, its hardiness in drought, heat, and wind, its zigzag branchlets and the way that it keeps its lower branches all the way to the ground. It is easily propagated from seed, sprouting the first year, and growing very rapidly. Yet it never grows so tall as to turn the hedge into a shade-casting wall harmful to crops.

[1] Charles Sprague Sargent, *Silva of North America.*

It meets the old demand that a hedge plant shall be "horse-high, bull-strong and pig-tight."

When the middle-western prairies were first settled, and before the coming of barbed wire in the seventies of the last century, the only method of fencing, in such a way as to hold stock, was by a pale of long wooden stakes — far too costly for any but small enclosures; and without fencing the settlers were forced to form broken and scattered settlements on the margins of groves and streams, treating the fertile prairies as common pasturage. Social organization, under such conditions, was kept to a primitive level, until the Osage Orange was first introduced in the fifties, into the Middle West by the efforts of John A. Wright, editor of the *Prairie Farmer,* and his friend Professor Jonathan B. Turner, who stumped the country for human betterment in general, Osage Orange in particular. The interesting story is told in detail in Lloyd Lewis's *John Wright, Prophet of the Prairies.* There is space here only to relate that thousands of miles were planted, in a few decades, to Hedgeplant, as these proponents called it, and to this day, especially in Missouri, one sees endless fields still hedged by this strange, glittering tree, producing a compartmental landscape almost like that of parts of Normandy and England. But many farmers are now grubbing out their picturesque and historic old Osage hedges. When they do so they are also destroying valuable cover without which game birds like bobwhite are left at the mercy of hunter and dog and hawk, and thus soon destroyed.

True, there are severe criticisms of Osage; it is not a gracious tree; it sends out, unless carefully tended, long sprawling shoots that render it shapeless and unsightly. The foliage is very tardy, not appearing until mid-May in the latitude of Chicago, and the unattractive flowers, which bloom in June and July, are wind-pollinated, and cause some hay fever; large quantities of pollen are on the air at flowering time wherever the tree is grown.

The leaves, very late in autumn, turn a clear, beautiful, shining yellow. The fruits are eaten by black-tailed deer in Texas, and devoured in the Middle West by fox squirrels, who carry them up in the trees and then drop them, allowing them to smash open. Crossbills are also said to peck the seeds out of the great fleshy green fruit. Recently it was announced by Professor George M. Toffel, chemist at the University of Alabama, that a single Osage Orange in a room will drive away cockroaches, apparently by its cedar-like aroma. A distillate, which was even stronger smelling, was found to be quite as effective as the fresh fruit in its pest-repellent qualities.

THE CALIFORNIA LAUREL

(*Umbellularia*)

THE EVERGREEN, Willow-like leaves are alternate and spicy-fragrant when crushed, as is the green bark of the twigs. The flowers, inclosed before opening in 4 bracts, are small and clustered in a tight head. The 6-parted calyx takes on a petal-like appearance, though true petals are none. The 9 stamens are arranged in equal series of 3, with the outer anthers facing outward, the inner inward. Three staminodia are present, alternating with 3 fleshy, stalked glands. The solitary pistil consists in a single, 1-celled ovary, a style, and a broad stigma. In fruit the carpel ripens into a drupe.

* * *

CALIFORNIA LAUREL

Umbellularia californica (Hooker and Arnott) Nuttall

OTHER NAMES: Oregon Myrtle. Spicetree. California or Green Baytree. California Olive. Mountain Laurel. California Sassafras. Pepperwood.

RANGE: Southwestern Oregon (South Fork of the Umpqua, Coos County, and in the Coast Ranges and Siskiyou Mountains) southward through the Coast Ranges of California to northern Baja California, and on the west slopes of the Sierra Nevada from 1200 to 4000 feet altitude.

DESCRIPTION: *Bark* of old trees thin, very dark brown, and scaly or warty but scarcely furrowed, that of young trees smooth and dull grayish brown. *Twigs* light green at first, soon becoming yellow-green and finally light brown tinged with red. *Leaves* 2 to 5 inches long, ½ to 1-½ inches wide thick, leathery and smooth, the upper surface shiny and deep yellow-green, the lower paler and dull, with light yellow slender midrib and conspicuous meshed veinlets, the margins curled under. *Flowers* in close clusters, the cluster on an axillary stalk 1 inch long, or the last clusters nearly stalkless, pale yellow, minute, the calyx divided almost to the base with 6 lobes; petals none; stamens inserted by their short, flattened filaments on the short calyx tube, arranged in 4 series or concentric rings, those of the fourth series reduced to sterile staminodia, the others bearing long, flattened pale yellow anthers; ovary contracted above with a stout columnar style with a simple stigma. *Fruit* olive-like, about 1 inch long, in clusters of 2 or 3, drooping on stout stalks in the axils of leaves, and surrounded at base by the enlarged, thickened calyx tube, the skin yellow-green sometimes tinged with purple, the flesh thin. *Seed* with a bony light brown coat. *Wood* hard, firm, fine-grained, very heavy when green, medium heavy when seasoned (40½ pounds per cubic foot, dry weight), with light, rich brown, and often mottled heartwood, and very thick paler and often streaked sapwood.

The many folk names of this tree tell a tale of the vivid impression it has made on the generations that have known it. To the Oregonians it is Oregon Myrtle, to the Californians it is California Laurel; though not strictly speaking either a Myrtle or a Laurel, it is at least in the Laurel family and, like the classic Laurel or Bay (*Laurus nobilis*) with which ancient victors and poets were crowned, it has a spicily aromatic and evergreen leaf. Hence the name of Green Baytree, Spice-tree, and Pepperwood. The little dark fruits are shaped like an olive; so it has been called California Olive.

Grand old trees have the noble stature of Oaks, and are surmised to be 200 and 300 years old. Young trees have all the elegant, formal charm of the true Laurel or Bay. The leaves are dark as some Magnolia's, yet graceful as a Willow's.

And always there is that pervading aroma, something like the true Baytree's, but much stronger, with a slight admixture of camphor and something peppery. One becomes aware of it after a few moments in a thick Laurel grove or under a great specimen, and the odor grows more, not less, insistent as you stay with it. Crush a leaf lightly and you will pronounce it delicious; but do not inhale it too much, for it may cause violent sneezing, even headache and dizziness.

If you travel south along the Pacific's shore you meet the green Baytree first in Oregon, keeping company with other hardwoods like the streamside Alders and Maples, becoming more and more abundant and beautiful. Indeed, it takes on there a special shape, seldom seen in California; at least along the highways, though not on the rich bottom-lands, it is a low tree with a short trunk, but broadened in crown to an almost globular mass. It looks then remarkably like some of the great old Box trees one sees in colonial gardens of Virginia, and so regular is its form that it is hard to believe it has not been clipped to an artificial perfection. A particularly lovely grove of such is Myrtle-wood Lane — some twenty miles of trees along Oregon State Highway 42, between Coquille and Myrtle Point. One would think they must have been planted here, when in fact the road is new, the trees are old. To preserve this species, Oregon has established a state park, the Maria Jackson Grove, on Brummet Creek, 26 miles from Myrtle Point, an area of 84 acres containing Myrtles of all shapes.

And almost everywhere along the roadsides of southwestern Oregon you see Myrtlewood for sale — platters and bowls, gavels and trays and cigarette boxes fashioned of it. Very light brown with lighter and darker streaks, or a lovely pale gray, Myrtlewood, when cut from burls, is of fancy and fanciful grain. Unfortunately too many of the objects offered for sale are in the souvenir class. The lumber has been cut for shipbuilding, interior finish, furniture, and the jaws, bits, cleats, and cross-trees of small boats. Formerly, at least, a volatile oil — limpid and straw-colored, with an odor resembling that of nutmeg and cardamom — was distilled from the wood and leaves and used hopefully in the treatment of catarrh and nervous headache, colic, diarrhea, and even meningitis. As a pharmaceutical product it seems not to be on the market at present.

Oregon's Myrtle becomes California Laurel as soon as you cross the state boundary. Now it assumes many other forms, as it adapts itself variously to growth upon sea bluffs forever swept by salt-laden winds, or in the profound shade of mighty Redwoods and Douglastrees, in the sun-scorched chaparral, on the open hills or in the depths of canyons. The typical woodland form is that of a tree taller (40 to 70 feet) than broad, with erect or ascending branches. In this form it resembles that of most forest-grown trees, and thus you see it in among Redwoods. In well-watered canyons, as on the slopes of Mount Tamalpais, dense jungles of Laurel form a dwarf forest, their boughs deeply covered with lichen and moss to make what children call a fairy-tale wood. There is also the pendulous form, seen only here and there, in isolated lofty trees whose branchlets drip in almost vine-like sprays. The thicket form is one where all the trees are of the same height and almost flat-topped, as if clipped off by pruning. Even when this form is found growing on the steep sides of a hill or canyon, the tops of the trees are apt to form an almost level expanse, for the trees higher up are mere shrubs, while lower trees may be 40 feet high. The wind, of course, is the sculptor of such groves — fast and constant breezes such as blow in from the ocean through the mouth of Tomales Bay, Marin County, California, modeling the trees of famed Laurel Hill. Where briny gales forever blow, as on Pacific bluffs, the Laurel becomes prostrate, crowding into any hollows it can find, and streaming along the ground like a green river. In the chaparral a dwarf form is found, as intricate and twiggy as every other tree that grows there. Where old, large specimens have been cut down, great numbers of shoots sprout up, a perfect fountain of many-jetted tree-life, bushy and luxuriant.

Great specimens are still numerous, despite the fact that in the pioneer days of agriculture the old and noble trees were as ruthlessly felled and grubbed out by the roots as the younger ones, in order to take over the soil for crops. In almost all parts of its range — in scores of California counties — the Laurel has specimens of unusual size and age, locally famous and often the object of deep affection. In the town of San Leandro there stands at 624 Lewelling Road a door-yard tree which is 70 feet high, has a crown 85 feet across, and a trunk 28 feet and 4 inches in girth. But its great table-like base is 49 feet in circumference. At eight feet from the ground it gives off five gigantic forks, the largest of them, in itself, 14 feet in circumference. Old inhabitants say that it was once a much larger tree than now in its old age, and that it was an Indian meeting place. Old Spanish coins have been found buried under it, or so runs the local legend, and this is not impossible, for the present town was all once the property of José Joaquín Estudillo whose rancho was one of the finest in Alta California, famous for its white cattle. Squatters in the eighteen-fifties tried to drive the Estudillos from their land and for some time the family was in danger of its lives as well as its fortunes; perhaps the coins were buried here then. At one period there was a great hollow in the base of the trunk and in it a little girl had her play-house. The bark has now grown completely over it.

On the old San Marcos Road near Santa Barbara grows another great Laurel; above its immensely swollen butt, the trunk is 23 feet in circumference. The total height is 82 feet, and it casts a pool of shade 104 feet across. In many respects this is the finest specimen which has been precisely measured in all its parts — a temple of a tree, breathing aromatic incense.

The little umbel of greenish-white flowers passes almost unnoticed when the blossoms appear in spring. But the foliage is at all times conspicuous, as freshly gleaming on the dark upper surface as if sparkling with dew, the undersides beautifully pale. The new growth of foliage pushes off the old leaves, which turn, a leaf here and there, a soft butter-yellow no matter at what season, but there is never a time when all the tree is golden nor when it stands all bare. Indeed, few trees cast so deep and constant a shade as this one, and when you get a mixture of bushy young Laurel with densely growing Redwoods or broad-leaved Alders and Maples, the darkness of the underwood is amazing. No eastern woods and none in Europe are so astonishingly dim. The light, for some unexplained reason, is often a golden-brown like that in the backgrounds of the old Dutch masters and in the intense umbrage only a few lush wood ferns are content to grow.

THE SYCAMORES
(*Platanus*)

SYCAMORES have thin, scaly bark, on the branches and young trunk, which constantly drops, in large thin plates, exhibiting the inner bark of contrasting colors; the pithy twigs, which grow by prolongation from an upper axillary bud, are zigzag. The smooth and shining winter buds, axillary in position, appear nearly surrounded at base by the narrow leaf scars and are covered by 3 deciduous, strap-shaped scales, which, falling at maturity, mark the base of the branchlets with narrow, ring-like scars; the outer scale splits longitudinally as the buds expand, the second scale, light green, exudes a fragrant gummy secretion and encloses a bud in its axil, while the third remains coated with long rusty hairs.

Alternate and deciduous, the leaves display 5 principal nerves, all arising from the point of attachment to the stalk and running out to the tips of the broad shallow lobe; a few large low teeth with shallow sinuses between them mark the margin between the points of the lobes. The veinlets branch and arch, becoming united near the margin, and are connected by still finer veinlets which are intricately meshed. When young, the leaf blades are clothed like the twigs, in branching, star-shaped, gray or rusty or silvery hairs. In winter the leaves turn dull yellow or merely brown before falling.

Appearing at the time of the unfolding of the leaves, the minute flowers are clustered into dense, unisexual, stalked spherical heads, the male and female heads usually on separate stalks. The male flowers have each a minute calyx divided into 3 to 6 scale-like sepals and 3 to 6 papery petals, the stamens as numerous as the petals and alternate with them. The female flower heads, on long terminal stalks, have each a calyx divided into usually 4 sepals, and show the same number of petals; the ovaries are as many as the divisions of the calyx and are gradually narrowed upward into bright red styles and surrounded at base by a tuft of hairs. In fruit the head of female flowers becomes a "button ball," each nutlet deeply buried among woolly hairs; at the time of the breaking up of the fruiting head at maturity, the nutlets, surrounded by the down, disperse upon the wind.

*   *   *

WESTERN SYCAMORE

Platanus racemosa Nuttall

OTHER NAMES: Buttonwood. Buttonball-tree. Planetree.

RANGE: Banks of streams in the Great Central Valley of California and canyons of the Coast Ranges from Monterey south to Baja California; also in the western foothills of the Sierra Nevada; ascending the southern slopes of the San Bernardino Mountains to 4000 feet. The variety *Wrightii,* here included, ranges through central Arizona south into Mexico and eastward to southern New Mexico.

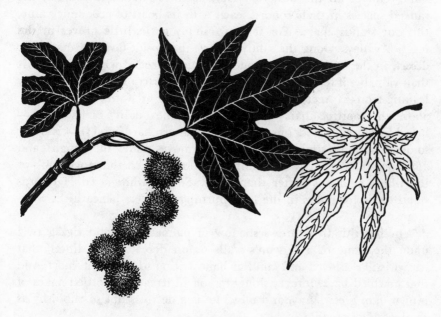

DESCRIPTION: *Bark* at the base of old trunks very thick, dark brown, deeply furrowed, with broad rounded ridges separating into small scales, that of younger and upper trunks smooth, close, flaking off and in consequence showing mottled colors of whitish, gray, yellowish or brownish, and pale green; bark high on the tree and limbs often nearly white. *Twigs* light reddish brown at first and clothed in rusty woolly hairs and flecked, by the first winter, with small lenticels, becoming gradually darker in their second and third years. *Winter buds* nearly ½ inch long, conic, smooth and shining and nearly surrounded at base by the dark conspicuous leaf scars. *Leaves* as broad as long (6 to 10 inches), thick and firm, light green above, the lower surface paler and more or less heavily coated in a deciduous rusty or yellowish mat of branched hairs, the blade with 3 to 5 acute palmate lobes, the base of the blade heart-shaped or sometimes truncate or wedge-shaped. *Flowers* in dense, spherical, unisexual heads arranged in a spike on a thick, hoary-pubescent stalk. The spikes of male flowers bear 4 or 5 heads of flowers, those of female flowers 2 to 7 heads with, usually, a single male head at the end of the spike. *Fruit* a seed-like akene ⅛ inch long, the tawny-hairy, fruiting heads ¾ inch in diameter, on slender drooping zigzag stalks 6 to 9 inches long. *Wood* cross-grained, difficult to split, pale brown and reddish-tinged, and medium-light (30½ pounds per cubic foot, dry weight).

Here is a tree that might have been created as the friend of mankind. Out of all the western sylva, the forests vast and somber, the ranked species in their cohorts, each with its boast of economic value, this one stands apart. For it grows singly or in little groves in the interior valleys, along the sandy washes, the upside-down rivers of the desert, in the cool of the canyon walls, more needed where you find it than valuable if felled, sawn, dressed, and exported. With its intimately leaning trunks it seems, even in the wild, to be pre-formed for bending above the rooftree that will come to it. The quality of its shade — broad but filmy-leaved (more like some eastern hardwood's) — is never so dense as to be stuffy; ever the breeze moves under the boughs, and any stir of air, in the warm habitats it chooses, even the rangeland's or the wheat field's, is better than none. So the white-faced Herefords stand or lie for hours in the long burning summers beneath the Sycamores.

Whether this tree throws shadow of palmate leaf and zigzag twig upon the stone of a canyon's walls or on doorstep and lintel, that scrawl is like a loved and familiar handwriting to the Westerner. And that marbled bark, forever sloughing off in irregular mottled flakes of brown, tan, green, gray, and off-white is a detritus not so rubbishy as comfortably homelike.

Certainly there is a pleasant quality about the shade cast by this, the outstanding shade tree of the Southwest. For one thing, the leaves are not glittering on the upper surface — a great relief in the hard-leaved evergreen woodlands of the desert and southern California where so many leaves are blades turned against the tired eyeballs. Sycamore leaves have at most a soft shine to them, when the down wears off, and

the undersides remain permanently coated in rusty or gray woolly hairs so that when the breeze spins the blades over they gleam silvery but cool. More, the shade, though so ample in summer, is taken down by Nature in the short period of Southwestern winter, allowing all the warmth and light in the sky to penetrate to soil or roof. Unlike the conifers, the Sycamore does not hold the cold, but scouts it.

All species of *Platanus* have as their outstanding beauty their massive trunks and mottled, smooth bark. The species *Platanus orientalis*, native from southern Europe to India, was thousands of years ago a favorite shade tree; it was planted in the Greek schoolyards just as Elms are the traditional academic trees of America, because its boughs were so wide, its shade so good, its trunks so like stout marble columns. Or perhaps, rather, the school came to the tree, at least the informal assemblies of Plato did so; under the tree that he called *platanos* (whence French, *platanier*, and English, Plane) he paced with his following, discoursing of his republic.

Call it Plane, or Sycamore, or Buttonwood, or *aliso* as the Spanish-speaking pioneers of the Southwest did, our Western *Platanus* cannot help falling into picturesque attitudes, and a Sycamore that looks regular, like a forest-grown type of tree, is a rarity. When growing on stream banks the tree is almost certain to lean, sprawl, or fork deeply, oftenest in a V-shape. But a trunk with a J-shape is common too, even well back from water, in the dry ranch-land grass, for there is something slouching about most bottom-land Sycamores. Indeed, some pasture specimens never stand up at all, but may be seen lying down on their backs, as it were, in a meadow, sending up vertical branches all from one side, like a horse scratching his back on the ground and kicking up his legs! But in general the trees on rich alluvial lands that, however, stand well up and away from the actual stream or gully bank, have very straight but short trunks clear of branches. As times goes on, this rapid-growing tree will thicken the base of the trunk into a great barrel-shaped affair, without pruning many of its lower branches, so that the true trunk ends abruptly in a perfect jet of trunk-like branches and these, in turn gracefully arching, may sweep low at the tips. This is the grandest, most lovable form of the tree, and it may perhaps be called the normal form.

In general, the Western Sycamore is about 40 or 50 feet high when mature, but specimens up to 80 feet are known, with trunks 5 feet in diameter. What must have been one of the biggest Sycamores in existence still stands, a truncated wreck, on Milpas Street, in Santa

Barbara. Though a quarter of a mile inland from the beach, it was once so lofty that, in the days when this city had no harbor and yet could be satisfactorily reached only by boat, a lantern was hung from this great tree's topmost boughs on stormy nights. Captain George Nidever, an old sailing master, reported that it was the mariners' custom to sight their course, by day, by this tree. That custom began back in 1800; today the tree is still alive though its top has been broken by storms and its great boughs were cut off some years ago to relieve their strain upon the hollow heart. In one respect only is it the tree it once was — in girth; it now measures 11 feet, 11 inches around at breast height.

Whitish woolly hairs on the undersides of the leaves are deciduous and so a nuisance to some persons. For several weeks they drift on the atmosphere, setting up an acute inflammation of the mucous membranes of sensitive noses. This is the only drawback to such a fine tree, unless we add the brittleness of the living wood. "Of its want of tenacity," said Dr. J. S. Newberry, surgeon-botanist of the Army reconnaissance that surveyed in 1855 for a railway from San Francisco to the Columbia River, "we had a striking illustration when we encamped under the tree. . . . Our beds were spread on the ground under its branches, nearly touching each other. During the evening — a fresh breeze blowing, but not a high wind — we were warned by a cracking overhead that danger was impending, and had just time to 'stand from under' when a branch about eight inches in diameter came crashing down directly where we had been lying."

The Sycamore's greatest moment of beauty comes to it in earliest spring or at the end of winter. For then the flowers bloom upon the crooked, golden-fuzzy twigs. The heads of the male flowers are no bigger than peas, and filled with long-haired scales, so that they seem like little greenish or yellow chenille balls. The female heads are the showy ones, the size of big marbles, with deep and bright brown and remarkably long and thread-thin styles bristling out all over them. Simultaneously the leaves begin to unfold, like opening hands; all covered with golden down the palmate blades shine in the sunlight as if rimed with a glow. Then in summer when the foliage is full but fresh, the female heads ripen into fruit, each tiny seed-like nutlet deeply imbedded in a tuft of silken gray hairs. In winter these break up like so many dandelion heads blowing, and so the nutlets go gliding away on the wind to some other canyon or pasture.

The Arizona and New Mexican specimens differ so markedly in leaf that they have been described as a separate form, variety *Wrightii* (Watson) Benson. It has deeply 5- to 7-lobed leaves, with slender and elongate lobes and the bases deeply heart shaped. This is a more beautiful foliage than the Californian, but as there are only leaf differences, the desert trees are not quite distinct enough for a separate species.

The Sycamore is the largest desert tree of Arizona, growing up to 80 feet in height. Sycamore Canyon is but one of the many places where one can see the Arizona variety, but it is certainly the most romantic, and still, because of the rugged nature of the country, little visited. It lies for some twenty-five miles in the deep-cut bed of Sycamore Creek, which flows into the Verde River in the Coconino National Forest. Indian caves are still found in it and once, according to local legend, it was a hide-out of badmen and renegade Indians. Today the great Sycamores throw their shadows on the canyon walls in peace. One specimen measures 17 feet in circumference, perhaps the doughtiest hardwood tree in the Southwest.

Many birds love the desert Sycamore. The red-tailed hawk will commonly nest in it and will perch all day in its groves on the lookout, sallying forth with its cry of *killee, killee!* Because Sycamores are so often hollow, Gila and Lewis and Arizona woodpeckers all delight to nest in it. And if ever you find yourself down on the Border, in the Chiricahua and Huachuca Mountains, in summer, watch for a tiny comet of a bird with bronzy green back, metallic purple cap, and emerald-green gorget. That will be the rare Rivioli hummingbird, up from Central America, who commonly nests in the canyon Sycamores, at 5000 to 7000 feet altitude, and sometimes lines its babies' cradle with down of the swinging fruit-balls plucked from the tree.

THE CATALINA
IRONWOODS

(*Lyonothamnus*)

Possessed of shreddy reddish-brown bark, these trees have long-stalked, opposite evergreen leaves of 2 sorts, some simple and un-toothed or merely scalloped on the margins, others pinnately compound. The perfect flowers occur in compound terminal clusters, the sepals 5 and the clawless petals of the same number; the 15 stamens line the rim of the calyx tube which is free from the twin pistils. These each consist in 2 spreading stout styles, a small nail-shaped stigma, and a glandular and hairy ovary. The fruit takes the form of a pair of woody carpels, each splitting along a ventral suture, and each with 4 oblong seeds.

❋   ❋   ❋

CATALINA IRONWOOD

Lyonothamnus floribundus Gray

OTHER NAMES: Western, Santa Cruz, or Island Ironwood. Lyontree.

RANGE: Santa Cruz and Santa Catalina Islands, off the coast of southern California.

DESCRIPTION: *Bark* thin, dark brown and shredding lengthwise in long, loose, smooth strips hanging persistently on the stem and weathering to silvery gray. *Twigs* stout, roundish, at first pale orange and pubescent, later smooth, bright red, shiny. *Leaves* opposite and long-stalked, thick and leathery, dark green and shining above, paler and sometimes pubescent below, transversely many-veined, with orange midrib; of 2 sorts: (*a*) simple, minutely toothed blades 4 to 8 inches long, ½ inch wide, and (*b*) fern-like and irregularly pinnately compound into 3 to 8 slender lobes or leaflets, the margins of these again deeply notched into little lobes. *Flowers* in loosely branched, compound, terminal, rather flat-topped clusters 4 to 8 inches across, the ultimate branches pubescent, slender, and beset with minute bracts, the individual flowers ⅛ to ¼ inch across; petals 5, white, small, roundish, not clawed at base; stamens 15, 2 opposite each petal, 1 opposite each sepal, as long as the petals or more so; ovary of 2 superior glandular carpels on the bottom of the calyx

tube, each carpel topped by a truncate stigma. *Fruit* of 2 woody glandular carpels about ³⁄₁₆ of an inch long, opening along the ventral suture. *Seeds* oval-oblong, pointed at the ends, with light brown and very thin coats. *Wood* close-grained, very hard, very strong and heavy (50 pounds per cubic foot, dry weight), bright clear red faintly tinged with orange.

Off the coast of southern California there lies a group of islands which were once connected in one great island or perhaps more exactly a long peninsula, called by the geologists "Catalinia." This land existed as early as mid-tertiary times, while fossilized plants and animals of these islands show that the period of their connection with each other and the mainland probably endured till Glacial times or shortly thereafter, when, perhaps, sea level was several hundred feet lower. With the melting of the continental ice caps the level of the sea rose again, drowning all but the highest mountains, and it is these water-girt peaks that we still see today from the mainland shore, several small ones and three big ones: Santa Catalina, Santa Cruz, and Santa Rosa. On these three islands many species are now isolated as endemics. Among them are a number of trees such as the Island Pine (*Pinus remorata*), Island Live Oak (*Quercus tomentella*), Catalina Cherry (*Prunus Lyonii*), Island Ceanothus (*Ceanothus arboreus*), and the present species which is unique.

For Island Ironwood is not closely related to any other tree on the mainland or elsewhere in the world, but stands in a singular genus, whose closest kin in our gardens would be our spiræa bushes. That, at least, is the current conjecture; botanists have variously placed this genus in the saxifrage, cuniono, and rose families.

And everything about this tree is distinctive. The great dense flat-topped clusters of white flowers which bloom in June and July have no counterpart among other western trees, except for a distant resemblance to Mountain Ash. The dark brown or red bark is forever exfoliating in long thin vertical strips and tatters and is usually weathered to a silvery gray through which the fresh inner bark shines softly. The foliage is the oddest feature of all, for it is of two most unlike sorts — a simple, almost peach-like blade with numerous minute teeth, or a compound, pinnately branched leaf, each leaflet coarsely cut, and the rachis winged, to look like the frond of some spleenwort fern, or still more like that shrub of the bayberry family called sweet fern. In general the trees of Santa Catalina Island display the first kind of foliage, the simple-bladed, while those of Santa Rosa and Santa Cruz Islands have only the compound foliage. These latter trees have been designated as a separate species but are best considered as variety *asplenifolius* (Greene) Brandegee. This is decidedly the more beautiful of the two forms.

William Lyon, a young forester, first discovered this strange tree on Santa Catalina Island in 1884, at the point called the Isthmus. It was naturally named in his honor and for many years was considered the rarest of North American trees. It is now known to grow in some abundance on Catalina especially beyond the Isthmus, and ranges in altitude from 500 to 2000 feet above sea level. Usually it grows quite by itself, forming small groves of half an acre or less on the north slopes of those steep rocky canyons that plunge toward the sea all around the island. Sometimes the trees are pole-like, with long clear stems branching only at the top, and trunks 3 to 6 inches in diameter. Again they are really imposing, widely branching specimens, up to 50 and 60 feet high, with trunks 1½ feet through. Commonly, though, especially in second growth, they are low, bushy, and branching much from the base, with picturesquely crooked stems, having the habit of manzanita shrubs.

The wood does not gain the name of Ironwood for nothing; it is as strong and tough as it is heavy and close-grained. Hence it has been used for fishing poles and canes by the white man, while the Canalino Indians who inhabited these islands employed it for spear handles and shaft wood. A beautiful pinkish tint when cut, the lumber might become fine cabinet wood if only Ironwood grew in abundance.

As an ornamental, Island Ironwood is an unsurpassed western hardwood, colorful and picturesque in every detail. Unfortunately, it seems difficult to propagate either from seeds or cuttings, though root sprouts are said to do fairly well. One still sees little of it, though, outside of botanical gardens and a few city parks in southern California.

THE APPLES
(*Malus*)

THESE TREES have scaly bark and branches marked with conspicuous ring-like scars of the overlapping bud scales and by the leafstalk scars which are narrow and horizontal. Alternate and deciduous, the leaves have toothed margins; on flowering shoots the blades are unlobed, but are more or less lobed or deeply double-toothed on vigorous sucker shoots. The flowers and fruit are borne on much shortened lateral spur-like branches which are sometimes terminated by a short spine. The tube of the calyx is inversely conical, its lobes reflexed in flower but erect on the fruit. The five petals are contracted at base into a claw. The stamens are numerous in several rows and inserted on the edge of a conspicuous disk that lines the bottom of the calyx tube. Inferior in position to the calyx, the ovary consists of five carpels united at base to form a 5-celled ovary. In the ripening fruit the carpels form the familiar apple core; they are tough, parchment-like, or papery, not bony or nut-like, and contain the acute shining seeds.

✳   ✳   ✳

OREGON CRAB APPLE

Malus fusca (Rafinesque) Schneider

RANGE: Aleutian Islands, southward along the coast and islands of southern Alaska and British Columbia, through western Washington, Oregon west of the Cascades, and in the northern Coast Ranges of California to Sonoma County.

DESCRIPTION: *Bark* of mature trunks with large, loose, plate-like, thin and pale red-brown scales. *Twigs* slender, at first coated with long pale hairs, becoming after the first winter smooth and shiny red and finally dark brown flecked with remote, minute, pale lenticels. *Winter buds* at first chestnut-brown, but the inner scales at maturity bright red and becoming ½ inch long. *Leaves* at maturity 1 to 4 inches long, ½ to 1½ inches wide, firm, thick, dark green above, paler below with prominent midrib and primary veins, the veinlets conspicuously meshed, the blades often slightly 3-lobed; stalks stout, stiff, 1 to 1½ inches long and pubescent. *Flowers* in short, many-flowered axillary clusters on slender stalks, the blossom ¾ inch across, the calyx lobes rather longer than the tube and hoary-woolly inside; petals white or rose, roundish or broadest near the end with wavy or irregularly notched margins and contracted to a short claw. *Fruit* an apple ½ to 1 inch long, longer than broad with nearly parallel sides, and drooping in clusters on slender stalks, the skin yellow flushed with red, or almost wholly red, the flesh dry and thin. *Wood* hard, close-grained, and heavy (52 pounds per cubic foot, dry weight), the heartwood light brown tinged with red, the sapwood paler and thick.

Most Crab Apples have charm and this one is no exception, with its lovely little waxen pink or white flowers breathing forth their exquisite fragrance in spring when the leaves, like those of the cultivated Apple, are half grown. In late summer its little pomes blush daintily upon their yellow-green cheeks, giving out a tart odor of green apples. In autumn the leaves turn scarlet and bright orange — a lovely sight along the stream banks of the Northwest. Oregon Crab reaches its largest size — 30 to 40 feet in height — in the valley of western Washington and Oregon, where it often forms pure thickets coming down almost to the sea along the mouths of rivers, or mingling with the creek-side Alders and Wax Myrtles. The flesh of the strangely oblong apples is rather dry and thin, and extremely sour but excellent for jams and jellies. The wood has been used, on account of its extreme toughness and ability to stand shock, for the wedges with which the Indians split Cedar wood for their lodges and by the white man for tool handles, mallets and mauls, and even for the bearings of machinery.

THE ROWANTREES
(*Sorbus*)

TREES of this group have smooth bark, the twigs marked by the conspicuous ring-like scars of the big bud scales. The alternate deciduous leaves are pinnately compound, with an odd number of leaflets which are seated in opposite pairs directly on the central axis, except for the long-stalked odd one at the tip of the frond. The flowers are numerous in broad, flat, terminal, leafy clusters, each flower with urn-shaped calyx tube, 20 stamens in 3 rows, and usually 3 carpels with 3 styles making up the compound pistil which is partly free from, partly united with, the calyx tube. The small, nearly round pomes are borne erect in broad, flat-topped clusters, while the seeds are enclosed in a core of rather tough carpels and have shining, chestnut-brown coats.

* * *

PACIFIC MOUNTAIN ASH

Sorbus sitchensis Roemer

OTHER NAMES: Sitka Mountain Ash. Western Rowantree.

RANGE: Coastal southwestern Alaska, south to the mountains of western Montana and Idaho and through Washington and Oregon to the Siskiyou, Salmon, and Trinity Mountains of northwestern California, and in the Sierra Nevada to Tulare and Mariposa Counties.

DESCRIPTION: *Bark* of trunks thin, light gray, smooth or scaly, the inner bark fragrant. *Twigs* stout, round in cross-section, red-brown at first and pubescent, becoming dark brown and glabrous, and marked by large leaf scars and oblong lenticels. *Winter buds* with a gummy exudation, dark red, hairy, the terminal buds ¼ to ¾ inch long, pointed. *Leaves* in over-all dimensions 4 to 6 inches long, with 7 to 13 leaflets each 2 to 4 inches long, ½ to 1 inch wide, hairless, shining and blue-green above but pale below, on stout red leafstalks 1½ to 2 inches long. *Flowers* regular and perfect, the flat-topped clusters 3 to 4 inches across, the corolla creamy white, ¼ inch across; stamens 20 in 3 rows; the 3 carpels united, at least at base, to the calyx tube and hence inferior. *Fruit* a berry-like pome ¼ to ½ inch thick, with orange-red skin, thin, acid, flesh and a core of papery carpels; seeds brown, ⅛ inch long. *Wood* soft, weak, light (34 pounds per cubic foot, dry weight), the heartwood pale brown, the sapwood thick and paler.

Amid all the lofty and ancient conifers of the Northwest, so somber and so important to man, a little tree like the Mountain Ash, which never grows over 40 feet high, is but a slight thing, measured by many standards. But beauty is never unimportant, and this tree is all grace, with its cleanly pale stems, feminine in its lovely fern-like fronds of foliage, in its compact masses of white flowers that are followed by a mass of shiny red fruits, gay in the autumn woods as holly berries at Christmas. So attractive it is that the mighty conifers seem as if they had as their first business the setting-off by contrast, with their unmoving darkness, the lively charms of this little tree that grows along the creek sides and tumbling white water, filling in all the sunny spaces between their crowding shadows.

If, as you wander the Northwest forests, you hear a deep booming voice, that seems to say *humph-humph-humph, ma humph-humph,* that will be the dark, secretive Richardson's grouse. And the rowan-berries, fruit of this tree, are his chief food, in season. The little bright pomes catch the cocked eyes of the varied thrushes (who never vary their monotonous notes), and of all the robins too, on their fall migrations, as the flocks travel, ravenous and gregarious, south before the gathering winter storms.

THE SHADBLOWS
(*Amelanchier*)

THESE TREES have scaly bark and slender twigs with acute buds, the inner scales bright-colored as they enlarge. The leaves, alternate and deciduous, are simple and never lobed or at most are only slightly double-toothed. From the axils of slender scales the long flower stalks develop, forming the nodding terminal spike. The cup-shaped calyx-tube adheres to the ovary, with the lobes reflexed in flower. The petals are 5 in number and long and slender, not clawed at base. There are 20 stamens in 3 rows; the 5-celled ovary bears 2 to 5 styles that are united below. The fruits, little pomes, contain a core of rather soft or papery carpels, and the 5 or 10 seeds bear dark chestnut-brown, leathery, mucilaginous coats.

* * *

PACIFIC SHADBLOW

Amelanchier florida Lindley

OTHER NAME: Serviceberry.

RANGE: Wrangell, Alaska, and valley of the Yukon River (near Dawson) southeastward to the Lake Superior region, South Dakota and Colorado, southward to central California and northwestern Arizona.

DESCRIPTION: *Bark* of trunks dull gray or light brown slightly tinged with red, thin and smooth or somewhat furrowed. *Twigs* slender, at first bright red-brown, becoming dark red-brown and finally ashen. *Winter buds* with dark chestnut-brown scales, the inner enlarging at maturity, becoming bright red-brown and coated with silky hairs. *Leaves* 1½ to 2½ inches long, 1 to 1½ inches wide, at maturity thin, dark green above, pale below. *Flowers* in short, crowded, erect spikes; blossoms ½ to ⅔ inch long, the calyx tube bell-shaped, the lobes hairy, soon reflexed; petals ⅛ to ¼ inch wide. *Fruit* a short-oblong or broadly elliptic pome ¼ to ½ inch thick with dark blue and glaucous skin and succulent sweet flesh. *Wood* close-grained, hard and heavy, with light brown heartwood and thick and paler sapwood.

In the somber forests of the Far Northwest, yes, even the Alaskan wilderness, it is almost startling to come upon a tree of such dainty, exquisite charm as this when, in earliest spring, sometimes before even the hardy Cottonwoods dare show a leaf, its naked boughs are decked out like a bride in a veil of white flowering. Tradition says that the Shadblow blooms when the shad begin to run. Certainly it flowers when the human eye begins to hunger most for just such a sight at the end of the long northern winter. Serviceberry is the preferred name of the tree, once the tiny apple-like fruits appear some time along in July. Sweet and succulent, they were an important part of the diet of many coast Indian tribes and are still a favorite food in season of that stentorian and mysterious bird of the North Woods, the sooty grouse. Indian tribes, wherever this tree grows, sought it out for arrow shafts, because, so slender and straight of branch, it is also so hard.

THE HAWTHORNS
(*Cratægus*)

THESE TREES or shrubs have dark scaly bark, and tough, zigzag, slender twigs, marked by pale, oblong lenticels and small leaf scars. Thorns are frequent and often long and slender; they are borne below or opposite the leaf, especially on sterile shoots. The winter buds have shining, light brown outer scales and enlarging green or rosy inner scales. The alternate deciduous foliage is simple or on sterile shoots sometimes distinctly lobed. The usually fetid white flowers occur in simple or branched round-topped clusters, the lowest flower stalks commonly arising from the axils of the uppermost leaves. Inversely conic, the calyx has lobes reflexed in flower. The petals are not clawed at the base; there are 5 to 25 stamens, and the ovary may have 1 to 5 carpels and adheres at base to the calyx tube. The fruit, a pome, contains a nest of as many nutlets as there are styles. Usually the nutlets appear flattened on the two inner faces and are rounded and ridged on the back.

※　　　※　　　※

WILLOW HAWTHORN

Cratægus saligna Greene

RANGE: Central Colorado, between 6000 and 9000 feet above sea level, along the banks of the Gunnison, San Juan, Cimarron, and other rivers.

DESCRIPTION: *Bark* of trunks bright reddish brown, separating on old trees into long, narrow, loosely attached scales. *Twigs* slender, bright red, smooth and shining, armed with numerous straight, slender spines ¾ to 1½ inches long. *Leaves* 1½ to 2 inches long, ¾ to 1 inch wide, more or less deeply lobed or doubly toothed along the sides, especially on enlarged leaves of vigorous sucker shoots, or quite unlobed and simply toothed with numerous fine teeth, the texture thick and firm, the upper surface dark green and shining, the lower paler; midrib stout, rosy on the upper side; veins dark and obscure; veinlets meshed. *Flowers* in compact, smooth, few- or many-flowered clusters; blossoms about ⅝ inch across, the calyx tube smooth, its lobes triangular, untoothed, bright red at tip; stamens 20, with small yellow anthers; styles 5. *Fruit* drooping on stout stalklets in compact clusters, ¼ inch thick, when full-grown shiny wine-red, but when ripe nearly black, the flesh thin, yellow, mealy but sweet; nutlets 5, thick, ⅛ to ³⁄₁₆ inch long, slightly ridged on the back.

The Willow Hawthorn takes its name not from the form of its leaves but from its switch-like branches gracefully drooping at the ends, and from the way that the slender stems spring from a single creeping root to form clumps and small thickets along the streams of many a Colorado mountain water course — like the roaring San Juan and the Gunnison in its gorges, the far-destined Cimarron, the White, the Eagle, and the Tomichi. The fruit, which ripens in late September, is unlike that of most Hawthorns in becoming ultimately a shiny blue-black, with sweet yellow flesh.

DOUGLAS HAWTHORN

Cratægus Douglasii Lindley

OTHER NAMES: Black Haw. Western Thorn Apple. Douglas Thorntree.

RANGE: Vancouver Island and southern and central British Columbia (as far north as the valley of the Parsnip River) south throughout the lower forests of Washington and Oregon to the Pit River in northern California, and through the Rockies of northern Idaho, Montana, and Wyoming to the Big Horns. East to northern Michigan and western Ontario.

DESCRIPTION: *Bark* of trunks reddish brown, slightly seamed. *Twigs* rigid, slender, smooth and shining, bright red or orange-red, armed with numerous stout, short (⅓ to 1 inch long), bright red (or finally ash-gray) blunt spines, or sometimes quite unarmed. *Winter buds* scaly, lustrous brown. *Leaves* 1 to 2 inches long, ½ to 1½ inches broad, usually somewhat lobed, the coarse teeth glandular; texture thin, smooth, dark and shiny green on the upper surface, paler below, the stalk slender but wing-margined near the blade, ½ to ¾ inch long. *Flowers* ½ inch across, in broad, open, few-flowered clusters; calyx tube top-shaped, red at apex; stamens usually 10 in number (rarely 5, 15, or 20), with small pale rose anthers and 2 to 5 styles surrounded by tufts of pale hairs. *Fruit* on slender stalklets, in drooping clusters, short-oblong, about ½ inch long, black and shining, crowned by the persistent calyx lobes; flesh light yellow, juicy and sweet; nutlets 5, about ¼ inch long, with a narrow ridge on the back, and shallow irregular cavities on the ventral surfaces.

Horticulture has taken up the Douglas Hawthorn as one of the outstanding beauties of that vast genus, *Cratægus,* to which all Hawthorns belong. In the eastern states there are hundreds of Hawthorns; very few have had the distinction of cultivation outside of botanical gardens. But the honors came easily to the present species, for its fine foliage, glossy and almost formal looking, for the wealth of its fair white blooms almost as dainty and charming as plum-blow. And above all for its little pomes, which hang in many-fruited clusters and, dark black and lustrous, look as tempting as so many black olives. Their flesh is sweet and juicy, highly appreciated by the various western quails, as well as those introduced game birds, the Hungarian partridge and ring-necked pheasant.

In the wild, Douglas Hawthorn mingles generally with other creekside trees of the West, and when not in flower or fruit it might be noticed only by the most discerning, amid all the splendors of the western forests. But sometimes it forms pretty little groves of its own; it invades abandoned fields, crowds around wet meadows where the deer step warily. It will even follow the streams far out of the forest belt on the rangelands and sagebrush mesas, charming the wilderness with its snows of bloom, its largesse of fruit.

THE MOUNTAIN
MAHOGANIES

(*Cercocarpus*)

THESE SMALL TREES with scaly bark, rigid but unarmed branches and short spur-like lateral twigs conspicuously roughened by horizontal leaf scars, possess simple, alternate, deciduous or evergreen leaves and small terminal or axillary flowers without petals. The calyx is tubular but expanded at the top with a cup-shaped flaring limb with 5 petal-like segments. The 15 to 45 stamens are inserted in 2 or 3 rows on the top of the throat of the calyx. The single pistil consists in a solitary ovary with 1 cell and 1 ovule and becomes in fruit a leathery, long-hairy akene included in the calyx tube and tipped with an elongated, twisted, feathery tail-like style. The single seed is long and narrow.

* * *

CURLLEAF MOUNTAIN MAHOGANY

Cercocarpus ledifolius Nuttall

OTHER NAMES: Desert Mountain Mahogany.

RANGE: Southeastern Washington, the Blue and Wallowa Mountains of Oregon, eastward to the Cascades and south to the high northern Coast Ranges of California (Scott and Snow Mountains) and along the east side of the Sierra Nevada (up to 9000 feet) and thence through the high southern Coast Ranges to San Diego County, California; in the Rockies from Idaho (Snake River Valley) and southwestern Montana almost throughout mountainous portions of Utah and Nevada, to the rim of the Grand Canyon in Arizona. Also in the Big Horn Mountains of Wyoming, and the San Pedro Mártirs of Baja California.

DESCRIPTION: *Bark* of old trunks thick, red-brown, firm and hard, becoming furrowed and scaly. *Twigs* rigid and stout, at first red-brown and pubescent, becoming ultimately smooth and dark brown, or weathering silvery. *Leaves* evergreen, thick and leathery, resinous, smooth, shining and dark green above, pale and minutely downy below, the margins curled under and not toothed. *Flowers* solitary or in pairs, seated in the axils of the leaves, ⅔ inch across; calyx tube long hoary-hairy; stamens 10 to 35, with smooth anthers. *Fruit* a leathery akene ¼ inch long, chestnut-brown, covered with long hairs and tipped with the persistent, hairy, tail-like style which is 2 to 3 inches long. *Wood* very hard and close-grained, extremely heavy (67 pounds per cubic foot), the heartwood clear red or dark brown, the sapwood very thin and yellow.

The name of Mountain Mahogany was given to these trees because of the rich dark brown color of the hard and heavy wood — so heavy that it will not float in water! Otherwise there is no slightest resemblance to the great tropical timber tree. For the present species is usually a shrub 3 to 15 feet high, or at most a contorted growth that manages to straggle up, sometimes, to a height of some 40 feet. The trunk is short and stout, sometimes as much as 2 feet through, the crown is rather compact and rounded, and the lower branches writhe in a tortured way. Everything about this tree is apt to be twisted and curled; even to the leaf margins that curl under, hence the common name of Curlleaf. Sometimes a grove will be encountered where all the specimens are straight-stemmed and quite as trim as other trees. But even then the stems are always twisted around some invisible axis of their own perversity.

The habitats over which Curlleaf is distributed are many, ranging from bunch-grass prairie through Pinyon and Oak woodland to Yellow Pine and Aspen, and even up to Lodgepole Pine and Spruce-Fir. In central Oregon, hundreds of square miles possess groves and thickets of Mahogany, as the ranchers call it (for short), covering the arid broken country, scrambling over slopes of talus and broken rocks where you would think only a lichen could endure. In California you see it most abundantly on the open rocky talus of the dry eastern side of the Sierra Nevada where the range plunges down toward the desert; and it turns up again on the remotest mountain ranges of the Mohave desert, as well as high in the southern Coast Ranges and even on the Channel Islands. At the Grand Canyon it grows right to the wind-swept rim and over it, dotting the desolate ledges and precipitous slopes.

Wherever it grows it has a wild, uncouth, but determined and indomitably hardy look. In its lack of shapeliness it is surely no beauty; it may be no lumber tree, though its close-grained wood would be worth cutting for cabinet work if it did not warp and split in drying. Though tough enough to turn a knifeblade, it is so brittle that you had best not reach for a branch of it to pull yourself up over a ledge, lest the bough snap off in your grasp. But it has its place, like everything else that natively grows.

For its leathery, aromatic leaves are a favorite food of the western deer, eaten, since they are evergreen, the year around. And deer find, in its intricate twiggy growth, refuge from our Nimrods. In autumn, herds of deer will often yard up in Mahogany thickets, and if you can penetrate its intensely secretive chaparral, you have a fine chance, in season, of jumping a buck.

The Gosiute Indians of Utah used to make their bows of this extremely stiff wood. The Navahoes formerly made a decoction of the roots, mixed with Juniper ashes and powdered Alder bark, to dye their wool blankets red. Souvenirs are sometimes cut for the tourist trade from the heavy wood since it takes so high a polish. Best of all, Mahogany makes a marvelous fuel, burning for a long time and giving off intense heat before it combusts completely to a fine white ash. Old-time Westerners know this well, and gather it, and vacationers and campers should learn to identify it.

The easiest way of recognizing any *Cercocarpus* (they all make good fuel) is by the beautiful, long silky "tails" — really the enlarged persistent styles of the female organs that in fruit become feathery. When moist, these plumes are straight or relatively so, but in dry weather they twist hygroscopically. As they go through the corkscrew motions of curling, they literally bore the seed right into the tough desert mountain soil.

BIRCHLEAF MOUNTAIN MAHOGANY

Cercocarpus montanus Rafinesque

OTHER NAMES: Hardtack. Sweetbrush.

RANGE: Mountains of central Oregon south to Baja California and the Channel Islands, and from the Black Hills of South Dakota and the Wasatch Mountains of Utah south to the Llano Estacado of Texas and the Cimarron desert of Oklahoma, and through the southern Rockies to Arizona, western Texas, and the mountains of Mexico.

DESCRIPTION: *Bark* gray to brown, and scaly-checkered and fissured on older trunks. *Twigs* slender, rigid, the lateral ones often spur-like, bright red-brown and at first hairy, finally ashen or reddish gray and smooth, flecked with big pale lenticels. *Leaves* deciduous, margins toothed, not curled under, veiny and pale beneath, gray-green above. *Flowers* solitary or in pairs or threes, seated in the axils of crowded leaves, the calyx tube slender and densely white-silky; stamens 22 to 44, with hairy anthers. *Fruit* a slender leathery akene included in the persistent red-brown calyx, ¼ inch long, covered with long white hairs and tipped by the elongate, silky style which is 1 to 3½ inches long. *Wood* very hard though brittle, extremely heavy, the heartwood red-brown, the sapwood paler.

Sweetbrush, one of the stockmen's names for this tall shrub or little tree (up to 20 feet high), indicates the high economic value of its foliage as browse for livestock of all classes, be they cattle, sheep, or goats. Its lowest official classification as browse is "good," varying to "very good" and "excellent." True that the foliage is deciduous and hence unavailable in winter, but the twigs are relished by stock the year around, and a twiggier tree there never was. Nothing but the danger from overgrazing limits the value of this growth to the stockman — that and its comparative sparseness of growth. Only in central and southern Utah and portions of Colorado is it a plant so abundant as to dominate wide landscapes.

In general its life zone is that of Gambel Oak, Juniper, Pinyon, and Yellow Pine. That is to say that it occurs between 4000 and 10,000 feet. Here it forms a favorite food, too, of the Rocky Mountain deer and the yellow-haired porcupine.

Painfully slow-growing, this straggling tree with its open crown casts but little shade, in lands of much heat and light. But if cut down or burned, it crown-sprouts freely and the lush foliage of sprout shoots is reported by stockmen and sheep herders as especially palatable to stock. You cannot seem to kill it with axe, drought, or fire. So this wiry, hardy species deserves its stouthearted name of Hardtack.

Blossoms, rather like those of our garden cotoneasters, come in May to sweeten, for two months, the Hardtack's hard-bitten physiognomy. But its real hour of beauty is in the summer and fall, when the fuzzy white styles, very like those of virgin's-bower and some other sorts of clematis, persist on the fruit as long silken whips, and shine on the branches like plumes streaming back in the wind. These plumose tails serve as parachutes and gliders to carry the seed far across the desert wastes to some other cliff, mesa, or mountain ledge. Once arrived there, the seed is screwed in as by a drill, for the tails in dry weather twist like corkscrews and so thrust the seed into the ground, in the same way as filaree, that bane of the cowboy's leg.

Because to the Navahoes white is the symbolic color of East, they employ the fruiting twigs of Mahogany, covered with these white plumes, as prayer sticks in some of their most sacred ceremonies. The handles of Navaho distaffs are made of it, probably because the wood never splinters, even invisibly, with use but on the contrary grows smoother; hence it can carry the spinning woman's most delicate floss without snagging it. Because it is bone-hard Mahogany is used for Navaho dice. The Navaho name for it is *tshe'estaazih,* meaning stone-heavy. The Spanish-speaking people of the Southwest call it *palo duro* — hard wood.

There is the greatest variation in this species, which is not surprising in view of the immense range that it covers, the many habitats and climes it occupies. So it has happened that botanists at various times have described fifteen species based on these variations. The latest monograph of the genus happily reduces nine of them to pure synonymy, while the other six are assigned the rank of varieties. Even most of these seem too slight for notice here. One exception is:

Variety *paucidentatus* (Watson) Martin, known from southern Arizona and New Mexico to northern Mexico, in chaparral and Oak woodland, on rocky mountainsides. It has slender leaves with only 3 to 5 teeth and these at the apex of the blade; the twigs are often spiny.

THE PLUMS AND CHERRIES

(*Prunus*)

THE MEMBERS of this group have astringent bark and simple alternate leaves. The flowers occur in spikes or branched and round-topped clusters, from buds borne separately from those of the leaf. The petals are usually clawed, and the stamens number 15 to 30, in 2 or 3 rows. There is a single ovary which is free from and superior in position to the calyx, and a single style. The fruit is a 1-seeded drupe, that is, a bony stone or nut filled with the seed, and enclosed in flesh and an outer skin.

*   *   *

PACIFIC PLUM

Prunus subcordata Bentham

OTHER NAMES: Western Wild, Klamath, Hog, or Sierra Plum.

RANGE: From central Oregon (east of the Coast Ranges) southward through northeastern California and the northern Sacramento Valley to the Yosemite Valley (up to 4000 feet) and south in the inner northern Coast Ranges to Lake County.

DESCRIPTION: *Bark* of trunks gray-brown, becoming deeply furrowed and divided into long, thick plates. *Twigs* short and rigid, finally becoming more or less spiny, bright red at first and flecked with a few pale small lenticels, becoming purplish and finally ashen or dark brown. *Winter buds* with chestnut-brown scales, the inner ones at maturity bright red. *Leaves* deciduous, 1 to 3 inches long, ½ to 2 inches wide, thickish, dark green above, paler below, with broad midrib and conspicuous veins. *Plum* short-oblong or broadly elliptical, ½ to 1¼ inches long, drooping on stout stalks; skin dark red or bright yellow; flesh juicy and acidulous; stone ⅓ to ½ inch long, somewhat flattened or turgid, the sides nearly smooth except for 2 or 3 low ridges, narrowly wing-margined on the ventral suture, grooved on the dorsal suture. *Wood* hard, close-grained, heavy (40 pounds per cubic foot, dry weight), the heartwood pale brown, the sapwood thin and paler.

There is only one kind of wild Plum in the Pacific coast states, and so the identity of this tree, in fruit at least, is simple to establish. Its favorite home is not on the coast, however, but on the east slopes of the Coast Ranges, and still more to the east of the Cascades — in the dry interior valleys of south central Oregon and northern California. You see quite a lot of it around the lumbering town of Bend, Oregon, and in the ranching country around Klamath Lake, where there are evidences that the ranch wife appreciates the fruits for her preserve shelves, for the trees are spared and protected. It is almost plentiful in that grand, exciting country around the base of glorious Shasta with its volcanic cone capped in eternal snows, and you encounter it again in the foothills of the northern Sierra Nevada.

In stature this is either a shrub or a little tree, only 15 to 20 feet high — but who wants a fruit tree to be a tall forester dangling its fruits tormentingly out of reach? It is often considerably broader than high, the typical orchard form, which seems to show a tendency inherent in so many fruit trees, and not induced by man's cultivation, though it may be increased by pruning.

The flowers appear precociously before the leaves and so bloom on the naked wood. For a couple of spring weeks they are an enchanting sight in the woods. In fall the leaves, especially in the colder and drier parts of its range, turn gorgeous scarlet and orange, or red and yellow; after these have fallen, the fruits mature in small loose clusters. Purplish or dark red, or a bright shining yellow of skin, they have a tangy, subacid flesh. One must not expect too much of any wild fruit, and this one is good for eating out of hand only if you do not make up your mouth for a garden plum but prepare to taste this offering of the wilderness "out of compliment to Nature," as Thoreau put it whimsically. But wild plums make more fragrant and delicious preserves than cultivated ones, as every good housewife knows, and this one cooks to a confection not inferior to the wild plum jams of the eastern states. Around Grass Valley and Sierra City and elsewhere in the Mother Lode country, you can often pick up a few jars set out for sale to the summer tourist and, whatever they cost, they will be worth it.

WILD RED PLUM

(Prunus americana Marshall)*

RANGE: Eastern parts of Montana and Wyoming, south at medium altitudes in the Rockies to the Sangre de Cristo Mountains of New Mexico, and south through the plains to eastern parts of Oklahoma and Texas to the Gulf of Mexico; eastward to the Atlantic coast, except northern New England and southern Florida.

DESCRIPTION: *Bark* dark brown, thick and rugged, exfoliating in little plate-like scales. *Twigs* chestnut-brown at first, turning gray, knotty or zigzag. *Leaves* 3 to 4 inches long, thick, firm, rather wrinkled, dark dull green above and pale beneath. *Flowers* white, in few-flowered, open clusters, the blossoms 1 inch across. *Plum* less than 1 inch thick, green at first, then orange with a red cheek, finally bright red, with thick, tough, bitter skin having numerous pale dots, the flesh yellowish, acid, and juicy. *Wood* hard, strong, with medium-rich red-brown heartwood and paler sapwood.

"We commenced following the Canadian [River]," writes Lieutenant James Abert, in his diary for September 3, 1853, as he led a reconnaissance party exploring for a railroad route across the continent along the thirty-eighth parallel, "meeting with scarcely any obstructions, although the road was strewn with broken axletrees of Spanish carts that had preceded us. On the way we found quantities of luscious plums." Next day the expedition, toiling over the Llano Estacado, crossed a line of burning dune sands at what is now the New Mexican–Texas line (at present-day Quay County, New Mexico) in that torment of thirst all western explorers knew. "The day was hot and as we held our course over the barren waste, without sign of water, we languished, and feared we should not find that necessary article. Our sufferings were greatly alleviated by the refreshing fruit of the plum-tree, which everywhere grew in great abundance; and we found the fruit equal to any of the cultivated varieties that we recollected to have tasted in the United States. . . . We reached a beautiful valley, where we found a clear, cold spring. . . . Our camp was formed under a grove of un- usually tall cotton-woods, the characteristic sylva of this region, and which heavily-timbered the course of the rill which flowed from the spring. A few yards north of our camp were a few low 'buttes,' covered with dwarf plum-trees, profusely laden with fruit." On September 6 Abert notes that "our road to-day was everywhere beautified by a luxuriant profusion of plum-trees and grape vines."

This little tree, so generous of its fruit to those thirsty explorers long ago, could be no other than the Wild Red Plum, beloved in spring and fall alike. For early in the year the Plum thickets foam with white blossoms upon the twigs that are naked still of leaves save for the first small blades, bronze and coppery-red, putting forth from the bud. In autumn the foliage turns a dull rich yellow, shading sometimes to salmon-pink, soft mauve, light scarlet.

To the Plains Indians, the Wild Red Plum was an important source of food. It was eaten by the Dakotans, Omaha-Poncas, and Pawnees, fresh and raw or cooked as a sauce. For preserving, it was first pitted and then dried. And still today every farm wife who lives in the range of the Red Plum will, if she is anything better than a human can- opener, make wild plum jam, as tart and tasty a preserve as ever came on the American table.

The Omahas used to plant their corn, beans, and squashes when the wild Plum came into bloom. They made bundles of Plum twigs into brooms to sweep the floor of the lodge, and boiled the bark of the roots to apply as a remedy for skin abrasions. The Navaho dyed wool red with an infusion of the root bark.

The Wild Red Plum has given rise to more pomological varieties than any other native species; at least the horticulturists list some three hundred names derived from this species.

FIRE CHERRY

Prunus pensylvanica Linnæus the Younger

OTHER NAMES: Bird, Pin, Pigeon, or Wild Red, Cherry.

RANGE: Eastern British Columbia east to Newfoundland, south to the mountains of Georgia, to Iowa, northwestern Nebraska, and the mountains of Colorado.

DESCRIPTION: *Bark* on trunks ½ inch thick, separating by horizontal strips into papery, mahogany-colored plates flecked with irregular bands of orange lenticels and covered with small scales. *Twigs* at first bright red and shining, with pale raised lenticels, becoming the second year thick, short, spur-like and dark red with light-orange lenticels, the outer bark peeling easily to show the brilliant green inner bark. *Winter buds* bright red-brown. *Leaves* 3 to 4½ inches long, ¾ to 1¼ inches wide, shining above, paler below, the leafstalks often glandular above the middle. *Flowers* appearing in midspring when the leaves are half grown (or late June at high altitudes), the calyx lobes red at tip and reflexed after the flowers open, petals creamy white, contracted into a short claw about ¼ inch long. *Fruit* ripening in summer, ¼ inch thick, with thick, light red skin and sour thin flesh, the stone thin-walled, only ³⁄₁₆ inch long, ridged on the upper suture and pointed at the apex. *Wood* soft, close-grained, medium-light (31 pounds to the cubic foot, dry weight), the heartwood light brown, sapwood thin and yellow.

Fire Cherry takes its name from its habit of springing up after forest fires, for its seedlings profit by the sudden access of sunlight, as do fireweed and brambles that accompany its early states, and apparently Fire Cherry does not suffer from burning-out of the humus. Later it may give way to valuable lumber trees, but in their coming it has played a useful rôle, giving them shade and doing a bit to restore the ruined humus of the burned-over lands. It is short-lived by nature and so, when it has grown 30 or 40 feet high at the most, it has completed its duty as a nurse tree.

It is not without charm when in full flower, with the little blossoms foaming all over the naked wood, and in autumn it is superb, with fiery red foliage. The tiny fruits, acid and tangy, are worthless for eating out of hand but are made into jelly by some farm wives.

For perhaps two centuries of lumbering, the Fire Cherry was considered a weed tree by all engaged in the wood industries, worthless in itself, and occupying good space that might be growing valuable timber species. True that it grows rapidly, trees 30 or 40 years of age reaching, under forest conditions, a height of 50 to 60 feet, with poles 6 to 12 inches in diameter. But maturity was no sooner attained at this age, foresters complained, than the trees would start breaking from trunk cankers and brown rot of the lower boughs. Yet a good stand of Fire Cherry will produce per acre from 12 to 20 cords of wood (for that is how it is measured), weak though that wood is, with no advantage except its lightness. Then in 1950, Cherry was experimentally cut, near Kingsport, Tennessee, peeled, and sent with Silverbell, Birch, and Sourwood to market as a pulpwood. Mixed with them, it is proving satisfactory, and this gives a hint that in the West, too, Fire Cherry might be profitably cut with other hardwood pulp species. "Any tree species attaining commercial size and producing wood at the rate of half a cord or more per acre per year cannot be written off as a worthless 'weed.' When a 'weed' tree goes to market and becomes useful to mankind, even in a small way, it should no longer be called a weed."[1]

[1] W. R. Paddock, "A Forest 'Weed' Goes to Market." *Southern Lumberman,* December 1950.

BITTER CHERRY

Prunus emarginata (Douglas) Dietrich

RANGE: Southern British Columbia and Vancouver Island, south almost throughout Washington and Oregon and the northern Coast Ranges of California to the north shore of San Francisco Bay and throughout the Sierra Nevada up to 8000 feet elevation, to the high mountains of southern California (up to 5000 feet in the San Rafael Mountains and to 9000 feet on San Jacinto Mountain and the San Bernardinos). Also in western parts of Idaho and Nevada and northwesternmost Montana; on the San Francisco Mountains of Arizona and through the Grand Canyon region, as well as the high mountains of southeastern Arizona and extreme western New Mexico (Mogollon and Black Mountains).

DESCRIPTION: *Bark* of trunks very bitter, thin, smooth, dark brown ringed by bands of light gray, the lenticels orange. *Twigs* slender, limber, round, at first greenish and pubescent, becoming smooth, bright red, and flecked with pale lenticels. *Winter buds* chestnut-brown, about ⅛ inch long. *Leaves* 1 to 3 inches long, ⅓ to 1½ inches wide, dark green above, paler below, the teeth glandular, the leafstalks very pubescent. *Flowers* in 6- to 12-flowered clusters on slender stalks; calyx tube bright orange in the throat; petals white tinged with green, the blossoms ⅓ to ½ inch across. *Cherry* ¼ to ½ inch in diameter, the skin bright red or turning almost black, the flesh thin, austere, and tannic; stone ⅛ inch long, egg-shaped, turgid and pointed, the walls pitted and grooved. *Wood* soft, brittle, and light (28 pounds per cubic foot, dry weight), the heartwood brown streaked with green, the sapwood paler.

The little Bitter Cherry is a dense, thicket-forming shrub except where it rises to a height of 25 or 30 feet in the rainy, tree-favoring climate of western Oregon and Washington; there the tall forests force it high for light and air, and specimens 40 and 60 feet tall have been found. Early in the spring, before or with the leaves, the white blossoms with conspicuous dark-tipped anthers foam daintily all over the naked twigs, and for a short time this is as pretty a woodland sprite of a tree as one could ask in all the somberness of the Northwest woods. The little red cherries are far from edible to human palates, but the birds, especially the cedar waxwings, love them and all summer hold great feasts among them. After a short span of life — less than the average man's — this little tree is old and dies; but there are always others coming along, for the birds void the uninjured seeds, and if they fall on the favorite site of this species — rich sandy or gravelly soils along streams — the new generation springs up abundantly.

SOUTHWESTERN CHOKE CHERRY

Prunus virens (Wooton and Standley) Shreve

RANGE: Mountains of interior northern Mexico, north to the Guadalupe Mountains of western Texas, throughout mountainous southern New Mexico (at 5000 to 8000 feet above sea level), and on the high mountains, mesas, and plateaux of southeastern and central Arizona.

DESCRIPTION: *Bark* of trunks thin, red-brown to black, scored with narrow, oblong, horizontal lenticels, becoming furrowed and scaly on old trunks. *Twigs* drooping, slender, round, smooth and red-brown to gray-brown, flecked with small pale lenticels. *Winter buds* terminal, very small, light brown and somewhat long-hairy. *Leaves* 1½ to 2 inches long, ¾ to 1 inch broad, the upper surface light green and shiny, the lower paler, smooth, with thin midrib and veins, and meshed veinlets; the stalk ¼ to ½ inch long, slender, smooth and without glands. *Flowers* ¼ inch across, in many-flowered, erect or spreading spikes 3 to 6 inches long; calyx tube saucer-shaped; petals pure white and broadly rounded. *Cherry* short-oblong to nearly spherical, ¼ to ½ inch thick, in erect or spreading spikes, the skin shiny purple-black, the flesh thin, juicy and acid; stone compressed, ¼ inch thick, calyx lobes persistent under the fruit. *Wood* close-grained, hard, strong and medium-light, with light brown heart-wood and yellowish sapwood.

The Southwestern Choke Cherry sometimes grows to a height of 40 feet in favorable sites along streams and in mountain canyons of the Oak woodland zone. You see it, for instance, as a fine forest tree, with glittering leaves, halfway up the Chiricahua Mountains and in the hardwood forests of Oak Creek Canyon, Arizona. Though the fruits look appetizing enough, glossy black and juicy as they are, nobody but an Indian cares to eat them — Indians and bears and such strong-palated inhabitants of the mountains down along the Border. The flowers are very charming in May, and the fruits are borne in fine pro-fusion in midsummer. The handsome foliage, somewhat browsed by deer and livestock, is nearly evergreen and hence of high value late in the season.

WESTERN CHOKE CHERRY

Prunus virginiana Linnæus, variety *demissa* (Nuttall) Torrey

RANGE: From British Columbia near sea level to San Diego County, California, in the Coast Ranges, the Sierra Nevada, and the high moun-tains of southern California, at increasingly high altitudes in the south (2000 to 3000 feet). Also in Idaho and occasionally eastward as far as the Indiana dunes of Lake Michigan.

DESCRIPTION: *Bark* on old trunks gray, slightly furrowed and scaly, but red-brown and smooth on young ones. *Twigs* slender, round, at first green, becoming red-brown or orange-brown, shining and flecked with pale lenticels, their bark when bruised having a disagreeable odor. *Winter buds* terminal, with pale chestnut-brown scales. *Leaves* 2 to 4 inches long, 1 to 2 inches wide, thick, the upper surface dark green, shining, not pubescent, the lower pale and pubescent, the stalk slender, ½ to 1 inch long with 2 glands near the apex. *Flowers* in many-flowered

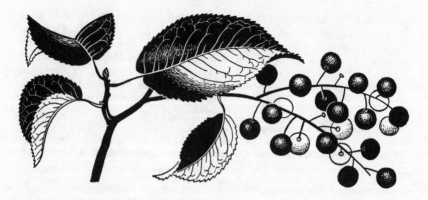

spikes, erect or nodding; calyx tube cup-shaped; petals white, broadly rounded, clawed at base; blossoms ⅓ to ½ inch across. *Cherry* borne on a short stalk, in drooping spikes, in shape globular, ¼ to ⅓ inch thick, the thick skin at first bright shiny red, becoming almost black when fully ripe, the flesh dark reddish purple, astringent; stone oblong-ovoid, one suture broadly ridged. *Wood* close-grained, hard, heavy, with light brown heartwood and thick, whitish sapwood.

It takes an Indian to eat choke cherries with a straight face, but eat them the red men did, and probably still do, however unpalatable to pale-faces except as a sweetened preserve. You will remember that it was while she was eating choke cherries at the Three Forks of the Missouri that the Shoshone child, Sacajawea, was captured by Mina-tarees and carried off to the Mandan villages of Dakota, where she was sold as a slave girl to the old French trapper Charbonneau. Thus when Lewis and Clark discovered her, they immediately appreciated her importance, despite her mere sixteen years, as a guide and "inter-pretress" to the Shoshone tribe with which, the explorers knew, they must do the important business of securing horses and guides over the Continental Divide. So she became the heroine of the momentous expedition — and all, you might say, from eating choke cherries in a lonely and dangerous spot!

The Cherries at Three Forks are only bushes, but this species rises 30 and 40 feet high in the more favorable climate and soil of Oregon and Washington with a fine clear trunk almost 1 foot thick, where it grows along streams and in cool canyons with rich soil. The manner of bearing the flowers and fruits — in long spikes instead of small axillary clusters — is so distinctive as to set this Cherry off unmis-takably from others, at least in the Northwest.

To the Navaho this is a sacred plant; its wood is used for making prayersticks, and because black is the color symbolic of the North, the black fruits are an important part of certain Navajo dances and chants. The Plains Indians too held it in esteem. The whole community was busy in the "black-cherry-moon" gathering and preparing the fruits while they lasted. Camps were pitched in groves of this tree and, since it was impractical to remove the tiny pits from the flesh, the whole fruits were pounded up in a mortar and made into small cakes baked by the sun. Dried cherries were kept as a sort of pemmican by the Dakotas.

Variety *melanocarpa* (Nelson) Rydberg, the BLACK CHOKE CHERRY, differs in having the leaves without hairs on the lower surface and the leafstalks without glands and only ¼ inch long. The dark purple or black fruit is but ¼ to ⅓ inch thick and has sweeter flesh than that of variety *denussa*. It is a tree or shrub up to 30 feet high and ranges from British Columbia and Alberta to North Dakota and Kansas.

ISLAY

Prunus ilicifolia (Nuttall) Dietrich

OTHER NAMES: California Laurel Cherry. Hollyleaf, Spanish Wild, or Mountain Evergreen Cherry.

RANGE: North shores of San Francisco Bay, south through the Coast Ranges of California to the San Pedro Mártir Mountains of Baja California, Mexico.

DESCRIPTION: *Bark* of trunks thin, dark red-brown, divided by shallow fissures and cross-checks into small square plates. *Twigs* at first orange or yellow-green, soon becoming gray or reddish-brown and conspicuously flecked with minute pale lenticels, and finally roughened by large leaf scars. *Winter buds* with dark red, slenderly pointed scales, the inner ones enlarging and persistent on the young twigs. *Leaves* evergreen, hollylike, thick, and leathery, 1 to 2½ inches long and 1 to 1½ inches wide, the margins with spiny teeth often tipped with dark glands, the upper surface dark green and glittering, the lower pale and yellow-green with slender midrib and faint veins, the stalk stout though short. *Flowers* ⅓ inch across, on short stalklets in dense, slender, erect spikes 1½ to 3 inches long; calyx tube cup-shaped, orange-brown, with very short, reflexed lobes; petals white, broadly rounded, short-clawed at base; stamens with minute yellow anthers; ovary abruptly contracted to a short, bent style which is capped by a large round stigma. *Cherry* dark red or finally purplish black, spherical or slightly compressed, large, ½ to ⅔ inch in diameter, the flesh thin and rather juicy; stone light yellow-brown, with 3 orange longitudinal bands along one suture, a single narrow one on the other, and meshed, vein-like, orange lines. *Wood* strong, hard, close-grained, extremely heavy (61 pounds per cubic foot, dry weight), the heartwood light brown, the sapwood thin and paler.

Islay is probably an Indian word; it comes to us, though, through the vocabulary of the Spanish pioneers of early California, who first appreciated this beautiful little tree. And amid its various names it is not wrong to choose this distinctive one, for the tree differs widely, with its glittering, evergreen, spiny-toothed leaves, from most of our ideas of what a Cherry should be. That is because it belongs to a group of the great genus *Prunus* known as the Laurel Cherries. Some species of Laurel Cherry grow wild in the Mediterranean region and have reached our gardens thence; others are native of the coastal plain in our South Atlantic states. This one is California's leading example, and like other Laurel Cherries it is so garden-worthy that one commonly sees it worked into horticulture. Formal, brilliant, hardy, it makes a fine show the year around. The white blooms are not especially conspicuous, but the bright cherry-red or mahogany-red or nearly black plump fruits in summer and fall are decidedly handsome. You may eat them freely, too; the flesh, though thin, is juicy and sweet. If the plant breeders would just put more flesh on those stones, or make the stones smaller, this would be an excellent fruit tree.

The California Indians certainly did not disdain to eat the fruits. The Coahuilla tribe, down Palm Springs way, gathered them and ate them out of hand. What they couldn't eat they dried in the desert sun, then extracted the stones, pounded them in a mortar, leached the mass with water, and of the mash made an *atole* or gruel.

Nobody has ever utilized the fine dark hard wood, but as a hedge plant Islay is ideal; it requires only a little pruning, rather than typical hedge-clipping, to make a lovely formal wall of shining green. The holly-like leaves substitute perfectly at Christmas time for the costly English holly; the red berries of the toyon can be wired in, a sprig at a time, to make a wreath that simulates the true Holly perfectly.

Presumably the foliage is poisonous like that of other Laurel Cherries. When you crush it, it gives off the characteristic almond odor of Laurel Cherries that indicates the presence of prussic acid. However, the leaves are not poisonous to handle, but only to eat, and livestock are wise enough to avoid this sort of bitter browse.

Islay grows to be about 35 feet tall in favorable situations, as in gardens, in cool canyons and on bottom-lands of streams. But it enters freely into the tough scrubbery known as chaparral and, reducing itself to a mere shrub, competes successfully with all the wiry, prickly species that compose this New World sort of *maquis*.

CATALINA CHERRY

Prunus Lyonii (Eastwood) Sargent

OTHER NAME: Island Laurel Cherry.

RANGE: Santa Cruz, Santa Catalina, and San Clemente Islands, off the coast of southern California.

DESCRIPTION: *Bark* of trunks thin, dark reddish, or gray-brown, becoming fissured in age. *Twigs* stout, light yellow-green when they first appear, becoming ultimately dark reddish brown and roughened by the elevated leaf scars. *Winter buds* acute or obtuse with dark reddish scales. *Leaves* 2 to 3 inches long, ½ to 2½ inches wide, evergreen, leathery, dark yellow-green and glittering above, paler below with stout midrib, obscure veins and meshed veinlets, the thick margins curled under, not toothed, or occasionally on vigorous sucker shoots remotely and minutely spiny-toothed. *Flowers* ¼ inch across, in densely-flowered spikes 3 to 4 inches long; calyx tube cup-shaped, orange-brown; petals wavy-margined, narrowed at base to a short claw; anthers small, yellow; ovary raised on a short stalk, the style bent near the middle, the stigma flat and circular. *Fruit* cherry-like, borne on stout stalklets in drooping few-fruited spikes, short-oblong to nearly spherical, 1 to 1¼ inches thick, the skin dark purple to nearly black, the flesh luscious and thick; stone about ¾ inch long, thin-walled, slightly compressed, pale yellow-brown, meshed with orange veinlets and banded by orange lines on the sutures. *Wood* very hard, close-grained, heavy, pale reddish brown.

The Catalina Cherry is a very close relative of the Islay, differing chiefly in its leaf margins which are not crinkled and prickly like that of the mainland tree. On Santa Catalina Island it forms beautiful groves of glittering little trees in Cherry and Descanso Canyons, which in spring burst with snowy bloom. It is found, too, on the mainland, but only in Baja California, and not within the limits of the United States. Its flowers and fruits are larger, its wood is lighter and softer, than those of the Islay. The Indians of these islands used to eat the fruit fresh and dried, just as they did with the Islay, and some people on the island of Catalina preserve it whole, to make a sort of wild cherry jam. Its value today, though, is an evergreen hedge plant; it requires no water, no real clipping, no sprays, no pampering of any sort but, ever fresh and shining, it is, once a year, quite lovely with its long spikes of flowers, followed by the ornamental fruits.

THE ACACIAS

(*Acacia*)

THE ACACIAS (at least the native species) possess slender branchlets beset with sharp spines just below the stalks of the ferny, evergreen leaves which are alternate, or on the older axils sometimes clustered. The leaves are twice-pinnate, our species of an even number with opposite pinnæ and small pinnules. The flowers occur either in spherical heads or interrupted or elongate spikes; they may be perfect or polygamous and are individually always very small, the minute calyx bell-shaped and 5- or 6-toothed, the petals also minute, 5 or 6 in number and somewhat united. The most conspicuous feature of the flower is the exserted tuft of usually 50 or more stamens which are inserted under or just above the base of the ovary. The filaments, united at base into a tube, are long and slender, and the anthers, though small, are showy in the mass. The ovary, which is superior, terminates in a long slender style and minute stigma. Taking the form of a jointed pod (legume), the fruit may be flat or cylindrical; it has no natural suture or opening; within it, the compressed seeds lie transversely. The seed possesses a thick bony coat marked on each face with an oval ring or depression.

*   *   *

SWEET ACACIA

Acacia Farnesiana (Linnæus) Willdenow

OTHER NAMES: Huisache. Cassie.

RANGE: From northern Chile northward in western South America and parts of Central America to the Big Bend country and the desert between the Rio Grande and Nueces Rivers in Texas; also apparently as a native, in the Baboquivari Mountains southwest of Tucson, Arizona. Cultivated all over the tropical world and naturalized in many places, as in Florida and extensively in Victoria County, Texas.

DESCRIPTION: *Bark* of trunks thin and peeling in large thin scales, reddish brown and irregularly broken by long braided ridges. *Twigs* slim, zigzag, the spines straight and rigid, not flattened, up to 1½ inches long. *Leaves* deciduous in our climate, in over-all dimensions 2 to 4 inches long, with 4 or 5 pairs of pinnæ, these in turn with 10 to 25 pairs of bright green leaflets only ⅛ to ¼ inch long. *Flowers* fragrant, a deep rich yellow, in spherical heads ⅔ inch thick, with 2 minute bracts under the head forming a cup-like involucre; stamens twice as long as the corolla; flower stalks 1 to 1½ inches long, 1 to 3 of them arising together from the axil of a leaf and thorn. *Pod* turgid but thin-walled and papery, oblong to spindle-shaped, 2 or 3 drooping together on short stalks, only slightly constricted between the seeds, 2 to 3 inches long, ½ to ⅔ inch wide, shiny and dark red-purple except for paler bands running along the broad sutures; each thin-walled compartment within filled with pulp. *Seeds* shiny light brown faintly marked by oval rings, ¼ inch long, oval, thick and flat, packed closely in the compartment in 2 rows. *Wood* hard, close-grained, and heavy (51½ pounds to the cubic foot dry weight), the heartwood rich reddish brown, the sapwood thin and pale.

"Farnesiana," one of the costliest scents distilled by the French perfumers, and worn by the most knowledgeable *exquises,* is derived from the flowers of this straggling, shrubby little tree which is so common throughout western Texas, as part of the thorn forest. Indeed, the Huisache, as the Texans like to call it, grows thickly around lakes and "tanks" (watering holes) and drainage ditches in the cattle country of the Lone-Star State. It grows abundantly on the Mesquite flats, taking over with especial vigor when Mesquite trees have been removed by agencies natural or human. Some will have it that it was

first brought to San Patrico County from Mexico by one of the
Mexican commissioners sent to represent the government in that
colony. He is supposed to have planted it out on his hacienda,
and it is a legend that all the Huisaches now growing in Texas have
sprung from that source. But this is probably as fictitious as the myth
that the bluebonnets (lupine) were brought here by friars and monks
from the Holy Land. The Huisache or Sweet Acacia is considered by
botanists to be a native of western Texas and also on the lonely
Baboquivari Mountains that rise from the desert and Mesquite
flats, southwest of Tucson, Arizona.

But long before the first white settlers reached Texas and Arizona
from Mexico, the Sweet Acacia was a favorite plant in the gardens of
Mediterranean Europe. It seems to have been brought in 1611 from
Santo Domingo and first cultivated in the gardens of Cardinal Odoardo
Farnese, where the exotic perfume of its little butterballs of bloom
was grateful to the exquisitely perceptive senses of that sensual and
gifted family, the Farnese. Intermarried with the Borgias and the
Medicis, the Farnese family filled the highest offices of the Church in
the sixteenth and seventeenth centuries, including the Papal throne.
It was a poor Farnese who was not a cardinal or at least a bishop, a
duke or at least a ruthless soldier of fortune, the daughter of a cardinal or at least the mistress of one. Alessandro Farnese, son of the
bastard son of Pope Paul III, was made a cardinal at the age of fourteen. He it was who founded at Catrarola, near Viterbo, the sumptuous villa and gardens that still bear the family name. Its very walls
are three miles in circumference, and the Cardinal's son and grandson
constantly enriched the flora of this garden with all that was new and
rare in plant life. When the garden belonged to Cardinal Odoardo
Farnese, he ordered Pietro Castello to draw up a description of its
botanical treasures, and in his rare publication of 1625 we find the
first mention of this American tree now known as *Acacia Farnesiana*.

Perhaps half a century later it was introduced into southern France,
and rapidly became one of the favorite dooryard trees of Provence.
With time it was found that the climate and soil of the Riviera, be-
teween Grasse and Cannes, and between the Esterels and the Var River,
precisely suited it, so that today that smiling district is a happy home
of the Sweet Acacia or *cassie,* as the French call it.

For *cassie* is one of the most important basic materials of a large
number of the mixed flower perfumes put out by the great Grasse
distilleries. A strain of this tree developed there produces two flower

crops a year; the best essence is derived from the flowers of September and October. On account of its cruelly pricking thorns, the *cassie* is no favorite with the peasant women who harvest the blossoms of this tree. They collect them in the morning as soon as the dew has burned off, and return two or three times a week for a new cutting. At the Grasse perfumeries the odor is generally extracted with oils, thus preparing a pomade which goes into extracts of violet and aromatic vinegar, into rouges and rice powders; a very concentrated form of extraction with alcohol is known as quintessence of *cassie*.

And what does it smell like, this wonderful perfume? But how can anyone describe an odor, to those who have never smelled it, save in terms of some other? The best one can say is that, compared with the fragrance of the Australian Acacias so familiar in the gardens of southern California, Sweet Acacia is far more honeyed and less dry and polleny. It is more intense and, by that same token, more cloying. Certainly it is an odor that once perceived will be identified forever after, so utterly unlike any other in the world it is.

In Texas there is no Grasse, no great perfume trade, yet the beekeepers there value Huisache highly, for it is an important pollen plant, even though it does not, like its relative the *huajillo,* produce the famous Uvalde honey. But bees must have a rich store of pollen to give their youngsters proper protein diet, particularly the future queens. And the pollen is the more precious to the bees because it comes at a time, usually January and February, when not many other plants are in bloom.

Under such names as Popinac and Opopanax, the Sweet Acacia has been grown almost around the world in tropical and subtropical countries. There are few where it has not escaped from cultivation, and in the Hawaiian Islands it has become practically a pest. But it is a pest with many charms, with its feathery foliage consisting in many sensitive leaflets and its butter-yellow blooms which make it, said a French poet, "a load of balm for every wind that stirs."

DESERT CAT'S–CLAW

Acacia Greggii Gray

OTHER NAMES: Paradise-flower. Texas Mimosa. Devil's-claws.

RANGE: Northern Mexico north to the valley of the Rio Grande and the Big Bend country of Texas, to southern New Mexico and throughout the low deserts of Arizona to southernmost Nevada and the low deserts of California.

DESCRIPTION: *Bark* light gray-brown, thin but furrowed and scaly. *Twigs* angled and slim, pale brown and beset with broad, stout recurved spines ¼ inch long. *Leaves* twice compound with 1 to 3 pairs of pinnæ, and 4 to 5 pairs of thick, rigid, hoary-pubescent leaflets, each leaflet 2- to 3-nerved and ⅟₁₆ to ¼ inch long, the main leafstalk marked near the middle by a little chestnut-brown gland. *Flowers* borne in long dense spikes, clustered, 2 or 3 spikes together, toward the ends of the branches; the calyx 5-lobed and very small, the 5 petals bright yellow, the numerous stamens pale yellow, ¼ inch long. *Pod* much contorted, light brown, 2 to 6 inches long, ½ to ¾ inch wide, constricted between the dark brown, compressed, shining seeds which are ¼ inch long. *Wood* very heavy (53 pounds per cubic foot, dry weight), very hard, strong, close-grained and durable, the heartwood red-brown, the sapwood thin and light yellow.

Desert Cat's-claw is the most detested and roundly cursed of all trees in the Southwest, for its ferocious armament of spines tears flesh and clothing of all who venture within its grasp. The name of Cat's-claw — *uña de gato,* as the Spanish-speaking Southwesterners call it — exactly describes its flattened and hooked talons, which, when they sink in, also curl under the skin or the cloth, making extraction worse than penetration. So "Devil's-claws" is one of the mildest epithets applied to this tree, and few creatures save honey bees are voluntarily intimate with it. To many small game animals, however, the dense thickets of Cat's-claw are precious. There the jack rabbit and the Gambel quail can find sanctuary from pitiless hawk and hunter.

Yet it is this hostile little tree that yields that white ambrosia known as Uvalde honey, the most celebrated in Texas. In Uvalde, honey is generally mixed with the nectar of another Acacia, a shrub called *huajillo;* their blooming times, though on the whole quite different, just overlap in April, and that is when the bees are most active at this tree, compounding a confection that is unequaled for fragrance and taste. The *huajillo's* flowers — that you may distinguish them in the field — are nearly white; those of Cat's-claw are greenish white with the petals creamy-margined, and they wear a fine tuft of some 50 golden stamens in each flower.

The young foliage is gingerly browsed by stock, afraid of the thorns perhaps, but eagerly taken by antelope. The ribbon-like pods are low in nutritive value but the seeds were eaten as pinole by the Pimas and Papagos, and Gambel quail still fatten on them. The very hard and durable wood, in our times made into trinkets and souvenirs, used to furnish the Southwest pioneers with all the singletrees and double-trees of their home-made wagons. As a fuel wood the Cat's-claw is almost peerless. It burns with a bluish flame, and long after most wood is reduced to ashes, Cat's-claw is still a bed of intense coals. In the very depths of the Grand Canyon, to which Devil's-claw descends, this is considered the best substitute for coal.

TREE CAT'S–CLAW

Acacia Wrightii Bentham

RANGE: From Nuevo Leon, Mexico, north to the Big Bend country of western Texas and to New Braunfels, central Texas.

DESCRIPTION: *Bark* narrowly seamed, with broad, flat ridges and thin, narrow scales. *Twigs* at first furrowed and angled and dark red-brown to pale yellow-brown, becoming in their second season gray and usually furnished with a few stout chestnut-brown spines. *Leaves* twice compound, on slender stalks 1 inch long or a little more, with 1 to 3 pairs of pinnæ each with 2 to 5 pairs of bright green, rigid leaflets measuring but ¼ to ⅝ inch long. *Flowers* light yellow, fragrant, in slender spikes 1½ inches long, which are borne on slender and often clustered stalks. *Fruit* 2 to 4 inches long, 1 to 1¼ inch wide, flattened, rather wrinkled and barely constricted between the seeds, the margins thick, the walls papery thin and mesh-veined. *Seeds* light brown, with large oval depressions, compressed, ¼ inch long. *Wood* close-grained, hard, very heavy (58 pounds per cubic foot, dry weight), with bright clear brown heartwood streaked with yellow and red, and thin, clear yellow sapwood.

The Tree Cat's-claw is a much less famous or infamous species than the Desert Cat's-claw, for it is armed scarcely at all, and so never brings down the curses of the Southwest stockman on its root and bough. The snow-white spikes of flowers are produced abundantly from March to May, and their nectar yields a high-grade honey. The wood makes a fine hot fire. In West Texas this beautiful little tree, with its ferny fronds, grows up to 30 feet in height, with a trunk 10 inches in diameter. Gradually its worth as an ornamental is coming to be appreciated, and it is now often cultivated in the Lone-Star State.

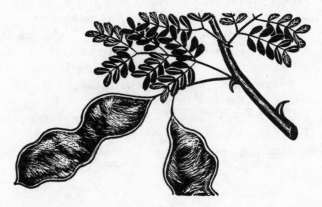

THE LEADTREES
(*Leucæna*)

THESE ARE thornless shrubs and small trees with slender branchlets and ferny, evergreen, alternate, twice-compound leaves, the pinnæ of an even number, in opposite pairs, the pinnules small, the long leaf-stalks often furnished with a conspicuous gland near the lower pinnæ. The minute flowers, mostly bisexual, are clustered in dense spherical heads in axillary clusters of leafless terminal spikes. The calyx has 5 minute lobes; the 5 petals are free from each other as are the 10 stamens which are inserted under the ovary and exserted from the petals. The ovary terminates in a slender style capped by a minute stigma. Many-seeded, the legume is stalked and slender, opening at length by a suture on the thick margin. The valves of the pod possess a papery dark outer coat and a pale brown, woody inner one. Compressed and transverse in the pod, the seeds have thin, shining brown and bony coats.

* * *

WAHOOTREE

Leucæna retusa Bentham

OTHER NAME: Littleleaf Leadtree.

RANGE: Texas, from Uvalde west to the Big Bend country (Jeff Davis County).

DESCRIPTION: *Bark* bright cinnamon-brown and persistently scaly. *Twigs* at first furrowed and covered with a deciduous wool, soon becoming rounded, pale cinnamon-brown, and minutely downy. *Leaves* twice compound on a main stalk and rachis with 2 to 4 pairs of long-stalked, remote pinnæ each 6 to 10 inches long in over-all dimensions, each pinna with 3 to 5 pairs of unsymmetrical thin, blue-green leaflets which are each ¾ to 1 inch long, ⅓ to ½ inch broad. *Flowers* in dense spherical heads ¾ inch thick and borne in clusters of 1 to 3 on slender often branched stalks 1½ to 3 inches long. *Pods* drooping on short stalks, 1 to 3 together, 3 to 5 inches long, ⅓ to ½ inch wide, thin, flattened and rigid, dark reddish brown with thickened margins. *Seeds* numerous, ⅓ inch long, ¼ inch wide.

Wahootree is the cattlemen's name for this beautiful little tree or tall shrub — it never grows more than 25 feet high — the northernmost representative of a fine genus of tropical plants related to *Acacia* and *Lysiloma*. But even the watchful cowboy does not see a great deal of it, for it shrinks away, like a pursued dryad, into the Live Oak groves that the Texan calls mottes and the Spanish-speaking ranchers refer to as the *encinal*. And the reason for its scarcity at present is that the cattle browse it to death, so ravenous are they for its evergreen yet highly palatable leaves. Most desert trees, like most cowboys, go armed; the Wahootree has no thorns to protect it. So it has grown very scarce in the open, on rocky hillsides and the tops of limestone cliffs.

In foliage the Wahootree much resembles Cat's-claw, but the pods are mere shoestrings in shape, compared to the Cat's-claw's ribbon-like fruits. The compact spheres into which the minute white flowers are headed much resemble their relative of the southern gardens, called there "Mimosa-tree," (*Albizzia Julibrissin*), for in both flowers the outstanding feature consists in the very long-exserted, delicate stamens that stand out like fairy dusters all over the flowering ball. The blooming season of the Wahootree begins in the spring and goes on intermittently till fall.

THE MESQUITES
(*Prosopis*)

Pairs of spines above the axils of the leafstalks, and growth not from terminal but from axillary buds, characterize these bushy small trees. The deciduous leaves are alternate on the new growth of the year, but clustered in the axils of older branches, and are twice-compound (rarely more), the primary divisions consisting in a pair of pinnæ forking from the common leafstalk; the slender pinnules or leaflets stand in remote pairs and are of an even number on the sometimes spiny rachis; the leafstalk bears a minute gland at its apex. In axilliary, stalked spikes the minute flowers occur densely; they possess a minute, deciduous, 5-toothed calyx and 5 petals which are united or free. The 10 stamens, inserted with the petals on the margin of a minute disk, are quite free of each other and exserted from the petals and sepals. The ovary adheres to the disk and calyx tube and terminates in a slender style and minute stigma. Slender and either flattened or thick, and sometimes twisting into a corkscrew spiral, the fruit — a legume — has a pale yellow and woody outer coat and a spongy inner coat of sweetish flesh in which the compressed seeds lie obliquely imbedded. The seeds are possessed of a shining, bony, outer coat; they escape by decay of the pod, since it has no natural sutures by which to open.

*   *   *

TRUE MESQUITE

Prosopis juliflora (Swartz) DeCandolle

OTHER NAMES: Western Honey Locust. Honeypod. Honey or Velvet Mesquite. Algarobo. Albarroba. Algaroba-tree. Texas Ironwood.

RANGE: Northern Mexico north to the low deserts of California, southern Nevada, and southwesternmost Utah, throughout the deserts of Arizona and New Mexico, and the arid parts of Texas and western Oklahoma, reaching southern Kansas and western Louisiana. Also on the island of Jamaica, south through Central America to Venezuela.

DESCRIPTION: *Bark* of trunks thick, dark reddish brown, furrowed and scaly. *Twigs* slim and smooth, round in cross-section but zigzag and usually armed with sharp spines ½ to 2 inches long. *Leaves* twice compound (or rarely more finely divided), with 12 to 30 crowded or well spaced deciduous leaflets each ¼ to 2 inches long; leafstalk glandular, spine-tipped where it forks. *Flowers* minute, fragrant, nearly regular and minute, bisexual, with greenish white petals which are half as long as the 10 free stamens. *Pod* flat or roundish, straight or curved, 4 to 9 inches long, ¼ to ½ inch wide, constricted between the 10 to 20 light brown, compressed, oblong seeds which are ¼ inch long and imbedded in the sweet pulp of the pod. *Wood* medium-heavy (48 pounds per cubic foot, dry weight), hard, close-grained, not strong but very durable, the heartwood dark brown or red, with clear yellow thin sapwood.

Of all the gold seekers who were misguided into Death Valley in 1849, the most pathetic was the Bennett-Manly party. For it was accompanied by the wives and children of this group of Middle Westerners. And the frailty of these hostages to fortune caused their menfolk to tarry beside the springs, hoping that strength would return to the emaciated bodies. Yet the longer they waited, the hotter grew the season, and the lower ran their food supplies. Eventually they escaped, after terrible hardships. But, all along, their sufferings could have been greatly lightened had they known enough to eat the sweet, nutritious pods which were swinging on the Mesquite trees right over their heads. The trees they knew were perhaps the very ones that still stand around the water hole that is known now, after this unhappy party, as Bennett Wells. But these courageous greenhorns —

these corn-and-beef-fed farmers, these small-townsmen whose food came out of barrels, sacks, and boxes — how could they guess that the Lord had appointed any manna in the valley and shadow of death?

Their ignorance was more pathetic than that of the Eastern tourist who, looking from the train window at the miles of Mesquite *bosque* between San Antonio and Uvalde, Texas, exclaimed that never had he seen such extensive Peach orchards. Texans slapped their thighs in glee as they told him what this growth really is, and taught him, no doubt, to pronounce it *"mez-keet"* [1] — for Texans decide these things for us. But indeed there is a remarkable resemblance in a Mesquite to a Peach, with its very short trunk, the deep V-shaped forks of its branches, its many twigs and low stature. Or when a Mesquite grows old it may come to look more like some ancient Apple tree, bent with years of bearing till its twigs grow knotty and its overborne boughs sweep downward at the ends. But on a second look the traveler sees there is something wrong with these "orchards." Those tough stems perversely twisted, those crooked twigs, those thorns set upon black and warty bases — they belong to no sweet Peach, no friendly Apple.

But do not compare this tree to such as grow by man's husbanding hand. Judge it rather by its peers, by all the thorn-set, hard-bitten desert flora. Then Mesquite appears as an astonishingly tall, um- brageous, and thrifty growth. For, where you would not think that any sort of tree could exist, in such arid soil, such flaming heat, or in the depths of the Grand Canyon with its raging floods, the Mesquite, when it comes to leaf, is a blessing on the earth that bears it.

Spring comes to the Mesquite first as a sudden rush of green to the twigs whose arthritic fingers seem to grow limber now; at this time the twigs are palatable browse to deer and cattle. Then the leaf buds burst and the foliage, at first an ethereal green, spreads over the thorny crown like a halo; swiftly each *bosque* catches the green fire, as the twice-compound leaves expand their ferny, frondose grace.

In spring, too, flowers appear for the first time — for there are two blooming seasons: April, after the winter rains, and again in June and July, continuing intermittently till fall. The flowers, really in the Mimosa family but looking like yellow catkins, do not make the magnificent display of such desert trees as the Palo Verde and the Ironwood, but they are delightfully fragrant, gently perfuming all the stern desert's airs. Bees come to them by the millions, especially

[1] From *mizquitl,* the Nahuatl Indian word for this tree, by way of Spanish *mesquite.*

in the honey-raising districts of west Texas. Mesquite honey is clear amber in color, and of good if not the highest quality.

In the lives of many Southwest Indian tribes, Mesquite was the most important of all trees. The Papago house was commonly built of it. Four to nine forked Mesquite posts made the pillars, and through the forks were laid light poles or horizontal stringers of Mesquite. Next, light slender rods of Saguaro were laid from pole to pole as a roofing. Then around the central core slender Mesquite poles were set in a circle, as siding, but standing about four feet from the posts. The tips were then bent over and tied to the horizontals with strips of soapweed (*Yucca glauca*) fiber. Thus was formed the skeleton of the dome-shaped hogan. Then the ribs or siding of Mesquite were bound to each other with withes of the ocotillo bush, to make a sort of lath.

"Kickball" was a Papago game, played with spheres of Mesquite wood, though how even an Indian toe could stand up to it is a matter of amazement. Paddles of Mesquite — one for the bottom, like a butter paddle, one for the sides, like a cleaver — were used to shape pottery. Cradle boards of Mesquite roots in the form of an elongated arch, shaped papooses. A snag of sharpened Mesquite was used as a plow from the coming of the Spanish to the coming of steel shares.

But it is the fruits — locust-like pods — that make this tree a blessing. Every Southwestern Indian tribe within its range made ample use of the pods, which could be eaten out of hand, or boiled, or stored in the ground, or even fermented to make a mild alcoholic drink. The handsome mottled seeds have always been of the highest importance as an Indian food, from our deserts all the way to South America, serving for flour for cakes and mush. As feed for horses, Mesquite pods were considered so valuable in the days when the United States Cavalry was out after Apaches, that the Army paid 3 cents a pound in New Mexico for Mesquite beans.

From the first introduction of livestock into the Southwest, the *algaroba,* as the Spanish-speaking pioneers called it, was ot recognized importance as browse. Not that the foliage is often touched, but the pods which contain 25 to 30 per cent grape sugar, are more than palatable to stock — they are devoured. Cattle reach as high for them as they can, or horn them down rather than risk tender muzzles among the thorns. Bulls sometimes batter off whole branches for their de-horned cows. Goats climb lightly into the Mesquite boughs, ventur-ing far out to devour pods, leaves, and twigs. Perhaps they even digest the thorns! At any rate it takes a goat but a short time to browse the toughest, dryest, wiriest Mesquite to death.

Over much of its range, Mesquite is but a shrub, the underground stems sending up many small shoots and these frequently branched right at the point where they leave the ground. But this is a species which passes the ill-defined border between tree and shrub, and through-out its range Mesquite is also arboreous, commonly 15 to 20 feet in height, often much more. "Old Geronimo" is a gigantic Mesquite on the grounds of the Santa Cruz Valley School, near Tumacacori, Ari-zona, with a trunk 14 feet and 11½ inches in circumference, that seems — to judge from its pollarded condition — to have furnished firewood and fence posts for over 200 years. On the same grounds stands another Mesquite 40 feet in height. The biological survey of Death Valley, made by the Department of Agriculture in 1891, found between Bennett Wells and Mesquite a specimen about 30 feet high, with a spread of branches 75 by 90 feet — quite a pool of shade for the hottest and most ill-reputed spot in all the annals of the desert!

The "Jail Tree," at the corner of Tegner and Center Streets in Wickenburg, Arizona, is an historic Mesquite to which badmen and suspects were chained, in lieu of any calaboose in the early days. To serve a sentence under its shade was perhaps more merciful than being locked in any jail the hell-raising frontiers would have provided.

Like the swallows in the Southwest, the Mesquite has a way of associating itself with ruins, such as the Tumacacori Mission near Nogales, Arizona, and Fort Richardson near Jacksboro, Texas. One of the most moving spots in Arizona is Fort Lowell, built of adobe in 1873 and then far outside the pueblo of Tucson with its temptations. Fine streets divided the company buildings, set with Mesquite and Mulberry trees; there were green lawns, and the deep verandahs, vine-clad and olla-hung, formed outdoor living rooms. Then there were balls and dress parades; visitors were lavishly entertained, and splendid cavalry mounts waited in the stables. Today all but a little is a crumbling ruin. For with the end of the Apache wars in 1886 the fort was abandoned and with every succeeding year fierce sun and rain and wind have done their work. Gone are the lawns, the flowers, the Mulberries, and the adobe arches are fallen. But everywhere the triumphant Mesquite invades, like the jungle tree it is, thrusting up through the very floors, rooting in crannies of the walls, aiding the tooth of the elements in the process of dissolution.

The good points of Mesquite are almost endless. It exudes a gum that was well known to the Indians, who chewed it, used it for wounds and sores as gum Arabic is employed in the Old World, mended pottery with it, and obtained from it a black dye. As early as 1871, more than 12,000 pounds of the gum were gathered in one Texas county alone and sent East for use in the preparation of gumdrops and mucilage. Several hundred pounds are exported annually to Australia, for what purpose is not known. The bark is useful in tanning and dyeing. The wood, almost as hard and beautifully colored as Mahogany and taking a high polish, would be precious cabinet wood if only the trees grew larger, the trunks taller and straighter. Even so it has served for years as a highly valuable fence post and corral stockade material, cheap to cut, and lasting in contact with the soil for years. The Navaho bow was made of the tough wood, and Mesquite beams were placed in that aboriginal apartment building, the Casa Grande, near Coolidge, Arizona. The Texas pioneers used Mesquite almost exclusively for the hubs and spokes of wagon wheels.

Though trunks and branches are used for fuel, the favorite part is the underground stems, erroneously called roots. These are still excavated for fuel wood where labor is cheap enough, and in the old days of exploration, survey-parties were dependent on Mesquite "root" for warmth and cooking. It burns with an intense heat, but very slowly and down to a long-lasting bed of coals, so that blacksmiths always preferred it to any other wood. Listen to the laconic praise that comes blowing out of the diaries of desert travelers: "Grama-grass good and abundant. There is here a sufficient quantity of mezquite to answer our purposes for cooking." "Mezquite root dry and good." "The mezquite wood is plenty and can be obtained without much labor." "The mezquite is green and grows in the utmost profusion; indeed one is cheated into the belief that he is passing through an orchard. This is the only growing timber we have seen since we left the pinery." "The Clear Fork traverses a very zigzag coarse, a beautiful and fertile valley, about three miles in width . . . covered by forests of mezquite."

Water and grass and Mesquite, Mesquite, grass and water — over and over, they are theme of the early Southwest travelers' prayers and thanks, till we feel as though we could still see the campfires of these courageous pioneer parties, and smell again the sweet incense of the burning Mesquite "root" — an odor as haunting as that of Pinyon.

Finally, the Mesquite is valuable because its great root system holds the banks of the dry stream courses and the washes of the southwestern streams down which, after summer thunderstorms, rush flash floods of water. And the root system of the Mesquite is a wondrous and a fearsome thing. Its branches may penetrate 50 or 60 feet to tap the deep veins of ground water that underlie much of our deserts. But they also come right up under the soil surface, to catch every possible drop of the light winter rains, and they spread laterally in a great circle. So the Mesquite is prepared to adapt itself to the benefits of the most passing shower, and yet survive the most prolonged periods of drought.

With all these wonderful qualities, Mesquite is yet the most feared and hated tree that grows, a menace that is every year extending its ravages, spreading desolation where once was wealth. In fifty years it has crossed Texas from the west and south, where it was always native, to southeastern Colorado and right over Oklahoma to southwestern Kansas — one of the most spectacular biological phenomena of this country. It is now beginning to become naturalized in Louisiana and Missouri and will probably not be stopped by anything except the isotherm of prolonged freezing. Carried to the Philippines in the days of the Manila treasure galleons, Mesquite is now firmly established there and, more recently, in the Hawaiian archipelago where it flourishes up to 60 feet in height. It has invaded the Bahamas from the West Indies, and is on the loose in South Africa, Australia, India, and Persia, where it was doubtless at first introduced only as a promising cultivated tree, but soon found itself able to elbow its way into the native plant cover and displace it.

How could all this come about, when the tree had for ages been a well-behaved species sticking closely to streams, washes, bottom-lands, arroyos and desert wells and springs? It seems that the cattle, devouring the fruits, void the seeds, often undigested and quite viable, on the upland range grasses. However, the Mesquite seedlings could not compete in the closed community of the range grasses but for the factor — reluctantly admitted or hotly denied by most stockmen — of over-grazing. In short, the rangelands were already broken down, ecologically, before the Mesquite began its jungle march. True, once established on grass land, Mesquite becomes co-villain in the plot by shading out the grass, and competing for soil moisture. So the vicious circle is closed. As a result, in the last few decades Texas has lost 37,000,000 acres to noxious brush of which Mesquite is the chief factor. Along U.S. highway 281, between Mineral Wells and Wichita Falls, the Texans — many of Norwegian, Polish, German, and Austrian descent — wage a constant warfare against the greedy trees that are always encroaching on their farms and ranches. Where the highway passes Gap Mountain, it is constantly being menaced by the thorny trees.

In Arizona in 1906 scientists could state that they saw no indications of danger from the increase in Mesquite; by 1936 the stockmen, so scornful of government interference, were begging their government for aid. The Mesquite jungles, stockmen found, were so extensive that cattle had to be hunted through them for days. The thorns are an agony to the cowboy and his horse.

Many methods of control were attempted. The first and most obvious one was to cut the Mesquites down. But since most of the stems are underground, this amounted to nothing better than lopping off the branches above ground. And, because Mesquite crown-sprouts, where one stem had been before, there were now twenty in its place. If you didn't cut it down, then the Mesquite increased by seeds. Gasoline blowtorches were used, but though the flame did wound the tree, a wounded Mesquite is something like a wounded tiger — if not so quick in its reactions. Next, poison injected through the wounds was tried. But even that didn't suffice.

In the end it was found best in Arizona to cut the tree down to the stump, then poison the stump with sodium arsenate applied from an engineer's oil can fitted with a small pump operated by the thumb.

The cost of the poison and that kind of labor is low; more, the felled trunks sold for enough as fence posts or fuel to pay off the cost of cutting and poisoning. And land cleared of Mesquite yields still further profit. For instance, it has been found that native uncleared Mesquite brush near Kingsville, Texas, will carry only one cow to every 25 to 30 acres, while cleared brushland will carry two.

Stockmen generally believe, however, that it will always be well to allow Mesquite to occupy some of their bottom-lands. The value of the tree for fence posts and fuel, the browse and shade it affords to livestock, are worth more than the same type of land would be if it were all range grass. So Mesquite is something more than a tree; it is almost an elemental force, comparable to fire — too valuable to extinguish completely and too dangerous to trust unwatched.

It is not surprising that, over its immense range in the West and South, Mesquite should show great variation. Indeed, many species have been proposed to express these variations; but probably all are synonyms or at the most varieties of one polymorphic species. Even these varieties are not all very clearly marked; at least for purposes of this book it will be reasonable to reduce them to the two following:

VELVET MESQUITE, variety *velutina* (Wooton) Standley, is clearly distinct by the fact that the entire foliage, twigs, and pods are covered with a short dense coat of hairs. Further, each compound leaf has two pairs, not one, of pinnæ, while the pinnules (ultimate leaflets) are less than ½ inch long. This variety is found from Mexico (states of Vera Cruz, Michoacan, and Baja California) north to the lower reaches of the Colorado River around Yuma, and up to 4500 feet in the Kofa

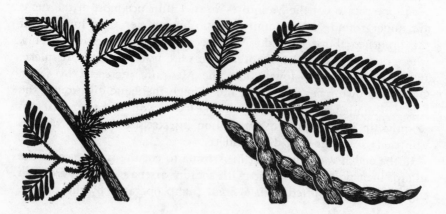

and Castle Dome Mountains, and almost throughout the southern tier of counties in Arizona. It recurs near El Paso, Texas.

HONEY MESQUITE, variety *glandulosa* (Torrey) Cockerell, has smooth foliage, twigs, and pods; each compound leaf consists in a single pair of pinnæ; the pinnules are more than ½ inch long. This variety (in which is included for the present the possibly distinct variety *Torreyana*, Benson) is, except in Arizona, the commoner one. It is found from northern Mexico north to Kansas, Colorado, New Mexico, southern Nevada and central Arizona. In California its distribution is most discontinuous: known from the eastern side of the Mohave desert, as in Death Valley and canyons of the Panamint and Funeral Mountains, it also occurs around Bakersfield and Taft in the Great Central Valley, and almost to the Pacific, in the Cuyama Valley of San Luis Obispo County.

TORNILLO

Prosopis pubescens Bentham

OTHER NAMES: Screwpod Mesquite. Frémont Screwbean. Screwbean Mesquite. Mescrew.

RANGE: Southern Nevada and extreme southeastern Utah south through the low deserts of California and western Arizona to northern Baja California and Sonora, also in extreme southeastern Arizona and the valley of the Rio Grande from central New Mexico, through the Big Bend area of Texas, south to northern parts of Chihuahua and Coahuila.

DESCRIPTION: *Bark* peeling into long, vertical, thin and shaggy strips, light brown tinged with red. *Twigs* slender, slightly zigzag, smooth and light red-brown, armed with persistent slender spines. *Leaves* deciduous, on a slender, glandular, spine-tipped stalk ⅓ to ⅔ inch long which forks to form two pinnæ, each of which is 1½ to 2 inches long and bears 10 to 16 leaflets each ⅓ to ⅔ inch long, ⅛ inch wide, and ashy-pubescent. *Flowers* from the axils of dry papery little bracts, borne in cylindrical spikes 2 to 3 inches long; nearly regular, the petals near the tip coated inwardly with thick white woolly hairs. *Pods* in dense spikes and twisted, by many screw-like turns, into a slender, curl-like spiral 1 to 2 inches long. *Seeds* light brown and shining, 1/16 inch long. *Wood* extremely hard but not strong, close-grained, heavy (47½ pounds per cubic foot, dry weight), the heartwood light brown, the sapwood thin and pale.

The Tornillo is a little tree or tall shrub that closely resembles its relative the True Mesquite, but can be distinguished as long as the pods are on the tree (and that is much of the year, since the flowers appear intermittently over a long season). For the pods have a spiral twist, like a corkscrew's, whence of course the names of Tornillo and Screwpod Mesquite. Very closely does this species follow the general range of the True Mesquite, save that it does not extend beyond western Texas into the southern and middle-western states. If anything, Tornillo is even hardier than its big relative, accepting an amount of drought and of bitter alkalinity that not even that tough tree seems able to endure. Tornillo reaches its large size — up to 30 feet in height, with a trunk a foot in diameter — along the Gila River in Arizona. Even in Death Valley, a specimen has been measured with a trunk 3½ feet in circumference.

It casts, with its small sparse leaves, even less shade for the traveler and the desert livestock. Yet it is perhaps more graceful, with its ascending branches and narrow outline, than the depressed form of True Mesquite with its crooked branches. The exceeding hard and durable wood has been used extensively for fence posts on the rangelands, and handles of tools are improvised of it. It burns with an intense flame. The pods are even sweeter for eating raw than those of True Mesquite. In consequence they have always been a favorite of the desert Indians. The Pimas cook the whole pods in pits covered with earth and left for three or four days. Then the pods are lifted out, dried in the sun and stored until the day when they are ground with pestle and mortar and eaten in the form of pinole. From the roots the Indians brew a concoction for dressing wounds.

THE SCREWBEANS
(*Parkinsonia*)

THIN, SMOOTH BARK and, in our species, short spines (either on the branches or the twigs or on the leafstalks) characterize these bushy trees with forked stems. The leaves are evergreen or deciduous, alternate or clustered in the axils of older growth, but always twice-compound with an even number of pinnæ and of the numerous pinnules (leaflets). The perfect flowers, remote from each other in slender axillary or solitary spikes, possess a 5-lobed calyx, 5-clawed petals much larger than the calyx, and 10 free stamens, of 2 alternate lengths, inserted in 2 rows on the rim of the disk. The single ovary is contracted above into a slender, incurved style capped with a minute stigma. The pod exhibits marked contractions between and beyond the bulging oblong seeds; these possess thin, light brown, hard coats.

*   *   *

RETAMA

Parkinsonia aculeata Linnæus

OTHER NAMES: Palo Verde. Horsebean. Jerusalem-Thorn.

RANGE: Widespread in Mexico except in the high mountains, north to the Gila desert of southwestern Arizona and the lower Rio Grande valley of Texas. Naturalized in California, Key West, and many tropical lands.

DESCRIPTION: *Bark* of trunks brown tinged with red, smooth or with small scales. *Twigs* slim, round, spine-like and beset with spines, at first yellow-green becoming orange or gray, and by the second year roughened with lenticels. *Leaves* evergreen, compound, of 2 forms: primary leaves on young branches with 2 to 4 pinnæ and a rachis which develops into a stout, inch-long, chestnut-brown, triple spine; secondary leaves, clustered in the axils of the primary, the very short stalk or rachis forking into 2 pinnæ 12 to 18 inches long in over-all dimensions, each with a round (not flattened) rachis and 2 or 3 pairs of light green leaflets each ¼ inch long. *Flowers* borne in long erect spikes 5 to 6 inches long, the stamens shorter than the bright yellow petals of which the uppermost is speckled at the base with red spots. *Pods* drooping in graceful spikes 2 to 4 inches long, dark orange-brown, compressed between the remote, bean-like seeds. *Wood* close-grained, hard, heavy (38 pounds per cubic foot, dry weight), with light brown heartwood and thick, paler, yellowish sapwood.

Retama is a Southwest Spanish name for this tree, more commonly called Palo Verde. But so many other trees lay claims, and better claim, to that title, that it is best to use the alternative name of Retama. Unlike other Palo Verdes, this one is not utterly naked most of the year, for its lurid, crooked, thorny twigs remain green with the odd drooping streamers of vertebra-like foliage — each leaf a long switch-like rachis beset with remote tiny leaflets. One cannot imagine a tree with any sort of leaves that could cast less shade. Yet the appeal of the tree is in this extremely airy and graceful foliage nonetheless, as well as in the shining yellow twigs and the pretty flowers which remind us that it is in the Cassia family. Gracefully borne on slim stalks, in loose zigzag spikes, they are slightly fragrant and quite striking, with the gold of the upper petals flecked with red spots.

Livestock seldom browse the sparse foliage protected by spines, but the hard wood makes a good desert fuel. The leaves, in Mexico, are steeped and made into home "remedies" for fever and epilepsy.

Because this little tree is so resistant to drought and alkali, it is widely cultivated and is commonly escaped from gardens to the deserts. But it is also native, at least on the foothills of the Coyote and Baboquivari Mountains, southwest of Tucson. There the flowers appear in the hottest part of the year, when few venture on the dusty washboard ranch roads. In cultivation flowering is almost continuous.

THE PALO VERDES
(*Cercidium*)

THE BRIGHT, smooth, light green bark of the tortuous stout branches, and the straight, slender axillary spines are conspicuous features of the Palo Verdes. The deciduous leaves are alternate and twice compound, the pinnæ or primary divisions only 2, the pinnules (leaflets) of an even and small number in opposite pairs. The bisexual flowers occur in solitary or clustered and few-flowered spikes, with 5-lobed calyx, and 5-clawed petals, the uppermost distinctly glandular at base of the claw and broader and longer-clawed than the other petals. The 10 stamens are inserted on the margin of the disk and stand quite free from each other, and, though distinctly exserted from the petals, are also somewhat declined in position. The ovary, inserted at the base of the calyx tube, stands, however, free of it, and terminates in a slender style with minute stigma. Straight or but slightly contracted between the seeds, turgid or compressed, the thin obliquely veined pod, a legume, opens tardily by a ventral suture. On long threads, the compressed seeds in their hard coats are suspended before falling.

✳ ✳ ✳

BLUE PALO VERDE

Cercidium floridum Bentham

OTHER NAME: Greenbark Acacia.

RANGE: Northern Mexico north to the Colorado Desert of southern California, in southern Arizona up to 3500 feet above sea level, and north to Mojave County in the Colorado River basin.

DESCRIPTION: *Bark* of trunks pale green, or, near the base, reddish brown and separating into thick, plate-like scales. *Twigs* glaucous, yellow to pale olive-green, beset with little spines ¼ inch long. *Leaves* few and scattered (when not lacking entirely), in over-all dimensions only 1 inch long; the stalk arising from the axil of a thorn, and soon branching to form the 2 pinnæ, these again compound with 2 or 3 pairs of glaucous leaflets, each one but 1/12 to 1/6 inch long. *Flowers* about ¾ inch across in 4- to 5-flowered, loosely branched clusters; calyx 5-lobed, the lobes reflexed; petals 5, clawed, bright yellow, the uppermost petal broadest and longest-clawed; stamens 10, free. *Pod* 3 to 4 inches long, ¼ to ⅓ inch wide. *Seeds* plump, ⅓ inch long. *Wood* close-grained, weak, medium-light (34 pounds per cubic foot, dry weight), the heartwood light brown, the sapwood clear light yellow.

As you go flying over the highways of southwestern Arizona, a very green, very twiggy, leafless little tree or tall Willow-like bush springs up

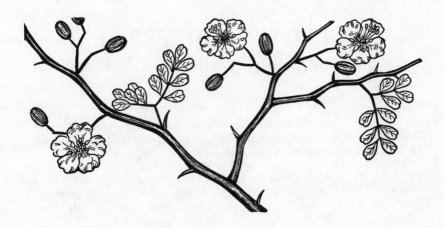

at you beside every culvert and bridge over the thousands of washes. Sometimes there are two trees — one at each side of the bridge; then you will see no more till you come to the next wash. Again the green tree leaps from a speck in the distance to a big bundle of switches, then drops behind in a flash. Summer, autumn, and winter, it stands like this, quite leafless but far from dead — its green, thin bark performing photosynthesis just as leaves would do.

But once a year, in the first warmth of the desert spring, the naked Palo Verde clothes itself in glory. The tiny leaves appear, but these pass almost unnoticed, for the whole tree fumes with glorious golden flowers. Nodding gracefully on their stalks, the flowers, each about ¾ of an inch long, are like those of their garden relatives, the Cassias, but borne in utmost profusion. Seen against the bald blue of the desert skies, they have won from the Spanish-speaking rancher the tribute poetry of *lluvia de oro* — "shower of gold."

The flowers and foliage droop together as the furnace breath of summer parches the desert. But there follow the big bean-like pods swollen by the plump seeds. The Pima and Papago Indians of Arizona eat them while they are still soft and immature, and cooked whole, like lima beans; they also grind the ripened seeds and cook the flour as atole or gruel.

The wood is soft and weak but the green limber twigs are a favorite browse of the little burro deer of the desert. Livestock will browse on them too, but only as an emergency, for the thorns, though not numerous, are ever troublesome.

YELLOW PALO VERDE

Cercidium microphyllum (Torrey) Rose and Johnston

OTHER NAME: Littleleaf Palo Verde.

RANGE: Mesas and rocky hills of southern and western Arizona (up to 4000 feet), deserts of southeastern California, and in Sonora and Sinaloa, Mexico, and northeastern Baja California.

DESCRIPTION: *Bark* of trunks dark orange and smooth, or on old trunks roughened by irregular, short, pale gray ridges. *Twigs* stout, pale yellow-green and rigid, and terminating in a stout spine, at first woolly, then

downy, in succeeding seasons, and frequently scaly. *Leaves* 1 inch long
in over-all dimensions, with 2 to 12 leaflets, each about ⅛ inch long,
densely woolly on unfolding, and always pubescent. *Flowers* pale yellow.
Pod 2 to 3 inches long, compressed between the 1 to 3 seeds, with long
and often curved tip. *Wood* close-grained, with orange-brown heartwood streaked with red, and thick light brown or yellow sapwood.

The Yellow Palo Verde is like its more noted relative, the Blue Palo
Verde, in being little more than a bundle of willowy green switches
for much of the year, then flowering profusely for a few brief weeks,
while the evanescent leaves also appear. The flowers of this species
come a few weeks later than the Blue Palo Verde's, however, when the
desert spring is already growing very hot. The blossoms are a pale,
not a golden, yellow and, by that much, less striking, but the banner
petal is somewhat differentiated by being white or green. While the
other species is almost always found near washes, this one is able to
subsist in more arid soil and will grow far up in the foothills and
even in the canyons of the driest desert ranges. The adjective "yellow"
applies to the yellowish-green of the bark of the twigs, as contrasted
with the blue-green of the branchlets of Blue Palo Verde. Like the
other species, this Palo Verde is a good honey plant, and its twigs
make important browse for wild animals, like the jack rabbit: in
times of great dearth, it is gnawed by livestock.

THE DESERT
SMOKETREES
(*Dalea*)

Naked, leafless, smoke-gray branches and rigid spine-tipped twigs characterize, for most of the year, this bushy desert tree. Only for a few weeks after the beginning of the rainy season is its foliage to be seen, and this consists in alternate and (in our species) simple and sparsely scattered little blades which are punctate with translucent dots (seen when held to the light). The wistaria-like flowers, appearing after the leaves, in short, few-flowered spikes, have a 5-toothed calyx and clawed petals. The short standard petal is heart-shaped, free of the other petals, and inserted in the bottom of the tubular disk, grown together with the calyx tube. The claws of the wing and keel petals are jointed upon and joined to the tube formed by the cohering filaments of the 10 stamens. The ovary is contracted into a slender style capped with a minute stigma. The 1-seeded small, capsule-like pod is more or less enclosed in the persistent calyx tube and has no natural suture for opening. The kidney-shaped seed possesses a bony coat.

✳   ✳   ✳

DESERT SMOKETREE

Dalea spinosa Gray

OTHER NAMES: Smokethorn Dalea. Indigobush.

RANGE: Low deserts of Sinaloa, Sonora, and Baja California, in Mexico, north in the basin of the Colorado River in western Arizona and eastern California (west to Palm Springs).

DESCRIPTION: *Bark* of trunks dark gray-brown, deeply furrowed on old trees, and roughened with scales. *Twigs* reduced to slender, finely pubescent spines developed from twiggy, rigid branches which in youth are silvery-gray pubescent but become bare when older; roughened with lenticels, and clothed in exfoliating brown bark which, as it peels, reveals the green inner bark. *Leaves* simple, early deciduous, few and irregularly scattered near the base of the branchlets, ¾ to 1 inch long, ⅛ to ⅓ inch wide, hoary-pubescent and usually with a few large glands. *Flowers* appearing in spikes 1 to 1½ inches long from the axils of minute bracts, on a slender hoary rachis; calyx tube 10-ribbed with 5 glands between the dorsal ribs; corolla dark violet blue, about ½ inch long, the standard petal heart-shaped, reflexed, glandular at the base; attached only at base to the wing petals and keel petals; ovary pubescent, with glandular dots. *Pod* thin, 1-seeded, very small, tipped with the remains of the style. *Seed* ⅛ inch long, kidney-shaped and pale brown, sometimes mottled. *Wood* coarse-grained, medium-soft, light (34½ pounds per cubic foot, dry weight), the heartwood rich brown, the sapwood nearly white.

Save for a few brief weeks in summer, when the little Smoketree puts forth the merest token of evanescent foliage — it stands perfectly leafless. But not unclothed or barren, for its twigs, up to their third year, are wrapped in a dense felting of translucent gray hairs. Sometimes the Smoketrees look almost like eastern deciduous trees coated in hoarfrost — but with no glitter to them, only a soft, smoky or silvery halo. Under the desert moon they are positively ghostly.

The Smoketree, which is seen at its best around Palm Springs and below sea level in the Salton Sink, is never much more than 20 feet high, and seldom that; nor does it usually stand up straight — how could it, with its inherent crookedness of growth? — and its thorny boughs are all zigzag. One would expect such a tree to be utterly shapeless, yet it cannot help falling into picturesque attitudes; in its wildly unsymmetrical form it somehow achieves a sort of Japanese artistry. Add to this the dramatic setting of canyon walls and boulder-strewn washes, of dreamy mesas or snow-capped peaks.

When the low deserts are flaming with full summer heat, and all the tourists have departed, the little Smoketree bears its profusion of deep violet-purple flowers, like so many tiny sweet peas in form. From them breathes out a tender fragrance to "waste its sweetness on the desert air," but with few then to praise it.

THE DESERT
IRONWOODS
(*Olneya*)

ARMED WITH stout spines beneath the leaves, the twigs are stout and
hoary-hairy, and the bark is thin and shreddy. The leaves, alternate or
clustered in the upper axils, are evergreen and once-compound with an
odd or even number (10 to 15) leaflets. The flowers, occuring in short,
few-flowered, axillary and hoary-hairy spikes, have a hoary-hairy, 5-
lobed calyx and a wistaria-like corolla with clawed petals which are inserted on the disk; the standard petal, reflexed and deeply notched at
the tip, is circular; the wing petals are oblique and oblong, while the
keel petals are broad, obtuse, and upcurved. There are 10 stamens, 9
of them united by their filaments into a tube. The ovary is surmounted by an inflexed style which is bearded along the middle and
bears a fleshy stigma. The oblique legume (pod) opens by 2 sutures,
the valves becoming thick, leathery and convex at maturity. The seeds
number 1 to 5 to a pod, with thin, light, shining brown coats.

❉   ❉   ❉

DESERT IRONWOOD

Olneya Tesota Gray

OTHER NAME: Tesota.

RANGE: From Sonora and Baja California in Mexico north in the valley of the Colorado River through southwestern Arizona and the low deserts of southeastern California (west to Palm Springs).

DESCRIPTION: *Bark* of trunks red-brown, thin, and peeling in long longitudinal strips. *Twigs* slender and at first coated in a heavy mat of ashen hairs, later in the second season becoming smooth, pale green more or less streaked with red, and in the third season pale brown and armed with very rigid and sharp spines ⅛ to ¼ inch long. *Leaves* once compound, in over-all dimensions 1 to 2½ inches long, ½ to ¾ inch broad, clothed in ashen-hoary pubescence, with 10 to 15 leaflets each ½ to ¾ inch long, broadest at the apex and there notched or coming to a minute tip. *Flowers* in short, axillary, hoary-haired spikes on stout stalklets longer than the hoary calyx; petals clawed, blue or purple, the standard petal flaring up and back and deeply notched, the wing petals free, oblique, oblong, as long as the obtuse, broad, incurved keel petals; stamens 10, 9 of them united at base by their filaments to form a slit tube, the slit filled by the tenth, free stamen; style inflexed and bearded above the middle, with a fleshy stigma. *Pod* 2 to 2½ inches long, light brown, glandular-coated, oblique, leathery, at first compressed, becoming at maturity irregularly convex or lumpy. *Seeds* 1 to 5 in a pod, with thin, shiny chestnut-brown coats. *Wood* extremely heavy (66 pounds per cubic foot, dry weight), hard and strong but brittle with rich dark brown heartwood sometimes streaked with red, and thin, clear yellow sapwood.

If you drop a block of Desert Ironwood into water, it sinks like a plummet of lead. For the specific gravity (that is, its weight compared with an equal volume of water) is 1.14. Or, expressed in terms of a balance scale, Ironwood weighs 66 pounds to the cubic foot. This is heavier than any other western wood, heavier indeed than any wood of North America except the Leadwood of southern Florida, which weighs 81 pounds to the cubic foot. Mahogany, which we think of as the heaviest wood in our ordinary experience, weighs only 45 pounds per cubic foot — something to remember next time you are asked to move furniture. And the specific gravity of this famous tropical timber is only 0.7832; it would float in water, at least when dried. The Desert Ironwood, of course, never, where it grows, meets enough water even to sink in!

Weight, to be sure, is no virtue in a wood, of itself; but it is usually associated with great strength and hardness. The strength of Desert Ironwood may never have been tested; this is said to be a brittle wood, though you will not think so if you try to break a limb off a living tree. But in hardness it is unexcelled, earning its name of Ironwood more thoroughly than any of the other trees that, in other parts of the country, claim the name. The ordinary knifeblade makes as much impression on it as it would on stone — minute slivers may be sliced off, but as for any attempt really to cut it, it defies the ordinary saw and axe driven by muscle. If you find a piece of steel sharp enough to cut Ironwood, the edge will be so fine that it will be turned by the refractory wood. Only a mechanically powered saw or lathe will cut through this wood in a precise plane, and even then the going is very slow.

Once the surface is planed, however, a beautiful figure appears on the quarter-section, the richest walnut-brown with darker brown lines; the tangential section looks much like the figure of Mahogany, though far deeper in tone. If only Desert Ironwood attained larger dimensions it would be a cabinet wood of great value. As it is, it is cut only for book ends and other novelties of the tourist trade. Formerly the desert Indians made arrowheads of it, but how they cut it with stone tools is a matter for wonder.

Ironwood grows more abundantly between Desert Center, California, and the Colorado River than anywhere else. You encounter it elsewhere, to be sure, but on the run from Parker or Blythe to Desert Center and Indio it is the dominant species, abundant at every one of the countless bridges and culverts that span the dry washes down which, a few times a year (or once in many years), the flash floods rush. For the most part it is a shrub, but again and again you see it grown to a tree's estate, sometimes 50 feet tall or more, and with a great spread of many-forked branches that may be 80 feet across. You couldn't, on the desert, ask for a finer pool of shade than is cast by the softly gray-green leaves. They have no cruel glitter to them, either; thickly set, the foliage bestows a deep shade, and that the year around, for it is evergreen. One specimen about 50 miles from Desert Center has a trunk that two men cannot put their arms around; this should make it about 15 feet in circumference. The age of such a giant can only be guessed; it must run into centuries.

Early in the summer, the Ironwood bursts into a glory which you would never expect from a tree that, at all other times, presents such a sober appearance — gray of bark and gray of leaf. For then the flowers appear, thousands of them on every bough, a beautiful deep indigo to rose-purple in shade, much like the corollas of Redbud in form. From the blossoms steals forth on the desert airs a subtle fragrance. Then, when the flowers have faded and fallen on the sands, the new leaves hastily push the old ones off; at this moment Ironwood is as near to being a naked deciduous tree as it ever gets, but it never looks barren, for the tender green of the young leaves clothes it coolly right in the height of the burning summer.

From the time it is young almost every Ironwood struggles with its arch-enemy the mistletoe, for infection often begins early and in the end may result in the death of the tree. The mistletoe berries are carried by that beautiful desert bird the silky flycatcher or phainopepla which devours the berries and then, sailing away on those wings that seem to have a translucent patch in them, alights on another bough where it voids the undigested and still living seeds. These lodge in the Ironwood's rough bark, sprout, and send down root-like suckers that parasitize the host tree. Immense tumor-like growths result; heavier even than normal Ironwood, the abnormal wood of these mistletoe tumors may weigh hundreds of pounds. Sometimes, for no explained reason, the Ironwood exudes great blobs of gummy or gelatinous sap, reddish in color, and said by those who have tasted it to have a pleasant flavor. Bees and hummingbirds come eagerly to sup upon it.

If ever you come upon a procession of rusty red ants marching to and from an Ironwood tree you may notice that those coming away from it are carrying each a tiny leaflet. For these creatures (*Atta desertorum*), are one of the many kinds of leaf-cutting ants, and the purpose of carrying the Ironwood foliage to the nest is not to devour it, but to allow it to molder and so become a culture medium for certain fungi. On the little spongy masses of the hyphal threads of the fungus the ant workers feed, and when the young "princesses" set out on their marriage flights they carry, in pouches in their mouths, a bit of the fungus with which to start the mushroom garden in their new homes. They do not, however, eat of it at all but carefully divide it, as a gardener divides rootstocks, nurturing each mass with a liquid from their bodies until they have raised a brood of worker-daughters. These, led by their instincts, search out an Ironwood tree and gather its leaves to begin manuring the mushroom garden, and so the strange cycle is complete.

THE LOCUSTS
(*Robinia*)

THE MEMBERS of this genus have zigzag twigs without a terminal bud, and small clusters of buds below the leafstalks which are protected by a scale-covering that embraces all the buds in clusters. The once-compound, alternate leaves have an odd number of medium-sized opposite leaflets (and one terminal one) which show untoothed margins and meshed veinlets. The drooping spikes of flowers are borne on long stalks from the leaf axils. The bell-shaped calyx tube is topped by unequal lobes; the wistaria-like corolla has the upper petal enclosing (not enclosed by) the lateral ones, in bud; the petals are short-clawed at base, the uppermost erect and reflexed at tip and, though large, barely longer than the other petals — the oblong-curved wing petals and the incurved, obtuse keel petals. Of the 10 stamens, 9 are united by their stalks into a tube surrounding the styles; the tenth one stands free. The slender style is inflexed and bearded along the inner side near the tip. The drooping pods are thin and papery, nearly stalkless, long and narrow and compressed. The hard-coated seeds are oblique and attached by a stout persistent stalk.

* * *

NEW MEXICAN LOCUST

Robinia neo-mexicana Gray

RANGE: Dry hills and stream banks from southernmost Nevada and south-eastern Utah (Zion National Park) south through northern, central and southeastern Arizona to the Sierra Madre of Sonora and Chihuahua, and from southern Colorado south through New Mexico to the mountains of western Texas.

DESCRIPTION: *Bark* of trunks light brown, thin and slightly furrowed, the ridges with small plate-like scales. *Twigs* slender, zigzag, spiny, at first clammy-hairy, becoming the next season smooth, red-brown, and flecked with scattered, small lenticels. *Leaves* with 15 to 21 short-stalked leaflets, these about 1½ inches long on a stout, pubescent rachis. *Flowers* in short, many-flowered, glandular-hairy spikes that droop on slender, glandular-hairy stalks; corolla pale rose or nearly white, with broad standard and wing petals. *Pods* 3 to 4 inches long, ⅓ inch wide, with a narrow wing. *Seeds* ⅟₁₆ inch long, dark brown and slightly mottled. *Wood* very hard, strong, heavy (50 pounds per cubic foot), the heartwood yellow streaked with brown, the sapwood lighter yellow and thin.

If the New Mexican Locust is but a spiny little tree, never over 25 feet tall, it is at least a beauty when from May to August it hangs out its fragrant, pale lavender or pink or purplish blossoms whose clusters look disproportionately large for so small a tree. Then the New Mexican species greatly resembles its famous eastern relative, the Rose-flowering Locust, one of the most delightful of horticultural subjects. But it looks even more like some sort of wistaria, though not of course a climbing plant. Our desert species is often cultivated in its native land, and because of its rapid growth and its tendencies to sprout from the underground stems and to form dense thickets, it is of great value in preventing erosion. To find it in the wild, seek out north-facing slopes of canyons and mountains where it keeps company with Pinyon, Juniper, Yellow Pine, and Rocky Mountain White Oak. The North Rim of the Grand Canyon is a favorite site, and there its foliage is a favorite browse of the mule deer of the Kaibab Plateau.

The Mescalero and Chiricahua Apaches used to gather the pods in fall and eat them either raw, or cooked and stored like Mesquite pods. The flowers, however, were considered a great delicacy as a vegetable and perhaps, with their store of nectar, we would like them too if we did not so disdain native plants.

THE MILKTREES
(*Sapium*)

THESE TREES are characterized by their leathery, evergreen, simple and alternate leaves and milky sap. The sexes are found in separate flowers on the same plant, each with 2 calyx lobes and no petals. The male flowers, borne in terminal spikes, possess 2 stamens of which the filaments are united at base; the female flowers, solitary or paired at the base of the male spikes, possess a 2-celled ovary. The fruit takes the form of a dry capsule containing large, nearly spherical seeds.

*　　　*　　　*

JUMPINGBEAN–TREE

Sapium biloculare (Watson) Pax

RANGE: Sonora and Baja California, Mexico, north to southwestern Arizona.

DESCRIPTION: *Leaves* leathery and smooth, long-pointed, ¾ to 2½ inches long, finely toothed. *Flowers* stalkless, in zigzag and slender clusters at the ends of the twigs, the male flowers occupying all but the lowest part of the cluster; female flowers one or two at the base of the cluster. *Fruit* a capsule, triangular-heart-shaped when viewed on the broad side, flattened dorsally, ½ inch broad, ultimately splitting. *Seeds* biconvex, 2 in number, ½ inch long, mottled brown and gray.

Who has not heard of the "deadly Upas tree" of the Near East, under whose shade, legend says, it is fatal to sleep? We have no Upas here, but we have the legend, and it is applied to the Jumpingbean-tree. Though it does not slay incautious sleepers with its poisonous breath, at least the smoke from its burning wood will cause sore, red, and swollen eyelids, and to get a drop of the intensely irritant sap into the eyes will be enough to put the sufferer into acute agony for hours. It is not, however, like poison oak irritating merely to touch; it may be handled with impunity as long as the milky sap does not come in contact with the mucous membranes or get into the stomach or blood stream.

The Pima Indians used to stupefy fish by macerating the twigs of this tree, then throwing them into the water. And the Apaches, in the days before they had guns, used to tip their arrows with the venomous juice. The Jumpingbean-tree belongs to a notoriously toxic order, the spurge family. Spurges are used for arrow poisons by the Brazilian Indians, and the related Manchineel tree of the West Indies poisoned the sailors of Columbus's second expedition the first day they went ashore.

If you are anxious to avoid this tree, or just as eager to see it, you will find it nowhere in the United States except from Gila Bend, Arizona, south through the Papago Indian reservation to the Border. Look for it on rocky slopes and in the dry desert washes, where it is fairly common and flowers from March to November, intermittently. But it is scarcely a conspicuous sort of bloom; there are no petals — only the green calyx and the tiny male and female parts. The male flowers give out a perfume, something like that of plumblow — which sounds better than it is; plum flowers are slightly on the fetid side. The flowering spikes have a curious way of ripening; the spike elongates, in the course of the season, flowering as it grows, near the tip, the lower flowers withering, the flowers in each cluster blooming successively.

The name of Jumpingbean comes from the fact that this is one of two sorts of seeds which are commonly inhabited by the restless grubs of the moth *Carpocapsa saltitans*. In their saltations they cause the pods to roll and jerk — to the delight of small boys who buy them at fairs.

THE ELEPHANT–TREES
(*Bursera*)

CHARACTERISTIC of this genus is the balsamic aroma of the resin that pervades the bark. The alternate aromatic leaves (deciduous in our species) are compound, with an odd number of leaflets (7 to 15 in the North American species). The perfect or polygamous or unisexual flowers are borne on clustered stalks in few-flowered clusters or spikes. The minute calyx is 4- or 5-lobed; inserted on the base of a ring-like disk, the 4 or 5 petals are reflexed above the middle. At the base of the disk are also inserted the 8 or 10 stamens; those found in the female flower are functionless. The 3-lobed ovary (rudimentary in the male flowers) terminates in a short style capped by a 3-lobed stigma. The fruit takes the form of a drupe, the outer coat red and 3-angled and splitting naturally into 3 valves; the flesh is leathery; the pit of the fruit (nutlet) is thin-coated and contains a thin-coated seed.

*　　　*　　　*

ELEPHANT–TREE

Bursera microphylla Gray

OTHER NAME: Elephant Bursera.

RANGE: Coasts of the Gulf of California in Mexico, north in the valley of the Colorado to the Gila desert of Arizona and the Imperial Valley of California.

DESCRIPTION: *Bark* of trunks resinous, thin, and firm, the outer layer pale gray, separating into thin red-brown scales; inner bark corky. *Twigs* slender, zigzag, and red, becoming roughened by crowded leaf scars. *Leaves* compound, in over-all dimensions 1 to 1¼ inches long, with some 10 to 20 pairs of thin, smooth, deciduous, opposite leaflets, these about ¼ inch long, 1½ inches wide. *Flowers* in mostly 3-flowered clusters, small (¼ inch long) with minute calyx and 5 white petals, 10 short stamens, and the united styles terminated by the 3-lobed stigma. *Fruit* a solitary, 3-angled drupe ¼ inch long, pendant on the thickened stalk, its skin red and splitting into 3 valves; the thin-walled, 3-angled nutlets gray. *Wood* hard, resinous, pale yellow.

This is not a rare tree in Mexico. There it is called *toroto* and *copal*. It was first discovered in 1860; but in the United States its occurrence was not suspected until about 1910. And the story of its finding goes back, as all good desert campfire stories should, to a mysterious old desert rat who makes a sudden appearance, telling of a strange tree he has found, while prospecting a gypsum mine — a tree with a gray bark bleached nearly white, and boughs like elephants' trunks, and a wood that bleeds like an animal when you cut it. Then, having delivered himself of this information, and leaving in the hands of his listeners a crude map sketched on a grimy slip of paper, the desert rat vanishes into the shimmering heat waves. You've heard the yarn before — connected with gold mines with a curse placed on them by their dead owners, with mysterious caves, and lost tribes of "white" Indians? Even if you have, you are asked, by an eminently grave and respectable scientific periodical, to believe it for this once. And to believe in the reality of Elephant-trees — even white Elephant-trees.

For it was by the near-whiteness of their bark that one Edward H. Davis — the bystander to whom the old desert rat confided the infor-

mation and the map — recognized them when he set forth to find them
and did — along a narrow arroyo tributary to Fish Creek, near Split
Mountain. Even today this is a difficult region, in the desertic eastern
part of San Diego County, California, to travel. It is best reached by
turning south off State Highway 78 at the sun-scorched settlement of
Ocotillo, continuing for about 12 miles to the site of a Navy air base
and about 5 miles further till you reach an area marked on the Automobile Club of Southern California's map of San Diego County "Elephant Tree Area" — wondrous botanical of them! And here it was
that Davis discovered the old desert rat's tree. And its boughs *did* look
like the upraised, curling snouts of elephants! And when stabbed
with a knife, it *did* exude a blood-red sap! And it proved to have not
merely one bark but three — a flaky white outer bark, a thin green
second layer and, under that, a thick mass of red cork.

Not content with one old desert rat, this drama is cast for two. For
though Mr. Davis was pleased enough with his discovery, the world
of science was still only dimly aware that *Busera microphylla* occurred
in the United States. Then, in the nineteen-twenties, another desert
rat — or the same one in disguise — appeared in San Diego and began
to tell tales of a grove of trees out in the remote eastern part of the
county, that looked like a herd of elephants. This old codger, however, vouchsafed no map; like others of his kind he hugged his secret,
and disappeared. But in the autumn of 1937, members of the Scripps
Institution of Oceanography, of the San Diego Museum of Natural
History, and of the state park system began to take rumor seriously
and set forth. A party so heavily weighted with intellect could not
miss of its quarry, and the Elephant-tree was soon rediscovered and
mapped in all of its sporadic occurrences in Fish Creek Canyon, Bow
Willow Canyon, and Canebrake Canyon. It is now known to occur in
Arizona too, from the Salt River Mountains, in Maricopa County, to
the Gila and Tinajas Atlas Mountains of Yuma County, up to 2500
feet above sea level. In Arizona it reaches its maximum development
— up to 20 feet high — within the borders of the United States.

But mere height, or lack of it, can give no idea of the great, fleshy,
dropsical-looking, smooth-barked trunks which start from cracks in
the blazing desert rocks without an apparent vestige of soil or moisture.
At the height of 3 or 4 feet these boles fork into sharply tapering,
brown-barked, curving branches. From these arise abruptly an intricate tangle of very slender, very crooked branchlets, and each of these
gives forth, almost at right angles, very rigid, almost thorn-fine bright

red twigs. Seen against the naked blue of that arid sky, the whole sprawling, half-absurd, half-lovely tree is hard to believe in even when you see it — as is, indeed, an elephant. The spicy-aromatic foliage is oddly delicate for such a ponderous vegetable — almost ferny, though so small and sparse as to cast but little shade. Equally surprising are the summer clusters of whitish or pink flowers and the red drupes, like choke cherries.

Obviously this tree is quite unlike what comes to our minds when we say the word tree. And no wonder, for Elephant-tree is the northernmost member of the Torchwood family, and our tree shows this tropical relationship in being very tender to frost. To this family belongs the plant that yields the frankincense mentioned in the Bible and still burned in Roman Catholic churches. Elephant-tree, too, is aromatic, and exudes a gum — that red blood mentioned by the anonymous prospector — used in Mexico for a great variety of handy purposes. — as a varnish base and a wood preservative, as a remedy in venereal diseases and an adhesive. A fragrant oil extracted from the wood is reported to be burned as incense in Mexican churches.

Bursera odorata T. S. Brandegee, is an extremely fragrant species of Mexico which crosses the frontier into Arizona and is found on the western foothills of the Baboquivari Mountains, where so many rare little tropical trees are found. The foliage has the odor of tangerine peel, while the bark of old trunks is gray-brown and peels off in thin papery sheets, like a Birch's. The flowers bloom in July.

THE MAPLES
(*Acer*)

MAPLE LEAVES are opposite on the twig and either simple and deeply lobed, with 3 to 7 principal nerves arising from the base, or, in the Box Elder group, pinnately compound. In falling, the leafstalks leave small U-shaped scars on the roundish twig. The buds are scaly, the inner scales marking the base of the twig with ring-like scars. The flowers are regular and usually have the sexes in separate flowers or on separate trees, or frequently some perfect or bisexual flowers are found amongst the unisexual. The calyx, which is generally colored, has 5 separate or united sepals. The petals are lacking, or, if present, are 5 in number and distinct from each other. In the center of the flower is a ring-like fleshy disk. The stamens number 4 to 10. The ovary is 2-lobed, with 2 styles between the lobes that are coherent below but divergent above into 2 stigmatic branches. The fruit is composed of 2 separable samaras (the familiar "keys" of Maples) which consist in nut-like, laterally flattened carpels furnished with a long, papery, veiny wing which is broader near the outer end.

*　　　*　　　*

BIGLEAF MAPLE

Acer macrophyllum Pursh

OTHER NAMES: Oregon, Broadleaf, or White Maple.

RANGE: Mountain valleys and rocky slopes, stream banks and bottom-
lands from the islands and mainland coasts of British Columbia through
Washington and Oregon west of the Cascade Mountains and south in
the Coast Ranges of California to San Diego County, and on the west
slopes of the Sierra Nevada between 2000 and 5000 feet; also on the south
slope of the San Bernardino Mountains.

DESCRIPTION: *Bark* of the trunk brown or bright reddish brown, deeply
furrowed, and broken into small scaly plates. *Twigs* stout and smooth,
at first pale green, becoming in their first winter bright green or dark
red and flecked with small white longitudinal lenticels, finally turning in
the second year gray or grayish brown. *Winter buds* obtuse, the terminal
with dark red, hairy-fringed, broad and spreading scales, the inner scales
becoming in spring green, leafy, and 1½ inches long. *Leaves* 8 to 12
inches wide and long, somewhat leathery at maturity and dark green and
shining above, pale below, deeply but unequally 5-lobed, the lowest
pair of lobes small, the terminal lobe sometimes again 3-lobed; stalks
10 to 12 inches long, their enlarged bases united in opposite pairs to
encircle the twig and sometimes with little tufts of white hairs on the
inside. *Flowers* in graceful, thickly flowered, drooping spikes 4 to 6
inches long, the male and female flowers in the same spike; blossoms ¼
inch long, bright yellow, fragrant; sepals petal-like, obtuse, a little larger
than the spatulate petals; stamens 9 to 10, their long slender filaments
hairy at base and bearing orange anthers; female flowers containing minute stamens and a hoary ovary bearing styles barely united at base, and
long stigmas. *Fruit* with wings 1½ inches long, ½ inch wide, slightly
divergent, the edges thickened; nutlets covered with long pale hairs,
containing the dark pitted seeds ¼ inch long. *Wood* close-grained, weak,
soft, and light (30½ pounds per cubic foot, dry weight), the heartwood
rich brown tinged with red, the sapwood very thick and nearly white.

There is not a finer part of the world than the country around Puget
Sound and the lower gorge of the Columbia River, where ocean and
snow-capped volcanic cones, a mighty river, river-like arms of the sea,
and magnificent forests all meet, so that every view is breath-taking in
its splendor. In summer, when the air is dry and glittering, the wind

is but a pleasant breeze, the light brilliant but softened everywhere by forest leaves, every step you take is easy, every breath you draw is exhilarating. And here it is that this noble Maple is at home. You see it lining the roadsides, growing in the streets of small towns and the dooryards of farms, following the windings of the clear cold streams, crowding the islands with its great domes of foliage.

Nor could there be a finer shade tree than this, for each leaf is frequently a foot long (and broad), and yet, deeply lobed as the blades are, they do not form an oppressive shade — windless and somber — but they act, rather, like lattices, letting the light through but not the heat of the day. On their very long stalks, the blades stir and spin vivaciously in the breeze. A great old tree, standing in the open with room to develop its full form, will so dispose each bough, each branch, each leaf, that all the leaves shade each other as little as possible, yet all together these immense leaves shade the resting cattle, the playing child, to the utmost.

In winter, when all the light and warmth available are most needed, this deciduous tree, of course, stands conveniently naked. Then we see the full perfection of its form, with short, sturdy trunks 2 and 3 feet in diameter, or even 5 feet in exceptional and venerable specimens, the boughs themselves the picture of strength and benignancy, the branches inclined to be upright, the twigs dark red or bright green against the winter sky. In early spring the big terminal winter buds begin to open, the outer red scales peeling back almost as brilliant as petals; then the green leafy inner scales begin to show, like the calyx of a flower. The leaves are at first downy and much crumpled and wrinkled, yet already possessed of their elegant, cut-leaved appearance. When the leaves are about three-fourths grown, in late April or early May, the flowers at last appear. They light up the tree with brilliant effect, bright yellow as they are, and drooping gracefully in long, heavy racemes. Summer finds the leaves fully expanded, a delicious light green becoming gradually darker. Then, in autumn, they turn color. The hue in the Pacific Northwest is a bright orange-yellow. In California it is a pale yellow, but even there it is a lovely note, translucent and, when the sunlight comes slanting through the mighty Redwoods overhead, almost angelic. So the annual cycle of this Maple's beauty is unbroken; when the tree again stands bare, it is seen at first to be covered with the fruits — the "keys" or winged samaras which, cut adrift at last, go gliding and twirling away on their errand of reproduction. In the cities, however, where the evening grosbeaks —

silent now, dull of plumage and heavy-billed — love to congregate in winter, the keys are usually stripped early from the trees. Squirrels are also persistent devourers of the fruits.

Naturally so fine a tree attracted the attention of all the early botanical explorers in the Northwest. Archibald Menzies, surgeon-botanist of the Vancouver Expedition, was the first scientist to collect specimens, Lewis and Clark were the first Americans to do so. It was David Douglas, however, who dispatched seeds of this tree to England where it soon became prized in cultivation. Thomas Nuttall, the shy and reclusive professor of botany at Harvard who yet undertook western exploration in the earliest days of penetration by the fur trade, was the first to describe its beauty and to give us an illustration of it in his *North American Sylva* — or, rather, the two volumes that he added to the work of that name begun by François André Michaux before the West was opened up for exploration.

The West is in general poor in hardwoods yielding high quality lumber, but Bigleaf Maple is an exception, producing several million board feet a year for use in furniture, interior finish, flooring, and boat-building. The best timber is not cut from trees in deep, coniferous woods, for these are apt to be spindling in competition with the mighty conifers, but from specimens grown in more open Maple groves. Curly and bird's-eye figures occasionally appear and are at once sent to the veneer knives for their high value. In the pioneering days in the Northwest, curly Maple gun stocks were highly prized, both by the Hudson Bay Company men and the Indians. Second-growth saplings were a favorite for single-trees in the days of wagon-building. And the Indians of Oregon and California made canoe paddles of this wood. Sugar has been made from the sap, and the nectar of the flowers is sought by honey bees.

WESTERN SUGAR MAPLE

Acer saccharum Marshall, variety *grandidentatum* (Nuttall) Sudworth

OTHER NAMES: Bigtooth, or Hard Maple.

RANGE: Mountains of northwestern Montana; mountains and sides of canyons of western Utah, extreme southeastern Idaho and southwestern

Wyoming; southern Colorado to western Texas and northern Mexico, and in Arizona quite general in the mountains (between 5000 and 8000 feet altitude) of the eastern and southeastern part of the state.

DESCRIPTION: *Bark* thin, dark brown, separating into plate-like scales. *Twigs* slender, bright red and smooth, encircled by narrow leaf scars bearing conspicuous bands of hairs. *Winter buds* terminal, sharp, bright red-brown, the outer scales hairy-margined. *Leaves* 2 to 5 inches across, 3- or 5-lobed, the lobes again distinctly lobed or large-toothed, dark green and shining above, pale and often pubescent below, on stout smooth stalks. *Flowers* polygamous, small, ¼ inch across, drooping on long slender stalklets in short-stalked clusters; petals none; sepals united into a yellow calyx; stamens 7 to 8; ovary usually smooth. *Fruit* ½ to 1 inch long, the wings divergent or nearly parallel, in summer rosy, but green at maturity; seed about ¼ inch long. *Wood* heavy, hard and close-grained, the heartwood light brown to nearly white, the sapwood white and thick.

This fine Maple, with its hard wood, its beautiful autumnal colors — red and yellow and orange — and its sweet sap, is the close western relative of the famed Sugar Maple of the eastern states. If it were as abundant as the true Sugar Maple and grew as accessibly, it would doubtless be an important hardwood lumber tree. But its habitat is in canyons and along the banks of mountain streams where it is unlikely that the saws will ever seek it while the eastern tree holds out.

This Maple grows as much as 60 feet high, with a short stout trunk 3 and 4 feet thick, and at all times makes a handsome appearance. The leaves, though not as large as those of the Bigleaf Maple, are nevertheless deliciously shady. The flowers appear with or even before the leaves in spring, drooping on the ends of the twigs, and are soon followed by the beautiful rose-colored "keys" — the double, winged samaras.

The SOUTHWESTERN MAPLE, *Acer brachypterum* Wooton and Standley, found in the San Luis Mountains of southwestern New Mexico, is distinguished by the only slightly lobed or nearly entire leaves, the glabrous leaf scars, and the shorter wing of the fruit (⅜ to ¾ inch long). It is a small tree, with very smooth pale bark, at least in the young trees.

VINE MAPLE

Acer circinatum Pursh

OTHER NAME: Mountain Maple.

RANGE: Coast of British Columbia (including Vancouver Island and the Fraser River Valley) south through the parts of Washington and Oregon lying west of the Cascades (up to 5000 feet in the Siskiyou Mountains) and in northern California (Mendocino County on the coast to Modoc County in the east), the Trinity Mountains and the headwaters of the Sacramento River.

DESCRIPTION: *Bark* of the trunk thin, smooth, bright red-brown and scored with many shallow seams. *Twigs* smooth from the first, pale green to reddish brown, sometimes flecked with a few lenticels. *Winter buds* blunt, with thin, bright red outer scales, the inner contracted to a long narrow claw and bright rose in hue, becoming in spring 2 inches long. *Leaves* 2 to 7 inches in diameter, almost circular in outline when fully expanded, with 7 to 9 palmate lobes of unequal size, the basal the smallest; thin and filmy in texture, completely hairless except for tufts in the axils of the veins on the pale undersides, the upper surface dull dark green; stalks 1 to 2 inches long, stout, grooved, clasping the twig by their enlarged bases. *Flowers* in loosely 10- to 20-flowered, branched clusters, drooping on long stems from the ends of slender, 2-leaved twigs; male and female blossoms produced in the same cluster; sepals purple or red and much longer than the greenish white, broadly heart-shaped petals; stamens 6 to 8, exserted beyond the petals in the male flowers, but much reduced in length in the female; ovary with spreading lobes and style divided nearly to the base into long stigmas. *Fruit* with thin wings 1½ inches long and diverging almost at right angles, red or rose color, as are the nutlets; seeds smooth, ⅛ to ¼ inch long, pale brown. *Wood* hard but not very strong, heavy (41½ pounds per cubic foot, dry weight), with light brown heartwood and thick pale sapwood.

The most gorgeous autumn colors of all the Northwest are those displayed by this little tree, which makes up in abundance what it lacks in stature — never more than 35 feet high. One hardly realizes, as one travels through the Northwest in summer, admiring the gigantic conifers and seeing everywhere the splendid Bigleaf Maples, that the interstices in the forest are filled with untold millions of Vine Maples. But when in fall they display their blazing red and gold against the blue October sky, with a high wind tearing at the leaves, the lake and river waters whipped to whiteness, the raucous clamor of crows ringing above the woods — then the Vine Maple becomes the very spirit of the bright, chill wilderness.

This tree gets its odd name from its intermittent habit of sprawling on the ground like a running lasso for sometimes 20 and 30 feet. The early French *coureurs du bois* in western Canada called it, for this reason, *bois du diable,* from its devilish habit of tripping up the canoemen as they plodded, heavily laden, weary and half unseeing where they stepped, along the portage trails.

The Vine Maple comes up abundantly in logged-off tracts, in old "burns," along abandoned lumber trails. Sometimes it entwines with its liana-like stems the abandoned logs and the trunks of other trees downed by windstorms, making the going doubly difficult. Again it stands erect, in little clumps, like young Aspens. Its star-shaped,

trembling, twinkling foliage has indeed something almost Aspen-like in quality if not in shape. But there is always a characteristic touch of red about the Vine Maple, for vigorous young shoots are constantly displaying their bright red twigs, and the "keys" or samaras are rosy red too. There has never been any utilization of this little tree by the lumber industry, despite the tough, close-grained, sometimes beautifully figured wood. Indeed the lumberman looks on it with contempt for its spindling stems; to him it is a weed tree. However, David Douglas, back in the early days of the Northwest, found that the Indians employed its slender branches in making the scoop nets with which they took salmon at the rapids and narrows of the rivers.

DWARF MAPLE

Acer glabrum Torrey

OTHER NAMES: Mountain, Rocky Mountain, Soft, Shrubby, Sierra, or Bark Maple.

RANGE: From southeastern coastal Alaska southward throughout the mountains of British Columbia and in the Rockies (including the Big Horns) to southwestern New Mexico, and southern Arizona; almost throughout the mountains of Washington; south through Oregon to the Siskiyou Mountains and Sierra Nevada of California (as far south as Kern County), but not in the Coast Ranges. Also in the Black Hills of South Dakota and Sioux County, Nebraska. At sea level in the northern part of its range, gradually ascending to higher altitudes in the south; at 5000 to 8000 feet in Arizona and southern California.

DESCRIPTION: *Bark* of the trunks smooth, thin, dark reddish brown. *Twigs* slender, smooth, many-angled, at first pale greenish brown, becoming in their first winter bright red-brown. *Winter buds* with scales of a yellow or bright red hue, the inner ones pale brown tinged with pink and hairy on the inner surface, becoming in spring 1½ inches long. *Leaves* thin, smooth, 3 to 5 inches broad, 3-lobed, sometimes broadly, sometimes narrowly so, sometimes shallowly, sometimes so deeply as to appear 3-leaved or "cutleaf," the middle lobe sometimes again 3-lobed or 3-parted or even divided into leaflets, the upper surface dark green and shining, the lower paler or even becoming glaucous, with conspicuous veinlets; leafstalk 1 to 6 inches long, often bright red, stout and grooved. *Flowers* in terminal, drooping, loosely few-flowered clusters; blossoms about ⅛ inch long; male and female flowers usually found on separate trees;

sepals petal-like **7** or **8**, with unequal smooth filaments shorter than the petals; ovary smooth, obtusely lobed, bearing a style divergent to the base into **2** stigmatic lobes as long as the petals. *Fruit* with erect (parallel) or slightly spreading wings ¾ to 1 inch long, ⅓ to ½ inch wide, in the summer slightly rose-colored; seeds ¼ inch long, bright chestnut-brown. *Wood* close-grained, hard, heavy (37½ pounds per cubic foot, dry weight), the heartwood light brown or nearly white, the sapwood thick and whitish.

Dwarf Maple in the Puget Sound region grows as much as 40 feet high, but much of the time it is much less impressive and is even reduced to the status of a shrub. As if crowded out by its mighty relative the Bigleaf Maple, this dwarf takes to poor, thin, gravelly soil in the mountains, clings to rocky cliffs and canyon sides, and joins the Alders along the mountain creeks. It seldom grows in groups, but scattered meekly among the bigger hardwoods and still mightier conifers. Never does it develop anything but a spindling trunk, and its life is probably very short — no more than the average man's. But no Maple can help being beautiful and even this one is no exception, with its bicolored leaves spinning gracefully on the long, slim, bright red stalks. In autumn the foliage is a clear gold and even in early spring there is a touch of color in the winter buds, a brilliant red as the outer scales begin to curl back.

BOX ELDER

Acer Negundo Linnæus

OTHER NAMES: Ash-leaved or Manitoba Maple. Sugar Ash.

RANGE: From central Texas north to southern Manitoba, western and southern New England, westward through southern Ontario to British Columbia and eastern Washington State, Nevada and Arizona, south to Florida, Texas and northern Mexico. Also in central and southern California.

DESCRIPTION: *Bark* thin, light brown or pale gray, soon scaly and furrowed. *Twigs* slender, limber, and pale green or bluish-gray or violet with scars left by winter buds encircling the twig. *Leaves* compound, with 3 to 11 leaflets, the terminal often very deeply 3-lobed; the leaflets 2½ to 4 inches long and 1½ to 2½ inches broad, light green above, paler and sometimes hairy on the veins of the lower surface. *Flowers* expanding just before or with the leaves, male and female always on separate trees, the female in drooping spikes, with the style separating from the base into 2 long stigmatic lobes, the male in close clusters each with 4 to 6 stamens; calyx greenish and 5-lobed. *Fruit* ("keys") drooping in long spikes, the nutlets narrow, the wings broad, veiny, and rather convergent. *Wood* soft, close-grained, weak, brittle, and very light (27 pounds to the cubic foot, dry weight), with sapwood and heartwood nearly white and scarcely distinguishable.

The Box Elder probably takes its name from its elder-like leaves and its white wood like that of Box. The foliage would make one think of some sort of cut-leaf Ash. Yet this tree's nearest relatives are undoubtedly the Maples, as is shown by its flowers, pendent on long stalks in early spring, and its autumnal crop of fruits, the typical double samara of the Maples.

In the states east of the Missouri, Box Elder is not considered a tree of any importance in the wild; it is simply one of the common trees of riverbanks, especially of slow and muddy streams, never associated with clear, cool rushing water; there it mingles with Willows, Cottonwoods, and Sycamores, most of which far outclass it in size and beauty and in the affections of eastern people. In cultivation it does rather better; the biggest Box Elder of record is one grown at White Plains, New York, having a spread of 102 feet, a height of 75 feet, and a circumference around the trunk at breast height of 19 feet, 11 inches — a very fine shade tree, by any standard. At one time Box Elder was extensively planted, indeed much over-planted, by persons seeking a quick and cheap effect for mushrooming Middle Western communities. But though it does soon begin to give a respectable amount of shade, it is a short-lived tree; its weak wood, worthless except for fuel, undistinguished in color and grain, all too easily splits when violated by wind and sleet storms; its leaves, in the eastern states, generally turn crisp and brown in fall, without ever assuming any of the beautiful autumnal tints of the Maples. Thus, in every respect, Box Elder in the East seems but a poor relation of the aristocratic Maples. Says the Kansas State Board of Agriculture in a bulletin on trees of that state: "There is no excuse for planting this tree." Yet excuses might be found, not the least of them that many people appreciate its resistance to heat, cold, drought, and ceaseless winds that would soon kill species with more exalted reputations. And even in winter it has its charms, with those smooth bright green twigs that bear, so precociously, in early spring the curious flowers.

But in the West, on the Great Plains and the southwestern deserts, in the hot interior valleys of California, any shade begins to look good — especially the wide-spreading, cool shade of a filmy-leaved deciduous tree like this one. The deciduous habit is valuable, of course, as admitting light and any warmth there is in the winter months, while providing a parasol in summer. No wonder that the Box Elder's name is pronounced gratefully wherever, in the West, it grows beside some watering spot for cattle, or at the ranch-house door, or along the roads and highways, in the school playground, or on the small-town street.

More, the Box Elder in its western varieties, especially in Colorado, New Mexico, Utah and Arizona, sometimes takes on a particularly lovely form. Probably this is indefinable, and partly subjective, or associated with the beauty of the surroundings. But its charms are real where in some of the gorges of the Colorado Rockies, for instance, the commonly sprawling habits of this tree seem corrected by the strictures of the sheer canyon walls and the competition of other trees, till the Box Elders stand straight and graceful as eastern forest-grown hardwoods, and the breezes that sweep above the dashing water set the frondose foliage to dancing in a way one never sees beside the lazy rivers of the lowlands.

In the West, Box Elder often taken on beautiful autumnal tints. In Arizona it is sometimes a rich red, almost worthy of one of the true Maples. A soft light yellow is not uncommon, and occasionally in some of the darker, moister canyons, or when closely pressed upon by conifers, Box Elder in Colorado will assume the very palest of translucent yellows, or almost a white, when, after an autumn rain, the sunlight steals through the foliage. Later you will see Box Elder leaves drifting into the trout pools of the mountain streams, piling up upon some rocky reef, swirling away like doomed galleons on the current.

Most Easterners would never imagine that Box Elder yields a sweet sap, like Maple syrup. Yet it does. The sugar is fine-grained and white, but is not so sweet as that of the Sugar Maple, and more is required to make the same quantity of sugar. However, writes Melvin Randolph Gilmore, "This tree was used also for sugar making by all the tribes [of the Missouri River basin]. The Dakota and Omaha and probably the other tribes used boxelder wood to make charcoal for ceremonial painting of the person and for tattooing. Previous information as to the making of sugar from sap of this tree pertained, among the Pawnee and Omaha, only to times now many years in the past; but it has been found that among some tribes sugar is still made from this source. In September, 1916, the writer found a grove of trees on the Standing Rock Reservation in North Dakota, of which every tree of any considerable size showed scars of tapping which had been done the previous spring in sugar making." [1]

The West boasts several varieties (hereinafter enumerated, as lawyers say), of the widespread Box Elder. The differences between them are genuine enough, but they are strictly botanical; they involve slight variations in the shape and size of the leaflets, in the texture and veininess of the foliage, in presence or absence of pubescence, but in no way do they affect the physiognomy of the trees. The most striking variation that one sees between one specimen of Box Elder and another is in the number of leaflets, which varies from 3 to 7, but this variation may be found in any part of the country and does not link up constantly with other variable characteristics, hence it does not serve well as a basis for distinguishing varieties. It has seemed best, therefore, to give above a generalized description that would fit all western Box Elders, leaving to the end a discussion of their distinguishing points:

WESTERN BOX ELDER, *Acer Negundo* variety *interius* (Britton) Sargent, is the most widespread of all the western varieties, ranging from southern parts of Alberta and Saskatchewan south, along riverbanks on the high plains of Montana, Wyoming and Colorado, and in the valleys, canyons, and foothills of the Rockies from Montana south

[1] "Uses of Plants by the Indians of the Missouri River Region," Bureau of American Ethnology, *Thirty-third Annual Report, 1911–1912.* (1919).

to New Mexico and Arizona. It also occurs in the Black Hills of South Dakota and Wyoming. It differs from the generalized description of the species, above, in having the twigs variously pubescent or hairy, and the fruit on pubescent stalks, while the leaflets, usually only 3 in number, are thickish in texture. This variety is most closely related to the California Box Elder, below, but the California tree differs in having the leafstalks and stalks of the leaflets hoary-woolly.

The CALIFORNIA BOX ELDER, *Acer Negundo* variety *californicum* (Torrey and Gray) Sargent, is a closely related variety, found in the valley of the Sacramento River, the western foothills of the

Sierra Nevada and the valleys of the central Coast Ranges to Santa Barbara County, and in the lower part of the canyons of the San Bernardino Mountains of southern California. It is a tree 20 to 50 feet high, with dark bark, hoary-hairy twigs and winter buds, the 3 leaflets long-oval to rhombic, long-acute at tip, wedge-shaped or unsymmetrically rounded at base, the margin coarsely toothed above the middle or almost without teeth or sometimes deeply lobed, the upper surface smooth except along the lightly downy midribs and nerves, the lower thickly coated with pale matted hairs and furnished in the axils of the veins with large tufts of long pale hairs. The texture of the foliage is thickish and veiny, just as in the Western Box Elder.

The EASTERN BOX ELDER, *Acer Negundo* (proper), occurs as far west as the western parts of the Dakotas, Nebraska and Kansas and occasionally in the Rockies (Colorado Springs, Colorado, and Nez Percé County, Idaho). It is distinguished from the foregoing varieties by the texture of the foliage which is thin, not thickish; there are 3 to 7 leaflets, and the margins, though sometimes intact or toothed only above the middle, are usually doubly toothed all around. Two and a half to 4 inches long and 1½ to 2½ inches wide, the leaflets are light green and smooth above at maturity and paler beneath and covered, especially along the veins and midribs with long soft hairs. The fruit hangs in drooping spikes 6 to 8 inches long. The Eastern Box Elder forms a tree up to 60 feet tall with brown, ultimately furrowed bark on the old trunks; the twigs are slender and either pale clear green or covered with a violet bloom.

THE HORSE CHESTNUTS

(*Æsculus*)

THE MEMBERS of this group have ill-smelling inner bark and opposite, palmately compound and deciduous leaves which in falling mark the stout twigs with big triangular leaf scars. The flowers are unisexual, the male and female found on the same tree but in separate flower clusters, though sometimes perfect or bisexual flowers are found near the base of the cluster. Usually the calyx is 5-lobed, the lobes often unequal, oblique, and inflated on the back. There are 4 or 5 petals, narrowed at base to a claw, and usually 6 to 8 stamens of unequal length but all free from each other and inserted on the disk. The ovary is 3-celled with a long, slender, curved style. Fruit takes the form of a roughened, leathery, thick-walled capsule, opening by 3 valves to allow the fall of the big chestnut-brown, dark, smooth and shining seed.

*　　　*　　　*

CALIFORNIA BUCKEYE

Æsculus california (Spach) Nuttall

OTHER NAME: Horse Chestnut.

RANGE: Foothills and valleys of the California Coast Ranges from Mendocino County south to San Luis Obispo County, and on the lower western slopes (up to 5000 feet) of the Sierra Nevada from the region of Mount Shasta in the north all the way to the Tehachapi Pass in the south and Antelope Valley and the Cañada de las Uvas near Fort Tejon.

DESCRIPTION: *Bark* of trunks smooth, light gray or nearly white. *Twigs* stout, hairless from the first, pale reddish brown becoming darker in the second season, marked with conspicuous triangular leaf scars. *Winter buds* large, sharp, with dark brown narrow scales rounded on the back and thickly coated with resin. *Leaves* on grooved slender stalks 3 to 4 inches long, with 5 (sometimes 4, 6, or 7) leaflets, these 4 to 6 inches long, 1½ to 2 inches wide, the upper surface dark green, the lower paler. *Flowers* 1 to 1¼ inches long, pale rose to white, in long-branched, long-stemmed, densely flowered, 1-sided, erect clusters 3 to 9 inches long; calyx 2-lobed, much shorter than the narrow petals; stamens 5 to 7, with long filaments extruded from the flower and bright orange anthers; ovary densely pubescent. *Pod* pear-shaped, 2 to 3 inches long, with thin, smooth, pale brown valves which split at last and release the solitary pale orange-brown seed. *Wood* very close-grained, soft, light (31 pounds per cubic foot, dry weight), white or faintly tinged with red.

This oddly beautiful little tree is an inhabitant of the Coast Ranges of central California and the dry foothills of the central Sierra Nevada, where the Forty-niners were the first English-speaking Americans to know it well. They gave it — for its great green pear-shaped pods — the name (perhaps derisive) of "California Pear." It is also, of course, a Horse Chestnut, generally speaking, and that too is possibly derisive, for the big, glossy seeds do indeed look like chestnuts, and look deceptively appetizing, but in fact are inedible and even poisonous unless properly cooked. The name of Buckeye is apt, though; well might one say that the seeds are like the great melting brown orbs of the deer.

And, under all names, this is an oddly lovely little tree. One sees it in abundance on the famed Skyline Drive that goes looping over the high grassy knobs which cap the Coast Ranges just south of San

Francisco, and in the shelters and hollows of the highlands, forever swept by the sea winds, of western Marin County just north of the Golden Gate. Probably the biggest and oldest specimens are to be seen on the Alder flats of the Point Reyes peninsula near Inverness, but there are fine groves of it along the lower course of the Kaweah River where that stream descends from the Sierra Nevada into the burning San Joaquin Valley.

Amid all the somber needle-leaved evergreens of central California, and the glittering broad-leaved evergreens, the Buckeye makes a striking contrast. Barren of leaves for one half of the year, like certain eastern hardwoods, the pale gray and crooked boughs are refreshing and always full of individual character, for no two Buckeyes are anything alike. Each is contorted in its own way. In general the outline of the tree is that of a low, broad dome, but wherever the sea winds reach it, they sculpture it or clip it with a sort of wild topiary, or force it to conform to the hollow of the hill where the tree seems to crouch in refuge.

A Buckeye 40 feet tall is unusually high, but that is not for lack of years. It is popularly said that it takes a Buckeye 100 years to mature, and that it lives at least another hundred without making much growth except the slow and subtle increase in thickness of trunk and boughs. Frequently, where conditions are arid, it never attains more than 12 feet in height and takes on the many-stemmed form of a shrub.

Unfortunately, most Californians do not appreciate the Buckeye as a domestic tree; the saying goes that you should never have one unless you like to rake leaves. The dropping of the big seeds — horse chest-nuts — and the still bigger green pods seems to annoy intensely those who want their Nature tidied like a drawing room, and some have the dooryard Buckeye hewn down and think they have made the world a better place.

Yet this is one of the most beautiful of western hardwoods, not only in its shining nakedness — which lasts from late summer to February — but in spring when the refreshing pale green of the quaint, com-pound leaves is first seen, and in early summer when the trees are covered with thousands of fragrant or rosy blossoms in great cande-labra-like spires, till in autumn the curious pods hang from the boughs, and, breaking open, let loose the seeds. Poisonous to cattle and hu-mans, these seeds were yet a staple in the diet of the California Indians. For, by leaching out the poisonous principle with boiling water, the Indians obtained an innocuous sweet starch of which a nutritious flour was made. The nectar of the flowers, however, has been charged with poisoning bees.

In autumn the leaves turn a dull sear brown, without any particu-lar glory, yet picturesque to the last. The wood, though it has no reputation in the lumber business, is very long-lasting, even in contact with the soil, and hence makes a fine fence-post material that has been appreciated for a century in the foothill ranching country where it delights to grow.

THE SOAPBERRIES

(*Sapindus*)

Growth of the Soapberries takes place from small axillary buds which are superposed in pairs, the upper bud larger. Fleshy thick roots, alternate, compound leaves, and minute unisexual flowers in erect, open, branched and ample clusters characterize these trees. Sometimes a few flowers are bisexual. The 4 or 5 unequal calyx lobes are slightly united at base but free from the ovary, which terminates in a columnar style with 3 or 4 spreading stigma lobes. The petals, 4 or 5 in number, are regular and clawed at base. The fruit takes the form of a leathery berry containing 1 to 3 bony-coated, dark seeds, each with a tuft of silky hairs at the point of attachment.

❋ ❋ ❋

WESTERN SOAPBERRY

Sapindus Saponaria Linnæus, variety *Drummondi*
(Hooker and Arnot) Benson

OTHER NAMES: Wild Chinatree. Wild Ligustrum.

RANGE: From Southwestern Missouri west to southern Colorado and central Arizona and south to Louisiana and northern Mexico.

DESCRIPTION: *Bark* bitter and astringent, red-brown and thin, furrowed into long scaly plates. *Twigs* stout, round, with a large pithy cylinder, at first pale yellowish green, later gray and marked by many small lenticels and numerous inversely heart-shaped leaf scars. *Leaves* deciduous, compound, with an even number of leaflets (4 to 9 pairs) the leaflets 2 to 3 inches long, ½ to ⅔ inches wide, leathery, veiny, pale yellow-green. *Flowers* minute, in large, open, branched clusters 6 to 9 inches long; petals white, contracted into a claw and furnished with scales at base, hairy on the inner surface; male flowers with 8 to 10 stamens. *Fruit* a 1- to 3-seeded drupe-like berry ½ inch thick, containing the solitary dark brown seed in its smooth bony coat. *Wood* hard, strong, very heavy (52 pounds to the cubic foot, dry weight), with light brown heartwood and thick whitish sapwood.

Up from the sylva of old Mexico, all the way to Missouri extends the range of this odd tree, growing up to 50 feet high, with a trunk as much as two feet thick. It is not so odd in leaf, when the foliage puts out in March or April, nor as to its flowers, which bloom in May and

June. But its great erect clusters of translucent fruits, looking like yellow cherries or grapes, are indeed astonishing and handsome. Early explorers of the Southwest commonly took these for the fruits of the Chinaberry (*Melia Azedarach*) and refer to it as "Wild China" in their narratives.

These fruits yield ingredients used in the preparation of varnish and floor wax. Because they contain 37 per cent saponin,[1] the fruits, macerated in water, work up into powerful suds. The Spanish found the Indians already well acquainted with the saponifying properties of these fruits; the Aztecs washed their clothes with it, and Mexican women still do so at the village fountain. In popular medicine the fruits have been used as a febrifuge, and in the treatment of rheumatism and kidney disease, but are not official drugs of the American pharmacy. That they are poisonous is quite certain; they cause a dermatitis in some persons on mere contact, are left alone by cattle, and have been used for stupefying fish. The nectar of the flowers is also probably poisonous, since that of closely related species kills whole hives of bees that store it. The seeds, hard and dark as they are, are in Mexico often strung into rosaries. Because the wood splits easily, it has been used for the making of cotton picker's baskets and for the frames of pack saddles.

[1] According to Francisco Hernández in the *Historia de las Plantas de Nueva España* (1571–1575).

THE BUCKTHORNS

(*Rhamnus*)

Buckthorns display (in our species) no thorns, and have alternate, simple leaves, and bisexual small flowers in simple axillary clusters or spikes, the bell-shaped calyx 4- or 5-lobed, the minute petals inserted on the edge of the disk from which the ovary stands free. The styles, with their spreading, stigmatic lobes, are somewhat united at base. The fruit, a berry-like drupe, has thick, juicy flesh and contains 2 to 4 separable cartilaginous nutlets which enclose the grooved, thin-coated seeds.

*   *   *

CASCARA BUCKTHORN

Rhamnus Purshiana De Candolle

OTHER NAMES: Cascara Sagrada. Bearberry. Bearwood. Pigeonberry. Bayberry. Yellowwood. Shittimwood. Bitterbark. Wild, Western, or California Coffee. Coffeebark. Coffeeberry.

RANGE: Vancouver Island and southern British Columbia south in almost all the mountains of Washington, and, at moderate elevations, in all but the desert ranges of Oregon, south along the coast of California to Mendocino County and in the Sierra Nevada to Bear Valley, Nevada County; in the Bitterroot Mountains of Idaho.

DESCRIPTION: *Bark* thin, scaly, gray to dark brown often tinged with red. *Twigs* slender, yellow-green or red-brown, marked with oval, elevated, horizontal leaf scars. *Winter buds* all lateral, small, naked and hoary-hairy. *Leaves* 2½ to 8 inches long, thin, deciduous, prominently veiny. *Flowers* on slender stalks in small clusters in the axils of the shoots of the year, the small calyx bell-shaped with 5 spreading lobes, the 5 petals minute, deeply notched, folded around the short stamens; stigma 2- or 3-lobed. *Fruit* a berry-like black drupe ⅓ to ½ inch thick, with thin juicy flesh and 2 or 3 gray or greenish bony nutlets enclosing the seeds in their papery yellowish coats (bright orange on the inside). *Wood* soft, weak, light (36½ pounds per cubic foot, dry weight), the heartwood brown tinged with red, the sapwood thin and paler.

Far north on the California coast, where the Golden State begins to "feel" like Oregon, you first meet signs — bits of paper or board with hastily lettered words on them — offering employment to "cascara barkers." These increase in number as you go up the Oregon coast, especially on the side roads and lumber roads, and soon you may find old cars, with licenses from various states, driven just off the road. If you could track their owners, you would probably find them deep in the shadiest parts of the forest, stripping the bark from a modest little tree growing with other understory trees like Manzanita and Alder, beneath the lofty Maples and Oaks or the still taller Firs and Port Orford Cedars. For the Cascara Buckthorn rarely forms pure stands, but is scattered in with others, or grows along the fencerows and roadsides with Hawthorn, Crab Apple, and Serviceberry.

Cascara is a shrubby tree at best, 10 to 30 feet high, or sometimes in the very rainy Coast Ranges 50 to 60 feet tall; but so intensive has become the search for the valuable bark that such fine specimens are now rare. At best, this Buckthorn is rather an undistinguished tree in appearance; the foliage is dull, except when in late autumn it turns a rich cottonwood-yellow; the bark is thin and scaly, and the greenish flowers pass unnoticed. The little red fruits, which turn black late in the season, are soon gobbled by grouse, pigeons, black bears, raccoons, and ring-tailed cats, so that we humans see little enough of the berries.

But the importance of this tree is out of all proportion to its un-assuming appearance. From 4,000,000 to 5,000,000 pounds of bark are collected annually from trees sought out in the depths of the forest, or along the roadsides and even around the farmhouse. The method of decorticating is so simple that unskilled labor can quickly learn to perform it. The thin bark is girdled by a knife at two points, about three feet apart on a fair-sized stem; a vertical slit is then made between the two girdling cuts and with blade and fingers a sheet of bark is swiftly unwrapped. When all the bark within reach has been peeled off, the tree is cut down to a stump, and the rest of the bark removed. During World War II, when immense amounts of bark were in de-mand for use of fighting forces overseas, a "barker" earned about $1.73 an hour, during which time he could collect about 20 pounds of green bark. This usually dries down to about half that weight, but still it was enough to furnish one dose each of cascara to 2345 soldiers and sailors, who knew the medication as "CC pills" and were accus-tomed to say that that was all you got when reporting for sick call.

The bark is usually collected by itinerant or part-time labor, such as farmers, older men out of regular employment, and boys. Unfortunately, property rights are still widely disregarded by many barkers who, like the 'sang diggers of the Appalachians, go through anybody's land harvesting what they consider to be God's common bounty. Immense reserves of Cascara remain, however, on Forest Service lands, where the guardianship is efficient enough to prevent most trespass by the barkers.

By the collectors the bark is sold to local buyers who resell it, at about 17 cents a pound for dry bark, to the wholesalers. Sometimes farmers mistake, or an itinerant barker attempts to substitute, the bark of some other tree. Red Alder bark is the commonest source of confusion. If there is any doubt, the local buyer chews a bit of the bark. The intensely bitter flavor of Cascara bark is unmistakable, and lingers for hours in the mouth, numbing the taste buds of the tongue.

Cascara, of course, means nothing more than bark in Spanish, and tradition has it that the early Franciscan missionaries of California first learned of the medicinal properties of this bark from their Indian neophytes, and just as the bark of Cinchona, the quinine tree of Peru, was long known as Jesuit's bark, so the Buckthorn's cortex was at first known as *cascara sagrada* or "holy bark." However, it did not become generally known as a medication until 1877 when Dr. J. H. Bundy of Colusa, California, first published a paper on its therapeutic uses. The following year the Parke-Davis Company put it on the market as an open formula, since when it has been carried continuously in the official pharmacopoeia.

In the three quarters of a century which have elapsed, the exploitation has so increased that barkers are pressing further and further into the forest in their search for material. The ultimate amount of destruction, however, is not all dead loss. For if the tree is cut down, it sprouts freely from the stump, and in a few years the sprouts can be harvested. More, the quantity of fruit produced is great, and birds and other animals, by voiding the seeds at a distance from the parent tree, are constantly spreading and replacing this valuable species. Only if the decorticated trees are left standing in the forest will they die.

THE CALIFORNIA LILACS
(*Ceanothus*)

THESE blue- or white-flowering species have, when of tree size, evergreen and simple leaves (alternate in our species). Growth is from small axillary buds. The minute but usually very numerous flowers appear in profuse, branched axillary clusters, each floret borne on a colored stalklet. The small calyx, 5-lobed beyond the tube, is colored like the 5, clawed, separate petals that are inserted on the edge of the disk, the stamens more or less infolded in the tube-like claw. The ovary is partly adherent to the disk, and is 3-celled and sometimes 3-angled, the angles frequently crowned by a fleshy gland which persists on the 3-lobed, berry-like drupe with its thin, dry outer coat. The drupe contains 3 cartilaginous nutlets, each one longitudinally marked with 2 sutures along which it splits.

*   *   *

REDHEART

Ceanothus spinosus Nuttall

OTHER NAMES: Greenbark Ceanothus. California Lilac.

RANGE: Coast Ranges of southern California, from Davis Canyon (San Luis Obispo County) south to Baja California, Mexico.

DESCRIPTION: *Bark* thin, red-brown, separating at the surface into small, close scales. *Twigs* yellowish green, smooth, commonly becoming spiny or spine-tipped. *Leaves* alternate, evergreen, ½ to 1¼ inches long, ⅝ to ¾ inch broad, thick and leathery, typically with but one main vein from the base (3-nerved on vigorous sucker shoots), smooth and shining on both surfaces, the margins not toothed except on sucker leaves. *Flowers* in large, fluffy, compound clusters 1½ to 6 inches long, pale blue varying to almost white. *Fruit* globular, ¼ inch thick, sticky, scarcely lobed or crested.

Redheart, or Greenbark Ceanothus as horticulturists prefer to call it, straggles up in ungainly fashion to a height of 20 feet; again it may be but a shrub no more than 8 feet high. Nor are the flowers as beautiful as those of many other species of this large genus, for they are but a gray-blue varying to white; only rarely are deep blue blossoms found. Thus horticulturists do not think much of this species except as a sturdy stock on which to graft the exquisite but tender *Ceanothus cyaneus*. But it is a very important little tree in erosion control, springing up swiftly after the disastrous chaparral fires that have been sweeping the dry hills of coastal California for centuries and with increasing frequency as human settlement grows thicker. Yet Redheart is, though such a phoenix after fire, one of the most combustible in that vast mixed scrub or maquis known as chaparral. It burns with intense heat, and smolders long in its underground parts.

The name of Redheart is derived from the very dark, ruddy wood. The underground parts frequently produce heavy and knobby club-like burls, and these, when grubbed out, make wonderful firewood. True that they send out a continuous stream of minute sparks that thread their way up the chimney like fairy fireworks, or explode horizontally in broadsides. But there is no danger that they will set either chimney or hearthrug on fire, for the sparks die in midair. And indeed the sound of its sparkling logs, and the aromatic smoke, make Redheart a delightful fireplace wood. It is only obtainable, however, when some road-making or house-building development has required the grubbing-out of the chaparral.

BLUEBLOSSOM

Ceanothus thyrsiflorus Eschscholtz

OTHER NAMES: California Lilac. Blue Myrtle.

RANGE: Canyons of the outer Coast Ranges, from southern Oregon (Douglas County) south to Point Concepcion, Santa Barbara County, California.

DESCRIPTION: *Bark* thin, bright red-brown, separating at surface into small close scales. *Twigs* angled, green. *Leaves* alternate, evergreen, ¾ to 2 inches long, ½ to ¾ inch wide, prominently 3-nerved from the base, dark green and smooth above, the lower surface paler and smooth except for a few coarse hairs flattened to the prominently raised veins, the margins finely toothed, or curled under and then appearing untoothed. *Flowers* in roundish or cylindrical clusters 1 to 3 inches long, light or deep blue varying to almost white. *Fruit* ⅙ inch wide, only slightly lobed at the summit, glandular-sticky, eventually blackening.

The genus *Ceanothus* is a very large one in the West, but it is made up for the most part of shrubs which pass collectively under the name of Wild or California Lilac. Some have white flowers, some pale blue, some a very dark and beautiful blue, some a lavender, a violet, and even deep purple. These plants early attracted the attention of European gardeners, and much more tardily California gardeners have realized that they have in this genus a wealth of colorful species. During the blooming season in spring every part of the state, wherever there is chaparral, becomes a glorious wild garden — to the admiration of visitors even more than of natives, who take this splendid display too much for granted.

Only a few kinds reach tree size — just how many would be a matter of opinion, since no satisfactory definition divides trees from shrubs — but of those which do this species is the commonist. When shrubby, it is 4 to 8 feet high, but in many places it straggles up to 20 feet, with a single, if rather crooked, tree-like trunk. The flowers, which are light or deep blue, bloom from March to June, filling with their charming color numberless canyon slopes and foothills of the outer Coast Ranges, where the influence of the sea is felt, all the way from Point Conception to the coast of Oregon. It is abundant, above all, in the Redwood belt, where it is seen in fine style along California Highway 9 (the Big Basin road) in Santa Cruz County. There in late April and early May it blooms simultaneously with the deep purple-flowered *Ceanothus papillosus,* the two colors veiling with cloudy masses mile after mile of the roadside. In southern Oregon and northern California Blueblossom is associated in June along the Redwood Highway with the annual display of rhododendron and azalea. In the early days, before the Gold Rush and the mushrooming of San Francisco, this species formed jungle-like thickets on the hills where the city now stands. From California it was taken at an early date to England, where for a century it has been a great favorite, especially for pruning back against a wall to make a flowery evergreen screen. In its native land, however, it is usually regarded as so much "brush," to be grubbed out in favor of exotics.

ISLAND CEANOTHUS, *Ceanothus arboreus* Greene, also called Feltleaf Ceanothus, Tree Myrtle, and Island Lilac, grows on Santa Catalina, Santa Cruz, and Santa Rosa Islands, off the coast of southern California. It forms a small tree 15 to 25 feet high with smooth gray bark and softly pubescent twigs. The alternate leaves are evergreen, 1 to 3 inches long, ¾ to 1½ inches wide, 3-nerved from the base, dull dark green above, the lower surface usually finely but densely covered with soft white hairs, the margins toothed above. The pinkish-lavender flower buds are followed by great masses of pale or deep blue, sweet-scented bloom in compound and ample clusters, each up to half a foot long. They appear in February and March. The heartwood is a rich red, the sapwood yellow and very thin. This attractive tree has been much cultivated on the mainland of southern California since its first introduction in 1911.

THE SAGUAROS
(*Cereus*)

LIKE OTHER MEMBERS of the Cactus family, the Saguaros are succulent plants with copious watery juice and numerous spines arising from cushion-like tufts of small bristles. The large, elongated flowers are clustered near the top of the stem, and are seated in a circle of radial spines. The numerous leaf-like or scale-like sepals overlap in many rows, forming a sort of false tube (of free parts), the lowest (outer) sepals short, adhering to the consequently inferior and scale-covered ovary, the upper (inner) long and appearing like a collar beneath the flaring petals. Numerous, the petals are ranked in 2 rows; at their bases they cohere somewhat with the top of the calyx tube. The filaments (shorter than the corolla) of the very numerous stamens, adherent by their bases to the tube of the calyx, cohere with each other at base to form a tube. The several fine, radiating branches of the long columnar style are stigmatic along their inner faces. The fruit, a fleshy berry overlapped by the persistent sepals, splits down from the top into 2 or 3 sections and contains numerous minutely dark and shiny seeds imbedded in the red pulp.

❋　　❋　　❋

SAGUARO

Cereus giganteus Engelmann

OTHER NAMES: Pitahaya. Giant Cactus. Suharo. Suguaro. Suwarro. Suwarrow. Sajuaro. Zuwarrow.

RANGE: From western Sonora, Mexico (coast of the Gulf of California to 150 miles inland), north to central Arizona (Gila, Graham, and Yavapai Counties and southern Mohave County), usually between 3500 and 4500 feet altitude, sometimes at much lower altitudes near the Colorado River and its tributaries. Rare in California, on terraces above the Colorado River, near Palo Verde, Yuma Dam, Parker, and in the Riverside Mountains.

DESCRIPTION: *Stem* of mature trunks spiny and columnar, with bright green, barkless trunk regularly furrowed between the 12 to 34 high-rounded ridges. *Flowers* borne at the ends of stems and boughs, clustered amid radial spines and about 4 inches long and, when fully expanded, 2 to 3 inches wide, the tube green and scaly, the petals white and numerous in 2 rows; stamens about 3000, with white filaments and golden anthers, shorter than the petals; style creamy white, with 12 to 18 stigmatic lobes. *Fruit* a big, plump, red or purple berry 2¼ to 3½ inches long, with red pulp and innumerable minute shiny black seeds.

The most fascinating part of the American desert is that which lies around the ancient city of Tucson, set in a valley surrounded by rugged mountains, snow-topped in winter, cloud-capped in summer, crowned at all seasons by a forest of Cypress and Juniper, Pine and Fir. The magic of Arizona sunlight and the long shadows cast by the peaks, the strange form of sheer-walled mesas, the nostalgic views of the long *bajadas* or down-sloping plains, give all of central Arizona a quality unlike that of any other part of the world, so that many persons who have never seen the region can put their fingers unmistakably on a picture of it and say, "That is Arizona." But there is one feature of the landscape more characteristic than any other — the Giant Cactus or Saguaro. Sometimes 30 or 40 feet tall, with enormous branches weighing, themselves, hundreds of pounds, this tree looks like the vegetation of some other planet, and so do the thorny ocotillo bushes, the jumping chollas, the barrel cacti, that are its associates.

The Saguaro (pronounced su-wahr-ro) might, one could fancy, be a tree designed by someone who had never seen a tree. With its upraised arms and tall peaked "head," it has a goblin look enhanced by those woodpecker holes in the top that often appear like two eye sockets or slits in a magician's hood. Just as twice the Apaches besieged the walled city of Tucson, so it is beleagured still by this strange vegetable host armed with fierce spines. Saguaros are seen on most of the approaches to the city; to the east of the town there is a great forest of them set aside as the Saguaro National Monument, embracing 63,284 acres and doubtless several million of these fantastic giants. And as one sees them dotting the stony slopes, as if marching down hill, one is likely to remember the fable of the Sorcerer's Apprentice, who started one automaton to life, struck him with an axe, and so made two that divided spontaneously into four, then sixteen, then hundreds, and at last thousands.

One may ask if the Saguaro is rightly called a tree. True that it has at no time in its life any leaves, bark, or solid cylinder of wood. However, palms are trees, yet they have no solid cylinder of wood and no true bark. And the cortex of the Saguaro's green stems and branches is full of chlorophyll and carries on photosynthesis and respiration just as leaves do. One might say that the cortex of a Saguaro is all one vast leaf. Nor does this cactus lack for woody tissue. This is found in the form of long strands of wood, close together at the base of the stem, but spreading apart and tapering above, which might be compared to a bundle of fishing poles. So strong is the wood in these rods that they have been used for centuries in house construction by Indians and Mexicans; as ceiling beams they hold up the thatch of *carrizo* or reed stems; as lath in the walls they furnish a surface for the adobe mud plaster.

Yet there is something about the Saguaro that seems more animal than vegetable, for this strange creation, like a human being, has its skeleton *inside* its soft tissues and, just as with the human animal, when a Saguaro dies the soft parts decay and the skeleton emerges, the woody rods usually so hardened with deposition of mineral crystals as to turn the blade of a knife and appear more like bleached bones than wood.

Nothing, though, so invites the comparison to humanoid forms as the branches or arms of this tree and their strange gesticulations. Leaving the main trunk at eighteen to twenty feet above the ground, they are constricted near the point of attachment (so that, ponderous as they are, they rather easily break off) and they soon become, normally, erect instead of pendent like the boughs of other trees. It is this position that, above all others, gives the Saguaros their exclamatory expression, as if they were shouting *hosannah* and testifying to the miracle of their existence upon the desert.

In prolonged droughts, when the turgor of the cells is lowered by falling water pressure, the arms may droop and even curl and, in the case of heavy old branches, they are likely never to regain their erect position. As a result, the arms may seem to be hugging the ribs of the torso-trunk as if in convulsions of pain or mirth. Or they may touch the ground, like bandy legs, or like a man walking with a cane in each hand. Or they arch gently together, like a tranquil sage thrusting his hands up his sleeves. "Sage of the Desert" is a common allusion to these ancients. Despite their wild fantasies of form, their ponderous awkwardness, they have an inherent dignity. After sitting down amongst them and laughing at their attitudes till the tears come, one leaves the Saguaros with the feeling that, after all, there is about them something deeply wise, if unconsciously so.

The Saguaro lives in a desert with a peculiar climate, an extension of that of the central highlands of northern Mexico where the cactus family reaches its greatest development. Tucson, for instance, has an average rainfall of about eleven inches a year, but distributed in a special way, and to that odd distribution the Saguaro, which contains as much as nine tons of water, and is seldom less than 90 per cent water, must adapt itself both in its bodily form and life history. In the first three months of the year comes the little rainy season, when the weather is cool and the rains fall gently and intermittently to a total of two to three inches. This is followed by the little dry season of spring, when the winter annuals and bulbs send briefly up their carpet of wild flowers. By June it is hot and dry in the Saguaro groves, but in July great cumulus clouds gather on the mountains, and sweep over the *bajadas* in majestic thunderstorms that wheel and roll and make strange patterns of wet and dry upon the desert's face. In July and August fall about six inches of rain, accompanied by strong gusts of wind, flash floods in the arroyos, and slipping down of soil on slopes and banks. Then comes the big dry season, lasting through December, a time of fierce sunlight and drought slowly mitigated by declining temperatures.

To fit itself into this peculiar climate, quite unlike that of the Californian desert with winter rains only and of the New Mexican deserts with summer rains only, the Saguaro has certain equipments common to many cacti but carried out to their greatest expression in this arboreous member of the family. The root system is strangely shallow, but far-reaching, so as to catch the maximum of rainfall which, however, never penetrates deeply. Its roots have been followed by investigators for forty feet before they become so tenuous as to break when excavated, and doubtless their capillary rootlets extend much farther until, indeed, they reach the only competitor well able to halt them — the periphery of the root system of some other Saguaro.

Then, too, the stem of the Saguaro is, as women would say, accordion-pleated. That is, it is fluted in long vertical ridges with deep furrows between them. When low in water supply, these ridges shrink and seem withered; as soon as the rains return the roots send up to the great storage tank of the trunk enough water to see them through thousands of burning desert hours — and the flutes again expand, the plant that seemed miserable and dying is again bright green, plump, and full of life.

At the close of the little rainy season the flower buds begin to form at the tips of the branches and top of the stem. They grow slowly at first, and are ready to bloom when the first hot weather of the year has come, in late April and May. Then one night the great blossoms begin to open. Usually the eclosion commences about eight in the evening; unlike some nocturnal flowers such as the evening primrose of the garden which can actually be detected in the swift opening of its petals, the old sage of the desert discloses his secret with deliberation; two or three hours are required to complete the performance and now at last the marvelous blossom stands open to the desert stars. Two or three inches across, it is a very heavy blossom, looking with its thick petals as if carved out of wax, and from it there steals forth an odor that, if not a sweet perfume to us, since it is faint and a little like melons, may allure its nocturnal insect visitors.

There is no known relationship between waterlilies and cactus flowers, yet there is something oddly reminiscent, in this queen of the desert night, to the nymph of the tranquil streams, in the serenity of the bloom and the great profusion of the parts. For there are many sepals, many big creamy-white petals, and inside them a circle of innumerable heavy stamens wearing a golden rim of anthers. One botanist had the patience to count them and found 3482 in a single blossom. Inside the ovary he counted 1980 ovules. The golden chalice of the stamens contains the exquisite long columnar style cut into numerous branches at the tip, each branch stigmatic along its inner face. No wonder that the Saguaro has been chosen as Arizona's state flower.

When morning comes, the blossoms are still open. They are often borne so high as to be quite out of reach and only if a contorted old branch bends downward will the obliging plant put its bouquet in your hands. As the heat of the desert day advances the flowers begin to close and wither, and though there will be others tomorrow they will not be the same blossoms. For each individual bloom is queen of the night for one night only.

Within a month after flowering, and before the onset of the big rainy season of summer, the fruits — the *pitahayas* of the Spanish-speaking people — are ripe. About as big as goose eggs, they split open on the tree, disclosing their pulp, of a watermelon pink, with number-less little black and shiny seeds within them. This is one of the prin-cipal wild vegetable foods of the Arizona Indians. The Papagos date their New Year from the fruiting of this great cactus, and the Pimas call July the Saguaro Harvest Moon. To bring down the fruits they use long poles made of the Saguaro's own woody rods, lashed together and fitted with a hook at the top. When the plump fruits fall, the women place them in wide baskets or clay *ollas* which they carry away on their heads. Jam, syrup, and preserves are made from the fruits and kept in sealed clay jars, or some may be dried in the sun like figs, becoming candied in their own sugar, or left to ferment into a strong liquor. Of the fat and oily seeds the Papagos make a sort of butter. The white man prefers his *pitahayas* eaten out of hand; the flesh has much of the crispness of radishes or cucumbers, and is cool and sweet. Save for the skin, you devour them seeds and all.

Naturally a fruit so delicious is sought by many desert animals and usually you find they have first call upon them. Even the coyote is said to eat them, but they are the favorite food of that beautiful game bird, the white-winged dove whose *cook-karra-coo* sweetens the desert morns. What the doves and Indians do not eat, the fierce desert ants soon destroy. Not one seed in a million, it has been surmised, ever escapes to germinate. The great fertility of stamens and ovules is not one germ of life too many.

When a seed does sprout successfully in the high temperatures of the big rainy season, it is usually in the shade of some Mesquite, Palo Verde, or Cat's-claw tree, for the tiny seedling is very sensitive to drying winds and sun. Hence these thorny little leguminous trees are an essential to a Saguaro grove, and they are seldom absent. As a result, too, of this sheltered position, a seedling is seldom detected; by the time it has outgrown its nurse it is already almost as old as an old man.

For the growth of a Saguaro is at first painfully slow. At the end of the second year it is but a quarter of an inch high! A plant 4 inches high is, in general, about eight years old. When it is twenty it will still be only 10 inches high. The growth rate now quickens, but not much. A Saguaro that has seen thirty summers will be only a yard high, and by the time it is 15 feet tall it is some sixty years along in its life. Branching begins now if it has not done so a little earlier, and the first flowers and fruit are borne about this time. For a while growth may be a foot a year, but at 35 or 40 feet, a Saguaro has attained its maximum. It will then be 1 or 2 feet thick in the trunk and will weigh 5 or 6 tons, all precariously balanced on a constricted base (like a fat man with thin ankles and small feet) and a root system that is little effective for purposes of anchorage.

The age of the old Saguaros has been guessed by non-scientific writers as rivaling the Redwoods. But since this type of vegetable does not lay down annual growth rings in solid wood, the age can only be inferred from the growth rate, and how long an old Saguaro may live after growth has practically stopped is unknown. The Arizona botanists believe that 150 years is the average life span of a Saguaro which is not killed violently, with two centuries as exceptional longevity.

During the life of the Saguaro the spines change materially. In youth there is a ferocious armament of them, though old trees may, at base, be spineless where gnawing rodents have torn away the spines and left battle scars. For the first half or three-quarters of a century the cortex bears a crop of heavy reddish-brown spines that, with weathering, turn gray and finally black. But as the plant reaches bearing age the new growth puts forth finer needles of a yellowish-brown hue much felted with hoary hairs. If we miss the sound of rushing leaves in this leafless tree, the place of that natural music — you will find if you stand in a Saguaro grove when the desert wind is plowing by — is taken by the whistling of the millions of spines, a sound like the far-off seething of surf. So the Saguaro too lifts up its voice with thorny tongues.

All trees have their birds, and the Saguaro is no exception. It is the favorite nesting site of the Gila woodpecker and its relative the golden flicker. Both of them will nest in Willow and Cottonwood when they can find them in a decadent state. But the soft body of the giant cactus is "peckable" at all times. In a very few minutes these birds can thrash out there a globular home for themselves. Oddly, they do this not at the beginning but at the end of the nesting season. The reason seems to be that the very moist interior of the freshly excavated cactus stem is probably not habitable for months — until indeed the soft wet inner cells have formed scar tissue. When this is complete, the following spring, the architects of these apartments proceed to occupy them, providing they do not have to dispute them with some squatter, and here the eggs are laid directly on the hard dry floor of the hole. Sometimes the same nest is used for several years by a pair of birds.

When it is vacated at last it may be appropriated by the tiny elf owl, no bigger than a sparrow, or the Arizona screech owl, the ferruginous pigmy owl, the ash-throated and Arizona crested flycatchers. That sweet, companionable bird, the purple martin, greatly prefers an old woodpecker hole in a nice cool Saguaro to the stuffy, sunbaked bird houses and gourds that humans hang for him.

Later, as these tenements become older and perhaps more disreptuable, such unaristocratic society as rats and wild mice may move in, though how they run up the spiny stems is beyond imagining. When at last a Saguaro falls and decays, the scar tissue of these old bird homes will resist the elements as firmly as a wooden shoe, which they vaguely resemble in shape. The Indians then gather these up and use them as storage vessels for preserves and dried fruits of the *pitahaya*.

These holes made by the birds evidently do the tree no harm, but it is not so with some forms of injury. As a shallow stab may give a man blood-poisoning by carrying bacteria into the system, so the careless habit of shooting bullets into Saguaros, which idle boys sometimes do, or plunging a pocketknife into their succulent forms, may be fatal to this desert giant. A terrific outbreak of bacterial infection swept through the Saguaro groves some years ago, and the noble vegetables sloughed down in a putrid mass sad to see. Measures of every sort were taken to combat the disease; whether these were effective, or whether the disease ran its course and would have disappeared anyway, the Saguaros around Tucson, at least, are at the present writing apparently in the best of health.

More constant are the inroads of the jack rabbits and other desert rodents, frantic for the water in the soft tissues. Despite the tenderness of their noses, these little mammals are frequently driven to the fanatic courage of thrusting their snouts far enough into the horrid armament to insert their chisel teeth into the cortex. After the first chunk has been ripped out it is then easy to undermine the other thorn clusters. In this way a colossus may soon be gnawed till it topples in the first gust of wind.

Even when intact, the top-heavy, ill-based skyscraper of such a vegetable is subject to overturn by the elements. The summer rains drench and soften the adobe soil to a soft paste; accompanying these thunderstorms are violent gusts of wind. Sooner or later a Saguaro is bound to fall in this way if not laid low by all the other ills and foes that may beset it.

Are the Saguaros holding their own against all these odds? Many close observers are sadly inclined to doubt it. They believe that this species extended its range into Arizona from the great cactus forests of the north Mexican highlands in early post-Pleistocene times, when the climate was perhaps both milder and moister. Since then times have changed for the colder and drier on this desert. In Arizona the Saguaro does very poorly on the north sides of mountains where the frost is deeper and lasts longer in winter. It cannot ascend the mountains much above 4000 feet for similar reasons. However, it does not do well in *bajadas* either, on account of the heat and lack of soil seepage; in muddy or sandy soil it cannot keep itself upright through wind and rain. It is also unsuccessful on very steep slopes. So it strings out on gentle slopes with rocky soil, the long axis of the groves following the contours.

As you drive toward California, after leaving Tucson, you cross "the Gila desert, of dreadful memory" as John W. Audubon called it when his party made its way, starving and dying, in its level wastes. You have left the Saguaro behind and imagine you will never see it again. And then, just as you approach the low desert mountains bordering the valley of the Colorado, the friendly goblin shape of the Saguaro leaps up again. Here the long axis of the groves does not follow but crosses the elevation contours, for the trees are hugging the arroyos, trying to get what moisture they can from the rare freshets that run down these lonely desert ranges.

That will be practically the last of the Saguaros. Beyond Yuma lie the sand dunes, beyond that the soft oppressive airs of the Salton Sink below sea level, and after that come the date gardens of Indio, like a bit of Araby, and then the snows of the San Jacintos and of the strange desert lily at your feet. Beyond those mountains lie the Pacific and great cities — a world so far from the Saguaro forests that you can only wonder there how you imagined such unearthly vegetation.

THE CORNELS

(*Cornus*)

ALTERNATE or opposite, simple, deciduous leaves, mostly without teeth, round twigs bearing scaly buds, and perfect or unisexual flowers, characterize the Cornels. The 4- or 5-toothed calyx is minute, with short lobes; there are 4 or 5 separate petals, with the stamens inserted on the margin of the conspicuous disk. The inferior ovary terminates in a short style and broad stigma. The fruit, a drupe, contains 1 or 2 oblong-egg-shaped seeds with membranous coats. Sometimes the heads of flowers are enclosed in broad petal-like bracts.

✳   ✳   ✳

PACIFIC DOGWOOD

Cornus Nuttallii Audubon

OTHER NAMES: California, Nuttall, or Flowering Dogwood.

RANGE: Vancouver Island and the Puget Sound region generally, south through western Washington and Oregon, along the Coast Ranges of California to the San Bernardino Mountains (at 4000 to 5000 feet above sea level and south to the mountains of San Diego County) and on the western slopes of the Sierra Nevada, commonly in the Sequoia zone. Also reported from the valleys of northwestern Idaho.

DESCRIPTION: *Bark* thin, brown tinged with red, and divided into small, thin, close-fitting scales. *Twigs* slender, light green in youth and clothed in pale hairs, later becoming reddish purple and conspicuously marked by the crescent-shaped, elevated leaf scars, finally turning light red-brown and smooth. *Winter buds* acute, the terminal ones ½ inch long, covered by 2 opposite light green scales, and accompanied by 2 pairs of side buds each with but a single scale, only the upper pair developing in spring, as their scales thicken and turn dark purple, into small leaves. *Leaves* thin, deciduous, 4 to 5 inches long, 1½ to 3 inches wide, generally clustered toward the end of the branches, in pairs (opposite), the margins faintly

wavy-toothed, the upper surface bright green, the lower woolly-pubescent; midrib distinctly impressed above; veins about 5 pairs, connected by meshed veinlets. *Flowers* very small in dense heads surrounded by an involucre of 4 to 6 showy, petal-like bracts, the minute calyx yellow-green or purple, with dark purple lobes, the petals yellow-green and strap-shaped; involucral bracts 1½ to 3 inches long, 1½ to 2 inches wide, white or tinged with pink, conspicuously 8-nerved with meshed veinlets between the spreading nerves. *Fruit* in dense spherical heads of 30 to 40 bright red or orange berry-like stone fruits each about ½ inch long, much flattened, the flesh thin and mealy, the obtuse stone 1 or 2 in each drupe. *Wood* extremely hard, strong, close-grained, very heavy (46½ pounds per cubic foot, dry weight), the heartwood light brown tinged with red, the sapwood very thick and lighter.

As you motor up, in May, through the solemn coniferous woods to Sequoia National Park, the forest aisles are lighted by drifts of shining bloom — the Dogwood, holding out its still nearly leafless and naked branches that are yet clothed, as fair as any bride, in shining white. Each bloom is like a great white star and each bough is fairly snowed under beneath the gleaming flakes, and each little tree becomes an artful drift of blossoming whiteness. In the forests around Puget Sound the Dogwood is even more striking; the trees are taller, and more abundant; and by contrast with the glistening, joyous little Dogwood, the aisles of the coniferous woods are even more somber.

David Douglas was the first botanist to observe this tree, but he made an error in botanical judgment that was rare for so perspicacious a plantsman; he mistook it for eastern Dogwood, so that he did not bother to send seeds to England. It differs, though, in having the white bracts (which are often mistaken for petals) not notched and green-tipped, but wholly white and rounded out; where the eastern tree, *Cornus florida,* has regularly only 4 bracts, this one has 4 to 6, commonly 5, to make a 5-pointed "star" whose perfection surpasses that of even the eastern species.

The first scientist to recognize this as a new species was Thomas Nuttall, the botanist who, with Dr. John K. Townsend, a Philadelphia ornithologist, joined the second Wyeth Expedition to the Northwest, and Nuttall tells us of his first sight of this enchanting tree which he saw then in fruit when it is almost as brilliant as in flower: "On arriving, toward the close of September, in 1834, at Fort Vancouver, I hastened again on shore to examine the productions of the forests of the Far West; and nothing so surprised me as the magnificent appearance of some fine trees of this beautiful Cornus. Some of them growing in the rich lands near the fort were not less than fifty to seventy feet in height with large . . . *lucid* green leaves, which, taken with the *smooth* trunks and unusually-large clusters of crimson berries, led me, at first glance, to believe that I beheld some new Magnolia, until the flower buds, already advanced for the coming season, proved our plant to be a Cornus, allied, in fact, to the *Florida,* but with the flowers or colored involucres nearly six inches in diameter! These appeared in all their splendor, in May of the following year, of a pure white with a faint tinge of blush. . . . Though the berries are somewhat bitter they are still, in autumn, the favorite food of the Band-Tailed Pigeon." [1]

It was at Fort Vancouver that the ornithologist Townsend, as a physician, responded to a call of the Cowlitz Indians, in whose lodges two children lay sick with intermittent fever. "My stock of quinine being exhausted," he notes in his journal, "I determined to substitute an extract of the bark of the Dogwood (*Cornus Nuttallii*) and taking one of the parents into the wood with his blanket, I soon chipped off a plentiful supply, returned, boiled it down in his own kettle, and completed the preparation in his lodge, with most of the Indians standing by and staring at me to comprehend the process. This was exactly what I wished, and as I proceeded, I took some pains to explain the whole matter to them in order that they might at a future time be enabled to make use of a really valuable medicine which grows abundantly everywhere throughout the country. . . . I administered to each of the children about a scruple of the extract per day. The second day they escaped the paroxysm, and on the third were entirely well." [2]

Cornus Nuttallii was named by John James Audubon. One does not think of the great bird painter as a botanist, but he was Nuttall's friend, and the specimens of the band-tailed pigeon which he received through Dr. Townsend suggested to him, when he came to figure them, in his *Birds of America,* the thought of including their food plant, the Dogwood. He has represented them — the bird and tree together — in Plate 367, and in his *Ornithological Biography* he gives a complete description of the plant, "a superb species of Dogwood, discovered by our learned friend Thomas Nuttall, Esq., when on his march towards the shores of the Pacific Ocean, and which I have graced with his name!"

[1] *North American Sylva.*   [2] *Narrative of a Journey Across the Rocky Mountains to the Columbia River* (1839).

THE ELDERS
(*Sambucus*)

The Elders are shrubby little trees with soft-pithy twigs and opposite, long-stalked, compound leaves with an odd number of toothed and opposite leaflets. Small, regular, and perfect, the blossoms are borne in profuse, broad, branched clusters on the ends of the twigs. The minute calyx is 3- to 5-lobed, as is the flat little corolla on which are borne the 5 stamens. The ovary is at least partly inferior and is capped by the thick 3- to 5-lobed style. The fruit is berry-like, with bright, thin, shiny, succulent flesh, and nutlets filled by the seed.

Although usually placed much farther along in the taxonomic system, the Elders are so obviously related to the Cornels that it has seemed reasonable to treat them here.

*　　　*　　　*

BLUEBERRY ELDER

Sambucus glauca Nuttall

OTHER NAME: Blue Elderberry.

RANGE: Southern British Columbia and Vancouver Island and extreme southwestern Alberta south through the Rockies of Montana, Idaho and Utah to Arizona and southwestern New Mexico, and from the Coast Ranges and Cascades of Washington and Oregon, to the Sierra Nevada at low altitudes, the Great Central Valley and the Coast Ranges of California, to Baja California, Sonora, and Chihuahua, Mexico.

DESCRIPTION: *Bark* thin, dark brown tinged with red, irregularly furrowed and ridged. *Twigs* stout, pithy, somewhat angled, pubescent or smooth, and sometimes glaucous. *Leaves* in over-all dimensions 5 to 8 inches long, consisting of 5 to 9 leaflets each 1 to 6 inches long, ½ to 2 inches wide, the lower leaflets sometimes 3-parted or pinnate, thin and deciduous but firm, green above, paler beneath, and either pubescent or smooth. *Flowers* numerous in flat-topped clusters 2 to 8 inches across; petals creamy or white; the 5 stamens as long as the petals. *Fruit* about ¼ inch thick, a berry-like drupe about ¼ inch in diameter, blue to nearly black under a whitish bloom, and sweet juicy flesh, with 3 to 5 nutlets. *Wood* soft, weak, coarse-grained and light (31½ pounds per cubic foot, dry weight), but durable; heartwood yellow tinged with brown; sapwood thin and paler.

The Elder is often no more than a bush, but almost throughout its range it struggles or straggles up to the height of a little tree, as much as 20 feet, and with a single (if almost always bandy) trunk which may be as much as 2 feet in diameter. Its favorite sites are along the banks and washes of streams, in rocky pastures or chaparral, or overhanging the cut banks of roadsides, or in fencerows and on the edges of fields where the plow does not disturb it, as well as under telephone lines where birds have voided its seeds after devouring its berries. It is thus not a forest species at all, but a ruderal little tree, more familiar to the farm child than the forester who passes it by as insignificant. That it may be, but it is also a beauty in a rustic way, with its frondose leaves of cheerful green, its bonny, flat-topped clusters of creamy, sweetly fragrant flowers, and its wealth of berries (blue under a heavy

glaucous coating of waxen white), so tempting to birds and children. Its pithy stems furnish the country boy with whistle wood.

Indeed, the California Indians called it "the tree of music," for of it they made their flutes, and the flute was the instrument of the Indian when he went courting. The Elder sticks for flutes were cut when green in early spring and left to dry with the leaves on. Then four flute holes were bored with a red-hot stick, but at random, so that no two flutes had the same scale. Straight shoots of Elder were also used for the shafts of arrows. The berries were prized in Indian cookery, and the brewed bark was used as a remedy for fever.

Two other species of tree-sized Elder have been described by botanists from the western states, but they seem to be no more than varities of the Blueberry Elder. They are:

REDBERRY ELDER, variety *callicarpa* (Greene) Jepson. Instead of leathery leaflets, this variety has thin ones, with abruptly pointed tips which are toothed to the apex; the leaflets are 2½ to 7 inches long. The berries, instead of being blue beneath a white bloom, are bright red. This variety grows close to the sea from Marin County, California, north to Washington.

ARIZONA ELDER, variety *arizonica* Sargent. This variety has evergreen foliage with rather broader leaflets whose margins are finely rather than deeply toothed; the blue berries are only moderately glaucous. It ranges from Mexico north into Arizona, New Mexico, and western Texas.

THE MADRONOS
(*Arbutus*)

THE MADRONOS are especially characterized by their smooth red branches and thin, scaly bark which continually peels or sloughs off, like a Sycamore's, and by hard, thick roots. The foliage is alternate, simple, hard, and evergreen. The regular, perfect flowers appear in somewhat branched and open clusters that are terminal on the branches. The calyx is 5-parted, nearly to its base, is free from the ovary, papery, and persistent. The corolla is urn-shaped, with 5 short flaring lobes. The 10 short stamens are not exserted beyond the corolla as the style is, but are inserted at its base. The glandular-roughened, superior ovary seated on the 10-lobed, glandular disk terminates in the columnar style, which protrudes beyond the mouth of the corolla and bears the obscurely 5-lobed stigma. The berry-like or drupe-like fruit, spherical and roughened, has a very thin, bright-colored skin, and contains dry, mealy flesh and abundance of little stones in which are found the small compressed seeds.

*　　　*　　　*

COAST MADRONO

Arbutus Menziesii Pursh

Other Names: Pacific, or Menzies Madroño. Pacific Madrone. Madrone-tree. Arbute-tree. Tree Arbutus. Strawberry-tree. Madroña (alternative spelling and pronunciation).

Range: East coast of Vancouver Island and adjacent islands and immediate mainland coast of British Columbia; in Washington on the west and south shores of Puget Sound; in Oregon all along the coast and western slopes of the Coast Range and Siskiyou Mountains, also on the western slopes of the Cascades; southward in the California Coast Ranges, both inner and outer, from sea level to 3000 feet, as far south as the mountains of San Diego County; thence only at high altitudes to the San Gabriel Mountains (Mount Wilson); in the Salmon, Trinity, Hayfork, Siskiyou and other northern cross-ranges and in the foothills (2000 to 3000 feet) of the Sierra Nevada through the old gold-mining country south to the South Fork of the Tuolumne.

Description: *Bark* of young stems and branches separating into thin, large scales which peel away revealing the very smooth, bright red inner bark; on old trunks dark reddish brown and covered with thick, small, plate-like scales. *Twigs* slender and often mottled or varicolored — light red, pea-green or orange; becoming in their first winter bright reddish brown. *Winter buds* with numerous, overlapping, bright red-brown scales keeled on the back and sharp-tipped. *Leaves* 3 to 5 inches long, 1½ to 3 inches wide, the upper surface bright green and glossy, the lower whitish, with large pale midrib and conspicuously meshed veinlets; stalks stout, wing-margined, grooved, ½ to 1 inch long. *Flowers* jug-shaped, white, ⅓ inch long, nodding on tiny stalks in a spike of blooms, the spikes clustered to make a terminal inflorescence 5 to 6 inches long and broad. *Fruit* bright orange-red, spherical and warty or glandular, about ½ inch thick, with thin, pulpy flesh and a thin-walled stone containing several dark brown, compressed seeds. *Wood* hard, strong, close-grained, heavy (44 pounds per cubic foot, dry weight), the heartwood light brown, shaded with red, the sapwood thin and paler.

As characteristic of the North Coast Ranges of California as the Redwood itself is the Madroño. But it is less an inhabitant of the somber Redwood groves than of a forest belt lying just inland or east of the Redwoods, among the high grassy "balds." Here with the splendid Tan Oak, the California Black Oak with its bold jagged foliage, the bicolored Maul Oak, and the ponderous Oregon Oak, the Madroño enjoys the brilliant, fog-free sunshine of this region. And even in such distinguished aboreal company it outshines them all.

In midsummer the old foliage begins to drop off the tree, just when the new leaves are pushing out as if in haste to sustain the species' reputation for being evergreen. The old leaves, dejected in position, turn a brilliant scarlet and hang in bunches for a time, then gradually drop off and drift heavily to the ground where they form a deep litter for the wood wanderer to scuff in, like the foliage of eastern deciduous trees in fall. In the meantime the scales of the winter buds are curling back, large as the sepals of some big flower. And the new leaves, very pale green at first, are unfurling like a wrapped standard; then they become plane, and finally concave-convex with recurved margins.

At the same time, the bark of young trunks, of limbs and the upper parts of old trunks, is actively exfoliating. A deep terra-cotta or brownish-red, it gleams like the limbs of an Indian through the forest. The skin is tight on the crooked and seemingly muscle-bound limbs, and peels off in vertical strips and thin quills, revealing the beautiful green under-bark whose destiny it is at last to turn ruddy. It is the brilliance of the bicolored deciduous bark that is the tree's chief charm. But the great compound clusters of creamy white, jug-shaped flowers, which proclaim that this is a tree of the noble heath family, are glorious, high overhead, from March to May. In late summer and autumn they are replaced by the yellow and orange fruits — both colors are seen in the same cluster.

For a hardwood the Madroño is endowed with considerable longevity; the largest specimens are stated to be 200 to 250 years old. And generous indeed are their dimensions. Professor Jepson in his *Silva of California* (1910) enumerates many of the great specimens of his day, all of them in Sonoma, Mendocino, and Humboldt Counties. The Indians, he says, greatly venerated these immense Madroños, and he tells the story of what is perhaps the noblest specimen of its kind:

"From the lower Mattole country in southwestern Humboldt a wagon trail climbs to the Wilder Ridge, heavily wooded with Tan Oak, Douglas Fir and Madroño, and at the end of the ridge drops again to the ford of the Mattole River. On this downward slope a mile above the French and Pixton ranch-house the road passes around a little sharply-defined shoulder, on which, sixty feet from the wagon path, stands the 'Council Madroña.' It is an isolated individual with clean spaces around it and as seen from some little distance up grade the tree suggests an oak, merely on account of its exceptional size. The tree is 75 feet in height and its crown 99 feet wide in the longest direction. . . . The trunk of this tree is round and perfect, and without fire or axe-scars or traces of disease. At its narrowest part (16 inches from the ground), it has a girth of 24 feet 1¼ inches. . . . At ten feet the trunk parts into its main branches, giving rise to a broad but very rounded and symmetrical crown. Under its spreading limbs the coast tribes met the interior tribes in former days for the discussion of intertribal matters and for the conclusion of treaties. Situated on a little knoll on the mountain side it commands a view of the adjacent country and has been saved from destruction or injury by fires through its local isolation in the surrounding forest."

In southern Oregon, Madroños sometimes take on a remarkably symmetrical habit, but in California asymmetry is the rule, and the weirdest eccentricity is not unknown. This seems to be owing to competition with the mighty Tan Oak and the pushing Black Oak. Sometimes the trunk will curve away from its base in a long snaky growth for thirty feet, then, as it gets free of other trees' shade, will shoot up, spindling and narrow-spired, for sixty feet. Again, all the limbs will develop on one side of the trunk, producing a most lopsided crown; or the trunk may trail along the ground for many feet, giving off boughs and foliage all the while. Even when granted ample space, a Madroño is apt to have an oddly twisted stem, to develop irregular limbs, and to produce a crown broader than high and often canted over like an umbrella turned to slanting rain. Frequently a curving trunk is much flattened contrary to the direction of the curve, and commonly in old trees great root-like buttresses are sent out, and a big tabular base is developed just above the ground, much as in the case of the California Laurel. When a Madroño is felled close to the ground, hidden and forgotten buds in the stump spring to life and send up crown shoots, producing circles of sister trees much like the "goose-nests" of the Redwood.

The name Madroño was given this tree by the first white man who ever saw it — Father Juan Crespí, chronicler of the Portolá expedition which was exploring, in 1769, overland to discover the "lost bay" of Monterey. On November 5 Crespí notes "many madroños, though with smaller fruit than the Spanish." For the word Madroño means the Strawberry-tree, *Arbutus Unedo,* a sister species of the Mediterranean world, and Crespí, who referred every Californian plant to his Spanish frame of reference, perceived at once the resemblance. The Strawberry-tree is commonly grown in California today, and its fruits, which are brilliant red, are indeed larger than those of our Californian Madroño, but the tree is smaller and so are the leaves. The California Indians ate the fruits both raw and cooked. To the white palate they are just barely edible; they have a dry custardy taste that is marred by the sharp if tiny seeds. Overeating of them quickly produces cramps. But band-tailed pigeons devour them and in the hunting season the Madroño groves ring with the shots of their persecutors.

TEXAS MADRONO, *Arbutus texana* Buckley, is a closely related shrub or small tree seldom more than 8 feet high, with a short, crooked, slim trunk separating, a foot or more from the ground, into several thick, spreading branches. The leaves are small (1 to 3 inches long, ⅔ to 1½ inches wide), dark green and smooth above, pale and slightly pubescent on the lower surface with a thick hairy midrib. The flowers appear in March, in compact, hoary-hairy clusters about 2½ inches long. The dark red, scarce fruit is ⅓ inch thick, with thin glandular flesh and a thick stone containing numerous seeds. This little tree is found on the Edwards Plateau of Texas, in the Guadalupe and Eagle Mountains of Culberson and El Paso Counties; in southeastern New Mexico, and south in the mountains of Nuevo León to Monterrey, Mexico. The wood is hard and heavy and appears to have been used sometimes in the manufacture of mathematical instruments and small tools.

ARIZONA MADRONO

Arbutus arizonica (Gray) Sargent

OTHER NAMES: Madronetree. Tree Arbutus. Strawberry-tree.

RANGE: Southeastern Arizona and extreme southwestern New Mexico and south in the Sierra Madre of Mexico.

DESCRIPTION: *Bark* of young stems and branches thin, smooth, dark red, peeling in large thin scales; on old trunks thick, irregularly broken into square, close and plate-like, pale gray or nearly white scales. *Twigs* thick, contorted, when they first appear light purple or reddish brown and glaucous, becoming by the end of the first year bright red, the bark already beginning to peel off in thin scales. *Winter buds* ⅓ inch long, red, the scales ridged on the back. *Leaves* thin but firm, 1½ to 3 inches long, ½ to 1 inch wide, light green above, paler beneath, on stalks often 1 inch long. *Flowers* white, ¼ inch long, the corolla narrowed near the middle, on short stout hairy stalklets from the axils of conspicuous papery bracts, in loose clusters 2 to 2½ inches long. *Fruit* dark orange-red, ⅓ inch thick, with a granulated skin, thin sweet flesh, and a papery, undeveloped stone containing the compressed seeds. *Wood* soft and brittle, close-grained and heavy (44 pounds per cubic foot, dry weight), the heartwood light brown tinged with red, the sapwood thick and paler.

South of Tucson, Arizona, lie some of the most biologically interesting mountains in the United States — the Santa Ritas and Santa Catalinas, the Huachucas and Chiricahuas, where trees of the North find sanctuary from the burning desert heat, at high altitudes, and others from the highlands of Mexico come up from the south to mingle with them. One of the latter is the Arizona Madroño, a tree which has numerous relatives in Mexico, but none of the others crosses the

Boundary. This one, at 4000 to 8000 feet above sea level, mingles with the solemn-looking Gray and Emory Oaks and Apache Pines but stands out amongst them like a brightly dressed woman amongst uniformed soldiers. The pale gray, almost white, bark of the lower trunks and the pale green leaves would be enough to make it a lovely and shining tree-presence. But color is everywhere in the tree. The limbs are wrapped, skin-tight, in a dark red and glossy bark which exfoliates in thin scales, and young branchlets are at first reddish brown or light purple with a glaucous bloom. The new leaves, which appear in September, after the summer rains, are very thin and tinged with red, and remain for at least a year on the branches. From April to September are borne the branched clusters of creamy white, jug-shaped flowers, followed in October and November by an abundance, all over the tree, of the dark orange-red fruits. The sweetish flesh is palatable if not exactly delicious.

The origin of the word Madroño is explained elsewhere, in the remarks on the Californian species. A word may be said of the name Arbutus, since it so often gives rise to misunderstanding on the part of eastern visitors to whom an Arbutus is a little trailing sub-shrub, *Epigæa repens,* whose early vernal flowers breathe a sweet odor of Birch bark. When Westerners say that their Arbutus grows forty to fifty feet high, like this one, they are accused of transparent exaggeration. But the fact is that the lovely eastern wild flower is an Arbutus only by analogy and courtesy. The old Latin word *arbutus* (accent on the first syllable) was the classic one for the Strawberry-tree of the Mediterranean. The Arizona and California species are genuine relatives of the Strawberry-tree, and they have every right historic, philological, and botanical, to the lovely name of Arbutus, given to the genus by Linnæus himself.

THE MANZANITAS
(*Arctostaphylos*)

These shrubby small trees or bushes, with reddish or dark brown wood which is heavy, hard, tough and strong, are characterized by their crooked and often twisted branches, their purple bark which is sometimes smooth and even shining, or, again, rough or peeling in thin plates. The leaves are simple, alternate, evergreen, and firm. The white or pinkish bisexual flowers occur in terminal branched or simple clusters; the calyx is 4- or 2-parted, the corolla urn-shaped, 4- or 5-lobed at the top; the 10 stamens are included within the corolla, the anthers with 2 recurved appendages on the back; a 10-lobed disk surrounds the superior ovary. The berry-like or drupe-like fruit consists in a soft pulp surrounding several distinct or more or less united nutlets or a single fused stone.

*   *   *

COMMON MANZANITA

Arctostaphylos Manzanita Parry

RANGE: Middle and inner northern Coast Ranges of California from Mount Diablo (Contra Costa County) northward to Tehama, Trinity and Shasta Counties, and thence southward in the Sierra Nevada foothills to Mariposa County, in the Digger Pine belt.

DESCRIPTION: *Bark* thin, smooth, dark reddish brown. *Branches* long and crooked. *Leaves* 1 to 1¾ inches long, ¾ to 1½ inches wide, thick and firm, pale or dark green. *Flowers* ¼ inch long, white or pale pink, in drooping, wide-branched clusters, the stalklets ⅛ inch long. *Berry* 5⁄16 to 7⁄16 inch thick, spherical or depressed, smooth, in early summer white, becoming deep brown; nutlets roughened or ridged on the back.

There are some forty kinds of *Arctostaphylos* or Manzanita in the West (compared with a single species in eastern North America and northern Europe), and most of them are but shrubs; several, though, reach tree size occasionally. The one which most commonly does so is the present species.

Common Manzanita is generally an inhabitant of the valley flats and low hills of much of the Digger Pine belt which, like a big letter O, surrounds the Great Central Valley of California, inhabiting the inner Coast Ranges and the western foothills of the Sierra Nevada. Up to 35 feet tall in exceptional instances, the Common Manzanita may put forth a crown of evergreen foliage that is as broad as the tree is tall. In the case of trees growing close together, however, no such opulent symmetry is possible. The branches are always crooked, flattened this way or that, with twisted grain, so that when these little trees grow densely they lock their brawny red arms and arthritic, haggish fingers into an impenetrable thicket or low forest of the type that in California is sometimes called an elfin wood. In many places this and other Manzanitas completely dominate the chaparral — that intricate inflammable scrub which covers such immense areas in California.

The flowering of Common Manzanita begins early, in February, during the winter rainy season which is biologically not winter but spring. Only some of the wild currants, the golden-flowered bush poppy

(*Dendromecon*), and a white-flowered Ceanothus bloom so early, and the Manzanita surpasses them all, with its prettily blushed, jug-shaped flowers which show by their frosty perfection that they are members of the aristocratic *Ericaceæ* to which belong heather and heath, rhododendron, azalea, mountain laurel, Madroño and mayflower. The fruits, berry-like drupes, received from the Spanish-speaking pioneers of the Southwest the name of Manzanita, meaning little apple, but you will be reminded, rather, of blueberries and huckleberries. Bears and chipmunks are fond of them, and so were the California Indians, but to the white man's digestive tract the seeds are most unmerciful.

The Common Manzanita, like others of its tribe, has been commercially exploited of recent years, with no regard to its reproduction, its great importance as a check on erosion, or the property rights of landowners. Because of the fascinating asymmetry of the branches, and the highly colored bark which, skin-tight, follows every contorted twist in the grain, florists have used these branches, artificially redressed with glued-on foliage shellacked and repainted, and a false "moss," and putting the whole into a bowl with a cheap Chinese figurine, have sold the little horror as a "Ming-tree." Or department stores will sell you the parts so that you can make your own. You can even equip the grotesque affair with a lamp — all at excessive prices.

A less banal fancy in Manzanita is the search for "abstractions" — oddities in fragments of Manzanita stems, branches, and roots, which bear resemblance to anything (or nothing) else on earth. These bits of "mountain driftwood" as they are called, are collectors' items amongst hobbyists. In order to prevent the collectors from stealing surreptitiously into National Forest lands and breaking down the Manzanitas with violent hands (while setting the forest alight with cigarette stubs in a hundred places every Sunday), the Forest Service opened in the summer of 1951 a "Manzanita Area," up in the old Mother Lode country. Here where the Manzanitas are superabundant and a ranger is at hand to enforce certain restrictions, collectors may "pick" their mountain driftwood, providing they are amateurs and not florists' scouts. But a sharp saw or axe will be necessary to cut this immensely tough, hard wood.

BIGBERRY MANZANITA

Arctostaphylos glauca Lindley

RANGE: From Mount Hamilton and Mount Diablo, California, south through the Coast Ranges to Baja California, Mexico.

DESCRIPTION: *Bark* of trunks smooth, reddish brown. *Twigs* pale green, glaucous, and either smooth or finely pubescent or glandular-hairy. *Leaves* 1 to 1¾ inches long, ½ to 1 inch wide, evergreen, pale grayish green and glaucous on both sides, on stalks ¼ to ½ inch long. *Flowers* about ¾ inch long, white or tinged with pink, in terminal, branched clusters that are broader than long, stalklets stout and glandular, but principal stalk and branchlets smooth. *Fruit* about ½ inch long, light brown when mature, and very glandular-sticky; nutlets united into a solid stone.

The Bigberry Manzanita is one of the finest of all its large tribe, as one sees it growing on the north slopes of the Santa Ynez Mountains, north of Santa Barbara. Here it sometimes reaches a height of 25 feet, with a distinct but short trunk, the usual smooth red bark, but pale green and glaucous twigs and leaves so heavily glaucous that they appear almost white. The fruits are especially large and oddly sticky with viscid hairs, and provided with solid stones. The flowers, white or beautifully blushed with pink, first appear in early February, on one of those warm, bright winter days between rains, when all the chaparral is glistening and sending forth its commingled odors, and distant ranges seem to have marched miles nearer at a stride. At such a moment the flowering of this Manzanita, almost the first member of the heath to bloom, is especially grateful, and though one sees it year after year, it is always a little surprising that so tough a growth, with its red, naked-seeming wood and its wild, unkempt form, could produce this wealth of dainty bloom.

Like so many other chaparral plants, this one is woefully subject to fire, and does not crown-sprout after being burned, as some species do. On the other hand, its seeds seem positively to benefit by a good toasting so that though this little tree is an incendiary brand when alight, and at all times adds to the menace of brush fires, it is also a fire-type plant, much like some of the California Pines, in part or wholly dependent, for abundant reproduction, upon fire.

The pallid leaves of this Manzanita are generally turned edgewise to the sun, as is so often the case with xeric, or semi-desertic, plants. In this way the blade is saved from excessive exposure during the long cloudless summers. But as a result the shade cast by this little tree is almost nil, as any panting chaparral traveler has learned if he tried to find relief beneath its canted foliage.

The white man never eats the "little apples" — really berry-like drupes — that are the Manzanita's fruits, but the Indians of California esteemed them next to acorns and pinyons, amongst vegetable staples. Stephen Powers, the authority on California Indians, believed that an acre of selected Manzanita bushes was capable of furnishing the aborigines with as much solid nourishment as an acre of wheat yields us. How the Indians overcame the constipating effect of the mealy and seedy pulp is not clear; it certainly disagrees with more civilized digestive systems. The Indians knew, and country people still some-times enjoy, a cider made from the ripe fruit by first scalding it, then crushing it to a juicy pulp. An equal quantity of water is added and the watered pulp is then strained into a bowl which is cooled in a run-ning stream.

The extreme hardness of Manzanita wood caused it to be used by the Indians for spoons and tobacco pipes. When the Franciscan Fathers built Mission Dolores (San Francisco), they had no iron nails. Instead they fashioned wooden pegs of Manzanita wood with which to pin the joints in the Mission structure.

THE CHITTAMWOODS
(*Bumelia*)

THESE TREES and shrubs have milky sap, spiny twigs, and simple, alternate, or clustered leaves. The minute flowers are borne in many-flowered, crowded clusters in the axils of leaves, or, on older growth, below the foliage of the season. The calyx is 5-lobed, as is the bell-shaped corolla with flaring limb. The 5 stamens alternate with 5 petal-like staminodia. The hairy, superior ovary is furnished with a simple style that is stigmatic at the acute tip. The berry-like, dark-skinned fruit contains a bony-coated shining seed.

* * *

CHITTAMWOOD

Bumelia lanuginosa (Michaux) Persoon, variety *rigida* Gray

OTHER NAMES: Gum-elastic. Gum Bumelia. Woolly Buckthorn. Shittim-wood. Gum Woollybucket.

RANGE: Mountains of southeasternmost Arizona (4000 to 5000 feet altitude) and extreme southern New Mexico through western Texas and down the Rio Grande valley; also in Brown and Uvalde Counties, Texas; in northern Mexico: Sonora, Chihuahua, Coahuila, Nuevo León.

DESCRIPTION: *Bark* of trunks dark red-brown, divided by furrows into narrow ridges covered with thick scales. *Twigs* rigid, slender, zigzag, at first coated with thick rusty or pale hairs, red-brown to ashy gray during their first winter, marked by semi-circular leaf scars, very thorny. *Winter buds* obtuse, with rusty-hairy scales. *Leaves* 1½ to 2½ inches long, ⅓ inch wide, thick, firm and tardily deciduous in winter, upper surface dark green, the lower softly hairy. *Flowers* minute (⅛ inch long), in 16- to 18-flowered axillary clusters, on pubescent stalklets; calyx hairy, corolla white, bell-shaped, 5-lobed, anther-bearing stamens 5, alternating with 5 sterile filaments. *Fruit* a drupe, solitary or 2 or 3 together, ½ inch long, and tipped with the remnant of the style; skin black, flesh thick, the stone containing a shiny seed ¼ inch long. *Wood* heavy (41 pounds per cubic foot, dry weight), soft, weak, close-grained, with yellow or light brown heartwood and thick and paler sapwood.

Chittamwood has an exotic sound, and well it may, for this tropical tree was probably given its name in the British West Indies from the analogy of its very hard wood to that of the shittah, a tree mentioned in the Bible. The ancient Jews obtained from it the lumber they called shittimwood. "And thou shalt make staves of shittimwood and overlay them with gold," said the Almighty, commanding Moses to build the Tabernacle and the Ark of the Covenant. There has never been any doubt what tree was meant, since the Arabian desert produces but a single timber species, known to botanists now as *Acacia Seyal*. With its close-grained, hard, orange-brown wood, it was an ideal cabinet wood for the Jews, and it is found also as clamps on the coffins of ancient Egyptian burials.

Of course, the Chittam of our southwestern states is no *Acacia;* on the contrary, it is a member of the tropical Sapodilla family, from one member of which we get our chewing gum or chicle. And, indeed, this tree too yields a gummy exudation, gathered from cracks in the bark and chewed by Texas children who have their own name for it; they call it "chicady"; to their elders it is gum-elastic.

The Chittamwood grows on bottom-lands and rocky hillsides, along streams and washes, on sandy knolls, in desert grassland and Oak woodland forming small thorny groves, and with its glittering leaves and its compact crown of stiff spreading branches presenting a tropical or exotic appearance. Sometimes on the Texas Panhandle a single tree will stand alone, a landmark on the vast grassy plains. Again it climbs the lower slopes of the desert ranges, as far west as the lonely and half mysterious Baboquivaris of southern Arizona. There it is usually shrubby, and not more than 13 feet tall, but in sheltered canyons of western Texas it may be 30 and 40 feet high.

The minute, whitish flowers would never be noticed but for their sweet odor. The cherry-like fruits are conspicuous enough but they are considered by our race too insipid to be worth eating. Yet the vanished Kiowas and Comanches were so fond of them that almost all the groves on the plains were regularly visited by these fierce tribes in late autumn when the fruits were ripe and black.

THE EBONIES
(*Diospyros*)

THE PERSIMMONS — our American representative of the Ebony genus — display alternate, simple, untoothed leaves and unisexual flowers, commonly all of one sex on a single tree, but sometimes the sexes intermix on the same tree. Growth is by scaly axillary buds; no terminal bud is present. Generally the male flowers are found in 2-flowered, branched clusters while the female are solitary in the axils of the leaves. The 4-lobed calyx is persistent on the fruit. Four-lobed, too, the corolla is generally jug-shaped with a contracted throat and short, recurved lobes. Sixteen stamens, inserted on the bottom of the corolla in 2 rows and in pairs, show the outer row on longer stalks than those of the inner. The ovary is topped by 4 styles, each 2-lobed at the apex and bearing 2-lobed stigmas. The fruit, technically a several-seeded berry, appears somewhat like a plum; spherical or oblong, it is surrounded at base by the enlarged persistent calyx. The oblong, compressed seeds have dark, shining, thick, and bony coats.

* * *

PERSIMMON

Diospyros virginiana Linnæus

OTHER NAMES: Possumwood. Date Plum.

RANGE: Southern Florida, north to the neighborhood of New York City, the central parts of Ohio, Indiana, Illinois, and Missouri, and west to Kansas, Oklahoma, and the Panhandle of Texas.

DESCRIPTION: *Bark* thick, dark brown or dark gray tinged with red, and deeply divided into innumerable square plates. *Twigs* zigzag with very thick pith, at first light brown, becoming ashy gray by winter and marked with occasional orange-colored lenticels and elevated leaf scars with deep, horizontal, crescent-shaped depressions. *Winter buds* minute, with thick, overlapping dark red-brown or purple shining scales. *Leaves* 4 to 6 inches long, 2 to 3 inches wide, leathery, dark green and shining above, pale below, with broad flat midrib and about 6 pairs of conspicuous primary veins which arch and join near the margin, and meshed veinlets. *Flowers:* male in 2- to 3-flowered, stalked clusters, the female solitary on short recurved stalks; corolla of the male flower tubular, ½ inch long, and slightly contracted at the throat; the 8 stamens with short, slightly hairy stalks; female flowers with greenish-yellow or creamy-white corolla nearly ½ inch broad; the ovary conic and terminating in 4 slender, hairy styles. *Fruit* on a short thick stem, depressed-spherical or egg-shaped, rounded or pointed at the apex ¾ to 3 inches thick, with tough, puckery skin, at first green, then amber, then orange, and finally purple-black, the flesh thick, yellowish, very austere and astringent until dead ripe; seeds oblong, much flattened, straight on one edge and rounded on the other, ½ inch long, ⅓ inch wide, with thick, hard, pale-brown wrinkled coat. *Wood* very strong, extremely hard, very heavy (52 pounds to the cubic foot, dry weight), the heartwood dark brown, the very thick sapwood pale brown.

"If it be not ripe," wrote Captain John Smith, of the first persimmon he tasted, near Jamestown, Virginia, "it will draw a man's mouth awrie with much torment." And your own first bite into a persimmon fruit, unless you have been brought up in the region where it is a familiar article of diet, may unluckily be an unforgettable experience. A day may pass before you get the puckery taste out of your mouth, and in all probability you will be disposed never to make another trial. At first green, then amber, then glaucous orange, a persimmon is not ripe until the skin is wrinkled and unappetizing in appearance and the pulp is so mushy that one cannot eat it without washing the hands afterwards.

Close relative of the kaki, or Japanese persimmon, our native fruit is not usually so large or handsome or firm of flesh. Yet it is esteemed by connoisseurs, who will travel miles to gather the fruit of a particularly fine tree, and they tell you that the art of eating a persimmon consists in avoiding the skin altogether, for the intensely tannic taste never leaves that part of the fruit. Certain it is that some trees produce large, some small fruit; some fruits are delicious, some never good at any season; some ripen in August, some in December, and others hold their fruit until spring. Obviously amidst such variation there are strains well worth propagating and breeding.

But no matter how we humans may improve the breed, the persimmon will never mean to us what it does in the lives of wild animals. It is eaten by birds, notably the popular bobwhite, by raccoon and skunks and white-tailed deer, by the half-wild hogs that rove the Ozarks, by flying squirrels and foxes, and above all by the opossum. According to song and story, most 'possum hunts end at the foot of a 'simmon tree, and when Audubon came to paint his great picture of opossums, he showed them devouring these strange, puckery-looking fruits, high in the branches of this grand old tree.

Black bears, too, are extremely fond of persimmons, climbing the trees for them with a sort of ponderous agility, and according to old hunters' tales their ursine tempers are often very short when garnering 'simmons. Indeed, the first printed notice of the occurrence of the Persimmon within the circumscription of this book came from that famous hunting classic, *The Border and the Buffalo,* when its author, John R. Cook, was on the south fork of the Canadian River, in the Texas Panhandle during the autumn of 1874.

"On the north side of the river from the cabin," he relates, "and a half-mile or so from the river, was quite a grove of persimmon trees, some of them twenty-five feet or thirty feet high, and some with trunks eight inches in diameter. About the time we first commenced the building of the cabin the fruit must have been in its prime, but when we found them they were nearly gone.

"On this particular morning we [1] found it, we had crossed the river on horseback and were riding north toward the hills to look for chance

[1] That is to say, the narrator and Buchanan Wood, known in the narrative as "Buck."

buffaloes, when Buck's attention was attracted toward the grove, which was on our left about two hundred yards from us.

" 'Look! Look! See how that tree shakes.' We stopped, and presently saw a violent trembling or shaking of another tree some little distance from the first. 'John,' said he, 'that's a 'simmon grove and that's a bear in it.'

"We had seen bear-tracks along the river-bars several times while building the cabin. He told me to keep around the right of the grove between it and the hills. . . . I rode quartering toward the grove, and on my left I caught sight of a bear with its head turned toward me. I stopped, cocked my gun, had my trigger finger inside the trigger-guard, and was raising the gun to take aim, when [my horse] old Barney gave a snort, whirled so quickly that I and the gun both went off . . . and for the next twenty or more minutes it was the most exciting, busy and laughable hunt . . . I ever experienced." It included the descent of a Persimmon tree by an infuriated bear, and a hasty ascent of another one by a scared hunter, — but the reader should look up this fine old source-book of Panhandle history to learn all the details.

The Persimmon, it seems, still grows along the South Canadian

River, despite the fact that it is not given from that region in Sargent's *Silva* and *Manual,* or in Cory and Park's *Catalogue of the Flora of Texas.* L. F. Sheffy, executive secretary of the Panhandle-Plains Historical Society writes that "Mr. Floyd V. Studer [curator of archæology] . . . was born and reared at Canadian, Texas. His father owns a ranch on the north side of the Canadian River. . . . Mr. Studer tells me that there are hundreds of persimmon trees growing and producing fruit along the banks of the Canadian River . . . and that they have been growing along the river since his early childhood." [1]

Even so this famous eastern tree is yet too rare within the area covered by this book to justify the presentation of all the details given in the volume on the eastern trees. A few lines more must suffice here.

The Persimmon often forms dense thickets on dry, eroded slopes. Not only has the tree a deep taproot, but it sends out long stolons or subterranean runners which are both wide-spreading and deeply penetrating. Trees grown from stolons, however, are apt to be shrubby and are very difficult to eradicate, once they have penetrated the soil of an abandoned field. Naturally, the bushy growths are preferred by persimmon pickers, since a fruit growing high in a lofty tree is most unhandy. Although not a fast-growing tree, the Persimmon begins sometimes to bear fruit at an early age. It succeeds in a wide variety of habitats, and a more adaptable tree it would be hard to find.

Persimmon belongs to the same genus as the black tropical cabinet wood, Ebony, and betrays the relationship in its heartwood, so dark a brown as to be nearly black. This, however, sometimes does not develop until the tree is over a century old. Persimmon when green is not especially strong, but no other wood gains more in hardness when well seasoned, and in this respect belongs in the class of the Ironwoods. In weight, too, it is in the very heavy class. It shrinks greatly in drying and will crack unless the ends are protected by paint or paraffin. Difficult to glue, it is never used in plywood, but when once seasoned, it retains its shape, and the more it is used the higher becomes its polish.

Persimmon wood is cut selectively, mostly by farmers, and is usually sold by the cord. It finds its chief use in the shuttles for textile looms, where it endures intensive wear without cracking. It is also sought for the wooden lasts over which children's shoes are built, for the heads of golf sticks (since it does not crack under an impact load), and is used for billiard cues and parquet flooring.

[1] Letter to Peattie, December 9, 1951.

THE ASHES
(*Fraxinus*)

Ashes have opposite, deciduous, usually pinnately compound leaves, twigs with thick pith, compressed, obtuse terminal buds and unisexual flowers with the sexes on different trees (or perfect flowers sometimes mixed with unisexual), in slender-branched, vernal clusters that develop from large buds covered with 2 scales. The small bell-shaped calyx is free from the ovary; the corolla may be lacking; if present, there are 2 to 4 lobes or the petals may stand free. Generally the stamens number but 2. The ovary is contracted into a style terminated by a 2-lobed stigma. The fruit takes the form of a mostly 1-winged samara, the body of the fruit containing the compressed seed in its chestnut-brown coat.

*   *   *

RED ASH

Fraxinus pennsylvanica Marshall

OTHER NAMES: River, Bastard, Black, or Brown Ash.

RANGE: Nova Scotia and the Gaspé peninsula west to Manitoba, eastern Wyoming, central Kansas and northeastern Oklahoma, and south to northern parts of Mississippi, Alabama and Georgia, and central parts of the Carolinas.

DESCRIPTION: *Bark* thin, brown tinged with red, furrowed into numberless braided ridges. *Twigs* slender, ashy gray or light brown tinged with red and often with a glaucous bloom, flecked with pale lenticels and marked with semicircular leaf scars. *Winter buds* — the terminal small, with 2 pairs of rusty-woolly scales. *Leaves* in over-all dimensions 10 to 12 inches long, with 7 to 9 thin, firm, light yellow-green leaflets which are coated below with silky hairs, each 4 to 6 inches long, 1 to 1½ inches wide. *Flowers* with the sexes on different trees, covered in bud with rusty-woolly scales; petals none; male flowers with a minute, cup-shaped calyx and 2 stamens with pale green, purple-tinged anthers; female flowers with deeply divided, cup-shaped calyx and 2 green stigma lobes. *Fruit* 1 to 2½ inches long, ½ inch wide, the thin wing gradually tapered to the slender body. *Wood* medium-light (39 pounds to the cubic foot, dry weight), hard, rather strong, the heartwood light brown, the sapwood lighter brown streaked with yellow.

The Red Ash could take its name from the cinnamon-colored inner bark, or from the rusty woolliness of the hairs on the bud scales. In form, at least as grown in the open, it makes a good show, with its very handsomely braided ridges on the bole, and ascending branches forming a fine crown, both tall and fairly wide. Under the best conditions, Red Ash may grow 60 feet tall, with a trunk over a foot and a half in diameter. Streambanks and low ground are the favorite site of this tree. In pioneer times it was split for rail fences, but today it goes to market for prosaic uses — flooring and boxes, butter tubs and interior finish. It is unimportant compared to its close relative:

GREEN ASH, variety *subintegerrima* (Vahl) Fernald. The distinguishing points of this variety are the narrower, shorter, and more sharply toothed leaflets, which are shining on both surfaces, and not hairy beneath except sometimes on the midrib. The twigs are hairless, not downy as in the Red Ash. The range is much wider than in the typical species, from western Maine and the vicinity of the city of Quebec south to northern Florida and Brownsville, Texas, west to Alberta, central Montana, and south through the Rocky Mountain states (but not in the mountains) to southern Arizona and northwestern New Mexico. It is absent from the Appalachians above 2500 feet, and from central and western Texas. Fast-growing in its favorite site of stream banks, shallowly but widely rooting, extremely hardy with respect to climatic conditions — cold or heat, drought or flood — Green Ash is a ubiquitous sort of tree, which, if it will never win a prize in a beauty contest, is, like its close associates the Box Elder and the Cottonwood, an infinite number of times better than no tree at all, once one gets out on the Great Plains. No other Ash is so often planted, in the western states, as a dooryard and street tree.

The wood of Green Ash is much heavier (44 pounds to the cubic foot, dry weight), than that of Red Ash, and harder and stronger too. It is generally sent to market, though, as White Ash, which it most nearly resembles in the many fine qualities of that species, and as White Ash grows scarcer Green Ash supplants it in industry. For instance, almost all oars and paddles now are made of Green Ash instead of the costlier White Ash, for Green Ash has the same virtues of toughness, elasticity, straight grain, and great strength. Unfortunately Green Ash weighs more than White; rowing must have been easier in the days of White Ash oars!

Green Ash makes a quick, hot fire when used for fuel. Where there is not much Pine, as along the lower Mississippi, it was a favorite for stoking wood-burning engines of all sorts, for it splits easily and has a fuel value 90 per cent that of White Oak taken as a standard of one hundred.

VELVET ASH

Fraxinus velutina Torrey

OTHER NAMES: Arizona, Standley, or Leatherleaf Ash.

RANGE: Mountain canyons up to 6000 feet, from southwestern Utah and southernmost Nevada to southeastern Arizona and southern New Mexico;

around desert springs of southeastern California (Panamint Range, Owen's Lake, southwestern base of the San Jacinto Mountains) and west to interior San Diego County; also in El Paso County, Texas, and in northern parts of Sonora and Chihuahua, Mexico.

DESCRIPTION: *Bark* of the trunk thin, gray slightly tinged with red, and deeply seamed, with broad flat broken ridges covered with thin small scales. *Twigs* slender, round in cross-section, at first ashen, later marked with large, heart-shaped leaf scars. *Winter buds* terminal, acute, with 3 pairs of pointed, hairy scales. *Leaves* 4 to 5 inches long in over-all dimensions, with 3 to 5 or even 7 elliptic leaflets, these 1 to 1½ inches long, ¾ to 1 inch wide, thick and sometimes leathery, pale green below or sometimes glaucous, with prominent midrib and veins and conspicuously meshed veinlets. *Flowers* unisexual, the sexes on separate trees, appearing on slender stalks in elongated branched clusters; calyx cup-shaped, densely pubescent; petals lacking; stamens with short filaments but long anthers; ovary shorter than the lobes of the stigma, almost enclosed in the calyx. *Fruit* in many-fruited clusters, the body club-shaped and many-rayed and longer than the rounded, blunt, or notched wing. *Wood* heavy (42½ pounds to the cubic foot, dry weight), rather soft and not strong, the heartwood light brown, the sapwood thick and paler.

This is *the* common Ash tree of all the southwestern desert country. Other species of *Fraxinus* there are in this region, but most of them are shrubs, or only occasionally do they reach tree size. The Velvet Ash grows up to 40 feet tall, with a trunk a foot or more thick, and with its wide-spreading branches it produces a rounded crown, most generous of shade where shade is most needed.

The leaflets are quite variable, and this had led to the description of numerous varieties; some have the margins of the leaflets slightly toothed, while some are without teeth; some show leaflets with short points, others with long points; the leaves of some specimens are thick and leathery, of others filmy and thin. The foliage may be quite hairless, or it may be densely short-hairy at least beneath. But no two or three of these variations remain constantly linked together, so that it seems best to treat them all as phases of one admittedly variable species.

The flowers appear in March and April, before the leaves, with the sexes on separate trees. The male flowers are yellow, the female green. In autumn the leaves turn a dull yellow before falling.

Streambanks, cool mountain canyons (like delightful Oak Creek Canyon), and moist washes are the preferred habitats of this pleasing tree, but it will appear, rather surprisingly, in desert grassland, and up to 7000 feet above sea level in Oak woodland and Western Yellow Pine forest.

Most of the Ashes have notably strong hard wood, and in consequence are highly valuable timber trees. The present species is disappointing in having what is, for a *Fraxinus,* a rather weak soft wood. In consequence it is seldom lumbered, though occasionally cut for tool handles and, in the days of wagon-making, for axles and singletrees and the like. But it does fine duty as an oft-thanked shade tree in Arizona, southern California, and northwestern Mexico, both along the irrigation canals and in the streets of towns.

The Velvet Ash was first discovered by Lieutenant William Emory, in New Mexico, where in 1846 he crossed the country in the Mexican War. "Bold Emory," as his West Point brothers called him, found the time, and had the turn of mind, even while serving as an active soldier in war time, to collect a large series of plants, and so became the first discoverer of many Western trees, on this occasion and later when he commanded the Mexican Boundary Survey.

BERLANDIER ASH, *Fraxinus Berlandierana* A. De Candolle, is an Ash of Texas reported to enter the mountainous western portion of that state which falls within the circumscription of this book. It is certainly related to the Velvet Ash, but differs in that the fruit is up to 1¼ inches long and the leaves and twigs are always hairless. It forms a small tree up to 30 feet high, with round, slender twigs which, while bright green at first, become light brown tinged with red, flecked with occasional lenticels and roughened by the small, elevated, circular leaf scars. The leaves, 3 to 7 inches long in over-all dimensions, are pinnately compound, with 3 or 5 leaflets, these 3 to 4 inches long, ½ to 1½ inches wide, dark green above, the lower surface paler and smooth or furnished with small axillary tufts of white hairs. The unisexual flowers, with the sexes on separate trees, have a calyx but no petals. The fruit, 1 to 1½ inches long and ¼ inch wide, has a flattened and many-rayed body and a blunt wing which runs down the sides of the body almost to the base.

OREGON ASH

Fraxinus oregona Nuttall

OTHER NAME: Water or Black Ash.

RANGE: Coastal British Columbia southward through western Washington and Oregon and the California coast region to San Francisco Bay and the Santa Cruz Mountains and along the western foothills of the Sierra Nevada to the lower slopes of the San Bernardino Mountains and on the eastern slopes of the Sierra Nevada in Inyo County (Ash Creek, near Owens Lake). Also in the mountains of San Diego County.

DESCRIPTION: Bark of the trunk 1 to 1½ inches thick, dark gray or brown tinged with red, deeply seamed between the thinly scaly, broad, flat ridges. *Twigs* thick, round in cross-section, hairless or, at first, with

pale or rusty silky pubescence which persists into the second season of growth when the twigs become orange or light brown and flecked with remote pale lenticels; in the second winter roughened by large, elevated, semi-circular leaf scars. *Winter buds* — the terminal acute, with 4 pairs of palely or rusty hairy scales. *Leaves* 5 to 14 inches long in over-all dimensions, with a stout, angled and grooved stalk and usually 5 to 7 (rarely 3 or 9) leaflets, these 3 to 7 inches long, 1 to 1½ inches wide, light green on the upper surface, the lower paler, sometimes hairy, sometimes quite smooth, with broad pale midrib, the veins conspicuously curved near the margins, and the veinlets meshed. *Flowers* unisexual, the sexes on different trees, on compact, hairless, compound clusters; male flowers with minute calyx and short stamens; female flower with fringed or deeply cut calyx shorter than the ovary which is narrowed to a stout style with long stigmatic lobes. *Fruit* 1 to 2 inches long, ¼ to ⅓ inch wide, in dense clusters, the wing often notched at tip and decurrent along the sides of the many-rayed body for half its length. *Wood* hard, brittle, coarse-grained and light (35½ pounds per cubic foot, dry weight), the heartwood brown, the thick sapwood paler.

In the interior valleys of the three Pacific coast states, above all in the Willamette Valley of Oregon, every low, wet meadow and bit of swampy ground, every slough or swale, is likely to be ringed about by scattering growths of this fine Ash. It comes up abundantly on the stream banks, and along the creek sides, with the Alders and Maples. It grows on the benches and bottom-lands of the major streams in the Northwest along with Grand Fir and Black Cottonwood. It springs up along the fencerows and roadsides, in the north country, with the Elder and Birch, and is altogether one of the commonest, as it is one of the finest, hardwood trees in its range. It is but medium-sized, usually growing 60 to 80 feet tall, with trunks 2 to 3 feet thick at maturity, but sometimes, where plenty of moisture is available, and good fortune has permitted an individual to live out its full two centuries and more, an Oregon Ash will grow to be 150 feet high. Trees growing in the open have short thick trunks, low, benignant boughs, and they form beautiful, compact, broad crowns, very lovely as shade trees for the dooryard and the street and roadside. In the forest, where most of the lumbering of this tree is done, a long pole-like trunk is developed and, of course, an equally slender crown.

In April or May the leaves burst their buds and at the same time the flowers appear in dense clusters, the female and the male always on separate trees. In autumn the leaves turn a clear yellow, and then drop early, so that for more than half the year, in the northern part of its range, this tree stands bare, yet with its light bark and fine tracery of twigs, it is graceful and shining in its nakedness, not merely denuded.

When Thomas Nuttall, the English botanist, in the pioneering times of the old fur trade in the Northwest, first saw this tree, he found a curious belief about it current. "An opinion prevails in Oregon," he tells us in his classic *Sylva of North America,* "among the hunters and Indians that poisonous serpents are unknown in the same tract of country where this ash grows, and stories are related of a stick of the black ash causing the rattlesnake to retire with every mark of trepidation and fear; and that it would sooner go into the fire than creep over it [the stick]. It is singular to remark that a similar superstition concerning the ash prevailed even in the time of Pliny the natural historian."

The wood of this species is of considerable commercial importance in the West, not because it is so superior or even abundant in commercial sizes, but because here, in the kingdom of the softwoods or coniferous trees, any reasonably good hardwood is in demand for interior finish, furniture, tool handles and cooperage. The chief value of Oregon Ash, however, is as fuel. It splits easily, burns readily, and has a caloric value almost the equal of Eastern White Oak.

Fraxinus Lowellii Sargent, the little-known LOWELL ASH is found on rocky slopes of Oak Creek Canyon near Flagstaff, and in Copper Canyon near Camp Verde in Yavapai County, Arizona. It forms a tree 20 to 25 feet tall, with dark, deeply furrowed trunks, and stout, square, and often wing-margined twigs, and compound leaves of 5 leaflets, these 2¼ to 3 inches long, 1 to 1½ inches wide, yellow-green and smooth above, the thin primary veins uniting near the thickened and curled-under margins. Occasionally a vigorous sucker shoot will bear simple leaves. The fruit, which ripens in July, has a flattened, many-rayed seed cavity and is surrounded to the base by the wing.

SINGLELEAF ASH

Fraxinus anomala Torrey

OTHER NAME: Dwarf Ash.

RANGE: From northwestern New Mexico and southeastern Colorado, throughout northern Arizona to southernmost Nevada and adjacent parts of the California desert.

DESCRIPTION: *Bark* of trunks thin, dark brown slightly tinged with red, divided by shallow seams into scaly narrow ridges. *Twigs* square in cross-section, slightly winged and at first orange and minutely hairy, becoming ashen and marked by pale lenticels and crescent-shaped leaf scars. *Winter buds* terminal, blunt, covered with orange hairs. *Leaves* usually simple, sometimes pinnately compound with 2 to 5 leaflets, 1 to 2 inches long, 1 to 2 inches wide (though smaller when compound), thin but rather leathery, the upper surface smooth and dark green, the lower paler, on a leafstalk ½ to 1½ inches long. *Flowers* in short, compact, pubescent, branched clusters, perfect or sometimes unisexual (flowers of both sorts borne together), with minutely 4-toothed, cup-shaped calyx and no petals; anthers orange, their slender filaments almost the length of the stout style. *Fruit* ½ inch long, with the wing surrounding the flattened seed cavity and notched at apex. *Wood* hard, close-grained and heavy (41 pounds per cubic foot, dry weight), the heartwood light brown, the sapwood paler and thick.

Down in Bright Angel Canyon, under the north rim of the Grand Canyon of the Colorado, this odd little tree grows up to 20 feet in height. And in the Havasu Canyon, where live the Havasupai Indians (the only peoples with a permanent habitation within the Grand Canyon itself), it is reported by observers to grow up to 30 feet in height.

Unlike most other sorts of Ash, which have pinnately compound leaves, this species, which is perhaps ancestral, has often only a simple blade, with a somewhat rounded or almost heart-shaped base, and hence looks most un-Ash-like; rather would one think it belonged to some sort of Poplar. Again, it may have 3 leaflets (variety *triphylla* Jones). The greenish flowers bloom when the leaves are about two-thirds open in spring. Sometimes the flowers are perfect — that is, with both sexes occurring in the same flower, as is normal for most plants but unusual in the Ashes; again, flowers will be wholly female or wholly male. All three sorts may occur in the same cluster.

The habitat of this odd little tree is along the banks of streams and on sandstone escarpments of the desert country. If it grew taller and were less rare, it might be a valuable hardwood timber tree. But as it is, no one ever troubles it, in the depths of the Grand Canyon, in the washes of the lonely Panamint Mountains above Death Valley, or in Labyrinth Canyon of southern Utah where it was first discovered in 1859 by Dr. John Newberry, surgeon-botanist of one of the famed Pacific Railway Surveys.

LITTLELEAF ASH

Fraxinus Greggii Gray

OTHER NAMES: Gregg, or Sierra Madre Ash.

RANGE: From the Sierra Madre of Nuevo León, Mexico, north into western Texas and Santa Clara County, southern Arizona.

DESCRIPTION: *Bark* thin, gray or light brown tinged with red, and papery-scaly. *Twigs* slender, round in cross-section, dark green and minutely downy at first, soon becoming ashen, and roughened by many minute, pale, elevated leaf scars, later turning dark gray or brown. *Winter buds* terminal, obtuse, with numerous light brown and pubescent scales which are rounded on the back. *Leaves* 1½ to 3 inches long in over-all dimen-

sions with a wing-margined stalk and rachis and 3 to 7 small, slim,
spatulate, thick and leathery leaflets, dark green above, pale below and
covered with dark dots. *Flowers* unisexual or perfect, on slender stalks
in pubescent, compound clusters ½ to ¾ inch long, from the axils of
rusty-pubescent bracts; calyx bell-shaped and papery, petals none; stamens
1 or 2; filaments longer than the calyx; the style surmounting a broad
ovary, and terminating in large, reflexed, stigmatic lobes. *Fruit* ½ to ⅔
inch long, ¼ inch wide, the body containing the seed roundish, not
flattened, in cross-section, with the blunt or notched wing somewhat decurrent along the sides of the seed cavity. *Wood* hard, close-grained,
heavy (49 pounds per cubic foot, dry weight), the heartwood brown, the
sapwood thick and paler.

Dry limestone cliffs are the habitat of this little tree which grows
only 20 to 30 feet tall. It is fairly common in western Texas, occurring
in the Big Bend National Park on the Pinnacle Mountains, in Boot
Canyon, and along Blue Creek. Completely lacking in New Mexico, it
recurs far to the westward at a single locality — famed Sycamore
Canyon — near Ruby, Arizona, where it was discovered in 1936 by
the inveterate plantsman of Arizona, Leslie N. Goodding. Possibly
the Arizona trees are a different variety, as noted by Kearney and
Peebles in their excellent *Arizona Flora*. They find that the twigs of
the Arizona plant are minutely downy, and some of the leaves are 7-
foliate; compared with the Texan and Mexican specimens, the leaflets
are broad and more distinctly toothed, while the body of the fruit is
longer and thinner and less obtuse, with the wing extending further
toward the base of the fruit.

Fraxinus Greggii is named for Josiah Gregg, of Independence, Missouri, one of the finest of the early American pioneers of the West.
Fluent in Spanish, scholarly enough to research the archives of New

Spain, he was perhaps the first English-speaking American to appreciate the cultural and historical importance of New Mexico. Going west with one of the Santa Fe trading expeditions, he soon became an authority on the famed route and everything connected with it, and his *Commerce of the Prairies* has been many times reprinted and remains a classic. His plant specimens he usually sent to his friend Dr. George Engelmann of St. Louis, while his literary work was transmitted to John Bigelow, the editor of the *New York Evening Post*. In 1849 Gregg successfully guided a party of gold searchers in the Trinity mining region of northern California out of a perilous position, but in attempting to return to the settlements for further help, he became so worn out by fatigue and hunger that he fell from his horse and was killed.

THE DESERT CATALPAS
(*Chilopsis*)

These crooked little trees, which grow by axillary buds, bear very slender, untoothed, 3-nerved leaves that, in our species, are alternate and at length deciduous. The showy perfect flowers are borne terminally on leafy branches of the year, in short, crowded spikes. The calyx, splitting on the opening of the bud to the base into 2 lobes, an upper and a lower, appears like 2 persistent bud scales beneath the ample, catalpa-like, slightly oblique or irregular corolla with its gaping throat and flaring, 5-lobed limb, the upper part 2-lobed, the lower lip unequally 3-lobed, the central lobe markedly the longest. The 4 inwardly facing stamens are inserted in the throat of the corolla, near its base, in pairs; there is a solitary staminodium. The conic ovary is gradually narrowed into a slender 2-lobed style which is stigmatic at the apex. The fruit is a very slender pod, tapered at each end and splitting along 2 sutures. The numerous seeds, inserted on the woody partition between the 2 cells of the pod, are made buoyant and wind-borne by narrow lateral wings and tufts of silky hairs.

＊　　　＊　　　＊

DESERT CATALPA

Chilopsis linearis (Cavanilles) Sweet

OTHER NAME: Desert, Flowering, or Bow Willow.

RANGE: Low deserts of Mexico, north to the valley of Rio Grande throughout its length in Texas, and well into southern Arizona, generally below 5000 feet altitude, and north in the Colorado River valley to extreme southern Nevada, extreme southwestern Utah, and the Colorado desert of California (but not the Mohave desert), inland to Palm Springs and along the Mexican boundary within 40 miles of the sea in San Diego County.

DESCRIPTION: *Bark* thin, dark brown, and seamed. *Twigs* slender, light chestnut-brown in the first season, turning darker in the second. *Leaves* opposite, or alternate, or both on the same twig, 5 to 12 inches long, ¼ to 1 inch wide, 3-nerved, thin and light green, sometimes sticky to the touch, sometimes smooth, very short-stalked. *Flowers* in showy spikes or branched clusters 3 to 4 inches long, the calyx palely pubescent, corolla irregularly trumpet-shaped (more or less 2-lipped), bisexual, pink, or white tinged with purple and with yellow spots in the throat, ¾ to 1½ inches long and almost as broad; stamens 4, inserted on the corolla. *Fruit* a very elongated, thin-walled capsule 7 to 12 inches long, only ¼ inch thick, splitting into 2 concave valves and persisting (like the leaves) on the tree over winter. *Seeds* numerous, ⅓ inch long, and ⅛ inch wide, slightly flattened and provided with broad, flat, round, papery wings. *Wood* soft, weak, close-grained and light (36½ pounds per cubic foot, dry weight), the heartwood brown with yellow streaks, the sapwood thin and paler.

As you go flying over the southwestern deserts, anywhere in the vast arid domain from the Big Bend of Texas to the Salton Sea of California, you may see, at the culverts and along the washes, this little tree, which never grows over 30 feet tall. It is often called Desert Willow from its long narrow leaves; yet, close relative of the true Catalpa and the trumpetvine, it is at the opposite end of the evolutionary scale from the primitive Willows. Perhaps there is something willowy in the way it overleans the banks of washes, but there is nothing kin to the weak-limbed Willows about the sinewy branches of this desert tree. So stiff is its wood that it is, or was, a favorite with the Indians for the making of bows. And Bow Willow Canyon in eastern San Diego County, California, is named for this tree, for here the Indians used to come to cut their bow wood.

Most visitors go to the deserts in winter, when this tree stands naked save for a few long, empty pods swinging disconsolately and weathered silver, on the twigs. Then in early spring the leaves appear. The flowers, though, do not open until most of the tourists have gone to their far-off homes, when the sound of the grinding of gears is low, and the wrangler of dudes has fallen asleep at his post. Then the lovely blossoms, much like those of the true Catalpa, pink, or whitish with purple veins, and yellow spots in the throat, open in stately masses, each flower a silent trumpet. So all summer, off and on, the flowers bloom, with few to praise them.

If anyone has read this book in something like sequence, he may have wondered, unless botanically trained, at the order of succession of the more than two hundred species which comprise the sylva of western North America. That sequence is the one usually followed by botanists who assume (or hope) that it represents the order of evolution from olden types of trees to the most modern. If that is so, one may ask in what way this spindling and unimportant little tree is "higher" than the mighty conifers, which endure for centuries and tower above all other trees in majesty, as they do in utility to man.

But biological order is not a question of splendor or worth; what sets the noble conifers in an early rank is the primitive naked flowers, which have no petals or sepals, and not even ovaries, for their ovules are borne naked on the scales of the female conelets. Obviously, the highly developed, tubular corolla of the Desert Catalpa is far more complex and perhaps more efficient, and it is believed, from fossil evidence, to represent millions of years of advance over the coniferous flower.

More — if we think of such titanic trees as the Sequoias in terms of modern conditions in western North America, it seems that, for all their stature and their years, they are adapted to no more than a narrow range of conditions. Such were perhaps found more widely in other geologic times, when Sequoias were widespread and the sylva of the West consisted in somewhat different assemblage of species. Today, though, it is in but two restricted localities that the Sequoias have survived. Quite the contrary with the Desert Catalpa; this modest little tree occupies a vast tract of the West as it is in our times. Call it a world of harsh contrasts, filled with wind and drought, heat and cold. But here this drought-resistant little tree holds its own remarkably well. It is even able to utilize the gusts of the desert that sear the land and make it uninhabitable for many trees with great reputations; for on the winds go sailing, from the Desert Catalpa's opened pods, the tiny seeds that are flat and light as bits of confetti and borne on silken wings. Thus they cross vast arid spaces, to populate the sands of other waterless washes, the cobbles of other arroyos. Swiftly the new seedlings spring up, enduring as readily as a Papago the long blazing summer days that know no shade until, from the lunar and jagged ranges, the sundown shadows rush forth across the long *bajadas* to the edge of the world. When the summer stars come forth, and hot Antares blazes in the Scorpion, then and then only there steals forth from the lips of the Desert Catalpa's blossoms the odor of sweet violets.

*

KEYS TO SPECIES
AND GENERA

GLOSSARY

INDEX OF
SCIENTIFIC NAMES

INDEX OF COMMON NAMES

KEYS TO SPECIES AND GENERA

THE SO-CALLED KEYS used by botanists and zoologists are devices for finding one's way to the name of an organism without having to compare an unknown specimen with every description and illustration in the book. Keys are most easily employed by those who have had a little classroom training in their use, but there is no reason why the botanically untaught should not "work" a key, with the help of the glossary and the following instructions.

A glance at the beginning of the Key on page 709 shows that it contrasts certain points, just as we do in the children's game of "twenty questions" or "animal, mineral, or vegetable?" Suppose that the object of such a guessing game were a Pine tree planted by George Washington at "Mount Vernon," and still living; the game would proceed something as follows: QUESTION: Is it animal? ANSWER: No. Q: Is it vegetable? A: Yes. Q: Is it now living? A: Yes. Q: Is it edible? A: No. Q: Is it a woody plant? A: Yes. One may imagine the continuation of this game to the point where the particular tree is finally pigeonholed or cornered (botanists would say keyed-out) satisfactorily.

Suppose now, that you have in hand a specimen from a Pine, and wish to know what its name is. You refer to the beginning of the General Key and find on page 709 that the first of the pair (both lettered "A") of alternatives put up to you is: "Leaves none at any time or present only evanescently in spring." This is plainly wrong, so you turn to the alternative "A" which reads: "Leaves present at all seasons," etc. This is correct, so you now proceed to the next choices, both lettered "B." The first reads: "Leaves very large (1 to 6 feet long and at least an inch wide at base," etc. While there are a few Pines with needles a foot long, none are as much as 1 inch wide at base. Obviously then this is the wrong category, so we turn to the alternative "B" which sets forth: "Leaves usually less than 1 foot long," etc. This corresponds with our specimen, so we continue to the next choice — that between the two "Cs." The first reads: "Leaves needle-like or scale-like, never more than ½ inch wide, usually evergreen and often resinous and aromatic (conifers)." Plainly this fits admirably, and we find that we are referred to "SECTION III, p. 710." Turning to that page, where all the conifers are keyed-out, we arrive, by the same process, at "PINES (see Key A, p. 716)." Referring to that page we repeat the same method and eventually come to the exact specific name of whatever Pine — Yellow, Sugar, Lodgepole, Whitebark, etc. — we may happen to have in hand.

The student then turns to the page where that pine is described in detail and represented by a picture, in order to verify the identity of a specimen; for keys, though handy devices, are very subject to error, both on their author's part and on the part of the student. A tree name is not satisfactorily settled merely by a hasty using of the key. In many cases the "determination" of a species cannot be made for certain until the student has had a chance to collect or study flowers, fruits, and young as well as mature leaves. If time is wanting for so much care, it is more accurate and helpful, if identification eludes a first attempt, not to know — and to say so — than to make a guess or a hasty decision.

GENERAL KEY

A. Leaves none at any time or present only evanescently in spring (*thorny desert trees*) SECTION I, p. 709
A. Leaves present at all seasons (evergreen) or in all but the winter (deciduous). B.
  B. Leaves very large (1 to 6 feet long and at least 1 inch wide at the base), the living ones fan-like and borne in a congested crown of foliage at the top of the unbranched stem or else sword-like and crowded at the ends of the branches; the dead leaves reflexed as a persistent dry thatch on trunk or boughs (*palms and yuccas*) SECTION II, p. 710
  B. Leaves usually less than 1 foot long or if so then the foliage not borne in a congested crown or clustered at the ends of the branches; dead leaves not reflexed and persistent as a thatch. C.
    C. Leaves needle-like or scale-like, never more than ½ inch wide, usually evergreen (except in Larches) and often resinous and aromatic (*conifers*) SECTION III, p. 709
    C. Leaves not needle-like or scale-like (*broadleaf hardwoods*). D.
      D. Leaves opposite in pairs or in whorls of 3. SECTION IV, p. 711
      D. Leaves alternate or clustered, but not in opposite pairs or whorls of 3. E.
        E. Leaves compound SECTION V, p. 712
        E. Leaves simple. F.
          F. Leaves evergreen SECTION VI, p. 713
          F. Leaves deciduous SECTION VII, p. 714

GENERAL KEY: Section I, *Leaves none at any time or present only evanescently in spring* (thorny desert trees)

Stems and branches succulent SAGUARO, p. 643
Stem and branches woody
  Young twigs with bright green and sometimes glaucous smooth bark
    BLUE PALO VERDE, p. 575
  Young twigs covered with a close, ashy pubescence
    DESERT SMOKETREE, p. 581

GENERAL KEY: Section II. *Leaves very large (1 to 6 feet long and at*
least 1 inch wide at base), the living ones fan-like and borne in a congested
crown of foliage at the top of the unbranched stem, or else sword-like and
crowded at the ends of the branches; dead leaves reflexed as a persistent dry
thatch on trunk or boughs (palms and yuccas)

Leaves 5 to 6 feet long, 4 to 5 feet broad, and palmately lobed, all borne in a congested crown at the top of the unbranched stem   DESERT PALM, p. 295
Leaves 1 to 4 feet long, relatively narrow, sword-like or stiletto-like, borne at the
ends of the branches   JOSHUATREE, p. 303

GENERAL KEY: Section III. *Leaves needle-like or scale-like, never*
more than ½ inch wide, usually evergreen (except in Larches) and often resin-
ous and aromatic (conifers)

A. Leaves needle-like. B.
  B. Leaves in clusters of 2 or more. C.
    C. Leaves evergreen, in 2- to 5-needled clusters, their bases enclosed (at least
          in youth) in a papery sheath   PINES (see Key A, p. 716)
    C. Leaves deciduous in winter, more than 5 to a cluster, not enclosed in a
          sheath at any time but borne on the end of a knob-like short-shoot
          Leaves 4-angled   ALPINE LARCH, p. 128
          Leaves in cross-section triangular
              Bark of old trunks thin and scaly; a tree of n. Can. and the Yukon
                R. basin in Alaska   EASTERN LARCH, p. 130
              Bark of old trunks thick (5 to 6 inches), deeply furrowed; a tree of
                Pac. coastal regions of Can., Ore., and Wash., and e. to Ida.
                and nw. Mont.   WESTERN LARCH, p. 125

  B. Leaves solitary, not clustered. D.
    D. Leaf enclosed at base in a papery sheath, this partly but never wholly
          deciduous   ONE–LEAF NUT PINE, p. 73
    D. Leaf not enclosed in a papery sheath. E.
      E. Margins of needles not curled under. F.
        F. Leaves not stalked
              Cones pendulous, their scales not deciduous from the central
                axis; needles usually sharp-pointed
                                             SPRUCES (see Key B, p. 719)
              Cones erect or spreading, their scales at length deciduous from
                the central stalk; needles (except in one species) blunt at tip
                                             BALSAM FIRS (see Key C, p. 719)
        F. Leaves stalked. G.
          G. Leaves affixed to short persistent bases
                Leaves flat, obtuse or notched at the tip and lying in one plane;
                  stomata on the lower surface
                                             WESTERN HEMLOCK, p. 157
                Leaves convex or keeled above, bluntly pointed, and bristling
                  all around the stem; stomata on both surfaces

MOUNTAIN HEMLOCK, p. 162

G. Leaves not affixed to short persistent bases

Leaves rounded and obtuse at apex, dark yellow-green or blue-green COMMON DOUGLAS FIR, p. 169

Leaves slenderly pointed, grayish green

BIGCONE DOUGLAS FIR, p. 182

E. Margins curled under

Blades abruptly contracted at base

CALIFORNIA NUTMEG, p. 313

Blades gradually narrowed to the base and partially decurrent on the twig

Leaves ½ to 1 inch long, 1/16 inch wide, thick, paler green below

WESTERN YEW, p. 285

Leaves ¼ to A inch long, ⅛ inch wide, thin, whitish below

COAST REDWOOD, p. 14

A. Leaves (at least on the more mature and fertile branches) more or less closely flattened to the twig and overlapping on it, scale-like or awl-shaped. (Those on vigorous sucker shoots and young individuals often more or less erect or scattered.) H.

H. Leaves alternate and somewhat scattered, not in opposite pairs or whorls of three GIANT SEQUOIA, p. 3

H. Leaves in opposite pairs or whorls of 3. I.

I. Twigs usually flattened (sometimes becoming roundish after several years) and lying mostly in one plane, forming a flat spray of foliage. J.

J. Leaves appearing in whorls of 4 INCENSE CEDAR, p. 211

J. Leaves obviously opposite, in pairs, not in whorls of 4. K.

K. Leaves with a distinct gland pit on the back

PORT ORFORD CEDAR, p. 255

K. Leaves with no gland pit, or only an obscure one

Leaves long-pointed, dull dark blue-green above, paler beneath, bronze at tip, limp and drooping almost as if wilted

ALASKA CEDAR, p. 211

Leaves short-pointed, yellow-green and shining above, paler below, half drooping in fringe-like sprays of foliage

CANOE CEDAR, p. 217

I. Twigs for the most part roundish or squarish, not flattened and not usually lying all in one plane

Fruit a spherical cone with a few shield-shaped or wedge-shaped woody scales CYPRESSES (see Key D, p. 720)

Fruit a cone transformed into a berry, sometimes showing a few woody projecting remnants of scales JUNIPERS (see Key E, p. 721)

GENERAL KEY, SECTION IV: *Leaves opposite*

A. Leaves simple, though sometimes deeply lobed. B.

B. Blades very long and narrow (more than 10 times as long as broad)

DESERT CATALPA, p. 701

B. Blades not more than thrice as long as broad. **C.**
  C. Leaves palmately veined   MAPLES (see Key N, p. 603)
  C. Leaves pinnately veined
      Leaves evergreen; bark shredding ISLAND IRONWOOD, p. 499
      Leaves deciduous; bark not shredding
         Blades 3 to 4 inches long   PACIFIC DOGWOOD, p. 653
         Blades 1 to 2 inches long   SINGLELEAF ASH, p. 653
A. Leaves compound. **D.**
  D. Blades with 4 to 7 palmate leaflets
                       CALIFORNIA BUCKEYE, p. 621
  D. Blades pinnately compound. **E.**
    E. Leaflets numerous. **F.**
      F. Rachis heavily winged or leaf-like, the leaflets deeply slashed or pinnat-
          ifid, making a fern-like frond ISLAND IRONWOOD, p. 499
      F. Rachis not, or only slightly, winged
         Margins not toothed or only finely so
                       ASHES (see Key O, p. 730)
         Margins sharply and coarsely toothed
            Leaflets not more than 3 times as long as broad
                      EASTERN BOX ELDER, p. 617
            Leaflets 4 or more times as long as broad
               Pith of twigs white   BLUEBERRY ELDER, p. 659
               Pith of twigs brownish   REDBERRY ELDER, p. 660
    E. Leaves with, generally, only 3 leaflets
      Leaflets without stalklets, seated directly on the rachis
                      DWARF MAPLE, p. 611
      Leaflets stalked on the rachis
      Leaflets finely toothed, never lobed; foliage evergreen
                      ARIZONA ELDER, p. 66
      Leaflets coarsely toothed, or not toothed at all, but never finely
      toothed; often lobed; foliage deciduous
               BOX ELDERS (see Key N, p. 729)

GENERAL KEY: Section V. *Leaves alternate and compound*

A. Branches more or less spiny. **B.**
  B. Leaves once-pinnate
      Leaflets 5 to 21 in number; flowers white or pink; pod compressed
               NEW MEXICAN LOCUST, p. 591
      Leaflets 7 to 15 in number; flowers purplish; pod round in cross-section
               DESERT IRONWOOD, p. 585
  B. Leaves twice- or more-pinnate. **C.**
  C. Leaflets numbering 1 to 6 pairs to a pinna. **D.**
    D. Leaflets crowded
      Leaflets green, hairless, with meshed veins
                    TREE CAT'S–CLAW, p. 552

Leaflets blue-green, pubescent, with obscure veins
DESERT CAT'S–CLAW, p. 550
D. Leaflets not crowded
Leaflets 2 to 3 pairs YELLOW PALO VERDE, p. 576
Leaflets 4 to 6 pairs BLUE PALO VERDE, p. 575
C. Leaflets numbering 10 to 25 pairs to a pinna
Rachis of the pinna flattened RETAMA, p. 571
Rachis of the pinna round
Leaflets ⅛ to ¼ inch long, very crowded
SWEET ACACIA, p. 547
Leaflets ⅓ to 2 inches long, usually not crowded
Leaflets pubescent TORNILLO, p. 567
Leaflets smooth TRUE MESQUITE, p. 559
A. Branches not spiny
Leaves twice-pinnate WAHOO–TREE, p. 535
Leaves once-pinnate
Leaflets ⅛ to 1½ inches long
Leaflets ⅛ to ⁵⁄₁₆ inch long ELEPHANT–TREE, p. 599
Leaflets ½ to 1½ inches long *Bursera odorata*, p. 601
Leaflets 2 inches long or more
Pith of twigs chambered (seen in a longitudinal cut); fruit a nut in a
husk WALNUTS (see Key H, p. 725)
Pith solid; fruit not a nut
Leaflets of an even number WESTERN SOAPBERRY, p. 627
Leaflets of an odd number
PACIFIC MOUNTAIN ASH, p. 509

GENERAL KEY, Section VI: *Leaves alternate or clustered, simple, and*
evergreen

A. Margins not at all toothed, wavy, or lobed, or only slightly so on leaves of
vigorous young shoots. B.
B. Blades with 3 principal nerves arising from the base.
BLUEBLOSSOM, p. 638
B. Blades with only a single principal nerve from the base. C.
C. Twigs usually spiny
Sap milky; tree of the SW. CHITTAMWOOD, p. 677
Sap watery; tree of Calif. REDHEART, p. 637
C. Twigs not, or not usually, spiny. D.
D. Foliage spicy-aromatic CALIFORNIA LAUREL, p. 485
D. Foliage not spicy-aromatic. E.
E. Veins running straight from midrib to margin
Leaves scattered; fruit a nut enclosed in a bur
WESTERN CHINQUAPIN, p. 409
Leaves clustered, except on vigorous new shoots; fruit a long-tailed
silky akene
CURLLEAF MOUNTAIN MAHOGANY, p. 523

E. Veins more or less curved before reaching the margin. F.
　　F. Leaves, in our species, mostly gray-green; surface of fruit smooth
　　　　Leaves glaucous on both sides
　　　　　　　　　　　　　　BIGBERRY MANZANITA, p. 673
　　　　Leaves sometimes pale or grayish green but never glaucous
　　　　　　　　　　　　　　COMMON MANZANITA, p. 671
　　F. Leaves dark green; surface of fruit granular
　　　　Bark of old trunks ashy gray; tree of Ariz. and N.M.
　　　　　　　　　　　　　　ARIZONA MADROÑO, p. 667
　　　　Bark of old trunks red-brown; trees of Tex. or Pac. coast
　　　　　　Ovary smooth; tree of Pac. coast
　　　　　　　　　　　　　　COAST MADROÑO, p. 663
　　　　　　Ovary pubescent; tree of w. Tex.
　　　　　　　　　　　　　　TEXAS MADROÑO, p. 666
A. Margin toothed or wavy. G.
　　G. Blades with 3 principal nerves arising from the base
　　　　Twigs angled or ridged; blades grayish downy beneath
　　　　　　　　　　　　　　BLUEBLOSSOM, p. 638
　　　　Twigs not angled or ridged; blades not grayish downy below
　　　　　　　　　　　　　　ISLAND CEANOTHUS, p. 640
　　G. Blades with only 1 principal nerve from the base. H.
　　　　H. Undersurfaces of leaves minutely dotted with black glands
　　　　　　　　　　　　　　CALIFORNIA WAX MYRTLE, p. 313
　　　　H. Undersurfaces not black-dotted. I.
　　　　　　I. Leaves 6 or more times as long as wide, silvery-silky beneath, the
　　　　　　　　margins curled under　　　　BONPLAND WILLOW, p. 351
　　　　　　I. Leaves less than 6 times as long as wide. J.
　　　　　　　　J. Primary veins extending straight from midrib to margins of leaves;
　　　　　　　　　　fruit an acorn
　　　　　　　　　　Acorns seated in a bristly cup; margins of blades merely wavy
　　　　　　　　　　　　with numerous, regular, rounded lobes　TAN OAK, p. 413
　　　　　　　　　　Acorns seated in a scaly or at most a "mossy" cup; margins of
　　　　　　　　　　　　blades sharply and often irregularly toothed, or intact, but
　　　　　　　　　　　　not merely wavy　　　　　　OAKS (see Key K, p. 727)
　　　　　　　　J. Veins arching and meeting before reaching the margin
　　　　　　　　　　Upper surface of foliage dark dull green
　　　　　　　　　　　　　　TEXAS MADROÑO, p. 666
　　　　　　　　　　Upper surfaces glittering
　　　　　　　　　　　　LAUREL CHERRIES (see Key M, p. 729)

GENERAL KEY, Section VII: *Leaves alternate or clustered, simple,
deciduous, leaving the tree at least briefly bare during winter*

A. Sap milky
　　Blades 3 or 4 times as long as broad　JUMPINGBEAN–TREE, p. 545
　　Blades not so narrow
　　　　Twigs thorny; leaves shining above, not toothed
　　　　　　　　　　　　　　OSAGE ORANGE, p. 479

Twigs not thorny; leaves dull above; margins finely toothed
WESTERN MULBERRY, p. 475

A. Sap not milky. B.
  B. Margins not toothed, though sometimes 3- or 4-lobed. C.
    C. Blades at least 24 times as long as broad DESERT CATALPA, p. 701
    C. Blades not so narrow
      Leaves with 3 or 5 principle nerves from the base
HACKBERRIES (see Key L, p. 728)
      Leaves with a single prominent midnerve
        Leaves without stipules; flowers solitary, fragrant, with creamy petals; fruit a several-chambered berry
EASTERN PERSIMMON, p. 681
        Leaves with stipules at least when young; flowers in catkins, without petals or scent; fruit a small green capsule
WILLOWS (see Key G, p. 723)
  B. Margins of leaves more or less toothed. D.
    D. Blades deeply lobed
      Leaves pinnately lobed   OAKS (see Key K, p. 727)
      Leaves palmately lobed   WESTERN SYCAMORE, p. 491
    D. Leaves not deeply lobed though sometimes doubly toothed. E.
      E. Scales of the winter buds none, the buds naked though downy
CASCARA BUCKTHORN, p. 631
      E. Scales present on the winter buds
        F. Scales of winter buds only a single pair
          Primary veins arching and uniting within the margin
WILLOWS (see Key F, p. 723)
          Primary veins running straight from midrib to margin
ALDERS (see Key J, p. 726)
        F. Scales of winter buds more than 2. G.
          G. Blades with 3 to 5 primary ribs from the base
HACKBERRIES (see Key L, p. 728)
          G. Blades with a single midrib. H.
            H. Fruit more or less fleshy — either a pome (apple-like) or a drupe (cherry- or plum-like)
              Fruit a drupe
PLUMS AND CHERRIES (see Key M, p. 729)
              Fruit a pome
                Twigs unarmed; winter buds sharply pointed
PACIFIC SHADBLOW, p. 513
                Twigs (in our species) more or less thorny; winter buds obtuse
                  Petals clawed; carpels (segments of the core) cartilaginous   OREGON CRAB APPLE, p. 505
                  Petals not clawed; carpels represented by a nest of nutlets in the center of the pome
                    Veins of leaves extending to the apex of each sinus as well as the point of each lobe
WILLOW HAWTHORN, p. 517
                    Veins of leaves extending to the points of the lobes only DOUGLAS HAWTHORN, p. 518

H. Fruit not fleshy, taking the form of a nut, or samara, or long-
tailed akene
Leaves markedly unsymmetrical at base; fruit a samara
WHITE ELM, p. 461
Leaves not or only slightly unsymmetrical at base; fruit a
nut or akene
Leafstalks ¼ to 1 inch long; foliage often resinous-
dotted, at least when young
BIRCHES (see Key I, p. 726)
Leafstalks ⅛ to ¼ inch long or shorter
Blades rounded or wedge-shaped at base, toothed only
above the middle; fruit a long-tailed, silky akene
BIRCHLEAF MOUNTAIN MA-
HOGANY, p. 525
Blades more or less heart-shaped at base, toothed all
around; fruit a nutlet enclosed in a bag-like or
hop-like involucre
Blades distinctly long-acute at apex
EASTERN IRONWOOD, p. 378
Blades barely acute, or bluntish at apex
CANYON IRONWOOD, p. 377

Key A: Pines

A. Sheaths at the base of the leaf clusters completely deciduous at maturity
B. Needles 3 in a bundle, slender, pale, glaucous green with conspicuous stomata on all 3 faces; cones long-stalked, 1½ to 2 inches long, the scales
scarcely thickened, light shining brown with pale umbos armed with
recurved deciduous prickles   CHIHUAHUA PINE, p. 76
B. Needles 5 in a bundle (SOFT PINES)
C. Cones long-stalked, light brown at maturity, their scales thin, with terminal unarmed umbos (*White Pines*)
Bark of young stem and branches thin, dark green; leaves slender and
flexible, 3½ to 4 inches long, with conspicuous white lines on the
back; cones 12 to 18 inches long   SUGAR PINE, p. 48
Bark of young stems and branches light gray; leaves stout and rigid,
with white lines on the ventral (less often also on the dorsal) face
WESTERN WHITE PINE, p. 39
C. Cones short-stalked, green or purple at maturity, their scales thick; bark
of young stems and branches often milky or silvery white (*Alpine
Pines*)
D. Leaves not shining on the back, not or but slightly incurved; cones
cylindric to nearly globular, their scales with terminal umbos. **E.**
E. Bark of the trunks whitish, and smooth, except sometimes at the very
base of old trees; cones ½ to 3 inches long, their scales remain-
ing closed at maturity; seeds wingless
WHITE–BARKED PINE, p. 31

E. Bark of trunks brown and furrowed or checked; cones 3 to 10 inches long, their scales open at maturity; seeds winged

Foliage yellow-green LIMBER PINE, p. 34

Foliage bluish green MEXICAN WHITE PINE, p. 37

D. Leaves shining on the dorsal surface, distinctly incurved toward the twig and densely tufted into a brush; cones oval or oval-oblong, their scales with dorsal umbos armed with slender prickles; seeds shorter than their wings

Needles ¾ to 1 inch long; cones armed with minute, incurved prickles FOXTAIL PINE, p. 62

Needles 1 to 1½ inches long; cones armed with long slender prickles BRISTLECONE PINE, p. 59

A. Sheaths persistent or incompletely deciduous at the base of the leaf clusters

F. Leaves much incurved toward the twig; cones nearly spherical and, when fully opened, 2 to 2½ inches wide, with few scales, only the middle scales fertile, the upper breaking away at maturity; seeds large (½ to ¾ inch long), rather triangular, nearly black on the lower side, chocolate-brown mottled with pink on the upper, the margins of the outer seed coat adhering to the cone scale (*Pinyon or Nut Pines*)

Needles flexible, comparatively long and slender (1½ to 2¾ inches long, only ½₂ inch wide), the edges minutely toothed, blue-green though whitened by stomatal lines on all 3 faces, usually 3 in a cluster (sometimes 5); shell of seed very hard

MEXICAN PINYON PINE, p. 65

Needles rigid and comparatively short and thick (1½ to 2 inches long, ½₂ to ½₄ inch thick), the edges not toothed, the clusters usually of some other number than 3; shell of nut fragile

Leaves usually solitary and thus in cross-section round, with stomata on all the faces ONE–LEAVED NUT PINE, p. 73

Leaves in bundles of 2 or 4 (rarely 5) needles; only the inner faces with stomata

Needles dominantly 2 to a bundle, 1¼ to 1¾ inches long, almost ½₆ inch wide; cones globose

NEW MEXICAN PINYON, p. 67

Needles dominantly 4 to a cluster, at least on flowering or cone-bearing shoots, ⅞ to 1¼ inches long, ½₂ inch wide; cones sub-globose

FOUR–LEAVED NUT PINE, p. 72

F. Leaves not incurved toward the twig; cones many-scaled; seeds usually strongly winged (HARD OR PITCH PINES). G.

G. Cones very large (4½ to 12 inches long, 4 to 7 inches thick) and heavy (1 to 8 pounds), with very thick scales having strongly hooked tips; wing of seed thick and short; needles 6 to 13 inches long (*Bigcone Pines*)

Needles gray-green, glaucous and drooping DIGGER PINE, p. 91

Needles dark or olive green but not grayish or glaucous or drooping

Needles 5 in a bundle TORREY PINE, p. 95

Needles 3 in a bundle BIGCONE PINE, p. 98

G. Cones not so large, or if over 6 inches long then not heavy, nor with very thick hooks on the scales; wing of seed thin and long. H.

H. Cones at maturity unsymmetrically developed, at least as to their basal scales; usually remaining unopened on the tree for years (*Closed-cone Pines*). I.

     I. Needles 2 in a bundle, thick and rigid. J.

         J. Cones at maturity incurved or appearing hump-backed

             Needles strongly divergent, ¾ to 1½ inches long; cones apparently unarmed   EASTERN JACK PINE, p. 108

             Needles not very divergent, 4 to 6 inches long; cones with distinct prickles   BISHOP PINE, p. 113

         J. Cones not incurved

             Leaves dark green, slender (less than 1⁄16 inch wide)
                 BEACH PINE, p. 100

             Leaves yellow-green, thickish (more than 1⁄16 inch wide)
                 LODGEPOLE PINE, p. 102

     I. Needles usually 3 in a bundle, slender and flexible

         Prickles of the cone scales minute; cones oval; needles 1½ to 4¼ inches long, rich bright green, a little shiny on the back, plane on the inner face   MONTEREY PINE, p. 116

         Prickles on the outer side of the cone thick, flattened, and incurved, those on the inner side slender, small, recurved; cones long-conic; needles 4 to 6¼ inches long, dull blue-green, the inner face concave
                 KNOBCONE PINE, p. 110

H. Cones essentially symmetrical. K.

     K. Tree found solely on the islands off the Santa Barbara coast, the needles 1¾ to 3¼ inches long, only 2 in a bundle; cones lateral, remaining unopened on the tree for years
                 ISLAND PINE, p. 115

     K. Trees of the mainland and, chiefly, of the interior; leaves 4 to 13 (rarely 3) inches long, numbering 3 to a bundle (or less commonly 2 or 5); cones subterminal, usually opening promptly, at least as to the upper scales which fall soon after shedding of the seeds; lower scales often persistent (*Longleaf, Yellow, or Lumber Pines*). L.

         L. Twigs (at least at the tip) glaucous or appearing frosted

             Leaves 3¾ to 4½ inches long; cones 5 to 15 inches long. Tree of Calif.   JEFFREY PINE, p. 98

             Leaves 5 to 7 inches long; cones 2 to 2½ inches long. Tree of Ariz.   ARIZONA PINE, p. 86

         L. Twigs not glaucous

             Leaves usually more than 10 (up to 15) inches long, about 1⁄12 inch wide; sheaths at base of leaf clusters ¾ to 1½ inches long   APACHE PINE, p. 87

             Leaves 3 to 8 (rarely 10) inches long, about 1⁄16 inch wide; sheaths mostly ⅜ to ¾ inch long

                 Needles mostly in clusters of 3, sometimes of 2; cones 3 to 6 inches long; prickles not backwardly hooked
                 WESTERN YELLOW PINE, p. 79

Needles mostly in clusters of 2, sometimes of 3; cones 2 to 3 inches long, with backwardly hooked prickles

ROCK PINE, p. 86

Key B: Spruces

Needles flat
    Foliage bright bluish green, the needles stiff and acute at tip to a prickly point
        SITKA SPRUCE, p. 147
    Foliage deep yellow-green, the needles flexible, and obtuse at tip
        WEEPING SPRUCE, p. 145
Needles at tip 4-sided
    Leaves of fertile branches slender, soft and flexible
        ENGELMANN SPRUCE, p. 135
    Leaves of fertile branches stout and rigid
        Twigs without downiness from the first; leaves unpleasantly scented, appearing (by a twist at the base) brushed forward to the upper side of the branchlet   WHITE SPRUCE, p. 140
        Twigs of the first season's growth downy; leaves pleasantly scented, bristling all around the stem
            Leaves strongly incurved, especially those on the upper side of the branch, gradually narrowed to long callous sharp points
                COLORADO BLUE SPRUCE, p. 137
            Leaves at most only slightly incurved and abruptly narrowed to a sharp callous point   BLACK SPRUCE, p. 143

Key C: Balsam Firs

A. Needles bristle-tipped, flat and rigid, 1½ to 2¼ inches long; cones with long, spiny bracts exserted ¾ to 1¾ inches   SANTA LUCIA FIR, p. 205
A. Needles not bristle-tipped; cones without spiny-tipped bracts. B.
  B. Needles of lower branches flattened; cones 2 to 5 inches long, and slender. C.
    C. Needles 1½ to 3 inches long; cones green-purple to yellow
        Needles spreading in all directions around the twig or only obscurely 2-ranked, 2 to 3 inches long, pale green and bearing whitened lines of stomata on both surfaces   WHITE FIR, p. 194
        Needles distinctly 2-ranked, lying all in one plane, 1½ to 2 inches long, the upper surface dark green, the lower whitened with stomatal lines   LOWLAND FIR, p. 193
    C. Needles of lower branches ¾ to 1¾ inches long; cones dark purple. D.
    D. Needles bearing whitened lines of stomata on the lower surface, the upper surface shining dark green
        Needles on lower branches lying all in one plane, and the spray of foliage thus flat on both sides
            EASTERN BALSAM FIR, p. 187

Needles on lower branches growing flat on the lower side of the twig, but brushy above, thus giving a thick-foliaged, ruffled appearance   SILVER FIR, p. 196
D. Needles whitened with stomatal lines on both surfaces
Bark of trunks hard, tough, smooth and gray   ALPINE FIR, p. 188
Bark of mature trunks soft, corky, yellowish white   CORKBARK FIR, p. 192
B. Needles 4-sided, bearing stomatal and whitened lines on all surfaces and thus usually more or less glaucous
Needles with a distinct groove on the upper surface only; cones 4 to 6 inches long, their scales much shorter than the papery bracts   NOBLE FIR, p. 198
Needles grooved both above and below; cones 6 to 9 inches long, their woody scales shorter than the papery bracts   CALIFORNIA RED FIR, p. 201

Key D: Cypresses

(Adapted from Carl B. Wolf: *The New World Cypresses*)

A. Dorsal surface of mature leaves usually bearing a gland or pit frequently exuding clear resin drops which turn gray or whitish on drying; foliage gray, glaucous, gray-green or a dusty dull green, never bright. B.
B. Twigs growing out in 1 plane, forming a flat spray of foliage   MCNAB CYPRESS, p. 227
B. Twigs disposed all around the branch. C.
C. Branchlets (apart from the foliage) slender (less than $\frac{1}{16}$ inch thick); crown of branches rather compact; male cones only $\frac{1}{8}$ inch long or less, of 6–10 scales; female cones $\frac{3}{8}$–$\frac{3}{4}$ inch long, warty-surfaced   MODOC CYPRESS, p. 228
C. Branchlets thicker (more than $\frac{1}{16}$ inch in diameter); crown of branches rather open; male cones more than $\frac{1}{8}$ inch long; female cones over $\frac{3}{4}$ inch long. D.
D. Trunks of mature trees with rough, fissured, fibrous, gray or dark brown, non-exfoliating bark, at least at the base of the trunk though that of branches, young trunks, and upper portion of main trunk may be exfoliating and smooth
Bark of branches of upper portion of main trunk and of saplings exfoliating in thin, non-fibrous plates, leaving a smooth cherry-red or mahogany-brown, polished surface; glands of leaves, when present, not exuding copious resin   ROUGH-BARKED ARIZONA CYPRESS, p. 230
Bark of branches and of upper portion of main trunk gray or red-brown, not exfoliating; almost all leaves with glands actively secreting resin   PAIUTE CYPRESS, p. 280

D. Trunks of mature trees with a smooth, polished, cherry-red or mahogany-brown bark which exfoliates annually in thin, curling, essentially non-fibrous plates
  Glands of leaves comparatively inactive; seeds mostly over ⅟₁₆ inch long, with a rather broad wing, the surface not glaucous
  CUYAMACA CYPRESS, p. 234
  Glands of leaves generally very active; seeds mostly ⅟₁₆ inch or less long, with wing usually rather narrow; surface very glaucous
  SMOOTH ARIZONA CYPRESS, p. 234
A. Dorsal surface of leaves essentially without apparent glands or pits; foliage either bright green, dark green or rarely somewhat dusty green or blue-green but never a real gray. E.
E. Trunks of larger branches with a cherry-red or mahogany-brown, smooth, polished bark which exfoliates in thin non-fibrous plates; foliage bright to slightly dull green; mature trees less than 30 feet high, cones with 10 to 14 scales TECATE CYPRESS, p. 237
E. Trunks and longer branches with fibrous, non-exfoliating bark or, if smooth (as on young trees and branches) not at all cherry-red or mahogany-brown. F.
F. Foliage dull dusty green or rarely a little glaucous; branchlets rather thick and bushy; dorsal pits evident and sometimes actively secreting resin SARGENT CYPRESS, p. 247
F. Foliage bright green or dark green, not at all dusty green or glaucous; dorsal pits of leaves apparently absent or if present never exuding resin
  Twigs rather thick and harsh; female cones 1 to 1½ inches long, with 8 to 12 scales MONTEREY CYPRESS, p. 238
  Twigs usually thin, not harsh; female cones mostly ⅞ inch or less long
    Tree with long slender whip-like leader; foliage deep dull dark blackish-green MENDOCINO CYPRESS, p. 245
    Tree with compact conical crown, or at least without a long whip-like leader; foliage a light bright green or sometimes slightly yellow to dull green
      Female cones ⁷⁄₁₆ to ¹¹⁄₁₆ inch long GOWEN CYPRESS, p. 244
      Female cones usually over ¹¹⁄₁₆ inch long
      SANTA CRUZ CYPRESS, p. 240

Key E: Junipers

A. Fruit red or reddish brown. B.
B. Bark of trunk separating into long-persistent scales. C.
C. Leaves closely appressed to the twig, obtusely pointed
  Leaves in whorls of three, rarely opposite; fruit ¼ to ½ inch thick, short-oblong CALIFORNIA JUNIPER, p. 266
  Leaves opposite, in pairs, rarely in threes; fruit ½ to ¾ inch thick
  UTAH JUNIPER, p. 263

C. Leaves not closely pressed to the twig, spreading at the apex, long-pointed, sometimes glandular; fruit roundish, ⅓ to ½ inch thick
DROOPING JUNIPER, p. 267

B. Bark of trunk divided into thick, nearly square plates; leaves without, or only rarely with, glands; fruit roundish to short-oblong, ½ inch in diameter, ripening at the end of the second season
ALLIGATOR JUNIPER, p. 268

A. Fruit blue, or blue-black, but often covered externally with a glaucous bloom, nearly spherical to short-oblong, ½ to ⅓ inch thick; seeds 1 to 4. D.

D. Leaves fringed with minute teeth, opposite or in whorls of three; fruit maturing in 1 season
Branchlets about ¹⁄₁₂ inch thick; leaves acute, conspicuously glandular; fruit short-oblong, ¼ to ⅓ inch thick; seeds 2 or 3
SIERRA JUNIPER, p. 271
Branchlets only ¹⁄₂₄ inch thick; leaves usually in threes; fruit short-oblong
Berries glaucous, ⅛ to ¼ inch thick
CHERRYSTONE JUNIPER, p. 274
Berries not glaucous, ⅜ to ⅝ inch thick   TEXAS JUNIPER, p. 278

D. Leaves not fringed on the margins, mostly opposite, without or with glands; fruit sub-globose
Twigs roundish in cross-section; fruit dark blue under a glaucous bloom
EASTERN RED JUNIPER, p. 281
Twigs 4-angled, fruit bright blue under a glaucous bloom
ROCKY MOUNTAIN JUNIPER, p. 280

Key F: Poplars

A. Leafstalks round in cross-section, or a little flattened above. B.

B. Leaves oval or broader than wide, and more or less rounded and heart-shaped at base. C.

C. Leaves oval, with gradually narrowed, long tips; terminal winter buds 1 inch long, ½ inch broad, with 5 chestnut-brown, shining scales saturated in a yellow, balsamic fluid   BALSAM POPLAR, p. 324

C. Leaves broadly oval with merely acute tips; terminal winter buds ¾ inch long, ¼ inch thick, with 6 or 7 light orange-brown, merely resinous scales   BLACK COTTONWOOD, p. 326

B. Leaves narrow (2 to 2½ times as long as broad, wedge-shaped at base
NARROWLEAF COTTONWOOD, p. 228

A. Leafstalks flattened along their sides. D.

D. Stalks not furnished with glands at the top. E.

E. Teeth of the leaves fine and numerous
Blades thin, light green and smooth above, the lower surface with inconspicuous meshed veinlets   TREMBLING ASPEN, p. 317
Blades thick, dark green and rough to the touch above, the lower surface with conspicuous, meshed veinlets
VANCOUVER ASPEN, p. 323

E. Teeth of the leaves coarse and few

    Twigs at first light green, becoming light yellow and finally light gray or yellow-brown; leaves oval or delta-shaped or kidney-shaped, the tips not toothed   FREMONT COTTONWOOD, p. 330

    Twigs light orange; leaves broadly delta-shaped, the tips toothed like the rest of the blade

            RIO GRANDE COTTONWOOD, p. 337

D. Stalks furnished with glands near the tip

    Twigs slender; blades thin; margins finely toothed

            PALMER COTTONWOOD, p. 339

    Twigs stout; blades thick; margins coarsely toothed

            PLAINS COTTONWOOD, p. 334

Key G: Willows

Part 1. KEY TO FLOWERING SPECIMENS

A. Scales of the flowers pale straw-color and deciduous. B.

  B. Flowers appearing with the leaves. C.

    C. Twigs brittle at base. D.

      D. Twigs light orange or yellow, or yellowish brown or yellowish gray

        Scales densely hoary-woolly on both sides; species of the Pac. coast and SW.   VALLEY WILLOW, p. 343

        Scales sparingly hairy on the outer face, densely so on the inner, with long soft hairs but not hoary-woolly; species ranging from east of the Rockies and over them to the interior Pac. NW.

            PEACH WILLOW, p. 346

      D. Twigs dark orange or red-brown or reddish purple or grayish purple

        Stamens 3 to 5; ovary egg-shaped; species of the Gt. Plains and east.

        EASTERN BLACK WILLOW, p. 345

        Stamens 5 to 9; ovary oblong-conic; species ranging from w. Tex. to s. Ariz.   WRIGHT WILLOW, p. 347

    C. Twigs not brittle at base

      Leafstalks glandular near the junction with the blade; winter buds acute; ovary long-stalked   YELLOW WILLOW, p. 349

      Leafstalks not glandular; winter buds obtuse; ovary short-stalked

            RED WILLOW, p. 347

  B. Flowers appearing after the leaves. E.

    E. Catkins only ¼ to ½ inch long; leaves only 1¼ inches long or less

        YEWLEAF WILLOW, p. 355

    E. Catkins 1 inch long or more when full-grown; leaves 1½ inches long or more. F.

      F. Ovary stalked, smooth; stamens 3 to 9; leafstalks ⅛ inch long or more

        Twigs with scattered hairs; leafstalks glandular near the blade; species ranging from the Yukon Valley to the n. parts of Ariz. and N.M.   YELLOW WILLOW, p. 349

Twigs smooth; leafstalks not glandular near the blade; species ranging through the s. parts of Ariz. and N.M.

BONPLAND WILLOW, p. 351

F. Ovary not stalked, hairy; stamens 2; leafstalks none or less than ⅛ inch long

Catkins borne on smooth twigs; stigmas short, hardly 2 or 3 times longer than broad   COYOTE WILLOW, p. 354

Catkins on hairy twigs; stigmas narrow, 4 or 5 times longer than broad

Twigs long-hairy; leaf blades ½ inch or more wide

SILVERLEAF WILLOW, p. 353

Twigs merely downy; leaf blades never more than ⅓ inch wide

SANDBAR WILLOW, p. 352

A. Scales of the flowers dark and persistent. G.

  G. Flowers appearing before the leaves

Branches (not twigs or trunks) with whitish bark

FIRE WILLOW, p. 360

Branches with dark or grayish bark, but not whitish

Catkins borne on short stalks   BEACH WILLOW, p. 358

Catkins stalkless, borne directly on the twig

ARROYO WILLOW, p. 356

  G. Flowers appearing with the leaves. H.

Style none, the yellow stigmas seated directly on the apex of the ovary

BEBB WILLOW, p. 359

Style present (long or short)

Twigs brittle at base; ovary pubescent; stamen solitary in each male floret   SITKA WILLOW, p. 362

Twigs not brittle; ovary smooth; stamens 2

BEACH WILLOW, p. 358

Part 2. KEY TO MATURE LEAVES

A. Leafstalks none or very short (⅛ inch or less long)

Blades ½ inch or more wide   SILVERLEAF WILLOW, p. 352

Blades never more than ⅜ inch wide, usually less

Leaves not over 1¼ inches long   YEWLEAF WILLOW, p. 355

Leaves 1½ inches long or more

Capsules smooth   COYOTE WILLOW, p. 354

Capsules white-hairy   SANDBAR WILLOW, p. 352

A. Leafstalks ⅛ inch long or more. B.

  B. Margins of the leaves not or almost not toothed (at least to the naked eye), the teeth, if any, minute or else remote and irregular. C.

    C. Upper leaf surface pubescent, not shiny   BEBB WILLOW, p. 359

    C. Upper leaf surface smooth or nearly so, the midrib sometimes pubescent. D.

      D. Leaves elliptic or oval, the tip roundish or merely acutish.

Undersides of leaves clothed below with long silvery white hairs

SITKA WILLOW, p. 362

Undersides of leaves smooth or variously pubescent, not as above
FIRE WILLOW, p. 360

D. Leaves long and slender, the tips acute or drawn out to a narrow (long or short) tip

Leaves prevailingly broadest above the middle, the tip acute or drawn out to a short point
ARROYO WILLOW, p. 356

Leaves prevailingly broadest at or below the middle, the tip drawn out to a long point RED WILLOW, p. 347

B. Margins of the leaves appearing to the naked eye as distinctly and regularly (though sometimes finely) toothed. E.

E. Lower surface of the foliage green, not or only slightly paler than the upper

Leaves 3 to 6 inches long, shining above; twigs reddish or grayish purple EASTERN BLACK WILLOW, p. 345

Leaves 1½ to 3 inches long, dull above; twigs yellowish gray
VALLEY WILLOW, p. 343

E. Lower surface of the foliage decidedly paler than the upper and often glaucous, silvery, or bluish. F.

F. Blades commonly not more than 3 times as long as wide

Twigs brittle at base PEACH WILLOW, p. 346

Twigs not brittle at base BEACH WILLOW, p. 358

F. Blades commonly 4 times as long as wide or longer

Margins of leaves and of leafstalks near the apex bearing conspicuous yellow glands; twigs and upper leaf surfaces very shiny
YELLOW WILLOW, p. 349

Margins of leaves and leafstalks not conspicuously glandular; upper surface of blades not or only slightly shiny

Leaves less than 6 times as long as wide, the tip distinctly long-acute but not drawn out to an extremely long narrow point
RED WILLOW, p. 347

Leaves 6 or more times as long as wide, drawn out to an extremely long slender tip

Twigs brittle at base WRIGHT WILLOW, p. 347

Twigs not brittle

Lower surface pale or glaucous and downy, at least minutely so ARROYO WILLOW, p. 356

Lower surface silvery white and smooth
BONPLAND WILLOW, p. 351

Key H: Walnuts

Leaflets 5 to 6 times as long as broad TEXAS BLACK WALNUT, p. 368

Leaflets less than 5 times as long as broad

Upper surface lustrous; leaflets 15 to 19 and long-pointed
NORTHERN CALIFORNIA WALNUT, p. 372

Upper surface not shining; leaflets 9 to 15 in number and acute but not long-
pointed
    Margins coarsely serrate; tree of Tex., N.M. and Ariz.
ARIZONA WALNUT, p. 367
    Margins finely toothed; tree of Calif.
SOUTHERN CALIFORNIA WALNUT, p. 370

Key I: Birches

A. Bark freely separable into thin layers. B.
  B. Leaves broadly oval to oblong-oval or narrower; leafstalk yellow. C.
    C. Leaves 1½ to 3 inches long; bases of the strobile scales broad at the tip,
        gradually narrowed; middle lobes of strobile scales as long as or
        longer than the lateral
        Leafstalks stout, ½ to ¾ inch long; leaf blades oval and a little long-
            pointed   PAPER BIRCH, p. 383
        Leafstalks slender, ¾ to 1 inch long; blades broadly oval and not at all
            long-pointed; middle lobe of the strobile scales shorter than the
            lateral lobes   ALASKA COAST BIRCH, p. 385
    C. Leaves 3 to 5 inches long; strobile scales abruptly contracted to the nar-
      row base; strobiles minutely downy, 2 to 2¼ inches wide
BROWN BIRCH, p. 386
  B. Leaves broadly oval-triangular or rhombic in shape; leafstalk bright red;
    strobile scales with large lateral lobes, a slender middle lobe equalling
    the lateral ones in length, and with a slender base or claw
YUKON BIRCH, p. 387
A. Bark not freely separable into thin layers; twigs permanently glandular
  Leaf bases broad and truncate or rounded   WATER BIRCH, p. 389
  Leaf bases narrowly wedge-shaped   DAWSON BIRCH, p. 391

Key J: Alders

Foliage lustrous on the lower surface; flowers opening in midspring, with the leaves
    or after them   SITKA ADLER, p. 395
Foliage not lustrous on the undersides; flowers opening in winter or early spring
    before the unfolding of the leaves
    Leaves rusty-pubescent on the lower surface; wing of the nut broad
OREGON ALDER, p. 396
    Leaves not rusty-pubescent below (except sometimes for a few tufts of hairs
      in the axils of the veins); wing of nut reduced to a narrow border
    Leaves shiny on the upper surface; stamens 4 in each male floret
THINLEAF ALDER, p. 401
    Leaves not lustrous above; stamens 2 or 3 in each male floret
      Leaves oval, barely acute at apex; Pac. coast species
WHITE ALDER, p. 402

Leaves oblong, distinctly acute at tip; SW. species
ARIZONA ALDER, p. 404

Key K: Oaks

A. Leaves, if toothed, not bristly from the veins running out beyond the margin; bark commonly gray, and scaly or flaky; inside of the acorn shell not downy; cup of the acorn with scales much thickened at base, narrowed at tip. B.

B. Foliage more or less hard or leathery. C.

    C. Upper surface of leaves lustrous

        Blades ½ to ¾ inch long, ¼ to ½ inch wide; cup saucer-shaped
TOUMEY OAK, p. 441

        Blades 1 to 2 inches long, ½ to ¾ inch wide; cup cup-shaped
MEXICAN BLUE OAK, p. 437

    C. Leaves dull or at most a little shiny on the upper surface. D.

        D. Blades coarsely net-veined and thickly coated on the underside with fulvous pubescence, the thick margins curled under. Trees of N.M. and Ariz. ARIZONA. WHITE OAK, p. 438

        D. Blades not, or only obscurely, net-veined; pubescence of lower surface of scattered light-brown hairs. Tree of Calif.
MESA LIVE OAK, p. 436

B. Foliage more or less thin and soft. E.

    E. Leaves not or but very shallowly lobed, though sometimes with lobe-like wavy teeth

        Margins with numerous, regular, somewhat lobe-like, wavy teeth
YELLOW OAK, p. 432

        Margins variously toothed or intact or if with somewhat wavy teeth then these few, not numerous

        Tree of Calif., with leaves 2 to 5 inches long
BLUE OAK, p. 434

        Tree of Tex., N.M. and Ariz. with leaves usually less than 2 inches long GRAY OAK, p. 440

    E. Leaves distinctly lobed

        Lower surface white-downy BUR OAK, p. 429

        Lower surface smooth or merely pubescent on the undersides, not white-downy

        Acorn long-conic, acute, 1¼ to 2¼ inches long
VALLEY OAK, p. 419

        Acorn oval, blunt, ½ to 1¼ inches long

        Tree of the Pac. coast; acorn cup shallowly cup-shaped
OREGON WHITE OAK, p. 425

        Tree of interior W. states; cup hemispheric
ROCKY MOUNTAIN WHITE OAK, p. 427

A. Leaves, if toothed, having the veins running out beyond the margins as bristles; bark commonly black or very dark, hard, and deeply furrowed; insides of acorn shells decidedly downy; acorn cup with thin or flat scales. F.

F. Leaves deciduous, distinctly lobed (except sometimes in *Q. graciliformis*), more or less soft and thin. G.

    G. Leaves only ¾ to 1¼ inches wide   *Quercus graciliformis*, p. 455

    G. Leaves 2 to 4 inches wide

      Trees of western Texas   CHISOS RED OAK, p. 454

      Tree of California   CALIFORNIA BLACK OAK, p. 457

F. Leaves evergreen, hard or leathery, lobed or entire

  H. Bark of trunks commonly gray, white or whitish, smooth or flaky but not with many deep furrows and narrow ridges

    Leaves 1 to 2 inches long, the lower surface lead-colored or when young covered with a golden or silvery fuzz

                         CANYON LIVE OAK, p. 444

    Leaves ⅔ to ½ inches long, densely woolly when young, with prominent regular parallel veins.   ISLAND LIVE OAK, p. 446

  H. Bark of old trunks dark or blackish and rough, often becoming deeply furrowed and narrowly ridged

    Lower surface coated with dense, woolly, white hairs

                         SILVERLEAF OAK, p. 456

    Lower surface smooth or merely pubescent, not densely white woolly

    Leaves convex-concave   COAST LIVE OAK, p. 447

    Leaves plane

      Lower surface with conspicuous, meshed veinlets, and hairless

                    INTERIOR LIVE OAK, p. 453

      Lower surfaces with obscurely meshed veins and 2 large tufts of white hairs on each side of the midrib at base

                        EMORY OAK, p. 442

Key L: Hackberries

A. Leaves not conspicuously mesh-veined beneath

    Leaves finely or coarsely toothed   THICKLEAF HACKBERRY, p. 466

    Leaves with intact margins or only sparingly and irregularly toothed

                    TEXAS HACKBERRY, p. 465

A. Leaves conspicuously mesh-veined below

    Leaves pale on the lower surface, coarsely toothed, smooth or only slightly pubescent below along the midrib and veins; fruit light orange-brown, on stalks often 3 or 4 times longer than the leafstalks

                    CANYON HACKBERRY, p. 471

    Leaves not pale on the lower surface, the margins intact; pubescent along the midrib and veins below and usually on the upper surfaces; fruit dark orange-red, on stalks not more than twice as long as the leafstalks

                    NETLEAF HACKBERRY, p. 468

Key M: Plums and Cherries

A. Flowers and fruits in axillary clusters. B.

B.˙ Fruit usually slightly 2-lobed by a ventral groove, usually more than ½ inch
long (*Plums*)

Leaves rolled in bud, merely acute at tip   PACIFIC PLUM, p. 529

Leaves folded in bud, coming to a long narrow tip
WILD RED PLUM, p. 531

B. Fruit not or scarcely grooved on the ventral face (*Cherries*)

Leaves oblong-lanceshape, gradually narrowed to a long tip
FIRE CHERRY, p. 535

Leaves broadest above the middle, usually obtuse at tip or merely acute
BITTER CHERRY, p. 537

A. Flowers and fruits in terminal spikes. C.

C. Leaves deciduous; flowers and fruits on branches of the year (*Choke Cherries*)

Leafstalks with 2 glands near the apex
WESTERN CHOKE CHERRY, p. 539

Leafstalks without glands
SOUTHWESTERN CHOKE CHERRY, p. 538

C. Leaves evergreen; flowers and fruits from the axils of the previous year
(*Laurel Cherries*)

Blades merely acute at tip, conspicuously spiny-toothed   ISLAY, p. 541

Blades at tip drawn out to a long point; margins usually not toothed
CATALINA CHERRY, p. 543

Key N: Maples and Box Elders

A. Leaves simple and palmately veined though often deeply lobed as well as often
toothed (*Maples*). B.

B. Lobes practically none   SOUTHWESTERN MAPLE, p. 609

B. Lobes present and distinct. C.

C. Teeth numerous and fine

Blades 7- to 9-lobed   VINE MAPLE, p. 609

Blades 3- to 5-lobed   DWARF MAPLE, p. 611

C. Teeth few, usually large

Blades 5-lobed, 8 to 12 inches long   BIGLEAF MAPLE, p. 605

Blades 3-lobed, 2 to 5 inches long
WESTERN SUGAR MAPLE, p. 607

A. Leaves pinnately compound (*Box Elders*)

Twigs smooth, shining green or glaucous violet; blades thinnish in texture;
leaflets 3 to 9, but generally 5 or 7, in number
EASTERN BOX ELDER, p. 617

Twigs at maturity pubescent or hairy, as are also the fruit stalks; blades
thickish in texture; leaflets 3 in number

Rachis and winter buds hoary-woolly
>>> CALIFORNIA BOX ELDER, p. 617
Rachis and winter buds variously pubescent or smooth but not hoary-woolly
>>> WESTERN BOX ELDER, p. 616

Key O: Ashes

A. Leaflets only ½ to ¾ inch long, spatulate; leaves in over-all dimensions 1½ to 3 inches long >>> LITTLELEAF ASH, p. 695
A. Leaflets 1 to 6 inches long; leaves (unless simple and not compound) 3 or more inches long. B.
>> B. Twigs 4-angled; fruit compressed, with oblong wing extending to its base Leaflets 5 (rarely 3); fruit 1 to 1½ inches long
>>>> LOWELL ASH, p. 693
>>> Leaves simple (rarely compound with 2 or 3 leaflets); fruit ½ inch long
>>>> SINGLELEAF ASH, p. 694
>> B. Twigs roundish in cross-section. C.
>>> C. Lateral leaflets not stalked >>> OREGON ASH, p. 691
>>> C. Lateral leaflets all stalked, at least slightly so. D.
>>>> D. Leaves in over-all dimensions 9 to 18 inches long; leaflets 7 to 9 in number
>>>>> Leaves, stalks, and twigs hairy >>> RED ASH, p. 687
>>>>> Leaves, stalks, and twigs smooth >>> GREEN ASH, p. 687
>>>> D. Leaves 3 to 7 inches long in over-all dimensions; leaflets 3 to 7 in number
>>>>> Leaflets thin, dark green above; tree of w. Tex.
>>>>>> BERLANDIER ASH, p. 690
>>>>> Leaflets thick, pale green above; tree of the SW. except Tex.
>>>>>> VELVET ASH, p. 698

GLOSSARY

Aborted. Incompletely developed, defective in form.

Acidulous. Having acid properties and taste.

Akene (achene). A dry, often seed-like fruit not opening or splitting by any natural sutures. Example: the fruits of Mountain Mahogany, the "seeds" or "straws" of strawberries.

Alternate. Growing singly at the nodes (*q.v.*) of the stem or axis or rachis; not opposite (*q.v.*) nor in whorls (*q.v.*).

Anther. The part of a stamen which contains the pollen. Anthers consist in 1 or more pollen sacks opening variously by pores or slits. If there is no stalk or filament, then the anther of itself constitutes the entire stamen (*q.v.*) and is exactly synonymous with it.

Apetalous. Without petals.

Apex. The tip; the upper or outer end, farthest removed from the stalk, axis, or stem.

Appressed. Closely and flatly pressed against.

Aril. An appendage or outer covering of a seed, an outgrowth of the hilum (*q.v.*), sometimes appearing pulpy: Example, the Yew.

Awl-shaped. Sharp-pointed and narrow.

Axil. The inner (upper) angle of a leaf with the stem, or of a scale with the axis.

Axillary. In the position of an axil.

Axis. The central shoot of a compound leaf, cone, inflorescence, or root, etc.

Balsamic. Having the qualities of balsam, soft, mucilaginous, often aromatic.

Bark. The outermost, often more or less corky or leathery cell layers on stems, branches, twigs, and roots, formed by the cambium cells. The bark of trees usually has at least two layers, the outer and the inner, more or less distinct in structure, texture, color, etc.

Base. The lower end of an organ, that is, the part nearest the stalk, stem, or axis on which an organ is borne.

Bast. The soft tissue of the fibers of the inner bark, which are often employed in making thread and rope.

Beard. Long, bristle-like hairs, especially upon petals or styles.

Bearded. Having a beard (*q.v.*).

Berry. As defined by botanists (only), a fleshy fruit proceeding from the ripening of a single pistil but with more than one seed, the seeds not enclosed in a "stone." Example: Madroño, Soapberry, Saguaro. The berries of the Juniper are really cones whose scales have become fused and pulpy but are in effect, if not in origin, berries.

Biconvex. Convex on both surfaces.

Bisexual. Having the parts or organs of both sexes simultaneously, as a flower which contains both pollen and ovules.

Blade. The expanded leaf, apart from its stalk.

Board foot. A unit of lumber measurement 1 foot long, 1 foot wide, and 1 inch thick, or an equivalent volume.

Bole. A tree trunk, especially that of a large tree.

Bract. A more or less modified leaf, generally subtending a flower, fruit, stalk, or flowering or fruit cluster, or head, or spike.

Branchlet. The ultimate division of a branch.

Bud. An embryonic shoot bearing embryonic leaves or flowers or both.

Bushy. Having the growth form of a bush; that is, with numerous branches or shoots from the base but little or no central trunk.

Calyx (pl. *calyces*). The outer envelope of a flower, generally green and more or less leaf-like but, in the absence of petals, sometimes petal-like. Usually the word calyx is used when the sepals are united.

Cambium. In trees, the thin layer of tissue just under the inner bark and just outside the wood, which by cell division increases the tree in diameter, giving off bark cells on the outside and wood cells on the inside.

Capsule. A compound pod (*q.v.*); a dry, few- or many-seeded fruit splitting at maturity by longitudinal sutures. Example: Poplar, Willow, Horse Chestnut.

Carpel. One of the units of a compound pistil (*q.v.*) or ovary — the basic ovule-bearing unit of the female reproductive organ. Example: the segments of an apple core; the fruits of Catalina Ironwood.

Cartilaginous. Parchment-like, hard and tough.

Catkin. A more or less compact spike of mostly unisexual flowers. A term used generally of the peculiar inflorescences of certain trees, such as the Willows, Poplars, Walnuts, Hickories, Oaks and, more loosely, of the conifers, having few or very reduced floral envelopes and those often consisting of bracts and scales rather than sepals and petals, while the flowers or florets are often reduced to the organs of one sex or the other.

Checked. Said of bark, when it is marked by horizontal cracks or grooves.

Claw. The narrowed or stalk-like base of the petals or sepals of certain flowers. Example: Plum.

Compound. Said of any organ composed of two or more similar parts. A compound leaf is one composed of 2 or more leaflets, as in the case of Walnuts and Locusts (see *Simple,* for contrast). A leaf is once-compound when the leaflets are arranged on a single, unbranched axis or rachis. They are twice-compound when the axis or rachis is branched. A compound leaf may be known from a twig bearing simple leaves by the fact that there is a bud in the axil of a leaf but not of a leaflet. A compound fruit is composed of many more or less united fruitlets. Example: Mulberry. A compound ovary is one composed of the union of two or more pistils and possesses two or more cells.

Cone. A dense and more or less conical mass of flowers or fruits, or (more strictly) of seed-bearing scales, on a central axis. Loosely used for the fruits of Alders, etc., but more specifically for the female inflorescence of the Pine family. The cones of Pines and their relatives consist in the more or less woody, leathery, papery, or fleshy seed-bearing scales of the female catkins after fertilization, these arranged on a central axis forming a homogeneous fruit which generally detaches as a unit.

Conelet. A small, or immature, or ungrown cone. Commonly said of the female catkin of the Pine family.

Confluent. Running together, or uniting, as the tissues of two organs.

Conifer. A member of the Pine family.

Coniferous. Of or pertaining to the conifers.

Corolla. The inner series (petals, *q.v.*) of floral envelopes; used especially where the petals are fused at base into a common tube. Examples: Madroño, Desert Catalpa.

Cortex. Surface, as of bark, or the bark-like rind of stems.

Deciduous. Naturally falling; said especially of the foliage of trees that become naked during the unfavorable seasons.

Declined. Bent downward.

Decurrent. Running down, as of the blades of leaves on their stalks.

Deflexed. Abruptly turned down.

Disc, disk. A more or less fleshy development of the receptacle (*q.v.*) of a flower around the pistil.

Dorsal. On the upper ("back") or outer face of an organ or part.

Drupe. A fleshy, 1-seeded fruit which contains a single stone which in turn contains the seed; a stone fruit. Examples: Plum, Cherry, Almond, Peach, Dogwood, etc.

Drupelet. A little drupe; more particularly one of a number of similar fruitlets in a compound fruit. Example: Mulberry.

Duct. A pit, chamber, or gland, usually filled with sap, resin or other secretion.

Ecological. Of or pertaining to ecology.

Ecologist. One who studies ecology.

Ecology. The life habits and interrelations of plants and animals with each other and with environmental influences.

Endophytic. Within the tissues of a plant. Said particularly of certain fungi living symbiotically in the root and other tissues of trees.

Epidermis. The thin layer of cells forming the outer coating of plants.

Evergreen. Remaining green through the seasons; never naked of foliage. All "evergreens" eventually shed their leaves but not as do deciduous trees — all at once or before new growth appears.

Exfoliating. Peeling away in papery plates or strips, as the bark of Sycamore, Birch, Eucalyptus, etc.

Exserted. Projecting beyond, as stamens which stand out beyond the corolla.

Female. Said of the flowers having only ovules and (except in the conifers) ovaries, but not male organs (stamens, pollen). Said of inflorescences or of trees bearing only female flowers.

Fertile. Capable of producing fruit. Sometimes used to denote flowers wholly female, or a pollen-bearing anther, as contrasted with a sterile one or staminodium. Also seed-bearing fruits.

Fertilization. Impregnation within the ovule of the egg cells by union with the sperm cells.

Filament. The stalk of an anther.

Flesh. The pulpy part of a fruit.

Flora. The plant population (or more strictly the flowering plants) of an area. Also a book dealing with their enumeration and identities.

Floral. Of or pertaining to flowers or inflorescences.

Floret. A little flower, especially when it is a part of a compact and specialized type of inflorescence such as a catkin (*q.v.*).

Flower. An axis bearing one or more anthers (male organs), or one or more female reproductive organs, or both sexes.

Fluted. Channeled or grooved.

Free. Not joined to other organs; said, for instance, of stamens free from the petals or an ovary free from the calyx.

Frond. Used sometimes for a compound leaf (as of a fern, palm, etc.) or for a spray of foliage.

Fruit. The seed-bearing organ; the ripened ovary or pistil and sometimes adjacent and cohering parts.

Fruitlet. A little fruit when it is a part of a compound fruit.

Fulvous. Dull brownish or reddish yellow; tawny.

Furrowed. Marked with longitudinal grooves.

Genus. A group of species (*q.v.*) which resemble each other more than they differ.

Gland. A secreting pore or part or prominence often exuding resinous, sticky, oily, or sweet substances; said also of hairs terminating in a knob-like tip, especially when exuding clammy substances, and of the teeth of leaves when gland-like in appearance (thickened and colored), and of any colored prominences of gland-like appearance — as those on the leaf-stalks of Plums and Cherries.

Glandular. Of or pertaining to a gland or of gland-like appearance.

Glaucous. With a bloom or cast of a bluish white appearance.

Globose. Approaching the form of a sphere.

Habit. The growth form of a plant.

Habitat. The situation, with regard to soil, light, temperature, and associated species, in which a plant grows.

Heartwood. The hard, inner cylinder of a woody stem, consisting of dead and heavy and more or less dense wood elements, usually darker, from the deposition of tannin, gums, resins, and pigments, than the sapwood.

Hilum. The scar or mark on a seed indicative of its point of attachment to the placenta of the parent plant.

Horizontal. At right angles to the (normally) up-and-down axis of growth.

Husk. The outermost covering of a fruit, usually of a heavy character — woody as in the case of the Walnut husk, leathery in the Locust pod, heavy in the hazlenut, and papery in the Hop Hornbeam's fruits.

Inferior. In a lower position. Said especially of ovaries which are adherent to, or surmounted by, the calyx, as in the case of Apples and Hawthorns.

Inflexed. Bent inwards.

Inflorescence. The flower cluster; the mode of bearing the flowers.

Integument. Covering or coat; outer tissues.

Involucre. A whorl (*q.v.*) of small

leaves or bracts subtending a flower or an inflorescence or fruit cluster. Example: Dogwood.

Irregular. Said of a flower when the parts or members of any one of the sets or series (particularly the petals) are unlike the others or eccentrically placed, or when the flower is bilaterally symmetrical, as in sweet pea, Locust and certain other flowers of the pea family.

Keel. A ridge like the keel of a boat, especially on a fruit or seed. Also the keel-shaped pair of united petals on the lower side of a flower of the pea family.

Lateral. On or at the side; not terminal.

Leader. A growing shoot, especially when extending beyond the rest of the crown of a tree.

Leaf. The lateral outgrowth of a stem or shoot, appearing from a bud, and usually flattened (but needle-like in Pines, Larches, etc.), veinous and, at maturity, green from the presence of chlorophyll; the principal photosynthetic organ of a tree. A leaf may consist in two parts, the stalk (when present) and the blade or leaf proper. Dimensions of leaves are usually given to include only the blade.

Leaflet. A single division of a compound leaf. The ultimate unit of division of a twice-compound leaf.

Legume. A pod opening by longitudinal sutures. Examples: the pod of a pea, bean, Mesquite, Locust.

Lenticel. A pore in the bark.

Limb. The flat or expanded part of an organ; in particular the flaring and lobed part of a corolla or calyx as distinct from its throat or tube.

Lobe. A segment of an organ usually separated from similar parts by a regular space or sinus, as in the lobed leaves of some Oaks, or the lobed corolla of Desert Catalpa.

Male. Said of flowers which bear pollen and, except in the Pine family, stamens. Said of a tree that bears only male flowers and never fruit.

Mammillate. Having the form of breast and nipple.

Medullary Ray. A vertical band or plate radiating between pith and bark.

Membranous. Thin and wide, membrane-like or filmy.

Midrib. The central or main and heaviest rib or nerve or vein, of a leaf or leaflet.

Needle. The peculiar, very long and narrow leaf, commonly triangular or piano-convex in cross-section, of Pines and (more loosely) of some of the relatives of Pines.

Nerve. A principal vein or slender rib of a leaf, especially when it is one of several arising from the base of the blade.

Node. The level, on a shoot, at which a branch, bud, leaf, or flower or other organ appears.

Nut. A dry, usually large, non-splitting fruit with thick, hard outer walls, produced from a 2- or more-celled ovary, but usually 1-seeded.

Nutlet. A small nut-like part, usually one of several, within a fruit.

Opposite. Said of leaves when they appear in pairs at the same node (*q.v.*) of the stem but on opposite sides of it; not alternate (*q.v.*) nor whorled (*q.v.*).

Ovary. The part of the pistil enclosing and bearing the ovules.

Ovule. The minute body, borne within the ovary and containing the female cells (eggs) which after fertilization become the seeds.

Palmate. Veined, lobed, or divided as the fingers of the hand or like the leaf of a fan palm. Examples: Sycamore, Horse Chestnut.

Perfect. Said of flowers when they are bisexual (*q.v.*).

Persistent. Remaining attached, not falling off.

Petal. A member of the inner series of floral envelopes, standing between the sepals and the stamens, and usually thin and colored (not green). See also *Corolla.*

Pinna (pl. *pinnæ*). The primary division of a compound leaf.

Pinnate. Said of a compound leaf with leaflets arranged along a common axis.

Pinnule. The secondary division of a pinna on a leaf which is twice or more compound.

Pistil. The ovule-bearing and seed-bearing organ of a flower, consisting in the ovary (*q.v.*), the stigma (*q.v.*), and, when present, the style (*q.v.*); the whole female organ.

Pith. The soft, spongy, loosely cellular tissue found within the woody cylinder of a stem, most characteristic of twigs and seedlings.

Placenta. Attachment point of ovules in an ovary.

Pod. A simple (not compound) usually thick-walled, dry fruit, splitting or otherwise opening at maturity.

Pollen. The spores or grains containing the male element (sperm) and originating in an anther (*q.v.*).

Pollination. The transfer of pollen from the anther to the stigma.

Polygamous. Bearing both perfect (*q.v.*) and unisexual flowers.

Pome. Fruit with papery or cartilaginous carpels (*q.v.*) at the center and fleshy outer tissue, of which the apple is a type; also pear, quince, and the fruits of Hawthorn, Mountain Ash, etc.

Polypetalous. Having separate, not united, petals.

Precocious. Coming to flower or fruit early in the year, or early in the life of a plant.

Pubescence. Soft short hairs.

Pubescent. Covered with short soft hair.

Punctate. Having translucent dots or pits.

Rachis. Axis shoot of a compound leaf or inflorescence; the central stalk or midrib.

Radial. Developed around a central axis.

Receptacle. The elongated or enlarged end of a shoot or flower axis on which some or all of the flower parts are borne.

Regular. Said of a flower when the parts of members in each series (as sepals, petals, stamens, pistils) are like each other and symmetrically disposed on 3 or more radii.

Resin. Secretions, usually formed in special passages or chambers, either hard or liquid, usually aromatic, insoluble in water, soluble in alcohol, ether, or carbon disulphide, and burning with a sooty flame.

Resinous. Containing, bearing, or impregnated with resin (*q.v*).

Ribbed. Having ribs (*q.v.*).

Ribs. Principal nerves, usually parallel or all arising from the base of a leaf, sometimes, also, the ridges between furrows on fruits, seeds, etc.

Rind. The firm close layer of cells covering many fruits and some trunks which do not have true bark, as palms.

Root. The usually underground part of a plant distinguished from a stem by its origin at the opposite end of the embryo, and by its generally downward growth.

Rosin. The hard brittle resin (*q.v.*) remaining after the oil of turpentine has been driven off by distillation.

Sack (sac). A pouch or receptacle or cavity in an organ, as the pollen sacks of an anther.

Samara. A dry, winged fruit not naturally splitting even at maturity. Examples: The fruits of Maples, Elms, Ashes.

Sapwood. The woody cylinder between the bark and the heartwood, usually paler than the heartwood, less heavy and dense, and more permeable.

Scale. A term used variously for different organs and appendages; often employed in connection with much reduced stem leaves and other thin, papery bodies, but in the cones of conifers denoting more or less woody, bract-like organs bearing the seeds.

Scurfy. Flaky.

Seed. The ovule (*q.v.*) after fertilization, containing the embryonic plant, within one or more coats, and often accompanied by a store (the endosperm or "meat") of fats, proteins, carbohydrates.

Sepal. One of the segments or lobes of the calyx (*q.v.*); usually said when the parts are not united at base.

Sheath. Any tubular structure surrounding an organ or part; the sheaths of Pines are short papery tubes enclosing the base of the bundle of needles.

Shoot. Any growing axis of a stem, or a new plant or branch growing from an old one.

Short-shoot. A shortened and condensed and usually thickened branch or twig usually bearing flowers, or a tuft of foliage, or spines.

Simple. Said of leaves that are not compound, that have a single unbranched midrib engaged continuously with the blade.

Sinus. The space or bay between two lobes of an organ.

Species. The unit of classification, composed, as a rule, of individuals which resemble each other more than they differ, are usually inter-fertile, are frequently sterile to other species, and breed true, reproducing their own kind.

Sperm. A male reproductive cell.

Spike. A simple elongated cluster.

Spore. A simple reproductive body, usually consisting in a detached cell.

Spreading. Standing outward or horizontally, not hanging deflexed or flattened to the stem.

Springwood. Growth made in the spring, as contrasted with the denser, darker summerwood.

Spur. A thickened short-shoot (*q.v.*), often bearing leaves, flowers or thorns.

Stalk. The stem of any organ as of a leaf, flower, inflorescence, anther, etc.

Stamen. The pollen-bearing or male organ. A single stamen, with or without floral envelopes, may, in the case of certain unisexual flowers, constitute a male flower. In bisexual flowers, the stamens usually stand outside the female organs but within or upon the floral envelopes.

Staminodium (pl. *staminodia*). A sterile or aborted stamen, without anthers or pollen, usually more or less modified in form (club-shaped, flattened, etc.) or even petal-like.

Standard. The upper petal of a flower of the pea family.

Stem. The main axis of growth above ground, bearing the buds, leaves, and flowers, as contrasted with the root-bearing axis.

Stigma. The part of the pistil that receives the pollen. Generally it is somewhat sticky and of a definite form, but it may occupy only an indefinite (see *Stigmatic*) area on the style.

Stigmatic. Of or pertaining to the stigma; often said of that portion of a style functioning as, but not clearly separated as, a stigma (*q.v.*).

Stipulate. Accompanied by stipules (*q.v.*).

Stipule. Generally a little appendage-like part of a leaf, growing one on each side of the base of the leafstalk and sometimes fused with it, sometimes deciduous.

Stoma (pl. *stomata*). A minute opening between two guard cells in the epidermis, especially on undersides of leaves, through which gaseous interchange between inner cells and atmosphere is effected.

Stomatal. Of or pertaining to stomata (see *Stoma*).

Style. The stalk-like or columnar part of the pistil surmounting the ovary and upholding the stigma (*q.v.*). Frequently the style is branched, thus representing a union of styles. Sometimes the styles are separate to the base, representing a union of carpels (*q.v.*). Sometimes no stigma is present, and the styles merely exhibit a stigmatic surface on one or more sides.

Subtend. To stand under, in a bract-like position.

Summerwood. Growth of darker, more compact wood made after the springwood.

Superior. Placed above; said of an ovary that is free from, and not surmounted by, the calyx. Example: Plum flowers.

Suture. A natural groove or line along which splitting takes place, especially in fruits, seeds, etc.

Sylva (silva). The forest trees of a region, collectively considered. A book dealing with the trees of an area.

Taproot. A vertical, strong, central root that continues growth, in line with the axis of the stem, straight down in the ground.

Terminal. At the end of a branch, shoot, style, etc.

Throat. The opening or orifice in a flower with united petals or united sepals at the point where the tube (*q.v.*) expands into the limb (*q.v.*).

Tortuous. Twisted, sinuous.

Transverse. Crosswise, across.

Tridentate. 3-toothed, especially at the apex of a part or organ.

Truncate. Appearing as if cut off along a straight or essentially straight margin. Example: the bases of the leaves of some Cottonwoods.

Tube. The unexpanded, more or less cylindrical and basal portion of a calyx (*q.v.*) or corolla (*q.v.*). See also *Throat* and *Limb*.

Tumid. Swollen.

Turgid. Distended by pressure from within.

Twig. A branchlet; the ultimate division of a woody shoot.

Umbo. The central boss on a cone scale.

Unarmed. Without thorns, prickles or spines.

Underbark. The inner, often brightly colored bark beneath the corky or scaly outer bark.

Unisexual. Composed of one sex only; said of a flower having pollen *or* ovules, but not both.

Valve. The separable part of a pod or capsule; the walls of such fruits, between the sutures (*q.v.*).

Variety. A fraction of the unit of classification (species, *q.v.*); a group of individuals within a species set aside from others by their exclusive resemblances in minor ways.

Vein. A branch of the sap-conducting tissue of a leaf, petal, scale, bract, seed coat, etc. See also *Veinlet, Midrib, Nerve.*

Veinlet. A secondary vein.

Veiny. With the veins heavily or darkly or intricately marked.

Venation. The system (variously patterned) of midribs, nerves, and veins in a leaf, petal, etc.

Venous. Of or pertaining to the veins or system of veins.

Ventral. On the under ("belly") or inner face of an organ or part. (See *Dorsal.*)

Vesicle. A chamber, blister, hollow, pit or duct, usually filled with sap, resin or other secretion.

Whorl. Three or more leaves or other organs arising in a circle from one node (*q.v.*) of a shoot.

Wing. A flat, thin expansion of an organ, as the papery wings of Elm and Maple fruits, or the winged seeds of Pines. The word is also used to denote the lateral petals of a flower of the pea family.

Winter Bud. A dormant, much condensed shoot formed during the previous season.

INDEX OF SCIENTIFIC NAMES

THE WORDS in bold-face represent valid specific names; those in italics are synonyms referred to valid names. These synonyms will not be found in the text of the book itself.

INDEX OF COMMON NAMES